ENVIRONMENTAL SCIENCE, ENGINEERING AND TECHNOLOGY

RAINFALL

BEHAVIOR, FORECASTING AND DISTRIBUTION

ENVIRONMENTAL SCIENCE, ENGINEERING AND TECHNOLOGY

Additional books in this series can be found on Nova's website under the Series tab.

Additional e-books in this series can be found on Nova's website under the e-book tab.

ENVIRONMENTAL SCIENCE, ENGINEERING AND TECHNOLOGY

RAINFALL

BEHAVIOR, FORECASTING AND DISTRIBUTION

OLGA E. MARTÍN
AND
TRICIA M. ROBERTS
EDITORS

nova publishers
New York

For permission to use material from this book please contact us:
Telephone 631-231-7269; Fax 631-231-8175
Web Site: http://www.novapublishers.com

Library of Congress Cataloging-in-Publication Data

Rainfall : behavior, forecasting, and distribution / [edited by] Olga E. Martmn and Tricia M. Roberts.
p. cm.
Includes bibliographical references and index.
ISBN 978-1-62081-551-9 (hardcover)
1. Rain and rainfall. 2. Rain and rainfall--Forecasting. 3. Rainfall anomalies. I. Martmn, Olga E. II. Roberts, Tricia M.
QC925.R226 2011
551.57'7--dc23

2012011763

Published by Nova Science Publishers, Inc. † New York

CONTENTS

PREFACE

In this book, the authors present topical research in the study of the behavior, forecasting and distribution of rainfall variability. Topics discussed in this compilation include coping strategies in relation to local rainfall variability in Tanzania; rainfall variability and changes in Bangladesh; non-parametric methods for forecasting time series from cumulative monthly rainfall; long term and interannual rainfall variability in the Argentinean Chaco plain region; study of wet scavenging of atmospheric aerosols using decay products in rainwater; spatial variability of rain and its erosivity in a tropical semi-arid area in Kenya; potential of the piezoelectric transducer for direct rainfall kinetic energy measurement and erosivity evaluation; climatology and rainfall in northeast Brazil; and the Kalman Filtering approach in the calibration of radar rainfall data.

Chapter 1 - This chapter explores a potential relationship between rainfall data and household self-reported harvest shocks and local (spatial) variability of harvest shocks and coping strategies based on a survey of 2700 rural households in the Kagera region of northern Tanzania. In addition, correlations of rainfall amounts across the districts in the region are estimated in order to assess the variations in rainfall patterns across the districts. The results show that rainfall patterns in the region are very location-specific, there are few correlations between rainfall events, and that the distribution of household reported harvest shocks differs significantly between districts and correspond to the observed variability in local climate patterns.

Coping strategies are focused on spreading risks and include reduced consumption, casual employment, new crops, external support and the selling of assets. There are no large differences in applied coping strategies across the region, but district-level data demonstrate how local strategies differ between localities within the districts. The results emphasize that in order to target rural policies and make them efficient, it is important to take into account the local conditions that rural households face when experiencing climate-related shocks.

Finally, shocks reported by households appear to correspond well with observed variability in rainfall patterns.

Chapter 2 - Rainfall variability in space and time is one of the most relevant characteristics of the climate of Bangladesh. Long-term annual average rainfall, coefficient of variation of annual rainfall, precipitation concentration and aridity indices at each station are computed and then interpolated using kriging method within a geographic information system to show the temporal and spatial variability of rainfall in Bangladesh. Mann-Kendall test is used to analyze the trends in rainfall at different confidence levels and the Sen's slope method is used to determine the magnitude of changes. The results show that rainfall in Bangladesh varies from 1527 mm in the west to 4197 mm in the east with a mean of 2488 mm. The gradient of rainfall from west to east is approximately 7 mm km^{-1}. The monthly distribution of rainfall shows that the rainfall is very much seasonal in Bangladesh, more than 89% of rainfall occurs during May to October. The aridity study over Bangladesh reveals three climate zones in Bangladesh viz. moist sub-humid, humid and wet. The climate in most of parts of Bangladesh is humid type. The northeastern side of the country belongs to wet climate and the central western part to moist sub-humid. Co-efficient of variation of annual rainfall shows a moderate inter-annual variability of rainfall in most parts of the country. The deviation of annual precipitation from mean precipitation is found to vary from +408 mm to -586 mm during the last fifty years. Highest inter-annual variation of rainfall is observed in northwest Bangladesh and lowest in the southern coastal region. The trend analysis using Mann-Kendall method reveals the presence of a positive trend in annual rainfall of Bangladesh at 90% level of confidence. The magnitude of change of annual rainfall estimated by Sen's slope estimator shows that the annual rainfall of Bangladesh has increased at a rate of +5.53 mm yr^{-1} in last fifty years. A significant increase in pre-monsoon rainfall at a rate of 2.47 mm yr^{-1} at 99% level of confidence is also observed over Bangladesh. However, there is no change in monsoon, post-monsoon and winter rainfalls. Spatial analysis of rainfall changes show significant increases in annual and pre-monsoon rainfall at more than one-third of stations mostly situated in the northern and southwestern parts of Bangladesh. The changes in rainfall during monsoon, post-monsoon and winter are significant only at few stations, mostly situated in the northern part of the country.

Chapter 3 - This chapter presents two non-parametric methods for designing algorithms to forecast time series from the cumulative monthly rainfall. Both approaches are based on artificial feed-forward neural networks (ANNs). The results are evaluated on high roughness time series from the Mackey-Glass Equation (MG), and from accumulated monthly historical rainfall data from one geographic location. In addition, both methods are compared with the classic non-linear moving average (NAR) predictor filter. The first case is an algorithm to forecast time series that set the parameters of a NAR model based on ANNs as function of the energy associated to the time series. The authors propose a tuning criterion, which consists of producing the values of the time series starting from the areas of the forecasted time series. These values are approximated by an ANN that generates a primitive calculated by a linear predictor filter. Depending on the roughness of the time series, the authors propose a heuristic law to establish the tuning process and the NN topology, assuming that the forecasted time series has the same Hurst parameter that the original data time series. In the second case, the methodology consists of generating time series by sampling the data time series, and each individual time series is associated with a predictor filter. Thus, depending on the data, others time series are obtained by sampling with an increasing interval. For each one of the time series generated, a specific ANN-based filter is adjusted, and each one generates a forecast that is then averaged among other subsamples time series, resulting in a mix of predictor filters. The tuning rule used in the adjustment process is based on the Levenberg-Marquardt method. From simulation results, it can be concluded that to achieve a more accurate forecast to reality of time series with high roughness, to smooth the time series is a good practice. The methodology proposed here proposes to divide the problem of time series forecasting by non-parametric methods by subdivision into stages of smoothing. The first was the subsampling method, which showed that restructuring is a good technique, and the second one, the integration of data time series that works with their primitive, which can be considered as the second case proposed in this chapter. The results are encouraging; deserving study and investment in implementation effort for the geographical locations of interest.

Chapter 4 - The Argentinean Chaco plain region has a relevant biodiversity and it has experienced an important increase in annual rainfall during the last century. However, there is evidence that some rainfall decrease has happened in some sub-regions since 1980; such decrease could be related to deforestation carried out in order to increase the farming area. In this paper rainfall variability was analyzed to better understand its behavior in scales greater than a year. There are indicators of a cycle of 22 years in the west of Chaco and other of 6,6 years in the east. The annual cycle is present all over the region and more pronounced towards the west. The interannual rainfall variability shows that there are three main rainfall anomaly leading patterns. The first is associated with the SST in the subtropical Atlantic Ocean, the second leading is related to ENSO and a high pressure system centered in central-southern Brazil and the third is associated with positive correlation in the west tropical and subtropical Pacific and with a wave train extended from the western Pacific Ocean towards South America. The results indicate that rainfall must be monitored in order to determine its future evolution and if deforestation has influenced the climate of the region. Likewise, the relation between climate and deforestation must be best studied in order to mitigate the negative impacts over the region. In order to describe a possible situation in the future some simulations are detailed. The regional model MM5 was nested within time slice global atmospheric model experiments conducted by the HadAM3H model. The simulations cover a 10-year period representing present-day climate (1981–1990) and two future scenarios for the SRESA2 and B2 emission scenarios for the period 2081–2090. Both the A2 and B2 simulations show a general increase in precipitation in northern and central Argentina especially in summer and fall and a general decrease in precipitation in winter and spring.

Chapter 5 - The consideration of rainfalls impact on water management is not new and started with the history of sanitation. At the beginning of the 20th century sewer networks in urban area were designed both for sewage and for stormwater management. In the 70's the impact of urban runoff on water quality was already studied (Pitt et al., 1977) and more recently the question of climate change impacts on water quality was considered with the effect of heavier rainy events. Commonly, categories of rain are defined by their intensity:light , moderate and heavy rain being characterised by the amount of mm of water/hour (respectively 2.5, 2.5 to 7.5, >7.5). According to the duration of a given rainfall, the same intensity can be observed during a short period (shower) or a longer one (storm). Consequences of these precipitations can result in so called extreme rain or flood respectively at local or regional scale. As reported by the 2007 IPCC report, it is likely that the frequency of heavy precipitation events has increased over most areas, particularly in Europe and North America, and that available research suggests a significant future increase in heavy rainfall events in many regions. Such phenomena, increasing in frequency and intensity, may have a strong impact on the quality of the waters. Indeed, resulting changes in flow regimes will influence the chemistry, hydromorphology and ecology of water bodies at the environmental level as well as, in urban area, the wastewater quality, the sewage treatment efficiency and the corresponding pollutants load (Roig et al., 2011). The effect of rainy events can also reach drinking water production system, impairing the quality of the distributed water (Figure 1).

Chapter 6 - The concentrations and the concentration ratios of individual short-lived ^{222}Rn decay products (^{214}Pb and ^{214}Bi) in rainwater were measured, and a scavenging model was designed for explaining the measurement results.

The measurement was done at Kumatori-cho (34.39° N, 135.35° E, approx. 70 m above sea level) in Osaka, Japan by gamma-ray spectrometry using a low-background Ge detector. The dependence of the time variations of the concentrations and their ratios on rainfall rate was investigated. It was observed that the concentrations were negatively correlated with the rainfall rate in some rainfall events, and that there was no clear correlation in other rainfall events. The changes in the dependence of the concentration on the rainfall rate occurred after the passage of a cold front during a single rainfall event. The concentration ratios showed a weak negative correlation with the rainfall rate for most of the observed rainfall events.

Based on the relationship between the concentrations of ^{214}Pb and ^{214}Bi in the rainwater and the rainfall rate for an individual rainfall event, the increase in the environmental gamma-ray dose rate from ^{214}Pb and ^{214}Bi deposited on the ground was calculated, and the calculated increase agreed well with that observed by the in situ measurement on flat ground.

Chapter 7 - Although precipitation is the key driver of water erosion processes, the spatial variability of rain depth and rain erosivity have never been studied in lakes Baringo-Bogoria catchment located in a semi-arid area that is under threat of desertification in Kenya. The objectives of this study were: to determine spatial variation of rain depth and how this is influenced by elevation, slope gradient, slope aspect and geographical position; and to analyze rain intensity and rain drop size that determine rain erosivity. Historical daily climatic data of a 15-44-year period from seven stations, spatially distributed in the study area, were considered. Recorded rain intensity data for three years was available in one station therefore rain drop size measurements was done in that station. Analysis of spatial variation of annual rainfall indicates that elevation and longitude, and to a lesser extent slope aspect and slope gradient determine the spatial distribution of mean annual rain. Rain intensity results indicate that most of the total rain volume (90.4%) falls with intensity <15mm/h, while a small amount (4.7%) falls with intensities >30mm/h. A relation between rain intensity and volume specific kinetic energy (Ek_{vol}) was developed and recommended for calculating Ek_{vol} of rain, as well as for computation of Universal Soil Loss Equation's rain erosivity factor on yearly basis.

Chapter 8 - Rainfall is the major driver of soil detachment in erosion processes. The potential of rainfall to detach soil has been defined as rainfall erosivity. Several indices have been suggested to quantify the rainfall erosivity based on both raindrop mass and fall velocity. However, the rainfall kinetic energy has been used widely in laboratory and field scales. The drop size distribution (DSD) of rainfall event is the primary rainfall data that can be used to quantify the rainfall erosivity; assuming that the raindrop fall velocity can be physically or empirically estimated from the raindrop mass. However, devices for continuous evaluation of rainfall DSD are not commonly used in conventional meteorological stations. In this study, piezoelectric transducers have been used to evaluate the natural rainfall erosivity and its relationship with rainfall intensity. Two piezoelectric sensors were installed on the roof of the Arid Land Research Center, Tottori University, Tottori city, Japan to measure the rainfall kinetic energy (KE) and drop size distribution (DSD). The output from the two sensors was logged in two notebook computers. The rainfall intensity was measured using tipping-bucket rain gauge installed beside the KE and DSD sensors. The direct measured KE has been compared to estimated KE using DSD data and four empirical fall velocity equations. The result from this study revealed that the piezoelectric transducer has a high potential for direct rainfall kinetic energy measurement and erosivity evaluation.

Chapter 9 - The Northeast of Brazil (NEB) shows high climate variability, ranging from semiarid regions with an annual rainfall below 500 mm to a rainy climate in the coastland with annual rainfall exceeding 1500 mm. The rainfall regimes are heterogeneous in space-temporal scales. According to the latest report of the Intergovernmental Panel on Climate Change (IPCC, AR4), the NEB is highly susceptible to climate change, and also heavy rainfall events (HRE). However, few climatology studies about these episodes were performed, thus the objective of the study was to compute the climatology of the episodes number and the daily rainfall rate associated with HRE; relate them to the normal rainfall events (NRE) and weak rainfall events (WRE). This study analyzed eight NEB states, excluding Bahia due to its different rainfall regime. The daily rainfall data of the hydrometeorological network managed by the Agência Nacional de Águas (ANA), from 1972 to 2002, contains accounting from 219 rain gauges. The authors applied the technique of quantiles to identify the rainfall episodes. The authors selected HRE, NRE and WRE where at least one rain gauge recorded precipitation above the 95th percentile, between 45th and 55th percentiles, and below the 5th percentile, respectively. The data distribution concerning the events was divided by seasons (DJF, MAM, JJA, SON). The linear trend in the number of events and the annual precipitation daily rate was analyzed using the Mann-Kendall. The results showed an increase in the number of cases and the intensity of WRE and the intensity of HRE, with a statistical confidence level above 95%. In addition the NRE showed a decrease in intensity during the JJA quarter (dry season). The results also suggest that climate change is altering the climatology of rainfall of the NEB, increasing extreme events (heavy and weak), weakening the normal events and increasing the HRE during the wet season.

Chapter 10 - In this chapter it is presented a comparative study of some methods to estimate radar rainfall in real time. Radar rainfall estimates have a poor performance comparatively to rain gauge estimates, due to errors of either meteorological or instrumental nature. Nevertheless, weather radar presents several advantages over rain gauges, namely by providing continuous measurements in real time, which it is not possible even in a dense telemetered rain gauge network, due to the large space-time variability of precipitation. Given these advantages, several approaches have been proposed to minimize radar errors. Namely, the combination of these two types of measurements via a state space representation associated to the Kalman filter has been investigated in recent years. However, recent literature presents different state space representations, and therefore their results are not directly comparable. This work intends to discuss and compare different state space formulations based on a same data set; for instance, the comparison between the modeling of the mean field radar rainfall logarithmic bias, a linear radar-rain gauge calibration model and a power law model. This investigation takes into account some issues associated to the state space approach: for instance, parameters estimation, the assessment of the accuracy estimates obtained by.

In: Rainfall: Behavior, Forecasting and Distribution
Editors: Olga E. Martín and Tricia M. Roberts
ISBN: 978-1-62081-551-9

Chapter 1

COPING WITH RAINFALL VARIABILITY IN NORTHERN TANZANIA

Sara Trærup*
UNEP Risø Centre, Denmark

ABSTRACT

This chapter explores a potential relationship between rainfall data and household self-reported harvest shocks and local (spatial) variability of harvest shocks and coping strategies based on a survey of 2700 rural households in the Kagera region of northern Tanzania. In addition, correlations of rainfall amounts across the districts in the region are estimated in order to assess the variations in rainfall patterns across the districts. The results show that rainfall patterns in the region are very location-specific, there are few correlations between rainfall events, and that the distribution of household reported harvest shocks differs significantly between districts and correspond to the observed variability in local climate patterns.

Coping strategies are focused on spreading risks and include reduced consumption, casual employment, new crops, external support and the selling of assets. There are no large differences in applied coping strategies across the region, but district-level data demonstrate how local strategies differ between localities within the districts. The results emphasize that in order to target rural policies and make them efficient, it is important to take into account the local conditions that rural households face when experiencing climate-related shocks.

Finally, shocks reported by households appear to correspond well with observed variability in rainfall patterns.

Keywords: climate variability, self-reported shocks, coping strategies, local rainfall distribution, Tanzania

---

* Corresponding Author:UNEP Risø Centre, P.O. Box 49, 4000 Roskilde, Denmark. Phone: +45 46775177. Email: slmt@dtu.dk

INTRODUCTION

Climate change presents a new type of challenge for development. It is by now widely acknowledged that climate change impacts amplify existing unfavourable conditions for developing countries (McCarthy et al. 2001). It is also acknowledged that poor populations are more vulnerable and have less adaptive capacity to confront such changes (Swart and Cohen 2003). Countries with a lack of resources, poor infrastructure, and unstable institutions have little capacity to adapt and are highly vulnerable (Smit and Pilifosova 2001). These factors are intrinsically linked with those promoting sustainable development that aims to improve living conditions and access to resources. Therefore, development planning and strategies have an important role in strengthening the adaptive capacities of societies at various levels.

Adverse effects of climate change are determined not only by the changing climate but also by the sensitivity of human and natural systems to these changes. The need for human (and natural) systems to adapt to changes in climate is not new, and humans are not powerless victims in response to changes and risks (Scoones et al. 1996; Christoplos et al. 2001; Roncoli et al. 2001). Climate variability and droughts are already important stress factors in Africa, where rural households have adapted to such factors for decades (Mortimore and Adams 2001; Mertz et al. 2009a), and in extreme dry regions households have even moved 'beyond climate' dependence (Nielsen and Reenberg 2010). Thomas et al. (2007) found that dry spells cause farmers to shift away from cropping to livestock holding. In Mali, Lacy et al. (2006) revealed a tendency for a shortening of the rainy season to induce farmers to shift some of their sorghum production to a variety with a shorter cycle than the traditional one. In a study from Burkina Faso, Nielsen and Reenberg (2010) found rain-fed cereal production to be declining due to a change in climate and a shift towards a higher level of dependence on migration, livestock, small-scale commerce and gardens. In East Africa, the sub-Saharan El Niño rains cause floods and destruction, while in the recent years droughts have also had catastrophic impacts. Consequently, harvest failure and incidents of food insecurity have become regular events occurring at least once or twice every decade and have been identified as consisting of a convergence of social and political as well as natural factors (Eriksen et al. 2005).

Rural households are likely to experience greater uncertainty in their rural production, and the negative shocks and trends from increased climate variability will affect rural livelihoods, thus exposing rural household welfare to greater levels of risk (Cooper et al. 2008; Paxson 1993; Udry 1994; Alderman 1996; Lim and Townsend 1998; Deaton 1991; Alderman and Paxson 1994; Fafchamps and Lund 2003; Kazianga and Udry 2006). Existing coping strategies, repeated over longer periods, can degenerate the asset base and even amplify households' vulnerability to climate change impacts. Consequently, household welfare is most likely to be depreciated.

Adger and Brooks (2003, p. 21) have interpreted the human ability to respond to climate change as involving 'socially determined futures over which there is a degree of space for action'. Determining the degree to which systems are sensitive and capable of adapting is the topic of a growing literature on both national and international agendas, though finding good indicators for the capacity to adapt to climate change has proved difficult (Vincent 2007). Singling out the driving forces and causalities that link vulnerability, poverty and climate variability remains a complex matter, and development policies aiming to reduce vulnerability to climate change variability still seem to be quite similar to traditional economic development policies. For example, studies aiming to identify measures that reduce rural households' vulnerability to climate variability often recommend drought preparedness, affordable grain, locally adapted seed varieties, improvement of access to markets for production inputs, promotion of investment incentives, weather forecasts and access to micro credit (Mortimore 2006; Roncoli et al. 2001; Lacy et al. 2006).

IPCC (2007) has defined vulnerability to climate change impacts as the degree to which a system is susceptible and unable to cope with the adverse effects of climate change. The key parameters of vulnerability are the stress to which a system is exposed, its sensitivity and its adaptive capacity. Thus, the vulnerability of a household will determine its ability to respond to and recover from the shocks. Usual household activities may not yield sufficient income when a large negative shock occurs, especially not if frequency of shocks increases. Studies have reported high income variability related to risks of various forms associated with fluctuations in crop yields (Townsend 1994; Kinsey et al. 1998). In a situation where all the households in a community, district or region are affected, the local income-earning activities are likely to be unavailable or insufficient. In such a situation, relying on the support of family members or others may not be possible unless they have migrated and can contribute with remittances. Here, formal or informal insurance transfers (credit or insurance) from outside the community are necessary, while inter-temporal transfers (e.g. the depletion of individual or community-level savings) are also possible. Besides seeking assistance, households may also pursue other activities as part of their coping strategies. Many examples, including temporary migration to find jobs, longer workdays, collecting wild foods and collecting forest products for sale are reported (e.g. Thornton et al. 2007; Davies 1996; De Waal 1987).

Based on these previous studies, it becomes evident that most households succeed in protecting their immediate consumption from the full effects of income shocks. In the long term, nevertheless, these shocks have consequences for low-income households, which are forced to, for example, reduce their investment in children's health and schooling, or sell productive assets in order to maintain consumption. Therefore, an argument can be raised for targeting policies to increase most vulnerable households' ability to resist and respond to income shocks. To provide targeted policies, it is necessary to identify, and differ between, conditions that make households vulnerable, besides being poor. Difference in access to basic resources such as water, infrastructure and public facilities are recognized as major contributors to differences in household welfare. Nevertheless, little work exists to explore the degree of variation from one locality to another. While these types of studies have been limited mainly by lack of adequate data and resources, studies by Merrey et al. (2005), Kristjanson et al. (2005) and Okwi et al. (2007) suggest that policies need to target local specificities to be effective. As a continuation of their work and recognizing that vulnerability of a society to climate variability is influenced by its development path, the physical exposures, the distribution of resources and the institutional setting, this chapter aims to explore local patterns of climate variability and potential impacts from this on local communities. Recognition of discrepancies in local factors may prove essential in designing both local and national policies with the aim to reduce poverty and improve households' ability to respond to climate variability and associated shocks. Research has also shown that there will be little divergence between the impacts due to climate variability and climate change. Therefore, studies of present-day vulnerabilities to climate variability contribute to improving the understanding of the impact of long-term climate change and of measures to facilitate adaptation (Smit et al. 2000; Kelly and Adger 2000).

To further explore the local discrepancies of rainfall patterns, the chapter further analyses the correlation between failures of rainfall in different localities within a limited geographical area. Moreover, the chapter will also compare households' self-reported harvest shocks against recorded rainfall data.

A growing body of literature contrasts local perceptions and scientific records on climate data in Africa. Ovuka and Lindquist (2000) identified coherence between Kenyan farmers' perceptions of decreasing trend in rainfall and recorded monthly and annual rainfall data. Also, Thomas et al. (2007) found rural households in South Africa to recognize changes in climate, and then respond to these changes. In Burkina Faso, West et al. (2008) found rural households' perceptions about a decrease over the last 30 years in both the overall seasonal rainfall and the number of 'big rains' during the rainy season to corroborate with rainfall record. Results from Senegal (Mertz et al. 2009b) also point in the direction of corroboration between actual and perceived evidence on rainfall. As a contrast to these studies, Meze-Hausken (2004) found no evidence of correlation between peoples' perceptions and recorded rainfall data from Ethiopia.

Consequently, the objective of this chapter is to explore to what extent rural households report shocks to income arising from rainfall variability and to explore how rainfall patterns vary and correlate from one locality to another. Furthermore, the chapter looks into the local spatial patterns of how households cope after a shock and links the spatial distribution of coping strategies with environmental conditions. This will provide some basic background which could benefit policy-makers in targeting interventions with regard to rural extension services etc. The chapter is organized as follows. Section 2 presents the local context of the research area. This includes an introduction of local conditions at district level. Section 3 introduces the applied data and methodology and section 4 analyses the results and provides a discussion of these. Finally, section 5 concludes.

Local Context

The Kagera region is the remotest region from the administrative center of Dar es Salaam in Tanzania, situated in the northwestern part of Tanzania by the shores of Lake Victoria and borders Rwanda, Burundi and Uganda (Figure 1). Kagera has a varied topography, with tropical vegetation, including forests and wide-open grasslands.

Large parts of the region are characterized by low soil fertility and – mainly in areas near and along the lake shores – soil erosion on sloping land is another problem (URT 2003). Nonetheless, the region produced between 1996/1995 and 2000/2001 an annual surplus of 681,000 tons of starch food (URT 2003). It is, however, the region in Tanzania with the lowest per capita GDP and 29 percent of all households in Kagera live below the basic needs poverty line (URT 2002b). The rainfall pattern in Kagera is bimodal, with annual rainfall ranging from 1000 to 2000 mm. The rainy seasons are defined as March-April-May (long rainy season) and October-November-December (short rainy season).

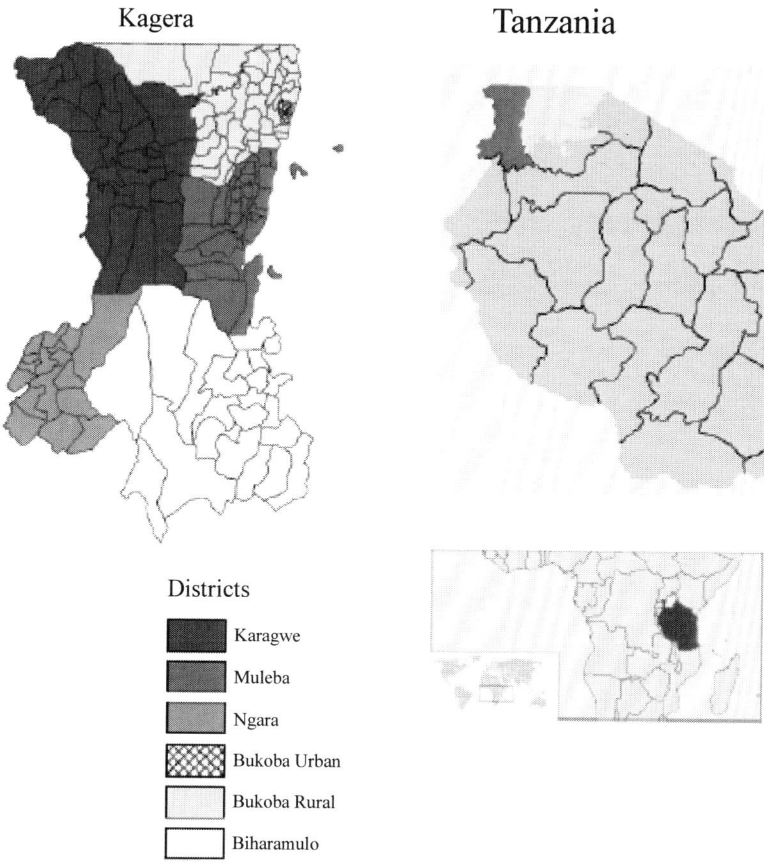

Figure 1. Districts in Kagera region.

In the long rainy season, the data used in this chapter shows that Kagera receives on average 41 percent of total annual rainfall, while the short rainy season receives on average 32 percent. The remaining 27 percent falls mainly in January and February. Table 1 presents a summary of the recorded rainfall data for Kagera as a total mean and for the respective districts. Rainfall varies in between the districts. Karagwe in the north experiences large variability from year to year, with a 1600 mm disparity, while Ngara in the south, on the contrary, receives significantly less average rainfall, but with less variability both within rain seasons and between years.

The population of Kagera is approximately two and a half million people (URT 2009). The population density varies between the six districts of Biharamulo, Bukoba Rural, Bukoba Urban, Karagwe, Muleba and Ngara (Figure 1 and Table 2). Bukoba Urban is excluded from the analysis in this chapter where the focus is on rural areas given that urban and rural households have different vulnerabilities and livelihood strategies.

The livelihoods of the rural population in Kagera are primarily based on a range of rain-fed annual crops such as maize, sorghum and tobacco in the south and bananas and coffee in the north. Capital investments are minimal and rural households use mainly traditional cultivation methods and tools, with land and labour as the principal factors of production. In some parts of Kagera, land ownership is customary. For example the land belongs to a clan and clan members approve any agreement related to selling of land.

Table 1. Recorded rainfall data in Kagera Region and districts from 1980 to 2003

	Bihara-mulo	Bukoba Rural	Karagwe	Muleba	Ngara	Kagera
Long season						
Mean rainfall	477	754	543	700	414	624
% total	38	42	39	43	41	41
Min rainfall	200	534	256	409	252	368
Max rainfall	975	1160	1038	1671	598	1106
Short season						
Mean rainfall	418	546	490	511	414	485
% total	34	30	35	31	41	32
Min rainfall	207	336	214	256	252	255
Max rainfall	724	777	1004	1023	598	862
Yearly						
Mean rainfall	1243	1799	1400	1637	1008	1508
Min rainfall	846	1109	795	1113	760	1024
Max rainfall	1390	2259	2338	3080	1387	2166

Source: own calculations based on Kagera Health and Development Survey (KHDS). The KHDS data and documents are available at http://www.worldbank.org/lsms/.

Table 2. Main characteristics of Rural Kagera region

	Bihara-mulo	Bukoba Rural	Karagwe	Muleba	Ngara	Rural Kagera total
Pop. density (person/km^2) [1]	46	73	56	155	76	81
Mean per capita annual expenditure (USD 2004) [2]	110	175	181	166	141	155
Cultivated area (ha.) per household [2]	0.39	0.95*	2.22	0.67	0.99	0.85
Estimated area under maize production (ha) of total area under food crop production (%)[5]	29.1	19.5	29.7	10.2	11.4	16.5
Literacy rate (%)[1]	51	68	61	61	50	58
Size (km^2) [1]	8,938	5,450	7,558	2,499	4,428	28,873
Weather stations [2]	2	7	5	4	2	20
Annual total rainfall (mm) [4]	1243	1708	1400	1637	1008	1400

The table shows total and district characteristic for Rural Kagera. Data is based on [1] URT (2002a), [2] KHDS, [4] long term average (1980 – 2003) based on KHDS, [5]URT (2003).

These aspects render agricultural production in the region, and thus rural livelihoods, highly dependent on the agricultural potential of land resources, water availability, the availability of land and access to local markets.

All these factors vary a great deal between the districts, with Ngara having the lowest degree of population density, agricultural potential and market access. The districts in rural Kagera are characterized by intra-district heterogeneity in livelihood vulnerabilities and opportunities (Kessy (2005), De Weerdt 2008, and EDI (2004)). Households in the northern district, Karagwe, may benefit economically from its geographical location. The slopes make transportation of agricultural products to the local markets burdensome, but roads leading into Uganda and market centers are relatively good. Karagwe is also the most highly populated district together with Bukoba Rural. After crop production, livestock keeping is the major income generating activity in Karagwe. Also households in Bukoba Rural gain from access to markets in Uganda where livelihoods are mainly based on banana and coffee growing. Because of the location next to Lake Victoria, households in Bukoba Rural have access to fishing, which is the second most important income generating activity in the district after agriculture. Likewise, households in Muleba districts also gain from fishing opportunities, as a supplement to agriculture, and have relatively good market access to the center in Bukoba Urban. At the same time population density is quite high and contributes to existence of local markets and trade.

The poorest district in Kagera is Biharamulo which is located in the southern part of the region. Soil quality is poor and rainfall is well below the Kagera average. As a contrast to households in the northern districts, who base their livelihoods to a large extent on banana/coffee farming systems, households in Biharamulo rely generally on sorghum/coffee/cotton farming systems. Tobacco production is increasing after a collapse of coffee and cotton markets. Ngara is the second poorest district in the region and it is the least populated district. It has little rainfall and low soil quality. These factors render agricultural production difficult in Ngara, but the district has the advantage of relatively good market access, not least to markets in Rwanda and Burundi. A livelihood system based on banana and coffee farming together with fishing activities enable households to sustain income and food security even during years with large anomalies in weather patterns. In districts where households mainly rely on agriculture for income and food intake, households would be expected to be more vulnerable to sudden or unexpected shocks to income and crops. Such heterogeneities surely exist not only between districts but also between households within each district.

In Tanzania, there are a number of key institutional structures and policy instruments in place at municipal level, including municipal land-use planning integrating perspectives on exposure to natural hazards, risk and emergency plans, and climate and energy plans. The proposed projects under the National Adaptation Programme of Action (NAPA) in Tanzania is planned to be implemented with high level ministries, such as Ministry of Agriculture and Food Security, but in cooperation with Local Government authority, Tanzania Meteorology Authority, local communities, and NGOs. This may provide a basis for an increase in capacity at local scales in order to cope with climate change as well as it could increase formal responsibilities for land-use and other planning. Local level vulnerability assessments could in this way be a key instrument for municipalities and may pave the way for integrating climate change perspectives in local governance. However, at this stage the NAPA assessment of vulnerabilities and adaptation strategies focus on country level factors and therefore may miss out on local complexity and lead to too generalized conclusions.

Data and Methodology

The analysis is based on household survey data from the Kagera Health and Development Survey (KHDS) for 2004, which covered over 2700 households. The KHDS data and documents are available at http://www.worldbank.org/lsms/. The KHDS was originally adapted from the World Bank's Living Standards Measurement Study (LSMS) questionnaires.

A concern arising from using the KHDS dataset for analyzing households' income shocks and coping strategies is that the section on income shocks in the KHDS is based on households' perceptions of a shock to income. Using self-reported shocks may contain some weaknesses, as self-reported shocks are by definition subjective and dependent on the perceptions of the individual included in the sample. This implies that one individual might report an occurrence of harvest failure, while another household in the same community, or even in the same household, might perceive the situation differently and thus not report any occurrence of harvest failure. Also, it is not possible to draw conclusions regarding the length of the hardship. And even though five opportunities for answers were provided regarding whether households had a good or bad year, the affirmative answers may still cover heterogeneous responses (Tesliuc and Lindert 2004). For example, some households in the same area may have lost most of their harvest and thereby a large potential income share due to heavy rains during or after the harvest season because they had only limited storage capacity. On the other hand, other households in the same area could also have reported the shock, but did not experience as large a negative impact to income and experienced less loss than the other households as they were able to store their harvest properly, away from the rains. These types of differences in responses cannot be extracted from the survey and will be a weakness that must be acknowledged in the analysis.

The analysis in this chapter was mainly carried out at district level, this being justified by the differences in rainfall patterns within the region and because rural households rely heavily on agricultural production, which is closely linked to rainfall quantity and distribution. The KHDS data refers to administrative districts before 2000 (after which Bukoba Rural and Biharamulo were subdivided).

To examine if intra-district differences in climate variability can be verified, an analysis is carried out to investigate correlation of weather events in between districts. Negative weather events can be related to minimum temperature for a specific period of time; amount of rainfall during a specific time period, whether there has been excess rain or a lack of rain; and lastly, reaching a certain wind speed related to hurricanes. Since rainfall is the main uncertainty in Kagera and water deficits adversely affect crop yields in rain-fed agriculture, a rainfall deficit of ten percent during short and long rains season respectively, will be used to reflect intra-district differences.

Monthly rainfall data was obtained from the KHDS. The data covers the period from 1980 to 2004 collected from a total of 20 rainfall stations distributed between the rural districts in the region. The stations are spatially distributed with 2 stations in Biharamulo, 7 in

Bukoba Rural, 5 in Karagwe, 4 in Muleba and 2 in Ngara. Comparison with longer time-series of rainfall and reports from FAO indicates well coherence with the KHDS rainfall data. The year 2004 lacks a number of observations from Biharamulo, Ngara and Muleba. In addition, Biharamulo lacks three observations from 1999 and one each from 1993, 1997 and 2000. Bukoba Rural lacks one observation each from 2001 and 2004. Based on this, year 2004 was removed from the analysis, while the remaining missing observations were accounted for during the analyses. Temperature is also important for agricultural production, but mainly for long-term changes in agricultural potential (Lobell et al. 2008; Liu et al. 2008). Therefore, temperature is omitted in this chapter, the focus being on short-term shocks.

RESULT AND DISCUSSION

Rainfall Variability and Shocks to Household Income

The shocks that households in Kagera have reported are primarily related to death, harvest failure and illness (Table 3). This chapter is limited to examining shocks defined as low income due to poor harvests of agricultural crops caused by unfavorable weather conditions, since these can be expected to be linked more or less directly to climate variability. This type of shock will hereafter be referred to as a harvest shock.

Shocks related to death, illness, low crop prices and lost wage employment can also be linked to climate variability, but the links are less direct and difficult to examine. Examples include increases in the incidence of malaria, which are major contributors to illness and deaths and have been attributed to increased climate variability in several studies (WHO 2003; Zhou et al. 2004; Wandiga et al. 2006; Abeko et al. 2003). Crop prices and employment opportunities are, among other things, influenced by agricultural productivity. Prices are affected by supply (crop yields and market access), while demands for labor are affected by seasonal fluctuations.

Table 3. Distribution of shocks reported by households in Kagera 1994-2003

	Death in family	Low harvest, weather	Serious illness	Loss of assets	Low crop prices	Wage employ-ment lost	Other	N
Biharamulo	20	28	37	4	2	2	7	50
Bukoba rural	48	14	14	3	3	3	14	385
Karagwe	26	33	16	4	6	2	13	140
Muleba	34	15	14	9	6	8	12	181
Ngara	24	40	16	5	1	1	13	146
Rural Kagera	31	22	18	6	5	5	13	
N	275	230	157	51	48	30	111	902

Source: own calculation based on KHDS 2004. The numbers are presented in percentage of total number of shocks within each district.

During the ten-year recall period for the KHDS, the overall distribution of reported harvest shocks by households in Kagera (Table 4) gives the impression that 2000 and 2003 were the years with the least favourable weather conditions for producing crops. The years 2000 and 2003 dominate, with almost fifty percent of the total number of recorded harvest shocks. Nevertheless, looking into the data at district-level it reveals a different tendency, with harvest shocks being unevenly distributed between the districts. The distribution of reported harvest shocks appears very much district-specific, with considerable variations between both years and districts (Table 4). Three districts in particular, Bukoba Rural, Karagwe and Ngara, have high frequencies of reported harvest shocks.

There may be a wide number of reasons for this, such as farm mismanagement, pest attacks, or even illnesses and deaths in the family. Nonetheless, if Table 4 is compared with Figure 2, it appears that the distribution of households reporting harvest shocks seems to be associated with variability in rainfall. Figure 2 shows rainfall anomalies on an annual and seasonal basis. The Figure also reflects the distribution of shocks presented in Table 4. Assuming that there is a correlation between the frequency of households reporting harvest shocks and rainfall patterns, harvest shocks seem to be associated with variability in terms of excessive rains in a season, dry spells and cumulated patterns, the latter meaning that excessive rains in one year can result in households reporting harvest shocks in the forthcoming year.

The rainfall data show large disparities in rainfall patterns between the districts. Overall, households reporting harvest-related income shocks are over-represented in districts with relatively large annual and seasonal variability: Karagwe, Bukoba Rural, Ngara and Muleba. In the district with relatively stable rainfall patterns, Biharamulo, the frequency of households reporting shocks is low. The trends in rainfall patterns based on the data from 1980 to 2004 point towards a shift in onset of rainfall and general patterns. With the exception of Biharamulo, where rainfall has remained almost stable, all districts have experienced an increase in amount of rainfall. The period outside the rainy seasons from June to September remains relatively dry, while, except for Biharamulo, the January-February rainfall trend shows a large increase especially in January rainfall. Especially Bukoba Rural has an increasing trend in amount of rainfall for the two rainy seasons as well as the January-February rains.

Table 4. District harvest shock distribution. The numbers represent percentage of actual number of households reporting very bad income shocks caused by harvest failure within each district

	1994	1995	1996	1997	1998	1999	2000	2001	2002	2003	N
Biharamulo	7	7	0	7	27	7	0	0	13	33	15
Bukoba R	5	5	4	16	16	5	10	3	4	32	77
Karagwe	9	9	13	2	7	7	33	7	4	11	46
Muleba	3	3	3	21	3	0	6	3	9	50	34
Ngara	5	2	0	5	2	3	54	8	12	8	59
Rural Kagera	6	5	4	10	9	4	25	5	7	25	231

Source: own calculations based on KHDS.

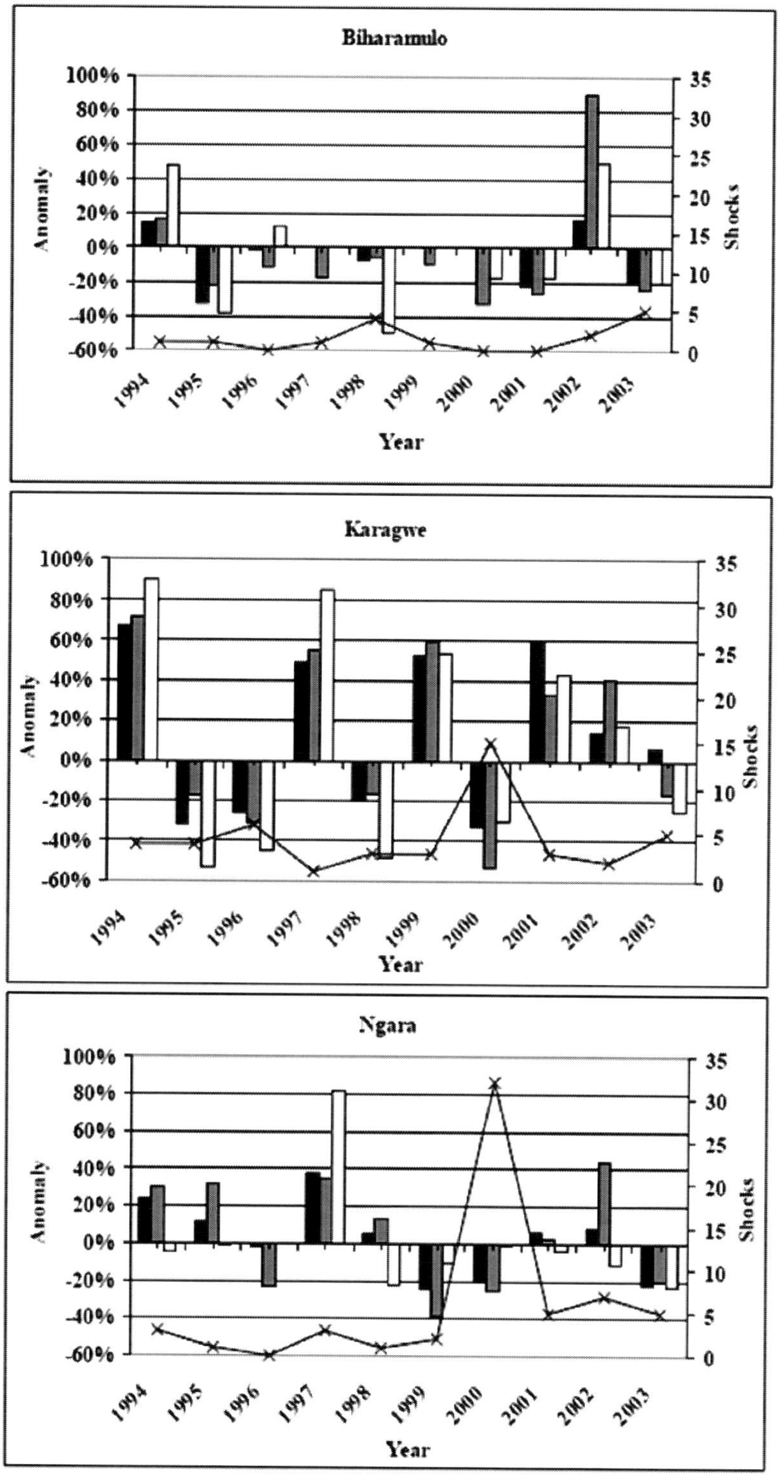

Figure 2. (Continued).

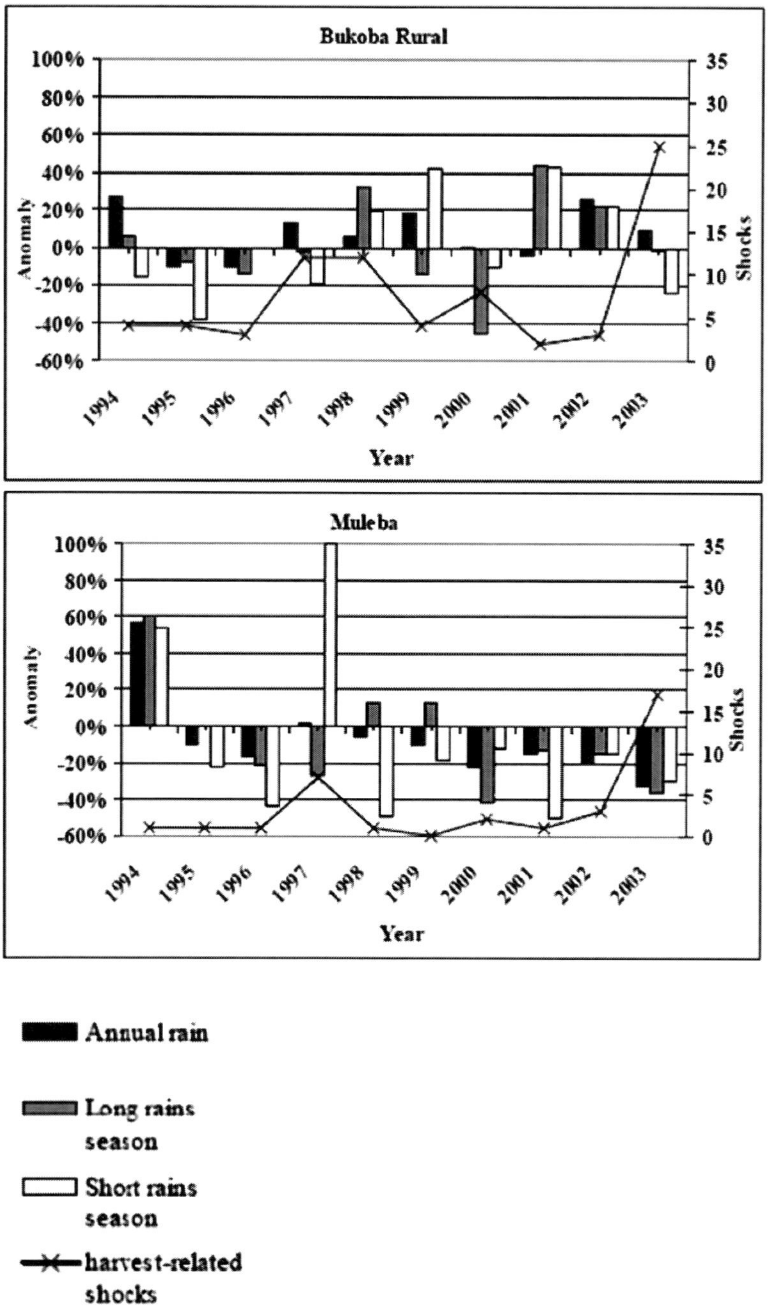

Figure 2. Rainfall anomalies.

District rainfall anomalies calculated based on deviation from the medium-term district mean rainfall records (1980-2003) received in any given year. The lines are associated with the secondary x-axis and show the frequency of households for each district who reported harvest shocks in respective years. Source: own calculations based on KHDS.

Unfortunately, the number of observations with regard to households reporting harvest shocks is too limited to allow a statistical analysis of the relationship between shocks and rainfall patterns. Nevertheless, it is possible to calculate the correlation of historical rainfall patterns at district level based on the available data from the district weather stations.

Generally, the rainfall statistics for Kagera showed the rainfall deficit to be correlated only among some of the districts in the region. This suggests that a lack of rainfall will only affect few districts at the same point in time. Table 5 and Table 6 provide the results of a correlation analysis for a ten percent deficit in rainfall compared to historical average (1980-2003) for the two rain seasons. The calculations show that shortfalls in rainfall in Ngara are only correlated with the amount of rainfall in Biharamulo. On the other hand, the rainfall amount in Muleba is correlated with amounts in two districts, Bukoba Rural and Karagwe.

Holding the results from the correlation analysis of rainfall patterns against the data on reported shocks gives the impression that there are other complementary factors than rainfall which play a role in households being vulnerable to rainfall deficit. This is also being seen in the light of the trend with an over-representation of households reporting harvest-related shocks with relatively large annual and seasonal variability in rainfall.

For example, rainfall in Biharamulo and Ngara is correlated, however it does not seem that frequency of reported shocks follows the same trend. This might be because rainfall in Biharamulo is relatively stable compared to Ngara. Even though rainfall patterns follow the same trend the anomalies might be smaller in Biharamulo.

Table 5. Correlation coefficients matrix for events with 10 percent deficit in rainfall, long rains season (March – May), Kagera districts 1980-2003

	Biharamulo	Bukoba Rural	Karagwe	Muleba	Ngara
Biharamulo	1.00	0.251	0.333	0.258	0.458*
Bukoba Rural	0.251	1.000	0.418*	0.669*	0.222
Karagwe	0.333	0.418*	1.000	0.430*	0.275
Muleba	0.258	0.669*	0.430*	1.000	0.118
Ngara	0.458*	0.222	0.275	0.118	1.00

Source: Own computations based on KHDS. The table is based on an analysis of 10 percent deficit in rainfall (mm) compared to long term average (1980 – 2003) for the same period. *means significance at 5 percent level.

Table 6. Correlation coefficients matrix for events with 10 percent deficit in rainfall, short rains season (October – December), Kagera districts 1980-2003

Parameter	Biharamulo	Bukoba Rural	Karagwe	Muleba	Ngara
Biharamulo	1.000	0.302	0.270	0.375	0.143
Bukoba Rural	0.302	1.000	0.302	0.389*	0.066
Karagwe	0.270	0.302	1.000	0.375	0.143
Muleba	0.375	0.389*	0.375	1.000	0.199
Ngara	0.143	0.066	0.143	0.199	1.000

Source: Own computations based on KHDS. The table is based on an analysis of 10 percent deficit in rainfall (mm) compared to long term average (1980 – 2003) for the same period. *means significance at 5 percent level.

In addition, Ngara might be less worse off in case of rainfall deficit because of the better market access households have in comparison to market access in Biharamulo. Better market access means that rural households may be able to sell the products that they have at a higher price at markets, if the supply is little, and they might also feel the hardship less, when they have access to alternative food supplies themselves.

One conclusion, which can be drawn from this, is that large local differences exist between the districts. Rainfall variability and shock distribution both vary, and aggregated data for Kagera does not provide valuable information at the regional level for policy-makers.

Household Coping Strategies

The term coping is sometimes used as a synonym for adaptation (Fankhauser, 1998), but coping measures are usually regarded as short-term responses to avert immediate threats (Berry 1989; Ellis 1998; Huq and Reid 2004; Vogel 1998), in opposition to adaptation, which requires adjustments in practices to continuous or permanent changes.

Over time, rural households develop a range of coping strategies as a buffer against uncertainties in their rural production induced by annual variations in rainfall combined with socio-economic drivers of change (Cooper et al. 2008). These coping strategies spread risk and aim to reduce the negative impacts on household welfare from income shocks due to harvest failures. In order to identify responses related to climate change impacts, coping must be considered in the context of extraordinary situations or extreme events that are the consequences of climate change. If coping strategies are integrated into a household's livelihood strategy, the household must be assumed not to be adapted to the conditions it is confronting. That said, it should be kept in mind that coping strategies are relative. Selling chickens in the market may be one household's livelihood strategy, while for another household it may be a coping strategy caused by harvest failure, forcing the household to sell off its productive assets.

Based on qualitative data, Kessy (2005) identified a number of strategies among households in rural Kagera for coping with a sudden or anticipated shock. Among the most important strategies were depletion of assets, namely selling livestock, especially goats and agricultural produce. Also mortgaging land was mentioned as a coping strategy, whereas selling land is very rare, partly due to the local land tenure in Kagera as described previously in this chapter. The majority of households in Kagera do not have many assets to deplete and depend on their land to counter shocks. For example, a respondent in Kessy (2005) experienced a severe storm that destroyed all his banana plants. As a coping strategy he planted short term crops such as sweet potatoes, and beans to take them through while waiting for the bananas to mature. Consequently, the dependency of land makes mortgaging of land problematic and may push households further down the poverty ladder. Lack of assets further contributes to the vulnerability of poor households since it is rarely possible to borrow money without collateral.

For an anticipated shock which provides households with time to react, households could either seek employment, make local brew or borrow money from relatives and friends. Alternatively, households who own cattle could go to nearby cattle markets to sell their cattle. At the market, the sellers get a better price compared to selling to a rich man in the village. In such a situation access to markets is of great importance. However, in case of a community wide shock, households would borrow money or seek remittances from households in nearby villages. The importance of remittances from children residing elsewhere has increased the interest among households in Kagera to invest in children's schooling as insurance for parents' old age. The majority of households also referred to "do nothing" in case of a community wide shock. Only a few households were found to accumulate savings.

Banks are absent, and keeping too much cash in the household is perceived as dangerous because of the risks of theft and fire. Lastly, assistance from government or non-governmental organizations was mentioned as inevitable during community wide shocks. Lundberg et al. (2005) found evidence that the poorer households in Kagera mainly rely on private remittance relative to the better off households who have better access to more formal credit institutions. Such evidence highlights the importance of improving access to formalized credit due to the risk of hardship not only affecting one village but several neighbouring villages which face the same climate conditions.

In the KHDS questionnaire, households were asked how they coped after a harvest shock. The responses are shown in Table 7 and correspond well with the strategies identified in Kessy (2005). In four of the six districts, reduced consumption is the most important coping strategy. Reduced consumption is most likely associated with the strategy of "do nothing" as mentioned by Kessy (2005). In the two remaining districts, Biharamulo and Muleba, casual employment is the most important strategy. In the four districts where reduced consumption is the most important strategy, casual employment is the second most reported strategy. Support from others, or remittances, shows up as an important coping strategy in most districts.

The introduction of alternative crops also plays an important role and must be considered a preventive strategy, one that assumes unfavourable production conditions for the next season. Looking into the data, again there are large disparities between the districts. Karagwe and Bukoba Rural, which are the main producers of banana and coffee, have the lowest percentages of households reporting the introduction of new crops as a coping strategy. In these districts fifty percent of nutrition intake comes from bananas (Gallez et al. 2004), while coffee production is a major cash crop contributing substantially to rural incomes (URT, 2003).

Table 7. Households' main coping strategies for harvest shocks in rural Kagera, 1994-2003

Coping strategy	Biharamulo	Bukoba Rural	Karagwe	Muleba	Ngara	Rural Kagera	N
Reduced consumption	33	40	37	24	69	44	102
Casual employment	47	35	30	41	37	36	84
Introduction of other crops	33	19	11	32	20	21	48
Support from others	13	21	22	18	14	18	42
Sale of assets	13	16	17	12	19	16	37
N	27	122	84	60	104		397

Source: Own calculation based on KHDS. The table gives percentages of total number of households in each district reporting a harvest-related shock.

Households in Kagera that produce bananas and coffee are less likely to diversify their farming activities and more prone to fall into poverty (DeWeerdt 2008). In the southern districts, where production mainly relies on annual rain-fed crops such as maize, sorghum and tobacco, which are easier to substitute than coffee and banana, there seems to be a tendency for households to be more likely to introduce new crops as a response to harvest failure. The available data do not permit us to identify the new crop varieties which are being introduced.

However, evidence from the literature suggests that uncertainty of rainfall patterns generally causes households to behave differently from how they would have done if the weather was known (Phillips et al. 2000; Mendelsohn et al. 2007). This uncertainty generally leads households to choose crops that will resist larger weather extremes and are tolerant of weather variations, but most often their yields are lower, and farmers invest in a lower level of inputs than the optimal, due to the risk of losing the investment. Lack of communication of seasonal forecasts and inadequate extension services in Kagera further contribute to inefficient agricultural practices.

Kessy (2005) notes that despite the presence of agricultural extension officers, information on good crop husbandry are generally not extended to a majority of farmers. Previous efforts from Africa have shown that access to climate information can be effective and contribute to reduce vulnerability of rural livelihoods to climate variability (Patt and Gwata 2002; Patt et al. 2007; Ziervogel 2004). Communication of seasonal forecasts should be addressed in any regional or district policy guidance, especially with a view towards mid-season review.

An extension officer can also draw attention to the role of the following year's soil and crop management subsequent to an abnormally wet or dry year. As a consequence of the different household responses between districts, the need to target policies to the local conditions that households are facing is emphasized.

In areas where households are likely to introduce new crops, improved information on future seasonal patterns and supervision of suitable crops with expected seasonal rainfall patterns could turn out to be beneficial. In areas where households are less likely to introduce other crops, policies on the management of current crops could prove valuable.

In both situations shorter-term seasonal weather forecasting would reduce the uncertainty of weather patterns and hence the risk of less beneficial decision making. It has been demonstrated that farmers in both East and West Africa see opportunities to benefit from seasonal weather forecasts (Rao and Okwach 2005; Roncoli et al. 2009).

Conclusion

This chapter has focused on rainfall variability and self-reported harvest shocks. With regards to shocks, the analysis indicated coherence between the number of shocks and anomalies in rainfall patterns with relatively large annual and seasonal variability both in terms of modest and excessive rains. Furthermore, the results of the analysis of harvest shocks showed large discrepancies between districts in the distribution of shocks. The rainfall data further revealed large local divergences in rainfall patterns, with dissimilarities in both magnitude and seasonal or annual variability between districts. This was further emphasized through a correlation analysis which revealed few correlations between rainfall patterns. Also, districts with more rainfall and large seasonal variability experienced more shocks than districts with less rainfall and less seasonal variability.

The conclusion of this analysis is that the timing of rainfall appears to affect the distribution of harvest shocks more than the magnitude of annual precipitation. However, this could not be statistically proven due to data limitations. A change in timing of rainfall would nonetheless encourage mid-season planning strategies to take advantage of the increasing trend in rainfall outside regular rainfall seasons. A change in timing of rainfall together with extreme rainfall events, including both drought and excessive rains, also emphasize the increasing need for multi-year planning.

The local differences between the districts are further emphasized in the analysis of coping strategies that households follow in response to harvest shocks. While the results for the region as a whole do not reveal great differences in applied strategies, district-level data demonstrates how local strategies differ between localities.

Breaking out of a low productivity–low income trap, which can be intensified by increased climate variability and inadequate coping strategies, requires a locally targeted approach to enable households to access fully and benefit from policies such as promoting improved technology, efficient markets and supportive strategies. The returns on policies and development initiatives in one locality will depend upon the respective challenges and conditions that households and institutions confront. For example, initiatives on rainfall harvesting for irrigation in crop production during dry seasons can be expected to result in a much higher return if the intervention is fitted to approximate local rainfall distribution.

REFERENCES

Abeku, T., van Oortmarssen, G., Borsboomde, G. J., Vlas, S. J., Habbema, J. D. F. (2003) Spatial and temporal variations of malaria epidemic risk in Ethiopia: factors involved and implications. *Acta Tropica* 87.

Adger, N. (2006) Vulnerability. Global Environmental Change 16: 268–281.

Adger, W.N., Brooks, N. (2003) Does Global Environmental Change Cause Vulnerability to Disaster? In: Pelling, M. (ed.) *Natural Disasters and Development in a Globalising World*, Routledge, London, 19-42.

Alderman, H. (1996) Saving and economic shocks in rural Pakistan. *Journal of Development Economics* 51: 343-365.

Alderman, H., Hoddinott, J., Kinsey, B. (2006) Long term consequences of early childhood malnutrition. *Oxford Economic Papers* 58: 450–474.

Alderman, H., Paxson, C. (1994) Do the poor insure? A Synthesis of the Literature on Risk and Consumption in Developing Countries. *International Economics Association Moscow* 4.

Antle, J. M., Capalbo, S., M., Elliott, E. T. (2004) Adaptation, spatial heterogeneity, and the vulnerability of agricultural systems to climate change and CO_2 fertilization: An integrated assessment approach. *Climatic Change* 64(3): 289-315.

Beegle, K., De Weerdt, J., Dercon, S. (2006) Kagera Health and Development Survey 2004 Basic Information Document Mimeo. The World Bank.

Berry, S. (1989) *Social Institutions and Access to Resources. Africa* 59(1), 41-55.

Churchill, C. (Ed.) (2006) Protecting the Poor: A Microinsurance Compendium. *International Labour Organization*, Geneva, 678 pp.

Cooper, P. J. M., Dimes, J., Rao, K. P. C., Shapiro, B., Shiferawa, B., Twomlow, S. (2008) Coping better with current climatic variability in the rain-fed farming systems of sub-Saharan Africa: an essential first step in adapting to future climate change? *Agriculture, Ecosystems and Environment* 126: 24–35.

Davies, S. (1996) Adaptable Livelihoods. London: Macmillan Press Ltd, UK.

De Waal, A. (1987) *Famines that kills: Darfur Sudan*, 1984-85. Oxford: Clarendon, UK.

De Weerdt, J. (2008) Defying Destiny and Moving out of Poverty: Evidence from a 10-year Panel with Linked Qualitative Data from Kagera, Tanzania. World Bank, *Moving out of Poverty project*.

Deaton, A. (1991) Saving and Liquidity Constraints. *Econometrica* 595: 221-1248.

Dercon, S. (2002) Income risk, coping strategies and safety nets. *World Bank Research Observer* 17(2): 141-166.

Eakin, H., Luers, A. L. (2006) Assessing the vulnerability of social environmental systems. *Annual Review of Environment and Resources* 31: 365–394.

EDI, Economic Development Initiative (2004) Kagera Rural CWIQ Baseline Survey on Poverty, Welfare and Services in Kagera Rural Districts. *Tanzania-Netherlands District Rural Development Programme*. Kagera, Tanzania. 188 pp.

Ellis, F. (1998) Household Strategies and Rural Livelihood Diversification. *Journal of Development Studies* 35(1), 1-38.

Eriksen, S. H., Brown, K., Kelly, P. M. (2005) The dynamics of vulnerability: locating coping strategies in Kenya and Tanzania. *The Geographical Journal* 171(4): 287–305.

Fafchamps, M., Lund, S. (2003) Risk-sharing networks in rural Philippines. *Journal of Development Economics* 71(2): 261-287.

Fankhauser, S. (1998) The Costs of Adapting to Climate Change. GEF *Working Paper* No 16. GEF: Washington DC, US.

Gallez, A., Runyoro, G., Mbehoma, C. B., Van den Houwe, I., Swennen, R. (2004) Rapid Mass Propagation and Diffusion of New Banana Varieties among Small-Scale Farmers in North Western Tanzania. *African Crop Science Journal* 12(1): 7-17.

Huq, S., Reid, H. (2004) Mainstreaming Adaptation in Development. IDS Bulletin: *Climate Change and Development* 35(3), 15-21.

IPCC (2007) Climate Change 2007: Impacts, adaptation and vulnerability. Contribution of Working Group II to the fourth assessment report of the *Intergovernmental Panel on Climate Change*. Cambridge University Press, Cambridge UK.

Kazianga, H., Udry, C. (2006) Consumption smoothing? Livestock, insurance and drought in rural Burkina Faso. *Journal of Development Economics* 79(2): 413-446.

Kelly, P. M., Adger, W. N. (2000) Theory and Practice in Assessing Vulnerability to Climate Change and Facilitating Adaptation. *Climatic Change* 47(4), 325–352.

Kessy, F. (2005) Rural Income Dynamics in Kagera Region, Tanzania. *A Report Prepared for the World Bank Economic and Social Research Foundation,* Dar es Salaam, Tanzania.

Kinsey, B., Burger, K., Gunning, J. W. (1998) Coping with drought in Zimbabwe: survey evidence on responses of rural households to risk. *World Development* 26(1): 89-110.

Kristjanson, P., Radeny, M., Baltenweck, I., Oguto, J., Notenbaert, A. (2005) Livelihood mapping and poverty correlates at a meso-level in Kenya. *Food Policy* 30: 568 – 583.

Lacy, S., Cleveland, D., Soleri, D. (2006) Farmer Choice of Sorghum Varieties in Southern Mali. *Human Ecology* 34, 331–353.

Lim, Y., Townsend, R. M. (1998) General equilibrium models of financial systems: theory and measurement in village economies. *Review of Economic Dynamics* 1: 59–118.

Liu, J., Fritz, S., van Wesenbeeck, C. F. A., Fuchs, M., You, L., Obersteiner, M., Yang, H. (2008) A spatially explicit assessment of current and future hotspots of hunger in Sub-Saharan Africa in the context of global change. *Global and Planetary Change* 64: 222-235.

Lobell, D. B., Burke, M. B., Tebaldi, C., Mastrandrea, M. D., Falcon, W. P., Naylor, R. L. (2008) Prioritizing Climate Change Adaptation Needs for Food Security in 2030. *Science* 319: 607-610.

Lundberg, M., Over, M., Mujinja, P. (2005) Sources of Financial assistance for households suffering an adult death in Kagera, Tanzania. *South African Journal of Economics* 68(5): 948 – 984.

McCarthy, J. J., Canziani, O., Leary, N. A., Dokken, D. J., White, K. S. (eds.) (2001) Climate Change 2001: Impacts, *Adaptation and Vulnerability*. IPCC Working Group II. Cambridge University Press, Cambridge.

Mendelsohn, R., Basist, A., Kurukulasuriya, P., Dinar, A. (2007) *Climate and rural income Climatic Change* 81(1): 101-118.

Merrey, D. J., Drechsel, P., Penning de Vries, F. W. T., Sally, H. (2005) Taking the integration paradigm to its logical next step for developing countries. *Regional Environmental Change* 5: 197-204.

Mertz, O., Halsnæs, K., Olesen, J. E., Rasmussen, K. (2009a) Adaptation to Climate Change in Developing Countries. *Environmental Management* 43: 43-752.

Mertz, O., Mbow, C., Reenberg, A., Diouf, A. (2009b) Farmers' perceptions of climate change and agricultural adaptation strategies in Rural Sahel. *Environmental Management* 43: 804 – 816.

Meze-Hausken, E. (2004) Contrasting climate variability and meteorological drought with perceived drought and climate change in northern Ethiopia. *Climate Research* 27: 19 – 31.

Mortimore, M. (2006) What are the Issues? Have the Issues Changed? In: Møllegaard, M. (ed.) Natural Resource Management in Sahel— Lessons Learnt. *Proceedings of the 17th Danish Sahel Workshop*. ReNED, Copenhagen, 10–18.

Mortimore, M. J., Adams, W. M. (2001) Farmer adaptation, change and 'crisis' in the Sahel. *Global Environmental Change-Human and Policy Dimensions* 11: 49-57.

Nearing, M. A., Pruski, F. F., O'Neal, M. R. (2004) Expected climate change impacts on soil erosion rates: a review. *Journal of Soil and Water Conservation* 59(1): 43-50.

Nielsen, J. Ø., Reenberg, A. (2010) Temporality and the problem with singling out climate as a current driver of change in a small West African village. *Journal of Arid Environments* 74: 464–474.

Niimi, Y., Thai, H. P., Reilly, B. (2009) Determinants of Remittances: Recent Evidence Using Data on Internal Migrants in Vietnam. *Asian Economic Journal* 23(1): 19-39.

Okwi, P., Ngeng'e, G. N., Kristjanson, P., Arunga, M., Notenbaert, A., Omolo, A., Henninger, N., Beson, T., Kariuki, P., Owuor, J. (2007) Spatial *Determinants of Poverty in Rural Kenya*. PNAS, 104(43), 16679-16774.

Ovuka, M., Lindqvist, S. (2000) Rainfall variability in Murang'a District, Kenya: meteorological data and farmers' perception. *Geografiske Annaler* 82 A (1): 107–119.

Patt, A. G., Gwata, C. (2002) Effective seasonal climate forecast applications - examining constraints for subsistence farmers in Zimbabwe. *Global Environmental Change* 12: 185-195.

Patt, A. G., Ogallo, L., Hellmuth, M. (2007) Learning from 10 Years of Climate Outlook Forums in Africa. *Science* 318: 49-50.

Paxson, C. (1993) Consumption and Income Seasonality in Thailand. *Journal of Political Economy* 101(1): 39-72.

Phillips, J., Unganai, L., Makauzde, E. (2000) Changes in crop management in response to the seasonal climate forecast in Zimbabwe during a La ninã year. In: proceedings of the International Forum on Climate Prediction, *Agriculture and Development*, Palisades, NY April 26–28, 2000, IRI, 213–216.

Porter, J. R., Semenov, M. A. (2005) *Crop responses to climatic variation Philosophical Transactions of the Royal Society B-Biological Sciences* 360(1463): 2021-2035.

Rao, K. P. C., Okwach, G. E. (2005) Enhancing productivity of water under variable Climate. In: *Proceedings of the East Africa Integrated River Basin Management Conference*, Sokione University of Agriculture, Morogoro, Tanzania, 7–9th March, pp. 2–9.

Roncoli, C., Ingram, K., Kirshen, P. (2001) The Costs and Risks of Coping With Drought: Livelihood Impacts and Farmers' Responses in Burkina Faso. *Climate Research* 19, 119–32.

Roncoli, C., Jost, C., Kirshen, P., Moussa, S., Ingram, K., Woodin, M., Somé, L., Ouattara, F., Sanfo, B., Sia, C., Yaka, P., Hoogenboom, G. (2009) From accessing to assessing forecasts: an end-to-end study of participatory climate forecast dissemination in Burkina Faso (West Africa). *Climatic Change* 92:433-460.

Rosenzweig, C., Tubiello, F. N., Goldberg, R. (2002) Increased crop damage in the US from excess precipitation under climate change. *Global Environmental Change-Human and Policy Dimensions* 12(3): 197-202.

Scoones, I., Chibudu, C., Chikura, S., Jeranyama, P., Machaka, D., Machanja, W., Mavedzenge, B., Mombeshora, B., Mudhara, M., Mudziwo, C., Murimbarimba, F., Zirereza, B. (1996) *Hazard and Opportunities: Farming Livelihoods in Dryland Africa: Lessons from Zimbabwe*. Zed Books and International Institute for Environment and Development, London.

Smit, B., Burton, I., Klein, R., Wandel, J. (2000) An Anatomy of Adaptation to Climate Change and Variability. *Climatic Change* 45, 223–251.

Smit, B., Pilifosova, O. (2001) Adaptation to Climate Change in the Context of Sustainable Development and Equity. Chapter 18 in McCarthy, J. J., Canziani, O., Leary, N. A., Dokken, D. J., White, K. S. (eds.), *Climate Change 2001: Impacts, Adaptation, and Vulnerability - Contribution of Working Group II to the Third Assessment Report of the Intergovernmental Panel on Climate Change*. Cambridge University Press, Cambridge, UK.

Swart, R., Robinson, J., Cohen, S. (2003) Climate Change and Sustainable Development: Expanding the Options. *Climate Policy* 3(1), S19-S40Tesliuc, E. D., Lindert, K. (2004) Risk and Vulnerability in Guatemala: A Quantitative and Qualitative Assessment. *World Bank Social Protection Discussion Paper No*. 0404. Washington DC, US.

Thomas, D. S. G., Twyman, C., Osbahr, H., Hewitson, B. (2007) Adaptation to climate change and variability: farmer responses to intra-seasonal Precipitation trends in South Africa. *Climatic Change* (83): 301–322.

Thornton, P. K., Boone, R. B., Galvin, K. A. (2007) Coping strategies in livestock-dependent households in east and southern Africa: a synthesis of four case studies. *Human Ecology* 35(4): 461-476.

Townsend, R. M. (1994) Risk and insurance in village India. *Econometrica* 62 no3: 539-591.

Udry, C. (1994) Risk and insurance in a rural credit market: *an empirical investigation of Northern Nigeria Review of Economic Studies* 61(3): 495-526.

URT, United Republic of Tanzania (2003) Kagera Region Socio-economic profile. *Joint Publication by Planning Commission*, Dar es Salaam, and Regional Commissioners Office, Kagera Dar es Salaam, Tanzania.

URT, United Republic of Tanzania (2002a) *Population and Housing Census* (2002).

URT, United Republic of Tanzania (2002b) The Economic Survey. Dar es Salaam: *President's Office—Planning and Privatization.*

URT, United Republic of Tanzania (2009) The Economic Survey. Dar es Salaam: *President's Office—Planning and Privatization.*

Vincent, K. (2007) *Uncertainty in adaptive capacity and the importance of scale Global Environmental Change* 17: 12-24.

Vogel, C. (1998) Vulnerability and Global Environmental Change. *LUCC Newsletter* 3, 15–19.

Wandiga, S. O., Opondo, M., Olago, D., Githeko, A., Githui, F., Marshall, M., Downs, T., Opere, A., Yanda, P. Z., Kangalawe, R., Kabumbuli, R., Kirumira, E., Kathuri, J., Apindi, E., Olaka, L., Ogallo, L., Mugambi, P., Sigalla, R., Nanyunja, R., Baguma, T., Achola, P. (2006) Vulnerability to climate induced highland malaria in East Africa. *AIACC Working Papers.*

West, C. T., Roncoli, C., Ouattara, F. (2008) Local perceptions and regional climate trends on the central plateau of Burkina Faso. *Land Degradation and Development* 19 (3): 289–304.

WHO, World Health Organization (2003) The Africa Malaria Report 2003. Malaria Control Unit, UNICEF, Geneva: *World Health Organization.*

Zhou, G., Minakawa, N., Githeko, A.K., Yan G (2004), Association between climate variability and malaria epidemics in the East African highlands. *Ecology* 101, No 8.

Ziervogel, G. (2004) Targeting seasonal climate forecasts for integration into household level decisions: the case of smallholder farmers in Lesotho. *Geographic Journal* 170: 6-21.

In: Rainfall: Behavior, Forecasting and Distribution
Editors: Olga E. Martín and Tricia M. Roberts ISBN: 978-1-62081-551-9

Chapter 2

RAINFALL VARIABILITY AND CHANGES IN BANGLADESH DURING THE LAST FIFTY YEARS

Shamsuddin Shahid*

Department of Hydraulics and Hydrology, Faculty of Civil Engineering, Universiti Teknologi Malaysia (UTM), Malaysia

ABSTRACT

Rainfall variability in space and time is one of the most relevant characteristics of the climate of Bangladesh. Long-term annual average rainfall, coefficient of variation of annual rainfall, precipitation concentration and aridity indices at each station are computed and then interpolated using kriging method within a geographic information system to show the temporal and spatial variability of rainfall in Bangladesh. Mann-Kendall test is used to analyze the trends in rainfall at different confidence levels and the Sen's slope method is used to determine the magnitude of changes. The results show that rainfall in Bangladesh varies from 1527 mm in the west to 4197 mm in the east with a mean of 2488 mm. The gradient of rainfall from west to east is approximately 7 mm km^{-1}. The monthly distribution of rainfall shows that the rainfall is very much seasonal in Bangladesh, more than 89% of rainfall occurs during May to October. The aridity study over Bangladesh reveals three climate zones in Bangladesh viz. moist sub-humid, humid and wet. The climate in most of parts of Bangladesh is humid type. The northeastern side of the country belongs to wet climate and the central western part to moist sub-humid. Co-efficient of variation of annual rainfall shows a moderate inter-annual variability of rainfall in most parts of the country. The deviation of annual precipitation from mean precipitation is found to vary from +408 mm to -586 mm during the last fifty years. Highest inter-annual variation of rainfall is observed in northwest Bangladesh and lowest in the southern coastal region. The trend analysis using Mann-Kendall method reveals the presence of a positive trend in annual rainfall of Bangladesh at 90% level of confidence. The magnitude of change of annual rainfall estimated by Sen's slope estimator shows that the annual rainfall of Bangladesh has increased at a rate of +5.53 mm yr^{-1} in last fifty years. A significant increase in pre-monsoon rainfall at a rate of 2.47 mm yr^{-1} at 99%

* Associate Professor, Department of Hydraulics and Hydrology, Faculty of Civil Engineering, Universiti Teknologi Malaysia (UTM), 81310 Johor Bahru, Malaysia, E-mail: *sshahid@utm.my*.

level of confidence is also observed over Bangladesh. However, there is no change in monsoon, post-monsoon and winter rainfalls. Spatial analysis of rainfall changes show significant increases in annual and pre-monsoon rainfall at more than one-third of stations mostly situated in the northern and southwestern parts of Bangladesh. The changes in rainfall during monsoon, post-monsoon and winter are significant only at few stations, mostly situated in the northern part of the country.

Keywords: Rainfall variability, Trends analysis, Aridity, Spatial distribution, Bangladesh

1. INTRODUCTION

Bangladesh is primarily a low-lying plain of about 144,000 km^2, situated on deltas of large rivers flowing from the Himalayas. Except the hilly southeast, most of the country is a low-lying plain land. Geographically, it extends from 20°34'N to 26°38'N latitude and from 88°01'E to 92°41'E longitude. Bangladesh has a tropical humid climate characterized by a seasonal reversal of surface winds and a distinct seasonality of precipitation. Four distinct seasons can be recognized in Bangladesh from climatic point of view: (i) the dry winter season from December to February, (ii) the pre-monsoon hot summer season from March to May, (iii) the rainy monsoon season from June to September, and (iv) the post-monsoon autumn season which lasts from October to November (Rashid, 1991). During the summer, winds blow from the Southern Hemisphere from mid-May to September, accumulating moisture and depositing copious amounts of precipitation over the South Asian continent. In the winter, dry winds blow from the cold land areas of Asia towards the warm southern ocean. The fundamental driving mechanisms of the monsoon cycle are the cross-equatorial pressure gradients established by thermal contrasts between the Asiatic landmass and the ocean modified by the rotation of the earth, and the exchange of moisture between the ocean, atmosphere, and land (Webster, 1987).

Climatic change due to global worming is a major concern in the recent years. It has been indicated that rainfall is changing due to global warming on both the global (Hulme *et al.*, 1998; Lambert *et al.*, 2003; Dore, 2005) and the regional scales (Rodriguez-Puebla *et al.*, 1998; Gemmer *et al.*, 2004; Kayano and Sansigolo, 2008). Future climate changes may involve modifications in climatic variability as well as changes in averages (Mearns *et al.*, 1996). The implications of these changes are particularly significant for areas already under stress, such as in Bangladesh where hydrological disasters of one kind or another is a common phenomenon. The country is one of the most flood prone countries in the world due to its geographic position. Severe floods in the years of 1974, 1984, 1987, 1988, 1998, 2004 and 2007 ravaged the country. Drought in the northern part of the country has also become a growing concern in the recent years. The country experienced eight droughts of severe magnitude in last forty years (Shahid, 2008; Shahid and Behrawan, 2008). Therefore, for disaster mitigation, agriculture and water resources planning and management in the context of global climatic change it is essential to study the characteristics and trends in rainfall in Bangladesh. Spatial and temporal variations and trends in rainfall of Bangladesh in the recent years have been analyzed in this article.

A number of literatures are available on climate (Ahmed and Karmaker, 1993; Ahmed et al., 1996; Hussain and Sultana, 1996; Kripalini et al., 1996; Ahmed and Kim, 2003; Shahid,

2008; Islam and Uyeda, 2008) and historical rainfall trends (Rahman et al., 1997; Singh, 2001; Jones, 1995; Shahid and Khairulmaini, 2009; Shahid, 2010) of Bangladesh. Climate models have also been used by a number of authors to predict the change in rainfall of Bangladesh (Manabe et al., 1991; May, 2004; Immerszeel, 2007; Kripalani et al., 2003, 2007; Stephenson et al., 2001; OECD, 2003; Das et al., 2006). However, consensus has not yet been arrived on the projected strength of monsoon circulation and the quantum of rainfall. May (2004) used climate model to study the rainfall pattern over the tropical Indian Ocean and predicted an increase in intensity of heavy rainfall events in Bangladesh. Immerzeel (2007) predicted seasonal increases in precipitation from 2000 to 2100 with more increases in monsoon compared to other seasons for the Brahmaputra basin. Kripalani et al. (2007) reported that although the projected summer monsoon circulation appears to weaken, the projected anomalous flow over the Bay of Bengal and Arabian Sea will support oceanic moisture convergence and more rainfall towards the southern parts of India. On the other hand, Stephenson *et al.* (2001) predicted a weakening of the monsoon circulation. Pal *et al.* (2001) suggested that the total rainfall may not change significantly but the temporal and spatial distributions over India are likely to change. Das et al. (2006) predicted weaker Indian summer monsoon and reduction of rainfall by about 30%. Kripalani et al. (2003) concluded that there seem to be no support for the intensification of the monsoon nor any support for the increased hydrological cycle as hypothesized by greenhouse warming scenario in model simulations nor the long historical observed data.

Several studies show that although the atmosphere-ocean couple models provide good representations of the synoptic scale feature, direct use of the model scenarios on regional scale suffers from the errors since GCMs do not capture the finer details of the spatial variation (Rupa Kumar and Ashrit, 2001; De, 2001; Kripalani et al., 2003). Therefore, investigation through observational data is required to seek independent confirmation of the findings obtained through the model simulations. Detail study of annual and seasonal variations in the rainfall of Bangladesh with long-term observational data can be helpful to understand the regional climate changes as well as to understand the broad features of the Asian coupled-land-atmospheric system.

Agriculture is the single largest producing sector of the economy of Bangladesh since it comprises about 18.6% of the country's GDP and employs around 45% of the total labor force (Bangladesh Bureau of Statistics, 2010). In the absence of other resources and in view of its large population and fertile agricultural land, Bangladesh must, of necessity, develop its agriculture potential more fully. Since agriculture is largely dependent on the natural rainfall, performance of rainfall has an overwhelming impact on food security as well as other major macroeconomic objectives like employment generation and poverty alleviation.

Spatial and temporal variability and trends in the annual and seasonal rainfall of Bangladesh are assessed in this paper through the analysis of fifty years (1958-2007) rainfall data. Daily rainfall data from 17 stations distributed throughout Bangladesh are used for this purpose. Aridity assessment using De Martonne's and Thornthwait's methods has been carried out for climate zoning of Bangladesh. Rainfall trends are computed for both annual and season rainfall time series. For seasonal analysis of rainfall, each year is divided into four seasons depending upon climatic conditions prevailing over the country. Non-parametric statistics are used to detect the trend as well as to determine the magnitude of change in rainfall.

2. Data and Methodology

2.1. Data

Bangladesh Meteorological Department (BMD) has more than 36 rain-gauges distributed over the country for measuring daily rainfall and other weather parameters. However, long-term (more than fifty years) daily rainfall records (1958-2007) are available only in seventeen stations which are selected for the present study. Location of the rain-gauges in the map of Bangladesh is shown in Figure 1.

2.2. Data Quality Control

Major problem to work with rainfall records of Bangladesh are missing data. A major portion of data is missing in 1971. Due to the independence war in 1971 most of meteorological stations of Bangladesh were unattended for many days. Number of missing days in 1971 varies between 57 and 207 days in the stations under study. Therefore, the record of 1971 is discarded from the set. After discarding 1971 records, percentage of missing data reduced to less than 2% in most of the stations. Though the stations with shorter records or high missing data are not selected in this study, they are used for assessing data quality and homogeneity at nearby stations.

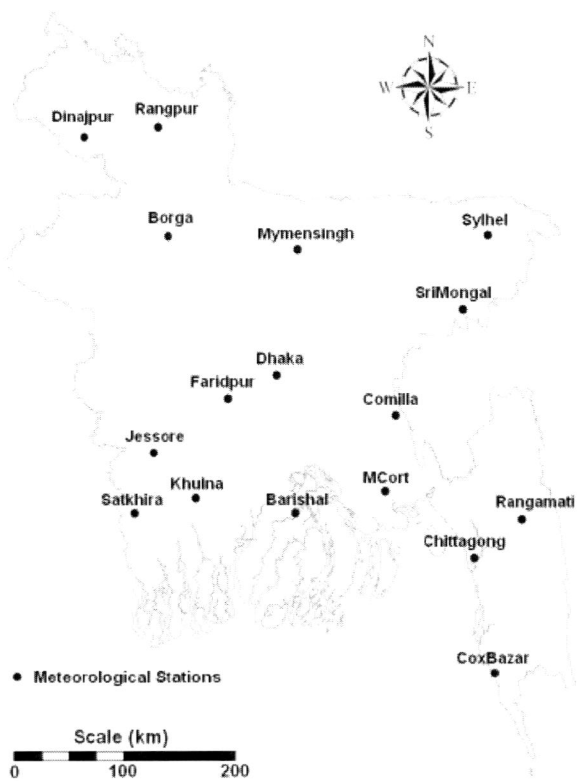

Figure 1. Location of rainfall stations used in the study.

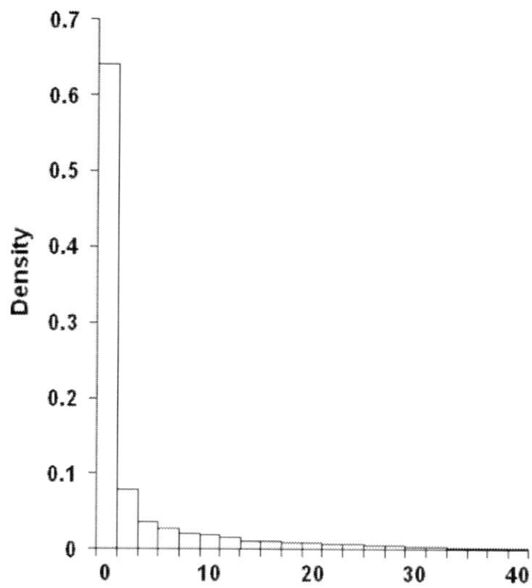

Figure 2. Precipitation histogram of Dhaka station.

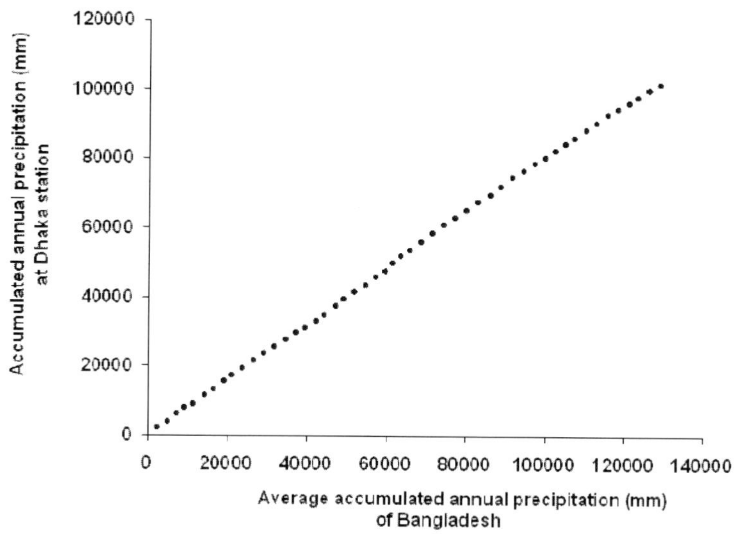

Figure 3. The double-mass curve of the rainfall series of Dhaka station.

A number of checks are carried out for quality controls of data such as precipitation values below 0 mm, winter rainfall higher than 100 mm, more than ten consecutive dry days in monsoon, etc. In some cases data are validated by the rainfall records of nearby stations. Histograms of the data are also created which reveal problems that show up when looking at the data set as a whole (Aguilar et al., 2005). An example plot of histogram of rainfall at Dhaka station used for data quality control is shown in Figure 2. It shows that precipitation data in the station is fine.

Several strategies have been described in the literature to detect non-homogeneities in the data series (Peterson et al., 1998). In this paper, both the subjective double mass curve method and the objective student T test were applied to the annual precipitation time series of each station. The double mass curve (Kohler, 1949) is a plot of the deviation from a station's accumulated values versus the average accumulation of the base group. Non-linearity or bends plots can be an indicator of changed conditions (Su et al., 2006). Results of the double mass curves of all stations are almost a straight line as displayed an example in Figure 3 for Dhaka station. No breakpoints are detected in the time series of precipitation.

Student's T test can also be used to assess homogeneity by determining whether or not various samples are derived from the same population (Panofsky and Brier, 1968). In a homogeneous series, variations are caused only by the variation in weather and climate (Conrad and Pollak, 1950). Thus, modified series obtained through the subtraction of the reference series from the original series of each station should be more capable of detecting any inhomogeneity resulting from non-climatic factors (Su et al., 2006). After filtering out the possible climatic abruption, T test is applied on each station. The results reveal a wide range of the 95% confidence interval of the difference including zero. So, it is clear that there is no statistically significant variation or break point existing in the rainfall time series.

2.3. Methodology

Different statistical characteristics of rainfall like mean rainfall over the year or different seasons, coefficients of inter-annual rainfall variation, precipitation concentration index (*PCI*), coefficient of variation of *PCI* are calculated for all the stations. The spatial distributions of these rainfall properties as well as trends of rainfall and *PCI* are mapped to analyze the spatio-temporal pattern of rainfall over Bangladesh. Methods used for analyzing rainfall data are discussed below.

2.3.1. Rainfall Characteristics Analysis

Precipitation Concentration Index (*PCI*) proposed by Oliver (1980) has been used to define temporal aspects of the rainfall distribution within a year. *PCI* is expressed as percentage in according to following formula:

$$PCI = 100 * \frac{\sum_{i=1}^{12} p_i^2}{P^2} \tag{1}$$

where, p_i = precipitation of i -th month, and P = annual precipitation.

PCI is very useful to evaluate the degree of seasonal concentration of precipitation. It provides information to compare different climates in terms of seasonality of precipitation regime. The more concentrated is precipitation, the more difficult is water management, irrigation control, soil erosion prevention and rainfed agriculture.

In order to show the spatial distribution of the intra- and inter- annual variability of rainfall in Bangladesh, *PCI* and the coefficient of variation of the annual rainfall(*R*) at each station are calculated and then interpolated.

2.3.2. Aridity Indices

Aridity index of an area gives an idea about its climate, bio-environment, soil moisture, drought vulnerability and erosion susceptibility. For aridity mapping of Bangladesh, De Martonne's aridity index and Thornthwait's precipitation effectiveness index are used. De Martonne (1926) proposed a method for calculating aridity index (AI) of an area using following equation:

$$AI = [P/(T+10) + 12p/(t+10)]/2 \qquad (2)$$

where:

P is the mean annual precipitation in mm,

T is the mean annual temperature in °C,

p the precipitation of the driest month in mm, and

t the mean temperature of the driest month in °C.

Thornthwaite (1931) classified the climatic regions into different classes based on the precipitation effectiveness index (*PE*), which is computed from the monthly values of precipitation and temperature by using following equation:

$$PE\ Index = \sum_{i=1}^{n} 115 * (P/(T\text{-}10))^{10/9} \qquad (3)$$

where, P = monthly precipitation in inches;

T = temperature in °F; and

n = months = 12.

2.3.3. Trend Analysis

Trends in data can be identified by using either parametric or non-parametric methods. In the recent past, both methods have been widely used for the detection of trends (e.g. WMO, 1988; Mitosek, 1992; Chiew and McMahon, 1993; Burn and Elnur 2002). The nonparametric tests are more suitable for non-normally distributed, censored data, including missing values, which are frequently encountered in hydrological time series (Hirsch and Slack, 1984). Mann-Kendall test is a non-parametric test which means it does not assume any priority distribution of the data, and is therefore robust in comparison to parametric tests (Shi, 2006). It has been found to be an excellent tool for trend detection in water resources time series (Hirsch et al., 1982; Helsel and Hirsch, 1992). Therefore, in the present study, Mann-Kendall test is applied to detect the trend in rainfall time series. Confidence levels of 90%, 95%, and 99% are taken as thresholds to classify the significance of positive and negative trends. The Sen's slope method (Sen, 1968) is used to determine the magnitude of change. Yue et al. (2002) found that Sen's slope is insensitive to outliers and can give a robust estimation of trend. A brief description of the methods used in the present study is discussed below.

2.3.3.1. Mann-Kendall Trend Test

In Mann-Kendall (MK) test the data values are evaluated as an ordered time series. Each data value is compared to all subsequent data values. The initial value of the Mann-Kendall statistic, S, is assumed to be 0 (*e.g.*, no trend). If a data value from a later time period is higher than a data value from an earlier time period, S is incremented by 1. On the other hand, if the data value from a later time period is lower than a data value sampled earlier, S is decremented by 1. The net result of all such increments and decrements yields the final value of S. If x_1, x_2, x_3 ..... x_i represent *n* data points where x_j represents the data point at time *j*, then *S* is given by,

$$S = \sum_{k=1}^{n-1} \sum_{j=k+1}^{n} sign(x_j - x_k) \tag{4}$$

where:

$$sign(x_j - x_k) = 1 \text{ if } x_j - x_k > 0$$

$$= 0 \text{ if } x_j - x_k = 0$$

$$= -1 \text{ if } x_j - x_k < 0$$

The probability associated with *S* and the sample size, *n*, are then computed to statistically quantify the significance of the trend. Normalized test statistic *Z* is computed as follows:

$$Z = \frac{S-1}{\sqrt{VAR(S)}} \text{ if } S > 0 \tag{5}$$

$$= 0 \text{ if } S = 0$$

$$= \frac{S+1}{\sqrt{VAR(S)}} \text{ if } S < 0$$

At the 99% significance level, the null hypothesis of no trend is rejected if $|Z| > 2.575$; at 95% significance level, the null hypothesis of no trend is rejected if $|Z| > 1.96$; and at 90%

significance level, the null hypothesis of no trend is rejected if $|Z| > 1.645$. Complete discussion of Mann–Kendall trend test can be found in Sneyers (1990).

2.3.3.2. Sen's Slope Model

Some trends may not be evaluated to be statistically significant while they might be of practical interest (Yue and Hashino, 2003; Basistha *et al.*, 2007). Even if climate change component is present, it may not be detected by statistical tests at a satisfactory significance level (Radziejewski and Kundzewicz, 2004). Therefore, in the present study, linear trend analysis is also carried out and the magnitude of trend is estimated by Sen's Slope method (Sen, 1968). Sen's Slope method gives a robust estimation of trend (Yue *et al.*, 2002). The method requires a time series of equally spaced data. The method proceeds by calculating the slope as a change in measurement per change in time,

$$Q' = \frac{x_{t'} - x_t}{t' - t} \tag{6}$$

where, Q' = slope between data points $x_{t'}$ and x_t, $x_{t'}$ = data measurement at time t', x_t = data measurement at time t.

Sen's estimator of slope is simply given by the median slope,

$$\begin{aligned} Q &= Q'_{[(N+1)/2]} \qquad \textit{if N is odd} \\ &= (Q'_{[N/2]} + Q'_{[(N+2)/2]})/2 \qquad \textit{if N is even} \end{aligned} \tag{7}$$

where, N is the number of calculated slopes.

2.2.4. Mapping Using GIS

For mapping of spatial characteristics of rainfall, mean annual rainfall, rainfall concentration index, their variation coefficients and trends are calculated for each station. Raster maps of rainfall characteristics are prepared from point data using kriging interpolation method. Geostatistical analysis tool of ArcGIS 9.0 (ESRI, 2003) has been used for this purpose. Kriging is a stochastic interpolation method (Isaaks and Srivastava, 1989), which is widely recognized as standard approach for surface interpolation based on scalar measurements at different points. Study showed that Kriging gives better global predictions than other methods (van Beers and Kleijnen, 2004). Therefore, kriging is used in this study for the interpolation of point data to prepare the raster maps of various rainfall parameters. Kriging is an optimal surface interpolation method based on spatially dependent variance, which is generally expressed as a semi-variogram. Surface interpolation using kriging depends on the selected semi-variogram model and the semi-variogram must be fitted with a mathematical function or model. Depending on the shape of semi-variograms, spherical and Guassian models are used in the present study for their fitting.

3. Results and Discussion

3. 1. Spatial Variability of Rainfall over Bangladesh

Precipitation climatology over Bangladesh or the mean of annual precipitation for the period 1958–2007 is shown in Figure 4(a). Rainfall in Bangladesh varies from 1527 mm in the west to 4197 mm in the east. The gradient of rainfall from west to east is approximately 7 mm km-1. The monthly distribution of rainfall over the country is shown by a graph in Figure 4(b). The left vertical axis of the graph represents rainfall in millimeter and the right vertical axis represents the rainfall as a percentage of annual total rainfall. The graph shows that the rainfall is very much seasonal in Bangladesh, more than 89% of rainfall occurs during May to October.

a)

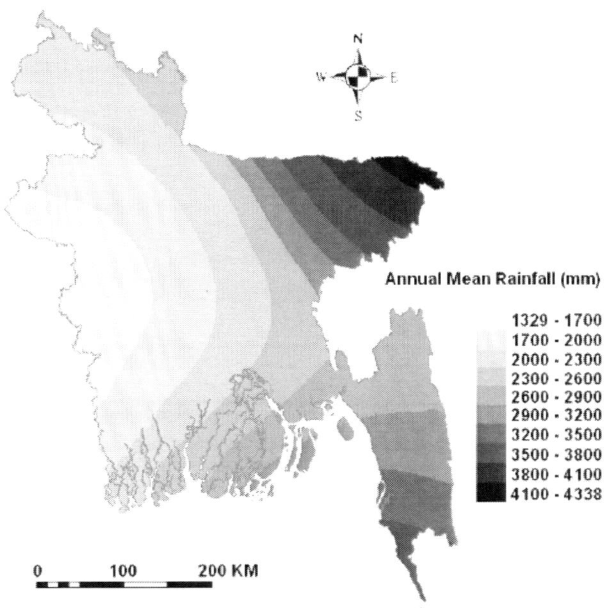

b)

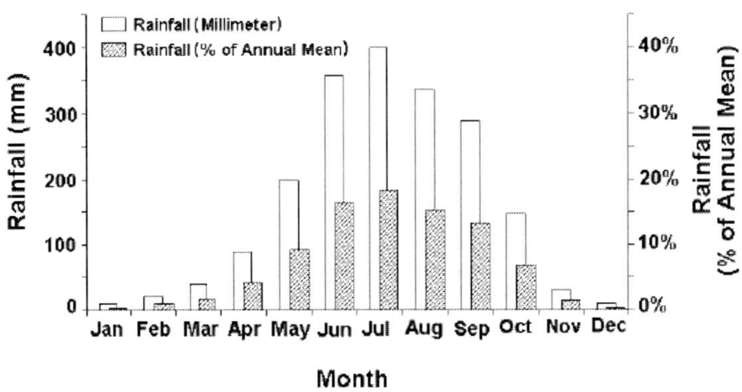

Figure 4: (a) Spatial; and (b) monthly distribution of rainfall in Bangladesh

a)

b)

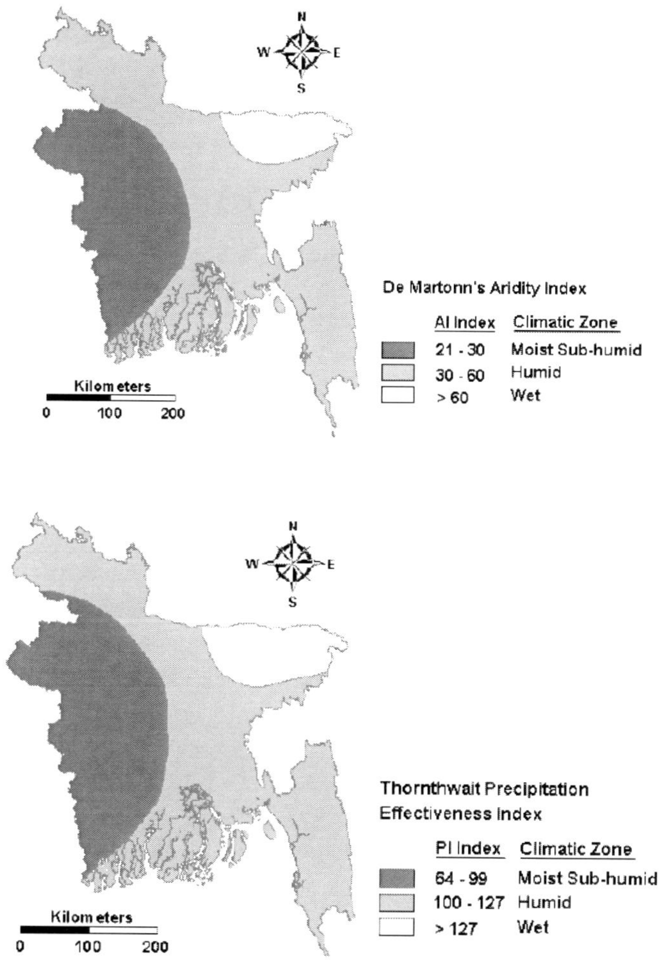

Figure 5. Dryness map of Bangladesh obtained by (a) De Martonne and (b) Thornwait models.

The main mechanism of the rainfall in Bangladesh during the summer monsoon season is caused by tropical depressions known as monsoon depression in the Bay of Bengal (Ahmed and Kim, 2003). The monsoon depressions move from the Bay of Bengal toward the monsoon trough, and produce enormous amounts of rainfall. Therefore, most of the rainfall in Bangladesh occurs in monsoon. The monsoon depressions enter Bangladesh from the Bay of Bengal with south-to-north trajectory and then turn toward the northwest and west being deflected by the Meghalaya Plateau. As these depressions move farther and farther inland, their moisture content decreases, resulting in decreasing rainfall toward the northwest and west of Bangladesh (Ahmed and Kim, 2003). On the other hand, the additional uplifting effect of the Meghalaya plateau increased the rainfall in northeast of Bangladesh.

3.2. Aridity Indices

De Martonne's aridity index and Thornthwait's precipitation effectiveness index maps of Bangladesh are shown in Figures 5(a) and (b) respectively. The aridity maps show that most of the area of Bangladesh is belong to humid class. The northeastern side of the country belongs to wet class and the central western part of the country belongs to sub-humid zone. Least index values obtained by De Martonne and Thornthwaite methods are 20.89 and 64.04 respectively in the northwestern sides of Bangladesh. As the dryness index values in the region is close to that of a 'dry zone', the climate of this region of Bangladesh is termed as 'dry climate'. The total annual evapotranspiration in this part of Bangladesh is also lower than or equal to annual rainfall in some years.

3.3. Inter-Annual Variability of Rainfall

Spatial pattern of the inter-annual variability of rainfall over Bangladesh is shown in Figure 6. A moderate to high variability of inter-annual rainfall is observed in Bangladesh. The maximum inter-annual variation is observed in northwestern part of the county. The value gradually decreases in all directions except in northeastern hilly region. High variability of rainfall in the northwester part of the country has made the region highly prone to droughts. The region experienced more than eight droughts of major magnitude in last forty years (Paul, 1998). Rainfall is comparatively reliable in the coastal region of Bangladesh which is highly prone to cyclones and storm surges.

The inter-annual variability of the Asian monsoon is linked with the El Niño Southern oscillation (ENSO).

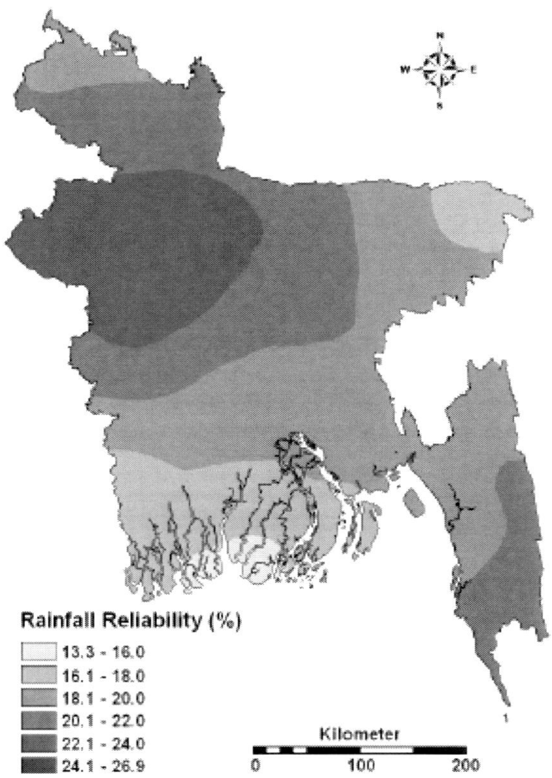

Figure 6. Map showing coefficient of variation of yearly rainfall over Bangladesh.

The general consensus is that during El Niño years anomalous subsidence suppresses convection over South Asia and results a weaker monsoon (Shahid, 2010). The troposheric temperature gradient between the Tibetan Plateau (TP) and the Indian Ocean also plays a critical role in inter-annual variation of Asian summer precipitation (Immerzeel, 2007). The snow depth on the TP affects the land surface thermodynamics and reduces this thermal gradient. There is an inverse relationship between the spring snow depth on the TP and monsoon precipitation in Bangladesh (Shaman et al., 2005).

3.4. Intra-Annual Distribution of Rainfall

Map of intra-annual distribution of rainfall or *PCI* in Bangladesh is shown in Figure 7(a). *PCI* values in most part of the country belong in the range of 13.4 to 16.0. According the classification proposed by Michiels and Gabriels (1996), this means that the rainfall of Bangladesh is moderately seasonal. Higher *PCI* values (*PCI*>16) in northern and southeastern part of the country means that rainfall in these region are seasonal. *PCI* only allow us to examine the variability of rainfall within a year. In order to measure the year-to-year variations of rainfall concentration, coefficient of variation of *PCI* is also calculated. The map of coefficient of variation of *PCI* of Bangladesh is shown in Figure 7(b). The map shows that irregular intra-annual rainfall distribution is mainly concentrated in the low rainfall zone. Higher values of coefficient of variation of *PCI* in western part of Bangladesh mean that seasonal variability of rainfall in the region is high.

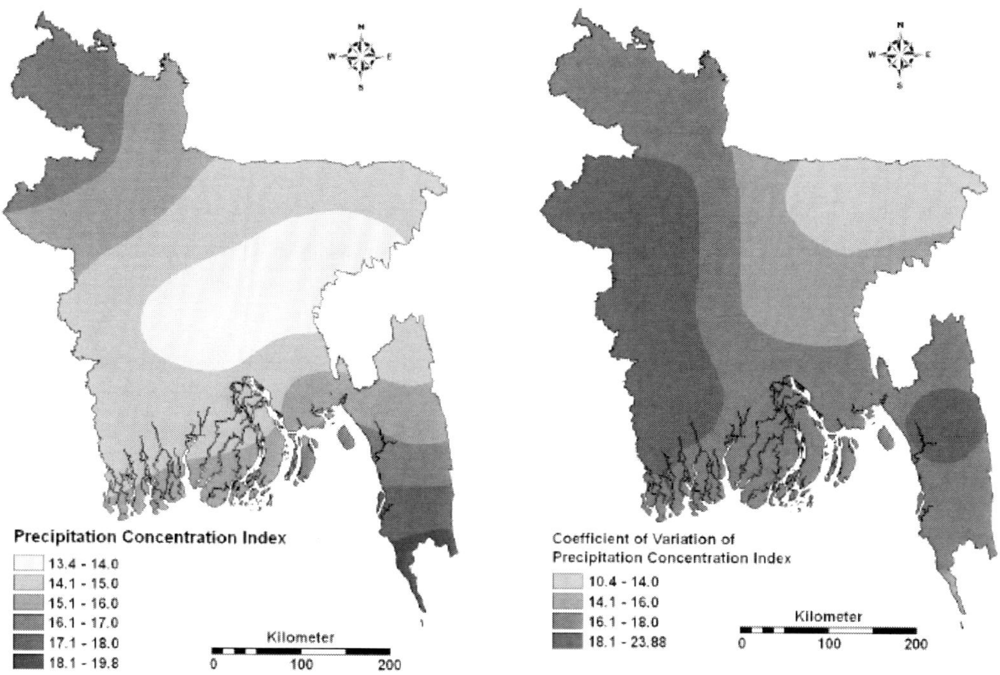

a) b)

Figure 7. Spatial distribution of (a) precipitation concentration index; and (b) coefficient of variation of precipitation concentration index.

3.5. Trend of Rainfall

Changes in both annual and seasonal rainfall of Bangladesh are considered for analysis in the present study. The results of trend analysis of annual and seasonal rainfall at each station as well as their average over Bangladesh are given in Table 1. The values in the table represent the change of rainfall in mm/year during the time period 1958-2007. The significant changes are presented by stars. Significant increases of annual and pre-monsoon rainfall are observed at more than one third stations of Bangladesh. The changes of rainfall in monsoon, post-monsoon and winter are significant only in few stations mostly situated in the western part of the country.

The annual and seasonal rainfalls of 17 stations of Bangladesh are averaged to get the time series of average annual and seasonal rainfalls of Bangladesh. The time series of annual rainfall of Bangladesh for the time period 1958-2007 is shown in Figure 8. The mean annual rainfall of Bangladesh is 2488 mm. The deviation of annual precipitation from mean precipitation is found to vary from +408 mm to -586 mm during the time period 1958-2007. The trend analysis over annual rainfall time series by Mann-Kendall test reveals the presence of a positive trend at 90% level of confidence. The Mann-Kendal normalized test statistic, Z of 1.957 means that the trend is very close to 95% level of confidence. The magnitude of change of annual rainfall estimated by Sen's slope estimator shows that the annual rainfall of Bangladesh is increasing at a rate of +5.53 mm/year during the time period 1958-2007.

Analysis of seasonal rainfall trends in Bangladesh shows significant increase of rainfall only in pre-monsoon at a rate of 2.47 mm/year at 99% level of confidence. The rate of increase is approximately 5.5% per decade during the time period 1958-2007. No change in monsoon rainfall is observed over Bangladesh like other parts of Indian subcontinent. Changes in post-monsoon and winter rainfalls are also not significant. OCDE (2003) study on changes in precipitation over Bangladesh using climate models projected increased precipitation in annual, pre-monsoon, monsoon and post-monsoon rainfall and no appreciable change in winter rainfall of Bangladesh. Study by using Geophysical Fluid Dynamics Laboratory transient model also estimated little change in winter precipitation and increase in precipitation in other seasons of Bangladesh (Ahmed and Alam, 1999).

The thunderstorms are the sources of pre-monsoon rainfall in Bangladesh (Sanderson and Ahmed, 1978). The thunderstorm season begins in the northeastern and eastern parts of the country by the first week of March. The thunderstorm activity gradually moves westward, and becomes significant in the western part of the country only before the advent of the summer monsoon in late May or early June. During the early part of the thunderstorm season, a zone of discontinuity crosses the country from southwest to northeast separates the hot dry air from the dry interior of India, and the warm moist air from the Bay of Bengal (Sanderson and Ahmed, 1978). The activity of the thunderstorms during the pre-monsoon season depends upon the supply of moist air from the Bay of Bengal. Stronger and more continuous winds from the Bay of Bengal during pre-monsoon months in the recent years due to the increase of sea surface temperature (Khan et al., 2000) might be the cause of increased pre-monsoon rainfall of Bangladesh.

Annual rainfall trends at each 17 station are interpolated to show the spatial pattern of annual rainfall trends in Bangladesh (Figure 9). The classes in the map are based on confidence levels. The numbers in the map show the amount of rainfall change in mm/year during the time period 1958-2007. The numbers in white color denote the trends are statistically significant. The spatial presentation of the detected precipitation trends enables a better understanding of climatic changes or variations in Bangladesh in the recent years. The map shows significant increase of annual rainfall in the western part of Bangladesh. The maximum increase is recorded in north Bangladesh by 16.45 mm/year at 99% level of confidence. Besides the western part of Bangladesh, rainfall is found to increase significantly at Rangamati station situated in southeastern hill region of Bangladesh at 95% level of confidence.

Table 1. Changes in annual and seasonal rainfall (mm/year) and *PCI* at different stations of Bangladesh

Station	Annual	Monsoon	Pre-Monsoon	Winter	PCI
Sylhet	8.11	2.00	2.20	0.22	0.023
Srimongal	-0.29	-2.24	-0.20	0.14	-0.042
Comilla	-2.97	-4.34	1.78	-0.60	0.009
Rangamati	11.38**	5.61	8.18**	0.00	-0.059
Chittagong	7.68	0.74	7.63***	0.53	-0.049
CoxBaz	4.82	3.18	8.14*	0.32	-0.072
M.Cort	0.00	-2.88	2.90	0.15	0.009
Faridpur	0.84	-0.91	0.07	0.72	-0.065**
Dhaka	4.33	1.12	1.05	1.55	-0.018
Mymen	7.86	0.20	2.69	2.73*	-0.101*
Khulna	7.79**	2.83	-1.15	1.80**	-0.151*
Barishal	0.89	0.89	1.23	-0.45	0.032
Satkhira	6.97**	2.93	1.93	0.18	-0.120*
Jessore	7.62**	4.70*	2.76*	1.50	-0.004
Bogra	6.47	2.50	4.18**	1.00	-0.093*
Dinajpur	14.39***	11.08***	7.44***	1.23	-0.117**
Rangpur	16.45***	11.15***	5.75**	2.65**	-0.064**
Average	5.53*	2.24	2.47***	1.03	-0.037

* 90% level of confidence; ** 95% level of confidence; *** 99% level of confidence.

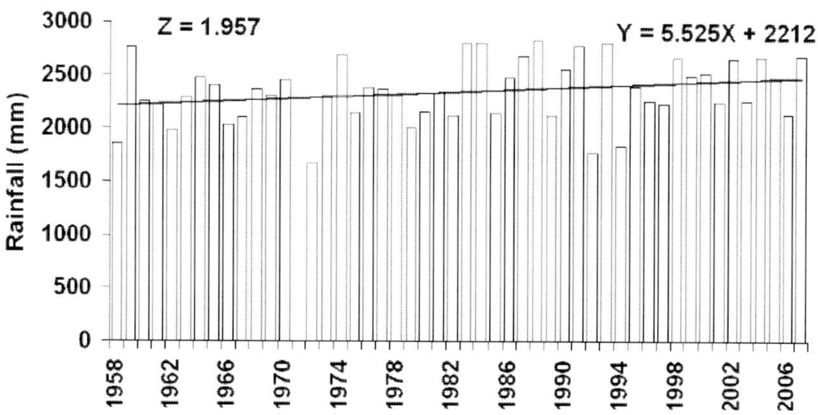

Figure 8. Trend in annual rainfall of Bangladesh shows a significant increase over the time period 1958-2007.

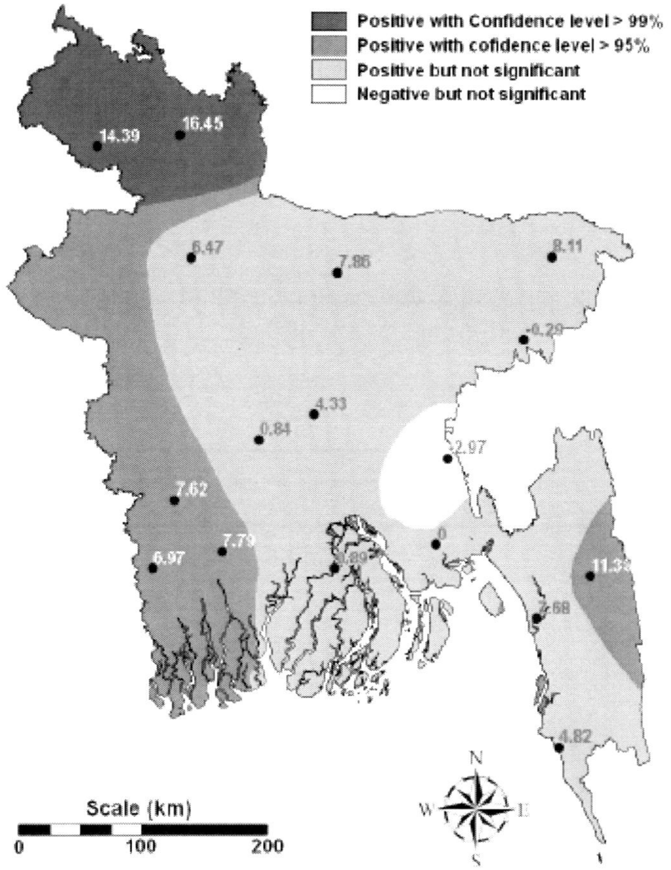

Figure 9. Spatial pattern of trends of annual rainfall in Bangladesh during the time period 1958-2007. The numbers in white color denote significant change.

As the monsoon and pre-monsoon rainfall are very important for Bangladesh, the spatial patterns of monsoon and pre-monsoon rainfall trends in Bangladesh are elaborated. Spatial pattern of monsoon rainfall trends in Bangladesh is shown in Figure 10(a). The map shows significant increase of monsoon rainfall only in the western part of Bangladesh. Maximum increase of rainfall is observed in northern Bangladesh by 11.15 mm/year at 99% level of confidence. Though the findings of present study agree with the result obtained by Rahman et al. (1997) that there is no change in monsoon rainfall over Bangladesh, it does not agree with the spatial pattern of monsoon rainfall trends in Bangladesh. Rahman et al. (1997) found changing pattern of monsoon rainfall in the stations located in the southeast hill region of Bangladesh on the contrary to the finding of the present study where changes are mostly observed in the stations located in northwest Bangladesh near the foot heel of Himalaya. However, the result is consistent with the finding of Krishna Kumar et al. (2003) in India. They noticed a statistically significant decreasing trend in the monsoon rainfall of northeast India (east of Bangladesh) at a rate of -6% - -8% of normal/100 years while statistically significant increasing trend over central India (west of Bangladesh) at a rate of +10% to +12% of normal/100 years.

a)

b)

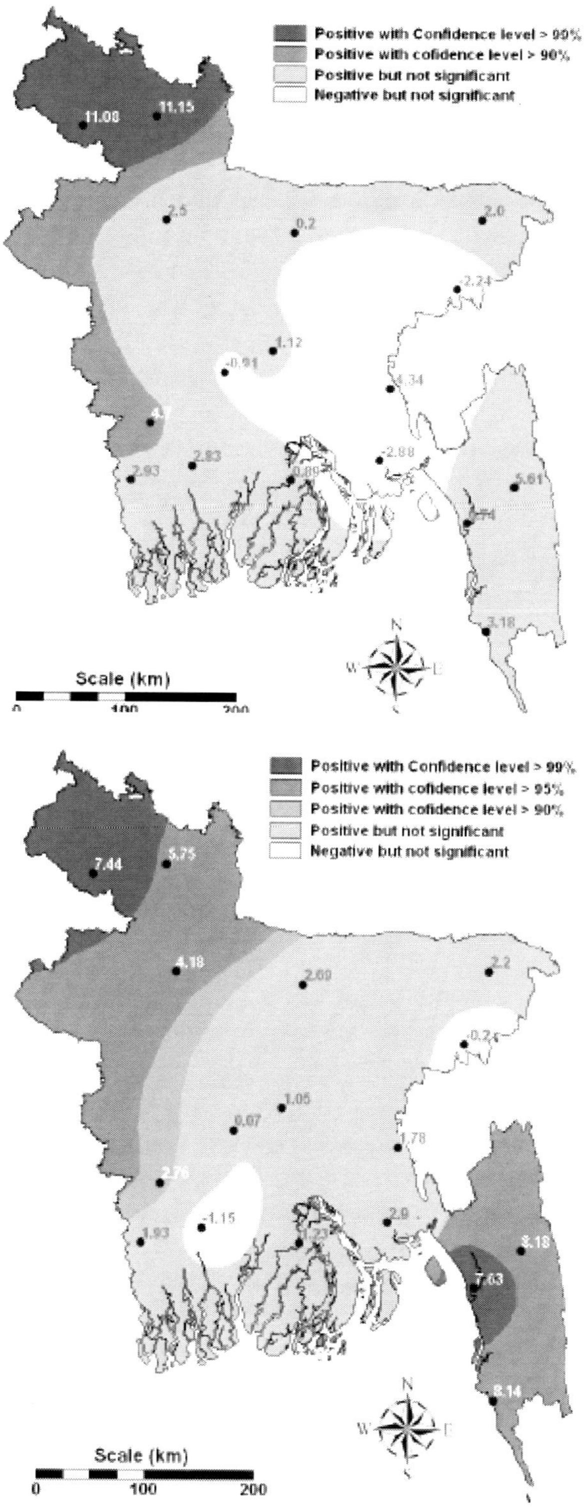

Figure 10. Spatial patterns of trends in (a) monsoon; and (b) pre-monsoon rainfall of Bangladesh during the time period 1958-2007. The numbers in white color denote significant change.

Spatial pattern of pre-monsoon rainfall trends in Bangladesh (Figure 10(b)) shows significant increase of pre-monsoon rainfall in northwestern and southeastern parts of Bangladesh. Maximum increase is observed in north Bangladesh by 7.44 mm/year at 99% level of confidence.

There exists a positive correlation between the sea surface temperature in the Bay of Bengal and the rainfall of Bangladesh (Salahuddin et al., 2006). The monsoon of Bangladesh flows in two branches, one of which strikes western India and the other travels up the Bay of Bengal and over eastern India and Bangladesh. The monsoon from the Bay of Bengal crosses the plain to the north and northeast before being turned to the west and northwest by the foothills of the Himalayas. Simulated increases in sea surface temperature in general circulation model (CGM) show that it alters wind patterns to the west of Bangladesh, leading to an accumulation of moisture in the region and greater rainfall during the summer monsoon season (Cash et al., 2007). Khan et al. (2000) found that sea surface temperature of Bay of Bengal has increased during the 14-year period from 1985–1998. Increase in sea surface temperature causes increase in precipitation due to the increase in convection (Alapaty, et al., 1995). Therefore, it can be remarked that increase in sea surface temperature of Bay of Bengal might be the cause of increased precipitation in Bangladesh. It is not possible to come to a decision about global climate change impact on rainfall of Bangladesh by analyzing the data presented in this chapter.

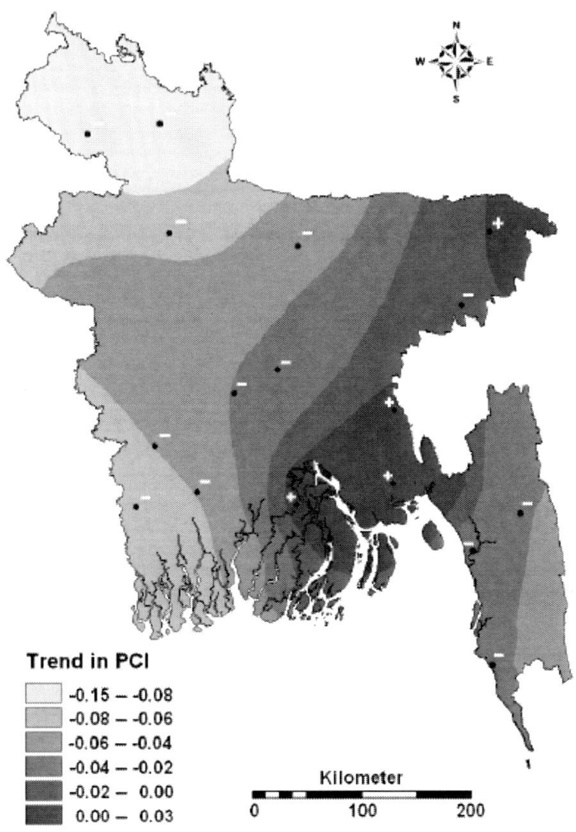

Figure 11. Spatial distribution of *PCI* trend over Bangladesh for the time period 1958-2007.

3.6. Trends in Precipitation Concentration Indices

No significant change in average *PCI* over Bangladesh is observed by Mann-Kendall test. Trend analysis of average *PCI* in each climate zone is also carried out. However, no statistically significant change of *PCI* in any climatic zone is observed. The trend analysis of *PCI* at each station is given in Table 1. *PCI* is found negative in 13 stations out of 17 stations of Bangladesh. Signification negative change of *PCI* is found in six stations. Spatial distribution of *PCI* trend over Bangladesh is shown in Figure 11. The figure shows a negative trend of *PCI* in all over Bangladesh except in northeastern corner.

CONCLUSION

Climate is an important factor in the economy of Bangladesh. Spatial and temporal variability of climate over Bangladesh in the recent years has been studied in this article. The result shows increasing annual and pre-monsoon rainfalls over Bangladesh. Spatial distribution of rainfall trends reveal that annual, monsoon and pre-monsoon rainfalls have been increased in north Bangladesh. Trend analysis of *PCI* shows that rainfall concentration has been decreased in few stations situated in the west part of Bangladesh. Most of the regional climate models also predict similar results – increasing annual rainfall in Bangladesh due to global climate change (IPCC, 2007). Though it is not possible to come to a concrete decision about climate change impact on rainfall in Bangladesh by analyzing the data presented, the results obtained in this study may be a first indication of the precipitation response to global warming – a hypothesis which needs to be further investigated by means of climate model projections.

REFERENCES

Aguilar E., Peterson TC., Ramırez Obando P. et al., (2005) Changes in precipitation and temperature extremes in CentralAmerica and northern South America, 1961–2003. *J. Geophy. Res. Doi.*:10.1029/2005JD006119.

Ahmed ASMS., Munim AA., Begum QN., Choudhury AM. (1996) El Niño Southern Oscillation and Rainfall Variation over Bangladesh. *MaUSm* 47(2): 157-162.

Ahmed AU., Alam M. (1999) Development of Climate Change Scenarios with General Circulation Models. In *Vulnerability and Adaptation to Climate Change for Bangladesh*, Huq S, Karim Z, Asaduzzaman M, Mahtab F(Eds.), Kluwer Academic Publishers, Dordrecht, 125-143.

Ahmed R., Karmakar S. (1993) Arrival and withdrawal dates of the summer monsoon in Bangladesh. *Internl. J. of Clim.* 13: 727–740.

Ahmed R., Kim I-K. (2003) Patterns of daily rainfall in Bangladesh during the summer monsoon season: case studies at three stations. *Phy. Geogr.* 24(4): 295–318.

Alapaty K., Raman S., Mohanty UC., Madala RV. (1995) Sensitivity of monsoon circulations to changes in sea surface temperatures. *Atmos. Env.* 29(16): 2139-2156.

Bangladesh Bureau of Statistics (2010) Census of Agriculture Bangladesh. Bureau of Statistics, Statistics Division, Ministry of Planning, Govt. of the People's Republic of Bangladesh, Dhaka.

Cash BA., Rodó X., Kinter JL. (2007) Links between tropical Pacific SST and the regional climate of Bangladesh: Role of the eastern and central tropical Pacific. *COLA Technical Report*, 236, 32pp, Center for Ocean-Land-Atmosphere Studies, Calverton, Maryland.

Conrad V., Pollak C. (1950) Methods in climatology. Harvard University Press, Cambridge.

Dash SK., Shekhar MS., Singh GP. (2006) Simulation of Indian summer monsoon circulation and rainfall using RegCM3. *Theor. and App. Clim.* 86(1-4): 161-172.

De Martonne E. (1926) Aérisme et indice d'aridité. *Comptes rendus de l'Académie des Sciences*, 182, 1395-1398.

Dore MHI. (2005) Climate change and changes in global precipitation patterns: What do we know. *Environ. Internl.* 31(8): 1167-1181.

ESRI. (2003) ArcGIS9: Getting Started with ArcGIS. Environmental System Research Institute, Redlands.

Gemmer M., Becker S., Jiang T. (2004) Observed monthly precipitation trends in China 1951–2002. *Theor. Appl. Climatol.*, 77, 39–45.

Hulme M., Osborn TJ., Johns TC. (1998) Precipitation sensitivity to global warming: comparison of observations with HADCM2 simulations. *Geophy. Res. Let.*, 25, 3379–3382.

Hussain AM., Sultana N. (1996) Rainfall distribution over Bangladesh stations during the monsoon months in the absence of depressions and cyclonic storms. *MaUSm* 47: 339–348.

Immerzeel W. (2007) Historical trends and future predictions of climate variability in the Brahmaputra basin. *Internl. J. of Clim.* 28(2): 243-254.

IPCC. (2007) Climate Change 2007: The Physical Science Basis. Summary for Policymakers. Contribution of the Working Group I to the Fourth Assessment Report of the Intergovernmental Panel on Climate Change, Cambridge University Press, Cambridge.

Isaaks HE., Srivastava RM. (1989) An Introduction to Applied Geostatisitics. New York: Oxford University Press.

Islam MN., Uyeda H. (2008) Vertical variations of rain intensity in different rainy periods in and around Bangladesh derived from TRMM observations. *Internl. J. of Clim.* 28(2): 273-279.

Jones PD. (1995) Maximum and minimum temperature trends in Ireland, Italy, Thailand, Turkey and Bangladesh. *Atmos. Res.* 37(1-3): 67-78.

Kayano MT., Sansígolo C. (2008) Interannual to decadal variations of precipitation and daily maximum and daily minimum temperatures in southern Brazil. *Theor. Appl. Climatol.*, DOI 10.1007/s00704-008-0050-4.

Kendall MG. (1975) Rank correlation methods. Griffin, London.

Khan TMA., Singh OP., Rahman MS. (2000) Recent Sea Level and Sea Surface Temperature Trends Along the Bangladesh Coast in Relation to the Frequency of Intense Cyclones. *Marine Geodesy* 23(2): 103-116.

Khan TMA., Singh OP., Rahman MS. (2000) Recent Sea Level and Sea Surface Temperature Trends Along the Bangladesh Coast in Relation to the Frequency of Intense Cyclones. *Marine Geodesy* 23(2): 103-116.

Kohler MA. (1949) Double-mass analysis for testing the consistency of records and for making adjustments. *Bull. Amer. Meteor. Soc.* 30: 188–189.

Kripalani RH., Kulkarni A., Sabade SS., Khandekar ML. (2003) Indian Monsoon Variability in a Global Warming Scenario. *Nat. Haz.* 29: 189–206.

Kripalani RH., Oh JH., Kulkarni A., Sabade SS., Chaudhari HS. (2007) South Asian summer monsoon precipitation variability: Coupled climate model simulations and projections under IPCC AR4. *Theor. and App. Clim.* 90(3-4): 133-159.

Kripalini RH., Inamdar S., Sontakke NA. (1996) Rainfall variability over Bangladesh and Nepal: Comparison and connections with features over India. *Internl. J. of Clim.* 16: 689–703.

Krishna Kumar R., Kumar KK., Prasanna V., Kamala K., Deshpande S., Patwardhan K., Pant GB. (2003) Future Climate Scenarios. In Shukla PR, Sharma SK, Ravindranath NH, Garg A, Bhattacharya S. (eds) Climate Change and India: Vulnerability Assessment and Adaptation, University Press, India.

Lambert F., Stott P., Allen M. (2003) Detection and attribution of changes in global terrestrial precipitation. *Geophy. Res. Abs.* 5: 06140.

Manabe S., Stouffer RJ., Spelman MJ., Bryan K. (1991) Transient responses of a coupled ocean-atmosphere model to gradual changes of atmospheric CO2. Part I: Annual mean response. *J. of Clim.* 4:785-818.

Mann HB. (1945) Nonparametric tests against trend. *Economet* 13: 245–259.

May W. (2004) Simulation of the variability and extremes of daily rainfall during the Indian summer monsoon for present and future times in a global time-slice experiment. *Clim. Dyn.* 22(2-3): 183-204.

Mearns LO., Rosenzweig C., Goldberg R. (1996) The effect of changes in daily and interannual climatic variability on CERES-wheat: a sensitivity study. *Clim. Change*, 32, 257–292.

Michiels P., Gabriels D. (1996) Rain variability indices for the assessment of rainfall erosivity in the Mediterranean region. In: Rubio, J.L., Calva, A. (ed) *Soil Degradation and Desertification in Mediterranean Environments*, 49-70, Spain/Logrono.

OECD. (2003) Development and Climate Change in Bangladesh: Focus on Coastal Flooding and the Sundarbans. In: Agrawala S, Ota T, Ahmed AU (ed) Organization for Economic Co-operation and Development (OECD) Report COM/ENV/EPOC/DCD/DAC(2003)3/FINAL, Paris, France.*www.oecd.org/dataoecd/46/55/21055658.pdf* Accessed on 25 March 2009.

Panofsky HA., Brier GW. (1968) Some applications of statistics to meteorology. Pennsylvania State University, Pennsylvania.

Paul BK. (1998) Coping mechanisms practiced by drought victims (1994/5) in North Bengal, Bangladesh. *Appl. Geogr.*, 18(4), 355-373.

Peterson TC., Easterling DR., Karl TR et al. (1998) Homogeneity adjustments of in situ atmospheric climate data: a review. *Int. J. Climatol.* 18: 1493–1517.

Rahman MR., Salehin M., Matsumoto J. (1997) Trends of monsoon rainfall pattern in Bangladesh. *Bangladesh J. of Wat Resour.* 14–18: 121–138.

Rashid HE. (1991) Geography of Bangladesh. University Press Ltd, Dhaka.

Rodrı´guez-Puebla C., Encinas AH., Nieto S., Garmendia J. (1998) Spatial and temporal patterns of annual precipitation variability over the Iberian Peninsula. *Int. J. of Climatol.*, 18, 299–316.

Rupa Kumar K., Ashrit RG. (2001) Regional aspects of global climate change simulations: Validation and assessment of climate response over Indian monsoon region to transient increase of greenhouse gases and sulphate aerosols. *MaUSm* 52: 229–244.

Salahuddin A., Isaac RH., Cutis S., Matsumoto J. (2006) Teleconnections between the sea surface temperature in the Bay of Bengal and monsoon rainfall in Bangladesh. *Global and Planetary Change* 53(3): 188-197.

Sanderson M., Ahmed R. (1979) Pre-monsoon rainfall and its variability in Bangladesh: a trend surface analysis. *Hydrol. Sci-Bull.* 24(3): 277-287.

Sen PK. (1968) Estimates of the regression coefficient based on Kendall's tau. *Journal of the American Statistical Association* 63: 1379-1389.

Shahid S. (2008) Spatial and Temporal Characteristics of Droughts in the Western Part of Bangladesh. *Hydrol. Proc.*, 22(13), 2235-2247.

Shahid S. (2010) Recent trends in the climate of Bangladesh. *Climate Res.*, 42, 185-193.

Shahid S., Behrawan H. (2008) Drought Risk Assessment in the Western Part of Bangladesh. *Nat. Haz.*, 46(3), 391-413.

Shahid S., Khairulmaini OS. (2009) Spatio-Temporal variability of Rainfall over Bangladesh during the time period 1969-2003. *Asia-Pacific J. Atmos. Sci.*, 45, 375-389.

Shaman J., Cane M., Kaplan A. (2005) The relationship between Tibetan snow depth, ENSO, river discharge and the monsoons of Bangladesh. *Intern. J. of Rem. Sens.* 26(17): 3735 – 3748.

Singh OP. (2001) Cause-effect relationships between sea surface temperature, precipitation and sea level along the Bangladesh coast. *Theor. Appl. Climatol.* 68: 233-243.

Sneyers R. (1990) On the statistical analysis of series of observation. WMO, Technical Note No. 143, Geneve, Switzerland.

Stephenson DB., Douville H., Rupa Kumar K. (2001) Searching for a fingerprint of global warming in the Asian summer monsoon. *MaUSm* 52: 213–220.

Su BD., Jiang T., Jin WB. (2006) Recent trends in observed temperature and precipitation extremes in the Yangtze River basin, China. *Theor. Appl. Climatol.* 83: 139–151.

Thornthwaite CW. (1931) The climate of North America according to a new classification. *Geog. Rev.*, 21 (4), 633-55.

Van Beers WCM., Kleijnen JPC. (2004) Kriging Interpolation in Simulation: A Survey. Ingalls, R.G., Rossetti, M.D., Smith, J.S., Peters, B.A. (ed) Proc. 2004 Winter Simulation Conference Washington.

Webster PJ. (1987) The Elementary Monsoon. Wiley: New York.

In: Rainfall: Behavior, Forecasting and Distribution
Editors: Olga E. Martín and Tricia M. Roberts
ISBN: 978-1-62081-551-9

Chapter 3

NON-PARAMETRIC METHODS FOR FORECASTING TIME SERIES FROM CUMULATIVE MONTHLY RAINFALL

Julián Pucheta[1]*, C. Rodríguez Rivero[1], Martín Herrera[2], Carlos Salas[2], Víctor Sauchelli[1] and H. Daniel Patiño[3]

[1]Departments of Electrical and Electronic Engineering, Mathematics Research Laboratory applied to control (LIMAC), at Faculty of Exact, Physical and Natural Sciences - National University of Córdoba, Córdoba, Argentina

[2]Departments of Electrical Engineering, at Faculty of Sciences and Applied Technologies - National University of Catamarca, Catamarca, Argentina

[3]Institute of Automatics (INAUT) Faculty of Engineering-National University of San Juan, San Juan, Argentina

ABSTRACT

This chapter presents two non-parametric methods for designing algorithms to forecast time series from the cumulative monthly rainfall. Both approaches are based on artificial feed-forward neural networks (ANNs). The results are evaluated on high roughness time series from the Mackey-Glass Equation (MG), and from accumulated monthly historical rainfall data from one geographic location. In addition, both methods are compared with the classic non-linear moving average (NAR) predictor filter. The first case is an algorithm to forecast time series that set the parameters of a NAR model based on ANNs as function of the energy associated to the time series. We propose a tuning criterion, which consists of producing the values of the time series starting from the areas of the forecasted time series. These values are approximated by an ANN that generates a primitive calculated by a linear predictor filter. Depending on the roughness of the time series, we propose a heuristic law to establish the tuning process and the NN topology, assuming that the forecasted time series has the same Hurst parameter that the original

* Email: limac@efn.uncor.edu

data time series. In the second case, the methodology consists of generating time series by sampling the data time series, and each individual time series is associated with a predictor filter. Thus, depending on the data, others time series are obtained by sampling with an increasing interval. For each one of the time series generated, a specific ANN-based filter is adjusted, and each one generates a forecast that is then averaged among other subsamples time series, resulting in a mix of predictor filters. The tuning rule used in the adjustment process is based on the Levenberg-Marquardt method. From simulation results, it can be concluded that to achieve a more accurate forecast to reality of time series with high roughness, to smooth the time series is a good practice. The methodology proposed here proposes to divide the problem of time series forecasting by non-parametric methods by subdivision into stages of smoothing. The first was the subsampling method, which showed that restructuring is a good technique, and the second one, the integration of data time series that works with their primitive, which can be considered as the second case proposed in this chapter. The results are encouraging; deserving study and investment in implementation effort for the geographical locations of interest.

Keywords: Time series forecast, sub-sampling decimation, integration, Hurst's parameter, Neural networks, Mackey-Glass

INTRODUCTION

The prediction of natural phenomena is a challenging topic, particularly the prediction of information about water availability, among other things, useful for control problems in agricultural activities. It is proposed to generate a methodology to design a system that is able to providing sequence of values that represent the future scenario of availability of rainfall.

The motivation to make this work arises from the need for know-how-based tools at the time the farmer must decide to plant one crop or another according to a desired profitability, then an information estimated by the system obtained needs to be reliable.

Thus, the purpose of the system is to estimate the availability of rainfall during the growth process before the farmer begins the process of planting the crop.

However, once they began the process of growth of the crop by a suitable control scheme [1], it is possible to making alterations in crop management to ensure the income of the operation.

There are several approaches based on artificial neural networks (ANN) for predictions [2], specifically rainfall [3], energy demands [4] and availability of water by taking a set of data points [5].

This chapter presents three case studies that provide an orientation to make a forecast. In the first case, we present results of a forecasting methodology based on classical ANN [6]. In the second and third cases, a series data is processed by generating a series in which it make possible an adjustment process of the filter, and finally compare the three results.

The predictor filters were tested from samples of MG equations and historical cumulative monthly rainfall time series from Santa Francisca, Cordoba, Argentina (-31.8670, -64.3655).

The chapter organization is as follows. After this introduction, the classic predictor filter based on neural networks called Case 1 is detailed. Subsequently, two predictor filters are listed called Case 2 and Case 3, each one with its partial results and discussions. Finally, we compare the three cases named and at the end it is described the conclusions of the chapter.

Motivations

The main motivations for this study follows the closed-loop control scheme [1], as shown in Figure 1, where the controller considers meteorological future conditions for designing the control law. These conditions are estimated by a system predictor, and the future scenarios are represented by the sequence $\{x_e\}$. The controller's portion concerning with the prediction system is presented by using a benchmark time series.

In this outline, the controller takes into account the actual state of the cumulative monthly rainfall in order to be used by the state observer. However, in this chapter, a part of the filter taking as starting point time series, respectively, is only introduced.

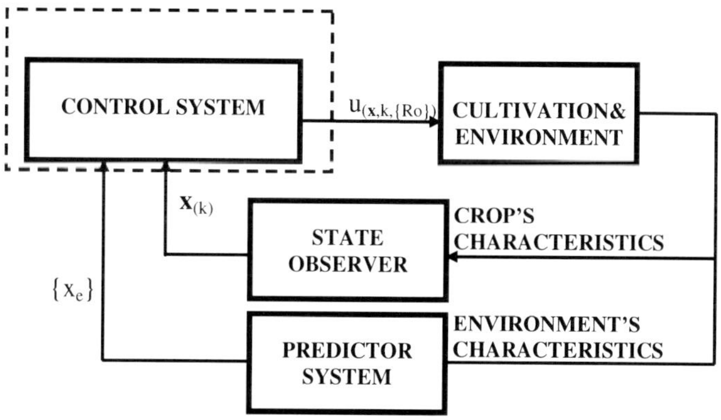

Figure 1. Control scheme that considers future values of a rainfall sequence.

Forecast Problem Statement

The classical prediction problem may be formulated as follows. Given past values of a process that are uniformly spaced in time, as shown by x(t-*T*), x(t-2*T*), .., x(t-*mT*), where T is the sampling period and m is the data length, it is desired to predict the present value x(t) of such process.

Therefore, to obtain the best prediction of the present values from a random (or pseudo-random) time series is desired. The predictor system may be implemented using an autoregressive model-based non-linear adaptive filter.

The ANNs are used as a non-linear model building, in the sense that the smaller the prediction error is (in a statistical sense), the better the ANN serves as a model of the underlying physical process responsible for generating the data. In this chapter, time lagged ANN are used.

The present value of the time series is used as the desired response for the adaptive filter and the past values of the signal serve as input of the adaptive filter. Then, the adaptive filter output will be the one-step prediction signal.

In Figure 2, the block diagram of the non-linear prediction scheme based on a NN filter is shown. Here, a prediction device is designed such that starting from a given sequence $\{x_n\}$ at time n corresponding to a time series it can be obtained the best prediction $\{x_e\}$ for the following sequence of 18 values.

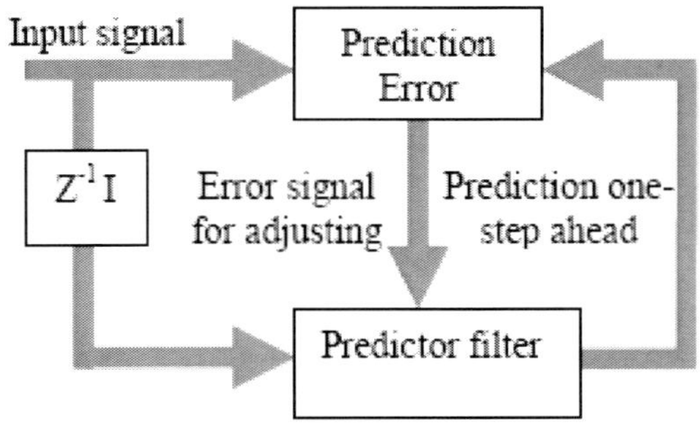

Figure 2. Block diagram of the predictor system.

Hence, a predictor filter is proposed with an input vector l_x, which is obtained by applying the delay operator, Z^{-1}, to the sequence $\{x_n\}$. Then, the filter output will generate x_e as the next value, that will be equal to the present value x_n. So, the prediction error at time *k* can be evaluated as:

$$e(k) = x_n(k) - x_e(k) \tag{1}$$

which is used for the learning rule to adjust the NN weights.

METHODS

In all of the predictions proposed by this work, soft tools commonly used in the literature as MG equation [9] useful for meteorological process modeling were employed [13]. The definition of the stochastic characteristic is related with the parameter H who gives an idea of roughness of the time series and the fractal dimensionality of the data set [10], in which the classical scope of forecast is based on ANN [6].

Samples of Mackey Glass Equation

The MG equation serves to model natural phenomena and has been used by different authors to perform comparisons between different techniques for prediction and regression models [7] [8].

Here we propose an algorithm to predict the data time series taken from the solution of the MG equation [9].

The MG equation is explained by the time delay differential equation defined as,

$$\dot{y}(t) = \frac{\alpha y(t-\tau)}{1 + y^c(t-\tau)} - \beta y(t) \tag{2}$$

where α, β, and c are parameters and τ is the delay time.

According as τ increases, the solution turns from periodic to chaotic. Equation (2) is solved by a standard fourth order Runge-Kutta integration step. The time series to forecast are composed by samples of a benchmark of MG solutions and the deterministic time series obtained varies according to its roughness.

Overview on Fractional Brownian Motion

The Hurst's parameter is used by the tuning algorithm to modify the number of patterns, the number of iterations, and the number of filter's inputs. This H gives an idea of roughness of a signal, and determines its stochastic dependence. The definition of the Hurst's parameter appears in the Brownian motion from generalizing an ordinary integral to a fractional integral.

The Fractional Brownian Motion (fBm) is defined in the pioneering work by [10], through its stochastic representation

$$B_H(t)=\frac{1}{\Gamma\left(H+\frac{1}{2}\right)}\left(\int\left((t-s)^{H-\frac{1}{2}}-(-s)^{H-\frac{1}{2}}\right)dB(s)\right.$$
$$\left.+\int(t-s)^{H-\frac{1}{2}}dB(s)\right) \tag{3}$$

where, $\Gamma(\cdot)$ represents the Gamma function

$$\Gamma(\alpha)=\int x^{\alpha-1}e^{-x}dx \tag{4}$$

and $0<H<1$ is called the Hurst parameter. The integrator B is a stochastic process, ordinary Brownian motion.

Note, that B is recovered by taking H=1/2 in (3). Here, it is assumed that B is defined on some probability space (Ω, F, P), where Ω, F and P are the sample space, the sigma algebra (event space) and the probability measure, respectively. So, a fBm is a continuous-time Gaussian process depending on the so-called Hurst parameter $0<H<1$. It generalizes the ordinary Brownian motion corresponding to H=0.5.

The fBm is self-similar in distribution and the variance of the increments is given by

$$\operatorname{Var}(B_H(t)-B_H(s))=v|t-s|^{2H} \tag{5}$$

where, v is a positive constant.

This special form of the variance of the increments suggests various ways to estimate the parameter H. In fact, there are different methods for computing the parameter H associated to Brownian motion [11]. In this chapter, the algorithms use a wavelet-based method for estimating H from a trace path of the fBm with parameter H [11] [12].

ANN-Based NAR Model

Along the three cases of study, we implement a classic NN-based NAR filter [6]. The ANN used is a time lagged feed-forward networks type. The ANN topology consists of l_x inputs, one hidden layer of H_o units, and one output unit as shown in Figure 3.

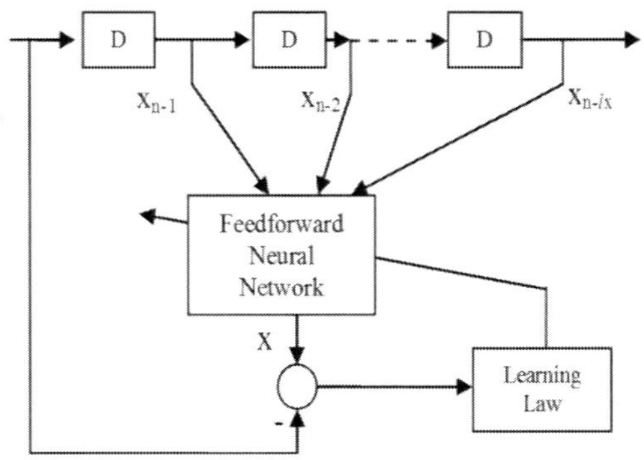

Figure 3. Neural Network-based nonlinear predictor filter. The one-step delay operator is denoted by D.

In order to predict the sequence $\{x_e\}$ one-step ahead, the first delay taken off from the tapped-line x_n is used as input. Therefore, the output prediction can be denoted by

$$x_e(n+1) = F_p\left(Z^{-1}I(\{x_n\})\right) \tag{6}$$

where, F_p is the non-linear predictor filter operator, and $x_e(n+1)$ the output prediction at n+1, and

$$I \in \Re^{lx} \times \Re^{lx}. \tag{7}$$

For the first case of study, we proposed a rule for the learning process based on the Levenberg-Marquardt method [14]. The learning rule modifies the number of patterns and the number of iterations at each iteration according to the Hurst's parameter H, which gives short and long term dependence of the sequence $\{x_n\}$ or —from a practical point of view, it gives the roughness of the time series. For the second case of study, we perform a smoothing process that consists of the use of subsampling techniques. At last, following the idea of smoothing the time series; we perform a transformation on the data series which consist of its integral function.

Performance Measure for Forecasting

In order to test the proposed design procedure of the NN-based non-linear predictor, an experiment with time series obtained from the MG solution was performed. The performance of the filter is evaluated using the Symmetric Mean Absolute Percent Error (SMAPE) proposed in the most of metric evaluation, defined by

$$SMAPE_S = \frac{1}{n}\sum_{t=1}^{n}\frac{|X_t - F_t|}{(X_t + F_t)/2}\cdot 100 \quad (7)$$

where t is the observation time, n is the size of the test set, s is each time series, X_t and F_t are the actual and the forecasted time series values at time t, respectively.

The SMAPE of each series s calculates the symmetric absolute error in percent between the actual X_t and its corresponding forecast value F_t, across all observations t of the test set of size n for each time series s.

CASE 1

The NN's weights are tuned by means of the Levenberg-Marquardt rule, which considers the long and short term stochastic dependence of the time series measured by the Hurst's parameter H.

The proposed learning approach consists of changing the number of patterns, the filter's length and the number of iterations in function of the parameter H for each corresponding time series. The learning process is performed using a batch model.

In this case, the weight updating is performed after the presentation of all training examples, which forms an epoch.

The pairs (i_t, N_p) are modified by the statistical dependence of the time series $\{x_n\}$, supposing that is an fBm. The dependence is evaluated by the Hurst's parameter H, which is computed using a wavelet-based method [11] [13].

Then, a heuristic adjustment for the pair (i_t, N_p) in function of H according to the membership functions is shown in Figure 4.

Finally, after each pass, the number of inputs of the non-linear filter is tuned —that is the length of tapped-delay line, according to the following heuristic criterion.

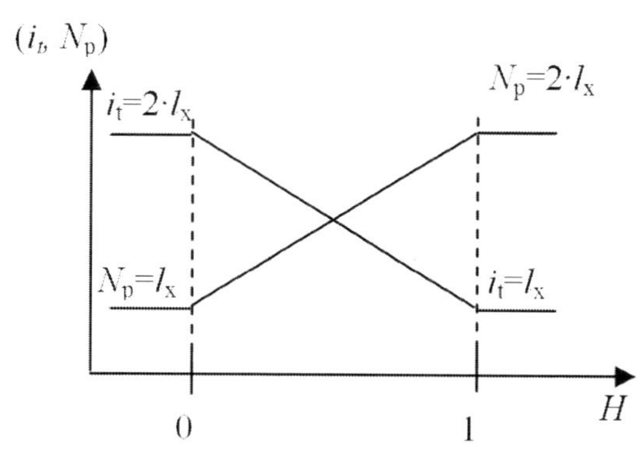

Figure 4. Heuristic adjustment of (i_t, N_p) in terms of H after each epoch.

After the training process is completed, both sequences —$\{x_n\}$ and $\{\{x_n\},\{x_e\}\}$, should have the same H parameter. If the error between $H(\{x_n\})$ and $H(\{\{x_n\},\{x_e\}\})$ is greater than a threshold parameter θ, the value of l_x is increased (or decreased), according to $l_x \pm 1$. Explicitly,

$$1_x = 1_x + \mathrm{sign}(\theta). \tag{8}$$

here, the threshold θ was set about 1%.

Set-Up of Model and Learning Process

The initial conditions for the ANN learning algorithm were set in function of the input quantity. These initial conditions of the learning algorithm were used for forecasting the time series, whose sizes have a length of 102 values each.

Prediction Results for the MG and Santa Francisca Time Series

Each time series are composed by sampling the MG solutions. However, there are two classes of data sets: one is those used for the algorithm in order to give the forecast, which are 102 values long. The other one is those used to compare if the forecast is acceptable or not where the 18 last values can be used to validate the performance of the prediction system. So, 102 values form the Data set, and the Forecasted and the Real sets have 120 values.

The results obtained are shown in Figure 5 and Figure 6 for the MG and Santa Francisca case, respectively.

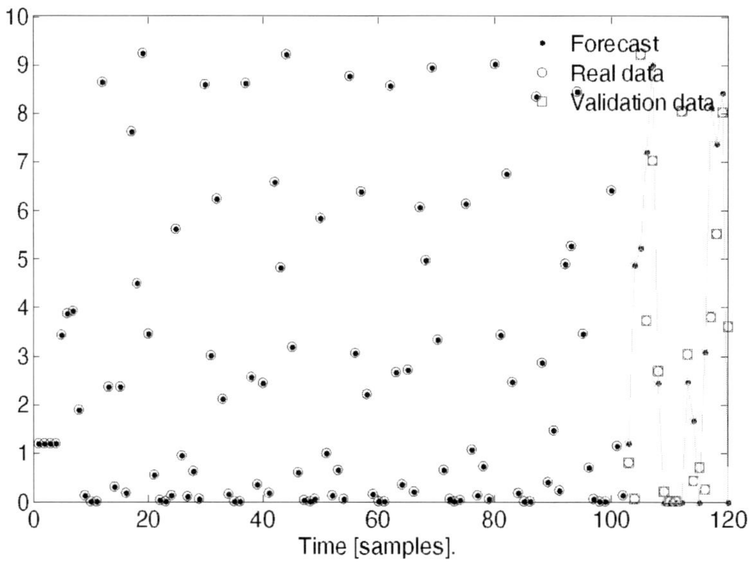

Figure 5. Forecast for MG time series where α=20, β=0.85, c=10 and τ=100.

The performance of the traditional NN-based predictor filter is evaluated through the SMAPE index, Equation (7), across the time series. In the analyzed cases, the generation of 18 future values from 102 present values was made by the algorithm. In Table 3 are the detailed results. Note that the computed value of the Hurst's parameter is denoted by either H_e or H when it is obtained from the Forecasted time series or from the Data series, respectively, since the Real (future time series) are unknown. Index SMAPE is computed between the complete Real series (it includes the Data series) and the Forecasted one, as indicates the Ec. (7) for each filter. Some the forecast's improvement may be attained by the algorithms detailed in the next two approaches, which exploited the stochastic characteristic for generates a deterministic result, such the prediction.

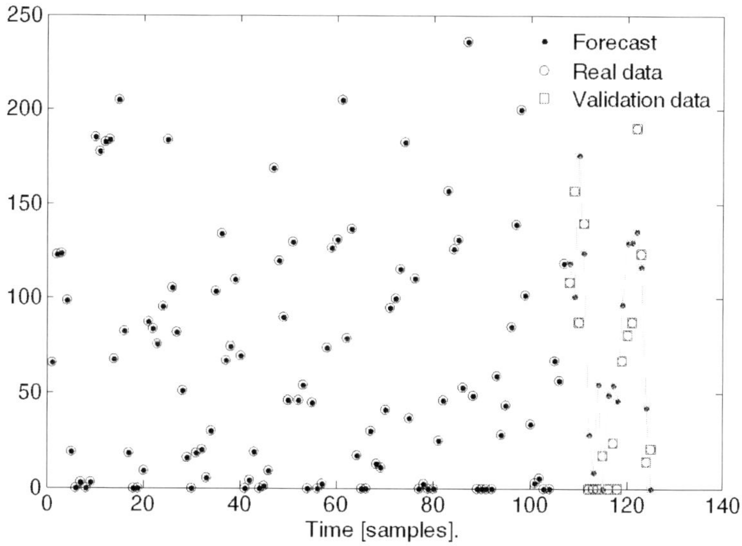

Figure 6. Forecast made without decimation of the classical ANN.

CASE 2

In this case, a proposal of a non-linear autoregressive model (NAR) based filter is shown using classic neural network for prediction, where it is intended to smooth the data series in order to be the prediction simpler. To achieve this issue, a proposed sub-sampling method is performed. The number of inputs in the filter is put in function on the amount of data available, so that when the data is subsampled, then the number of inputs is lower.

The methodology consists of generating time series starting from the original series subsamples, based on the latest available at the earliest. Thus, sampling with an interval it is obtained a time series, with two intervals another time series, and so on until for example 7 intervals, depending on data series allow.

For each of the series created by sub-sampling, it was adjusted to a different filter based on neural networks, and each one of them produces a forecast that is then averaged together. This average, which is a value for each future moment, is comprised of 18 values.

The adjustment rule used in the learning process is based on the Levenberg-Marquardt method. The proposed filter performance is evaluated using the index SMAPE.

There are some cases of MG time series that show an observable improvement, but in the case of Santa Francisca rainfall series, is more similar to the result obtained by the neural network based filter without down-sampling. It is concluded that it is better to smoothing time series with a sort roughness, which is very common in monthly accumulated rainfall series.

The algorithm proposed here separates into several predictor filters starting from sub-sampling the original series, and the outputs made by these filters are averaged straightforwardly without weighting up a filter over the other. It is encouraging to generate a criterion for merging the outputs of predictor filters instead of averaging only.

Sub-Sampling General Description

This paper implements a sampling of the data series to perform several different time series. In each of these series, it is intended to use the same predictor filter structure to determine the future values αk at one step. In Figure 7 and Figure 8, examples of a time series decimation, caused by MG and a monthly accumulated rainfall series, are shown

$$y_k = R(\alpha k), \quad k = 0, 1, 2 \ldots 120, \tag{9}$$

where αk varies from 0 to the end of series, and the original series α=1.

From the series of Equation (9), a second subset sampling at every odd k is generated, which results in

$$y_k^D = y_k, \; D = 2, \; k = 0, 2, 4, 6 \ldots 120, \tag{10}$$

where the number of steps subsampled is D, and in this article varies from 2 to 7.

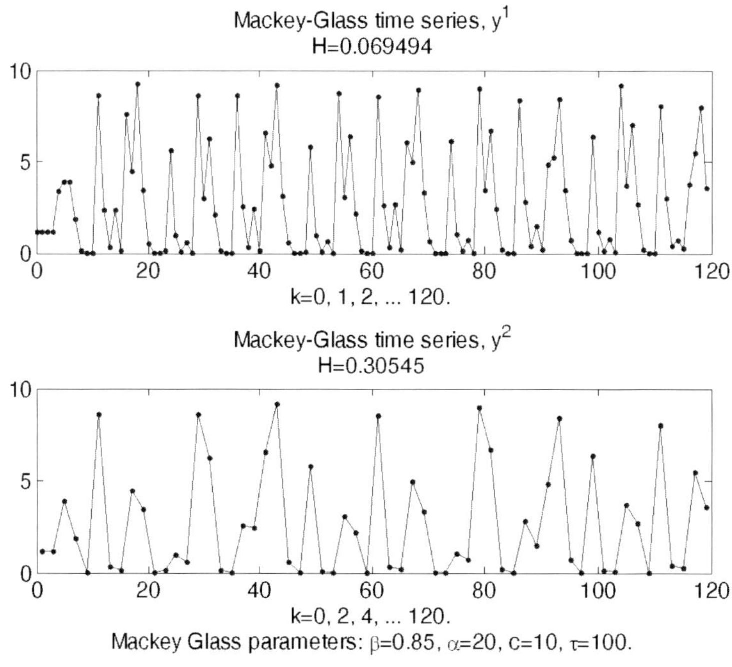

Figure 7. MG time series y^D, subsampled time series with decimation D of 1, 2 and 3.

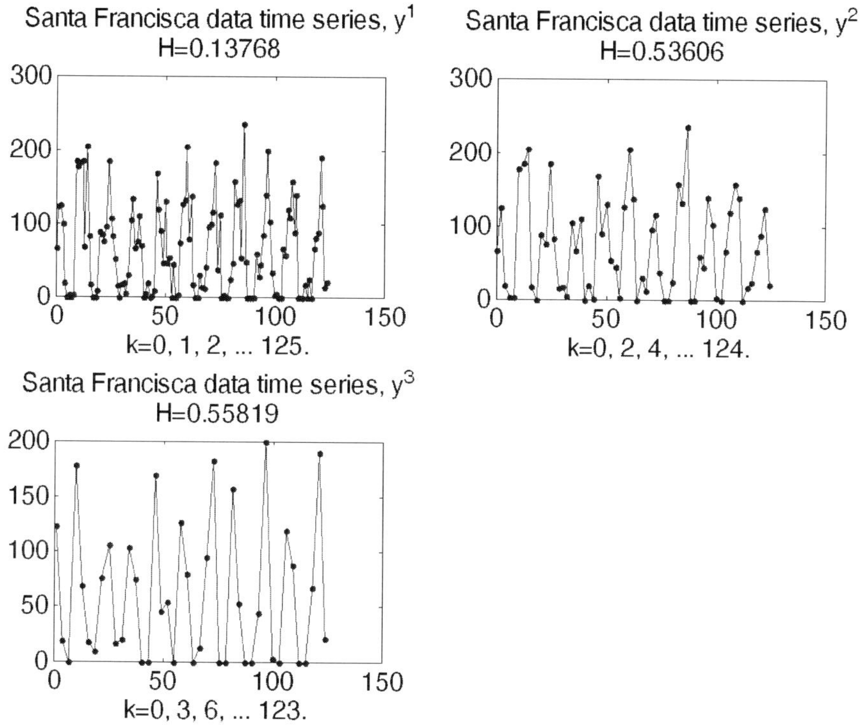

Figure 8. Original time series from Santa Francisca y^D, subsampled with decimation D of 1, 2 and 3.

However, in Figure 7, time series obtained when D varies from 1 to 2 for MG time series is shown. Note that a subsampled time series has its future value one step ahead, in which coincides with the original time series at each subsampled value, so the Δt goes 1 to 2, from the Δt of the original time series.

The H parameter associated with each serial changes from 0.069494 for the original, to 0.30545 for a subsample of 2, which it is highlighted that the time series obtained are smoother than the original. A similar situation can be observed for the Santa Francisca time series, as is shown in Figure 8.

Methodology Proposed

Some results have been obtained from an autoregressive linear approximation which is detailed in [17]. These results were promising and it is desired to be improved by more sophisticated filters. Now, it is proposed a NAR filter model NAR [2] [6] [15] where the ANN is fed back with time lag.

The topology of the ANN consist of lx inputs, one hidden layer of neurons H_o, and one output neuron, as shown in Figure 3. The learning algorithm used is the Levenberg-Marquardt method [16].

In order to predict the sequence $\{x_e\}$ one step ahead, the first value without delay taken from the line is x_n, which is used as an input. Thus, the predicted output can be expressed as

$$x_e(n+1) = F_p\left(Z^{-1}I(\{x_n\})\right) \tag{11}$$

where F_p is the non-linear operator of the predictor filter, and $x_e(n+1)$ the output of the predictor in n. To accomplish the forecasted time series, the generated value of $x(n+1)$ is used as an input to the filter F_p with a proper delay,

$$x_e(n+2) = F_p\left(Z^{-1}I(\{x_n, x_e(n+1)\})\right) \tag{12}$$

and this value $x_e(n+2)$ is achieved, at the same time is delayed again and entered as a new input to obtain the next value $x_e(n+3)$ by Eq. (11),

$$x_e(n+3) = F_p\left(Z^{-1}I(\{x_n, x_e(n+1), x_e(n+2)\})\right) \tag{13}$$

and so on until a value $x_e(n + D_e)$,

$$x_e(n+D_e) = F_p\left(Z^{-1}I(\{x_n, x_e(n+1), \ldots, x_e(n+D_e-1)\})\right) \tag{14}$$

in which of the case of the original time series, here it is intended to reach up to 18.

However, the use of time series $\{x_n\}$ requires the predictor filter F_p a great amplitude of response speed, since the sequence $\{x_n\}$ can have abrupt changes from one time interval to another. To face this issue of the prediction process, in this article it is proposed to implement a subsampling attempting to smooth the series $\{x_n\}$.

Proposed Solution

The methodology comprises to generate time series by subsample from the original time series $\{x_n\}$, based on the latest available value toward the oldest. Thus, sampling with an interval results in a time series, with two other intervals, and so on for example, 7 intervals, according to the data series allows. Thus, by subsampling each of the interval $\{x_n\}$, it is obtained the sequence $\{x_n\}^2$, which will have half of elements $\{x_n\}$, with decimation D = 2 decimation. Consequently, with D = 3, it is obtained $\{x_n\}^3$ and in general, D is obtained by the sequence $\{x_n\}^D$. Each of the sequences $\{x_n\}^D$ employed a specific filter F_p, which will generate predictions for each series according to Eq. (11). Thus, if a series exists for the sequence $\{x_n\}$, there will be s F_p filters that will implement the prediction of Equation (11).

The values obtained are used as a matrix P of input to an Adaline neural network (adaptive linear combiner element that receives all the inputs, weights up all these and produces an output), in which it is yielded a set of parameters $\{w_i\}$, to sum the output of the core network.

$$x_e^s(n+1) = \sum_s w_i F_p^s\left(Z^{-1}I(\{x_n\}^s)\right) \tag{15}$$

where x^s_e is the variable to predict whose argument $n+1$ is located in the time series with a decimation D as indicated by the index s. The sequence $\{x_n\}^s$ corresponds to $\{x_n\}^D$ with the appropriate change of indexes, and F^s_p is referred to the predictor filter for each sequence $\{x_n\}^s$.

It can be noted that every time the expression of Equation (11) is employed according to the subsampling procedure expressed by Equations (12)-(13)-(14) in the subsampled time series, the value of $D_e(n+1)$ will change, as it is decreasing according to D. Therefore, a set of subsampled time series are made of for s = 1 De = 18, for s = 2 De = 9, for s = 3 De = 6, and so forth.

They were defined two kinds of data in each series, one of these used by the algorithm for the adjustment of the filter, which contains 102 data. The other series data is used to validate the prediction of the system and a class validation to determine whether the prediction is acceptable or not is defined in the last 18 values. Thereby, the 102 values of the data series used for forecasting in addition to the 18 validation values, gives a real data set of 120 values. Something similar was done with Santa Francisca rainfall series, as it was intended to forecast the past 18 values.

Model Setup and Adjustment Process

The initial conditions of the filter and the learning algorithm are shown in Table 1.

Table 1. Adjustment algorithm parameters

Variable	Symbol	Value
Number of inputs	l_x	$D{\cdot}D_e$
Number of patterns	N_p	l_x
Number of neurons in hidden layer	H_o	l_x+3
Number of iterations	i_t	$4{\cdot}l_x+10$

Note that the number of neurons in the hidden layer and iterations are adjusted depending on the number of inputs. The initial conditions of the learning algorithm are used for time series forecasting, the length of the data set is 102 or 107 values each one.

Results of the Test with MG Series

The results obtained are shown in Figure 9 and Figure 10 for MG and Santa Francisca time series, respectively. In Figure 9, the forecast obtained for the case of the series $\{x_n\}^1$, $\{x_n\}^2$, $\{x_n\}^3$, and $\{x_n\}^4$ is shown , and in Figure 10, the validation detail of the algorithm is shown, where the actual and predicted time at one step are overlapped. Then the filter proposed by Equation (15) is implemented, where the result obtained is shown in Figure 10.

The results obtained in the test of the predictor filter of Equation (15) applied to Santa Francisca rainfall time series are shown in Figure 11 and Figure 12.

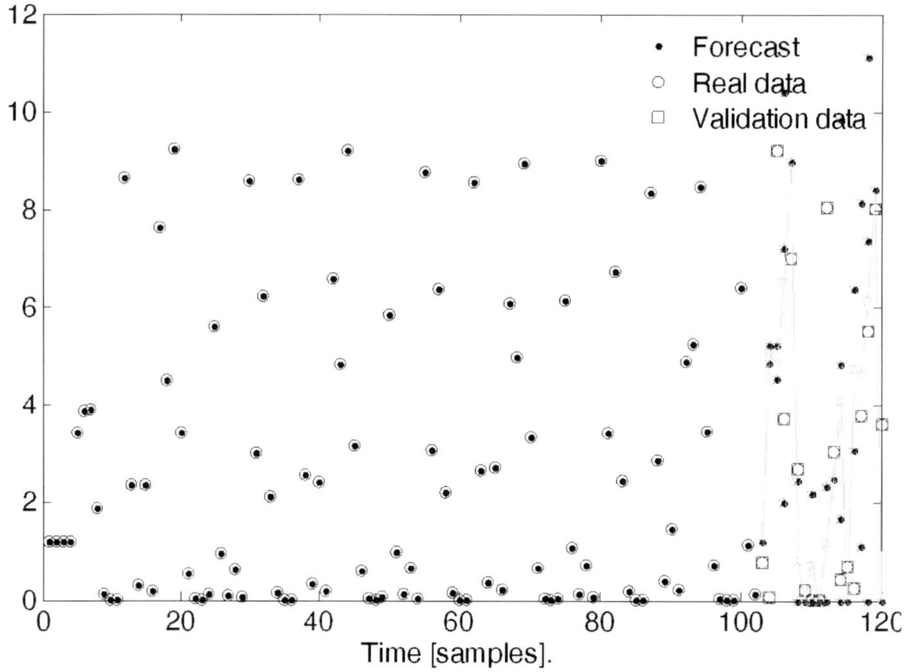

Figure 9. Forecast made with decimation D={1,2,3,4}.

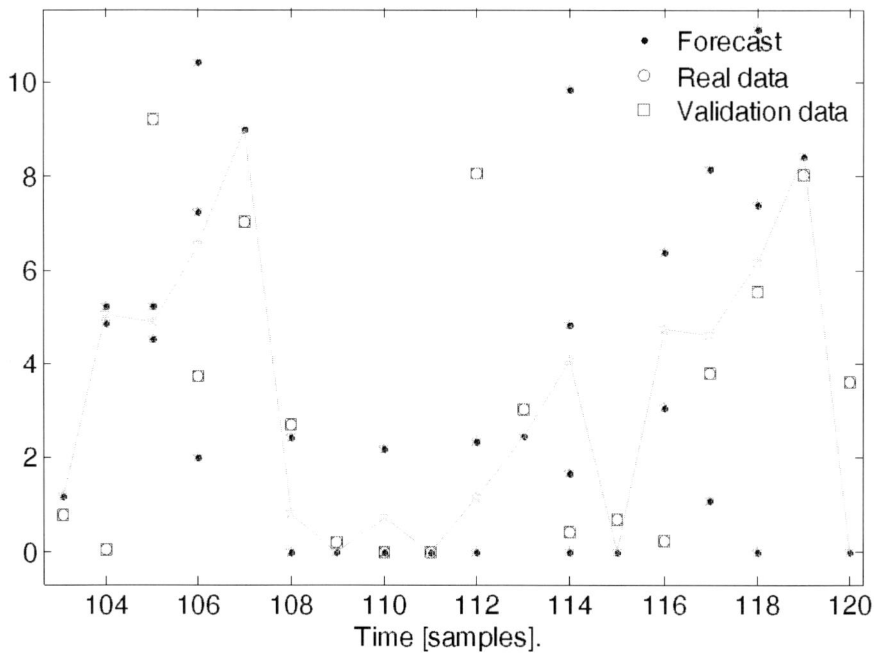

Figure 10. Forecast validation with D={1,2,3,4} by Eq. (15).

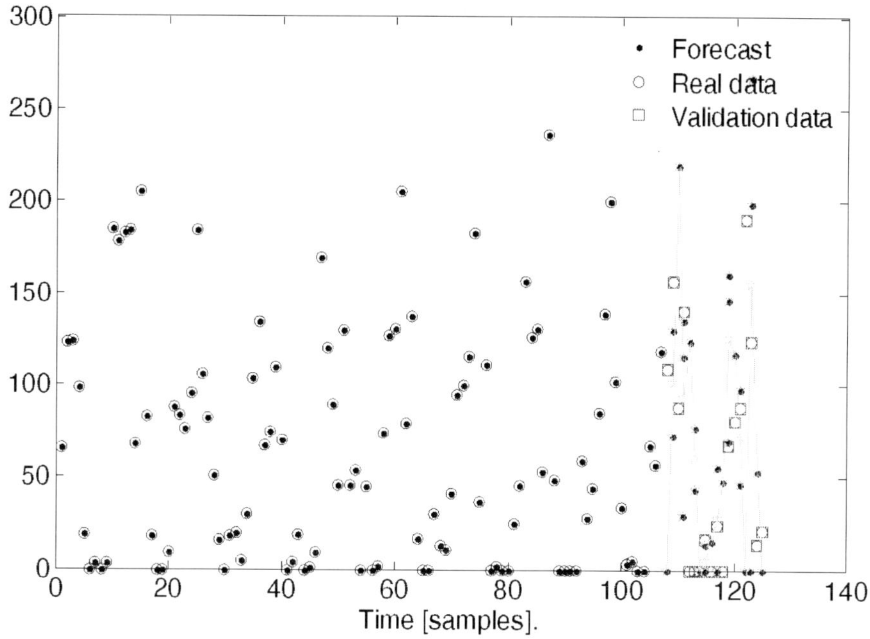

Figure 11. Forecast performed by evaluating Equation (15) with D={1,2,3} over the original time series.

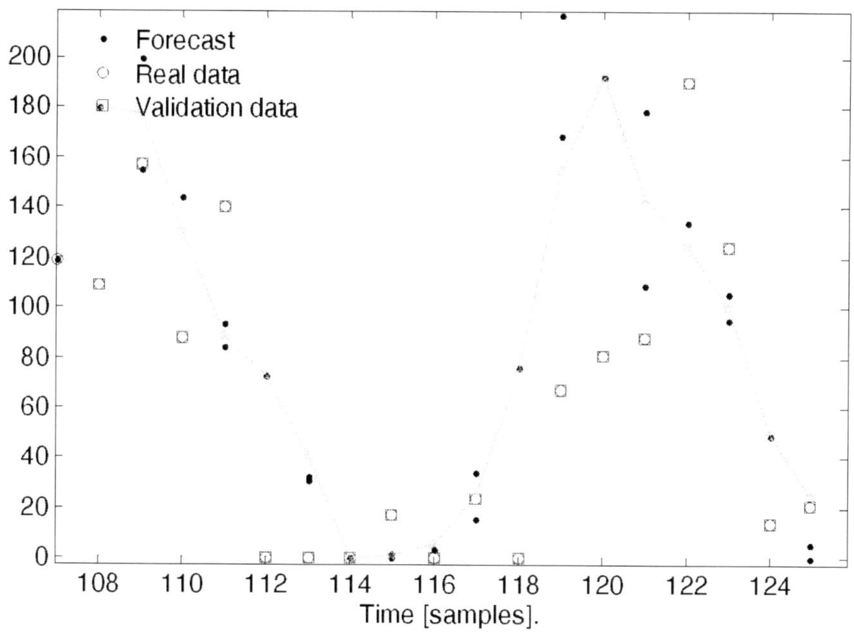

Figure 12. Validation of the forecast performed with D={1,2,3} by Eq. (15) over the original time series.

Comments and Remarks

Note that the results show that it is possible to enhance time series forecasting by a predictor filter that uses subsampling. The MG series was chosen because it has a mean and a roughness similar to Santa Francisca rainfall series. However, the filter performance was better in the Santa Francisca rainfall series. Other time series have been tested with MG series, in which good results were obtained but not added in this article to keep a little representative. The MG series was chosen because it is representative, according to these parameters, from Santa Francisca rainfall time series located in Alta Gracia, Cordoba. Various tests were performed in Santa Francisca series, and were displayed the best they represent the performance of the filter proposed here. It remains to prove combinations of {D}, for example {1,3} or {1,3,4} trying to improve performance. The concept that emphasized the proposed filter when forecasting is to use smooth time series, the performance is better when the series are rough. Hence, the effect sought by subsampled method is to smooth time series. Furthermore, the algorithm proposed here separates into several predictor filters starting from subsampling the original time series, and the outputs generated by these filters are weighted up, with averaging a filter over the other. The effect of weighting the average is a challenge that can produce a benefit in the performance of the filter.

In Table 3 shows the results obtained for two test series. Note that the goal is to reach the best approximation of the real mean by the forecasted mean, and this forescated series together with the series data should present a similar roughness.

It can be noted that in some MG time series are obtained an improvement in the SMAPE index, but in the case of the Santa Francisca time series, is more prominent the enhancement with respect to SMAPE index, the error in the forecasted mean tends to decrease, and the parameter of H roughness attempts to approximate to the data series.

CASE 3

In the latest proposal, it proceeds to smoothing the data time series by means of integration of the original time series. Then, a forecast of the integrated time series is performed in order for getting its roughness. By this estimated calculus, the filter predictor of the original time series is adjusted and is conjectured that the prediction result is better.

Approximation by Primitive

The basic assumption is the following. It is considered to take the area resulting of integrating the time series data. That primitive is obtained by considering each value of time series its derivate;

$$y_{t_k} = \int_{t_k}^{t_{k+1}} x_s ds \tag{16}$$

where y_t is the original time series value. The approximation area is assumed to be its periodical primitive

$$I_{t_n} = \int_{t_n}^{t_{n+p}} x_s ds = X_t \big|_{t_n}^{t_{n+p}}, n = 1,2,...N. \tag{17}$$

During the learning process, those primitives are calculated and serve as a new input for tuning by the algorithm of the ANN-based predictor. The prediction attempts to make the area's roughness of the forecasted times series equal to the primitive real area predicted. The tuning algorithm is detailed in Figure 4 and Equation (8).

In Figure 13 and Figure 14, two time series are shown where the energy associated to each one is depicted, altogether with the H parameter. Note that the roughness of both series is higher for the top series with respect to those of the bottom.

The real area is used in two instances. Firstly, from the real time series, an area is obtained and is run by the forecast algorithm. The algorithm is described in [14].

The H parameter of this data time series is called H_A. On the other hand, the data time series is forecasted by the filter, so the H parameter from energy associated to this time series is called H_S.

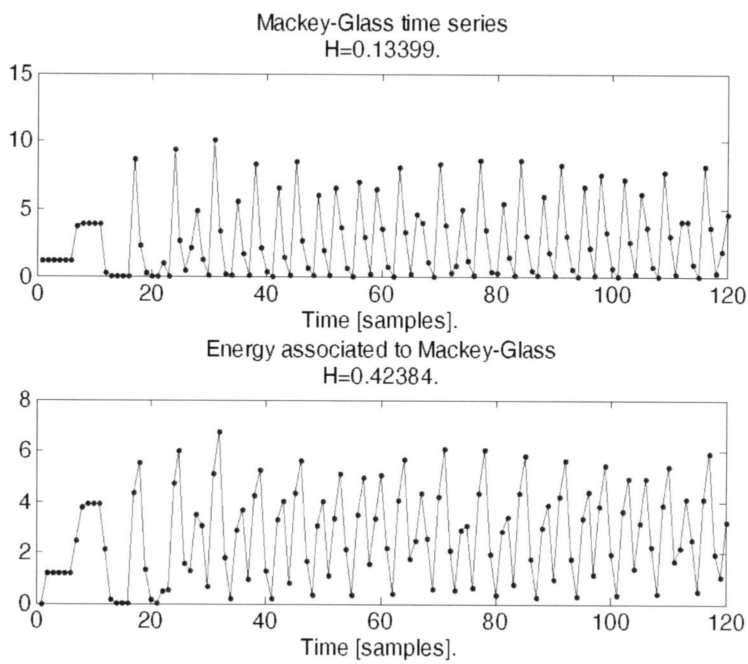

Figure 13. Time series from MG Eq. (2): top: original time series, bottom: energy associated to the MG series.

Finally, according to the heuristic criterion detailed in Figure 4 and Equation (8), after each pass the number of inputs of the non-linear filter is tuned that is the length of tapped-delay line. After the training process is completed, both sequences are analyzed -

$\{\int\{\{x_{n,}\},\{x_e\}\}\}$ and $\{\int\{x_{n,}\}\}$, in accordance with the hypothesis, they should have the same H parameter. If the error between H_A and H_S is greater than a threshold parameter θ, the value of l_x is either increased or decreased according to l_x ±1, as in Equation (8) with the same threshold.

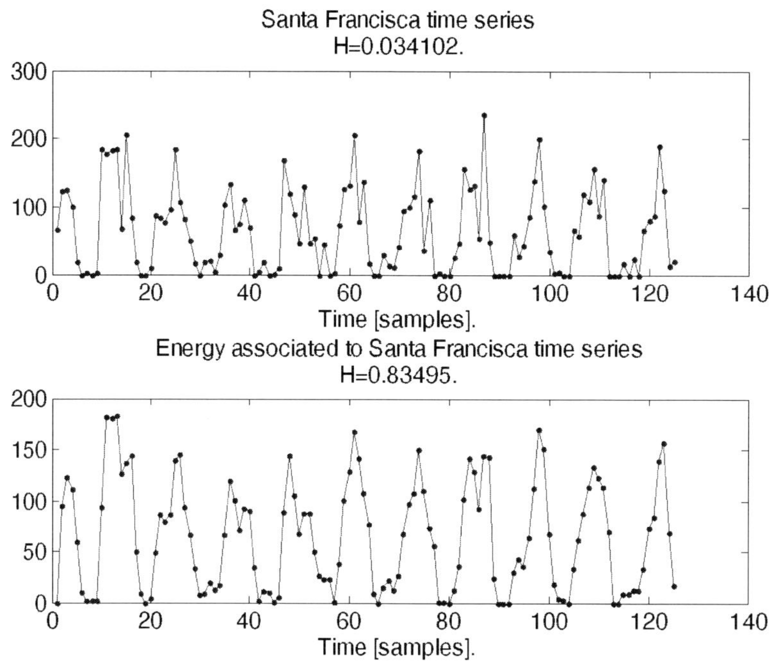

Figure 14. Cumulative monthly rainfall time series: above, the original series, bottom, the energy associated of series.

Model Setup and Adjustment Process

The initial conditions for the filter and learning algorithm are shown in Table 2. Note that the first number of hidden neurons and iteration are set in function of the input number. These initiatory conditions of the learning algorithm were used to forecast the primitive of the time series, whose length is 102 and 107 values.

Table 2. Initial conditions of the parameters

Variable	Initial condition
l_x	15
H_o	$l_x/2$
i_t	l_x
H	0.5

Prediction Results with MG and Santa Francisca Time Series

For each time series, there are three classes of data sets: one is the original time series used for the algorithm in order to give the forecast, which comprises 102 and 107 values for MG and Santa Francisca time series, respectively. The second one is the primitive obtained by integrating the values of original time series. The last one is used to compare if the forecast is acceptable or not where the 18 last values are used to validate the performance of the prediction system, which 102 or 107 values form the data set, and 120 or 125 values constitute the Forecasted and the Real ones depending on MG or Santa Francisca time series. The second class is the primitive data obtained by integrating the values of the original time series.

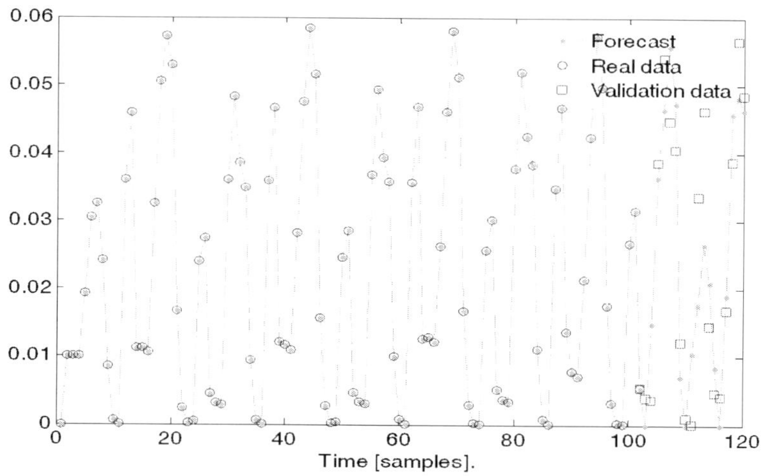

Figure 15. Forecast obtained for MG time series where the tuning algorithm considers its energy associated.

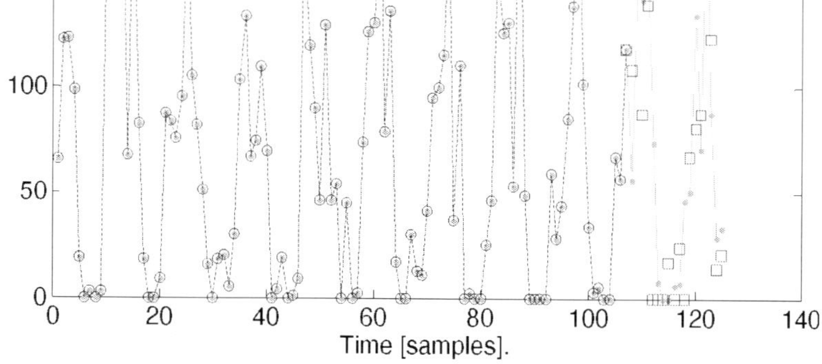

Figure 16. Forecast obtained for Santa Francisca time series where the tuning algorithm considers its energy associated.

Equation (6) is used iteratively to forecast the next 18 values of the MG and Rainfall time series and their primitive obtained by integration.

In Figure 15, the legend "Forecast" represents the values obtained by Equation (6), and the legend "Real data" denotes the actual values -not available in practice- used here for verification purposes only.

From time k equal 103 to time 120 the inputs of Equation (6) include the outputs delayed one time interval. The obtained time series has a mean value, which is indicated at the foot of the figure by "Forecasted Mean".

The "Real Mean" it is not available at time 102. They are displayed at the foot of the figures.

Comments and Remarks

The assessments of the obtained results by comparing the performance of the proposed filter with the classic filter, both are based on NN are shown in Table 3. Although the difference between both filters resides only in the adjustment algorithm, the coefficients that each filter has, each one performs different behaviors.

In the two analyzed cases, the generation of 18 future values from 102 or 107 present values was made by each algorithm.

The same initial parameters were used for each algorithm, but these parameters and the filter's structure are changed by the proposed algorithm that is not modified by the classic algorithm.

In the adjustment of the proposed filter, its coefficients and structure are tuned by considering their stochastic dependency. It can be noted that in each of the figures —Figure 15, Figure 16 in Table 3— the computed value of the Hurst's parameter is denoted either by H_e or H, both taken from the Forecasted time series or from the Data time series, respectively, since the Real time series (future time series) are unknown. Index SMAPE is computed between the complete Real time series (it includes the series Data) and the Forecasted one, as indicates the Equation (16) for each filter. Note that there is an improvement of the forecast for both time series.

Obtained Results

The performance of the entire ANN-based predictor filter was evaluated through the SMAPE index, and is shown in Table 3 along the time series. In addition, if it were used a classical linear filter, like historical mean since December 2008 to May 2010, the forecasted mean would be 74.57 while the actual is 65.18.

The comparison between the Case 1, Case 2 and Case 3 predictor filters series is shown in Table 3.

The results involve the SMAPE index, the Forecasted mean, the H_e parameter associated to the data time series data with the forecasted.

Table 3. Results obtained by the three algorithms. The Real Mean for the MG time series is 3.1778 and 62.2222 for the Santa Francisca time series. The roughness H for MG is 0.2626 and 0.0205 for Santa Francisca

	MG				Santa Francisca	
Variable	Case 1 Figure 5	Case 2 Figure 9	Case 3 Figure 15	Case 1 Figure 6	Case 2 Figure 11	Case 3 Figure 16
Forecasted mean	3.3945	3.3258	3.1702	78.5024	67.6638	69.5113
H_e	0.3102	0.27088	0.2626	0.4678	0.0205	0.0659
SMAPE	55.8234	58.8763	36.5261	76.6024	64.5416	51.5059

CONCLUSION

In this chapter, three methods based on neural networks for forecasting time series have been presented. All of them use an ANNs algorithm based on a heuristic law for tuning their parameters. The learning rule proposed to adjust the ANN's coefficients was based on the Levenberg-Marquardt method.

Furthermore, in function of the long or short term stochastic dependence of the time series assessed by the Hurst parameter H, an on-line heuristic adaptive law was proposed to update the ANNs topology at each time-stage, the number of input taps, the number of patterns and the number of iterations. The main result shows a good performance of the ANNs predictor system applied to time series forecasting when the observations are taken from a single point due to similar roughness for both, the original and the forecasted time series, evaluated by H and H_e, respectively.

In the second case, a model of a non-linear filter for high roughness time series forecasting using sub-sampling was presented. Its main contribution lies in generating smooth time series from a data series, which allows adjust the filter parameters for each subseries and then it is averaged over all of the outputs.

The time series data set was subsampled uniformly, by integer values, this procedure showed to be straightforward and simple, although perfectible. The roughness of the resulting forecasted time series was again evaluated by the Hurst parameter H. The main results show a good performance of the predictor system, applied to time series obtained from solution of the MG equation, considering the roughness and average of the time series to representing rainfall time series such as those presented here of Santa Francisca, Cordoba, Argentina. These results encouraged us to continue working on new machine learning algorithms and downsampling, using other methods.

In Case 3, a filter was presented for time series forecasting based on the energy associated of series with a non-linear autoregressive model based on ANNs. Furthermore, according to the stochastic dependency of long or short range of the energy associated of series indicated by the Hurst parameter H, the topology of ANNs was updated in each stage with a heuristic adaptation law. The main result shows that the area prediction system for time series forecasting has a good performance for a sort of MG series, especially in a series in which the H parameter is small, less than 0.3. This indicates that the series has a high roughness, which is evaluated by H_S and H_A, respectively. Its extrapolation to rainfall time series of Santa Francisca was also very acceptable.

These results encourage us to work with new learning algorithm to be applied to other NN models.

REFERENCES

[1] Pucheta, J., Patiño, H., Schugurensky, C., Fullana, R., Kuchen, B. Optimal Control-Based Neurocontroller to Guide the Crop Growth under Perturbations. Dynamics Of Continuous, Discrete And Impulsive Systems Special Volume Advances in Neural Networks-Theory and Applications. DCDIS A Supplement, Advances in Neural Networks, *Watam Press,* Vol. 14(S1), pp. 618—623. 2007.

[2] Zhang, G.; B.E. Patuwo, and M. Y. Hu. *"Forecasting with artificial neural networks: The state of art"*. J. Int. Forecasting, vol. 14, pp. 35-62. 1998.

[3] Masulli, F., Baratta, D., Cicione, G., Studer, L. *"Daily Rainfall Forecasting using an Ensemble Technique based on Singular Spectrum Analysis"*. In Proceedings of the International Joint Conference on Neural Networks IJCNN 01, pp. 263-268, vol. 1, IEEE, Piscataway, NJ, USA, 2001.

[4] Chow, T.W.S.; Leung, C.T. *"Neural network based short-term load forecasting using weather compensation"*. Power Systems, *IEEE Transactions on,* Vol.11, Iss.4, Nov 1996, Pp. 1736-1742.

[5] Liu, J.N.K.; Lee, R.S.T. *"Rainfall forecasting from multiple point sources using neural networks"*. In *proc. of the International Conference on Systems, Man, and Cybernetics*, Pages:429-434 Vol.3.1999.

[6] Haykin, S. Neural Networks: A Comprehensive Foundation. 2nd Edition, Prentice Hall. 1999.

[7] Espinoza Contreras, Adriana Eliza. El Caos y la caracterización de series de tiempo a través de técnicas de la dinámica no lineal. Universidad Autónoma de Mexico. *Campus Aragón*. 2004.

[8] Velásquez Henao, Juan David, Dyna, Red. Pronóstico de la serie de Mackey glass usando modelos de regresión no-lineal. Universidad Autónoma de Mexico. *Campus Aragón*. 2004.

[9] Glass, L. and M. C. Mackey. From Clocks to Chaos, The Rhythms of Life. Princeton University Press, Princeton, NJ, 1988.

[10] Mandelbrot, B. B., (1983), The Fractal Geometry of Nature, Freeman, San Francisco, CA. 1983.

[11] Flandrin, P., (1992) Wavelet analysis and synthesis of fractional Brownian motion" *IEEE Trans. on Information Theory*, 38, pp. 910-917.

[12] Abry, P.; P. Flandrin, M.S. Taqqu, D. Veitch. (2003), Self-similarity and long-range dependence through the wavelet lens. Theory and applications of long-range dependence, Birkhäuser, pp. 527-556.

[13] Pucheta, J., Herrera, M., Salas C., Patiño, H.D., and B. Kuchen. (2009) "A Neural Network-Based Approach for Forecasting Time Series from Mackey-Glass Equations". In proc. Of the XIII RPIC, Rosario, Argentina.

[14] Bishop, C. (1995). Neural Networks for Pattern Recognition. University Press. Oxford.

[15] Mozer, M. C. (1993) Neural Net Architectures for Temporal Sequence Processing. A. S. Weigend and N. A. Gershenfeld, eds. Time Series Predictions: Forecasting the Future and Understanding the Past. pp. 243-264. Reading, M.A.: Addison-Wesley. 1993.

[16] Bishop, C. Pattern Recognition and Machine Learning. Boston: Springer, 2006.

[17] Pucheta, J., Patiño, H. D., Kuchen, B. (2008) *"A Statistically Dependent Approach for the Monthly Rainfall Forecast from One Point Observations"*. In Proc. of the Second IFIP Conference on Computer and Computing Technologies in Agriculture (CCTA2008) October 18-20. Beijing, China. 2008.

In: Rainfall: Behavior, Forecasting and Distribution
Editors: Olga E. Martín and Tricia M. Roberts
ISBN: 978-1-62081-551-9

Chapter 4

LONG TERM AND INTERANNUAL RAINFALL VARIABILITY IN ARGENTINEAN CHACO PLAIN REGION

Marcela H. González,[1,2] Diana Dominguez[1] and Mario N. Nuñez[1,2]

Departamento de Ciencias de la Atmósfera y los Océanos - FCEN-UBA, CIMA - 2º piso, Pabellón II, Ciudad Universitaria, Buenos Aires, Argentina[1]
Centro de Investigaciones del Mar y la Atmósfera – CONICET/UBA; UMI-IFAECI/CNRS, CIMA - 2º piso, Pabellón II, Ciudad Universitaria, Buenos Aires, Argentina[2]

ABSTRACT

The Argentinean Chaco plain region has a relevant biodiversity and it has experienced an important increase in annual rainfall during the last century. However, there is evidence that some rainfall decrease has happened in some sub-regions since 1980; such decrease could be related to deforestation carried out in order to increase the farming area. In this paper rainfall variability was analyzed to better understand its behavior in scales greater than a year. There are indicators of a cycle of 22 years in the west of Chaco and other of 6,6 years in the east. The annual cycle is present all over the region and more pronounced towards the west. The interannual rainfall variability shows that there are three main rainfall anomaly leading patterns. The first is associated with the SST in the subtropical Atlantic Ocean, the second leading is related to ENSO and a high pressure system centered in central-southern Brazil and the third is associated with positive correlation in the west tropical and subtropical Pacific and with a wave train extended from the western Pacific Ocean towards South America. The results indicate that rainfall must be monitored in order to determine its future evolution and if deforestation has influenced the climate of the region. Likewise, the relation between climate and deforestation must be best studied in order to mitigate the negative impacts over the region. In order to describe a possible situation in the future some simulations are detailed. The regional model MM5 was nested within time slice global atmospheric model experiments conducted by the HadAM3H model. The simulations cover a 10-year period representing present-day climate (1981–1990) and two future scenarios for the SRESA2 and B2 emission scenarios for the period 2081–2090. Both the A2 and B2 simulations show a general increase in precipitation in northern and central Argentina especially in summer and fall and a general decrease in precipitation in winter and spring.

Keywords: rainfall trends, variability, Chaco region, atmospheric circulation pattern, climatic change

1. INTRODUCTION

Chaco plain region is located in the north of Argentina and eastward the Andes Mountain Range and includes the ecosystems of dry Chaco in the west, wet Chaco in the east and forest yungas, which are discontinuously scattered in Salta, Jujuy and Tucumán, as a part of the sub-Andean Hills. In the east fertile area of this region, there are performed important agricultural activities that have expanded to the west in the sub-wet area and towards the west Chaco where there is the so-called "El Impenetrable" thick forest. In this region, the use of soil (Adamoli et al 2004) has been significantly modified and so, the weather has probably been affected because of the extension of the agricultural border westwards (Barros et al, 2000) on one hand, and of the monoculture soya crops, on the other. Grau et al (2005) estimate that 20% of the semi-arid Chaco forest was deforested since 1972. The initial deforestation was associated to black bean crops that were grown after an increase of rainfall during the 1970s and due to high soybean prices. These stimulated further deforestation in drier areas because the climatic limitations were overcome by technological improvements. Vegetation changes affect water fluxes between the ecosystems and groundwater and can lead to accumulation of salt in soils and aquifers, as a consequence of conversion of native grassland to tree plantations in the plains of Argentina (Nosetto et al 2008, IAI 2010). Besides, forests use precipitation inputs in deep, generating small drainage fluxes and maintaining deep groundwater levels (Jobbagy et al 2008). In Argentina annual crops showed the fastest expansion, from 4% to 14,3% between 1988 and 2002. Paruelo et al (2006) created a conceptual framework to understand the process that determines land use changes which included environmental, economic, social and political causes.

Many studies have focused in investigating the evolution of annual rainfall during last century (Barros et al 2008 and 2000; Barros and Castañeda 2001; Liebmann et al 2004; Gonzalez et al 2005) and the most relevant conclusion is that rainfall has increased all over the northeast and central Argentina. However, there is some evidence that these trends could be reversing (Flores and Gonzalez 2009) and it is important to determine the truth of this conclusion and the possible causes which are related to these observed changes. Also, the interannual variability of rainfall must be studied because of the great agricultural activities which are carried out in the region, specially the understanding of spatial rainfall patterns in summer when rainfall is greater than in the rest of the year.

The great interannual rainfall variability makes it necessary understand the large circulation patterns associated with different hydric situations. There is evidence of the relationship between the interannual rainfall variability and the El Niño-Southern Oscillation (ENSO) in this region (Ropelewsky and Halpert 1987; Vargas et al 1999, Grimm et al 2000). For example, the summer rainfall in the eastern Argentina increases during the ENSO warm phase. However, ENSO does not explain the whole variability, and so, many authors have investigated other large scale atmospheric forcing in the region of study. For example, Barros and Doyle (2002) found a significant relation between the sea surface temperature in the southwest of the Atlantic Ocean in summer and the incoming of humid air into the continent, Silvestri and Vera (2003) related rainfall in autumn and spring with the Antarctic Oscillation. Gonzalez and Barros (2002) explored the relation between the interannual variability of the austral South American monsoon onset date and the interannual variability of spring rainfall in subtropical South America. They found that an early (delayed) onset is associated with decreased (enhanced) rainfall only in southern Brazil, while in Argentina and Uruguay there is an opposite signal and the delay was related to sea surface temperature in the Caribbean Sea region. All these results are important for planning forest and agricultural activities.

The objective of this chapter is to improve the knowledge of rainfall variability in the Chaco region of Argentina using rainfall measurements from different sources. This chapter is organized as follows: Section 2 describes the dataset and the methodology; Section 3 presents the observed rainfall trends, the annual cycle and other rainfall variability; Section 4 shows the description of the leading patterns of summer rainfall anomalies and their relation with large scale circulation features; Section 5 describes the future probable situation and Section 6 presents the main conclusions.

2. DATA AND METHODOLOGY

Monthly rainfall data derived from 53 stations from different sources: the National Meteorological Service (SMN), the Secretary of Hydrology of Argentina (SRH), the Regional Commission of Bermejo River (COREBE) and the Provincial Water Administration of Chaco (APA) were used in this study. The area of study is located between 22°S and 30°S and between 66ºW and 57ºW, including the Argentinean provinces of Chaco, Formosa, Tucumán, east of Salta and Jujuy, and north of Santiago del Estero and Santa Fe (Figure 1, Table I). Stations data records were different over 1900-2007. All the selected stations have less than 20% of missing monthly rainfall data and their quality has been carefully proved.

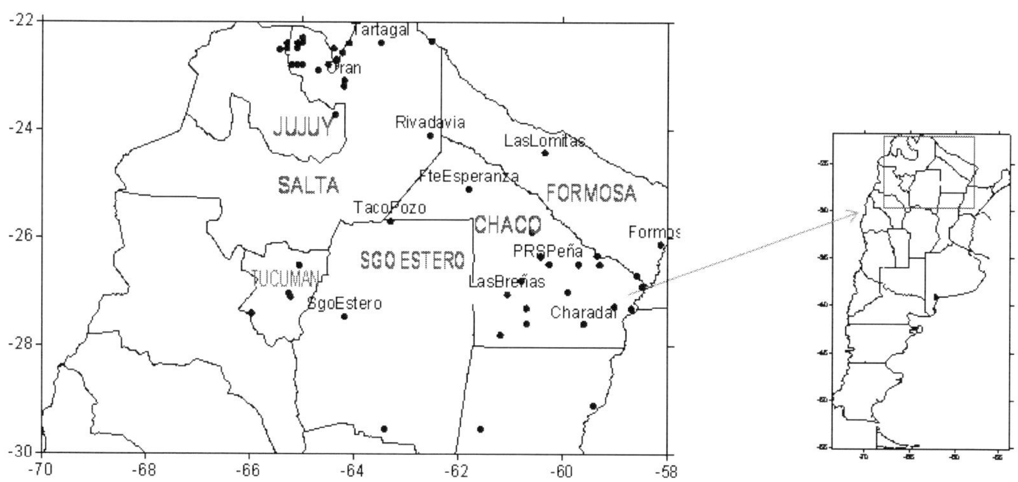

Figure 1. Area of study. Provinces (in red) and some stations mentioned in the text are detailed.

Annual precipitation low frequency variability was analyzed using a linear trend method of minimum squares, and statistics significance was tested using a T-Student test. The dominant frequencies related with the variability of the leading patterns were identified through spectral analysis.

Table I. Linear trend calculated for the complete record (left panel) and for maximum record in the period 1980-2007 (right panel). Significant (95%) correlation coefficient (r) in italics and shaded

complete record						1980-2007		
station	lon	lat	n° years	trend (mm/year)	r	n° years	trend (mm/year)	r
aguas blancas	-64.35	-22.71	43	7.05	0.326	27	1.13	0.03
balapuca	-64.4	-22.5	36	-1.11	0.039	28	-2.7	0.075
caimancito	-64.36	-23.73	36	-2.48	0.111	26	-16.18	0.51
campo largo	-60.8	-26.8	51	-3.06	0.174	28	-20.4	0.562
castelli	-60.6	-25.9	53	-2.08	0.164	28	-5.6	0.215
ceres	-61.57	-29.53	108	1.2	0.176	28	-2.86	0.114
charaday	-59.6	-27.6	52	5.15	0.271	28	-2.56	0.078
cnia benitez	-58.7	-27.3	52	1.33	0.063	28	-7.27	0.167
el colorado	-59.35	-26.33	39	-3.86	0.146	27	-21.5	0.524
el pabellón	-65.3	-22.5				24	-8.75	0.545
Famailla	-65.25	-27.03	39	2.03	0.089	28	-2.11	0.067
formosa	-58.14	-26.12	104	2.56	0.263	28	-7.04	0.196
fte esperanza	-61.8	-25.1				28	5.47	0.234
gral san martin	-59.3	-26.5	52	-3.31	0.203	28	-12.74	0.391
iruya	-65.2	-22.8				26	-2.1	0.209
la paz	-62.51	-22.36	43	0.95	0.075	27	-5.93	0.31
la sosa	-65.22	-27.1	54	12.03	0.407	28	-4.73	0.093
laguna limpia	-59.7	-26.5	52	0.43	0.022	28	-16.85	0.44
las breñas	-61.07	-27.05	70	2.47	0.221	28	-7.31	0.244
las cañas	-65.96	-27.4	55	4.88	0.321	28	-1.14	0.036
las higueras	-65.1	-22.8				26	-3.37	0.298
las lomitas	-60.35	-24.42	71	-0.15	0.014	28	-11.81	0.411
nazareno	-65.1	-22.5				25	-18.3	0.485
oran	-64.19	-23.09	48	4.46	0.299	28	-4.4	0.161
paltorco	-65.1	-22.4				24	-12.98	0.567
pcia dela plaza	-59.9	-27	53	4.49	0.208	28	7.34	0.165
pescado	-64.5	-22.8	44	8.31	0.366	28	-6.2	0.179
poscaya	-65.1	-22.5				24	-2.43	0.148
pozo sarmiento	-64.2	-23.2	63	6.36	0.589	28	5.82	0.361
prsp	-60.27	-26.49	82	2.9	0.263	28	-7.75	0.235
pto bermejo	-58.5	-26.9	51	-2.15	0.093	28	-8.22	0.18
pto pilcomayo	-57.7	-25.4				20	-38.46	0.598

complete record						1980-2007		
station	lon	station	lon	station	lon	station	lon	station
pto velaz	-58.6	-26.7				20	5.21	0.112
reconquista	-59.42	-29.11	60	0.67	0.042	28	-10.98	0.282
resistencia	-59.03	-27.27	42	7.65	0.347	28	-10.17	0.247
rivadavia	-62.54	-24.1	86	0.69	0.104	28	-16.18	0.719
san antonio	-65.0	-22.8				26	-1.4	0.2
san bernardo	-60.7	-27.3	48	3.32	0.167	28	-7.7	0.202
san isidro	-65.2	-22.8				25	-14.8	0.648
san jose	-64.7	-22.9				28	-9.6	0.225
san telmo	-64.23	-22.58	27	0.74	0.022	19	-7.89	0.154
sgo estero	-64.18	-27.46	92	1.08	0.165	28	-2.53	0.119
sta sylvina	-61.2	-27.8	53	-2.45	0.159	28	-12.42	0.38
sta victoria	-65.0	-22.3				26	-5.2	0.25
taco pozo	-63.3	-25.7	51	1.16	0.109	28	3.85	0.166
tarija	-64.1	-22.4	37	2.14	0.063	28	2.15	0.046
tartagal	-63.49	-22.39	40	1.87	0.125	28	3.42	0.129
tres isletas	-60.43	-26.35	53	0.61	0.035	28	-13.89	0.355
trigo huaico	-65.0	-22.4				24	-2.05	0.096
tuc tuca	-65.3	-22.4				26	-9.83	0.399
tucuman	-65.06	-26.51	56	0.56	0.045	28	-2.013	0.084
villa angela	-60.7	-27.6	53	2.32	0.106	28	-19.39	0.41
villa maria	-63.41	-29.54	77	3.03	0.388	28	-5.82	0.293

The spectral analysis and its significance, depending on the spectrum adjusted a white or red noise model, were performed using the Blackman-Tukey method (Mitchell el al 1966, Blackman and Tukey 1958). The spectral analysis was applied to series after filtering the annual cycle and a confidence level of 95% was used to detect significant peaks. When analyzing actual data, one would like to find the frequencies with the greatest spectral densities, that is, the frequency regions, consisting of many adjacent frequencies that contribute most to the overall periodic behaviour of the series. This can be accomplished by smoothing the spectral values using a weighted moving average transformation. In this paper a Tukey window (Blackman and Tukey 1958) was used for that purpose. It implies that the weights for the weighted moving average of the spectral values are computed as:

$$w_j = 0.5 + 0.5*\cos(p*j/p) \quad (\text{for } j=0 \text{ to } p)$$

$$w_{-j} = w_j \quad (\text{for } j = 0)$$

where p = (m-1)/2).

Summer rainfall was defined as the accumulated anomalies rainfall from October to April. The anomaly summer rainfall leading patterns were obtained through a Principal Component Analysis (PCA), in the T-mode (Green 1978). Therefore, the principal scores (PC) describe the spatial patterns while the loadings provide the temporal evolution of the patterns. Monthly sea surface temperatures (SST), 500 HPa (G500), 1000 HPa (G1000) and 200 HPa (G200) geopotential heights from the National Center of Environmental Prediction (NCEP) reanalysis were also used (Kalnay et al 1996) in order to describe their relation with summer rainfall anomaly. Monthly anomalies were determined removing the climatological monthly means from the original values. Simultaneous correlations between summer rainfall loadings and SST and G1000, G500 and G200, were calculated. The results allow describing some relations between the summer rainfall leading patterns and both, SST and large circulation features.

3. Long Term and other Rainfall Variability

Linear trend approximation was used to evaluate the observed change in annual rainfall time series (Wilks 1995) for the maximum record of each station (Table I, left panel). The same was evaluated for the maximum record included in the period 1980-2007 (Table I, right panel). When they were both the same, only the values in the right panel of Table I were detailed. A former conclusion derived from Table I is that most locations show positive trends for a complete period (left panel). This result agrees with Barros and Castañeda (2001) who calculated linear trends using a shorter period, ending in 1996 and with Liebmann et al (2004) who detected an increase in summer rainfall in southeastern South America. However, there is a tendency to negative trends when the period 1980-2007 is considered (right panel). Meanwhile, only three stations (Tartagal, Taco Pozo and Fuerte Esperanza) maintain and ever increase the positive trend of the complete record.

To better understand the spatial distribution of annual rainfall evolution, annual trends were calculated for the periods (1980-2007) in 53 stations (figure 2, top panel), for (1970-2007) in 36 stations (figure 2, central panel) and for (1960-2007) in 28 stations (figure 2, bottom panel). The number of stations surveyed in each period depends on the record of the stations. The main result is that most of the area (Formosa, central and east Chaco, Tucuman and east of Salta and Jujuy) showed a tendency to lower rainfall in the 1980s (figure 2, top panel) when compared with the observed 1960-2007 (figure 2, bottom panel). Meanwhile, the east of Chaco shows an increase of rainfall in the 1960s, even greater in the 1970s but a decrease in the 1980s, although it decrease is not significant. The only sub-region with different behavior is the west of Chaco in "El Impenetrable", where Taco Pozo station was located. It is the only station that reveals regular increase of rainfall since 1960. Unfortunately, there are no stations with long record in this area to evaluate if the behavior of Taco Pozo is an exception or if it is a regional pattern. The nearest station is Fuerte Esperanza, in the west of Chaco, which shows a great positive trend of 5.4 mm/year in the period 1980-2007 but it has no data before 1980.

LechuSA programme (Land Ecosystem change utility for South America, http://lechusa.unsl.edu.ar/) (Baldi et al 2008) is an enterprise whose main objective is to understand the changes of ecosystems in South America, specially, those derived from changes in land uses. They analyze temporal series of normalized difference vegetation index (NDVI) derived from satellites measurements in the period 1982-1999 and identified "hotspots" representative of intense changes. One of the hotspots identified by Baldi et al (2008) agrees with the area analyzed in the present paper that reveals rainfall decrease in the

1980s (Formosa, central and east Chaco, Tucuman and east of Salta and Jujuy). Besides, Sorensson and Menendez (2010) calculated a coupling strength between soil moisture (associated to different land covers) and precipitation in South America and they also identified a main hotspot in our region of study.

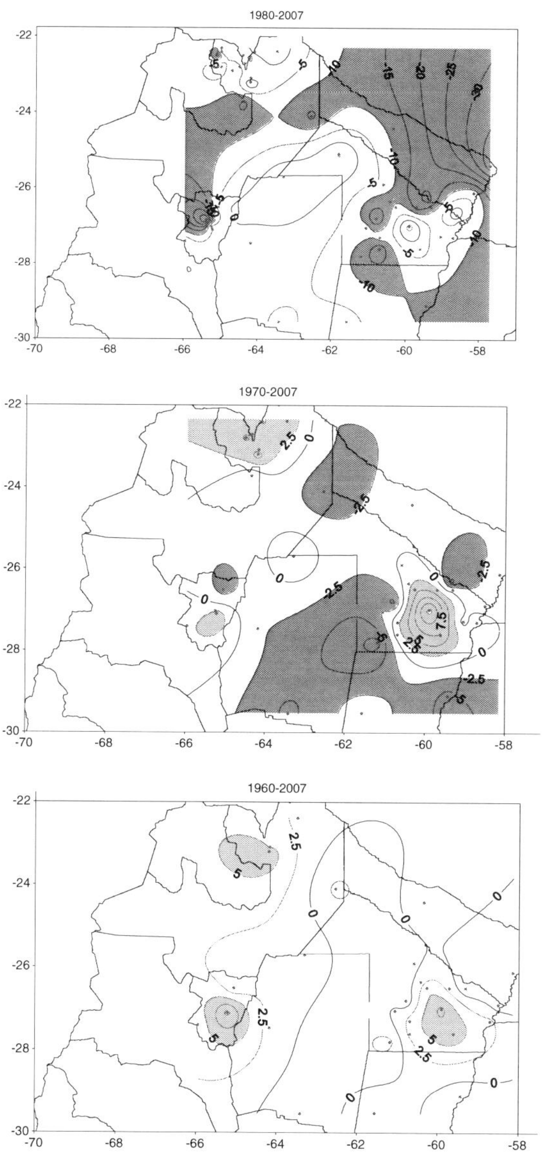

Figure 2. Trends (mm/year) calculated in (1980-2007) (top panel, lines every 5 mm), in (1970-2007) (central panel, lines every 2,5 mm) and in (1960-2007) (bottom panel, lines every 2,5 mm). Stations used to perform the graphics are superimposed. Shadow areas were significant at the 95% confidence level. Red (blue) lines are positive (negative).

Although there is some controversy about the actual causes of those changes and their relation with observed rainfall trends, some authors have analyzed the impact of land cover over climate (Lee 2010, Lee and Berbery 2010; Jin et al 2000; Mabuchi et al 2005, among others) and they found promising results. Lee (2010), Lee and Berbery (2010) and Collini et al (2008) studied these impacts in the La Plata Basin, where the region considered in this chapter is included. They concluded that areas where croplands replace forests, would experience an overall increase in albedo and reduced surface friction. These facts lead to a reduction of sensible heat and surface temperature, higher evapotranspiration and stronger low winds. They also pointed out that the effect on sensible heat seems to dominate and leads to a reduction in convective instability and the stronger low level winds due to reduced friction also imply a larger amount of moisture advected out of the basin, and thus resulting in reduced moisture flux convergence within the basin. The two effects, increased stability and reduced moisture flux, result in a reduction of precipitation.

Therefore, most of the area of study in this paper has undergone changes in land use because of deforestation and, at the same time, a decrease in annual rainfall has been observed. As it was detailed in previous paragraph, changes in land cover and rainfall might be related each other. Hence, the area studied in this chapter, must be monitored, changes must be evaluated and more sustainable forestry policies must be regulated.

Some periodicities of monthly rainfall were studied and the more relevant results will be detailed in the present chapter. The main periodicity of monthly rainfall is the annual cycle. 39 out of the 53 stations were considered in order to calculate the mean monthly rainfall evolution during the maximum common period: 1968-2007 (more recent 30 years period). The differences among them let us define three sub-regions (west, central and east) and the mean precipitation series were calculated using 13, 6 and 20 stations, respectively (figure 3). The main feature is a defined annual cycle with a peak in summer. The west region has the most defined cycle; the central region has less rainfall in summer than the west one and almost no rainfall in winter. The east region tends to have two relative peaks: in autumn and in late spring.

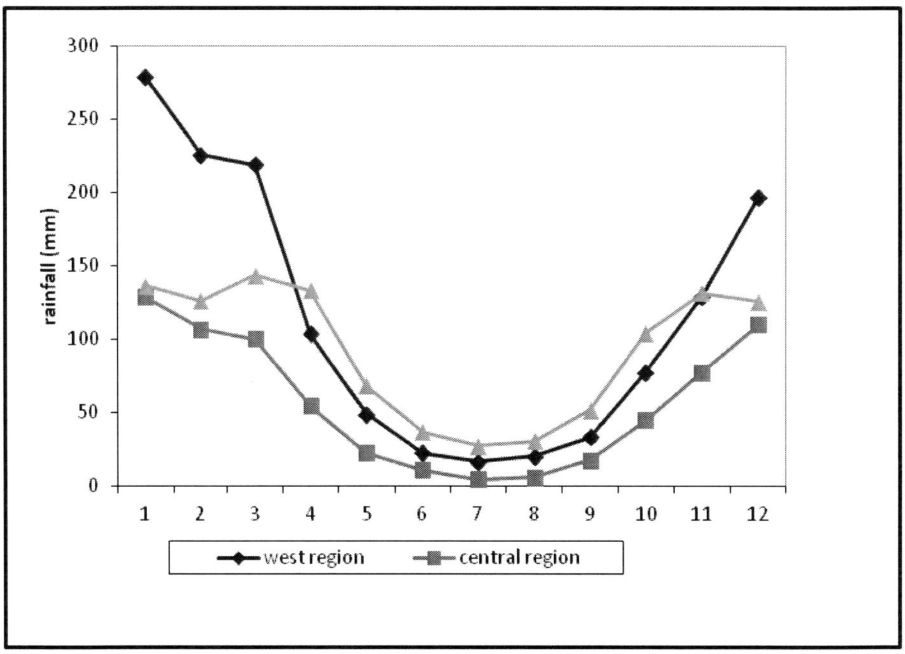

Figure 3. Mean annual cycle in three sub-regions defined (1968-2007): west region (blue line), central region (pink line) and east region (green line).

Stations with more than 45 years of record were considered to perform a spectrum analysis in order to analyze significant variability greater than one year. A peak at about 22 years is detected for two stations in the east of Salta and west of Formosa (Rivadavia and Las Lomitas). For example, Figure 4 shows the spectrum for Rivadavia, which has a record of 86 years (1920-2005). A peak at 22 years (frequency of 0,0038) and the rest of annual cycle (about frequency of 0,08) are the only significant peak of variability greater than a year.

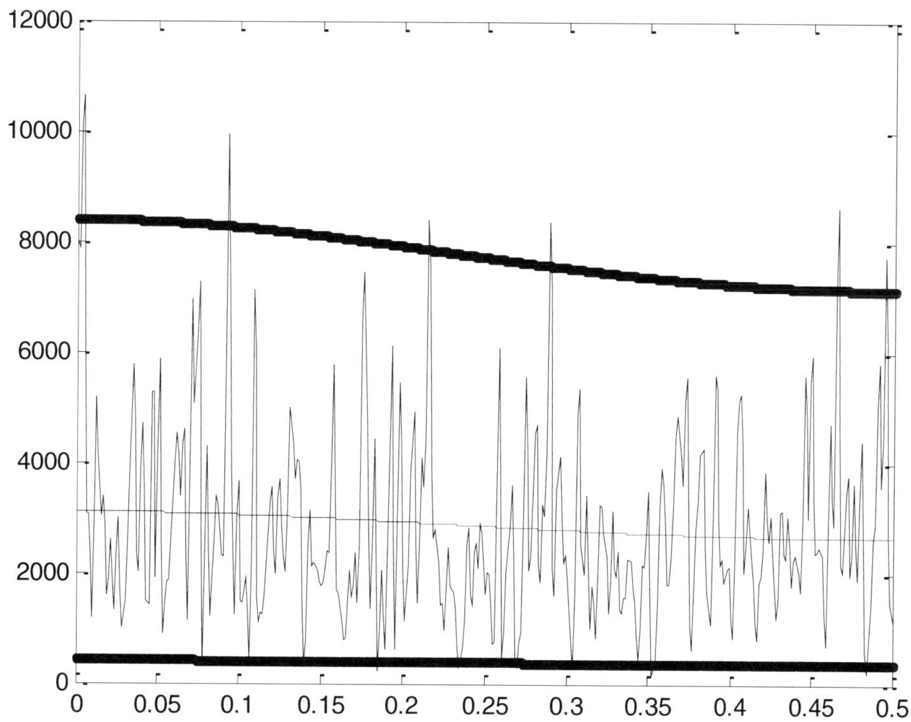

Figure 4. Spectrum for monthly rainfall in Rivadavia (1920-2005).

Figure 5a shows the evolution of annual rainfall in Rivadavia where the negative trend in the period 1980-2005 can be appreciated. But it might be related to the 22 years variability from the spectrum. Although 10 out of the 53 stations have records of more than 60 years, only in two of them the 22 year peak was detected. An harmonic analysis was applied to monthly rainfall anomalies in Rivadavia and the harmonics which explained the great percentage of variance were the corresponding to 26, 6, 20 and 16 years. Probably, the rainfall variance associated with these peaks is related to the 22 year peak encountered when using spectral techniques. In fact, Figure 5b shows the rainfall monthly anomalies and the reconstructed wave using the harmonic corresponding to 26, 6, 20 and 16 years. There, it is important to point out that the reconstructed wave seems to represent a great part of the behavior of the rainfall anomaly series.

Significant variability of 6,6 years (frequency of 0,0125) is detected in the east of Chaco (Las Breñas, PRS Peña, Charadai). For example, Figure 6 shows the spectrum for Las Breñas, which has a record of 70 years (1938-2000). Significant peaks of 8,8 years are found in stations in the Tucumán province. Also, a 2 years peak is present in the northeast of the study region (Las Lomitas, Formosa, PRS Peña).

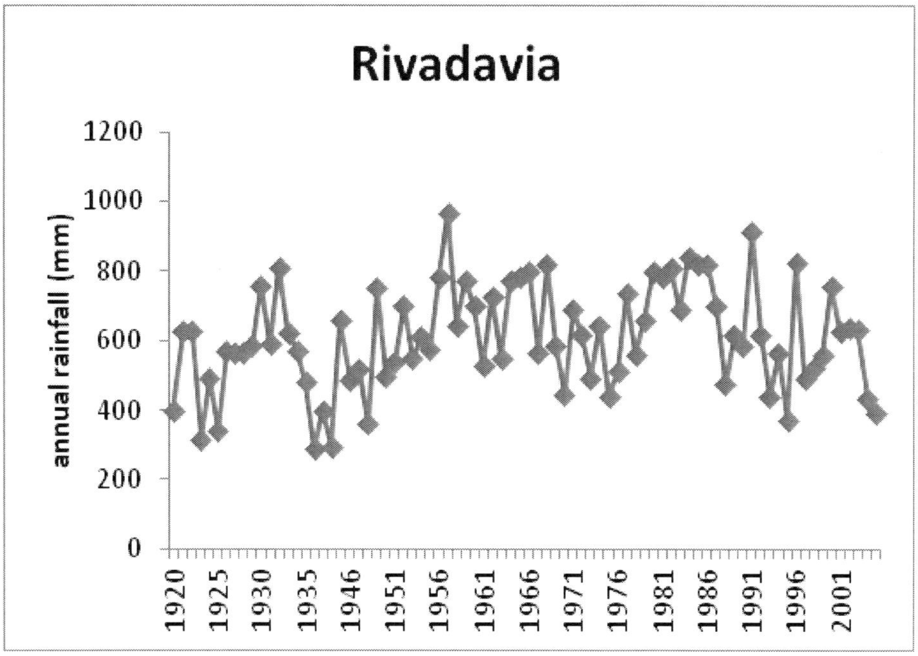

(a)

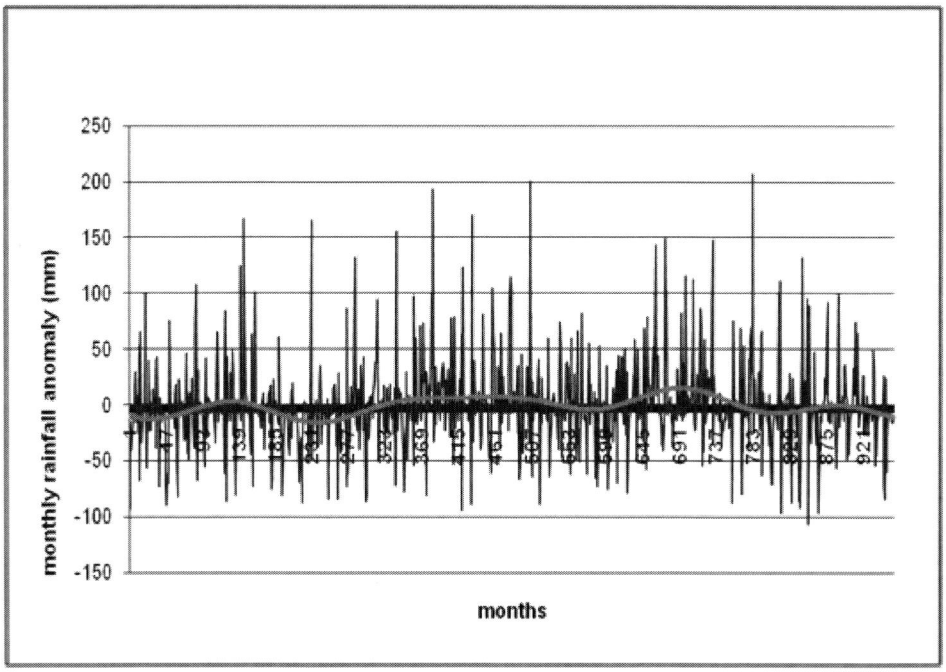

(b)

Figure 5. (a) Accumulated annual rainfall in Rivadavia (1920-2005), (b) monthly rainfall anomalies (blue line) and the reconstructed wave with 26,6, 20 and 16 years harmonics (pink line).

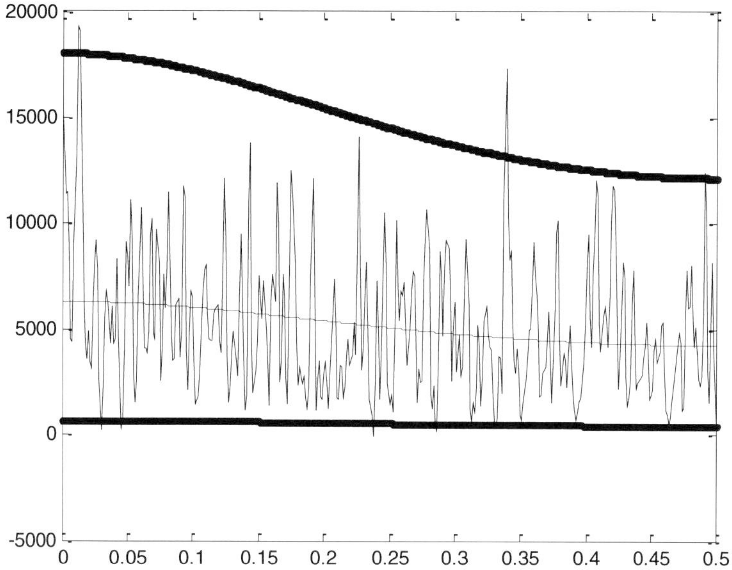

Figure 6. Spectrum for Las Breñas, in the east of Chaco (1938-2007).

4. Analysis of Interannual Variability of Summer Rainfall

The same 39 out of the 53 stations used to calculate the annual cycle in the previous section were considered to analyze the behavior of the summer rainfall anomalies during the period 1968-2007. Due to the fact that the whole region shows a rainfall season extended from October to April, the "summer" rainfall was calculated as the accumulated rainfall all over this period. These values are standardized with the mean summer rainfall of the period and expressed as percentage. A PCA is applied to summer rainfall anomalies for the period 1968-2007. Three leading patterns are retained following the Kaiser´s criterion (Kaiser 1958), where the PC with eigenvalues greater than one are considered.

The first three leading patterns (PC1, PC2, PC3) explain 21%, 9,3% and 9,1%, of the variance respectively, being statistically significant at the 95% confidence level. Figure 7 shows the spatial patterns. PC1 describes years when summer rainfall anomalies in the east are of opposite sign to the west. On the other hand, PC2 mostly describes the variability of anomalies of opposite sign between the north and the south regions with an area of maximum variability in west Formosa and east Salta. PC3 represents years when summer rainfall anomalies were of opposite sign in the southwest and northeast regions.

In order to relate these leading patterns to large scale circulation features, simultaneous correlations were calculated among the latter and the mean SST and geopotential height at different levels over the same period (from October to April). Correlations greater than 0,31 are significant at 95% confidence level. Figure 8 shows the correlation map between SST and PC1 time series. A positive correlation area above the subtropical Atlantic Ocean, at about 20° southwards on the Brazilian coast, is observed, which indicates that PC1 pattern is associated with the warming in this area of the Atlantic Ocean. In fact, when SST is high, the evaporation is enhanced and the incoming of wet air to the continent through the Atlantic High can be intensified generating rainfall in the northeast of the study region.

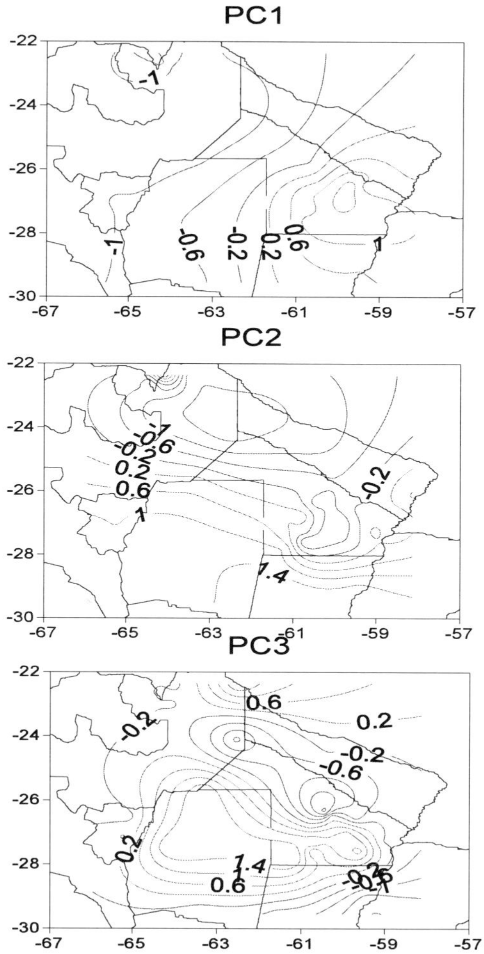

Figure 7. The three leading pattern of anomaly summer (rainfall accumulated from October to April) rainfall (1968-2007).

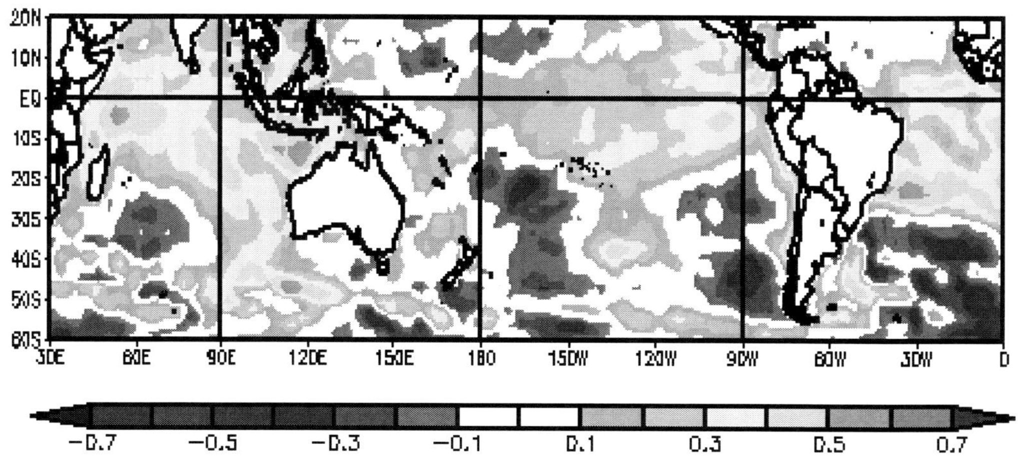

Figure 8. Map correlation between mean SST between October and April and PC1 for the period 1968-2007. Correlations greater than 0,31 are significant at 95% confidence level.

The correlation between PC1 and G1000 (figure 9) shows that the maximum rainfall in the east study region is related to low pressure systems at low levels as well as a high pressure system in G200 (figure 10) in southeastern Brazil and east of the area of study. The low pressure in low levels over the east of the study region, favors the development of precipitating systems. The correlation map between G500 and PC1 (figure 11) shows an annular-like pattern at high latitudes similar to that associated with the Southern Antarctic Oscillation (SAO) (Mo 2000), combined with light wave-like patterns at middle latitudes. This feature can also be observed in G200 (figure 10) and it is indicative that a positive phase of SAO (increment of zonal wind and decrease of connection between low and middle latitudes) is related to negative rainfall anomalies in the north of Argentina, except for the northeastern of the studied region. In fact, previous papers have shown SAO influence on rainfall variability in some regions of South America. For example, Silvestri and Vera (2003) showed such influence on precipitation interannual variability in southeastern South America particularly during November and December; Reboita et al (2009) detected a decrease of frontal activity when positive phase of SAO is present. In other regions of the Southern Hemisphere some authors have detected relation between rainfall and SAO, too.

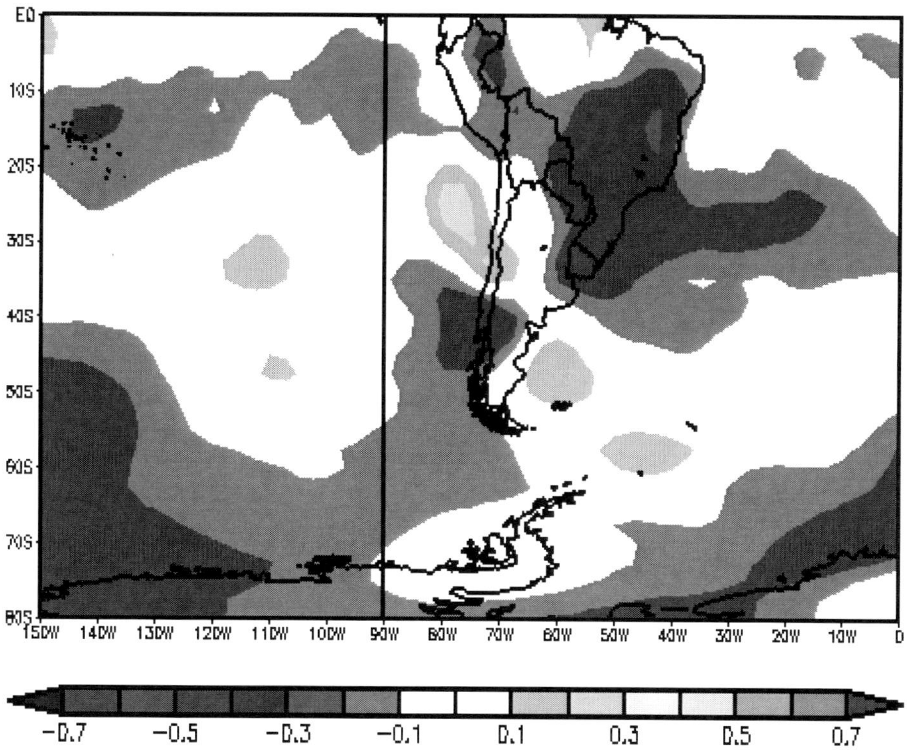

Figure 9. Map correlation between mean G1000 between October and April and PC1 for the period 1968-2007. Correlations greater than 0,31 are significant at 95% confidence level.

For example, Zheng and Frederiksen (2006) showed that this signal affects summer rainfall variability in the New Zealand sector and Reason and Rouault (2005) showed that wetter (drier) winters in western South Africa occur during the negative (positive) SAO phase. Also, the 6,6 year significant peak in spectrums of stations in the east of Chaco might be explained by the fact that PC1 variability is related to the SAO, which exhibit a peak of variability at around that period (e.g. Mo, 2000).

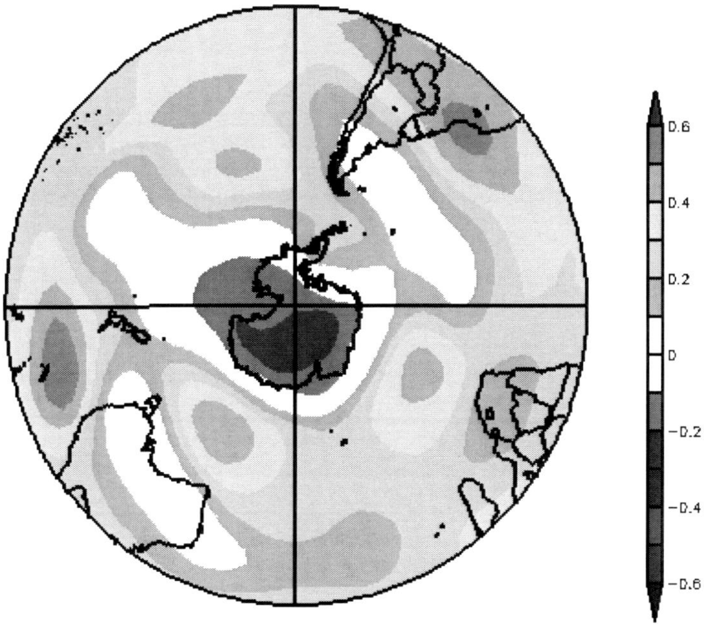

Figure 10. Map correlation between mean G200 between October and April and PC1 for the period 1968-2007. Correlations greater than 0,31 are significant at 95% confidence level.

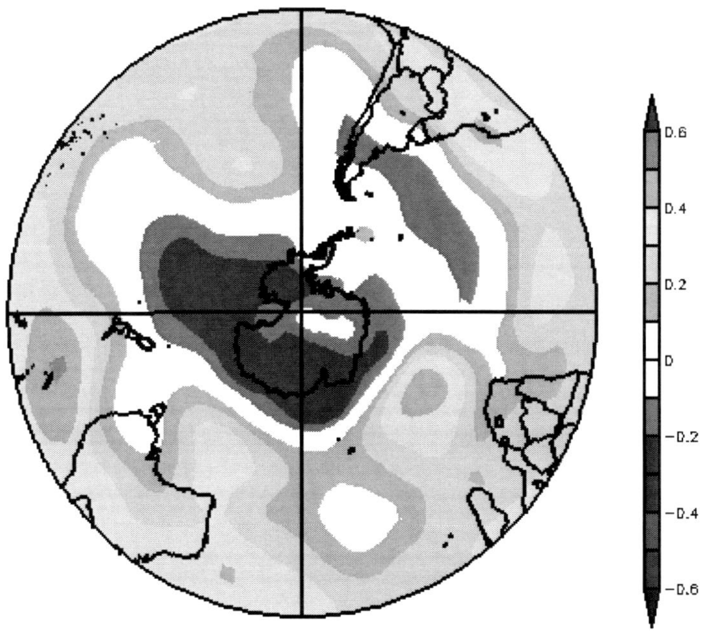

Figure 11. Map correlation between mean G500 between October and April and PC1 for the period 1968-2007. Correlations greater than 0,31 are significant at 95% confidence level.

Correlation maps between PC2 time series and both SST and G1000 anomalies were performed and displayed in figures 12 and 13. Positive correlations values along the tropical band with higher values in the Pacific Ocean (between 150°W and South America coast) are detected between SST anomalies and PC2, resembling an ENSO like pattern, meanwhile no significant correlation appears in the Atlantic Ocean (figure 12). Therefore, a positive phase of ENSO (El Niño) is associated with lower than normal rainfall in east of Salta and west Formosa, where PC2 shows its maximum expression. This agrees with Grimm et al (2000) who observed rainfall below normal in the northwest of Argentina during positive ENSO phase. The correlation map between the G1000 and PC2 (Figure 13) shows a negative area in the Atlantic Ocean (30°S) and a positive area in southern Brazil over the continent.

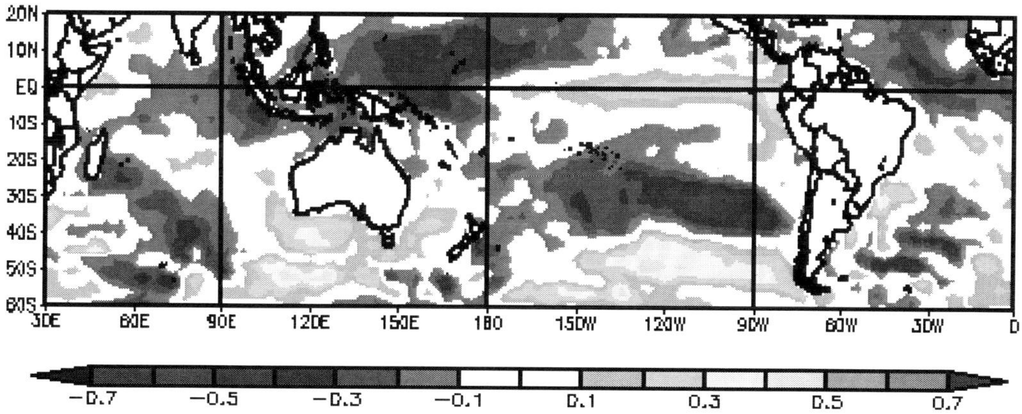

Figure 12. Map correlation between mean SST between October and April and PC2 for the period 1968-2007. Correlations greater than 0,31 are significant at 95% confidence level.

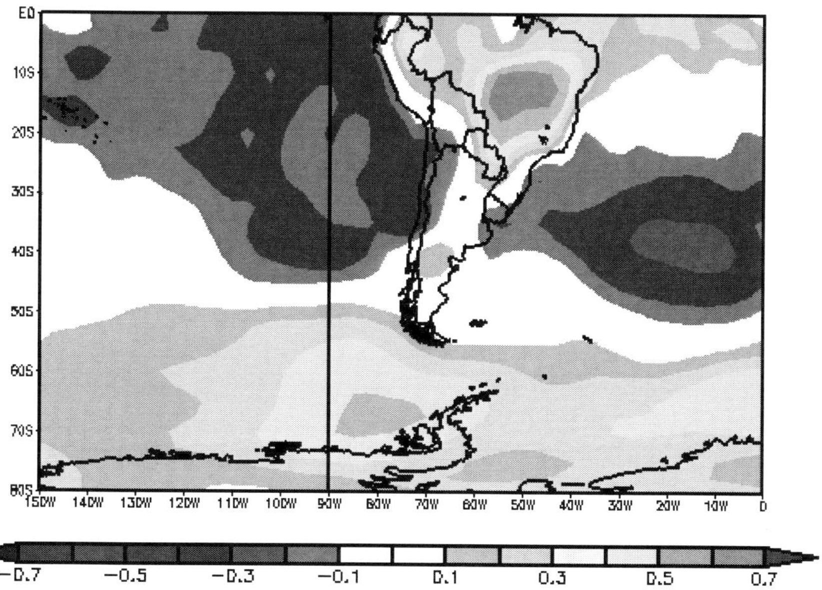

Figure 13. Map correlation between mean G1000 between October and April and PC2 for the period 1968-2007. Correlations greater than 0,31 are significant at 95% confidence level.

This feature indicates that the high pressure system in southern Brazil prevents that precipitating systems can be developed over the area, and the weaken Atlantic high, contributes to decrease the incoming of wet air from the Atlantic Ocean. As a consequence of both effects, the humidity flux from the north is reduced and, therefore, lower than normal rainfall in the north of Argentina, especially in west east Salta and west Formosa is expected.

PC3 enhances the differences between the northeast and the southwest behavior. The correlation map between PC3 and SST (figure 14) shows an area of significant positive correlation in the west subtropical Pacific, even extending towards the eastern Indian Ocean, and the correlation map between G500 (figure 15) and PC3, shows a wave train extended from the western Pacific Ocean towards South America. It is important to notice that remote forcing can influence the rainfall pattern because it can be extended out to longer ranges based on the influences of slowly evolving boundary conditions on the atmospheric circulation, such as the SST, and hence, seasonal climate can tilt in a specific direction. The pattern shown in figure 15 is similar to one described by Mo (2000) which is called the "Pacific South American Pattern" and shows that it was characterized by a wave train emanating from the tropical western Pacific. This pattern is associated with the tropical Indian Ocean SST anomalies on quasi-biennial timescales (Mo 2000). In fact, in Southern South America, the Andes chain prevents the access of humidity from the Pacific Ocean north of 38°S but low pressure systems enter Argentina south of 38°S and air mass eruptions from polar regions have trajectories towards the northeast. Therefore, intermittent eruptions of polar fronts from the south can develop rainfall events in the southwest of the region of study. Besides, it is important to notice that the area of greater variability of PC3 is the northeastern part of the area of study. The spectrum analysis has shown a 2-year peak (see section 3) in stations located in these regions (Las Lomitas, PRS Peña and Formosa) and this fact can be associated with the SST anomalies in the Indian Ocean on quasi-biennial timescales, described by Mo (2000).

The results, presented here, confirm that such combined influence of SST, position of dynamics systems and SAO can also affect the rainfall variability in the Argentinean Chaco plain region.

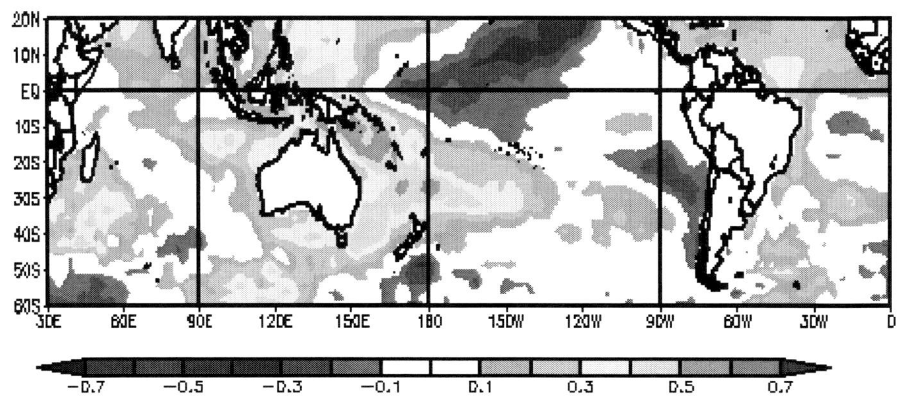

Figure 14. Map correlation between mean SST between October and April and PC3 for the period 1968-2007. Correlations greater than 0,31 are significant at 95% confidence level.

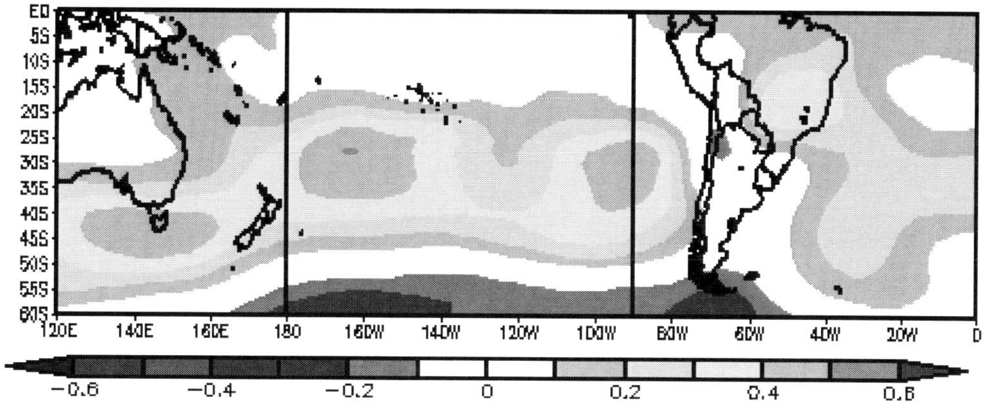

Figure 15. Map correlation between mean G500 between October and April and PC3 for the period 1968-2007. Correlations greater than 0,31 are significant at 95% confidence level.

5. Climate Change in the Chaco Plain Region

The Second National Communication of Argentina for Climate Change aimed to advance the climate impact research for the region. In this context, climate change simulations of southern South America climate were performed using a regional climate model (RCM) nested in time slice atmospheric general circulation model (AGCM) experiments. Several results were published and some of them can be consulted to have a more complete vision of the possible climate change in Argentina. As examples can be cited here the papers of Solman et al. (2008) and Nuñez et al. (2009).

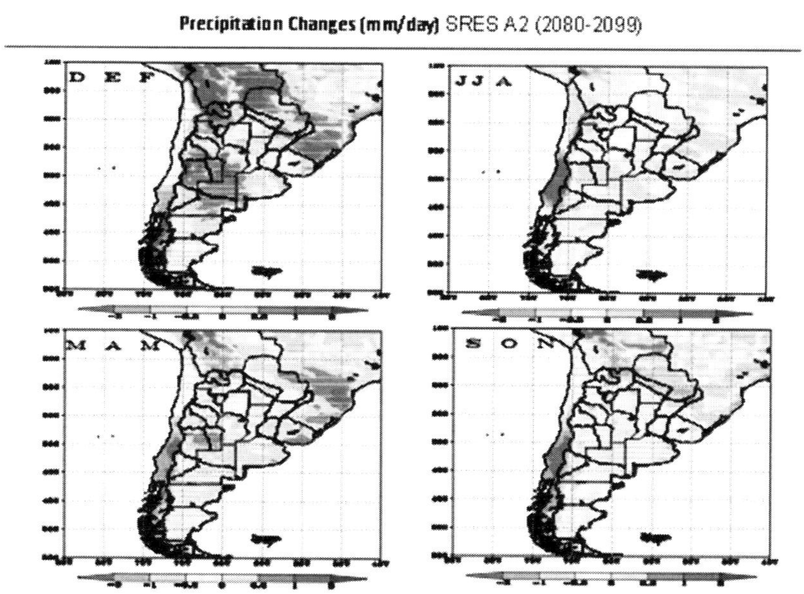

Figure 16. top left summer precipitation, top right winter precipitation, bottom left fall precipitation and bottom right spring precipitation.

In order to describe a possible situation in the future some simulations are broadly explained. The regional model MM5 was nested within time slice global atmospheric model experiments conducted by the HadAM3H model. The simulations cover a 10-year period representing present-day climate (1981–1990) and two future scenarios for the SRESA2 and B2 emission scenarios for the period 2081–2090. The changes in mean precipitation for summer (DEF), winter (JJA), autumn (MAM) and spring (SON) are shown in Figure 16. There are large seasonal and geographical variations in the change, as can be seen in the figure. The A2 scenario simulation shows a significant broad area of precipitation increase over central Argentina including Chaco Plains, especially in summer and fall and a general decrease in precipitation in winter and spring.

Conclusion

The Argentinean Chaco plains region has experienced a relevant annual rainfall increase during the last century but these trends have begun to change since 1980 in some stations of the study area where the most important deforestation took place. Cycles greater than one year were determined: a cycle of 22 years was found in some stations in the west of Chaco and east of Salta. There is a large annual cycle all over the region but it is more pronounced towards the west. The interannual rainfall variability shows that there are three main rainfall anomaly leading patterns. The first shows the difference between the east and the west of the area and it is associated with the SST in the subtropical Atlantic Ocean, the low pressure systems over the area and SAO. The area of greater variability shows a 6,6 year cycle as it is observed for SAO. The second leading pattern shows the difference between rainfall in the north and in the south of the study area, with maximum expression in west Formosa and east Salta and is related to ENSO, and with the decrease of humidity flux from the north. The third leading pattern enhances the contrast between the northeast and the southwest. It is associated with the heating of subtropical Pacific SST and a wave train extended from the western Pacific Ocean towards South America, on quasi biennial timescale (Mo 2000). In this chapter rainfall variability was analyzed to better understand its behavior in scales greater than a year. The results indicate that rainfall must be monitored in order to determine its future evolution and if deforestation has influenced the climate of the region. Likewise, the relation between climate and deforestation must be best studied in order to mitigate the negative impacts over the region.

Acknowledgments

Rainfall data were provided by the National Meteorological Service (SMN), the Secretary of Hydrology of Argentina (SRH) and the Provincial Water Administration of Chaco (APA) and the Regional Commission of Bermejo River (COREBE). Images from figures 9 to 16 were provided by the NOAA/ESRL Physical Sciences Division, Boulder Colorado from their web site: http://www.cdc.noaa.gov. This research was supported by UBACyT 2010-2012 CC02, UBACyT 2011-2014 1028, CONICET PIP 112-200801-00195 and CLARIS LPB.

REFERENCES

Adamoli J., S. Torrela, and R. Ginzburg, 2004. Diagnóstico Ambiental del Chaco Argentino. Gestión Integrada y Desarrollo Sostenible para reducir la degradación social, económica y ambiental del Gran Chaco Americano. *Informe de la Secretaría de Ambiente y Desarrollo Sustentable de la Nación Argentina.*

Baldi G, M. Nosetto and E. Jobbagy, 2008. The effect of tree plantations on south American ecosystems functioning. *Ambiencia*, V.4, 23-34.

Barros V., M.E. Castañeda and M. Doyle, 2000. Precipitation trends in Southern South America, east of the Andes: An indication of climate variability. *Southern Hemisphere Paleo-and Neoclimates: Key Sites, Methods, Data and Models,* 187-208, Springer.

Barros V. and M. E. Castañeda. 2001. Tendencias de la precipitación en el oeste de Argentina. *Meteorologica* 26, 5-24.

Barros V. and M. Doyle, 2002. Mid-summer low level circulation and precipitation in subtropical South America and related sea surface temperature anomalies in the South Atlantic. *J.Climate*, 15, 3394-3410.

Barros V., M. Doyle and I. Camilloni, 2008. Precipitation trends in southeastern South America: relationship with ENSO phases and the low-level circulation. *Theoretical and Appl. Climatology*. 93,1-2, 19-33.

Blackman, R. B. and J. Tukey, 1958. *The measurement of power spectral from the point of view of communication engineering*. New York, Dover.

Collini, E.A., Berbery, E.H., Barros, V. R. and Pyle, M.E. 2008. How does soil ñoisture influence the early stages of the South American Monsoon? *J. Climate*, 21, 195-213

Flores O.K. and M. Gonzalez, 2009. Análisis de la precipitación en la llanura chaqueña argentina y su relación con el comportamiento de la circulación atmosférica y las temperaturas de la superficie del mar. Preprint *CONGREMET X, CLIMET XIII*, Buenos Aires, October 2009, 16pp.

González M., M.E. Castañeda, and J. Texeira Neri, 2005. Evolución de la precipitación en el noreste de Argentina y sur de Brasil. *Preprint Congremet IX*, 3-7 octubre, Buenos Aires, Argentina, ISBN 987-22411-0-4.

González M. and V. Barros, 2002. On the forecast of the onset and end of convective season in the Amazon", *Theoretical and Applied Climatology*, 73, 3-4, 169-188.

Grau H.R., N.I. Gasparri and T. Mitchell Aide, 2005. Agriculture expansion and deforestation in seasonally dry forest of north-west Argentina. *Environmental Conservation* 32, 140-148.

Green P. 1978. *Analysing Multivariate Data*. Dryden Press, pp 341-387.

Grimm A.M, V.R. Barros and M.E. Doyle, 2000. Climate Variability in Southern South America associated with El Niño and La Niña events. *J. Climate*, 13, 35-58.

IAI, 2010. Alimentos e inundaciones. Aguas subterráneas someras y manejo de tierras de cultivo en la region pampeana. *Instantáneas de la Ciencia 7.* IAI

Jin J., S. Lu, S. Li, and N.L.Miller, 2000.Impact of Land Use Change on the Local Climate over the Tibetan Plateau. *Advances in Meteorology*, 2010, ID 837480, 6 pages, doi:10.1155/2010/837480

Jobbagy E.G., M Nosetto, C. Santoni and G. Baldi, 2008. El desafío ecohidrológico de las transiciones entre sistemas leñosos y herbáceos en la llanura Chaco-Pampeana. *Ecologia Austral* 18, 305-322.

Kaiser H.F. 1958. The varimax criterion for analytic rotation in factor analysis. *Psychometrica*. 23, 187-200.

Kalnay E., M. Kanamitsu, R. Kistler, W. Collins, D. Deaven, L. Gandin, M. Iredell, S. Saha, G. White, J. Woollen, I. Zhu, M. Chelliah, W. Ebisuzaki, W. Higgings, J. Janowiak, K.C. Mo, C. Ropelewski, J. Wang, A. Leetmaa, R. Reynolds, R. Jenne, D. Joseph, 1996. The NCEP/NCAR Reanalysis 40 years- project. *Bull. Amer. Meteor. Soc.* 77, 437-471.

Lee S.J. 2010.Impact of land surface vegetation change over the La Plata Basin on the regional climatic environmental: A study using conventional land cover/land use and newly developed ecosystem functional types. *Doctoral Thesis.* University of Maryland.

Lee S.J. and E.H. Berbery, 2010. On the effects of land cover change on the climate of La Plata Basin. *Submitted J. Hydrometeor.* In press.

Liebmann B., C. Vera, L. Carvalho, I. Camilloni,M. Hoerling, D. Allured, V. Barros, J. Báez, and M. Bidegain, 2004. An Observed Trend in Central South American Precipitation. *J. Climate,* 17, 22, 4357-4367.

Mabuchi K., Y. Sato and H. Kida, 2005. Climatic Impact of Vegetation Change in the Asian Tropical Region. Part I: Case of the Northern Hemisphere Summer. *J. Climate*, 18, 410-428.

Mitchell J.M., Dzerdzeevskii, B., Flohn, H., Hofmeyr, W.L., Lamb, H.H., Rao, K.N., Walléen, C.C. 1966. Technical Note No. 79. Climatic Change. *(Report of a working group of the Commission for Climatology). WMO* 195, 79pp.

Mo K. 2000. Relationships between low frequency variability in the Southern Hemisphere and sea surface temperature anomalies. *J. Climate* 13, 3599-3610.

Nosetto M.D. and E. Jobbagy, T.Toth and R.B. Jackson, 2008. Regional patterns and controls of ecosystem salinization with grassland afforestation along a rainfall gradient. *Global Biochemical Cycles*, 22, GB2015, doi: 10.1029/2007GB003000.

Nuñez M.N., S. Solman and M.F. Cabré, 2009. Regional Climate change experiments over Southern South America. II: Climate change scenarios in the late twenty first century. *Climate Dynamics*, 32, 7-8, 901-1186.

Paruelo J.M., J.P. Guerschman, G. Piñeiro, E. Jobbagy, S.R. Veron, G. Baldi and S. Baeza, 2006. Cambios en el uso de la tierra en Argentina y Uruguay: marcos conceptuales para su análisis. *Agrociencia* X, 2, 47-61.

Reason C. and Rouault, M. 2005. Links between the Antartic Oscillation and winter rainfall over western South Africa. *Geophys. Res. Lett.* 32, L07705 DOI: 10.1029/2005GL022419.

Reboita M.S., T. Ambrizzi and R.P. Da Rocha, 2009. Relationship between the Southern Annular Mode and souther hemisphere atmospheric systems. *Revista Brasilera de Meteorologia*, 24, 1, 48-55.

Ropelewsky C. and M. Halpert, 1987. Global and regional scale precipitation patterns associated with El Niño/Southern Oscillation. *Monthly Weather Review,* 115, 2161-2165.

Silvestri G., and C. Vera, 2003. Antarctic Oscillation signal on precipitation anomalies over southeastern South America. *Geophysical Research Letters*, 30 (21), 21-15.

Solman, S., M.N. Nuñez and M.F. Cabré, 2008. Climate change experiments over southern South America. I: Present climate. *Climate Dynamics*, 30, 5.

Sorensson A. and C. Menendez, 2010. Summer soil-precipitation coupling in South America. *Tellus*. DOI: 10.1111/j.1600-0870.2010.00468.x

Vargas W., O. Penalba and J. Minetti, 1999. Las precipitaciones mensuales en zonas de la Argentina y el ENOS. Un enfoque hacia problemas de decisión. *Meteorologica*, 24, 3-22.

Wilks D. S., 1995. Statistical methods in the atmospheric sciences (An introduction). *International Geophysics series*. Academic Press, San Diego, California, USA, 467 pp.

Zheng X. and Renwick J. 2003. A regression scheme based for seasonal forecasting of New Zealand temperature. *J. Climate* 16:1843-1853.

In: Rainfall: Behavior, Forecasting and Distribution ISBN: 978-1-62081-551-9
Editors: Olga E. Martín and Tricia M. Roberts

Chapter 5

RAINFALL AND WATER QUALITY

Benoit Roig[1,2,*], Estelle Baures[1,2], Aude-Valérie Jung[1,3], Ianis Delpla[1,2] and Olivier Thomas[1,2]
[1]Advanced School of Public Health (EHESP), LERES, Rennes Cedex, France
[2]INSERM U1085, LERES, Rennes Cedex, France
[3]School of Environmental Engineering (EME), Campus de Ker Lann, Avenue Robert Schumann, Bruz, France

1. INTRODUCTION

The consideration of rainfalls impact on water management is not new and started with the history of sanitation. At the beginning of the 20th century sewer networks in urban area were designed both for sewage and for stormwater management. In the 70's the impact of urban runoff on water quality was already studied (Pitt et al., 1977) and more recently the question of climate change impacts on water quality was considered with the effect of heavier rainy events. Commonly, categories of rain are defined by their intensity:light , moderate and heavy rain being characterised by the amount of mm of water/hour (respectively 2.5, 2.5 to 7.5, >7.5). According to the duration of a given rainfall, the same intensity can be observed during a short period (shower) or a longer one (storm). Consequences of these precipitations can result in so called extreme rain or flood respectively at local or regional scale. As reported by the 2007 IPCC report, it is likely that the frequency of heavy precipitation events has increased over most areas, particularly in Europe and North America, and that available research suggests a significant future increase in heavy rainfall events in many regions. Such phenomena, increasing in frequency and intensity, may have a strong impact on the quality of the waters. Indeed, resulting changes in flow regimes will influence the chemistry, hydromorphology and ecology of water bodies at the environmental level as well as, in urban area, the wastewater quality, the sewage treatment efficiency and the corresponding pollutants load (Roig et al., 2011). The effect of rainy events can also reach drinking water production system, impairing the quality of the distributed water (Figure 1)

* E-mail: benoit.roig@ehesp.fr

This chapter aims to make an overview of the impact of rainfall on water quality, by considering, within the water life cycle, chemical, biological and physico-chemical parameters of water quality.

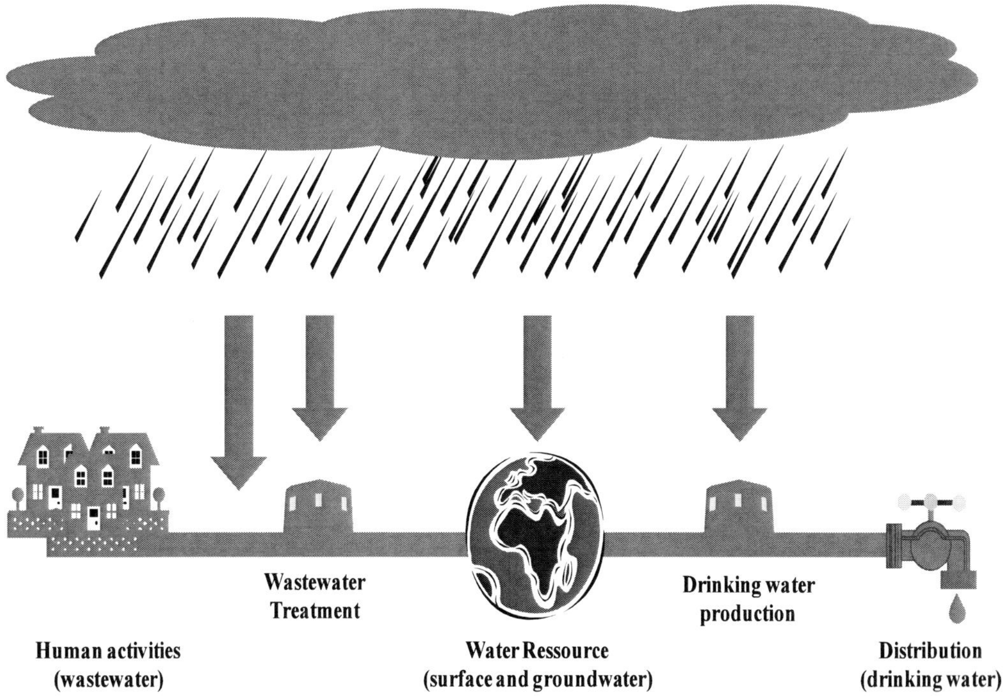

Figure 1. Impact of heavy events on water life cycle.

2. Water Quality

Water bodies are characterised regarding their chemical and biological status. A number of parameters are used to analyse water quality. European water regulations (Drinking-water Directive (DWD) and the Water Framework Directive (WFD)) have been established, since the end of the 1990s, to ensure public health security for water intended for human consumption by promoting a policy for the management and protection of European Member state's water resources. More recently, a new preventive risk management approach was initiated by WHO and water suppliers, via the implementation of Water Safety Plans (Bartram et al., 2009), the aim of which is to guarantee the safety of a drinking-water supply through the use of a comprehensive risk assessment and risk management approach. Despite this regulatory framework, numerous water bodies are often of impaired quality and non-compliant with European regulations (Bloech, 2011).

In general, raw water quality is influenced by both 'natural' and anthropogenic driving forces. The former include spatial and temporal variation in water availability, wildlife, topography, geology, vegetation and the future impact of climate change, particularly with respect to the frequency and severity of droughts or rainfalls. Anthropogenic driving forces come from each of the key sectors that use water (industry, energy production, public water supply and agriculture) and include point sources (e.g. wastewater discharges) and non-point sources (e.g. surface runoff). In general, water quality degradation is directly linked to anthropogenic pressure, and climate change acts as an indirect aggravating factor for these pressures on the environment. In particular, the main determinants of climate change having a direct or indirect impact on water quality are air temperature and extreme water events (flood, drought) (Delpla et al., 2009). Resource availability is linked to these parameters, and it becomes important to consider extreme events in assessing both evolution of water stress and efficiency of the treatment processes (sanitation and sewage treatment).

3. Impact of Rainfall on Urban Water Cycle (From Wastewater to the Environment)

The historical question of rainfall impact on urban water cycle is linked to urban runoff, well studied since the 70's. For instance, Pitt et al. (1977) studied the water-quality effects from urban runoff for a hypothetical city of 100,000 inhabitants. Total solids concentration and oxygen consumption were calculated for receiving waters using various storms simulated in the study.

Cities are becoming increasingly vulnerable to flooding because of rapid urbanization, installation of complex infrastructure and changes in the precipitation patterns caused by anthropogenic climate change (Willems et al, 2012). For more than a century, sewer systems have been constructed at large scale across cities worldwide. These sewer systems could make the cities more vulnerable to extreme rainfall, partly due to the lack of consideration to what occurs when the design criteria are exceeded. Next to this increase in the vulnerability, there is strong evidence that, due to global warming, the probabilities and risk to sewer surcharge and flooding are under discussion. But impacts of climate change on urban drainage are still weakly investigated (Willems et al., 2012).

In AMWA report (2007), the different impacts of climate changes on water suppliers are identified and described as follow:

i. direct impacts resulting from the effects of climate change on water utility functions and operations,
ii. indirect impact resulting from the effects of climate change on the baseline environment in which water utility functions and operations are carried out and
iii. compound impact resulting from the cumulative effect of the direct and indirect impacts which affect the same natural systems or utility systems.

Among the direct impacts, more frequent and intense rainfall events are intended to increase turbidity, sedimentation, risk of direct flood and consequently damage water utility facilities: for example, loss of reservoir capacity storage (shallower, warmer water, increased evaporation and eutrophication and potential conflicts with flood control objectives) with consequences on water treatment (AMWA, 2007). However for urban watercourses, there is often "flashy" hydraulic regimes and poor water quality, making them potential hazards.

Furthermore, the knowledge of impact of intense rainfall events on urban river water discharge and, in particular, fine particles transport is limited (Old et al., 2003). The washed off pollutants such as suspended solids increases the turbidity of the receiving water, thereby reducing the penetration of light, resulting in decreased activity and growth of photosynthetic organisms. Clogging of fish gills has also been attributed to the presence of suspended solids. These ones settle in receiving water pose long-term threats resulting from increased oxygen demand and gradual accumulation of toxic pollutants. Such detrimental effects have made suspended solid concentration one of the pollutant measurement indices (Aryal, 2009).

Moreover, Old et al. (2003) demonstrated that this extremely large and urban flux of fine sediment is likely to have a major downstream impact on water quality in the river.

Brodie and Egodawatta (2011) have shown that suspended particles in stormwater runoff generated from road surfaces loads increase linearly with average rainfall intensity. Above a threshold intensity, there is evidence to suggest that a constant or plateau particles load is reached.

Cheng et al (2009) have studied the impact of four different intensity rainfall (light rain, moderate rain, heavy rain and storm) on water quality of urban combined sewerage system (CSS) in highly urbanized region and the correlations of parameters with both rainfall intensity and runoff graph. Basic parameters and metals concentrations were monitored and shown good relation between them and runoff.

Temporal evolution of microbiological, physical, and chemical quality of stormwater runoff from a stormwater drain was studied by He et al. (2010) in an urban residential area in Calgary, Canada. Intensive rainfall events produced highly polluted stormwater runoff when pollutant source limitation did not occur. Inconsistent event-based correlations between total suspended solids (TSS) concentrations and water quality parameters were observed. During storms, the loading of TSS exhibited a flow-dependent nature, whereas microorganism discharge appeared to be governed by a flow-independent mechanism. No strong first-flush effect was observed in either TSS or microorganisms, on average. No correlation of first-flush loads of TSS with rainfall characteristics was identified.

Rainfall events can also play an important role regarding micropollutants load at sewage treatment works (STWs). In general, urban runoff tends to originate from five main categories: transportation (i.e. roads and vehicles), roofing materials, construction activities, vegetation and soil. There may be many variables within a given source, e.g. runoff from roads and associated traffic emissions may contain vehicle lubricants, exhaust emissions, degradation from tyres and brake linings, road maintenance and surface degradation, accidental spillages and road salting in winter. The extent of urban runoff is dependent on levels of contaminants deposited on urban surfaces through wet and dry deposition, the length of the preceding dry spell and the characteristics and size of the urban catchment. Assessing the effects of rainfall STW influent has produced results that suggest that with short rainfall incidences the level of most micropollutants will increase due to "first flushing" events, whereas continuous high levels of rainfall will result in a dilution effect on micropollutant levels (Rowsell et al., 2010).

Another consequence of runoff on water quality may be ecotoxicological impact linked to the presence of contaminants. Meland et al. (2010), exposed brown trout (Salmo trutta L.) to highway runoff samples during 24 h. The metabolism of the fish through reduced condition factor was affected and the observed effects were likely caused by multiple stressors and not by a single contaminant. A sedimentation pond clearly reduced the toxicity of the highway runoff. But even in the least polluted exposure condition signs of physiological disturbances were evident.

Considering the threats originating from wastewater utilities, the type of wastewater system is of crucial importance. Moreoften a combined wastewater system is prevalent in urban area, with domestic wastewater and stormwater runoff from impervious surfaces (streets, roofs etc.) collected in the same sewer system.

During rain events, the wastewater treatment plants as well as the sewer systems have to cope with a high load of combined wastewater that may exceed the systems' capacity. Thus, certain volumes of wastewater must be stored or discharged. This may be achieved by storm water overflow basins or stormwater tanks, with both retention and treatment functions (Heins, 2009). Combined sewage overflows, which were previously designed to directly discharge the exceeding flow, tend to be removed from wastewater networks.

In case of heavy rainfall, the wastewater treatment plant (WWTP) temporarily receives low concentrated sewage and high hydraulic loading. Prolonged exposure to stormwater conditions will negatively affect all treatment steps by decreasing the residential time and particularly the settling processes (primary and secondary) as well as the biological part of the treatment with activated sludge, and possibly denitrification and phosphorus removal processes. For this last step, it is still not clear whether this is due to inhibition of phosphorous-removing bacteria (PRB) or that the low chemical oxygen demand (COD) concentrations in the influent are causing the problem. It has been reported that, for example, the deterioration of PRB efficiency regularly occurred at some WWTPs after heavy rainfall. The phenomenon was attributed to low plant loading that took place during such events (Brdjanovic et al., 1998).

An observatory of urban pollutants was created in France for the purpose of assessing the dynamic of wastewater and wet weather flow (WWF). The magnitude of WWF pollutant loads characterized by physical-chemical parameters: TSS, dissolved organic carbon (DOC), heavy metals (Cu, Zn), polycyclic aromatic hydrocarbons (PAHs), and their subsequent acute impact on receiving waters have been extensively studied since 1970 (Suarez and Puertas, 2005; Gasperi et al., 2010). Some studies have observed the becoming of specific pollutants concentrations during wet weather flows in wastewater. Gilbert et al., (2011) for instance showed that alkylphenols (AP) and polybromodiphenylether (PBDE) concentrations are 1.5 to 5 fold higher under wet weather flows.

The removal rates of several antiphlogistics and lipid regulating agents were investigated during a rainfall event (Ternes, 1998). The elimination rates of drugs like bezafibrate, diclofenac, naproxen and clofibric acid were significantly reduced on the rainfall day. For bezafibrate a reduced elimination rate (<5%) was observed the last day of the investigation period. These results indicate that the rainfall event may be presumably responsible for the decreased drugs elimination rates by the sewage treatment plant probably due to a reduced microbial activity and/or altered sorption and flocculation conditions within this rain period (Ternes, 1998).

4. Rainfall and Water Resource (Quality Modification of Natural Water)

Water quality depends on stressors among which climate-related parameters such as water temperature and river flows (Murdoch et al., 2000). According to these authors, changes in water quality are related to hydrological factors (e.g. limited dilution of point sources during low river flows, or increased runoff from agricultural area during rainstorms), terrestrial factors (e.g. changes in vegetation and soil structure) and resource-use factors (e.g. increased water use, increased demand for cooling capacity of industrial processes). More recently, bibliographic reviews and case studies (Delpla et al., 2009; Zwolsman and van Bokhoven, 2007; Van Vliet and Zwolsman, 2008) concluded that climate change has a negative impact on water quality. Depending on the season, the same impact (increase of water pollution) may be related to different conditions. During winter rainfall, water and air temperatures are low, river flows generally high and soil leaching and runoff increase, contrary to summertime where very high air temperature may lead to drought (e.g. Krysanova et al., 2005). Both cases may give a high pollution level either by runoff (heavy rain in winter) or by physical conditions (drought in summer).

According to Bates et al. (2008) and Brunetti et al. (2001), climate change in temperate area will lead to a decrease of the number of rainy days, with however a significant increase of the mean volume for each event. Consequently, the drought and re-humidification cycles for the soils will allow the decomposition and leaching of the organic matter to the surface waters and thus impact water quality as a whole (Evans et al., 2005). Heavy rainfall events could lead to an increase in DOC concentration (Evans et al., 2005; Fellman et al., 2009) which is known to play an important role concerning the transport and release of pollutants (Lennartz and Louchart, 2007; Pédrot et al., 2008).

Nutrients concentrations (nitrate, phosphate) and obviously particulate and colloidal suspended matter are directly correlated with rainy events (Prathumratana et al., 2008; Bhat et al., 2007; Drewry et al., 2009) and could consequently exceed water quality regulated limits.

For heavy rainy events leading to an increase of river flows, the major risk is also certainly the transport of pollutants by runoff (such as pesticides and pharmaceuticals). It was often acknowledged that the timing and magnitude of rainfall events are significant on pesticide transport through rapid flow processes (Leonard, 1990; Flury, 1996; Kladivko et al., 2001; McGrath et al., 2010) with in general an increase of pesticide leaching with increasing rainfall amount (Tiktak et al., 2004; Jiang et al., 2012). Pharmaceuticals considered as « emerging substances » are of a special importance because they are not yet regulated. Some studies specifically show significant correlations between some of these compounds (carbamazepine, monensin, clofibric acid, iopromide, sulfamethoxazole, trimethoprim, flumequine) and flow rates variation during rainfall events (Oppel et al., 2004; Lissemore et al., 2006; Tamtam et al., 2008).

Variations of temperature, pH and water composition occurring during rainfall events could also have an influence on contaminants by impacting their sorption on mineral phases. Moreover, the influence of soils properties has to be taken into account for the leaching behaviour assessment of anthropogenic compounds (Oppel et al., 2004; Yu et al., 2009).

Neal et al. (2004) studied the water quality of rainfall and runoff for two catchments of different characteristics. Average water quality concentrations and fluxes vary across the sites, typically by about 30% but stream chemistry is much less variable due to water coming from aquifer sources of high storage. Moreover, the catchments appear to retain both P and N coming from agricultural practices and sewage inputs to the streams.

Some studies on coastal water quality impacts of rainfall like Coulliette et al. (2008) have shown the effect of non-point source contamination linked to stormwater. Fecal coliforms concentrations increased with rainfall intensity but higher than expected values existed during conditions of negligible rainfall (< 2.5 mm), indicating a possible reservoir population in the sediment.

Liu et al. (2010) worked on the occurrence and distribution of three typical endocrine-disrupting chemicals (EDCs), nonylphenol mixture (NPs), bisphenol A (BPA), and 17-ethynilestradiol (EE2), in the coastal water, suspended solid, and sediment. With the increasing rainfall, the concentrations of target EDCs decreased in water and sediment and increased in suspended solid.

The genotoxic impact on fish of heavy rainfall following herbicide application has been investigated by Polard et al. (2011). For three hydrological conditions (basal flow, winter flood, and spring flood), chemical analysis of the water samples confirmed the higher contamination of the spring flood water, mainly explained by a peak of metolachlor. Genotoxicity was evaluated on Crucian carp and exposure to spring flood water resulted in the highest damage induction. Further experiments on pesticides mixture add on water flood revealed a mutagenic impact of water contamination during the spring flood, emphasizing the need to consider these transient events in water quality monitoring programs.

Concerning pathogens, floods frequently lead to a faecal contamination of surface and deep waters and also to waterborne diseases (Beaudeau et al., 2010). As an example, very elevated levels of bacteria E. Coli (2000 – 7000 CFU/mL) have been measured downstream Milwaukee river basin after rainfall events (Patz et al., 2008). Curriero et al. (2001) have shown that half of the waterborne diseases outbreaks in United States during the second half of the 20th century followed a period of extreme rainfall (defined as the excess of the 90th percentile based on 50-year distribution).

Finally changes in rainfalls patterns and temperature could also have an effect on occurrence of cyanobacteria (blooms). Althought intense rainfalls could interrupt bloom development in a water body by flushing and mixing at the event scale, they could also increase the nutrients load and the rate of eutrophication which favour cyanobacteria at a longer time scale (Reichwaldt and Ghadouani, 2011).

5. Impact on Drinking Water Production

Rainfalls events could lead to elevated levels of turbidity and organic matter in river waters which in turn could cause a decline in treatment performance. Mineral particles leaching could lead to high concentrations in natural waters, having a direct impact on coagulant demand during water treatment (Shin et al., 2008) and on Disinfection By-Products (DBPs) formation. However, this decrease in efficiency could be also due to a combination of a change in the nature and increased concentrations of Natural Organic Matter (NOM) and lower water temperatures in the natural water (Hurst et al., 2004). This could explain why seasonal differences have a significant impact on process robustness which is independent of the raw water turbidity. Moreover, in the distribution system, the highest spatial variation in Trihalomethans concentration (from 2 to 4 times) is measured for elevated water temperatures (>18°C) typically during the summer season, whereas this variation is small for water temperature lower than 15°C during the spring or fall seasons (Rodriguez and Serodes, 2001).

Although very few studies reported the relationship between algae and DBPs precursors, some authors pointed out the algal contribution to some DPBs formation such as Haloacetic Acids (Chen and Zhang, 2008).

Heavy rainfall and associated floods could flush biological contaminants into waterways and aquifers, for example with combined sewer systems overflowing and agricultural lands leaching. Greater water flow contributes to increase the pathogen load and the penetration speed of pathogens into resource waters and the drinking-water supply (Unc and Goss, 2003). A significant number of waterborne disease outbreaks have involved the transport of bacteria, viruses, or small parasites into water systems or well-heads during a heavy rainfall event (Auld et al., 2004; Thomas et al., 2006). As an example, heavy rainfalls contributed to the Milwaukee (United States) outbreak of Cryptosporidium in 1993 (54 deaths, 403000 cases) and the Walkerton (Canada) E. Coli O157:H7 outbreak in 2000 (7 deaths, 4300 cases). Monitoring the change of the biological charge with adequate and rapid tools is very important to ensure maximum efficiency of the treatment and protection of the population after rainfall events. This is of primary importance regarding the fact that routine monitoring programs mainly use techniques that are time consuming and not allow a representative picture of the wide range of biological contaminants that could be present in water.

The main recent studies dealing with the occurrence and fate of micropollutants with respect to drinking water treatment are related to pharmaceuticals. Actually, the majority of studies on pharmaceuticals focused on wastewater treatment, for which the insuficient removal efficiency may affect the quality of water resources downstream to a treated effluent discharge. Although they are partially removed, residual quantities may remain in treated water and contaminate drinking water resources (Al-Ahmad et al., 1999; Hernando et al., 2006). Actually, more than 20 substances (parent compound and residues) have been found in drinking water (Mompelat et al., 2009).

The efficiency of pharmaceuticals removal varies with treatment processes and also with temperature and weather (Choi et al., 2008). For instance, diclofenac showed largely different elimination rates whose range, comprised between 17% (Heberer et al., 2002), 69% (Ternes et al., 1998), and 100% (Thomas and Foster, 2004) depends on these two last parameters. Pharmaceuticals removal could only be achieved with advanced processes as ozonation, activated carbon adsorption, membrane filtration (Ternes et al., 2002) or UV treatment (Canonica et al., 2008). Finally, only some lipophilic pesticides are removed adequately in conventional physico-chemical drinking water treatment processes, such as flocculation, sedimentation, filtration, or lime softening (Baldauf, 2006).

Concerning natural micropollutants, mainly represented by cyanotoxins, chlorination, micro/ultra-filtration and especially ozonation are the most effective water treatment procedures in destroying cyanobacteria and in removing microcystins (Hitzfeld et al., 2000). Lots of studies concerning removal of cyanobacterial toxins from water showed that the effectiveness of the oxidation process is not only dependant on the reactant concentration, but also on temperature, pH, ionic composition (Rositano et al., 1998; Shawwa and Smith, 2001) and NOM concentration (Al Momani et al., 2008). Moreover, some studies tried to improve by-products identification and toxicity assessment for cyanotoxins (Rodriguez et al., 2007; Mérel et al., 2009). Although DBPs formation has largely not been investigated, the few studies conducted have concluded to a decrease in cyanotoxins toxicity (microcystin, cylindrospermopsin, saxitoxin) after chlorination (Mérel et al., 2010).

Extreme weather events could affect the efficiency of drinking water treatment processes, leading to a possible degradation of quality in distributed drinking water (Sinisi and Aertgeerts, 2010). These concerns are of primary importance for small-scale water suppliers (SSWSs), private, community-based or public, which usually prevail in rural areas. A significant part of the population living in these areas (16 million people in Europe (WHO, 2010) do not have access to improved drinking water resources). This vulnerability of SSWSs is due to an insufficient sanitary protection of resources, agricultural pressures, limited water treatment technologies, relatively greater capital costs of technical installations and larger per unit costs of materials and construction. By considering these existing pressures, and the indirect risks posed by climate change, SSWSs are facing several challenges, including their regulatory environment, administration, management, operation, and their available technical, human and financial resources (Sinisi and Aertgeerts, 2010).

Conclusion

Rainfall can be a significant source of variation in water quality. In urban area, depending on its intensity, rainfall can have an effect on utility functions and operations as well as water discharge due to runoff (road, roof ...). The relation between water quality and runoff is in particular well known since the 70's as an increase of turbidity, sedimentation, transport of more or less fine particles and pollutants (conventional and/or emerging). The main outcomes were the improvement of sewer and rainstorm networks design with in situ settling systems for TSS removal and flow storage. More recently the effect of rainfall on soil erosion has been also highlighted, in particular the suspended solid exportation and increase of nutrient in surface water.

Water resource is also stressed by rainfall. Changes in water quality rely in particular to hydrological, terrestrial and resource-use factors as well as climate. Climate changes are more and more studied with consequences on micropollutants transportation and cyanobacteria crisis

One important point of the relation between water quality and rainfall is the duration and intensity of transient effect, in particular regarding toxicity and ecotoxicity and sanitary water.

References

Al-Ahmad, A; Daschner, FD; Kummerer, K. Biodegradability of cefotiam, ciprofloxacin, meropenem, penicillin G, and sulfamethoxazole and inhibition of waste water bacteria. *Arch Environ Contam Toxicol* 1999, 37,158–63.

Al Momani, F; Smith, DW; El-Din, MG. Degradation of cyanobacteria toxin by advanced oxidation process. *J Hazard Mater* 2008, 150, 238–49.

AMWA (Association of metropolitan water agencies), *Implications of climate change for urban water utilities,* Washington DC, December 2007, 18 p.

Aryal, RK; Lee, B.-K. Characteristics of Suspended Solids and Micropollutants in First-Flush Highway Runoff. *Water Air Soil Pollut: Focus* 2009, 9, 339–346.

Auld, H; MacIver, D; Klaassen, J. Heavy rainfall and waterborne disease outbreaks: the Walkerton example. *J. Toxicol. Environ. Health* A 2004, 67, 1879-1887.

Baldauf, G. Removal of pesticides in drinking water treatment. *Acta Hydrochim Hydrobiol* 2006, 21, 203–8.

Bartram, J; Corrales, L; Davison, A; Deere, D; Drury, D; Gordon, B; Howard, G; Rinehold, A; Stevens, M. Water Safety Plan Manual: Step-By-Step Risk Management for Drinking-Water Suppliers, *World Health Organization*, Geneva, Switzerland, 108p, 2009.

Bates, B; Kundzewickz, ZW; Wu, S; Palutikof, J. (Editors) Climate Change and Water. *Technical Paper of the Intergovernmental Panel on Climate Change, IPPC Secretariat,* Geneva, Switzerland, 210 p., 2008.

Beaudeau, P; Valdes, D; Mouly, D; Stempfelet, M; Seux, R. Natural and technical factors in faecal contamination incidents of driniking water in small distribution networks, France, 2003-2004: a geographical study. J. *Water Health* 2010, 08.1, 20-34.

Bhat, S; Hatfield, K; Jacobs, JM; Lowrance, R; Williams, R. Surface runoff contribution of nitrogen during storm events in a forested watershed. *Biogeochemistry* 2007, 85, 253-262.

Bloech, H. *Summary Record of the Meeting of the Committee under Article 12 of Directive* 98/83/EC, DG ENV, 22/02/2011.

Brdjanovic, D; Slamet, A; Van Loosdercht, MCM; Hooijmans, CM; Alaerts, GJ; Heijnen, JJ. Impact of excessive aeration on biological phosphorus removal from wastewater. *Water Research* 1998, 32, 200-208.

Brodie, IM; Egodawatta, P. Relationships between rainfall intensity, duration and suspended particle washoff from an urban road surface. *Hydrology Research 2011, 42,* 239-249.

Brunetti, M; Maugeri, M; Nanni, T. Changes in total precipitation rainy days and extreme events in Northeastern Italy. *Int. J. Climatol.* 2001, 21, 861-871.

Canonica, S; Meunier, L; von Gunten, V. Phototransformation of selected pharmaceuticals during UV treatment of drinking water. *Water Res.* 2008, 42, 121-128.

Chen, C; Zhang, X-J; Zhu, L-x; Liu, J; He, W-j; Han, H-d. Disinfection by-products and their precursors in awater treatment plant in North China: seasonal changes and fraction analysis. *Sci Total Environ* 2008, 397, 140–147.

Cheng, J; Yang, K; Huang, X-F; Lue, Y-P. Hydrology and Water Quality of Rainfall-Runoff in Combined Sewerage System Along Suzhou Creek in Central Shanghai. *Environmental Science* 2009, 30, 1893-1900.

Choi, K; Kima, Y; Park, J; Park, CK; Kim, M; Kim, HS; Kim, P. Seasonal variations of several pharmaceutical residues in surface water and sewage treatment plants of Han River. *Sci Total Environ* 2008, 405, 102–28.

Coulliette, AD; Noble, RT. Impacts of rainfall on the water quality of the Newport River Estuary (Eastern North Carolina, USA). *Journal of Water and Health* 2008, 6, 473-482.

Curriero, FC; Patz, JA; Rose, JB; Lele, S. The association between extreme precipitation and waterborne disease outbreaks in the United States, 1948-1994. *Am. J. Public Health* 2001, 91, 1194-1199.

Delpla, I; Jung, A-V; Baures, E; Clement, M; Thomas, O. Impacts of climate change on surface water quality in relation to drinking water production. *Environment International* 2009, 35, 1225-1233.

Drewry, JJ; Newham, LTH; Croke, BFW. Suspended sediment, nitrogen and phosphorus concentrations and exports during storm-events to the Tuross estuary, Australia. *J. Environ. Manag.* 2009, 90, 879-887.

Evans, CD; Monteith, DT; Cooper, DM. Long-term increases in surface water dissolved organic carbon: observations, possible causes and environmental impacts. *Environment Pollution* 2005, 137, 55–71.

Fellman, B; Hood, E; Edwards, RT; D'Amore, DV. Changes in the concentration, biodegradability, and fluorescent properties of dissolved organic matter during stormflows in coastal temperate watersheds. *Journal of Geophysical Research* 2009, 114, G01021, doi:10.1029/ 2008JG000790.

Flury, M. Experimental evidence of transport of pesticides through field soils — a review. *J. Environ. Qual.* 1996, 25, 25–45.

Gasperi, J; Gromaire, MC; Kafi, M; Moilleron, R; Chebbo, G. Contributions of watewater, runoff and sewer deposit erosion to wet weather pollutant load in combined sewer systems. *Water Research* 2010, 44, 5875-5886.

Gilbert, DS; Gasperi, J; Rocher, V; Lorgeoux, C; Chebbo, G. Efficiency of the seine centre wastewater treatment plant during wet weather periods regarding conventional wastewater parameters, alkylphenols and polybromodiphenylethers. *Techniques Sciences et Méthodes* 2011, 4, 63-72.

He, J; Valeo, C; Chu, A; Neumann, NF. Characteristics of Suspended Solids, Microorganisms, and Chemical Water Quality in Event-Based Stormwater Runoff from an Urban Residential Area. *Water Environment Research* 2010, 82, 2333-2345.

Heberer, T; Reddersen, K; Mechlinski, A. From municipal sewage to drinking water: fate and removal of pharmaceutical residues in the aquatic environment in urban areas. *Water Sci Technol 2002*, 46, 81–88.

Heinz, B; Birk, S; Liedl, R; Geyer, T; Straub, KL; Andresen, J; Bester, K; Kappler, A. Water quality deterioration at a karst spring (Gallusquelle, Germany) due to combined sewer overflow: evidence of bacterial and micro-pollutant contamination. *Environmental Geology* 2009, 57, 797-808.

Hernando, MD; Mezcua, M; Fernandez-Alba, AR; Barceló, D. Environmental risk assessment of pharmaceutical residues in wastewater effluents, surface waters and sediments. *Talanta* 2006, 69, 334–342.

Hitzfeld, BC; Höger, SJ; Dietrich, DR. Cyanobacterial toxins removal during drinking water treatment and human risk assessment. *Environ Health Perspect* 2000, 108, 113–122.

Hurst, AM; Edwards, MJ; Chipps, M, Jefferson, B; Parsons, SA. The impact of rainstorm events on coagulation and clarifier performance in potable water treatment. *Sci Total Environ* 2004, 321, 219–230.

Jiang, W; Haver, D; Rust, M; Gan, J. Runoff of pyrethroid insecticides from concrete surfaces following simulated and natural rainfalls. *Water Res.* 2012, 46, 645-52.

Kladivko, EJ; Brown, LC; Baker, JL. Pesticide transport to subsurface tile drains in humid regions of north America. *Crit. Rev. Environ. Sci. Tech.* 2001, 31, 1–62.

Krysanova, V; Hattermann, F, Habeck, A. Expected changes in water resources availability and water quality with respect to climate change in the Elbe River basin (Germany). *Nordic Hydrology* 2005, 36, 321-333.

Lennartz, B; Louchart, X. Effect of drying on the desorption of diuron and terbuthylazine from natural soils. *Environmental Pollution* 2007, 146, 180-187.

Leonard, R.. Movement of pesticides into surface waters. In: Cheng, H.H. (Ed.), Pesticides in the Soil Environment. *Soil Science Society of America,* Madison, USA, 1990, pp. 303–349.

Lissemore, L; Hao, C; Yang, P; Sibley, PK; Mabury, S; Solomon, KR. An exposure assessment for selected pharmaceuticals within a watershed in Southern Ontario. *Chemosphere* 2006, 64, 717–729.

Liu, Y; Guan, Y; Tam, NFY; Mizuno, T; Tsuno, H; Zhu, W. *Influence of Rainfall and Basic Water Quality Parameters on the Distribution of Endocrine-Disrupting Chemicals in Coastal Area. Water, Air, & Soil Pollution* 2010, 209 333-343.

Meland, S; Salbu, B; Rosseland, BO. Ecotoxicological impact of highway runoff using brown trout (Salmo trutta L.) as an indicator model. *Journal of Environmental Monitoring* 2010, 12, 654-664.

Mérel, S; Lebot, B; Clement, M; Seux, R; Thomas, O. MS identification of microcystin-LR chlorination by-products. *Chemosphere* 2009, 74, 832–9.

McGrath, G; Hinz, C; Sivapalan, M. Assessing the impact of regional rainfall variability on rapid pesticide leaching potential. *J Contam Hydrol.* 2010, 113, 56-65.

Mérel, S; Clément, M; Thomas, O. State of the art on cyanotoxins in water and their behaviour towards chlorine. *Toxicon* 2010, 55, 677-691.

Mompelat, S; Le Bot, B; Thomas, O. Occurrence and fate of pharmaceutical products and by-products, from resource to drinking water. *Environ Int.* 2009, 35, 803-814.

Murdoch, PS; Baron, JS; Miller, TL. Potential effects of climate chance on surface water quality in North America. *Journal of the American Water Resources Association* 2000, 36, 347-366.

Neal, C; Skeffington, R; Neal, M; Wyatt, R; Wickham, H; Hill, L; Hewitt, N. Rainfall and runoff water quality of the Pang and Lambourn, tributaries of the River Thames, south-eastern England. *Hydrology and Earth System Sciences* 2004, 8, 601-613.

Old, GH; Leeks, GJL; Packman, JC; Smith, BPG; Lewis, S; Hewitt, EJ; Homles, M; Young, A. The impact of convectional summer rainfall event on river flow on fine sediment transport in a highly urbanized catchment: Bradford, West Yorkshire, *The Science of the Total Environment* 2003, 314-316, 495-512.

Oppel, J; Broll, G; Löffler, D; Meller, M; Römbke, J; Ternes, T. Leaching behaviour of pharmaceuticals in soil testing systems: a part of an environmental risk assessment for groundwater contamination. *Sci Total Environ* 2004, 328, 265–273.

Patz, JA; Vavrus, SJ; Uejio, CK; McLellan, SL. Climate change and waterborne disease risk in the Great Lakes region of the US. *Am J Prev Med* 2008, 35, 451–458.

Pédrot, M; Dia, A; Davranche, M; Bouhnik-Le Coz, M; Henin, O; Gruau, G. Insights into colloid-mediated trace element release at the soil/water interface. *J Colloid Interface Science* 2008, 325, 187–197.

Pitt, R; Field, R. Water-Quality Effects from Urban Runoff. *J. Amer Water Works Assoc.* 1977, 69, 432-436.

Polard, T; Jean, S; Gauthier, L; Laplanche, C; Merlina, G; Sanchez-Perez, JM; Pinelli, E. Mutagenic impact on fish of runoff events in agricultural areas in south-west France. *Aquatic Toxicology* 2011, 101, 126-134.

Prathumratana, L; Sthiannopkao, S; Kim, KW. The relationship of climatic and hydrological parameters to surface water quality in the lower Mekong *River. Environ. Int.* 2008, 34, 860-866.

Reichwaldt, ES; Ghadouani, A. Effects of rainfall patterns on toxic cyanobacterial blooms in a changing climate: Between simplistic scenarios and complex dynamics. *Water Research* 2012, 46, 1372-1393.

Rodriguez, MJ; Serodes, JB. Spatial and temporal evolution of trihalomethanes in three water distribution systems. *Water Res* 2001, 35, 1572–1586.

Rodriguez, E; Sordo, A; Metcalf, JS; Acero, JL. Kinetics of the oxidation of cylindospermopsin and anatoxin-a with chlorine, monochloramine and permanganate. *Water Res* 2007, 41, 2048–2056.

Roig B, Delpla, I., Baurès, E., Jung, A.V., Thomas, O. Analytical issues for drinking water contamination monitoring related to short term intense rainy events, *Trends in Analytical Chemistry* 2011, 30, 1243-1251.

Rositano, J; Nicholson, BC; Pieronne, P. Destruction of cyanobacterial toxins by ozone. *Ozone-Sci Eng* 1998, 20, 223–38.

Rowsell, VF; Tangney, P; Hunt, C; Voulvoulis, N. Estimating levels of micropollutants in municipal wastewater. *Water, air and soil pollution* 2010, 206, 357-368.

Shawwa, AR; Smith, DW. Kinetics of microcystin-LR oxidation by ozone. *Ozone-Sci Eng* 2001, 23, 161–170.

Shin, JY; Spinette, RF; O'melia, CR. Stoichiometry of coagulation revisited. *Environ Sci Technol* 2008, 42, 2582–2589.

Sinisi, L; Aertgeerts, R. *Guidance on Water Supply and Sanitation in Extreme Weather Events,* World Health Organization, Geneva, Switzerland, 2010.

Suarez, J; Puertas, J. Determination of COD, BOD and suspended solids loads during combined sewer overflow (CSO) event in some combined catchments in Spain. *Ecological engineering* 2005, 24, 199-217.

Tamtam, F; Mercier, F; Le Bot, B; Eurin, J; Tuc Dinh, Q; Clément, M; Chevreuil, M. Occurrence and fate of antibiotics in the Seine River in various hydrological conditions. *Sci Tot Env* 2008, 393, 84 – 95.

Ternes, TA. Occurrence of drugs in German sewage treatment plant and rivers. *Water Research* 1998, 32, 3245-3260.

Ternes, T; Hirsch, R; Mueller, J; Haberer, K. Methods for the determination of neutral drugs as well as betablockers and alpha2-sympathomimetics in aqueous matrices using GC/MS and LC/MS/MS. *Fresen J Anal Chem* 1998, 362, 329–40.

Ternes, T; Meisenheimer, M; McDowell, D; Sacher, F; Brauch, H-J; Haist-Glude, B; Preuss, G; Wilme, U; Zulei-Seibert, N. Removal of pharmaceuticals during drinking water treatment. *Environ Sci Technol.* 2002, 36, 3855-3863.

Thomas, KM; Charron, DF; Waltner-Toews, D; Schuster, C; Maarouf, AR; Holt, JD. A role of high impact weather events in waterborne disease outbreaks in Canada, 1975 – 2001. *Int. J. Environ. Health Res.* 2006, 16, 167-180.

Thomas, PM; Foster, GD. Determination of nonsteroidal anti-inflammatory drugs, caffeine, and triclosan in wastewater by gas chromatography-mass spectrometry. *J Environ Sci Health* A *Tox Hazard Subst Environ Eng*. 2004, 39, 1969–1678.

Tiktak, A; de Nie, DS; Piñeros Garcet, J; Jones, A; Vanclooster, M. Assessment of the pesticide leaching risk at the pan-European level: the EuroPEARL approach. *J. Hydrol.* 2004, 289, 222–238.

Unc, A; Goss, M. Movement of Faecal Bacteria through the Vadose Zone. *Water Air Soil Pollut.* 2003, 149, 327-337.

Van Vliet, MTH; Zwolsman, JJG. Impact of Summer Droughts on the Water Quality of the Meuse River. *Journal of Hydrology* 2008, 353, 1-17.

Willems, P; Arnbjerg-Nielsen, K; Olsson, J; Nguyen, VTV. Climate change impact assessment on urban rainfall extremes and urban drainage: methods and shortcomings. *Atmosperic Research* 2012, 103, 106-118

World Health Organization (WHO), Vision 2030 – *The Resilience of Water Supply and Sanitation in the Face of Climate Change,* World Health Organization/Department for International Development, Geneva, Switzerland, 2010 (http://www.who.int/water_sanitation_health/publi-cations/9789241598422_cdrom/en/ index.html, accessed 5 January 2011).

Yu, L; Fink, G ; Wintgens, T ; Melin, T ; Ternes, TA. Sorption behaviour of potential organic wastewater indicators with soils. *Water Res* 2009, 43, 951–60.

Zwolsman, JJG; Van Bokhoven, A. Impact of summer droughts on the water quality of the Rhine River - a preview of climate change? *Water Science & Technology,* 2007, 56, 45–55.

In: Rainfall: Behavior, Forecasting and Distribution
Editors: Olga E. Martín and Tricia M. Roberts ISBN: 978-1-62081-551-9

Chapter 6

STUDY OF WET SCAVENGING OF ATMOSPHERIC AEROSOLS USING ^{222}RN DECAY PRODUCTS IN RAINWATER

Masanori Takeyasu*
Radiation Protection Department,
Nuclear Fuel Cycle Engineering Laboratories,
Tokai Research and Development Center,
Japan Atomic Energy Agency, Ibaraki, Japan

ABSTRACT

The concentrations and the concentration ratios of individual short-lived ^{222}Rn decay products (^{214}Pb and ^{214}Bi) in rainwater were measured, and a scavenging model was designed for explaining the measurement results.

The measurement was done at Kumatori-cho (34.39° N, 135.35° E, approx. 70 m above sea level) in Osaka, Japan by gamma-ray spectrometry using a low-background Ge detector. The dependence of the time variations of the concentrations and their ratios on rainfall rate was investigated. It was observed that the concentrations were negatively correlated with the rainfall rate in some rainfall events, and that there was no clear correlation in other rainfall events. The changes in the dependence of the concentration on the rainfall rate occurred after the passage of a cold front during a single rainfall event. The concentration ratios showed a weak negative correlation with the rainfall rate for most of the observed rainfall events.

Based on the relationship between the concentrations of ^{214}Pb and ^{214}Bi in the rainwater and the rainfall rate for an individual rainfall event, the increase in the environmental gamma-ray dose rate from ^{214}Pb and ^{214}Bi deposited on the ground was calculated, and the calculated increase agreed well with that observed by the in situ measurement on flat ground.

* Corresponding author: Radiation Protection Department, Nuclear Fuel Cycle Engineering Laboratories, Tokai Research and Development Center, Japan Atomic Energy Agency, 4-33 Muramatsu, Tokai-mura, Naka-gun, Ibaraki 319-1194, Japan, Tel.: +81-29-282-1111; fax: +81-29-282-3838, E-mail address: takeyasu.masanori@jaea.go.jp

Keywords: ^{222}Rn decay products; rainwater; rainfall rate; scavenging model; environmental gamma-ray dose rate

1. INTRODUCTION

Rainfall scavenges atmospheric aerosol particles. In general, the scavenging mechanisms of the aerosol particles by rainfall include rainout (in-cloud scavenging) and washout(below-cloud scavenging) [Engelmann, 1968]. To investigate these mechanisms is important for solving the dynamics of aerosols in the atmosphere.

The Radon (^{222}Rn), which has a half-life of 3.82 d, is the gaseous radionuclide that may diffuse into the atmosphere after being produced by the decay of ^{226}Ra in soil. The ^{222}Rn in the atmosphere disperses with advection and diffusion, and decays to radionuclides including ^{218}Po (half-life: 3.10 min), ^{214}Pb (half-life: 26.8 min), ^{214}Bi (half-life: 19.9 min) and etc., according to the decay scheme. The ^{222}Rn decay products in the atmosphere are trasnported to the ground by the scavenging effects of rainfall. ^{222}Rn decay products in rainwater are useful tracers for investigating the scavenging mechanism of aerosols in the atmosphere, because the decay products behave as tracers that reveal the dynamics of the process. For example, the concentration ratio between ^{222}Rn decay products in rainwater changes with time after the capture of ^{222}Rn decay products by rain, and becomes a useful indicator of the scavenging effects of rainfall. For this reason, the investigation of ^{222}Rn decay products, especially short-lived decay products, which are transported by rainfall is necessary.

In this capter, the following are discussed:

i. Measurement of concentrations of ^{222}Rn decay products in rainwater
ii. Scavenging model of atmospheric ^{222}Rn decay products by rainfall
iii. Analysis of increase in environmental gamma-ray dose rate by rainfall

2. MEASUREMENT OF CONCENTRATIONS OF ^{222}RN DECAY PRODUCTS IN RAINWATER

2.1. Previous Study

A number of studies have examined the concentration of short-lived ^{222}Rn decay products in rainwater. Damon and Kuroda (1954) measured the concentration of ^{222}Rn decay products in rainwater samples using a GM detector. Bhandari and Rama (1963) and Nishikawa et al. (1985) measured the concentration of ^{222}Rn decay products in rainwater samples using NaI (Tl) scintillation detectors. Finck and Persson (1980), Katase et al. (1982), and Horng and Jiang (2004) used Ge detectors to perform in situ measurements of the environmental gamma-ray intensity associated with rainfall. However, most previous measurements of ^{222}Rn decay products in rainwater concerned the total concentration of ^{222}Rn decay products in the rainwater, with few measurements performed with the objective of examining the concentrations of individual ^{222}Rn decay products. The concentration ratio between ^{222}Rn decay products in rainwater becomes a useful indicator of the scavenging effects of rainfall, because the ratio changes with time after the capture of ^{222}Rn decay products by rain. For this reason, measuring the concentrations of individual ^{222}Rn decay products, and the concentration ratio is useful.

2.2. Measurement in This Study

In the present study, rainwater was sampled while rain was falling, with the gamma ray spectra of the sampled water being measured using a Ge detector. The measurements were used to determine the concentrations of individual short-lived ^{222}Rn decay products in the rainwater and their concentration ratio.

The concentrations of ^{222}Rn decay products were measured in rainwater from 24 rainfall events on the campus of the Research Reactor Institute of Kyoto University at Kumatori-cho (34.39° N, 135.35° E, approx. 70 m high above sea level) in Osaka, Japan from March 1992 to March 1993.

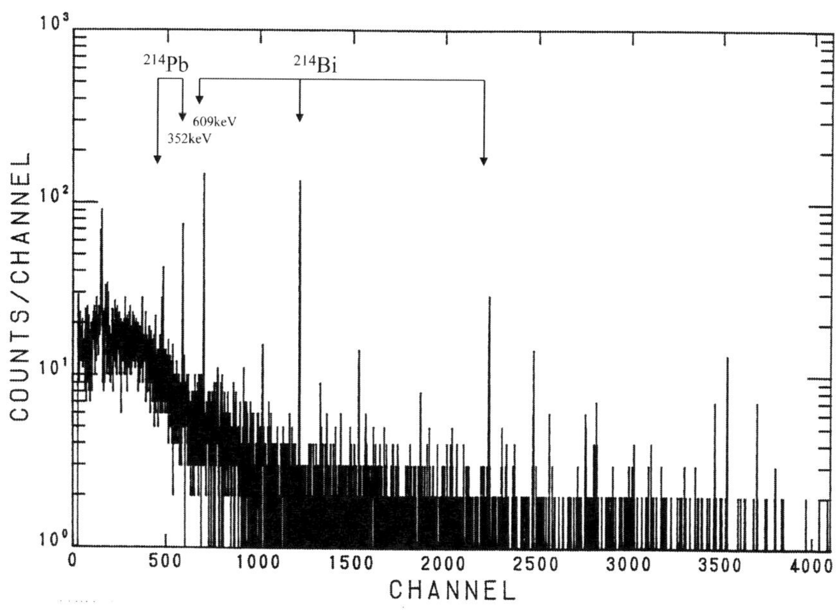

Figure 1. Example of the gamma-ray spectrum of rainwater (data of measurement: December 7, 1992; sampling amount of rainwater: 250 cm^3, measuring time: 30 min). (This figure is reprinted with permission from the *J. Environ. Radioactivity*, published by the Elsevier Ltd., 2006, Vol. 88, pp74-89)

A rainwater sample of about 250 cm^3 was collected using a 1 m × 1 m Teflon funnel sampler. The collection time, from which the rainfall rate was obtained, was less than 30 min. At about 3 min after the end of the collection, the rainwater sample was subjected to gamma-ray spectrometry using a low-background Ge detector with a measuring time of 30 min. As the sampling of rainwater was possible, these procedures were repeated, and the gamma-ray spectra for multiple rainwater samples were measured during one rainfall event. A high-purity Ge detector (the Toshiba Corp.) used for the measurement had a diameter of 50 mm and the height of 60 mm and a relative efficiency of about 32.4%, compared to the efficiency of a NaI (Tl) scintillation detector with a diameter of 76 mm (3 in) and height of 76 mm (3 in), and the resolution was 1.75 keV for the 1.33 MeV gamma-ray from ^{60}Co. The peak gamma-ray count was calculated using a gamma-ray radionuclide analysis program made by Nippon Atomic Industry Group Co. Ltd. The counting efficiency of the Ge detector was determined using a standard point source containing known amounts of radioisotopes, such as ^{60}Co and ^{137}Cs, and was corrected using the counting efficiencies at the ^{40}K gamma-ray peak (1.46 keV) for the volume source, the shape of which was the same as that of the rainwater sample container and which contained a known amount of ^{40}K. An example of the gamma-ray spectrum of the rainwater is shown in Fig.1. From Fig.1, it is shown that the most of the large gamma-ray peaks are due to the ^{222}Rn decay products, namely, ^{214}Pb and ^{214}Bi. These radionuclides have their maximum gamma-ray emission at 352 keV and 609 keV, respectively. From the peak counts of these gamma-rays, the individual concentrations of ^{222}Rn decay products were calculated.

The concentrations were calculated using the following assumptions:

a) The rainwater does not contain ^{218}Po produced by the decay of ^{222}Rn. The reason is that, with a half-life as short as 3 min, any ^{218}Po atoms have probably already decayed by the time that the rainwater reaches at the ground surface.
b) It is assumed that the concentrations of ^{214}Pb and ^{214}Bi contained in rainwater that reached at the ground surface and the rainfall rate during the sampling of the rainwater are constant.

Letting T_s (s) denote the rainwater collection time, the following equations give the radioactivities of ^{214}Pb and ^{214}Bi in the sampling container at the end of the collection time for each sample:

$$\lambda_{Pb} N_{Pb}(T_s) = N_{Pb}^0 S\left(1 - e^{-\lambda_{Pb} T_s}\right), \tag{1}$$

$$\lambda_{Bi} N_{Bi}(T_s) = \left(N_{Pb}^0 + N_{Bi}^0\right) S\left(1 - e^{-\lambda_{Bi} T_s}\right) + \frac{\lambda_{Bi} N_{Pb}^0 S}{\lambda_{Pb} - \lambda_{Bi}}\left(e^{-\lambda_{Pb} T_s} - e^{-\lambda_{Bi} T_s}\right), \tag{2}$$

where λ_{Pb} and λ_{Bi} denote the respective decay constants (s^{-1}), $\lambda_{Pb}N_{Pb}(T_s)$ and $\lambda_{Bi}N_{Bi}(T_s)$ denote the radioactivities in the sampling container at the end of the collection time, T_s, for each rainwater sample (Bq), N_{Pb}^0 and N_{Bi}^0 denote the number of atoms of ^{214}Pb and ^{214}Bi contained in rainwater that reached at the ground surface (cm^{-3}) and are assumed to be constant based on assumption (b), and S denotes the rainwater sampling rate (cm^3 s^{-1}), obtained by multiplying the rainfall rate (cm s^{-1}) by the area of the rainwater sampler (1×10^4 cm^2), which is constant because of the constant rainfall rate based on assumption (b).

The radioactivities after the end of the collection for each rainwater sample ($\lambda_{Pb}N_{Pb}(t)$ and $\lambda_{Bi}N_{Bi}(t)$, where t_c (s) is the elapsed time from the end of the collection) are given by the following equations:

$$\lambda_{Pb} N_{Pb}(t_c) = \lambda_{Pb} N_{Pb}(T_s) e^{-\lambda_{Pb} t_c}, \tag{3}$$

$$\lambda_{Bi} N_{Bi}(t_c) = \lambda_{Bi} N_{Bi}(T_s) e^{-\lambda_{Bi} t_c} + \lambda_{Pb} N_{Pb}(T_s) \frac{\lambda_{Bi}}{\lambda_{Bi} - \lambda_{Pb}} \left(e^{-\lambda_{Pb} t_c} - e^{-\lambda_{Bi} t_c} \right) \quad . \tag{4}$$

The measurement of the gamma-ray spectra for the time duration t_m (s) starting at t_c (s) gives the gamma-ray peak counts, C_{Pb} and C_{Bi}, for ^{214}Pb and ^{214}Bi, respectively, in the form of the following equations:

$$C_{Pb} = \varepsilon_{Pb} a_{Pb} N_{Pb}(T_s)\left(1 - e^{-\lambda_{Pb} t_m}\right) e^{-\lambda_{Pb} t_c} \quad , \tag{5}$$

$$C_{Bi} = \varepsilon_{Bi} a_{Bi} N_{Bi}(T_s)\left(1 - e^{-\lambda_{Bi} t_m}\right) e^{-\lambda_{Bi} t_c} + \varepsilon_{Bi} a_{Bi} N_{Pb}(T_s) \frac{1}{\lambda_{Bi} - \lambda_{Pb}} \left\{ \lambda_{Bi}\left(1 - e^{-\lambda_{Pb} t_m}\right) e^{-\lambda_{Pb} t_c} - \lambda_{Pb}\left(1 - e^{-\lambda_{Bi} t_m}\right) e^{-\lambda_{Bi} t_c} \right\} \quad , \tag{6}$$

where ε_{Pb} and ε_{Bi} denote the detection efficiency of the detector for the 352 keV gamma-ray of ^{214}Pb and for the 609 keV gamma-ray of ^{214}Bi, respectively, and a_{Pb} and a_{Bi} denote the respective gamma-ray emission rates.

The concentrations of ^{214}Pb and ^{214}Bi contained in rainwater that reached at the ground surface, $\lambda_{Pb} N_{Pb}^0$ and $\lambda_{Bi} N_{Bi}^0$ (Bq cm^{-3}), were obtained from these gamma-ray peak counting rates, taking into account the rainwater collection time, the elapsed time from the end of collection to the start of the measurement, and the measurement time. The detection limits were 6.7×10^{-3} Bq cm^{-3} for ^{214}Pb and 9.2×10^{-3} Bq cm^{-3} for ^{214}Bi.

2.3. Results and Discussion

Table 1 shows the number of concentration measurements per rainfall event and the ranges of the rainfall rate, the ^{214}Pb and ^{214}Bi concentrations and the ratio of the ^{214}Bi to ^{214}Pb concentrations. It should be noted that a "rainfall event" refers to a continuous period starting after an immediately preceding period of 6 h or more in which no rainfall has occurred. The number of concentration measurements per rainfall event depends on the period of continuous rainfall, and ranged from 1 to 12 times. The rainfall rate varied during each rainfall event, ranging from 0.4 mm h^{-1} for the rainfall event on August 3, 1992 to 39.9 mm h^{-1} for the rainfall event on May 8 to 9, 1992.

Table 1 also shows that the concentrations of ^{214}Pb and ^{214}Bi ranged from 0.1 Bq cm^{-3} to several Bq cm^{-3} for single rainfall events. In most cases, the relative error in concentration was within 10 % for ^{214}Pb and within 20 % for ^{214}Bi. These concentrations are about the same as those measured in Nagoya-shi located in Japan's Chubu region [Ikebe et al., 1985]. Ikebe et al. also reported a seasonal variation in which the concentration was higher in winter and lower in summer [Ikebe et al., 1985]. In the present study, higher concentrations of ^{214}Pb in the rainfall of April 1992 and January 1993 and higher concentrations of ^{214}Bi in the rainfall of April and June 1992, and January 1993 were observed, compared with those in the summer rainfall events, indicating higher concentrations over the period from winter to early spring, which is in agreement with the results of Ikebe et al. These results can be explained by the fact that, as has been suggested in previous studies [Shimo and Ikebe, 1979], the wind in winter, which blows in principally from the north and northwest, i.e., from Siberia, carries a large amount of continental ^{222}Rn to Japan, increasing the air concentrations of ^{222}Rn decay products that are transported to the ground through the scavenging effects of rainfall.

The ratio of the ^{214}Bi to ^{214}Pb concentrations was distributed over a range from 0.1 to about 2 for single rainfall events, and there was no apparent seasonal variation, which is similar to the results reported [Ikebe *et al.*, 1985].

Table 1. The number of measurements, the ranges of the rainfall rate, the ^{214}Pb and ^{214}Bi concentrations and the ratio of the ^{214}Bi to ^{214}Pb concentrations in the rainwater. Uncertainties are 1 standard deviation. (This table is reprinted with permission from the *J. Environ. Radioactivity*, published by the Elsevier Ltd., 2006, Vol. 88, pp74-89)

Date	Number of measurements	Range of rainfall rate (mm h^{-1})	Range of ^{214}Pb concentration in rainwater (Bq cm^{-3})	Range of ^{214}Bi concentration in rainwater (Bq cm^{-3})	Range of the ratio of ^{214}Bi to ^{214}Pb concentrations
Mar. 15, 92	2	2.6~4.0	0.34±0.031~0.44±0.035	0.16±0.079~0.24±0.062	0.46±0.050~0.66±0.08
Apr. 15-16, 92	3	0.79~4.4	1.2±0.055~2.1±0.074	0.70±0.068~1.1±0.11	0.48±0.050~0.97±0.11
Apr. 22, 92	7	2.3~26.7	0.31±0.018~2.2±0.051	0.11±0.02~2.2±0.078	0.35±0.070~1.0±0.04
Apr. 24, 92	1	1.8	2.3±0.045	1.7±0.15	0.75±0.07
May 2, 92	1	4.1	1.6±0.043	0.93±0.071	0.58±0.05
May 8-9, 92	12	1.4~39.9	0.078±0.010~1.4±0.05	0.13±0.031~1.1±0.088	0.43±0.11~1.4±0.13
May 9, 92	3	1.6~5.3	1.4±0.039~1.7±0.045	0.63±0.064~0.97±0.11	0.36±0.18~0.71±0.19
May 13-14, 92	4	3.9~10	1.1±0.037~1.8±0.048	0.82±0.049~1.2±0.065	0.65±0.040~0.72±0.05
May 30, 92	3	2.6~8.4	0.31±0.021~0.88±0.033	0.22±0.031~0.27±0.053	0.31±0.060~0.74±0.14
June 7, 92	8	1.5~15	0.18±0.013~1.7±0.043	0.12±0.019~2.0±0.075	0.67±0.12~1.3±0.13
July 11, 92	1	1.9	0.67±0.021	0.38±0.04	0.57±0.06
Aug. 3, 92	1	0.4	0.35±0.019	0.22±0.047	0.63±0.14
Sep. 14, 92	1	0.75	0.75±0.029	0.96±0.058	1.3±0.09
Sep. 25, 92	3	0.75~2.0	0.93±0.031~1.2±0.038	0.71±0.049~0.91±0.059	0.67±0.060~0.88±0.06
Sep. 29, 92	7	2.3~22	0.21±0.014~0.60±0.023	0.094±0.021~0.70±0.039	0.28±0.070~1.3±0.09
Oct. 8-9, 92	5	2.1~4	0.16±0.013~0.40±0.02	0.27±0.024~0.47±0.035	1.0±0.11~1.7±0.20
Oct. 14, 92	2	0.64~2.5	0.21±0.016~0.21±0.015	0.16±0.031~0.28±0.0326	0.76±0.16~1.3±0.016
Nov. 9, 92	7	1.3~5.6	0.29±0.019~0.58±0.025	0.39±0.031~0.77±0.041	1.2±0.09~1.7±0.16
Nov. 20, 92	10	1.3~17	0.098±0.011~0.99±0.036	0.035±0.011~1.4±0.062	0.36±0.12~1.4±0.08
Dec. 7, 92	3	0.97~7.1	0.16±0.013~0.19±0.013	0.11±0.018~0.35±0.03	0.58±0.10~1.9±0.24
Jan. 10, 93	2	3.2~4.2	1.3±0.040~2.7±0.061	1.9±0.11~2.2±0.066	0.69±0.040~1.7±0.07
Jan. 15, 93	1	0.54	0.89±0.034	1.1±0.069	1.2±0.09
Feb. 21, 93	1	0.78	0.58±0.031	1.1±0.061	2.0±0.15
Mar. 15, 93	4	2.3~3.7	0.12±0.015~0.22±0.018	0.22±0.023~0.42±0.03	1.8±0.23~2.4±0.37

Figure 2 shows the time variations of the concentrations of ^{214}Pb and ^{214}Bi, the ratio of their concentrations, and the rainfall rate for two rainfall events where the measurements were consecutively repeated for single events. Figures 2(a) and (b) show the variations on May 8 to 9, 1992, and on Nov. 20, 1992, respectively. From Fig. 2, the concentrations of ^{214}Pb and ^{214}Bi and the concentration ratio varied with time, as did the rainfall rate, and notably the higher concentrations were not observed at the beginning of the rainfall events, which is in agreement with the results reported by Fujinami (1996). In the measurement illustrated in Fig. 2(a), the atmospheric air temperature rapidly dropped from 21° to 19° around 20:00 on May 8, and the concentration changed around that time. It was reported that the drop in temperature of atmospheric air caused the diffusion of ^{222}Rn and its decay products in the atmospheric boundary layer to decrease and consequently the concentrations of these radionuclides in the atmospheric air to increase [Silva and Claro, 2005]. When it is higher in the atmospheric air, it can be expected that the concentrations of ^{222}Rn decay products may be higher in the rainwater. The reason why the concentrations became higher after around 20:00 in Fig. 2(a) could be the change of the temperature of atmospheric air. In the measurement illustrated in Fig. 2(b), a cold front passed across the area at around 14:30 during the rain that fell on Nov. 20, 1992, and this was accompanied by a change in wind direction from south to northwest. The concentrations of both ^{214}Pb and ^{214}Bi were below 0.2 Bq cm^{-3} before the passage of the front, but rose to about 1 Bq cm^{-3} after it had passed. As reported by Nishikawa et al. (1985), the occurrence of this phenomenon is probably due to a change in the concentration of ^{222}Rn in the atmosphere following the change in the air masses after the passage of the cold front. The south wind blowing before the passage of the cold front was from the sea, with a lower atmospheric concentration of ^{222}Rn, whereas the northwest wind blowing after the passage was from the continent and had a higher atmospheric concentration of ^{222}Rn. In contrast, the concentration ratio of ^{214}Bi to ^{214}Pb was higher after the passage of the cold front than before it passed, as shown in Fig. 2(b). A possible explanation follows. It is thought that the rainfall before the passage of the cold front is due to a preceding warm front, namely the stratiform clouds, and that the rainfall after the front is due to the cold front, namely the cumulous clouds. In the stratiform cloud, the movement of the cloud liquid water might be smaller than that in the cumulous clouds. This means the time from the attachment of the ^{222}Rn decay products to the cloud liquid water and its arrival at the ground is shorter for the stratiform clouds than for the cumulous clouds. When the time is shorter, the decay of ^{214}Pb is reduced, with a corresponding reduction in the quantity of ^{214}Bi produced by the decay of ^{214}Pb.

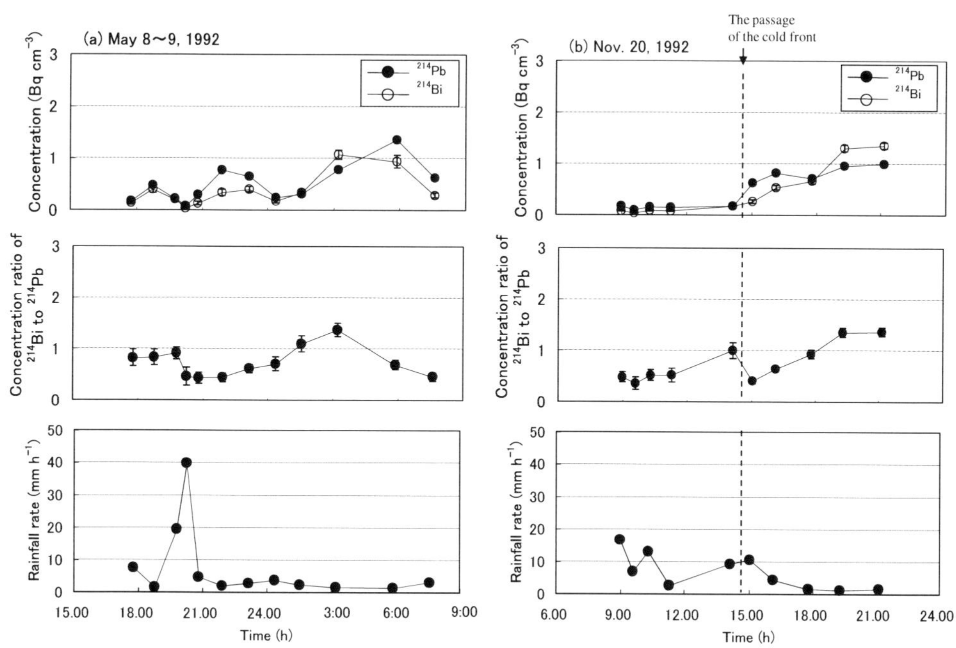

Figure 2. Time variations of the concentrations and its ratio of ^{214}Pb and ^{214}Bi in the rainwater, and rainfall rate during one rainfall event. Uncertainties are 1 standard deviation. (This figure is reprinted with permission from the *J. Environ. Radioactivity*, published by the Elsevier Ltd., 2006, Vol. 88, pp74-89)

The relationships between concentration and rainfall rate for the same rainfall events used in Fig. 2 are shown in Fig. 3, in which the calculated relationship is also shown, and discribed in the section 3. Figure 3(a) shows a negative correlation of the concentrations of ^{214}Pb and ^{214}Bi with the rainfall rate for the rainfall event on May 8 to 9, 1992, and the correlation coefficients (Pearson's coefficient) were –0.53 and –0.47 for ^{214}Pb and ^{214}Bi, respectively, at the 95% confidence level (according to the null hypothesis test). Figures 3(b) and (c) show that the dependency of concentration on rainfall rate was not clearly apparent for the rainfall event before the passage of the cold front, and that there was a negative correlation between concentrations and rainfall rate after the passage of the front on Nov. 20, 1992. The correlation coefficients were –0.72 and –0.78 (95% confidence level) for ^{214}Pb and ^{214}Bi, respectively. The changes in the dependence of the concentration on the rainfall rate occurred after the passage of the cold front, as shown in Figs. 3(b) and (c). Nishikawa et al. (1985) reported that a change in the dependence of the concentration on the rainfall rate occurred halfway through a single rainfall event. The result of the present study is consistent with their study. For the 14 rainfall events in which the rainwater was sampled and measured three times or more, the results of the dependency of the concentration on the rainfall rate were fitted to power functions by the least square method. Among the 14 rainfall events, there were 8 events in which the concentration was negatively correlated with the rainfall rate, and 6 events in which the correlation between the concentration and the rainfall rate was not clearly apparent at the 95% confidence level.

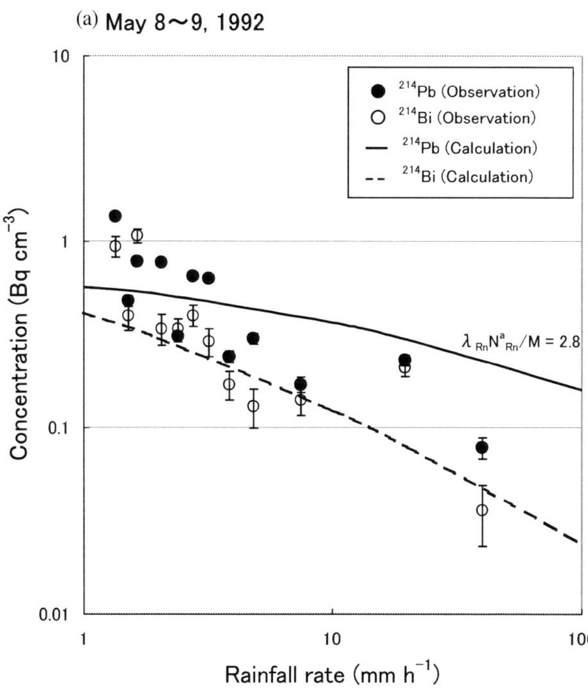

Figure 3. (a) Rainfall rate dependency of the concentrations of ^{214}Pb and ^{214}Bi in the rainwater. Uncertainties are 1 standard deviation. (This figure is reprinted with permission from the *J. Environ. Radioactivity*, published by the Elsevier Ltd., 2006, Vol. 88, pp74-89)

A number of reports have examined the negative correlation between the concentration of ^{222}Rn decay products in rainwater and the rainfall rate [e.g., Minato, 1980a; Damon and Kuroda, 1954]. On the other hand, Nishikawa et al. (1985) reported that the concentrations were distributed widely between the high and low values for lower rainfall rates, and that the concentrations were found to be lower for the higher rainfall rates. Nishikawa et al. (1985) also studied the relationship between the amount of ^{222}Rn decay products deposited on the ground surface and the rainfall rate, thus producing a positive correlation. In the present study, it was observed that the relation between the concentrations and the rainfall rate was not clearly apparent for some rainfall events. However, when the concentration is constant regardless of the rainfall rate, the deposition on the ground surface correlates positively with the rainfall rate. This is consistent with the observations made by Nishikawa et al. (1985).

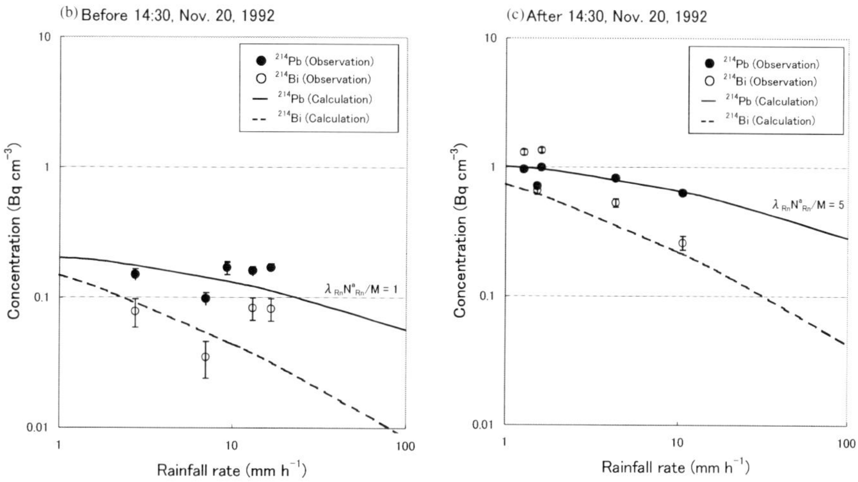

Figure 3. (b) and (c) Rainfall rate dependency of the concentrations of ^{214}Pb and ^{214}Bi in the rainwater. Uncertainties are 1 standard deviation. (This figure is reprinted with permission from the *J. Environ. Radioactivity*, published by the Elsevier Ltd., 2006, Vol. 88, pp74-89)

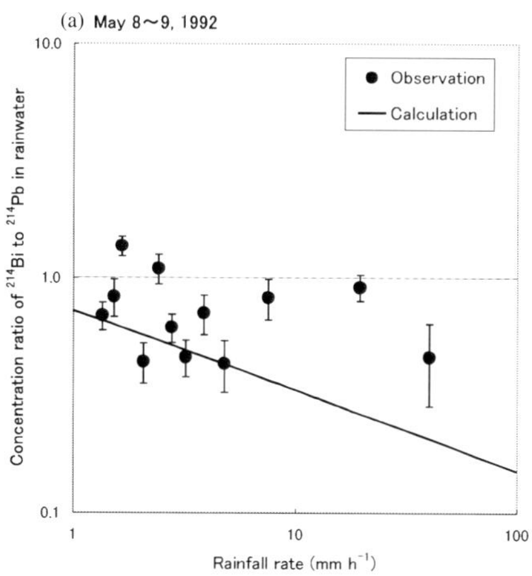

Figure 4. (a) Rainfall rate dependency of the concentration ratio of ^{214}Bi to ^{214}Pb in the rainwater. Uncertainties are 1 standard deviation. (This figure is reprinted with permission from the *J. Environ. Radioactivity*, published by the Elsevier Ltd., 2006, Vol. 88, pp74-89)

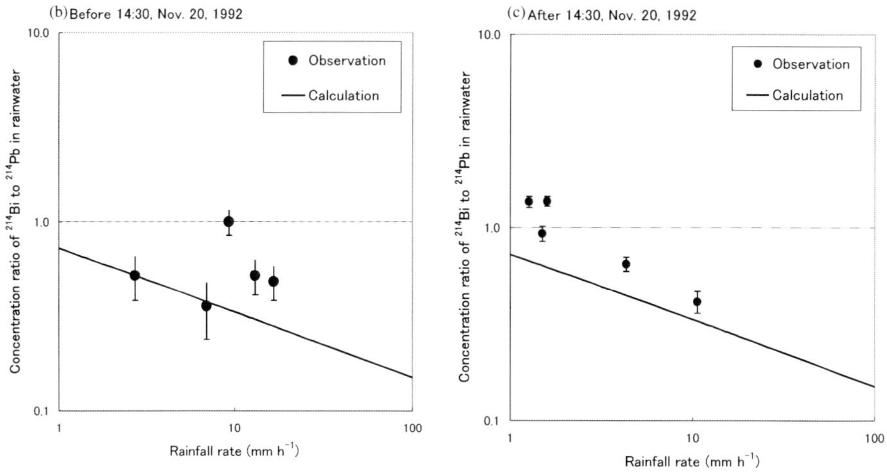

Figure 4. (b) and (c) Rainfall rate dependency of the concentration ratio of ^{214}Bi to ^{214}Pb in the rainwater. Uncertainties are 1 standard deviation. (This figure is reprinted with permission from the *J. Environ. Radioactivity*, published by the Elsevier Ltd., 2006, Vol. 88, pp74-89)

The relationship between the concentration ratio and the rainfall rate is shown in Fig. 4, for the same rainfall events as those in Fig. 2. From Figs. 4 (a) and (c), the dependence of the concentration ratio on the rainfall rate showed a weak negative correlation. From Fig. 4(a), the correlation coefficients were –0.23 (95% confidence level); and from Fig 4(c), -0.85 (95% confidence level). From Fig. 4 (b), the dependence was not clearly apparent at the 95% confidence level. A weak negative correlation was observed for most of the other rainfall events at the 95% confidence level. It is thought that with an increase in the rainfall rate, the time during which raindrops dwell in a cloud and the time over which the raindrops fall from the cloud base to the ground surface are shortened. When the time is shorter, the decay of ^{214}Pb is reduced, with a corresponding reduction in the quantity of ^{214}Bi produced by the decay of ^{214}Pb. This might be the reason for the weak negative correlation.

3. Scavenging Model of Atmospheric ^{222}Rn Decay Products by Rainfall

3.1. Previous Study

Takeuchi and Katase (1982), Minato (1983) and Ikebe et al. (1985) proposed models for the scavenging of ^{222}Rn decay products in air by rainfall. The models by Takeuchi and Katase (1982) and Minato (1983) included the rainout (in-cloud scavenging) and washout (below-cloud scavenging). Their models showed that ^{222}Rn decay products contained in rainwater are mainly removed by rainout. The model by Ikebe et al. (1985) included the rainout. Fujinami et al. (1993) proposed a model for estimating the cloud parameters from the observation results showing the dependency of the amount of ground surface deposition of ^{222}Rn decay products on rainfall rate. Fujinami et al. (1993) have designed a simplified model with some assumptions such that ^{222}Rn decayed to ^{214}Pb and ^{214}Bi directly, instead of ^{218}Po, and that ^{214}Pb and ^{214}Bi were treated as a single radionuclide.

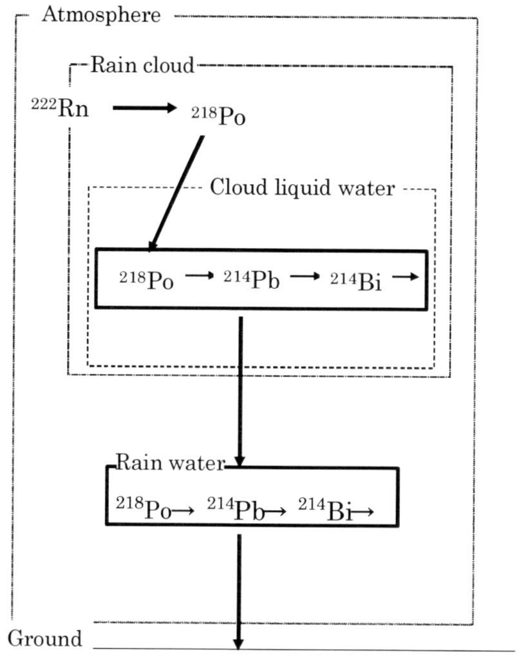

Figure 5. Outline of the proposed scavenging model by rainfall for ^{222}Rn decay products in the atmosphere.

3.2. Model in This Study

In this study, a more detailed rainout model was designed in which the concentrations of individual ^{222}Rn decay products and their ratio were discussed, and compared with the observation results for the dependencies on rainfall rate of concentration and the ratio of ^{214}Pb and ^{214}Bi in rainwater. The model was shown in Fig. 5[Takeyasu and Takeishi, 2010]. The conditions of rain clouds were set as follows.

a) The ^{222}Rn is distributed uniformly in the atmosphere at the height of rain clouds.
b) The ^{222}Rn in the atmosphere decays to ^{218}Po, ^{214}Pb, ^{214}Bi, etc., according to the decay scheme.
c) The rain cloud is a homogeneous liquid-water column.
d) A radioactive equilibrium is established between the ^{222}Rn decay products contained in the cloud liquid-water.
e) All the cloud liquid-water removed from rain clouds is transported to the ground as rainwater.
f) The transport time of the liquid water from the cloud base to the ground was set in relation to the rainfall rate.

Under these conditions, the concentrations of ^{222}Rn decay products in the cloud liquid water or the rainwater are given by the following.

3.2.1. In the Rain Clouds

The concentrations of ^{222}Rn decay products absorbed into the cloud liquid water varies with time according to the following equations:

$$\frac{dN_{Po}^{w}}{dT} = \Lambda N_{Po}^{a} - (\lambda_{Po} + \psi) N_{Po}^{w}, \tag{7}$$

$$\frac{dN_{Pb}^{w}}{dT} = \lambda_{Po} N_{Po}^{w} - (\lambda_{Pb} + \psi) N_{Pb}^{w}, \tag{8}$$

$$\frac{dN_{Bi}^{w}}{dT} = \lambda_{Pb} N_{Pb}^{w} - (\lambda_{Bi} + \psi) N_{Bi}^{w}, \tag{9}$$

where N_{Po}^{w}, N_{Pb}^{w} and N_{Bi}^{w} are the number of atoms of ^{218}Po, ^{214}Pb and ^{214}Bi, respectively, in the cloud liquid water (m^{-3} of the cloud air), Λ the transport coefficient of ^{218}Po between the air and the liquid water in the cloud (s^{-1}), N_{Po}^{a} the number of atoms of atmospheric ^{218}Po (m^{-3}), λ_i the decay constant of the ^{222}Rn decay product i (s^{-1}), and Ψ the removal rate of the cloud liquid-water from rain clouds (s^{-1}). Wilkening (1990) showed that ^{218}Po that was produced by the decay of ^{222}Rn in the atmosphere attached to cloud particles rather than to atmospheric aerosols. Therefore,

$$\Lambda N_{Po}^{a} = \lambda_{Rn} N_{Rn}^{a}, \tag{10}$$

where λ_{Rn} is the decay constant of ^{222}Rn (s^{-1}), N_{Rn}^{a} the number of atoms of atmospheric ^{222}Rn (m^{-3}), which is constant according to condition (a).

According to assumption (d), the equations from (7) to (9) are solved under the equilibrium condition, that is, $\frac{dN_{Po}^{w}}{dT} = \frac{dN_{Pb}^{w}}{dT} = \frac{dN_{Bi}^{w}}{dT} = 0$, and the number of atoms of ^{222}Rn decay products in the cloud liquid water, $N_i^{w}(\infty)$ ($i = Po, Pb, Bi$) (m^{-3} of the cloud air) are obtained.

3.2.2. Below the Rain Clouds

During the period when the liquid water that was removed from rain clouds is being transported from the cloud base to the ground, the concentrations of ^{222}Rn decay products in the falling liquid water are represented by the following equations:

$$\frac{dN_{Po}^{r}}{dt} = -\lambda_{Po} N_{Po}^{r}, \tag{11}$$

$$\frac{dN^r_{Pb}}{dt} = \lambda_{Po} N^r_{Po} - \lambda_{Pb} N^r_{Pb}, \tag{12}$$

$$\frac{dN^r_{Bi}}{dt} = \lambda_{Pb} N^r_{Pb} - \lambda_{Bi} N^r_{Bi}, \tag{13}$$

where N^r_i is the number of atoms of the ^{222}Rn decay product i in the falling liquid water (m^{-3} in the air), and $N^r_i(0) = N^w_i(\infty)$. According to assumption (e), the falling liquid water that was removed from rain clouds becomes rainwater, and the number of atoms of the ^{222}Rn decay product i in the falling liquid water is converted to that in the rainwater, n^r_i (cm^{-3} in the rainwater) using the following equation:

$$\lambda_i n^r_i = \frac{\lambda_i N^r_i}{M}, \tag{14}$$

where M is the liquid water content of rain clouds (cm^3 m^{-3} (in the cloud air)).

By solving the equations from (11) to (14), the concentrations and the ratio of ^{222}Rn decay products in the rainwater are obtained.

3.2.3. Determination of the Values of Several Parameters

The removal rate, Ψ, of the liquid water from various types of clouds was found to correlate well with the rainfall rate, according to the radar observation carried out [Takeda and Natsuki, 1982]. The time, t (s), is the transport time of the falling liquid water from the cloud base to the ground, and is calculated with the cloud base height and the speed at which the liquid water falls. The cloud base height was set at 3000 m, which was adopted as the mean height of stratiform clouds by Ikebe et al. (1985). Mason (1971) gave the relationship between the mean raindrop diameter and the rainfall rate and that between the raindrop diameter and the terminal speed of the raindrop. From the cloud base height and Mason's relationships, the falling time of the liquid water can be represented as a function of the rainfall rate. When the rainfall rate is 1 mm h^{-1}, the falling time is about 20 min, and when the rainfall rate is 10 mm h^{-1}, the falling time is about 10 min.

3.3. Results and Discussion

The dependency of concentration and the ratios of ^{214}Pb and ^{214}Bi in the rainwater on the rainfall rate as calculated using the above model were compared with the observation. A comparison of the dependency of concentration is shown in Fig.3, and that for the concentration ratio of ^{214}Bi to ^{214}Pb is shown in Fig.4. The atmospheric ^{222}Rn concentration and the liquid water content in rain clouds are variable, and the atmospheric ^{222}Rn concentration divided by the liquid-water content in rain clouds was normalized in the comparison in Fig. 3, to make the calculated concentration of ^{214}Pb agree with the observed value. From the comparison in Fig.3, there was good agreement between the calculation and the observation for the dependency of the concentration of ^{214}Bi on rainfall rate, and from the comparison in Fig. 4, the dependency of the concentration ratio on rainfall rate were in agreement. However, from the comparison in Fig. 4, it can be seen that some observation results are larger than the calculation results. One of the factors affecting the agreement between the calculation and the observation is considered to be the cloud base height that was set at 3000 m as the mean height of stratiform clouds in this study. The cloud base is likely to be different with every rainfall event, which is another parameter that should be investigated in the next study.

In the comparison between the calculation and the observation as shown in Fig. 3, the atmospheric ^{222}Rn concentration divided by the liquid water contents in rain clouds was normalized. If the liquid-water content of rain clouds is known, the atmospheric ^{222}Rn concentration can be calculated from the observation results. Fujinami et al. (1993) assumed the liquid-water content of rain clouds to be 0.8 cm^3 m^{-3} (in the cloud air), and the same value was used in this study. From a comparison of the results for the dependency of the concentration of ^{214}Pb in the rainwater on rainfall rate for each of the rainfall events, the atmospheric ^{222}Rn concentration was calculated to range from 1 Bq m^{-3} to the order of 10 Bq m^{-3}, which showed a seasonal variation such that the concentration was lower in summer and higher in winter. This calculated concentration was comparable to that measured at a height of a few kilometers around central Japan by aircraft [Iida et al., 2003], and the seasonal variation agreed with that of the atmospheric ^{222}Rn concentration near the ground surface in the previous study [Shimo and Ikebe, 1979].

4. Analysis of Increase in Environmental Gamma-Ray Dose Rate by Rainfall

The transportation of atmospheric ^{222}Rn decay products to the ground by the scavenging effects of the rainfall causes the environmental gamma-ray intensity at the ground surface to increase significantly, anywhere from several percent to several tens of percent of intensity compared to the dry conditions with no rain. The variations in environmental gamma-ray dose rates can seriously interfere with the monitoring of unexpected releases of radioactivity from nuclear facilities [e.g., Toyama *et al.*, 2005].

Based on the relationship between the concentrations of ^{214}Pb and ^{214}Bi in the rainwater and the rainfall rate in an individual rainfall event, the amounts of ^{214}Pb and ^{214}Bi deposited on the ground surface due to the rainfall were determined using the rainfall rate data that were observed continuously using a 0.5 mm tipping bucket rain gauge. The ground deposition amounts of the decay products i (i=^{214}Pb, ^{214}Bi) by the rainfall during the time from t_j-5 to t_j+5 (min), D_{ji} (atom $cm^{-2}s^{-1}$) were obtained by multiplying the concentrations of the decay products in rainwater by rainfall, shown in the equation of (15). The value of j corresponds to the period of rainfall, and t_1 the start time of rainfall. For example, if the rainfall period is 60 min, the value of j is from 1 to 6.

$$D_{ji} = \frac{2.8\times 10^{-5} A_{ji} P_j}{\lambda_i}, \tag{15}$$

where A_{ji} is the concentrations of the decay products i in rainwater (Bq cm^{-3}) which falled between the period of t_j-5 to t_j+5 (min), P_j the rainfall (mm h^{-1}) and λ_i the decay constant of the decay products i (s^{-1}).

The decay products that deposited to the ground were assumed to be not losed by surface runoff. The amount of the decay products i on the ground (N_{Ji}; atom cm^{-2}) which falled by rainfall from the time of t_j-5 to t_j+5 (min) changed according to the following equations;

(1) for the time of t (t_j-5< t < t_j+5)

$$\frac{dN_{jPb}}{dt} = D_{jPb} - \lambda_{Pb} N_{jPb}, \tag{16}$$

$$\frac{dN_{jBi}}{dt} = D_{jBi} + \lambda_{Pb} N_{Pbj} - \lambda_{Bi} N_{Bij}, \tag{17}$$

(2) for the time of t (t_j+5 < t)

$$\frac{dN_{jPb}}{dt} = -\lambda_{Pb} N_{jPb}, \tag{18}$$

$$\frac{dN_{jBi}}{dt} = \lambda_{Pb} N_{Pbj} - \lambda_{Bi} N_{Bij}. \tag{19}$$

The amount of the decay product i (S_{ji}; atom cm^{-2}) at the time of t (t_j+5 < t) (min) resulting from the deposition amount by the rainfall until the time of t_j+5 (min) is given by the following equation;

$$S_{ji} = \sum_{k=1}^{j} N_{ki} \tag{20}$$

The increase in the environmental gamma-ray dose rate from ^{214}Pb and ^{214}Bi deposited on the ground was calculated using conversion factors under the assumption that the deposited ^{214}Pb and ^{214}Bi form infinite plane sources on the ground surface [Minato, 1980b]. Figure 6 shows the calculated increase in the dose rate compared with that observed by the in situ measurement using a NaI(Tl) scintillation detector with a diameter and height of 25 mm (1 in) mounted 1 m above flat ground during the rainfall event on Nov. 9, 1992. The observed increase in the dose rate due to the rainfall was determined by subtracting the normal background dose rates before and after the rainfall from that during the rainfall. From Fig. 6, it can be seen that there is good agreement between the calculated and observed variations.

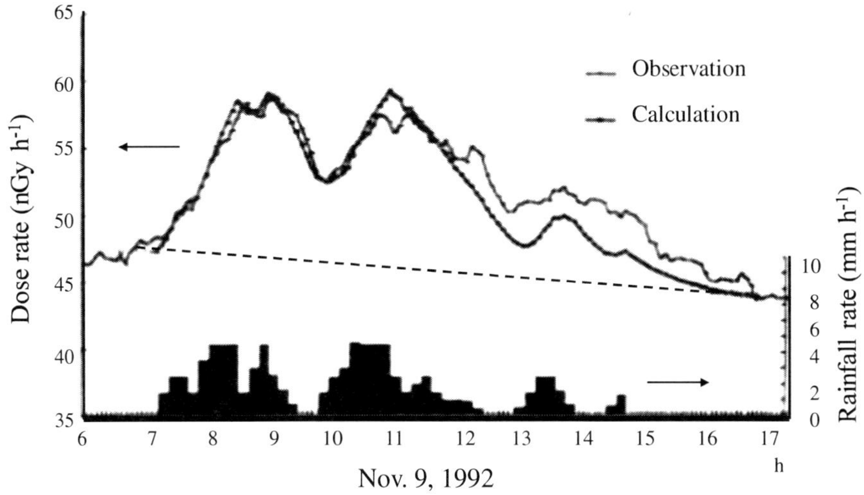

Figure 6. Comparison between the calculated and the observed increases in the dose rate during the rainfall. (This figure is reprinted with permission from the *J. Environ. Radioactivity*, published by the Elsevier Ltd., 2006, Vol. 88, pp74-89)

REFERENCES

Bhandari, N., Rama, 1963. Study of atmospheric washout processes by means of radon decay products. *J. Gephys. Res.*, 68, 3823-3836.

Damon, P. E., Kuroda, P. K., 1954. On the natural radioactivity of rainfall. *Trans. Am. Geophys. Union,* 35, 208-216

Engelmann, R. J., 1968. *The calculation of precipitation scavenging, in meteorology and atomic energy*. Slade, D. H. (Ed.), USAEC Rep. TID-24190.

Finck, R. R., Persson, B. R. R., 1980. In situ Ge(Li)-spectrometric measurements of gamma radiation from radon daughters under different weather conditions. *Proceedings of the Natural Radiation Environment III*, CONF-780422, Springfield, VA, 357-369.

Fujinami, N., Esaka, S., Minato, S., 1993. Estimation of cloud parameters from short-lived Rn daughter activities of rainwater. *Nucl. Geophys.* 7, 359-366.

Fujinami, N., 1996. Observational study of the scavenging of radon duaghters by precipitation from the atmosphere. *Environment International*. 22, 181-185.

Horng, M. C., Jiang, S. H., 2004. In situ measurements of gamma-ray intensity from radon progeny in rainwater. *Radiat. Meas.*, 38, 23-30

Iida. T., Moriizumi, J., Yamada, K., Ishizaka, T., Nagao, I. and Iwasaka, Y., 2003. *Vertical profile of radon concentrations in the atmosphere, in radioecology and environmental dosimetry*. Inaba, J., Tsukada, H. and Takeda, A. (Eds.), Institute for Environmental Sciences, Japan.

Ikebe, Y., Saijo, K., Iida, T., Nagai, H., Takeda, T., 1985. A model for precipitation scavenging of short-lived Rn-222 daughters. *Res. Lett. Atmos. Electric.*, 5, 17-21

Katase, A., Narahara, Y., Ishihara, Y., Tanaka, K., Matsuyama, H., 1982. Variation of intensity of environmental gamma rays measured with Ge(Li) spectrometer. *J. Nucl. Sci. Technol.* 19, 918-927.

Mason B. J. (1971) *The Physics of Clouds*. Oxford University Press, London.

Minato, S., 1980a. Some observations of the variations in natural gamma radiation due to rainfall. *Proceedings of the Natural Radiation Environment III,* Conf-780422, Springfield, VA, 370-382

Minato, S., 1980b. Monte carlo calculation of gamma radiation field due to precipitation washout of radon daughters from the atmosphere to the ground surface. *Jpn. J. Health Phys.*, 15, 19-24.

Minato, S., 1983. Estimate of radon-222 concentrations in rainclouds from radioactivity of rainwater observed at ground level. *J. Radioanal. Chem.* 78, 199-207.

Nishikawa, T., Aoki, M., Okabe, S., 1985. Time variation of ^{222}Rn progeny concentration in rainwater. *Health Phys.* 49, 1284-1289.

Shimo, M. and Ikebe, Y., 1979. ^{222}Rn , ^{220}Rn and their short lived daughters products concentrations in the atmosphere. *Jpn. J. Health Phys.*, 14, 251-259 (in Japanese).

Silva, A. A. and Claro, L. H., 2005. Surface air radon progeny at São Jos é dos Campos, Brazil. *Atmos. Environ.* 39, 4619-4625.

Takeda T. and S. Natsuki (1982) Estimation of liquid matter amount in an extended cloud by Nimbus-5 microwaves data. *J. Meteor. Soc. Japan*, 60, 1153-1164.

Takeuchi, N., Katase, A., 1982. Rainout-washout model for variation of environmental gamma-ray intensity by precipitation. *J. Nucl. Sci. Technol.* 19, 393-409.

Takeyasu, M., Takeishi, M., 2010. Estimation of ^{222}Rn concentration in the lower troposphere during precipitation using wet scavenging model for its decay products. *Asian J. Atmos. Environ.* 4-1, 20-25.

Toyama, K., Takeda, A. and Okawa, T., 2005. *On the case correspondence in continuous monitoring of the environmental radiation, in bulletin of the environmental pollution research center of Ibaraki prefecture*, Environmental pollution research center of Ibaraki prefecture, Japan, 14, 1-8 (in Japanese).

Wilkening M. (1990) *Radon in the Environment*. Elsevier Science Publishers, Amsterdam.

In: Rainfall: Behavior, Forecasting and Distribution
Editors: Olga E. Martín and Tricia M. Roberts

ISBN: 978-1-62081-551-9

Chapter 7

SPATIAL VARIABILITY OF RAIN AND ITS EROSIVITY IN A TROPICAL SEMI-ARID AREA IN KENYA

E. C. Kipkorir*, C. K. Songok and A. K. Toromo
Chepkoilel University College, School
of Engineering, Eldoret, Kenya

ABSTRACT

Although precipitation is the key driver of water erosion processes, the spatial variability of rain depth and rain erosivity have never been studied in lakes Baringo-Bogoria catchment located in a semi-arid area that is under threat of desertification in Kenya. The objectives of this study were: to determine spatial variation of rain depth and how this is influenced by elevation, slope gradient, slope aspect and geographical position; and to analyze rain intensity and rain drop size that determine rain erosivity. Historical daily climatic data of a 15-44-year period from seven stations, spatially distributed in the study area, were considered. Recorded rain intensity data for three years was available in one station therefore rain drop size measurements was done in that station. Analysis of spatial variation of annual rainfall indicates that elevation and longitude, and to a lesser extent slope aspect and slope gradient determine the spatial distribution of mean annual rain. Rain intensity results indicate that most of the total rain volume (90.4%) falls with intensity <15mm/h, while a small amount (4.7%) falls with intensities >30mm/h. A relation between rain intensity and volume specific kinetic energy (Ek_{vol}) was developed and recommended for calculating Ek_{vol} of rain, as well as for computation of Universal Soil Loss Equation's rain erosivity factor on yearly basis.

Keywords: Rain, drop size, intensity, kinetic energy, Lakes Baringo-Bogoria catchment

* E-mail*: emmanuel_kipkorir@yahoo.co.uk

1. Introduction

Precipitation is the driving force of most water erosion processes, through the detachment of soil particles and creation of surface runoff (Moore, 1979). Rain is also the triggering factor for mass movements. The upper size limit of raindrops seems to be 5-6 mm, with larger drops being unstable and disintegrating due to turbulence (Hudson, 1971; Maidment, 1993). Raindrop impact dislodges soil particles and forms a crust (Ellison, 1945), which seals the surface and limits the infiltration. In semi-arid tropics where totals alternate with periods of no or little rainfall, Van dijk et al. (2002), notes that rainfall events are of high intensity and often yield very strong erosivity forces (Nyssen et al. 2005). In lakes Baringo-Bogoria catchment, a tropical semi-arid area in Kenya, high plateaux and ranges influence the penetration of erratic rain-producing storms.

Attempts to regionalize rainfall patterns were made by Suzuki (1967), Troll (1970), Gamachu (1977) and Goebel and Odenyo (1984). Krauer (1988) showed that variability of rain patterns results in yearly rain depths being almost independent of elevation at the country scale. At above 1,500 m above sea level, other factors, including slope aspect and characteristics of dominant air masses, mask the possible relationship between elevation and mean annual rain. Eklundh and Pilesjo (1990) regionalised the explanatory factors of rain depth in Ethiopia, using principle component analysis (PCA). Results showed that in most regions, elevation is not an explanatory factor. In Kenya, no in-depth studies of explanatory factors of rain distribution have been conducted at a local scale.

Rain erosivity is a function of the rain's physical characteristics. In tropical semi-arid regions, rains are intense and sometimes short in duration. These characteristics, in addition to rain depth, drop size distribution, terminal fall velocity, wind speed and rain inclination determine rain erosivity (Obi and Salako, 1995). Studies on raindrop size measurements and analysis in Africa exist for Zimbabwe (Hudson, 1965; Kinnell, 1981), Nigeria (Kowal and Kassam, 1976; Aina et al., 1977; Lal, 1998) and Ethiopia (Nyssen et al., 2004). Drop size distribution, for a given intensity, is unimodal and slightly skewed to the left (Brandt, 1990). Often, a relationship of the type Equation (1) is expected between the median volume drop diameter (D_{50}) and rain intensity (I), with a and b as constants in a given region (Hudson, 1971).

$$D_{50} = aI^b \tag{1}$$

The calculation of kinetic energy (E_k) of a raindrop involves transformation of average drop diameter into mass (m), assuming that raindrops are spherical, and an assessment of the terminal fall velocity (v) of raindrops of different sizes in Equation (2), as experimentally obtained by Laws (1941).

$$E_k = (mv^2)/2 \tag{2}$$

Calculations of kinetic energy generally show that there is an increase up to an intensity of about 75 mm/h, above which E_k remains constant (Wischmeier and Smith, 1958; Hudson, 1971; Jayawardena and Rezaur, 2000; Salles et al., 2002). Measurements of kinetic energy and raindrop sizes are in most cases not readily available, hence the development of empirical relationships between rain intensity and kinetic energy, which is generally considered volume-specific, and expressed in $Jm^{-2}mm^{1}$. Time-specific kinetic energy in Equation (3) gives generally better correlation with rain intensity (Salles et al., 2002).

$$E_{k\ time} = E_{k\ volume}\, I \tag{3}$$

This study analysed the spatial variability of rain and its erosivity in lakes Baringo-Bogoria catchment. Of particular interest was (i) the spatial variation of rain in the study area, and how this is influenced by elevation, slope aspect, slope gradient and geographical position; and (ii) rain erosivity and the different factors determining it, such as rain intensity and rain drop size.

2. Materials and Methods

2.1. Study Area

Lake Baringo-Bogoria catchment is located in Rift Valley Province of Kenya, and occupies about 7000 km² (Figure 1).

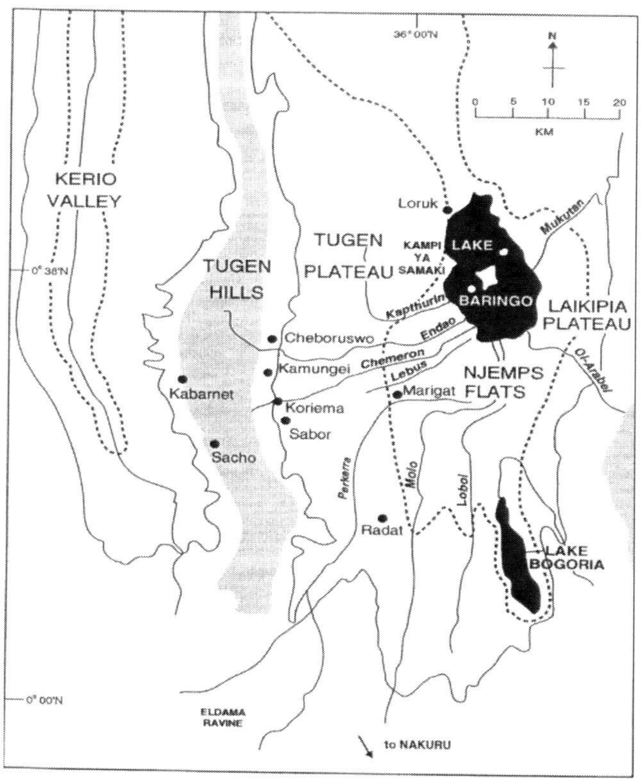

Figure 1. Location of the study area.

The two lakes, Baringo and Bogoria are situated in a subsiding half-graben of the central Kenya Rift Valley just north of the equator. An alluvial plain, the Loboi Plain, which is approximately 22 km long by up to 20 km wide and Njemps flats separate the lakes (Renaut et al., 2000). The land surface rises abruptly from about 950 m above sea level at the shores of the lakes to 2000-3000 m above Tugen plateau and Njemps flats as a series of distinct fault-blocks that form the Laikipia Escarpment on the east and Tugen Hills on the west. The block faulting and the high rugged relief are related to east-west extensional tectonics associated with the East African Rift. Significant volcanic activity has been associated with the crustal extension and volcanic activity is still prevalent evidenced by numerous hot springs, steam jets, and tremors; the latest volcanic eruption occurred in 1895 (Lewis, 1998; Renaut et al., 2000).

The climate in the Tugen plateau and Njemps flats is dry and hot (average temperature is 30°C) and mean annual evapotranspiration is estimated to be 2500 mm. The mean annual rainfall is lowest in the flats (650 mm) and nearly doubles (1300 mm) on the summit of Tugen hills. The rainfall in the study area is influenced by twice-yearly passage of the Intertropical Convergence Zone (ITCZ). Easterly trade winds carry moisture to the rift valley from the Indian Ocean located 650 km away (Griffiths, 1972; Nicholson, 1996).

In general, there is one rainy season from April to August, with some evidence of bimodality (Kipkorir, 2002; Sutherland et al., 1991), and a prolonged dry spell. However, rainstorm activity is very varied and over the period of measured records, nine different months have provided the peak rainfall (Kipkorir, 2002). Rainstorms are sporadic, localised and usually of low moderate intensity, but some high intensity storms occur in most years and peak intensities exceeding 100 mm/h have been recorded (BSAAP, 1984). Rainfall patterns are strongly influenced by local topography.

Like in most semi-arid regions, rainfall variability in the study area is very high. The rainfall pattern for the flats shows irregular but frequent drought with sub-normal rainfall every 3-4 years. Severe droughts occur at least once every decade, and show no consistent trend of decline (Kipkorir, 2002). This general pattern simplifies the actual pattern where rainfall is so localised and sporadic, and there are probably very few years when drought is not a problem in some parts of the study area. High rainfall is equally problematic with flooding and severe erosion, as in 1917 and 2002 when irrigation structures were destroyed in Marigat, and 1947 when the Njemps flats where flooded.

There are seven operational meteorological stations in the study area. The characteristics of the seven meteorological stations located within the catchments are presented in Table 1. All stations are located within one degree of latitude and longitude of each other and between 950-2800 m above sea level (Table 1). The data sets range from 15 to 44 consecutive years of precipitation.

The soil texture found in the Njemps flats and Tugen plateau ranges from silt loam to clay with silt loam dominating the surface soils. Although potentially fertile, the silt loam crust readily and encourages surface runoff. Some fertile soils occur on the upper hills, but extremely steep slopes and high erosion hazard limit agricultural potential. Due to population pressure and to poverty-induced agriculture, cultivation is practiced in areas with steep slopes, resulting in soil erosion related problems in the study area.

Table 1. Characteristics of the meteorological stations (α is the standard deviation)

Station	Elevation (m)	Latitude	Longitude	Record (years)	Mean annual rainfall (mm)
Equator	2762	0° 00' 00" N	35° 33' 00"E	44	1205 (α=299)
Kabarnet	1971	0° 29' 36"N	35° 44' 07"E	39	1300 (α=368)
Talai	2241	0° 34' 58" N	35° 48' 46"E	44	1322 (α=338)
Kimose	1515	0° 14' 01" N	35° 53' 08"E	28	938 (α=237)
Lake Bogoria	1020	0° 20' 38" N	36° 03' 55"E	15	708 (α=152)
Perkerra	1008	0° 28' 01" N	35° 59' 50"E	38	638 (α=146)
Snake farm	987	0° 39' 44" N	35° 54' 39"E	32	674 (α=181)

2.2. Rain Gauge Network

One automatic recording rain gauge station with three years data located at Kenya Agricultural Research Institute (KARI) in Perkerra, Marigat (Figure 1) as well as seven non-recording rain gauges (Table 1) were considered in this study. Obtained data from the automatic recording rain gauge station was used to characterise rain intensity of Njemps flats in the study area. Historical daily rainfall data for the seven operational rainfall stations was acquired from Kenya Meteorological Department (KMD).

2.3 Raindrop Size Measurements

Raindrop sizes were measured during five months (May - September) of the long rains season in 2008 by the blotting paper method (Poesen, 1983). The recording rain gauge was functional at about ten metres distance from the place where the drop size measurements was done, which allowed linking rain intensity to each measurement of raindrop sizes. Other methods, such as the optical spectropluviometre (Salles and Poesen, 1999), though less time consuming, were not used due to logistic reasons. Blotting paper (280 g/m^2) was cut into cards of 9 by 15 cm. During a rain event, cards were held in the rain until the stains start overlapping. During transfer period from inside the site office to the measuring place, and back to the site office again, the cards were covered by a tray. Time was registered on the card and stains were immediately outlined using a pencil by a team of three people working inside the KARI site office in Marigat.

The underlying principle for this method is that a drop falling on a uniformly absorbing surface creates a stain with a diameter that is proportional to the drop diameter. Poesen (1983) established a calibration curve (Equation 4) for stains 0.6-6.0 mm on blotting paper of 280g/m^2.

$$\phi_{st} = 2.44\phi_{dr}^{1.34} \tag{4}$$

where $Ø_{st}$ = diameter of stain on blotting paper (mm) and $Ø_{dr}$ = diameter of water drop (mm).

2.4. Statistical and Mapping Methods

The degree of association between variables was measured by regression and calculation of the Pearson correlation coefficient (r).

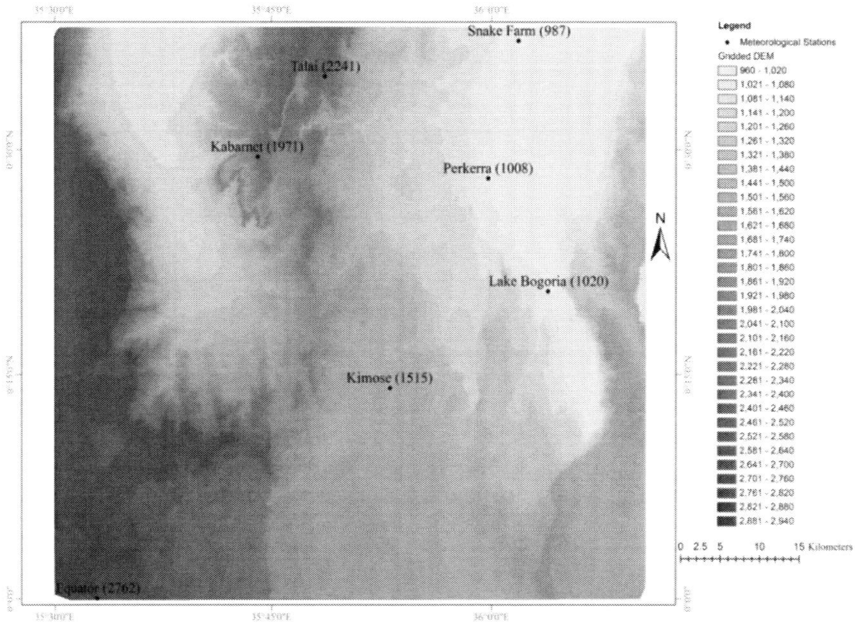

Figure 2. Digital Terrain Model (DTM) of the area with indication of the location of the rainfall stations.

Significance of these coefficients was tested at different probability levels by F-test. Rain distribution was modelled by a non-linear multiple regression; the type of model was first determined, and then a "best fit" was calculated using SPSS software. Contours, digitized at 20-m interval from topographic maps at a scale of 1:50,000 were interpolated to derive a Digital Terrain Model (DTM) of the study area (Figure 2). Using the DTM, local or valley slope gradients and aspect (in degree, turning right from the N) were computed.

3. Results and Discussion

3.1. Spatial Variation of Rain

Observed mean (15-44-year period) rainfall, computed from measured annual rain depth in the study area for 7 stations varies between 638 mm in the flats and 1322 mm in the highlands (Table 1). Between the highest and the lowest rain gauge, there is a difference in elevation of 1775 m. However, correlation analysis shows that there is strong positive correlation between elevation and mean annual rain ($r = 0.96$; $P<0.05$), moderate positive correlation between slope gradient and mean annual rain ($r= 0.60$; $P<0.01$) and strong negative correlations between longitude and mean annual rain ($r = -0.91$; $P<0.01$) and significant at the specified levels.

Given that slope aspect can take all trigonometrical directions, the relationship of local slope aspect or orientation of the valley to rain depth was expected to be best represented by a waveform function (Nyssen et al., 2005) expressed by the model:

$$P_{ann} = p_1 + p_2(\sin(a - p_3)) \quad (5)$$

where P_{ann} is the expected mean annual precipitation (mm); a is local or valley slope aspect (degree, turning right from N). The three parameters are: p_1 expected average annual rain depth (mm); p_2 amplitude of the sinusoidal function (mm) and p_3 aspect (deg) where average rain is expected.

In this study, correlation analysis between slope aspect represented as $\sin(a-p_3)$ and mean annual rain for the seven stations indicate a moderate correlation (r=0.45) and not significant at level 0.01. In the analysis parameter, p_3 representing aspect (in deg) was estimated at 112^0 by iteration.

The results shown previously indicate that, elevation and longitude are major factors, and to a lesser extent both slope-gradient and slope aspect determine spatial mean annual rain in the study area. In the second step, multiple regression analysis was done with mean annual rain as the dependent variable and elevation, slope gradient, slope aspect and longitude as independent variables and the model in Equation(6) was developed:

$$P_{ann} = 13.13s - 0.07z - 1466.66long + 89.66\sin(a - 112^0) + 53492.89 \ (R^2=0.95) \quad (6)$$

where s is slope gradient (%), z is elevation (m a.s.l.) and long is the longitude (UTM).

As can be observed from the earlier results, there is evidence of significant rainfall increase with elevation as one moves westwards from the plains. These observations are important for geomorphic processes and for agriculture. This is because, those parts of the highlands in the study area that are oriented more to the East and in the neighbourhood of important topographic height differences, have better agricultural productivity or forest growth, but are also more susceptible to erosion and landslide risk due to extremely steep slopes (Figure 2). Equation (6) can be used for prediction purposes within the study area.

3.2. Rain Intensity

Based on data recorded by the automatic recording rain gauge, with 5 minute time step intervals, during three years (2006-2008), it was found that the intensity during events is quite variable. High intensity storms show no clear regular pattern. Generally, rain intensity is low during most of a storm and high during a small part of it; this high intensity period can be situated at the beginning, in the middle or at the end of the storm. Overall, rain intensity is not very high. Most of the total rain volume (90.4%) falls with an intensity <15 mm h^{-1}, while 4.9 and 4.7% of the total rain falls with intensities of 15-30 and >30mm h^{-1}, respectively.

From the automatic recording rain gauge data, maximum rain depths for the three years for the given time spans were calculated (Table 2) and their corresponding maximum intensities compared to values defined by Greer (1971) as excessive. Rain intensities beyond these thresholds caused >50% of total soil loss on runoff plots (Krauer, 1988). A stabilisation in maximum rain depth do not take place, however maximum rain depth occurs at the 1.5 h time span, indicating that high intensities do not last long. It should however be noted that these maxima intensities exceed by thrice to twice the threshold values for excessive rain, both for short time span (10 min) and 1 – 1.5 h time span, respectively. These maxima are highest in the rainy season, but even exceptional rains during the dry season can be very intensive (Kipkorir, 2002).

Table 2. Maximum recorded rain depth in the study area (2006–2008) for different time spans, compared to thresholds for excessive rain, as defined by Greer (1971)

Time span	Maximum rain depth (mm)	Corresponding maximum intensity (mm h^{-1})	Threshold values for excessive rain (mm h^{-1})
5 min	1.4	16.8	76
10 min	9.6	98.4	36
30 min	8.8	33.6	25
45 min	24.2	62.4	
1 hr	16.6	50.4	20
1.5 hr	33.6	86.4	
2 hr	17.4	24.0	
3 hr	14.4	19.2	
4 hr	5.6	9.6	
5 hr	17.2	14.4	
7 hr	11.2	9.6	

3.3. Raindrop Size and Rain Intensity

Measured raindrops during the five months period were classified according to their size and to rain intensity (Table 3). For each of the observed rain intensity, D_{50} or median volume drop diameter was determined. The observed maximum drop diameter size was 6.1mm. Theoretically, some 10,000 drops should be sampled for every intensity class to have a D_{50} with low standard deviation (Salles et al., 1999). While this could not be realised due to logistical constraints, it might not have seriously affected the results since standard deviations for the classes (Table 3) is not that big. The relation between D_{50} and rain intensity (Figure 3), unlike the often found power model in Equation (1), can in this study area best be represented by a logarithmic regression (Vandenreyken, 2001; Nyssen, et al., 2005) as indicated in Equation (7).

$$r^2 = 0.85;\ n=10;\ P<0.001 \qquad (7)$$

where D_{50} is median volume drop diameter (mm) and I is rain intensity (mm h^{-1}).

Kurtosis of drop-size analysis (Table 3), representing rain intensities as a function of drop size was done and results indicate that small intensities (< 8mm h^{-1}) had more peaked distribution (+Kurtosis) than larger intensities that had a relatively flat distribution (-Kurtosis).

Table 3. Median volume drop diameter (D_{50}) for each rain intensity and Kurtosis of drop-size distribution

Rain intensity (mm h^{-1})	Number of drops	D_{50} (mm)	Standard Deviation (mm)	Kurtosis coefficient of drop-size
2.4	8423	2.1	0.8	2.21
4.8	3467	2.2	0.9	2.01
7.2	1732	2.1	0.9	1.76
9.6	986	2.4	0.7	-0.02
12.0	830	2.5	0.9	-0.54
14.4	1259	2.3	1.1	-0.14
16.8	463	2.5	1.3	-0.95
24.0	257	2.6	1.0	-0.44
50.4	263	2.8	0.4	-0.62
52.8	297	2.7	0.7	-0.86

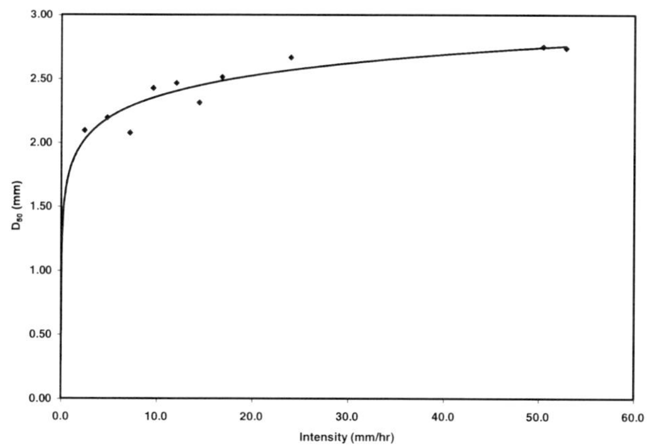

Figure 3. Median volume drop diameter (D_{50}) versus rain intensity (I) for KARI metrological station in the Njemps flats.

3.4. Rain Kinetic Energy

Foreach rain intensity, the kinetic energy per drop size class was determined using Equation (2). The different classes were then summed to obtain the total volume specific kinetic energy (in J m^{-2} mm^{-1}), and regression analysis of Ek_{vol} on I yielded Equation (8):

$$(r^2 = 0.86; n=10) \quad (8)$$

A regression of the 'classic' Ek_{vol} on rain intensity can be made either by the commonly used logarithmic regression Equation (8), or by adopting a model of the type $Ek_{vol}=a(1-b/I)$ which for the data from the study area yielded Equation (9):

$$(\text{for } I>1.49 \text{ mm } h^{-1}) \ (r^2 = 0.87; n=10) \quad (9)$$

Equation (9) can be used to describe the relation between kinetic energy and rain intensity in the Njemps flats within the study area. It is however very different from relations found elsewhere (Hudson, 1963). Furthermore, the adoption of a model of the type $Ek_{vol}=a(1-b/I)$ allows a better representation of kinetic energy for lower intensities. However, from a physical standpoint, any value of $I>0$ must have a value of $Ek_{vol}>0$ so that Equation (9) is a pragmatic approximation that is not valid at very low rainfall intensities less than 1.5 mm h^{-1}.

Equation (9) has important implications for the calculation of rain erosivity factor R of the (Revised) Universal Soil Loss Equation ((R)USLE) (Renard et al., 1997):

$$R = \sum(EI_{30})/N \tag{10}$$

where, E is total storm energy, I_{30} is the maximum 30-min intensity and N is the period of observation in years. Since the direct measurement of E is difficult and based on the present study, which includes the only raindrop size measurement ever carried out in Kenya, it is recommended to use Equation (9), in calculating the rain erosivity factor (R) for stations in the Kenyan semi-arid area of Njemps flats within Lakes Baringo-Bogoria catchment. Given the fact that there are slightly high standard deviations on median volume drop diameter at some intensities (Table 3), a high scatter in Equation (9) can be expected when using short-term data; hence this equation is only destined to be used in calculating yearly R values.

CONCLUSION

Analysis of the spatial variability of rain and its erosivity in lakes Baringo-Bogoria catchment shows that despite the short observation period of only five months for raindrop size measurements, several conclusions can be drawn. The major factors that control spatial distribution of annual rain depth are elevation and longitude and to a lesser extent slope aspect and slope gradient. A non-linear multiple regression model (Equation 6) represents this rainfall distribution. Rain depth is highest in the highlands with important differences in elevation. Next to factors related to the land and its cover, the observed differences of more than 700 mm in yearly rain can have important repercussions on erosion processes and agricultural productivity. If rain intensity is lower than expected, 90.4% falls with an intensity of less than 15 mm h^{-1}, but a stabilisation in maximum rain depth do not take place, however maximum rain depth takes place at the 1.5 h time span, indicating that high intensities do not last long. These maxima are highest in the rainy season, but even exceptional rains during the dry season can be very intensive. Analysis of rain intensities as a function of drop diameters (D50) was done and results indicate that small intensities (< 8 mm h^{-1}) had more peaked distribution than larger intensities. However, it should be noted that large rain erosivity is due to large drop sizes, rather than to high rain intensities. A new relation between rain intensity and kinetic energy was developed (Equation 9). This relationship (Equation 9) is suggested for use in calculating average Ek_{vol} values in the Kenyan semi-arid area of Njemps flats within Lakes Baringo-Bogoria catchment and for computing yearly (R)USLE's rain erosivity factor.

ACKNOWLEDGMENTS

Financial support by Moi University through the 4th Annual Research Grant is acknowledged. Many thanks go to the research assistants who did rain catching and rain drop outlining.

REFERENCES

Aina P.O., Lal R. and Taylor GS (1977). Soil and crop management in relation to soil erosion in rainforest of Western Nigeria. In: Foster, G.R. (ed.), Soil erosion: prediction and control. Ankey, *Soil Cons. Soc. Am.*, pp. 75-82.

BPSAAP (1984). Baringo Pilot semi-arid area project. Interim report, Ministry of Agriculture, *Nairobi*, 441pp.

Brandt CJ (1990). Simulation of the size distribution and erosivity of raindrops and through fall drops. *Earth Surface Processes and Landforms*, 15: 687-698.

Eklundh L and Pilesjo P (1990). Regionalisation and spatial estimation of Ethiopian mean annual rainfall. *International Journal of Climatology*, 10: 473-494.

Ellison WA (1945). Some effects of raindrops and surface flow on soil erosion and infiltration. *Transactions of the American Geophysical Union*, 26: 415-29.

Gamachu D (1977). Aspects of climate and water budget in Ethiopia. Addis Ababa University Press, 71pp.

Goebel W and Odenyo V (1984). Ethiopia. Agroclimatic resources inventory for land use planning. Ministry of Agriculture, Land Use Planning and Regulatory Department, UNDP, FAO. Technical report DP/ETH/78/003, Vol. I, 208pp; Vol. II, 95pp.

Greer J (1971). Effect of excessive-rate rainstorms on erosion. *J. Soil Water Conserv.*, 5: 196–197.

Griffiths JF (1972). Climates of Africa. World Survey of Climatology; v.10. Elsevier Publishing Co. Amsterdam, New York, 604 pp.

Hudson NW (1963). Raindrop size distribution in high intensity storms. *Rhodesian Journal of Agricultural Research*, 1:5-16.

Hudson N (1965). The influence of rainfall mechanics on soil erosion. Cape Town, Msc thesis. University of Cape Town, Cape Town, South Africa.

Hudson N (1971). Soil conservation. Great Britain, *Biling and Sons Ltd*, 320 pp.

Jayawardena AW and Rezaur RB (2000). Drop size distribution and kinetic energy load of rainstorms in Hong Kong. *Hydrological Processes*, 14:1069-1082.

Kinnell P (1981). Rainfall intensity kinetic-energy relationships for soil loss prediction. *Soil. Science Society of American Journal*, 45(1): 153-155.

Kipkorir EC (2002). Analysis of rainfall climate on the Njemps Flats, Baringo District, Kenya. *Journal of Arid Environments*. 50(3): 445-458.

Kowal JM and Kassam AH (1976). Energy and instruments intensity of rainstorms at Samary, Northern Nigeria. *Trop. Agric.*, 53: 185-198.

Krauer J (1988). Rainfall, erosivity and isoerodent map of Ethiopia. Switzerland, University of Berne, Soil Conservation Research Project, *Research Report*, 15, 132 pp.

Lal R (1998). Drop size distribution and energy load of rainstorms at Ibadan, Western Nigeria. *Soil and Tillage Research*, 48: 103-114.

Laws J (1941). Measurements of the fall velocity of water drops and raindrops. *Hydrology*, 22:709-721.

Lewis MN (1998). *A Guide to Lake Baringo and Lake Bogori*a. Horizon Books Ltd. 161pp.

Maidment DR (1993). Handbook of hydrology. Mcgraw-Hill, Inc.

Moore TR (1979). Rainfall erosivity in East Africa. *Geografiska Annaler*. 61A: 147-156.

Nicholson SE (1996). A review of climate dynamics and climate variability in Eastern Africa. In: Johnson, T.C. and Odada, E.O. (Eds.), *The Limnology, Climatology, and Paleoclimatology of the East African Lakes, pp. 25-56.* The Netherlands: Gordon and Breach Publishers.

Nyssen J, Poesen J, Vandenreyken H, Moeyersons J, Deckers J. Mitiku H and Salles C (2004). Spatial variability of rain and its erosivity in a tropical mountain catchment: Tigray, Northern Ethiopia. In: G. Demaree, M. De Dapper and J. Alexandre (Eds). Proceeding of the second International Conference "Tropical Climatology, Meteorology and Hydrology", Brussels, Belgium, 13-14 December 2001: pp. 95-119.

Nyssen J, Vandenreyken H, Poesen J, Moeyersons J, Deckers J., Mitiku H, Salles C, Govers G (2005). Rainfall erosivity and variability in the Northern Ethiopian Highlands. *Journal of Hydrology*, 311:172–187.

Obi ME and Salako FK (1995). Rainfall parameters influencing erosivity in Southern Nigeria. Catena. 24:275-287.

Poesen J (1983). Regenerosiemechanismen en bodemerosiegevoeligheid. PhD Thesis, Katholieke Universiteit Leuven, Department Geography—Geology.

Renaut RW, Tiercelin JJ and Owen RB (2000). Lake Baringo, Kenya Rift Valley, and its Pleistocene precursors. In: Gierlowski-Kordesch, E. and Kelts, K. (Eds). Lake Basins Through Space and Time. pp. 561-568. AAPG Studies in Geology, 46.

Renard KG, Foster GR, Weesies GA, McCool DK, Yoder DC (1997). Predicting soil erosion by water: a guide to conservation planning with the Revised Universal Soil Loss Equation (RUSLE). Agriculture Handbook 703. United States Department of Agriculture, Washington, p. 404.

Salles C and Poesen J (1999). Performance of an optical spectropluviometer in measuring basic rain erosivity characteristics. *Journal of Hydrology*, 218:142-156.

Salles C, Poesen J, Borselli L (1999). Measurement of simulated drop size distribution with an optical spectro pluviometer: sample size considerations. Earth Surf. Process. *Landforms*, 24: 545–556.

Salles C, Poesen J and Sempere-Torres D (2002). Kinetic energy of rain and its functional relationship with intensity. *Journal of Hydrology*, 257: 257-271.

Sutherland RA, Bryan RB and Oostwoud Wijdenes DJ (1991). Analysis of the monthly and annual rainfall climate in a semi-arid environment, Kenya. *Journal of Arid Environments*, 20:257-275.

Suzuki H (1967). Some aspects of Ethiopia climates. *Ethiopian Geographical Journal*, 5(2): 19-22.

Troll C (1970). Die naturraumliche Gliederung Eritreas. *Erdkunde*, 24(4): 249-269.

Van Dijk AIJM, Bruijnzeel LA, Rosewell CJ (2002). Rainfall intensity-kinetic energy relationships: a critical literature appraisal. *Journal of Hydrology*, 261: 1–23.

Vandenreyken H, Poesen J, Moeyersons J, Nyssen J (2001). Ruimtelijke en temporele variaties van neerslag en zijn erosiviteit in een tropisch berggebied in Noord-Ethiopie¨. *De Aardrijkskunde,* 25 (4): 13–24.

Wischmeier W and Smith D (1958). Rainfall energy and its relationship to soil loss. *Trans, AGU*, 39: 285-291.

In: Rainfall: Behavior, Forecasting and Distribution
Editors: Olga E. Martín and Tricia M. Roberts
ISBN: 978-1-62081-551-9

Chapter 8

RAINFALL EROSIVITY MEASUREMENT AND EVALUATION: POTENTIAL OF PIEZOELECTRIC TRANSDUCERS UNDER TOTTORI, JAPAN RAINFALL

Mohamed A. M. Abd Elbasit[1,2,*], Hiroshi Yasuda[1] and Atte Salmi[3]

[1]Arid Land Research Center, Tottori University, Tottori, Japan
[2]Desertification Research Institute, National Center for Research, Khartoum, Sudan
[3]Vaisala Oyj, Helsinki, Finland

ABSTRACT

Rainfall is the major driver of soil detachment in erosion processes. The potential of rainfall to detach soil has been defined as rainfall erosivity. Several indices have been suggested to quantify the rainfall erosivity based on both raindrop mass and fall velocity. However, the rainfall kinetic energy has been used widely in laboratory and field scales. The drop size distribution (DSD) of rainfall event is the primary rainfall data that can be used to quantify the rainfall erosivity; assuming that the raindrop fall velocity can be physically or empirically estimated from the raindrop mass. However, devices for continuous evaluation of rainfall DSD are not commonly used in conventional meteorological stations. In this study, piezoelectric transducers have been used to evaluate the natural rainfall erosivity and its relationship with rainfall intensity. Two piezoelectric sensors were installed on the roof of the Arid Land Research Center, Tottori University, Tottori city, Japan to measure the rainfall kinetic energy (KE) and drop size distribution (DSD). The output from the two sensors was logged in two notebook computers. The rainfall intensity was measured using tipping-bucket rain gauge installed beside the KE and DSD sensors. The direct measured KE has been compared to estimated KE using DSD data and four empirical fall velocity equations. The result from this study revealed that the piezoelectric transducer has a high potential for direct rainfall kinetic energy measurement and erosivity evaluation.

Keywords*:* Drop size distribution, rainfall kinetic energy, soil erosion

---

* E-mail: mbasit@alrc.tottori-u.ac.jp; m_abdelbasit@hotmail.com.

1. INTRODUCTION

Rainfall erosivity has been defined as the potential of rainfall to cause soil detachment and transport. The Rainfall erosivity is considered as a major factor in soil erosion processes and is not controlled directly by human modifications. However, some simulation studies present some changes in rainfall erosivity due to climate change (Nearing, 2001; Nearing et al., 2004; Zhang et al., 2005). IPCC (2007) reported the increase of extreme events due to clime change. However, these studies were based on monthly and annual erosivity indicators. The relationship between rainfall intensity and drop size distribution (DSD) controls various rainfall parameters including the rainfall erosivity (Abd Elbasit et al., 2010), and there is no evidence that the climate change may affect the rainfall DSD patterns.

Generally, high intensity rainfall events generate more sediment than low intensity rainfall. However, the relationships between rainfall intensity and soil erosion are highly related to the rainfall DSD and intensity relationship. For example, although the temperate regions receive higher rainfall amount than tropical regions, still erosion is higher in tropical than temperate areas due to rainfall intensification in tropical regions. This factor made the soil erosion in tropical areas is much sever than temperate areas beside other controlling parameters such as land cover, and topographical factors. Several rainfall erosivity indicators have been used in order to assess the total and event-based soil loss. These indicators can be classified into two major classes: micro-structural and macro-structural rainfall erosivity indices.

1.1. Micro-Structural Rainfall Erosivity Indices

The micro-structural rainfall erosivity indices are the indices that depend on raindrop parameters to assess the total rainfall erosivity (Table 1). The major raindrop parameters that control the micro-structural rainfall erosivity are raindrop mass and fall velocity. Thus, the micro-structural index must include one or both of these raindrop parameters. Epema and Riezebos (1983) reported the following generalized form of micro-structural rainfall erosivity index:

$$E \propto m^a \ v^b \tag{1}$$

where E is raindrop erosivity parameter, m is the raindrop mass, v is the raindrop fall velocity, and a, and b are exponential values. The most common rainfall micro-structural erosivity indices are rainfall kinetic energy (KE) (a =1, and b =2) and momentum (a, and b = 1). The advantage of the rainfall micro-structural erosivity indices is that it represents the actual dissipated raindrop power on the soil surface and can be directly related to soil detachment. However, the limitations of these micro-structural indices are that these drop parameters are not commonly available in weather stations and sophisticated equipments are needed for continuous measurement. Among these micro-structural indices the rainfall kinetic energy is widely used as erosivity indicator under natural and simulated rainfall. Mathematically, the KE has been defined as the product of half raindrop's mass multiply by its squired fall velocity. Several methods have been employed to quantify the rainfall KE. Implicitly, these methods can be categorized in direct and indirect methods from raindrop measured parameters side of view.

Directly, the rainfall KE has been measured by force transducers (Madden et al., 1998; Jayawardena and Rezaur, 2000a). This method can be considered as direct method because it attempts to evaluate the raindrops' KE by their impact or physical deformation of sensing materials. These kinds of sensing materials are usually inexpensive, easy to use but it needs to be calibrated with waterdrops with known kinetic energy. The advantage of the force transducer method is: it measures the actual impact without imposing any assumptions related to the drop shape. The major disadvantage is the measurement accuracy depends on the calibration accuracy and the calibration should be done by actual water droplets. Another direct method is the optical methods, where the drop size and velocity can be measured simultaneously (Salles and Poesen, 2000; Nanko et al., 2004). Several optical sensors have been developed commercially with different monitoring capacity related to rainfall intensity. The major disadvantages of optical method are it include some raindrop shape assumptions, and expensive. Indirectly, rainfall KE has been evaluated by measuring the drop size automatically (ex. Joss-Waldvogel disdrometer) or manually (ex. Filter-paper, and flour-pellet) and then estimate the raindrop velocity physically or empirically.

The error propagation in the indirect KE measurement methods can be generated from drop size and fall velocity evaluations.

1.2. Macro-Structural Rainfall Erosivity Indices

Rainfall macro-structural erosivity indices are indices employ rainfall data that describe rainfall bulk-parameters and rainfall measurements in course time intervals. The data that can be used to calculate these indices are annual, monthly, daily and hourly rainfall depth data. Zhang et al. (2002) reported method to calculate annual rainfall erosivity using summation of half-month rainfall erosivity estimated from daily rainfall as follow:

$$M_i = \alpha \sum_{j=1}^{k} (D_j)^{\beta} \tag{2}$$

where M_i is half-month rainfall erosivity (MJ mm ha-1 h-1 year-1); D_j is effective rainfall for day j in one half-month (mm); k is number of days in half month. The D_j must be greater than or equal to 12 mm day^{-1}. The terms α and β are empirical parameters calculated as follow:

$$\alpha = 21.586\beta^{-7.1891} \tag{3}$$

$$\beta = 0.8363 + \frac{18.144}{\overline{P}_{d12}} + \frac{24.455}{\overline{P}_{y12}} \tag{4}$$

where $\overline{P}_{d12}$ and $\overline{P}_{y12}$ are the average daily rainfall larger than 12 mm and average annual rainfall for days with rainfall higher than 12 mm (Zhongbao et al., 2010).

Fournier (1960) devised an index (Eq. 5), which was modified by Arnoldus (1980), referred to as modified Fournier index and denoted by MFI. It is defined by (Eq. 6)

$$F = \frac{p_i^2}{P} \tag{5}$$

$$MFI = \frac{\sum_{i=1}^{12} p_i^2}{P} \tag{6}$$

Oduro-Afriyie (1996) assessed another modification on the Fournier index, which is defined as follow:

$$MFI = \frac{p_{wettest}^2}{P} \tag{7}$$

where P_i is monthly rainfall; P is annual rainfall; $p_{wettest}$ is the maximum monthly rainfall (wettest month).

The MFI, generally, assesses the effect of erosion by rainwater. Higher index value indicates a greater aggressivity while lower values indicate lower aggressivity of rainfall. The MFI has erosivity categories as very low (MFI=0-60), moderate (MFI=90-120), high (MFI=120-160) and very high (MFI>160). For assessment of erosive potential, this index has been used by several researchers (e.g. Oduro-Afriyie, 1996; Apaydin et al. 2006; Munka et al., 2007; De Luis et al., 2010).

Table 1. Example of Rainfall Micro-Structural Erosivity Indices

Index	Symbol(a)	Formula(b)	References
Kinetic energy	KE	½ m v2	Al-Durrah and Bradford (1982), Riezebos and Epema (1985), Kinnell (2005)
Momentum	M	m v	Al-Durrah and Bradford (1982), Salles et al. (2000)
Kinetic energy x drop circumference	KEC	KE (π D)	Gilley and Finkner (1985)
Momentum x drop diameter	MD	M D	Salles et al. (2000), Nanko et al. (2008)
Drop impact pressure	Pe	4m v2/ π D3	Mouzai and Bouhadef (2003)

[a] *KE* is drop kinetic energy (J); *M* is drop momentum (kg m s^{-1}); *F* is impact force per impact perimeter (N m^{-1}); F_D drop stress (N cm^{-2}); P_e drop impact pressure (Pa). [b] *m* is drop mass (kg); *v* is drop fall velocity (m s^{-1}); *D* is drop diameter (mm).

1.3. Combined Rainfall Erosivity Indices

Combined rainfall erosivity indices are attempted to link between the rainfall bulk (macro-) parameters such as depth and rate, from one side and raindrop parameters on the other side. The widely used combined erosivity index is the rainfall and runoff erosivity (R-factor) of the Universal Soil Loss Equation (USLE) and its revised forms. This index represents a good example for these combined indices. Mathematically the R-factor can be calculated by the following equation:

$$R - factor = \frac{1}{n}\sum_{i=1}^{n}\sum_{j=1}^{e}\left(KE\, I_{30}\right)_e \qquad (8)$$

R-factor is average annual rainfall and runoff erosivity (MJ mm ha^{-1} h^{-1} $year^{-1}$); KE is total kinetic energy of single storm (MJ ha^{-1}); I_{30} is the maximum 30-min rainfall intensity (mm h^{-1}); e is the number of j erosive storms in each i year; n is the number of years used to obtain average R (Renard and Freimund, 1994). The existence of continuously measured KE for all rain storms provides the annual erosivity directly. However, in most cases, the availability of the KE data is limited. To solve this data availability problem of KE measurement, several studies have reported relationships between rainfall intensity and KE under different environments (Figure 1).

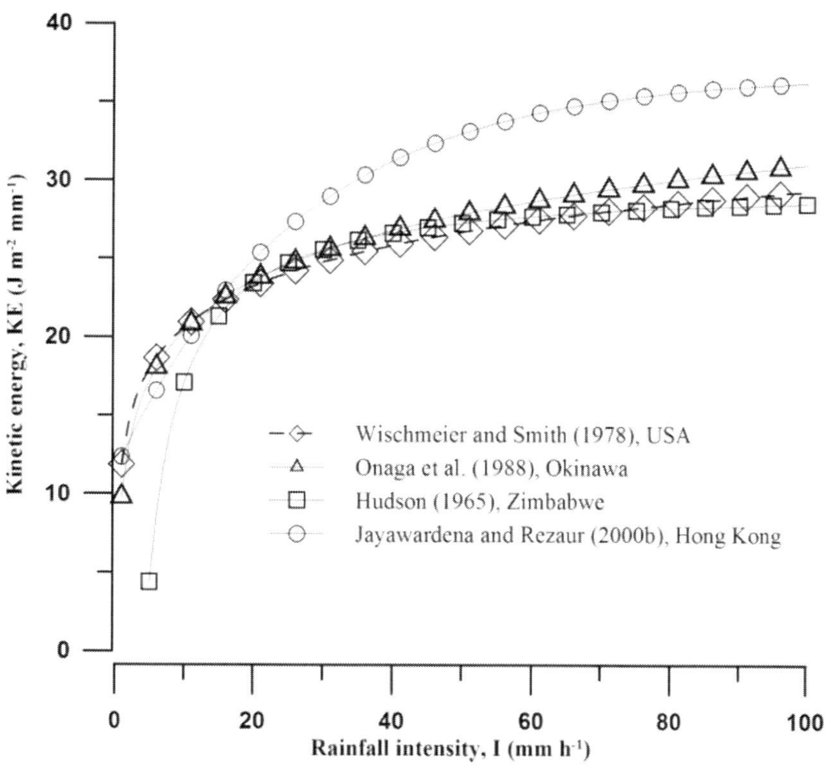

Figure 1. Example rainfall intensity-kinetic energy relationships (I-KE) under different geographical and environmental conditions.

1.4. Erosivity Measurement and Evaluation

Rainfall erosivity/aggressivity is a qualitative terms which does not imply physical nature of the rainfall. This made the measurement of indices that quantify the erosivity is the only possible way for assessment. The most direct index is the sediment that generated due to certain rainfall characteristics (rainfall type, intensity, duration, depth). In natural field, rainfall with similar characteristics is rarely repeated. Moreover, sediment measurement is scale dependent and the erosion processes involve several factors such as land use, land cover, soil characteristics, topography, and land management. Thus, evaluation of rainfall erosivity through indices measured at rainfall level is the most practical methodology for soil loss estimation. The rainfall kinetic energy is widely used in field and laboratory scales. Different methods have been used to evaluate the rainfall kinetic energy. In this study we aimed to assess the potential of using piezoelectric transducers in measuring the kinetic energy under natural rainfall at Tottori, Japan.

2. Piezoelectric Sensors for Rainfall Erosivity

The word piezoelectric is a compound of two words; "piezo" which is Greek word (*piezein*) means stress or squeeze and the word electric (Oxford Dictionaries, 2012). Piezoelectric materials are the materials that able to generate electric charge when it receives an stress. Generally, the piezoelectric effect can be defined as the electrical response to mechanical deformation. This phenomenon has been utilized in various fields and applications.

2.1. Study Area

The rainfall KE and DSD were observed for 24 days at Tottori, natural rainfall. The site was located at latitude 35.217°, longitude 134.533° and the altitude was 23 m above the sea level (Figure 2). Two piezoelectric sensors, and tipping-bucket rain gauge were installed on the roof of the Arid Land Research Center, Tottori University (Figure 2). The observation period was form November 29th 2006 to December 22nd 2006. During the observation period, 14 rainfall events were selected for further analysis (Table 2). The 70 years annual average rainfall in Tottori, Japan is 1975 mm (± 270 mm) and the rainfall is approximately distributed evenly between the year months (Figure 3). Generally, due to the common tropical cyclones the highest rainy months can be considered as June, and July. However, these months are not suitable for our objective due to high wind velocity and turbulence which affect the raindrop velocity evaluation by empirical equations.

2.2. Piezoelectric Transducers

The KE (mJ) and DSD (mm) were measured under different rainfall intensities using piezoelectric transducers modified from the Vaisala RAINCAP® rain sensor (Vaisala,

Finland). Both measurements were curried out at 10-s intervals. The measurement principle of the RAINCAP® sensor is based on the acoustic detection of individual raindrop impact (Salmi and Ikonen, 2005). The drop impact generates acoustic waves to the piezoelectric detector (Figure 4). Resulting mechanical stresses in the piezoelectric material causes a voltage between the sensor electrodes (Abd Elbasit et al., 2010). Due to the well known relationship between raindrop terminal velocity and mass, the raindrop size can be determined from the voltage signal results from its impact.

The sensor is constructed from a piezoelectric transducer covered by stainless steel shell (Figure 4). The voltage pulses delivered by the piezoelectric transducer are filtered, amplified, digitized, and finally analyzed as to their selected parameters related to the raindrop size. Final computations are performed by the micro-processor system (Abd Elbasit et al., 2010).

The DSD sensor was calibrated at Vaisala Rain-Laboratory, Finland using controlled drop sizes falling from a height of 14 m and the velocity of each drop size was measured using two parallel laser beams and a prism (Abd Elbasit et al., 2010). The received optical signal was converted to a voltage signal, which was proportional to the area of the laser beam intercepted by the raindrops (Salmi and Elomaa, 2007). The software of the sensor divided the raindrop size into eight classes normalized to the mean drop size (Table 3). For example, all data in the drop size class 0.80 to 1.12 mm were normalized to 1.0 mm (Salmi et al., 2008). The DSD sensor was also compared with a Joss-Waldvogel RD-69 disdrometer under natural rainfall conditions in Finland (Pohjola et al., 2008) and the results of the two methods showed significant agreement for raindrop size greater than 0.80 mm.

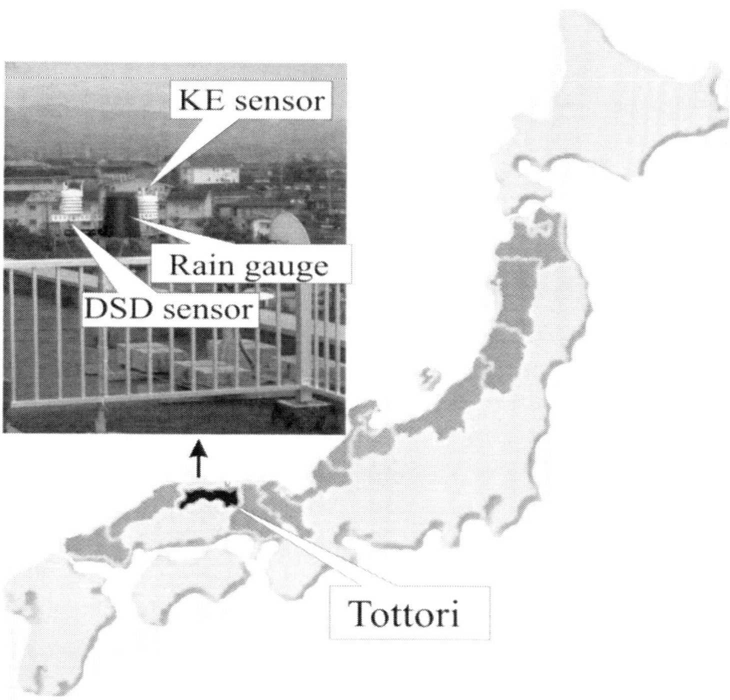

Figure 2. Location of observation site, and the photo show the rainfall kinetic energy, and drop size distribution sensors installed on the roof of the Arid Land Research Center, Tottori University, Japan.

Table 2. Selected Rainfall Event During the Observation Period

Event	Date	Depth	D (h)	I (mm h^{-1})	WD°	WS (m s^{-1})	T°C	RH %
1	11/30/06	2.00	1.40	1.43	195.76	1.48	8.91	83.31
2	11/30/06	1.80	0.32	5.63	233.32	1.68	8.38	86.43
3	12/2/06	2.00	0.23	8.70	178.77	2.03	5.59	81.64
4	12/2/06	2.60	1.10	2.36	148.53	1.62	4.83	87.37
5	12/3/06	6.20	2.80	2.21	136.19	0.92	3.73	87.91
6	12/8/06	4.80	7.80	0.62	157.29	1.07	9.81	93.25
7	12/8/06	1.60	1.30	1.23	249.37	2.04	10.41	93.19
8	12/8/06	2.20	1.80	1.22	298.49	2.81	9.80	90.89
9	12/10/06	4.40	1.80	2.44	142.96	0.61	9.48	93.46
10	12/10/06	10.60	3.00	3.53	232.26	1.49	9.64	89.02
11	12/10/06	3.60	2.35	1.53	78.71	1.01	7.40	88.54
12	12/13/06	2.80	2.25	1.24	104.00	1.09	9.17	91.46
13	12/18/06	12.20	4.00	3.05	252.41	3.82	4.73	82.00
14	12/18/06	1.80	1.05	1.71	124.38	1.76	3.00	93.64

WD, WS are wind direction and velocity, respectively. T and RH are temperature and relative humidity, respectively. D, I are rainfall duration and , average rainfall intensity, respectively.

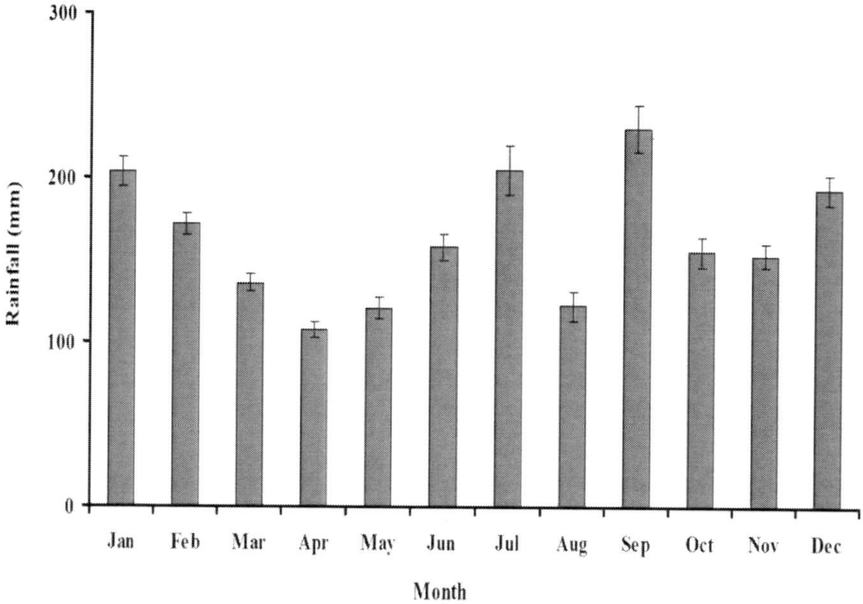

Figure 3. Average Monthly rainfall (70 years) at Tottori, Japan.

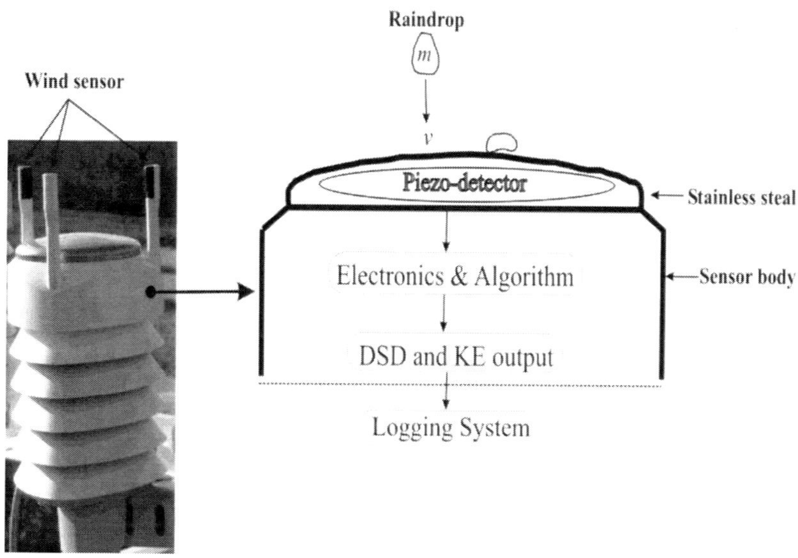

Figure 4. Schematic view of the piezoelectric sensor modified form Vaisala, RAINCAP® sensor.

The KE sensor was calibrated using rain drops with known kinetic energy values. The raindrop KE was determined form the raindrop mass and fall velocity measured by the optical method used for the DSD sensor calibration (Abd Elbasit et al., 2010). The raindrops' KE that was used for the KE sensor calibration was calculated from the raindrop size (controlled by the rainfall simulator) and fall velocity (measured using the optical method). The KE sensor was also validated under simulated rainfall and the sensor output (direct KE measurement) was compared with the calculated KE using rainfall DSD and empirically calculated velocity from drop size (Abd Elbasit et al., 2011). The correlation between directly measured KE using the KE sensor and estimated KE was statistically highly significant under different rainfall intensities and empirical relationships (Abd Elbasit et al., 2007; Abd Elbasit et al., 2011). Moreover, there was agreement between the two methods in terms of the shape of the relationship between rainfall intensity and measured and estimated KE (Abd Elbasit et al., 2007).

The signals from the two sensors were logged in two notebook computers using the RS-232 serial interface and data logging software. The rainfall intensity was measured using a tipping-bucket rain gauge (Davis rain collector II, CA, USA) with 0.2-mm resolution. The rain gauge was attached to event data logger (HOBO Event Logger; Onset Computer Corp., MA, USA) with 0.5 s interval recording accuracy.

2.3. Erosivity Evaluation

The rainfall kinetic energy was expressed in two ways: 1) kinetic energy rate where energy is a function of time (KE_t, J m^{-2} s^{-1}), and 2) kinetic energy content where energy is a function of rainfall depth (KE_c, J m^{-2} mm^{-1}). The KE_t was calculated from the piezoelectric sensor direct measurement of the *KE* using the following equation:

$$\mathrm{KE_t} = \left(\frac{1}{\mathrm{t}}\right)\left(\frac{10^4}{\mathrm{A}}\right)\sum_{\mathrm{i}=1}^{\mathrm{n}} \mathrm{KE_i} \tag{9}$$

where

KE_t = kinetic energy rate (J m^{-2} s^{-1})

t = sampling time (10 s)

A = piezoelectric sampling area (60 cm^2)

n = number of classes (eight drop size classes)

KE_i = kinetic energy measured at i class ranged from 1 to 8 (mJ).

The KE_c was determined from the KE_t and rainfall intensity using the following equation:

$$KE_c = c\,KE_t\,I^{-1} \tag{10}$$

where

KE_c = kinetic energy content (J m^{-2} mm^{-1})

I = rainfall intensity (mm h^{-1})

c = conversion factor equal to 3600

The KE_t was also estimated from the DSD information using the following equation:

$$KE_t = \left(\frac{\rho\pi}{12}\right)\left(\frac{1}{10^6}\right)\left(\frac{3600}{t}\right)\left(\frac{10^4}{A}\right)\sum_{i=1}^{n} N_i\, D_i^3\, v_{Di}^2 \tag{11}$$

where

N_i = number of drops in class *i* (drops)

D_i = drop diameter of class *i* (mm)

v_{Di} = drop fall velocity of drops in class i based on the drop sphere equivalent diameter (m s^{-1}).

The drop fall velocity was estimated using four empirical equations (Figure 5). The four empirical equation reported by Sekhon and Srivastava (1971), Beard (1976), Uplinger (1981), and Abd Elbasit et al. (2011).

The equations are shown in equations 12 to 16, respectively:

$$v_{Di} = 4.25D^{0.6} \tag{12}$$

$$v_{Di} = 0.0561D^3 - 0.912D^2 + 5.03D - 0.254 \tag{13}$$

$$v_{Di} = 4.854D\, e^{-0.195D} \tag{14}$$

$$v_{Di} = 9.5 \times \left(1 - \exp(-0.54\, D^{1.13})\right) \tag{15}$$

where D = drop sphere equivalent diameter (mm).

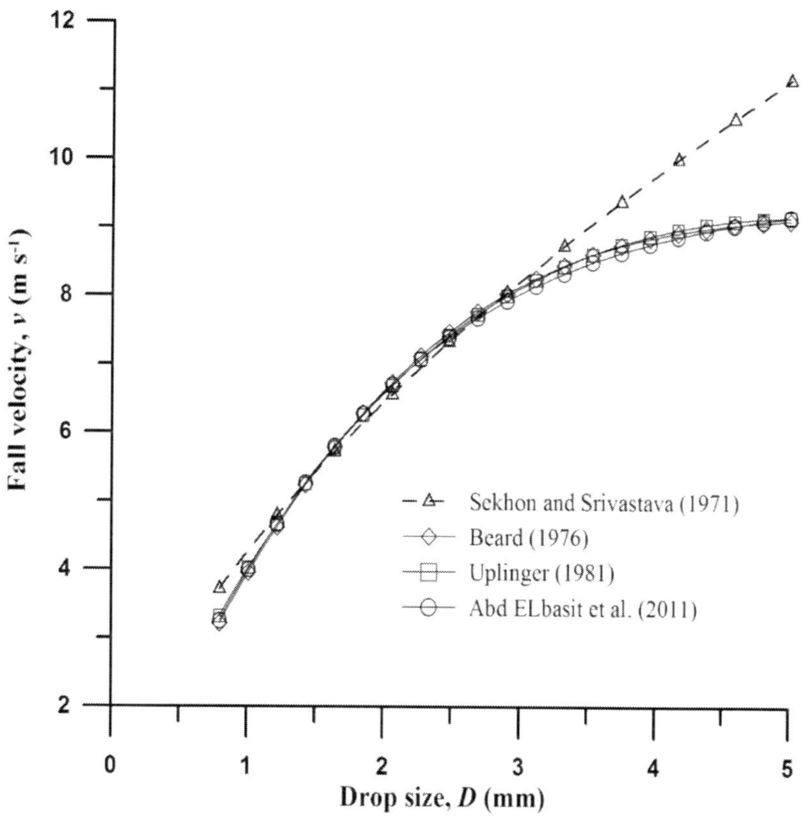

Figure 5. Example of empirical drop fall velocity equations.

Table 3. Drop Size Classes of the Piezoelectric Sensor

Class ID	Drop size range (mm)	Mean drop size (mm)
1	0.80-1.12	1.00
2	1.12-1.40	1.25
3	1.40-1.79	1.60
4	1.79-2.24	2.00
5	2.24-2.89	2.50
6	2.89-3.59	3.20
7	3.59-4.49	4.00
8	> 4.49	5.00

The Rainfall depth was calculated from the DSD data (P_{dsd}) and compared with the rain gauge (P_{rg}) measurements using the following equation:

$$P_{dsd} = \left(\frac{\pi}{6}\right)\left(\frac{3.6}{10^3}\right)\left(\frac{1}{At}\right)\sum_{i=1}^{8} N_i D_i^3 \qquad (16)$$

where P_{dsd} is the rainfall depth determined from the DSD measurements.

3. Piezoelectric Output

The DSD data under four representative rainfall intensities are shown in Figure 6. Generally, the percentage of large drops (D ≥ 2.5 mm) increase with intensity. The large drops percentage was 8, 30, 32, and 60% under 0.62, 1.42, 3.53, and 8.7 mm h^{-1} rainfall intensities, respectively. The typical output from the KE sensor under different rainfall events are shown in Figure 7. The 10s interval data show high variability in the total rainfall KE as the coefficient of variation under the four examined intensities was higher than 100%. However, the average kinetic energy increase with rainfall intensity (Figure 7). The sensor's signal variability was assessed by the coefficient of variation (CV). The CV was calculated as the ratio of the KE_t standard deviation to the KE_t mean (Abd Elbasit et al. 2011).

4. Rainfall Erosivity

The direct measured rainfall KE using the piezoelectric transducer was compared to DSD estimated KE_t (Figure 8). Four empirical relationships were used for raindrop fall velocity estimation. The correlation coefficient between the observed KE_t using the KE_t sensor and the estimated KE_t for the four relationships higher than 0.95 (P<0.001). This results indicate the potential use of the piezoelectric transducer sensor in direct measurement of the KE under the natural rainfall.

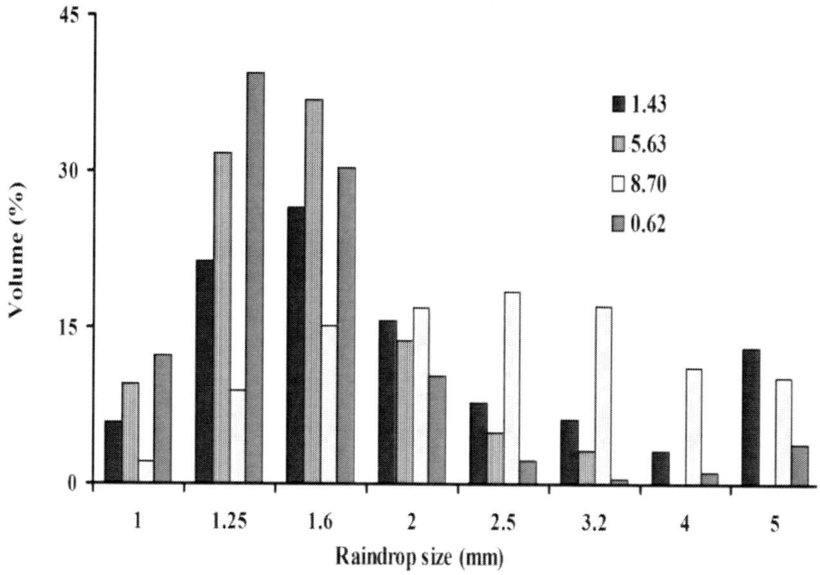

Figure 6. Raindrop size distribution under four representative rainfall intensities.

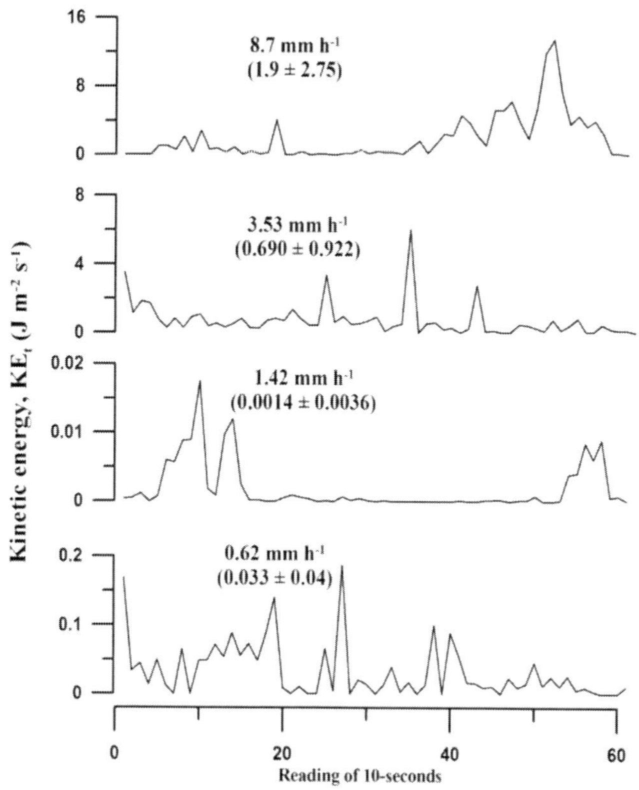

Figure 7. Typical output from the KE sensors (KE_t) in 10s intervals shown at four rainfall intensities. The mean value and standard deviation of KE_t are shown in brackets.

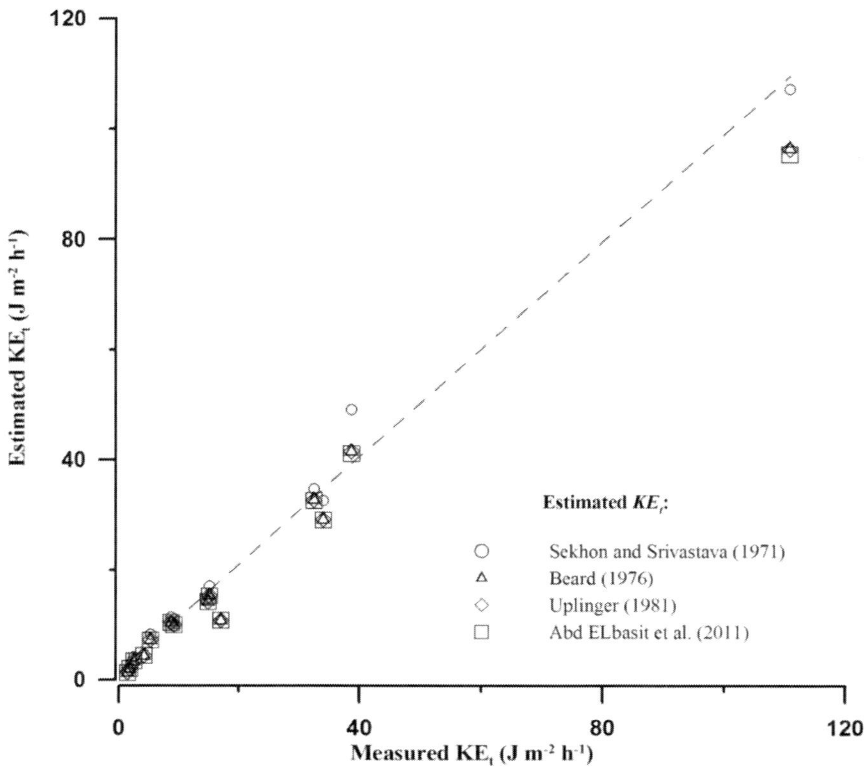

Figure 8. Relationship between the direct measured kinetic energy (KE_t) and estimated KE_t using the drop size distribution data and empirical fall velocity.

CONCLUSION

The natural rainfall kinetic energy and drop size distribution have been observed under Tottori, Japan environment. Two piezoelectric transducers have been used for KE and DSD measurement. The DSD pattern showed good agreement with the rainfall intensity. Specifically, the large drop percentage showed positive association with the rainfall intensity. The typical output from the KE sensor showed high variability with time. However, the average value has a significant correlation with rainfall intensity. The directly measured KE_t using KE sensor showed significant correlation with estimated KE_t using empirical fall velocity (>0.95, P<0.001).

ACKNOWLEDGMENTS

This work was financially supported by the Japan Society for the Promotion of Science (JSPS). The authors would like to thank Ms. Marreia Elamin Ugool for her help in data entry and analysis.

REFERENCES

Abd Elbasit MAM, Yasuda H, Salmi A, and Anyoji H. 2010. Characterization of rainfall generated by dripper-type rainfall simulator using piezoelectric transducers and its impact on splash soil erosion. *Earth Surf. Process. Landform.* 35(4): 466-475.

Abd Elbasit MAM, Yasuda H, Salmi A, Kopsala P, and Anyoji H. 2007. Characterization of rainfall generated by dripper-type rainfall simulator using piezoelectric transducer. Proceeding of the annual conference of Japan Society of Hydrology and Water Resources, 10-11. Nagoya, Japan.

Abd Elbasit MAM, Yasuda H, Salmi A. 2011. Application of piezoelectric transducers in simulated rainfall erosivity assessment. *Hydrological Science Journal.* 56(1): 187-194.

Al-Durrah, MM, Bradford JM. 1982. The mechanism of raindrop splash on soil surfaces. *Soil Science Society of America Journal.* 46: 1086-1090.

Apaydin H, Erpul G, Bayramin I, Gabriels G. 2006. Evaluation of indices for characterizing the distribution and concentration of precipitation: A case for the region of Southeastern Anatolia project, Turkey. *Journal of Hydrology.* 328: 726-732.

Arnoldus HM. 1980. An approximation of the rainfall factor in the universal soil loss equation, in De Boodt M, Gabriels D (Eds.) Assessment of Erosion. John Wiley and Sons, Inc., Chichsester, pp.127-132.

Bayramin U, Erpul G, Erdogan HE. 2006. Use of CORINE methodology to assess soil erosion risk in the semi-arid area of Beypazari, Ankara. Turkish *Journal of Agriculture and Forestry.* 30: 81-100.

Beard KV. 1976. Terminal velocity and shape of cloud and precipitation drops aloft. *Journal of Atmospheric Science.* 33: 851-864.

De Luis M, Brunetti M, Gonzlez-Hidalgo JC, Longares A. 2010. Is rainfall erosivity increasing in the Mediterranean Iberian Peninsula? *Land Degradation and Development.* 21: 139-144.

Epema GF, Riezebos HTh. 1983. Fall velocity of waterdrops at different heights as a factor influencing erosivity of simulated rain. In: DePloey, J (Ed.): Rainfall simulation runoff and soil erosion, Catena Supplement 4.

Fournier H. 1960. Climat et erosion. Presses Universitaires de France: Paris.

Gilley JE, Finkner SC. 1985. Estimating soil detachment caused by raindrop impact. *Transaction of the ASAE.* 28: 140-146.

Hudson NW. 1965. The influence of rainfall mechanics on soil erosion. MSc Thesis: Cape Town University, South Africa.

IPCC (2007). Climate change 2007: the physical Science bases. Cambridge University Press.

Jayawardena AW, and Rezaur RB. 2000a. Measuring drop size distribution and kinetic energy of rainfall using a force transducer. *Hydrological Processes.* 14: 37-49.

Jayawardena AW, Rezaur RB. 2000b. Drop size distribution and kinetic energy load of rainstorm in Hong Kong. *Hydrological Processes.* 14: 1069-1082.

Kinnell PIA. 2005. Sediment transport by Medium to large drops impacting flows at subterminal velocity. *Soil Science Society of America Journal.* 69: 902-905.

Madden LV, Wilson LL, Ntahimpera N. 1998. Calibration and evaluation of an electronic sensor for rainfall kinetic energy. *Phytopathology.* 88: 950-959.

Mouzai, L., and M. Bouhadef. 2003. Water drop erosivity: effect on soil splash. *Journal of Hydraulic Research.* 41: 61-68.

Munka C, Cruz, G, Caffera RM, 2007. Long term variation in rainfall erosivity in Uruguay: a preliminary Fournier approach. *GeoJournal.* 70, 257-262.

Nanko K, Mizugaki S, Onda Y. 2008. Estimation of soil detachment rates on the forest floor of an unmanaged Japanese cypress plantation based on field measurement of the throughfall drop sizes and velocities. *Catena* 72: 348-361.

Nanko, K., N. Hotta, and M. Suzuki. 2004. Assessing raindrop impact energy at the forest floor in a mature Japanese cypress plantation using continuous raindrop-sizing instruments. *Journal of Forest Research.* 9:157-164.

Nearing MA, Pruski FF, O'Neal MR. 2004. Expected climate change impacts on soil erosion rates: A review. *Journal of Soil and Water Conservation.* 59(1):43-50.

Nearing, M.A., 2001. Potential change in rainfall erosivity in the U.S. with climate change during the 21st century. *Journal of Soil and Water Conservation.* 56, 229-232.

Oduro-Afriyie, K., 1996. Rainfall erosivity map for Ghana. *Geoderma.* 74, 161-166.

Onaga, K., K. Shirai, and A. Yoshinaga. 1988. Rainfall erosion and how to control its effects on farmland in Okinawa. In: Rimwanich, S. (Ed.), Land Conservation for Future Generations, 627–639. Department of Land Development, Bangkok.

Oxford Dictionaries. oxforddictionaries.com. (Access Jan. 20th 2012)

Pohjola, H., L. Konkola, M. Hoikkanen, and D. M. Schultz. 2008. Adjusting radar-derived QPE with measured drop-size distribution at the surface. The fifth European conference on radar in meteorology and hydrology. Helsinki, Finland

Renard, K.G., Freimund, J.R., 1994. Using monthly precipitation data to estimate the R-factor in the revised USLE. *Journal of Hydrology.* 157: 287-306.

Riezebos, H. T. H., and G. F. Epema. 1985. Drop shape and erosivity part П: Splash detachment, transport and erosivity indices. *Earth Surface Processes Landform.* 10: 69-74.

Salles, C, and Poesen J. 2000. Rain properties controlling soil splash detachment. *Hydrological Processes.* 14: 271-282.

Salles, C., Poesen J, Sempere-Torres D. 2002. Kinetic energy of rain and its functional relationship with intensity. *Journal of Hydrology.* 257: 256-270.

Salmi A, Elomaa L. 2007. Measurement of the terminal velocity and shape of falling raindrops at Vaisala rain laboratory. Eighth European conference on application of meteorology (ECAM), San Lorenzo de El Escorial, Spain.

Salmi A, Ikonen J. 2005. Piezoelectric precipitation sensor from Vaisala. World Meteorology Organization technical conference on meteorological and environmental instruments and methods of observation (TECO 2005), Bucharest, Romania.

Salmi, A, Elomaa L,. Laukkanen E. 2008. Piezoelectric Vaisala RAINCAP® rain sensor applied to drop size distribution monitoring. WMO Technical Conference on Meteorological and Environmental Instruments and Methods of Observation (TECO 2008), St. Petersburg, Russian Federation.

Sekhon RS, Srivastava RS. 1971. Doppler radar observation of drop size distribution in a thunderstorm. *Journal of Atmospheric Science.* 28: 256-270.

Uplinger WG. 1981. A new formula for raindrop terminal velocity. In: Proceeding 20th Conference Radar Meteorology. *American Meteorological Society*, Boston: 389-391.

Van Dijk AIJM, Bruijnzeel LA, RosewellCJ. 2002. Rainfall intensity-kinetic energy relationship: a critical literature appraisal. *Journal of Hydrology*. 261: 1-23.

Wischmeier WH, Smith DD. 1978. Predicting rainfall erosion losses, Agricultural Handbook 537: Science and Education Administration, Washington, D. C.: USDA.

Zhang WB, Xie Y, Liu BY. 2002. Rainfall erosivity estimation using daily rainfall amounts. *Scientia Goegraphica Sinica*. 22, 705-711 (in Chinese).

Zhang GH, Nearing MA, Liu BY. 2005. Potential effects of climate change on rainfall erosivity in the Yellow River Basin of China. *Transaction of ASAE. 48(2), 511-517.*

Zhongbao, X., Xinxiao, Y., Qingyun, L., 2010. Spatiotemporal variation in rainfall erosivity on the Chinese Loess Plateau during the period 1956-2008. *Reg. Environ. Change*. 11, 149-159.

In: Rainfall: Behavior, Forecasting and Distribution
Editors: Olga E. Martín and Tricia M. Roberts ISBN: 978-1-62081-551-9

Chapter 9

TREND OF RAIN IN NORTHEAST BRAZIL

Priscilla Teles de Oliveira[1,4], Cláudio Moisés Santos Silva[1,2,4] and Kellen Carla Lima[1,3,4]
[1]Universidade Federal do Rio Grande do Norte (UFRN)
[2]Departamento de Física Teórica e Experimental (DFTE)
[3]Escola de Ciências e Tecnologia (ECT)
[4]Programa de Pós-Graduação em Ciências Climáticas (PPGCC)
Natal, RN, Brasil

ABSTRACT

The Northeast of Brazil (NEB) shows high climate variability, ranging from semiarid regions with an annual rainfall below 500 mm to a rainy climate in the coastland with annual rainfall exceeding 1500 mm. The rainfall regimes are heterogeneous in space-temporal scales. According to the latest report of the Intergovernmental Panel on Climate Change (IPCC, AR4), the NEB is highly susceptible to climate change, and also heavy rainfall events (HRE). However, few climatology studies about these episodes were performed, thus the objective of the study was to compute the climatology of the episodes number and the daily rainfall rate associated with HRE; relate them to the normal rainfall events (NRE) and weak rainfall events (WRE). This study analyzed eight NEB states, excluding Bahia due to its different rainfall regime. The daily rainfall data of the hydrometeorological network managed by the Agência Nacional de Águas (ANA), from 1972 to 2002, contains accounting from 219 rain gauges. We applied the technique of quantiles to identify the rainfall episodes. We selected HRE, NRE and WRE where at least one rain gauge recorded precipitation above the 95th percentile, between 45th and 55th percentiles, and below the 5th percentile, respectively. The data distribution concerning the events was divided by seasons (DJF, MAM, JJA, SON). The linear trend in the number of events and the annual precipitation daily rate was analyzed using the Mann-Kendall. The results showed an increase in the number of cases and the intensity of WRE and the intensity of HRE, with a statistical confidence level above 95%. In addition the NRE showed a decrease in intensity during the JJA quarter (dry season). The results also suggest that climate change is altering the climatology of rainfall of the NEB, increasing extreme events (heavy and weak), weakening the normal events and increasing the HRE during the wet season.

Keywords: extreme events, climatology

INTRODUCTION

Northeast Brazil (NEB) is composed by Alagoas, Bahia, Ceará, Maranhão, Paraíba, Pernambuco, Piauí, Rio Grande do Norte and Sergipe Brazilian states, occupying 1,588,196 km², which is equivalent to 18% of the Brazilian territory, situated between 1°N and 18°S and 34.5°W and 48.5°W. The NEB presents a high climatic variety since semi-arid regions (annual rainfall less than 500 mm), reaching the coastland (annual precipitation above 1500 mm), being influenced by extreme events on the time scale (precipitation excess) and climatic scale (dry episodes). The rainfall presents itself heterogeneously in the spatial-temporal scales.

The main atmospheric systems acting in the NEB are: the Intertropical Convergence Zone (ITCZ); the Upper Tropospheric Cyclonic Vortex (UTCV); the Easterly Waves Disturbances (EWD) and the Squall Lines (SL). The South of Bahia has actuation of the Front Systems (FS) and the South Atlantic Convergence Zone (SACZ). Specifically, the Semi-arid Northeast study verified that intense events are associated to mesoscale systems, which are embedded in dynamic-unstable synoptic environments (Barbosa e Correia 2005; Diniz et al. 2007; Silva et al. 2008).

The ITCZ is an atmospheric system located around the globe equatorial line, formatted by confluence between the northeast and southeast trade winds. The ITCZ showed a north-south displacement through the year, reaching maxima latitude around at 1° S (April), and 8° N (July), this variability to determinate the rainy and dry periods over the north NEB (Uvo, 1989).

According to Kayano et al. (1997) the UTCV are systems with a persistent and cold core, which influence the rainfall during the austral summer time in NEB. In the core the motion is descending, inhibiting the generation of clouds and in the UTCV periphery the wet air motion is ascending, causing potential kinetic energy conversion and keeping the UTCV motion (Gan and Kousky, 1986).

The EWD description was made by Riehl (1945) on the Caribbean region, which has oscillations in the pressure and wind fields in phase with the surface weather condition. They present the highest intensity in the medium tropospheric levels and move toward the NEB coastland, mainly during the end of summer time, which often presents the weakest cyclonic circulation (Hastenrath, 1988). During the trajectory the EWD causes impact in the weather conditions, being associated with cloudiness and heavy precipitation episodes, modifying the pressure and wind intensity on the surface (Tarakanov, 1966).

The SL's are agglomerated of cumulus clouds organized in line shape, associated to the sea breeze (Kousky, 1980; Cavalcanti, 1982; Cohen, 1989; Greco et al., 1990). Due to diurnal variability, the maxima convective activity occurs at late afternoon hours, being often observed in infrared satellite images.

System Front (SF) is the region that presents two air masses with different characteristics. The cold air mass advances over the given region, causing hot air to ascend. During the austral winter, these systems are formed by air masses originated from high latitudes, causing frost and rainfall episodes in different parts of Brazil, including the South NEB. During the cold fronts moving toward low latitudes, they interact with air producing hot and moist tropical deep convection (Cavalcanti and Kousky, 2009). The interaction between the FS and the convection due to the diabatic heating at the surface organizes a preferential region of convergence (SACZ) especially during the summer months. The SACZ is characterized by a band of cloudiness with a northwest-southeast orientation that extends from the Amazonia southwest to the Atlantic Ocean (Kousky, 1988). The SACZ presents a stationary characteristic, with a period of four or more days above the same region.

Although the different actuating atmospheric systems above all the NEB, the most climatologically rainy period occurs during the fall, on March, April and May (Carvalho et al., 2004).

According to the last report from the Intergovernmental Panel on Climate Change (IPCC; AR4), the NEB is an area highly susceptible to climatic changes, being susceptible to the occurrence of high precipitation events. An important question about these extreme events is the time tendency identification.

The climatic change influences the intensity and frequency extreme events depending not only on the rate of change of the environment variable, but of the statistical parameter changes that determine the variable distribution. The analysis of extreme precipitation is the most complex analyses, due to the low degree of correlation between the precipitation events (Marengo, 2009).

The reliable tendencies estimative of the precipitation events are possible in areas with a dense rain gauge dataset. The lack of high quality and homogeny weather observations is the greatest obstacle to quantify the extreme changes during the past century (Vincent et al., 2005, Haylock et al., 2006).

There is little research on the extreme events climatology in NEB, although there are important scientific efforts about the Amazonia and the regions South and Southeast (Liebmann et al., 2001; Haylock et al., 2006; Satyamurty et al., 2010; Lima et al., 2010; Teixeira e Satyamurty, 2011 e Marengo et al., 2011). In NEB the research is practically non-existent, having only results in global studies that involve the region (Groisman et al., 2005; Marengo et al., 2009).

The objective of this study regards the climatology and the tendency toward the number of events and the daily precipitation rate associated with Heavy Rainfall Events (HRE), Normal Rainfall Events (NRE) and Week Rainfall Events (WRE).

Material and Methods

1. Data

This study was performed with a rainfall dataset of the eight NEB states: Alagoas, Ceará, Maranhão, Paraíba, Pernambuco, Piauí, Rio Grande do Norte and Sergipe.

The Bahia was excluded due to its different rainfall regime. Daily precipitation data of the hydrometeorological network management by the National Water Agency of Brazil (Agência Nacional de Águas - ANA) was used. This included an accounting from 219 stations during the period from 1972 to 2002 (31 years).

A quality control was made to exclude spurious and missing data, thus only 81 rain gauges presented acceptable failure level. The distribution of rain gauges is shown in Figure 1. This total, 7% present missing, 70.7% were null data, and 22.3% of rainy days.

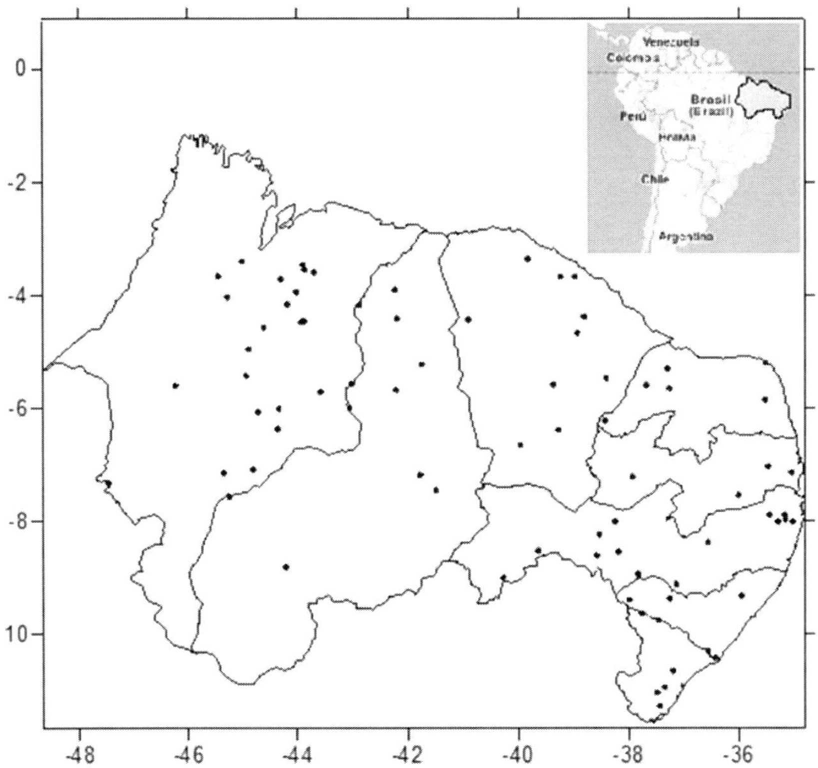

Figure 1. The rain gauge spatial distribution over the NEB.

2. Methodology

2.1. Quantiles Technique

The quantiles are points in regular intervals of a series of data. According to Wilks (2006), many statistical analyses were based on the quantiles technique. The main advantage of this technique with relation to the traditional methods (mean and standard deviation) is the independency on normalization hypothesis, which is not necessarily satisfied in rainfall data. In addition, the quantiles technique considers the characteristic of the precipitation distribution frequency of each meteorological station. Therefore, the quantiles are immune to eventual asymmetry on the density function of probabilities that describes a random phenomenon (Xavier, 1984).

To determine extreme events, many studies were developed in different regions, using the distribution of daily rainfall percentiles. Groisman et al. (2005) used the 90°, 95°, 99°, 99.7° and 99.9° percentiles in a global study, Zhai et al. (2005) applied the 95° percentile to China rainfall; Grimm and Tedeschi (2009) performed a study over South America, using the 90° percentile; Khishnamurthy et al. (2009) identified extreme events in the region of India from the 90° and 99° percentiles; Jones et al. (2011) used the 90° percentile in a study over the USA; finally, Gemmer et al. (2011), with rainfall data over China used the 90°, 95° and 99° percentiles.

In the present study we select extreme (weak and intense events) and the normal events only to nonzero daily rainfall. Each case is selected if at least one rain gauge was observed: Heavy Rainfall Event (HRE) presented precipitation great than 95° percentile; the Normal Rainfall Event (NRE), are between percentiles 45° and 55°; Week Rainfall Event (WRE) presented precipitation less than 5° percentile. The data was divided by seasons: summer DJF (December, January and February); autumn MAM (March, April and May); winter JJA (June, July, August); spring SON (September, October and November).

2.2. Trend Analyses

The nonparametric Mann-Kendall (Mann, 1945; Kendall, 1945) test was applied to analyze the trend of the number and intensity of rainfall. This test compares each value of the temporal series with the remaining values in sequential order, counting the number of times that the remaining terms are greater than the analyzed value. This test is generally used to calculate climatic and hydrological tendencies (Acero et al. 2001; Silva 2003; Santos et al. 2010). Goossens and Berger (1986) showed that the Mann-Kendall test is the most appropriate method to analyze weather tendencies in climatological series.

RESULTS AND DISCUSSION

Figure 2 presents the annual distribution of rainfall events during the studied period. Both NRE and HRE show a cyclic and correspondent variability. It is not possible to identify linear trends in this data. The year with maxima quantity of NRE and HRE were 1985, 1989 and 2000; and minimum quantity in 1976, 1981, 1983, 1993 and 1997, coincided with strong El Niño and La Niña events, respectively. According to Grimm and Tedeschi (2009) and Rodrigues et al. (2011), El Niño and La Niña events have direct influence on the NEB rainy season, and consequently on the NRE and HRE. During El Niño years the NRE and HRE events decrease, while in La Niña they increase; however, the El Niño actuation is more pronounced than La Niña events. The WRE do not present cyclic characteristics and the data presents a linear decrease from 1972 until 1982. Between 1983 and 1990 the distribution of WRE strongly corresponds to the variation of the NRE and HRE (El Niño and La Niña events). After 1990 the number of events increases significantly.

The seasonal climatology of rainfall is presented in Figure 3a. The period of highest rainfall is during autumn (MAM) and the minimum is in the spring (SON). Comparing with WRE, NRE and HRE seasonal climatology (Figure 3b) it is possible to verify consistent distributions. The HRE seasonal variation is more accentuated than the WRE and NRE one. The dry seasons (JJA and SON) contain fewer HRE in comparison with other events.

The interannual variation of the WRE, NRE and HRE is described in Figure 4. In Figure 4a it shows the distribution of summer Events, in which a cyclic variability is noted until

1993, after this the data presents a positive trend. The same occurs during MAM for the HRE and NRE (Figure 4b), with exception of the HRE, which presents a cyclic variation throughout the study period. During the winter and spring the variability of NRE and HRE do not present significant trends, whereas the WRE presents a positive trend.

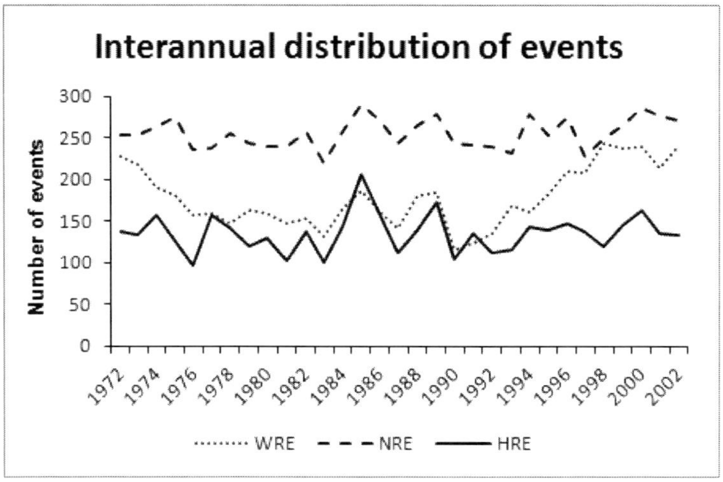

Figure 2. Interannual distribution of events.

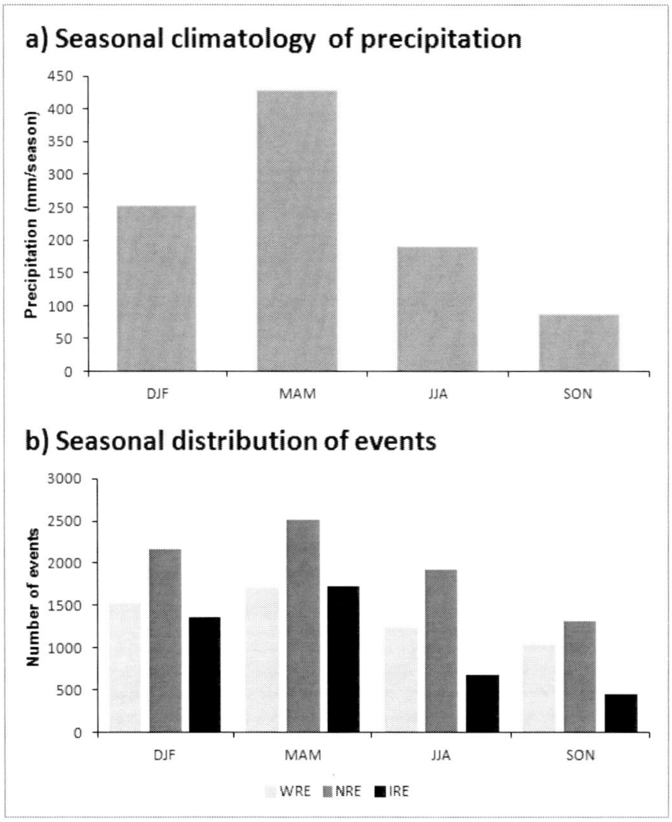

Figure 3. Seasonal climatology (1972 to 2002): of rainfall (a) and of the amount of rainfall events (b).

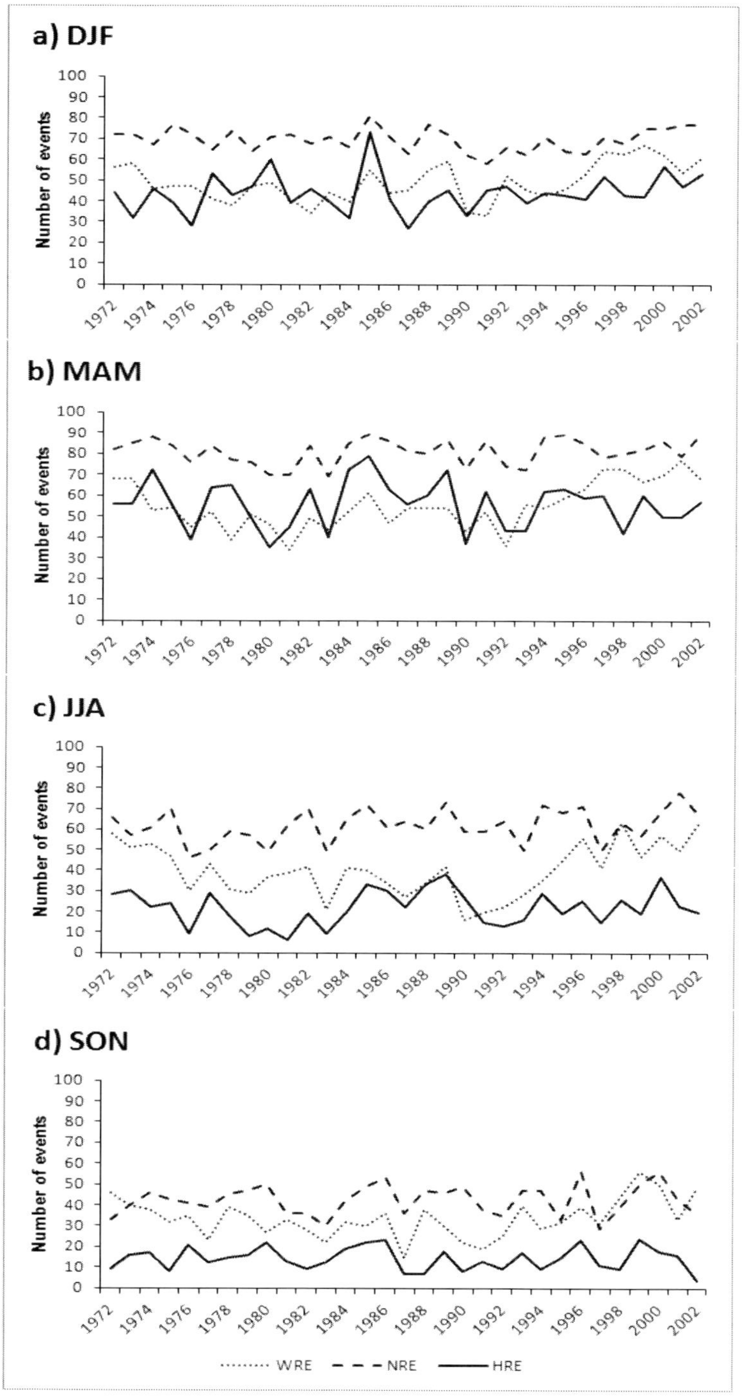

Figure 4. Interannual variation of the cases amount: DJF (a), MAM (b), JJA (c) e SON (d).

Figure 5 shows the daily interannual distribution of rainfall intensity. The WRE (Figure 5a) presents a strong positive trend for all seasons. In general, The NRE, Figure 5b, shows no positive or negative trend, with the exception of the winter season (JJA), which shows a negative trend. The HRE, Figure 5c, does not show a relevant trend, except during MAM, which shows a positive trend. The intensity variability is also correlated with El Niño and La Niña occurrences, but this variation is less sensitive to these phenomena than the variation in the number of events.

Tables 1 and 2 show the WRE, NRE and HRE statistical significance and tendency from the Mann Kendal test. With relation to the number of events, the WRE presents annual and summer (DJF) positive trends at 90%, and a 99% significance level for autumn (MAM). The NRE and HRE presented positive tendency during all seasons, but without statistical significance.

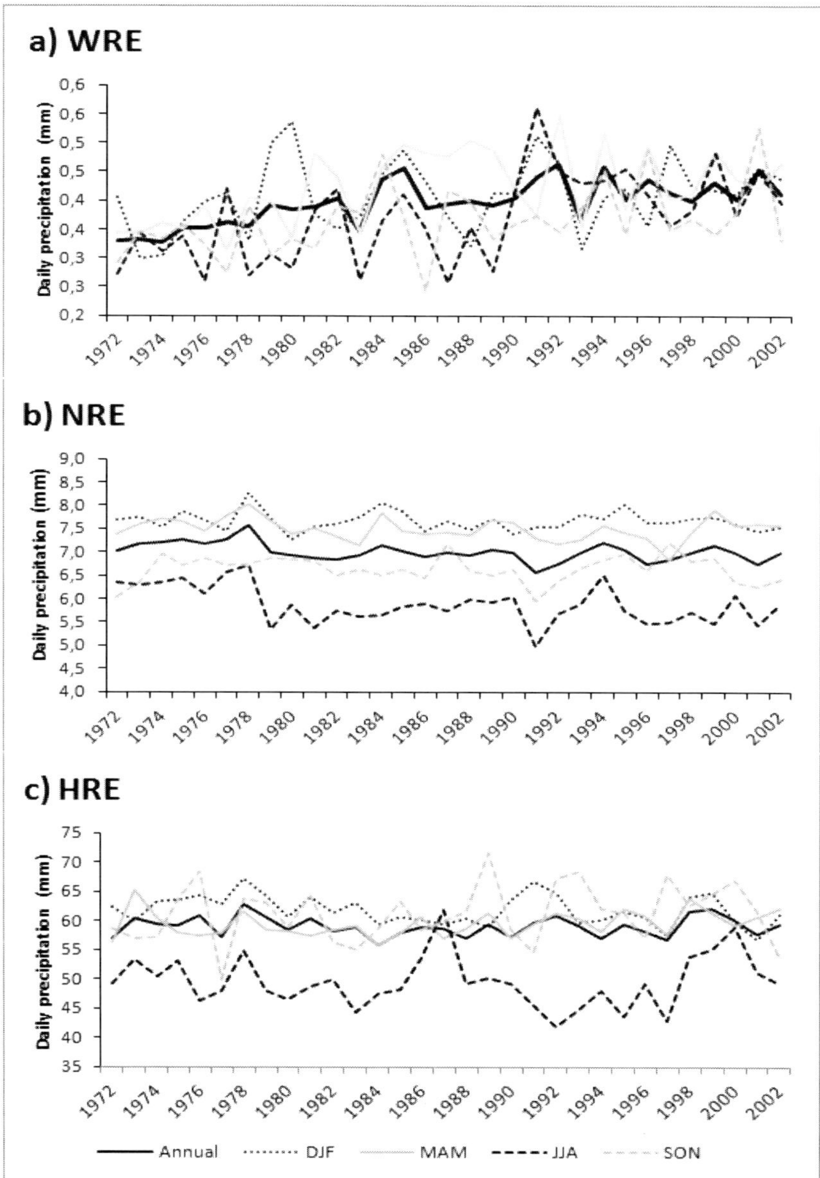

Figure 5. Daily interannual distribution of rainfall intensity: WRE (a), NRE (b) e HRE (c).

Table 1. Statistical significance (Sig.) and tendency (Tend.) of increase (+) or decrease (-), from Mann-Kendall test applied in variation of quantity Events

	WRE		NRE		HRE	
	Sig.	Trend	Sig.	Trend	Sig.	Trend
Annual	90%	+		+		+
DJF	90%	+		-		+
MAM	99%	+		+		-
JJA		+		+		+
SON		+		+		

Table 2. Statistical significance (Sig.) and tendency (Tend.) of increase (+) or decrease (-), from Mann-Kendall test applied in variation of intensity of daily rainfall

	WRE		NRE		HRE	
	Sig.	Trend	Sig.	Trend	Sig.	Trend
Annual	99.9%	+	95%	-		
DJF	90%	+		-		-
MAM	99%	+		-	95%	+
JJA	99%	+	95%	-		
SON	90%	+		-		+

With respect to rainfall intensity, the WRE presented a positive trend at 90% and 99.9% significance level. The NRE presented a negative trend in all cases, with statistical significance at 95% level for the annual variation and winter (JJA). The HRE showed a positive trend during the autumn (MAM) and spring (SON), however only in the autumn reaching 95% significance level. During the summer (DJF) a negative trend was observed, but without statistical significance. The HRE presented a positive trend in the number of events during the study period, but not significantly above 90%. A similar trend was observed by Groisman et al. (2005), who observed in the east of Brazil (almost all the NEB), there was an increase of 40% in the HRE annual frequency in the period between 1910 and 2000, however their results were statistically significant at 90% significance level.

In general, the quantity of events presented a positive trend over the NEB, mainly the WRE. With respect to intensity, there is an increase in the extremes, while mean precipitation cases presented a negative trend; in other words, the WRE and the HRE is becoming more intense whereas the NRE is becoming weaker.

CONCLUSION

A set of 81 rain gauges distributed over the NEB provided daily rainfall data, which were used to analyze the WRE, NRE and HRE. The main objective was to calculate the climatology of the number of cases and daily rainfall rate associated with these events.

Concerning the climatology aspects, it was observed that all cases presented a positive trend, but only the WRE with at least 90% statistical significance. With respect to rainfall intensity, the WRE and HRE show positive trends and the NRE negative trends, all with at least 90% statistical significance. It was verified that the extreme events (WRE and HRE) are becoming more intense, and the NRE weaker. The number of events is modulated by La Niña and El Niño occurrences, which were verified larger and smaller events, respectively. Furthermore, it was found that rainfall intensity is less sensitive to the La Niña and El Niño occurrence.

The HRE showed a positive trend at 95% statistical significance during the autumn (MAM), which is the rainy season of the NEB. However, a NRE decrease was observed at 95% statistical significance during the winter (JJA), which coincides with the dry season of the area. These results suggest alterations on the temporal rain distribution over the NEB, resulting in an increase of the seasonality amplitude.

Positive trends of HRE were also found over the South and Southeast Brazilian regions (Lima et al. 2010; Teixeira e Satyamurty 2011), therefore these results can be evidence of the global warming effects on the Brazil climate.

ACKNOWLEDGMENTS

To the Coordenação de Aperfeiçoamento de Pessoal de Nível Superior (CAPES) by doctoral scholarship of the first author and to the Agência Nacional de Águas (ANA) by daily rainfall data.

REFERENCES

Acero, F. J.; Gallego, M. C. and García, J. A. Multi-day rainfall trends over the Iberian Peninsula. *Theoretical and Applied Climatology,* 2011. DOI 10.1007/s00704-011-0534-5.

Barbosa, T.F. And Correia, M.F. Sistemas Convectivos Intensos no Semi-árido Brasileiro: O Controle da Grande Escala. *Revista Brasileira de Meteorologia*, v. 20, p. 395-410, 2005.

Carvalho, L. M. V.; Jones, C.; Liebmann, B. The South Atlantic Convergence Zone: intensity, form, persistence, and relationships with intraseasonal to interannual activity and extreme rainfall. *Journal of Climate*, v. 17, n. 1, p. 88-108, 2004.

Cavalcanti, I. F. A. Um estudo sobre interações entre sistemas de circulação de escala sinótica e circulações locais. 1982. 113 f. (INPE-2494-TDL/097). *Dissertação (Mestrado em Meteorologia)* – INPE, São José dos Campos, 1982.

Cavalcanti, I. F. A. and Kousky, E. V. Frentes Frias Sobre O Brasil, In: Cavalcanti, I. F. A.; Ferreira, N. J.; Justi Da Silva, M. G. A.; Silva Dias, M. A. F. *Tempo e clima no Brasil.* São Paulo: Ed. Oficina de Textos, Cap. 9, p.135-146, 2009.

Cohen, J. C. P. Um estudo observacional de linhas de instabilidade na Amazônia. 1989. 153 f. *Dissertação (Mestrado em Meteorologia)* – INPE, São José dos Campos, 1989.

Diniz, M.C.S.; Correia, M.F. and Silva Arago, M.R. Convecção profunda no submédio do Rio São Francisco: uma avaliação das condições atmosféricas na área do aeroporto de Petrolina-PE. *Revista Brasileira de Meteorologia*, V. 19, p. 273-286, 2004.

Gan, M.A. and Kousky, V.E. Vórtices Ciclônicos da alta troposfera no oceano Atlântico Sul. *Revista Brasileira de Meteorologia*, n.1, p.19-28, Jan. 1986.

Gemmer, M.; Fischer, T.; Jiang, T.; Su, B. and Liu, L.L. Trends in Precipitation Extremes in the Zhujiang River basin, South China. *Journal of Climate,* n.24, p.750-761, 2011.

Goossens, C. and Berger, A. Annual and seasonal climatic variations over the northern hemisphere and Europe during the last century. Annales Geophysicae, Berlin, v.4, n.B4, p.385-400, 1986.

Greco, S; Swap, R.; Garstang,M.; Ulanski, S.; Shipham, M. and Harris, R. C. Rainfall and surface kinematic conditions over central Amazonia ABLE 2B. *Journal of Geophysical Research*, v. 95-D10, p.17001-17014, 1990.

Grimm, A.M. and Tedeschi, R.G. Enso and extreme rainfall events in South America. *Journal of Climate*, v. 22, n. 7, p. 1589-1609, 2009.

Groisman, P. Y..; Knight, R.W.; Easterling, D.R.; Karl, T.R.; Hegerl, G.C. and Razuvaev, V.N. Trends in intense precipitation in the climate record. *Journal of Climate*, v.18, n. 9, p. 1326-1350, 2005.

Hastenrath, S. Climate and circulation of the tropics. New York: Atmospheric Sciences Library, 1988. 455p.

Haylock, M. R.; Peterson, T. C.; Alves, L. M.; Ambrizzi, T.; Anunciação, Y. M. T.; Baez, J.; Barros, V. R.; Berlato, M. A.; Bidegain, M.; Coronel, G.; Corradi, V.; Garcia, V. J.; Grimm, A. M.; Karoly, D.; Marengo, J. A.; Marino, M. B.; Moncunill, D. F.; Nechet, D.; Quintana, J.; Rebello, E.; Rusticucci, M.; Santos, J. L.; Trebejo, I. and Vincent, L. A. *Journal of Climate*, v.19, p.1490-1512, 2006.

Intergovernmental Panel On Climate Change (IPCC). *The scientific basis:* contribution of working group I to the fourth assessment report of the intergovernmental panel on climate change. Cambridge, UK: University Press, 2007. 996f. Edited by Solomon et al.

Jones, C.; Gottschalck, J.; Carvalho, L. M. V. and Higgins, W. Influence of the Madden–Julian Oscillation on Forecasts of Extreme Precipitation in the Contiguous United States. *Monthly Weather Review,* v. 139, p. 332-350, 2011.

Kayano, M.T.; Ferreira, N.J. and Ramírez, M.C.V. Summer circulation patterns related to the upper tropospheric vortices over the tropical South Atlantic. *Meteorology and Atmospheric Physics*. v.64, n.3-4, p.203-213. 1997.

Kendall, M. G. Rank correlation methods. London: Charles Griffin, 1975. 120p.

Kousky, V. E. Diurnal rainfall variation in Northeast Brazil. *Monthly Weather Review*, v. 108, p. 488-498, 1980.

Kousky, V. E., 1988, Pentad outgoing longwave radiation climatology for the South American Sector. *Revista Brasileira de Meteorologia*, 3, pp 217-231.

Krishnamurthy, C. K. B.; Lall, U. and Know, H. H. Changing Frequency and Intensity of Rainfall Extremes over India from 1951 to 2003. *Journal of climate*, v. 22, p. 4737-4746, 2009.

Liebmann, B.; Jones, C.; Carvalho, L. M. V. Interannual variability of daily extreme precipitation events in the state of São Paulo, Brazil. *Journal of Climate*, v.14, n. 2, p. 208-218, 2001.

Lima, K. C.; Satyamurty, P.; Fernández, J. P. R. Large-scale atmospheric conditions associated with heavy rainfall episodes in Southeast Brazil. *Theoretical and Applied Climatology*, v. 101, n. 1-2, p.121-135, 2010.

Mann, H. B. Nonparametric tests against trend. *Econometrica*, v.13, p.245-259, 1945.

Marengo, J. A.; Jones, R.; Alves, L. M. and Valcerde, M. C. Future change of temperature and precipitation extremes in South America as derived from the PRECIS regional climate modeling system. *International journal of climatology*, v. 29, p. 2241-2255, 2009.

Marengo, J. A.; Tomasella, J.; Soares, W. R.; Alves, L. M. and Nobre, C. A. Extreme climatic events in the Amazon basin. *Theoretical and applied climatology,* 2011. DOI 10.1007/s00704-011-0465-1.

Marengo, J.A. Mudanças climáticas, Condições meteorológicas extremas e eventos climáticos no Brasil. *Mudanças climáticas e eventos extremos no Brasil*. Fundação Brasileira para o Desenvolvimento Sustentável - FBDS, p.4-18, 2009.

Riehl, H. Waves in the easterlies and polar front in the tropics. Chicago: Chicago University, *Department of Meteorology*, 1945. 79p.

Rodrigues, R.R., R.J. Haarsma, E.J.D. Campos and T. Ambrizzi, The impacts of inter-El Nino variability on the Tropical Atlantic and Northeast Brazil climate. *Journal of Climate*, v. 24, p. 3402-3422, 2011.

Santos, D. dos S.; Silva, V. P. R.; Sousa, F. A.S. and Silva, R. A. Estudos de alguns cenários climáticos para o Nordeste do Brasil. Revista *Brasileira de Engenharia Agrícola e Ambiental*, v.14, n.5, p.492–500, 2010.

Satyamurty, P.; Castro, A. A.; Tota, J.; Gularte, L. E. S. and Manzi, A. O. Rainfall trends in the Brazilian Amazon Basin in the past eight decades. *Theoretical and applied climatology*, v. 99, p. 139-148, 2010.

Silva, F.D.S.; Correia, M F ; Aragão, M.R.S. and Silva, J.M. Convecção linearmente organizada na área de Petrolina, semi-árido do Nordeste do Brasil: aspectos em meso e grande escala. *Revista Brasileira de Meteorologia*, v. 23, p. 292-304, 2008.

Silva, V. P. R. On climate variability in Northeast of Brazil. *Journal of Arid Environments*, v. 58, p. 575-596, 2004.

Takaranov, G.G. Tropical Meteorology. URSS: Moscou: Mir, 1966. 150p.

Teixeira, M. S. and Satyamurty, P. Trends in the Frequency of Intense Precipitation Events in Southern and Southeastern Brazil during 1960–2004. *Journal of climate*, v. 24, p. 1913-1921, 2001.

Uvo, C.R.B. A Zona de Convergência Intertropical (ZCIT) e sua relação com a precipitação da região norte e nordeste brasileiro. São José dos Campos. 82 p.(INPE-4887-TDL/378). *Dissertação (Mestrado em Meteorologia)* – Instituto Nacional de Pesquisas Espaciais, 1989.

Vincent, L. A.; Peterson, T. C.; Barros, V. R.; Marino, M. B.; Rusticucci, M.; Carrasco, G.; Ramirez, E.; Alves, L. M.; Ambrizzi, T.; Berlato, M. A.; Grimm, A. M.; Marengo, J. A.; Molion, L.; Moncunill, D. F.; Rebello, E.; Anunciação, Y. M. T.; Quintana, J.; Santos, J. L.; Baez, J.; Coronel, G.; Garcia, J.; Trebejo, I.; Bidegain, M.; Haylock, M. R. and Karoly, D. *Journal of Climate*, vol. 18, p.5011-5023, 2005.

Wilks, D. S. *Statistical methods in the atmospheric sciences*. 2. ed. Amsterdam: Elsevier Academic Press, 2006. 627 p.

Xavier, T. M. B. S.; Xavier, A. F. S. Classificação de anos secos e chuvosos na região Nordeste do Brasil e sua distribuição espacial. In: CONGRESSO BRASILEIRO DE METEOROLOGIA, 3., Belo Horizonte. Anais...Rio de Janeiro: SBMet, 1984.

Zhai, P.; Zhang, X.; Wan, H. and Pan, X. Trends in Total Precipitation and Frequency of Daily Precipitation Extremes over China. *Journal of climate*, v. 18, p. 1096-1108, 2005.

In: Rainfall: Behavior, Forecasting and Distribution ISBN: 978-1-62081-551-9
Editors: Olga E. Martn and Tricia M. Roberts

Chapter 10

Kalman Filtering Approach in the Calibration of Radar Rainfall Data - A Comparative Analysis of State Space Representations

Marco A. S. Costa[1]*, ***Magda S. V. Monteiro***[2] ***and A. Manuela Gonçalves***[3]
[1] Escola Superior de Tecnologia e Gestão de Águeda,
Universidade de Aveiro, Portugal
Centro de Matemática e Aplicações Fundamentais da Universidade de Lisboa
[2] Escola Superior de Tecnologia e Gestão de Águeda,
Universidade de Aveiro, Portugal
Unidade de Investigação de Matemática e Aplicações
[3] Departamento de Matemática e Aplicações,
Universidade do Minho, Portugal
Centro de Matemática da Universidade do Minho, Portugal

Abstract

In this chapter it is presented a comparative study of some methods to estimate radar rainfall in real time. Radar rainfall estimates have a poor performance comparatively to rain gauge estimates, due to errors of either meteorological or instrumental nature. Nevertheless, weather radar presents several advantages over rain gauges, namely by providing continuous measurements in real time, which it is not possible even in a dense telemetered rain gauge network, due to the large space-time variability of precipitation. Given these advantages, several approaches have been proposed to minimize radar errors. Namely, the combination of these two types of measurements via a state space representation associated to the Kalman filter has been investigated in recent years. However, recent literature presents different state space representations, and therefore their results are not directly comparable. This work intends to discuss and compare different state space formulations based on a same data set; for instance, the comparison between the modeling of the mean field radar rainfall logarithmic bias

*E-mail address: marco@ua.pt

(Chumchean et al., 2006), a linear radar-rain gauge calibration model (Alpuim & Barbosa, 1999; Costa & Alpuim, 2011) and a power law model (Brown et al., 2001). This investigation takes into account some issues associated to the state space approach: for instance, parameters estimation, the assessment of the accuracy estimates obtained by each model. Another question worth investigating is the impact of the number of rain gauges used in the improvement of radar calibration estimates. It is useful to analyze the behavior of different state space representations associated to different rain gauge network densities. The data set consists of a set of storms between September 1998 and November 2000 in an area located around 40Km upnorth of the weather radar located in Cruz do Leão, in the Lisbon region. This region has been used in several works of the Portuguese Institute of Meteorology since this area presents the highest rain gauge density under the radar umbrella.

Keywords: Kalman filter, state space model, rainfall estimates, weather radar, calibration, nonparametric estimation

AMS Subject Classification: 60G35, 62M10, 62M05

1. Introduction

The weather radar allows the monitoring of the rainfall in area, thus constituting one of its main advantages. However, precipitation radar estimates contain errors associated with the reflectivity measurement errors or with the reflectivity rainfall rate (Z-R) conversion errors (Jordan et al., 2000). Nevertheless, even if these two sources of error have been corrected based on an understanding of the physical processes, there remain errors in the radar rainfall estimates when compared with rain gauge measurements (Chumchean et al., 2006). A suitable mechanism to reduce errors is to combine both weather radar and rain gauge network data. On the one hand, the weather radar provides precipitation data in a large area, for instance in a 300Km radial distance from the radar (Figure 1). On the other hand, a rain gauge network gives accurate point measurements in its location. The differences between radar and rain gauges are understandable because these are two different types of rainfall measuring sensors.

There are several ways to tackle with radar estimates bias when compared with accurate rain gauge estimates. Krajewski (1987) and Severino & Alpuim (2005) apply an optimal interpolation method based on Kriging and CoKriging. An alternative way to merge the radar and rain gauge measurements is to relate the two types of measurements through a state space representation associated to the Kalman filter algorithm. In this chapter it is performed a discussion of three models based on the Kalman filter framework. Chumchean et al. (2006) formulated a model with the assumption-which was also considered in Anagnostou et al. (1998) and Krajewski & Smith (2002)-that radar errors produce a uniform bias in radar rainfall estimation when compared to rain gauge data. Brown et al. (2001) proposed a single-site modeling approach with a power law model to describe the relationship between gauge and radar data, which needs a linearization procedure with the logarithmic function. Alpuim & Barbosa (1999) and Costa & Alpuim (2011) used a multiplicative calibration factor model. Whereas Alpuim & Barbosa (1999) compared the mean area prediction in a univariate and multivariate point of view, Costa & Alpuim (2010) evaluated the models

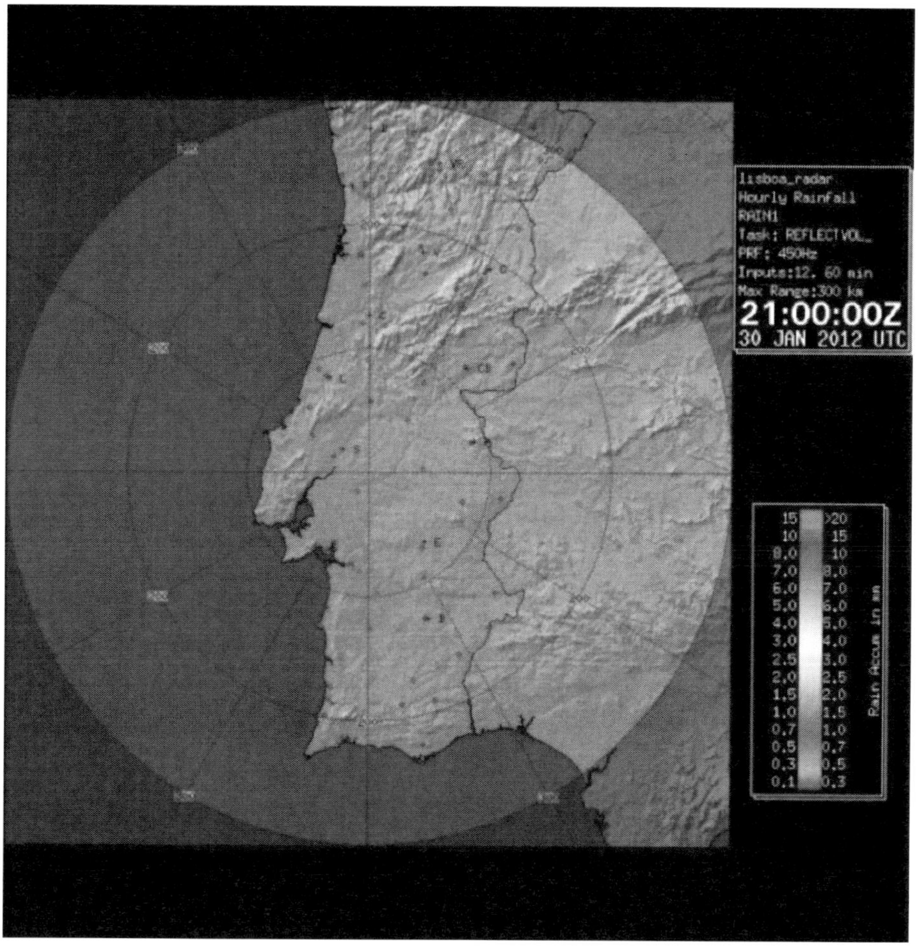

Figure 1. Radar umbrella of the weather radar located in Cruz do Leão, Coruche, Portugal.

performance when its parameters are estimated by Gaussian likelihood and nonparametric estimators.

The comparison of the three models is achieved based on a single data set. However, the data set is divided in two subsets: one for the parameters estimation and the remaining data for the assessment procedure. The parameter estimation is performed by using the nonparametric estimators suggested in Costa & Alpuim (2010), which had achieved good results in the radar calibration (Costa & Alpuim, 2011).

2. Kalman Filtering Approach

The Kalman filtering approach has the main advantage of providing a real-time scheme to calibrate radar rainfall estimates based on rain gauge measurements. This algorithm is an iterative procedure to update unknown stochastic variables predictions taking into account the observed variables at each time, and provides an estimate of the error variance in the computed prediction. This potential has encouraged the application of the Kalman filter techniques in the radar rainfall estimates calibration in several forms. For simplicity, in this chapter the modeling procedure of the relation between rain gauge and radar estimates of the precipitation is based on a single site modeling approach associated to interpolation methods, if needed.

2.1. State space models and the Kalman filter

The Kalman filter (Kalman, 1960) is applied to a class of models that admits a state space representation. In this chapter, it will be considered, in general, the state space representation as follows

$$A_t = \beta_t B_t + e_t \tag{1}$$

$$\beta_t = \mu + \phi(\beta_{t-1} - \mu) + \varepsilon_t. \tag{2}$$

Equation (1) is called the measurement equation and relates the observable variable A_t with the unobservable variable β_t, called the state. The coefficient B_t is known and e_t is a white noise, called the measurement error, with variance σ_e^2. Furthermore, the state β_t varies in time according to Eq. (2), the transition or state equation, i.e., a stationary AR(1) process with mean μ. Here, ϕ is an autoregressive coefficient, $|\phi| < 1$, and ε_t is a white noise with variance σ_ε^2. The disturbances e_t and ε_t are assumed to be uncorrelated, that is, $E(e_t\varepsilon_s) = 0$, for all t and s. The model (1)-(2) can be seen as a dynamic linear regression where the slope is an AR(1) process.

Notice also that no assumption is made about the errors distributions. Indeed, it is usual to consider the model (1)-(2) as a standard linear Gaussian state space time series model, that is, the errors e_t and ε_t follow Gaussians distributions. However, in general precipitation data deviates from the normal curve. Moreover, in Brown et al. (2001) it is indicated that the distribution of residuals is somewhat longer tailed than the normal distribution, which reinforces that the assumption of the normality of the errors may not be a good choice. Alternatively, in this chapter, are considered nonparametric estimators for the parameters, following the work of Costa & Alpuim (2010).

Assuming that parameters of a state-space model are known, the Kalman filter recursions give the best linear predictors to filter, forecast, and smoothing the prediction of vector of states. Let $\widehat{\beta}_{t|t-1}$ represent the predictor of β_t based on the information up to time $t-1$ and let $P_{t|t-1}$ be its mean square error (MSE). As the orthogonal projection is a linear estimator, the predictor for the observable at time t, A_t, is given by

$$\widehat{A}_{t|t-1} = B_t \widehat{\beta}_{t|t-1}.$$

When, at time t, A_t is available, the prediction error or innovation, $\eta_t = A_t - \widehat{A}_{t|t-1}$, is used to update the estimate of A_t, through the equation

$$\widehat{\beta}_{t|t} = \widehat{\beta}_{t|t-1} + K_t \eta_t$$

where K_t is called the Kalman gain matrix and is given by

$$K_t = P_{t|t-1} A_t \left(A_t^2 P_{t|t-1} + \sigma_e^2\right)^{-1}.$$

Furthermore, the MSE of the update predictor $\widehat{\beta}_{t|t}$ verifies the relationship

$$P_{t|t} = P_{t|t-1} - K_t A_t P_{t|t-1}.$$

In turn, at time t, the forecast for the state vector β_{t+1} is given by the equation

$$\widehat{\beta}_{t+1|t} = \mu + \phi(\widehat{\beta}_{t|t} - \mu)$$

with MSE $P_{t+1|t} = \phi^2 P_{t|t} + \sigma_\epsilon^2$. The recursive process needs initial values for the state $\beta_{1|0}$ and for its variance $P_{1|0}$, which in this case, as the state process is assumed to be a stationary AR(1) process, it is given by

$$\widehat{\beta}_{1|0} = \mu \text{ and } P_{1|0} = \sigma_\beta^2 = \frac{\sigma_\varepsilon^2}{1-\phi^2}.$$

2.2. Models

In this chapter are considered three models to perform the radar rainfall estimates calibration proposed in the Kalman filtering approach literature. Although the three models are real-time procedures based on Kalman filter recursions, different models are taken into consideration to relate rain gauges and radar measurements. The next sections briefly present the models as well as their assumptions.

2.2.1. Linear calibration (LC)

Alpuim & Barbosa (1999) and Costa & Alpuim (2010) proposed a state space representation that relates rain gauges and radar measurements by a multiplicative factor of calibration between these two estimates, as follows

$$\begin{aligned} G_t &= \beta_t R_t + e_t \\ \beta_t &= \mu + \phi(\beta_{t-1} - \mu) + \varepsilon_t \end{aligned}$$

where G_t is the rain gauge observation in time t, R_t is the radar measurement at the same time and location, and β_t is the corresponding calibration factor for each pair of values. The model has the assumptions of the general model (1)-(2), with the necessary adaptations. This formulation assumes a local linear relation between radar and rain gauge estimates since it is considered, for each time, that rain gauge measurement is proportional to radar observation added to an error.

The linear calibration model has the advantage of not presenting restrictions to the radar and rain gauge measurements, that is, it can be formulated even in the cases when radar or rain gauges present null estimates. As will be seen later on, other models present this type of restriction.

As the modeling procedure is the single-site approach, it will be necessary to interpolate the predicted calibration factors β_t to other sites where it is intended to correct radar measurements.

2.2.2. Mean field radar rainfall logarithmic bias modeling (FB)

The second model, designated by mean field radar rainfall logarithm bias, was proposed in Chumchean et al. (2006) and is based on the assumption that there is a consistent bias between radar and rain gauge measurements. This assumption is supported by Austin (1987), who concludes that when the radar adjustment schemes force agreement at a few gauges sites these are inappropriate due to large random discrepancies between radar and gauge measurements as a result of sampling errors. However, Costa & Alpuim (2010), in a comparative analysis between one calibration factor and a single site approach, concluded that the single site approach produces better results (minimum mean square error).

Assuming that is reasonable to admit a single bias, Chumchean et al. (2006) defined the mean field radar rainfall logarithmic bias at time t as

$$\beta_t = \frac{1}{k}\sum_{i=1}^{k}\log_{10}\left(\frac{G_{i,t}}{R_{i,t}}\right) \tag{3}$$

where k is the number of radar-gauge pairs data available in time t, and $G_{i,t}$ and $R_{i,t}$ are the rainfall and unfiltered radar rainfall at time t at location i. The temporal evolution of the logarithmic mean field bias is modeled through the state space model

$$Y_t = \beta_t + e_t \tag{4}$$

$$\beta_t = \mu + \phi(\beta_{t-1} - \mu) + \varepsilon_t. \tag{5}$$

where Y_t is the observed mean field logarithmic bias at time t and is computed by Eq. (3). While in the original work of Chumchean et al. (2006) the state β_t is taken as a stationary AR(1) process with zero mean, in this chapter this assumption is not considered, since it seems that there is no reason for imposing a zero mean for the state process, therefore it is considered the mean μ. Indeed, if the state with zero mean is imposed, it would imply admitting that the ratios G/R are, in average, equal to one, that is, $G = R$. However, as is largely accepted, in general the weather radar underestimates precipitation intensity. The model (4)-(5) assumes that both radar and gauges measurements are nonzero due to the logarithmic function.

2.2.3. Power law modelling (PL)

Brown et al. (2001) make the assumption that the relationship between gauge and radar reflectance measurements can be described by a power law, as previously mentioned in Collinge & Young (1993),

$$G_t = bR_t^a \tag{6}$$

In a first proposition, Brown et al. (2001) consider a linearization of Eq. (6) where the parameters a and b are not necessarily fixed quantities but may vary stochastically over time. That is,

$$\begin{aligned} Y_t &= \alpha_t U_t + \beta_t + e_t \\ \alpha_t &= \mu_\alpha + \phi_\alpha(\alpha_{t-1} - \mu_\alpha) + \varepsilon_{\alpha,t} \\ \beta_t &= \mu_\beta + \phi_\beta(\beta_{t-1} - \mu_\beta) + \varepsilon_{\beta,t} \end{aligned}$$

where $Y_t = \log_{10}(G_t)$, $U_t = \log_{10}(R_t)$ and e_t is a white noise error. However, Brown et al. (2001) concluded that the prediction intervals on the parameter α remain quite wide most of the time, suggesting that it is poorly identified; therefore, they treated this parameter as if it is constant.

Thus, in this chapter will be taken the model

$$\begin{aligned} Y_t &= \alpha U_t + \beta_t + e_t \\ \beta_t &= \mu + \phi(\beta_{t-1} - \mu) + \varepsilon_t \end{aligned}$$

where α is previously estimated by the method of least squares as the slope of the usual linear regression between Y_t and U_t. As this approach is a single-site modeling procedure, it also needs interpolation methods to calibrate radar estimates in other sites.

2.3. Estimation of the parameters

As mentioned before, the estimation of the parameters is performed by nonparametric estimators based on the method of moments, which does not assume any distribution for the errors. Costa & Alpuim (2010) proposed consistent estimators for the parameters of the model (1)-(2) whose performance was compared to the usual maximum likelihood estimators considering Gaussian errors in a Monte Carlo study. The nonparametric estimators presented a good performance even when errors were simulated with normal distribution. It is possible to obtain the maximum likelihood estimates by maximizing the log-likelihood function in order to estimate unknown parameters by using numerical methods, namely the EM algorithm (Shumway & Stoffer, 1982), or the Newton-Raphson algorithm (Harvey, 1996). However, the maximum likelihood method may not converge at all and produces estimates that fall outside the parameters space more frequently than the non-parametric estimators, particularly for small values of the autoregressive coefficient (Costa & Alpuim, 2010).

The estimation of the mean μ of the state process $\{\beta_t\}$ is performed as the average of the ratios A_t/B_t, that is

$$\widehat{\mu} = \frac{1}{n}\sum_{t=1}^{n}\frac{A_t}{B_t}.$$

The remaining parameters of the state process $\{\beta_t\}$ are estimated based on the autocovariance structure of an AR(1) stationary process. Indeed, if $\{\beta_t\}$ follows an AR(1) stationary process, it verifies the recursive equation $\gamma_k = \phi\gamma_{k-1}$, for any $k \geqslant 2$, where γ_k is the autocovariance function, whose empirical estimator is

$$\widehat{\gamma}_k = \frac{1}{n}\sum_{t=1}^{n-k}\left(\frac{A_{t+k}}{B_{t+k}} - \widehat{\mu}\right)\left(\frac{A_t}{B_t} - \widehat{\mu}\right).$$

The estimator for the autoregressive parameter ϕ is obtained by the least square method taking into account the autocovariances $\widehat{\gamma}_k$, with $k = 1, ..., \ell$, that is, considering $\ell - 1$ equations of the form $\gamma_k = \phi\gamma_{k-1}$, which produce the estimator

$$\widehat{\phi} = \sum_{k=2}^{\ell}\widehat{\gamma}_k\widehat{\gamma}_{k-1}\left(\sum_{k=2}^{\ell}\widehat{\gamma}_k^2\right)^{-1}.$$

The choice of ℓ depends on sample dimension, as proposed in Costa & Alpuim (2010). Notice that $\{\beta_t\}$ is an AR(1) stationary process, so the noise variance in the state equation

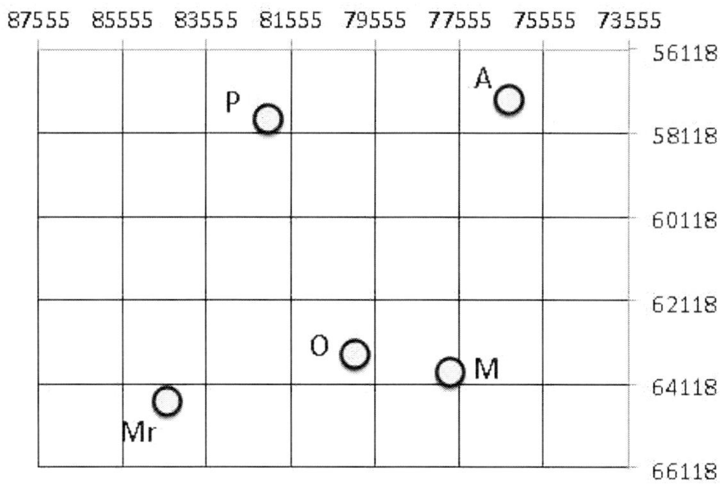

Figure 2. Location of the five rain gauges in the Portuguese system of coordinates and in the grid of 35 cells used in this chapter.

σ_ε^2 is estimated using the explicit formula

$$\widehat{\sigma}_\varepsilon^2 = \frac{1-\widehat{\phi}^2}{\widehat{\phi}}\widehat{\gamma}_1.$$

The variance of the measurement equation is done by using the relationship $var(A_t/B_t) = \sigma_\beta^2 + B_t^{-2}\sigma_e^2$, where $\sigma_\beta^2 = \frac{\sigma_\varepsilon^2}{1-\phi^2}$, that produces the estimator

$$\widehat{\sigma}_e^2 = \left[\sum_{t=1}^{n}\left(\frac{A_t}{B_t} - \widehat{\mu}\right)^2 - n\widehat{\sigma}_\beta^2\right]\left(\sum_{t=1}^{n} B_t^{-2}\right)^{-1}.$$

3. Comparative Study

The models have been proposed in the literature accompanied by case studies to illustrate their benefits and advantages. However, as in each case is used a different data set, it is not possible to compare their performances. In this chapter it is performed a modeling work based on a data set of radar and gauge estimates, where the three models above described are applied. This approach allows to compare the performances of these models based on the same data and with the same conditions, namely, the same density gauge/Km^2.

3.1. Experiment description

The models comparison is done considering a data set of 17 stratiform storms between September 1998 and November 2000 (in a total of 178 hourly precipitation estimates) in a 10×14 Km^2 area (Figure 2), including the Alenquer River basin, located around 40 Km north of Lisbon and between 31 and 44 Km of distance from the weather radar in Cruz do Leão. This area has been studied by meteorologists of the Institute of Meteorology of

Table 1. Descriptive statistics of radar and rain gauges data in the five locations

descriptives	Rain gauges					Radar				
	Mr	M	O	P	A	Mr	M	O	P	A
average	1.60	1.45	1.51	1.64	1.60	1.06	0.95	0.95	0.91	1.04
median	1.00	0.85	1.05	1.00	1.00	0.52	0.45	0.50	0.43	0.49
std. deviation	1.78	1.73	1.62	1.86	1.72	1.48	1.22	1.24	1.25	1.34
kurtosis	5.67	6.69	4.32	4.03	2.96	10.61	4.68	6.08	8.02	5.10
skewness	2.03	2.27	1.91	1.89	1.61	2.88	2.07	2.28	2.58	2.12

Portugal due to the fact that there are five rain gauges located in this area: Merceana (Mr), Meca (M), Olhalvo (O), Penedos (P) and Abrigada (A). These rain gauges correspond to a reasonable high density ($\sim$ 1 gauge/28Km^2) and present the highest gauge density under the radar umbrella. Furthermore, this area is associated to a very low concentration time (about 3 h), which makes this region particularly prone to flash floods, making it especially appropriated to study models. Since about 90% of the region is below 400 m, it might be considered homogeneous from the point of view of the climatology of precipitation, and it was not deemed necessary to explicitly correct the orography effect on the precipitation values (Alpuim & Barbosa, 1999).

Previous works in this area have considered smaller or larger areas (Alpuim & Barbosa, 1999; Severino & Alpuim, 2005; Costa & Alpuim, 2011) but without significant differences in the area size. This small river basin, prone to flash floods and intensively instrumented, was selected for studies of precipitation measurement by radar, as well as for other hydrometeorological and hydrological studies and for testing different hydrological models by using radar data (Rossa et al., 2005). Costa & Alpuim (2011) used this data set in order to compare the impact between the nonparametric estimator and the Gaussian maximum likelihood estimators in view of the area rainfall estimation. As usual in this type of studies, the radar resolution is 2×2 Km; however, the nominal resolution of the radar is 1×1 Km that was transformed in the resolution 2×2 Km. The radar and rain gauge estimates were converted to hourly measurements, in this case to each cell of 2×2 Km.

The available data from Cruz do Leão weather radar was collected in an important period time testing since this radar was installed in 1995. Therefore, it is expected to observe a significant variability in this initial period of the radar's work.

Table 1 shows the main descriptive statistics of radar and gauges measurements. In a preliminary analysis, it is clear that radar measurements underestimate, since radar samples have lower averages than the respective gauge averages. Another relevant conclusion from Table 1 is the confirmation that the precipitation data is not Gaussian distributed. Indeed, the sample kurtosis and skewness clearly deviated from the excepted Gaussian values for these statistics. On the other hand, the same conclusion is achieved through the analysis of the histograms, Q-Q plots and Kolmogorov-Smirnov test, which are omitted for simplicity.

Additionally, Figure 3 shows the boxplots of gauge and radar measurements, ratios G_t/R_t and $\log_{10}(G_t/R_t)$. The transformation of ratios G_t/R_t through the logarithmic function clearly normalized data; however, as it will be mentioned later on, the model based on this procedure does not produce the best results. As expected, the data set has several outliers, which is very common in this type of data. Only the severe outliers were

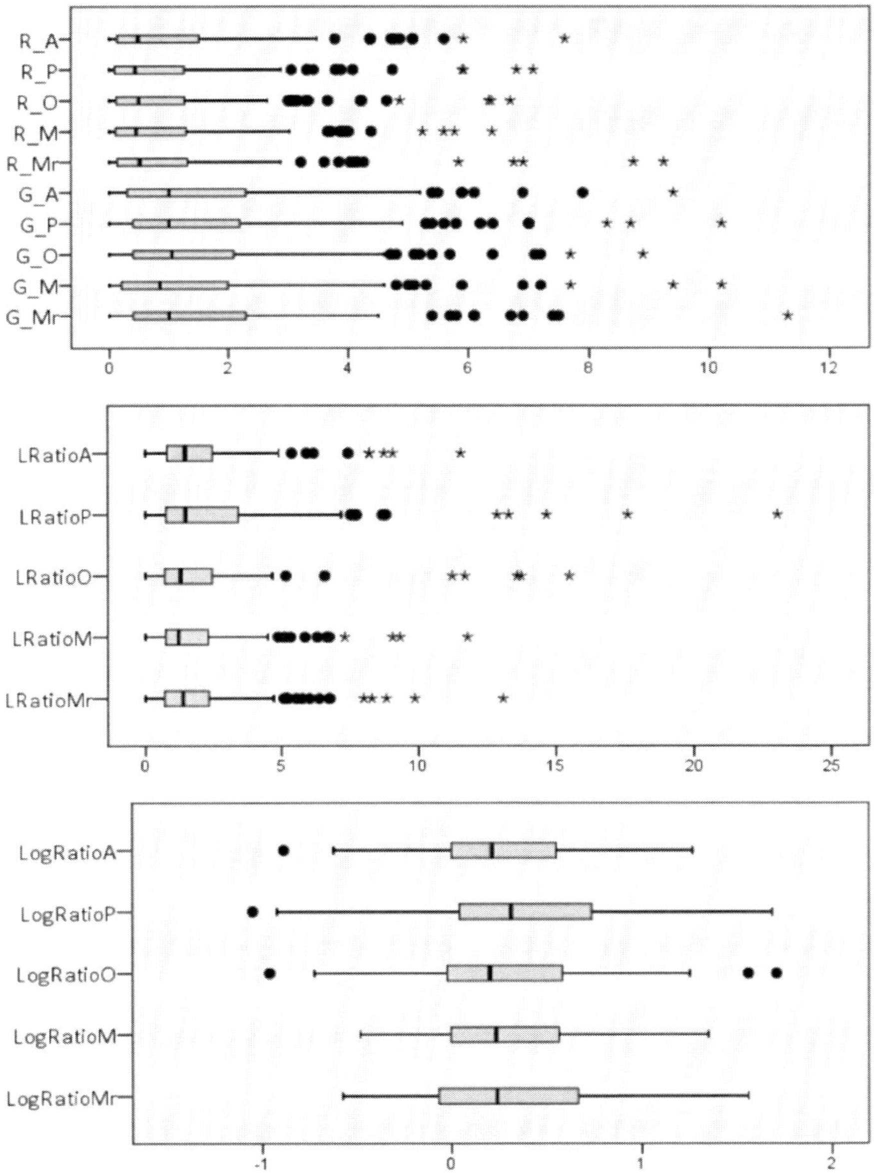

Figure 3. (Top) Boxplots of radar (R) and gauges (G) measurements of the precipitation in the five locations with rain gauges; (Center) Boxplots of linear ratios (LRatios) G_t/R_t; (Bottom) Boxplots of the $\log_{10}(G_t/R_t)$ values.

not considered in the parameters estimation procedure because they may distort their estimates. Nevertheless, the remaining outliers were kept because they are important, mainly to estimate correctly the variances of the errors.

In order to ensure the independence between parameters estimation and the calibration modeling, three storms occurred in January 13, April 28 and October 19, 2000 (62 hours) are used to estimate the models parameters, while the remaining storms are used in the assessment of calibration performance. The calibration performances of the three models

Table 2. Combination of rain gauges considered for each number of rain gauges taken in the calibration procedure

number of rain gauges					
1	2		3		4
Mr	MrM	MP	MrMO	MrPA	MOPA
M	MrO	MA	MrMP	MOP	MrOPA
O	MrP	OP	MrMA	MOA	MrMPA
P	MrA	OA	MrOP	MPA	MrMOA
A	MO	PA	MrOA	OPA	MrMOP

are compared in a set of scenarios considering 1, 2, 3 or 4 rain gauges to calibrate the radar estimates in the remaining gauges not used in the parameters estimation procedure. Table 2 shows all scenarios considered in the calibration procedure.

3.2. Models specification

Before the prediction of the calibrated radar estimates, it is necessary to fit each of the three models to the data relatively to the five locations where the rain gauges are located. This adjustment is performed by using only the three storms mentioned above in order to separate the parameters estimation from the radar calibration procedure.

Notice that, as it was previously seen, precipitation data is usually not normally distributed. This puts the assumption of normality into question if it is intended to obtain Gaussian maximum likelihood estimates. Furthermore, the data set used in this chapter consists of a set of disjoint storms with a short length in general. This data structure is not the most suitable structure to implement numerical algorithms since, in practice, the log-likelihood is the sum of log-likelihood of small samples, which may also contain missing values. Thus, the selected nonparametric estimators seem to be adequate for this type of data because they are less influenced by missing values or by non-sequential data. Hence, the nonparametric estimators for the state equation's parameters are constructed on the lags of observations: for instance, the autocovariance γ_k is computed based on the observed lags k, which may not present the same number of observations than the other γ_s.

Table 3 presents the parameters estimates for the single site models of each of the three models. Notice that it was followed the suggestion of Costa & Alpuim (2010) to choose ℓ, in this case $\ell = 15$, since the storms are very short. Both LC and FB models confirm that, in average, radar measurements are lower than gauges estimates, but in a different magnitude. It is possible to analyze and interpret the estimates of averages μ in models LC and FB. These estimates can be compared approximately if the conversion of the estimate of μ of the model FB is performed as 10^{μ}. By performing this conversion, the results are 1.406, 1.285, 1.211, 1.268 and 1.396, respectively, which represent that model FB tends to produce lower calibration factors between G_t and R_t than LC model, that is, the first model is more conservative.

The LC model presents an advantage in the interpretation of errors variance. Indeed, the variance σ_e^2 can be interpreted as the variability associated to the rain gauge, while the variance σ_ε^2 can be interpreted as a component of the variability associated to the radar. Con-

Table 3. Parameters estimates for the single-site models for each of the three models LC, FB and PL

model	LC				FB			
gauge	μ	ϕ	σ_ε^2	σ_e^2	μ	ϕ	σ_ε^2	σ_e^2
Mr	1.76	0.608	0.863	0.00372	0.148	0.247	0.0640	0.0619
M	1.43	0.691	0.229	0.00112	0.109	0.751	0.0098	0.0940
O	1.33	0.505	0.187	0.00112	0.083	0.485	0.0078	0.0917
P	1.63	0.657	0.650	0.01110	0.103	0.552	0.0335	0.1192
A	1.53	0.768	0.325	0.00126	0.145	0.714	0.0093	0.0599

model	PL				
gauge	α	μ	ϕ	σ_ε^2	σ_e^2
Mr	0.695	0.116	0.172	0.0418	0.0643
M	0.660	0.123	0.866	0.0129	0.0735
O	0.662	0.078	0.609	0.0066	0.0819
P	0.235	0.175	0.591	0.0561	0.0611
A	0.712	0.158	0.576	0.0239	0.0356

sidering this interpretation, the errors variances estimates obtained in the LC model indicate that the rain gauges located in Merceana (Mr) and Penedos (P) have the highest variability. This is possibly due to the fact that these two rain gauges are of the bascule type, while the remaining gauges are of the syphon type. The models residuals were analyzed in order to perform a diagnostic checking of the models adjustment. As it is assumed that errors are a white noise process, both autocorrelations (ACF) and partial autocorrelations (PACF) functions were drawn. For instance, Figure 4 shows samples ACF and PACF functions for the Abrigada rain gauge. In general, samples ACF and PACF functions have the expected behaviour of a white noise with no significant serial correlation, which validates this initial assumption. On the other hand, this check supports that the nonparametric estimators are proper to this type of data.

3.3. Calibration procedure

The radar calibration procedure focus on the remaining fourteen storms not used in the parameter estimation (116 hourly measurements). The calibration procedure in the scenarios with more than one rain gauge requires the interpolation of its calibration factors to other locations. The FB model does not need interpolation procedures since it assumes a single mean field bias in the radar umbrella.

The Kalman filter equations were implemented for each scenario of Table 2 in order to predict the state β_t at each hour t. Since the aim is to consider a real-time procedure, the needed prediction is the filtered prediction of β_t, that is, $\widehat{\beta}_{t|t}$. Notice that in the beginning of each storm the Kalman filter algorithm is initialized with the initial values $\widehat{\beta}_{1|0}$ and $P_{1|0}$. For instance, Figure 5 shows the filtered calibration factors $\widehat{\beta}_{t|t}$, with the empirical pointwise intervals with semi-amplitude $\pm 2\sqrt{P_{t|t}}$ for the single-site model of Meca by using the model LC for the fourteen storms. When the calibration procedure includes only a single rain gauge, the process of extending the calibration to other location is a straightforward

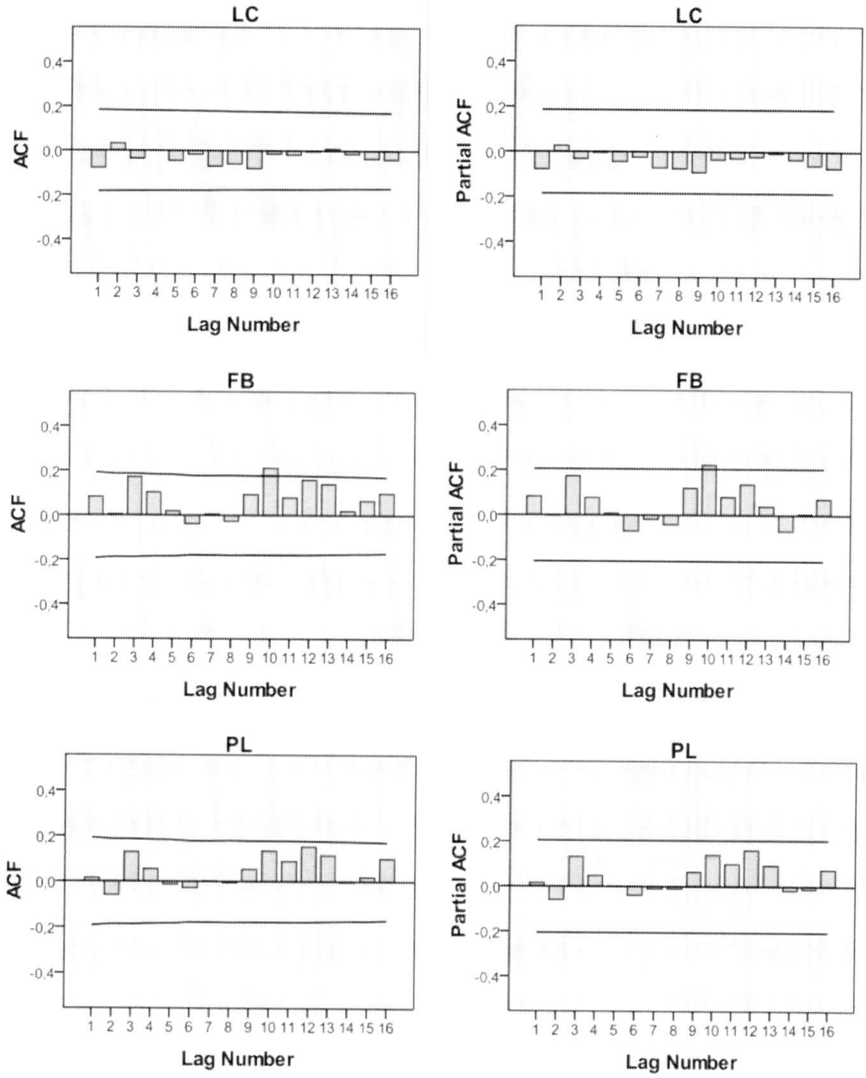

Figure 4. Estimates of autocorrelation function (ACF) and partial autocorrelation function for the rain gauge located in Abrigada.

procedure. This remains true even if the model applied is the FB, since this model assumes a single mean field bias of calibration. In this case, Chumchean et al. (2006) used the equation $B_t = 10^{\widehat{\beta}^{(FB)}_{t|t}+0.5P_{t|t}}$ to convert the predicted state $\beta^{(FB)}_t$ into B_t, which is the calibration factor used for correcting the radar measurements in other locations, that is,

$$\widehat{R}^{(FB)}_t = R_t 10^{\widehat{\beta}^{(FB)}_{t|t}+0.5P_{t|t}}.$$

In the case of model LC, the radar calibration is obtained by multiplying the radar estimate R_t by the filtered calibration factor $\widehat{\beta}^{(LC)}_{t|t}$, that is,

$$\widehat{R}^{(LC)}_t = R_t \widehat{\beta}^{(LC)}_{t|t}.$$

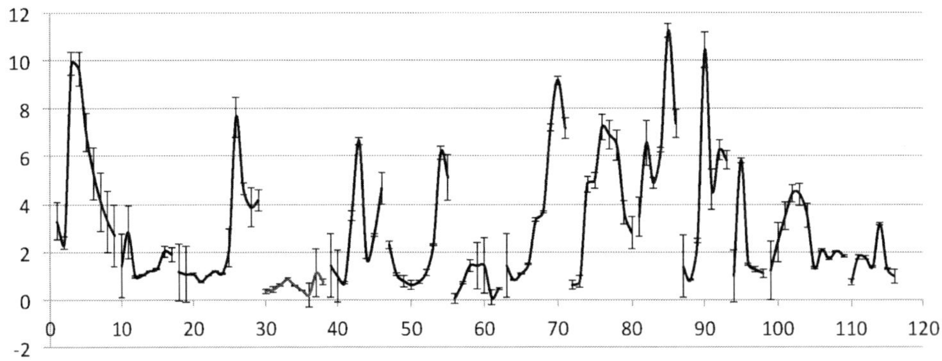

Figure 5. Calibration factors $\widehat{\beta}_{t|t}$ with the empirical pointwise intervals $\pm 2\sqrt{P_{t|t}}$ relatively to the rain gauge located in Meca using the single-site model LC.

The prediction of the states of model PL, $\beta_{t|t}^{(PL)}$ allows to obtain the radar calibration by using the expression

$$\widehat{R}_t^{(PL)} = 10^{\widehat{\beta}_{t|t}^{(PL)}} R_t^{\widehat{\alpha}}.$$

Interpolation methods are needed when the correction of radar measurements is based on more than one rain gauge and the modeling procedure assumes one of the models LC or PL. When the set of rain gauges is sufficiently representative to fit a model of spatial continuity into the spatial process of calibration factors, it is suitable to use stochastic methods of interpolation in space, as the Kriging method. However, the available data has few rain gauges to allow the adjustment of spatial continuity models. In the literature there are several alternative methods such as the Thiessen polygons, the multiquadratic interpolation or the inverse square distance methods (for instance, Haberlandt, 2007; Babak & Deutsch, 2008). In this case it is considered the inverse square distance method, which takes into consideration all available rain gauges to calibrate radar estimates. In this method, the estimate of the surface function $f(\cdot)$ in a point s_0, knowing the function in the points s_i, with i =1, 2,..., k, is the weighted average.

$$\widehat{f}(s_0) = \frac{\sum_{i=1}^{k} d^{-2}(s_0, s_i) f(s_i)}{\sum_{i=1}^{k} d^{-2}(s_0, s_i)}$$

where $d(s_0, s_i)$ is the Euclidian distance between the points s_0 and s_i.

3.4. Models performance assessment

The models performance assessment is done according to the empirical square root of the mean square error of point prediction by using the fourteen storms data (116 hourly observations) kept for this purpose. That is, for each gauge not used in the calibration procedure, it is compared the gauge rainfall estimates G_t with the calibrated radar cell measurement

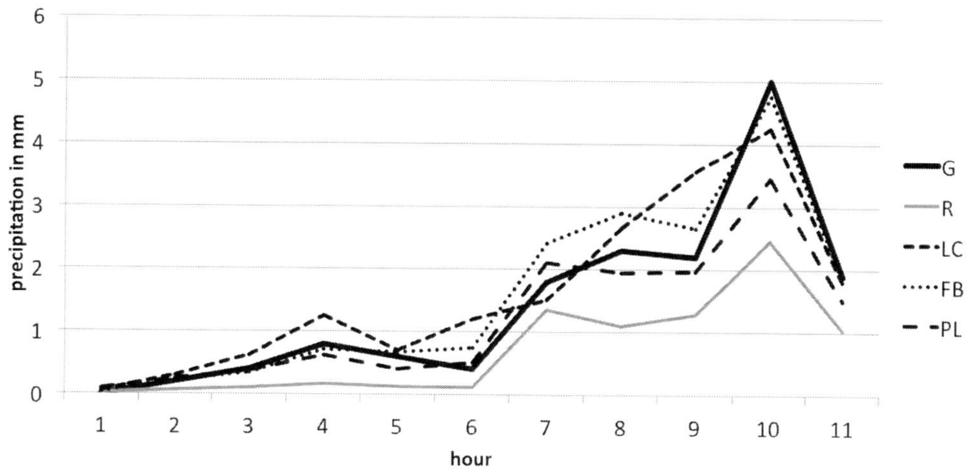

Figure 6. Validation rain gauge of Meca calibrated using Olhalvo and Abrigada gauges for the storm of November 2, 2000.

Table 4. Comparing square roots of the empirical mean square errors of the three models. In brackets is indicated the % of RMSE reduction in comparison to the reference value

number of rain gauges	Model LC	FB	PL
1	1.38 (-3%)	1.30 (-9%)	1.19 (-16%)
2	1.21 (-16%)	1.23 (-14%)	1.10 (-23%)
3	1.16 (-19%)	1.16 (-19%)	1.11 (-22%)
4	1.09 (-23%)	1.07 (-25%)	1.11 (-22%)
global	1.21 (-15%)	1.19 (-16%)	1.13 (-21%)

$\widehat{R}_t^{(m)}$, with m = LC, FB and PL, at the same location. As there are five rain gauges available in the area under study, it is considered systems with 1, 2, 3 or 4 gauges for the calibration process, and for each of these schemes is computed the empirical square root of the mean square error for all combination of each number of gauges.

The empirical square root of the mean square error $\mathrm{RMSE}_k^{(m)}$ for the scheme modeled based on k rain gauges with the model m is computed by

$$\mathrm{RMSE}_k^{(m)} = \sqrt{\frac{1}{116(5-k)} \sum_{i=1}^{5-k} \sum_{t=1}^{116} \left(G_t^i - \widehat{R}_t^{(m),i} \right)^2}.$$

Table 4 compares the square roots of the empirical MSE between the three models by considering different numbers of rain gauges in the calibration process. The pre-calibration RMSE of the five rain gauges is taken as the reference value to analyze the impact of the calibration procedures. For the data set under the calibration procedure (the fourteen events) this value is 1.43. Thereby, it is possible to compare the models performance in view of the percentage of the reference value reduction (indicated in Table 4 in brackets). These results have to be interpreted as a global measure of the models performance since these values do not take into consideration the relative position of both rain gauges of calibration and calibrated radar predictions.

It can be stated that the models lead to a significant reduction in the error of the radar estimates of precipitation. However, an interesting conclusion that may be drawn is that the model PL is less sensitive to the number of rain gauges used in the calibration process. RMSE of both models LC and FB decrease significantly when more gauges are added to the calibration process. When the rain gauge density is the lowest (1 gauge per 140Km^2) the PL model performed the largest RMSE reduction with a strong difference to other models. On the other hand, when the higher density (1 gauge per 35Km^2) is considered, the models present similar performances. Nevertheless, the FB model produces the greatest RMSE reduction.

4. Conclusion

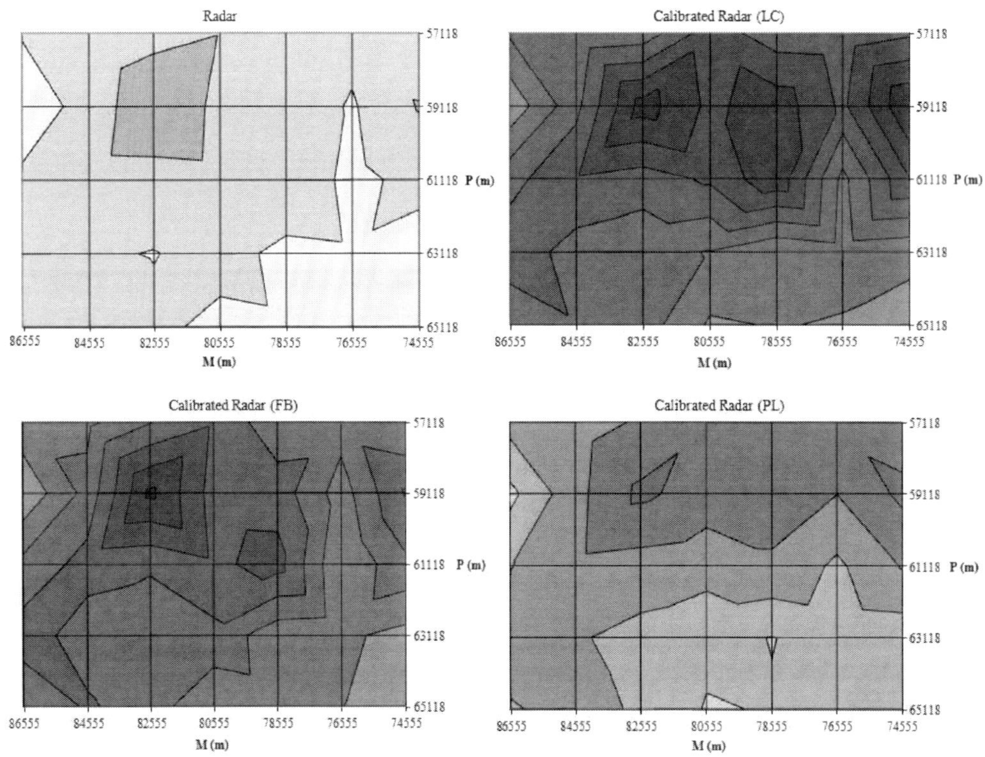

Figure 7. Accumulated precipitation isopleths, in mm, for the storm of November 2, 2000 for the radar non calibrated estimates and for the calibrated estimates considering the five rain gauges and the three models LC, FB and PL.

It can be stated that the Kalman filter approach with any of the three models leads to a significant reduction of point estimation of the precipitation. The state space models employed in this approach, have shown to be a useful tool in the improvement of radar data accuracy. The combination of the two sensors (radar and rain gauges) allows conjugating the advantage of the area estimation of the radar with the accuracy of the point prediction of the rain gauges.

The primary objective in this chapter has been to provide a fair comparison between three alternative models that have been applied in the calibration radar estimates of precipitation by using the Kalman filter algorithm. Taking a single data set in the modeling process for all models allows to assess the models performances with equal conditions. Both the linear calibration model and the mean field radar rainfall logarithmic bias model were more sensitive to gauge density. These models performances have improved with the increase in the number of gauges in the calibration procedure. On the other hand, the performance of the power law model was smoother as the gauge density was increased. Figure 7 illustrates the radar calibration based on the accumulated precipitation of one storm by using all available rain gauges in the area.

In summary, the use of state space models associated to the Kalman filter algorithm is an efficient approach to increase the accuracy of weather radar estimates. Moreover, this approach may be implemented in a real-time scheme where models are established based on an independent data set of the calibration process, which continues to develop as new data is available.

Acknowledgments

Marco Costa was partially supported by Fundação para a Ciência e a Tecnologia, PEst OE/MAT/UI0209/2011. A. Manuela Gonçalves was partially financed by FEDER Funds through "Programa Operacional Factores de Competitividade – COMPETE" and by Portuguese Funds through FCT - "Fundação para a Ciência e a Tecnologia", within the Project Est-C/MAT/UI0013/2011. Magda Monteiro was partially supported by *FEDER* funds through *COMPETE*–Operational Programme Factors of Competitiveness ("Programa Operacional Factores de Competitividade") and by Portuguese funds through the *Center for Research and Development in Mathematics and Applications* (University of Aveiro) and the Portuguese Foundation for Science and Technology ("FCT–Fundação para a Ciência e a Tecnologia"), within project PEst-C/MAT/UI4106/2011 with COMPETE number FCOMP-01-0124-FEDER-022690.

References

[1] Alpuim T. & Barbosa S. (1999). The Kalman filter in the estimation of area precipitation. *Environmetrics*, 10:377-394.

[2] Anagnostou, E.N. & Krajewski, W.F. (1998). Calibration of the WSR-88D precipitation processing system. *Weather Forecasting*, 13:396-404.

[3] Austin, P. (1987). Relation between measured radar reflectivity and surface rainfall. *Monthly Weather Review*, 115: 1053-1071.

[4] Babak, O. & Deutsch C.V. (2008). Statistical approach to inverse distance interpolation. *Environmental Research and Risk Assessment*, 23: 543-553.

[5] Brown M., Diggle P., Lord M. & Young P. (2001). Space-Time Calibration of Radar Rainfall Data. *Journal of the Royal Statistical Society, Series C (Applied Statistics)*, 50(2):221-241.

[6] Chumchean S., Seed A. & Sharma A. (2006). Correcting of real-time radar rainfall bias using a Kalman filtering approach. *Journal of Hydrology*, 317:123-137.

[7] Collinge V.K. & Young P.C. (1993). The calibration of weather radars using a time series approach. In *Concise Encyclopaedia of Environmental Systems* (ed. P.C. Young), 706-710. Oxford: Pergamon.

[8] Costa M. & Alpuim T. (2010). Parameter estimation of state space models for univariate observations. *Journal of Statistical Planning and Inference*, 140: 1889-1902.

[9] Costa M. & Alpuim T. (2011). Adjustment of state space models in view of area rainfall estimation. *Environmetrics*, 22:530-540.

[10] Haberlandt, U. (2007). Geostatistical interpolation of hourly precipitation from rain gauges and radar for a large-scale extreme rainfall event. *Journal of Hydrology*, 332:144-157.

[11] Harvey, A.C. (1996). *Forecasting Structural Time Series Models and the Kalman Filter*. Cambridge University Press: Cambridge.

[12] Jordan P., Seed A. & Austin G. (2000). Sampling errors in radar estimates rainfall. *Journal of Geophysical Research*, 105(D2):2247-2257.

[13] Kalman, R.E. (1960). A new approach to linear filtering and prediction problems. *Journal of Basic Engineering, Transactions ASME*, 82(Series D):35-45.

[14] Krajewski W. (1987). Cokriging radar-rainfall and rain gauge data. *Journal of Geophysical Research*, 92(D8):9571-9580.

[15] Krajewski W.F. & Smith, J.A. (2002). Radar hydrology: rainfall estimation. *Advances in Water Resources*, 25:1387-1394.

[16] Rossa A., Bruen M., Fruehwald D., Macpherson B., Holleman I., Michelson D. & Michaelides S. (2005). Use of Radar Observations in Hydrology and NWP models. Document external project: 2005, COST 717 Final Report, EUR 21954, 292 pp, Brussels.

[17] Severino J. & Alpuim T. (2005). Spatiotemporal models in the estimation of area precipitation. *Environmetrics*, 16:773-802.

[18] Shumway R., Stoffer, D. (1982). An approach to time series smoothing and forecasting using EM algorithm. *Journal of Time Series Analysis*, 3:253-264.

INDEX

A

B

C

D

E

F

L

M

N

O

P

Q

R

S

T

U

V

W

Y

Z

Innovations in the Legal Services

PUBLICATION OF THE SCIENCE CENTER BERLIN
Volume 10
SCHRIFTEN DES WISSENSCHAFTSZENTRUMS BERLIN
Band 10

Innovations in the Legal Services

Research on Service Delivery
Volume I

Edited by
Erhard Blankenburg

Oelgeschlager, Gunn & Hain, *Publishers,* Inc.
Cambridge, Massachusetts

Verlag Anton Hain · Königstein/Ts.

International Standard Book Number. 0-89946-010-0 (U.S.A.)
3-445-01976-2 (Germany)

Library of Congress Catalog Card Number: 79-24923

Printed in the United States of America

Library of Congress Cataloging in Publication Data
Main entry under title:

Innovations in the legal services.

Bibliography: p. 251.

1. Legal services—Addresses, essays, lectures.
2. Public Interest law—Addresses, essays, lectures.
3. Legal aid—Addresses, essays, lectures.
I. Blankenburg, Erhard, 1938–
K133.Z9I56 345'.01 79-24923
ISBN 0-89946-010-0

Contents

Foreword

This is the first publication of the Science Center Berlin on research on service delivery. It is one of the Science Center's main tasks to venture into new research fields relating to urgent social and political problems. Public services are a major problem area. In the Federal Republic of Germany, as in other Western countries, the proportion of the service industries in the labor force as well as in the GNP is steadily increasing. Accordingly, the expansion of the service sector is becoming more and more subject to criticism and analysis. The criticism is primarily directed at the quantitative and qualitative expansion of services and the financial and personal resources they require. However, these evident trends must be interpreted in the wider context of social changes in highly industrialized countries. A report of the Organization for Economic Cooperation and Development (OECD), *Innovations in the Social Services,* took up this problem and encouraged research in the field.

Within the framework of the research program of the International Institute of Management at the Science Center Berlin, a number of activities were initiated in the past few years in the problem area of "service delivery." They soon went beyond the scope of single projects and became a research program in their own right. The scientists involved in these projects decided to unite their efforts with researchers at the University of Bielefeld working in

the same field; together, they formulated an integrated research program covering problems of health services, legal services, and social services. This integrated research concept may lead to the institutionalization of "service delivery" as a research priority at the Science Center Berlin.

As part of the initial research and stimulated by the above-mentioned OECD report, the Science Center held, in cooperation with the OECD, an international conference on "Innovations in Service Delivery" in the summer of 1978. I am very pleased to include these conference proceedings in our publication series; the discussion and results of this conference demonstrate the relevance of the approaches developed at the Science Center in the research field of service delivery.

Needless to say, the responsibility for the data, results and conclusions presented rests solely with the authors.

Helmut G. Meier
Secretary General
Science Center Berlin

Berlin, July 1979

Innovations in the Legal Services

Introduction

Erhard Blankenburg

Law and the legal profession are usually stereotyped as bringing stability rather than innovation to institutional structures. However, the development of legal services since the 1960s demonstrates that this stereotype is not true. In many Western industrialized countries the use of law and of litigation has undergone basic changes, initiated by the movement to provide legal aid for people with traditionally limited access to the law. The most extensive innovations have been in Great Britain, where legal aid was introduced as early as 1949 and has been growing ever since. In the United States the War on Poverty of the 1960s initiated a wave of legal advice centers and legal actions intending to help minority groups, especially those slum areas in large American cities. Lawyers were the vehicle of social change in the 1960s, and by using legal institutions that are appropriate to their skills, they have shaped the form this change has taken.

This movement has been favored by the increase in the number of lawyers that all Western industrialized countries have experienced in the last two decades. The increasing size of the legal profession and its increasing engagement in social change activities have transformed the legal profession as a result. Although this movement took different forms in each of the countries studied (according to the specific national

legal cultures), innovative forms of legal services sprang up during the 1970s in Scandinavia and the Netherlands and found imitators throughout the French-speaking countries. Like other social movements, this one is a product of both imitation effects as well as converging conditions calling for change.

Research has been an important part of this process. Studies on "legal need" in the 1960s fostered an awareness of the traditionally selective activity of lawyers. Research findings have been used to legitimize the expansion of legal services into fields that previously were the prerogative of social policy rather than legal policy. It would be hard to say, however, which came first, research into legal needs or the actual extension of legal services. Most likely, both have reinforced each other mutually. There would not have been as much interest in scientific research if there had not been some public awareness of the problem, and there would not have been such a drastic change of lawyers' self-understanding without some of the provocations of scientific findings.

This volume presents some of the discussions that are central to this remarkable legal change movement. Researchers from England, the United States, the Netherlands, and Norway assembled at the Science Center Berlin in order to help set up research on legal services in the Federal Republic of Germany as well as to confront the German legal profession with an international discussion that it has largely been unaware of until now. The contributions fell into three parts, which Cappelletti (1968) has aptly ordered into three "waves" of a social change movement:

- The first wave consisting of an attempt to provide *legal aid* to lower classes and minority groups who have so far been barred from access to the legal system
- The second wave of (predominantly American) lawyers campaigning for *public interest issues* of a much wider social spectrum
- The third wave of looking for *alternative forms of law* in order to avoid some of the dysfunctions of legalization that have been increased by the legal aid movement as well as the public interest law campaigns

In this book these contributions are presented in the form of a discussion as it took place in Berlin in June 1978. Some of the contributions were papers presented at this meeting and others were formulated in the discussion responding to the papers. I hope that the readers will find the arguments as stimulating as we did. I also hope that they will find the common thread that ran through the deliberations of our meeting. As a guide to the development of these arguments, they might use the simplified but suggestive way of ordering the discussion into three waves.

THE FIRST WAVE: LEGAL NEED RESEARCH AND THE LEGAL AID MOVEMENT

An important factor in the scientific discussion has been the international imitation effect. These contributions document some stages of this discussion. In Chapter 1, Barbara Curran presents an extensive survey on the use that Americans make of lawyers, showing that people take certain problems only to certain lawyers: those they think competent to handle the problems. The conclusions of Jon Johnsen in his survey checking on a list of problems that experts rated as being legally relevant shows the other extreme. Here the definition of "legal" is provided by the team of researchers, the survey mainly serving to find out how many of such problems do occur and how they are socially distributed. Thus, a profile of potential legal needs is defined by the researchers, based on their normative assumption about what would be "legally relevant." However, there is no empirical statement as to what conditions would have to be met either to make claimants aware of their claims or to activate them.

It is not surprising, therefore, that the policy conclusions of this research meet with heavy scepticism. For example, Griffiths challenges the normative assumptions of the "need" concept, maintaining that there is no scientific basis for concluding that noninvocation of the law implies an underlying need for it. In fact, Reifner shows that for certain socially underprivileged groups alternatives to legal action such as solidary action and preventive interest articulation might be more desirable. Both of these authors, Griffiths arguing from the point of view of positivistic separation of scientific statement and normative assumption and Reifner arguing from the point of view of certain interests, conclude that there are limits to legal action (either as a matter of fact or as a matter of desirability).

THE SECOND WAVE: PUBLIC INTEREST LAW

Arguing from the point of view of certain interests takes away some of the problems of defining "need." If legal aid teams and law centers in deprived neighborhoods lower some of the barriers to access to legal aid, they also provide a legal infrastructure for specified groups who are socially deprived. Arguing from the point of view of the interests of the socially deprived leads to a more radical strategy; that is, where traditional jurisdiction does not provide for any rights, the legal

strategy implies a drive for creating new laws and for changing the traditional jurisdiction. Therefore, recent protest movements use combined legal and political strategies, such as aiming at court decisions (especially in common law countries) while lobbying in the legislative arena at the same time and also negotiating for administrative rules or devising self-help institutions.

The "public interest law movement" in the United States provides many examples of using legal strategies, such as filing court cases, using political influence, boycotting administrative practice, or avoiding conflict by bypassing public institutions by self-organization. In contrast to legal aid policies, public interest law has not exclusively devoted its efforts to lower-class or minority interests. For example, broad-scale interests such as consumer protection or control of the medical profession are also of concern to the middle class. However, the individual consumer of industrial products or of professional services is usually not sufficiently affected to fight an issue singlehandedly against an established industry or profession. Organization of such "diffuse interests" calls for new modes of articulation through political as well as legal channels. "Public interest law firms" have found a unique way of mixing strategies. As a rule, they use public funds and foundation financing, and they also receive money from providing further education as well as a little from court work. They engage volunteers as well as young professionals, and they use the network of the professional as well as political community as much as it is accessible to them. The chapters by Joel Handler and David Trubek give examples of some of the most well-known aspects of public interest law.

Although the specific mixture of academic entrepreneurism and populist legality in American public interest law might not be transferable to European institutions, the chapter by Kees Groenendijk from Holland shows that some diffusion effects of the use of political-legal strategies can be observed in the climate of continental legal cultures if there is a propensity for institutional innovation. While we hope to increase the receptiveness for institutional innovation by scientific exchanges like ours, the likelihood for innovation in the legal services nevertheless relies on structural features of the legal profession (see Chapter 13 on the conditions restricting innovativeness in the German legal profession).

THE THIRD WAVE: LOOKING FOR ALTERNATIVE FORMS OF LAW

A quantitative factor that makes the legal profession receptive

to changes is the increase in the number of lawyers in all Western industrial countries as a result of the extension of the educational system. In addition, social change toward increasing public organization and bureaucratization has turned many areas of social self-regulation into legally controlled systems. Public interest law has had an influence on legalizing the relationship of doctors, teachers or bureaucrats to their clientele. Therefore, it is common for professionals to avoid risks and for bureaucrats to adopt rigid rules rather than use discretion. In Philippe Nonet's terms, citizens lose in responsibility of public bureaucracy what they gain in legal controls. Thus, we find a strong movement among American law-and-society scholars for delegalization in some social areas at the same time as the same academic community is effectively legalizing others. Paul Geerts provides an overview of the intellectual currents that form the "delegalization" issue—a topic that simultaneously is a contribution to the general theme of the social definition of what is perceived as "legal problems" in our societies.

The effectiveness of legal rights depends on a particular party mobilizing the law, which is mediated by institutions such as lawyers, legal aid, or legal information. The way in which institutions perform their services determines to what degree the social barriers to access to the law can be lowered. How this is achieved differs from one legal culture to another.

In surveying legal institutions in West Germany, we found the following types:

Private lawyers, whose clientele and services may differ considerably
Public counseling services
Interest groups providing legal counsel for their members, sometimes combining this service with political strategies

Depending on the legal fields, social distribution of legal needs, and the organizing ability of legal interests, the likelihood and success of these types of institutions may differ. Certainly, the Scandinavian and Anglo-Saxon countries developed a greater variety of mediating institutions than did Germany.

Nevertheless, there is a similarity in innovations in legal aid in all of the countries surveyed. In England, legal aid societies, which have developed since the late 1940s, have changed continuously. In the United States, the "War on Poverty" gave rise to a number of innovations, although some of them were short-lived. In the Scandinavian countries and the Netherlands, there was a major innovative movement in the early 1970s, whereas in the Federal Republic of Germany there has been a vivid discussion until now, but only few attempts at actual

reform. Examining foreign experiences will serve as a stimulus in this situation. This book presents contributions by social scientists as well as jurists about institutions for legal counseling as a system of organization determining the effectiveness of law and analyzing changes of social functions of the courts if innovations in the system of legal counsel are introduced.

PART I

Research into Legal Needs and the Legal Services

Chapter 1

Research on Legal Needs: Patterns of Lawyer Use and Factors Affecting Use

Barbara A. Curran

The 1960s was a period in which the attention of the legal community in the United States focused on delivery of legal services to the poor, that is, the 10 to 20 percent of the U.S. population whose annual incomes fell below the level determined by the U.S. government to be necessary for a minimal standard of living in keeping with basic "American consumption patterns." Interest in the legal needs of this segment of the population had been stimulated by two developments. The first (occurring in 1962) was the U.S. Supreme Court decision that persons accused of serious crimes were entitled to legal representation as a matter of right and, therefore, it was the responsibility of the trial court in each case to insure that counsel was provided for any person who could not afford to hire a lawyer.[1] In response to this mandate, a variety of programs were established throughout the country that made free legal counsel available to indigent accused persons.[2] The second and contemporaneous development was the introduction in 1965 of a national program for funding free legal services for the poor in civil matters. This program, created as part of President Lyndon Johnson's War on Poverty, provided massive amounts of financial aid to local legal assistance plans established to serve the civil legal needs of the poor. The result of this infusion of funds into both the criminal and civil areas was a quantum jump in the amount of free legal service available to the poverty population.[3]

The funding of these action programs was accompanied by a series of grants for research. Consistent with the objectives and priorities of the national funding program, much of the financial support, particularly in the civil area, went to research on substantive issues, such as consumer law, that would provide backup support to free legal service attorneys in serving their constituencies. Financial support was also provided, however, for research aimed at broadening understanding about the legal needs of the target population, with particular emphasis on explorations of the impact of the new and expanded legal assistance programs on such needs.[4] By the close of the 1960s a substantial, if unintegrated, body of empirical investigation into the various aspects of delivery of legal services to the poor was emerging.[5]

The concentration of effort on delivery of free service to persons below the poverty line provided a stark contrast to what was being done, planned for, or indeed even known about the legal needs of other income groups, particularly those whose incomes were only marginally above the eligibility limits established for the free programs.[6] The few empirical studies conducted before and during the 1960s that had examined legal needs of groups above the poverty level were limited in population coverage or scope of inquiry. Although some suggested the reasons for particular variations in legal need among different economic groups, none attempted a comprehensive exploration of the legal needs of the public.[7]

In 1971, work began on a general survey of the legal needs of the public. Undertaken at the American Bar Foundation, a research institute created in 1952 by the American Bar Association, the study was sponsored by a special committee of the association and was funded in part by a grant from the American Bar Endowment and in part from grants from other private foundations and groups not affiliated with the bar association.[8] In the period from October to March, 1973–1974, 2064 persons constituting a representative sample of the noninstitutionalized adult (i.e., eighteen years or older) population of the United States were surveyed. The questionnaire, administered in personal interviews averaging about one and one-half hours in length, inquired into the kinds of legal problems and situations respondents had encountered during their lives, how they had dealt with these matters, their experiences in consulting lawyers, and their perceptions and opinions about lawyers and their work, the courts, and the legal system generally. In December of 1977, the first full report on the survey results was published.[9]

One of the principal objectives of the study was to determine the extent to which private citizens consult lawyers in dealing with personal nonbusiness legal matters and to identify what factors affect the

determination to seek or not to seek the help or advice of a lawyer in such matters. In the following section, I will discuss the circumstances under which lawyers' services are utilized and in the next section after that I will examine some of the considerations that seem to shape these patterns of lawyer usage.

PATTERNS OF USE OF LAWYERS' SERVICES

Each person's life consists of myriad exchanges, interactions, and relationships, some of which are planned or expected while others are accidental or unanticipated. From time to time the individual may enlist the advice or help of someone else either in planning for, or understanding the nature of, any such process or in dealing with the process or problems that emerge from it. That most people work through the major part of life's situations without legal counsel or assistance is reflected in the fact that approximately one-quarter of U.S. citizens over forty-five years of age at the time of the survey had never consulted a lawyer, almost one-third had consulted a lawyer two or three times, and only 10 percent of this age group had consulted a lawyer more than three times.[10]

The advice or help of a lawyer is seldom sought when planning for the future. The principal exception is arranging for disposition of one's possessions and property after death. Between one-quarter and one-third of the adult population had executed a will as of the time of the survey. As might be expected, older persons were far more likely to have done so: about one-half of those over fifty-five had wills compared to about one-quarter of those between thirty-five and fifty-five and less than 10 percent of adults under thirty-four. Lawyers are almost always consulted for estate planning: 85 percent of persons with wills had sought a lawyer's help, 9 percent wrote their own wills, and only 6 percent turned to other sources of help.

Most exchanges are made, obligations entered into, and relationships established without the advice or counsel of a lawyer. Eighty-three percent of the adult population had been married at least once as of the survey date and most had not consulted a lawyer about the marriage. The same was true for the 76 percent of the population who had undertaken one or more credit obligations, the 85 percent who had rented property, and the 90 percent who had entered into an employment contract. Although individuals typically acquire most consumable goods and services in the marketplace without seeking the advice or counsel of a lawyer, a lawyer's help may well be sought when the transaction involves real property. As of the survey date, 71 percent of the adult population

had acquired real property at least once and almost 40 percent of those who had done so consulted a lawyer for the most recent acquisition. Approximately the same proportion (i.e., almost 40 percent) handled such acquisitions without enlisting any help or advice and one-quarter sought assistance from other sources.

By and large, it is only when difficulties have emerged in a relationship or problems are encountered in the course of, or as an aftermath of, an exchange or other interaction that a lawyer's advice or help is likely to be enlisted. Even in such circumstances, however, the extent to which lawyers may be consulted varies widely by the nature of the difficulty. One such circumstance in which a lawyer is likely to be contacted is when marriages terminate. About 70 percent of persons involved in divorce proceedings consulted a lawyer and about 60 percent of persons experiencing postdivorce problems associated with custody of children or with payment of support or alimony sought legal help. On the other hand, when marriage was terminated by death, only about one-third of surviving spouses enlisted the help of a lawyer. For all matters relating to marriage terminations, however, individuals who do not consult lawyers rarely seek out alternative sources of help; they simply try to handle the matter themselves or take a passive role in the proceedings.

Lawyer use is generally substantially lower for difficulties arising out of marketplace exchanges or relationships emanating from such exchanges, for example, creditor-debtor or landlord-tenant relationships. A lawyer's help is most often sought in matters where an individual's income is threatened, such as a wage garnishment by a creditor, or where real property is involved, such as a difficulty with a home builder or a problem with a real property mortgage. Between one-quarter and one-third of those with such problems consulted lawyers. On the other hand, less than 10 percent of persons involved in a dispute with a seller of consumable goods over a major purchase seek legal help. Ironically, it is these latter disputes that account for the major share of problems encountered in the marketplace. Generally speaking, the use of lawyers' services is somewhat greater when the difficulty involves an ongoing obligation by the consumer. Thus, the advice or help of a lawyer is sought in 10 percent to 20 percent of cases involving landlords and creditors. No general alternative resources emerged for problems encountered in the marketplace. Indeed, except where real property was involved or wages threatened, approximately three-quarters of the consumers either tried to handle such matters on their own without legal or other help or simply did nothing at all about such problems.

Individuals are somewhat more inclined to seek advice or help in encounters with governmental bureaucracy but such help is not

necessarily from lawyers. Although about 50 percent of those who had difficulties with governmental agencies or services sought assistance of some kind, less than 10 percent of those with complaints about municipal services (such as fire and police protection) enlisted the help of a lawyer, and only about 18 percent consulted lawyers when problems arose with other governmental agencies. Principal alternative resources used in governmental problems are, interestingly, elected officials and representatives.

The extent to which lawyer assistance is sought in claims for damage or injury arising out of chance or unpredicted encounters varies to some extent by the presence or absence of insurance coverage. One-half of the persons confronted with serious injury or property damage through the fault of someone else either sought the help of their insurer or a lawyer. For personal injury, about 35 percent consulted lawyers and 15 percent relied on insurers, while in property damage matters, 7 percent consulted lawyers and 45 percent dealt with their insurers. An even greater proportion of problem-havers seek the help of one of these two resources when a complaint is made against them by someone else.

In such cases, 20 percent of problem-havers consulted lawyers about the complaint made against them and 55 percent had their insurers handle such matters for them—a combined total of 75 percent of problem-havers.

Persons complaining of less tangible injuries like job discrimination (because of race or sex or other personal characteristics) or infringement of constitutional rights are least likely to take remedial action of any kind including even self-help measures. Only a little over one-quarter did anything at all about job discrimination problems and less than 1 percent consulted a lawyer in such matters. Just over 55 percent took any kind of action in constitutional rights matters. This was far less than was the case for most problems, in which between 70 percent and 95 percent of problem-havers took some kind of action—either on their own or with the help of lawyers. Although constitutional problems are among the most clearly "legal" problems likely to be encountered by private citizens and most people would probably agree that such problems, if they are to be dealt with at all, are most effectively handled by lawyers, it is surprising that more people did not seek legal help.

FACTORS RELATED TO LAWYER USE PATTERNS

As discussed above, lawyer use varied widely by problem type, from less than 1 percent by persons confronted with job discrimination to

85 percent for will preparation. Highest lawyer use was associated with estate planning and divorce matters. More than 50 percent of persons in such situations consulted lawyers. The level of lawyer use was, however, substantially lower for most other problems. From a high of 37 percent lawyer use for all real property matters combined, the proportion of problem-havers who consulted lawyers moves inexorably downward: 31 percent for settlement of spouse's estate, 16 percent for personal injury and property damage matters combined, 15 percent for problems with governmental agencies and services, 12 percent for difficulties arising out of the consumer transactions, and 12 percent for constitutional violations. Within each of these general problem categories there was also considerable variability in lawyer use patterns as demonstrated by consumer problems in which lawyer use ranged from 30 percent of problem-havers for wage garnishments to 7 percent for major difficulties with sellers of consumer goods.[11] In the following paragraphs I shall discuss some of the factors that seem to account for variations in lawyer use observed for different kinds of problems.

To examine why patterns of lawyer use are as they are, I begin with the premise that there is a generally shared predilection by the public not to seek advice or help from lawyers in problem solving. This general disinclination to consult lawyers is, I think, grounded in a fundamental inertia that may be accompanied in some individuals by a generally positive orientation toward lawyers and in others by a generally negative view of lawyers. The data suggest that this inertia is more likely to be disrupted for some kinds of problems than for others, and the nature of these variations indicate that the relevant factors affecting inertia are (1) the intensity of concern that the person has about the outcome of the problem and (2) the probable effectiveness of the lawyer in achieving the desired outcome at a cost reasonably related to the potential benefit.

The stake that a person has in the outcome of a legal problem is often economic. In some cases, the economic interest lies primarily in the value of the subject matter involved and in other cases it inheres in the economic impact of the problem resolution. The relatively greater use of lawyers in all matters involving real property than for problems involving consumable goods is undoubtedly related to the substantially greater value and importance placed on ownership of real property by the consumer. Another example of the significance of the value of the subject matter can be found in the use of lawyers for the settlement of a spouse's estate; only 15 percent of surviving spouses consulted a lawyer when the estate was valued at less than $5000 (excluding insurance).[12] The importance of the economic consequences of the outcome may be found in the use of lawyers for wage garnishments. The proportion of

problem-havers (30 percent) who consulted lawyers about garnishments was substantially higher than the 7 percent to 23 percent who consulted lawyers for other consumer matters.

Concern about outcome is not necessarily exclusively of economic importance. For example, only one-third of respondents in divorce proceedings were represented by counsel when there were no minor children at the time of the divorce, but 60 percent of respondents sought legal help when minor children were involved. In part, the difference between the two groups may be attributed to economics to the extent that the presence of children raised issues of postdivorce child support. But the issue is not entirely economic to the extent that basic questions about child custody are also implied. Another example of the noneconomic dimensions of an individual's concern about outcome involves evictions. Over one-half of blacks threatened with eviction by a landlord consulted a lawyer about the matter in an effort to resist the eviction compared to only 18 percent of whites who contacted a lawyer when confronted with eviction proceedings. Indeed, while almost two-thirds of whites simply moved out when served with an eviction notice, only 17 percent of blacks complied without some resistance. One possible explanation for the different behavior of the two groups in the face of possible eviction may be that fewer housing alternatives are available to blacks than to whites.

The concern of the problem-haver about outcome is not the sole determinant of lawyer use in most cases. But the level or intensity of concern coupled with the probable effectiveness of the lawyer in achieving the desired outcome at some realistic and rational cost are probably compelling factors in the decision to seek the advice or help of a lawyer. The survey shows that there are correlations between the probability of lawyer use for various problem types and the likely outcome at the close of the lawyer's involvement in each such matter.

As might be expected, a client's objective in consulting a lawyer is most likely to be achieved in those cases in which it is well within the control of the lawyer to provide the results the client wants, that is, where the matter does not involve other participants with conflicting interests. These areas are estate planning (e.g., wills), real property acquisitions, and most estate settlements. And, in over 90 percent of these kinds of cases, clients report that they obtained the results they hoped to achieve when they initially contacted a lawyer.

In marital matters (mostly divorce) optimal results were achieved by the lawyer three-quarters of the time, but a substantial proportion of the remaining 25 percent of marital cases were dropped by the client when he or she settled differences with the spouse. A client's objective was less likely to be achieved in other more clearly adversarial or contested matters either because the lawyer did not carry the case to completion or,

if work was completed, the lawyer was unable to achieve the result the client wanted. Thus, results in about one-fifth of the torts problems about which lawyers were consulted were either adverse to the client or the lawyer discontinued work on the matter prematurely; in 25 percent of torts cases the lawyer achieved optimal results for the client; and in the majority of such cases (56 percent), a settlement or compromise was arranged.

While marital problems and torts matters are distinguishable from the first group of cases in which optimal results were achieved more than 90 percent of the time, the lawyer achieved optimal results or at least a settlement in 80 percent of marital cases and 80 percent of torts cases. The outcomes in consumer and governmental cases brought to lawyers differ markedly from other matters. In both governmental matters and consumer problems, each of which have a low probability of lawyer use by problem-havers, approximately 40 percent of cases actually brought to lawyers either terminated prematurely or with adverse results. In consumer matters, clients reported that they obtained the results they wanted about half the time; in about 10 percent of the cases a compromise or settlement was arranged; in 7 percent the results were adverse; and in 35 percent of the cases the lawyer terminated work prematurely. The pattern was similar for problems arising out of difficulties with governmental agencies. In about one-half of the cases the lawyer obtained optimal results; 11 percent were settled; 7 percent had adverse outcomes; and 25 percent of the cases were dropped or not completed.

In both governmental and consumer matters, work was often discontinued or not undertaken because the lawyer and client agreed that the cost of pursuing the matter further was too high or the chances of a successful outcome were too slim, or both. In many of these cases, the advice of the lawyer was simply to drop the matter. Sometimes this was the extent of the lawyer's contribution to problem solving; however, in other cases the adversary would be contacted in a limited attempt to help the client.

There are other elements that undoubtedly interact with intensity of concern about the outcome and the perceived cost-effectiveness of a lawyer's help and thus help to shape people's responses to legal problems. Some are specific to particular problem types and others are general. Factors specific to particular problems include the availability of alternative problem-solving resources. For example, the presence or absence of insurance coverage is a crucial element in the way in which personal injury and property damage matters are solved; in job discrimination matters, the availability of a governmental agency established to handle such claims is an important alternative; in real property acquisitions, financial institutions and real estate agents are

perceived by many consumers as reasonable alternative sources of advice.

At a more general level, the opinions and perceptions held by problem-havers about lawyers, the courts, and the legal system may also influence the decision to consult a lawyer. The effect of general views held by any problem-haver on these matters may well be incremental. Thus, in a marginal case, a generally positive view about lawyers when added to particular levels of concern and estimates of probable lawyer effectiveness may be just enough to move the problem-haver toward seeking legal help. Conversely, negative views of lawyers and their work in certain circumstances may tip the scales in the direction of no action or self-help or use of alternative resources.

Perhaps one of the major contributions of this survey is that it demonstrates the fundamental reasonableness with which most people deal with their legal problems. It suggests that unmet legal needs, particularly in consumer matters and problems with governmental agencies, are an important measure attributable to problems within the system and not ineptness in problem solving by the public. The data show that people have a remarkable perceptiveness about what may be expected from lawyers both in terms of what lawyers can deliver and the ways in which they relate to their clients.

NOTES

1. *Gideon* v. *Wainwright*, 372 U.S. 335 (1963). Also see *Argersinger* v. *Hamlin*, 407 U.S. 25 (1971) extending guarantee to all crimes involving imprisonment. For history see Barbara A. Curran, "Legal Services for Special Groups," in the *Encyclopedia of Social Work* (New York: National Association of Social Workers, 1977), pp. 828–835.
2. *The Criminal Justice Act in the Federal District Courts*, Report of the Subcommittee on Constitutional Rights, Committee of the Judiciary, U.S. Senate, 1968 (Washington, D.C.: U.S. Government Printing Office, 1969). Also Curran, supra note 1, p. 830.
3. *Statistics of Legal Aid and Defender Work in the United States and Canada* (Chicago: National Legal Aid and Defender Association, 1969). Also Earl Johnson, Jr., *Justice and Reform: The Formative Years of the OEO Legal Services Program* (New York: Russell Sage Foundation, 1974), xiii + 416 pp.
4. For materials on programs funded by the national program, see *Poverty Law Reporter* (Chicago: Commerce Clearing House, 1970), §§ 6000–6176. Also, Johnson, supra note 3, pp. 180–182.
5. See Chilton Research Services, *Legal Services Evaluation Study: Literature Search Report*. Prepared for Office of Planning, Research and Evaluation, Office of Economic Opportunity (Philadelphia: Chilton Research Services, 1971), 429 pp.
6. B. F. Christensen, *Lawyers for People of Moderate Means: Some Problems of Availability of Legal Services* (Chicago: American Bar Foundation, 1971), 313 pp.
7. See discussion in B. A. Curran, *The Legal Needs of the Public: The Final Report of a National Survey* (Chicago: American Bar Foundation, 1977), pp. 1–9.

8. Including Carnegie Corporation of New York; The Edna McConnell Clark Foundation; International Foundation of Employee Benefit Plans; International Union, United Automobile, Aerospace and Agricultural Implement Workers of America (UAW); and Russell Sage Foundation.
9. B. A. Curran, *Legal Needs,* supra note 7, pp. xxxvi and 382.
10. The proportions of lawyer users were, of course, smaller for those 18 to 44 years of age as of the survey date: never used a lawyer, 44 percent; used lawyer once only, 26 percent; used lawyer two or three times, 21 percent; used lawyer more than three times, 9 percent.
    See id. at pp. 186–203.
11. The following shows the proportion of problem-havers who consulted lawyers for selected problems. Also see Curran, supra note 7, at pp. 143–146.

Problem Type	*Percent of Problem-havers Who Consulted Lawyer for Most Recent Occurrence of Problem*
Wills ($N = 557$)	85
Divorce ($N = 310$)	69
Postdivorce ($N = 61$)	61
Real property acquisition ($N = 1451$)	39
Personal injury ($N = 245$)	34
Spouse's estate ($N = 202$)	31
Garnishment ($N = 50$)	30
Interference with real property ($N = 105$)	28
Dispute with home builder ($N = 43$)	27
Injury to own child ($N = 160$)	25
Problem with mortgage ($N = 40$)	24
Eviction ($N = 81$)	23
Problem with local government agency ($N = 10$)	21
Problem with state government agency ($N = 84$)	20
Claim by another for injury or damage ($N = 107$)	20
Dispute with home repair contractor ($N = 81$)	19
Repossession ($N = 58$)	14
Problem with federal government agency ($N = 104$)	14
Creditor ($N = 90$)	13
Constitutional ($N = 145$)	12
Landlord ($N = 172$)	10
Property damage ($N = 825$)	8
Problem with municipal services ($N = 137$)	7
Dispute with seller ($N = 283$)	7
Job discrimination ($N = 171$)	1

12. The following shows the proportion of surviving spouses who consulted lawyers in relation to size of estate.

Size of Estate, Exclusive of Insurance	*Percent of Surviving Spouses Who Consulted Lawyer*
Less than \$5,000 ($N = 80$)	15
\$5,000-\$9,999 ($N = 21$)	30
\$10,000-\$24,999 ($N = 87$)	54
\$25,000-\$49,999 ($N = 23$)	51
\$50,000 and over ($N = 13$)	64

Chapter 2

Problems in Planning Legal Services

Jon T. Johnsen

HOW TO ESTIMATE EXISTING NEEDS

Although current legal aid research shows a widespread need for legal services among all classes of society, the uncertainty in estimating this need is an obstacle to planning reforms. On what estimates should planning be based? Unrealistic premises would create a continuous problem of unexpected costs, lack of capacity, and poor assistance. Therefore, the calculations of estimated need should be based on empirical research; but existing research also leaves room for a wide range of interpretations, which means that planning is of necessity uncertain.

Not only is making an empirical assessment of need uncertain, but the definition of legal need itself is also troublesome. There is no general agreement about the concept, and therefore definitions will necessarily be somewhat arbitrary. Ultimately, the researcher decides on the definition.

In my opinion, a broad definition of legal need is required if reforms are to be planned realistically. This does not mean that *all* needs should

Note: This chapter is based on Jon T. Johnsen, *Rettshjelp i utkantstrok (Legal aid in the outskirts)* (Oslo: Institute for Sociology of Law, University of Oslo, 1978).

be covered by public legal aid schemes. However, a broad understanding of the problems is important in making decisions of political priority in the field.

In my own research, I have defined legal aid as legal assistance in clarifying, avoiding, obtaining, or utilizing existing legal positions. For an *unmet need,* both a client and a legal expert have to find legal assistance important in treating an existing problem. The expert judgment has to be based on a concrete evaluation of the client's problem as well as the client's understanding of the situation. The client's desire for assistance should be measured against the condition that the assistance is free, includes help in identifying the legal problems, and is available at the client's home.

In our project in Northern Norway, we tested the concept of "unmet legal need" by selecting two local communities and asking all households to participate in an open-ended interview on legal problems. Each respondent was asked to present his or her legal problems. In addition, we prepared a questionnaire tracing unknown legal problems about property and housing, working situation (with special questions for each of the following subgroups: employees, fishermen and farmers, housewives, and pensioners), economic situation, health, damages and compensation, and family situation. All households were offered free legal assistance for the problems discovered. More than 60 percent of the interviews uncovered problems that were defined as an unmet legal need according to my criteria, with an average of more than two cases per household.

Using this definition, I have made an estimate—based on existing legal aid research—of the total need for legal assistance among households with taxable incomes below 60,000 Nkr. in 1974 (80 percent of all households). The probable figure was approximately two million cases per year.

It cannot be assumed that the existing needs represent a temporary phenomenon. Legal problems are closely connected to processes of societal change and control in industrialized societies. For example, although the divorce rate in Norway in 1971 was only one-third of that in Denmark and Sweden, it will not be long before we reach the same level. The last five years have shown an increase of almost 50 percent. Current Norwegian welfare research indicates that a marked rise in the use of social security in urban areas will occur in the future, owing to structural changes in industry. If the present economic crisis continues, an increase in the unemployment rate will also occur. It is easy to predict that such social changes will also increase the need for legal services.

Actually, it is difficult to find trends in ongoing development

processes that indicate a decrease in future needs. The most realistic hope seems to lie in the rise of the educational level, which means that the individual would become more competent in handling his own legal problems. However, major changes cannot be expected in the coming decade.

Nor can planning be based on the assumption that most of the needs are accumulated over many years and that a developed system may be expected to handle a continuous need of much smaller dimensions. My own findings in Northern Norway show that more than half of the registered legal problems have come into existence during the last year. These findings indicate that legal problems in the population are created continuously and that most of them exist as such for a relatively short time.

Although the results of legal aid research may be uncertain, the need for reform should not be underestimated. Four main obstacles to a more extensive use of legal services can be pointed out:

1. *Costs.* The economic consequences of seeking legal assistance represent a major obstacle. Probably less than 20 percent of the Norwegian population is covered by the existing legal aid scheme and important types of cases are also excluded. The fees for an average case normally mean a severe blow to the economy of most low- and middle-income households, if they have to pay themselves. In addition, there is considerable uncertainty connected with hiring a lawyer, both in regard to costs and outcome of the case.
2. *Alienation.* Legal aid research shows a widespread alienation toward legal institutions among ordinary people. They fear bad treatment and doubt their own capacity to make use of lawyers. This obstacle is reinforced by lack of knowledge of how to get and use legal assistance and of the possibilities of reimbursement from the legal aid scheme.
3. *Distance.* The necessity of traveling to visit legal institutions also represents a barrier. Much of a working day may be lost by seeing a lawyer. Both travel costs and loss of income make it unprofitable to use legal assistance. The problem of traveling to seek legal aid may be especially great for invalids and women confined at home caring for young children. Because most legal services are located in towns and in larger community centers, the effects of distance are most strongly felt in sparsely populated areas.
4. *Capacity.* Legal aid research in Norway also indicates an important fourth obstacle, *namely, lack of capacity.* Today, how-

> ever, this represents only a potential problem because the demand for legal services is so low. But the legal profession in Norway would not be able to meet a sharp rise in the demand for legal assistance among ordinary people.

There are about 1700 lawyers in private practice in Norway out of a total population of four million. The average time spent on legal aid cases in 1976 was approximately thirty hours per lawyer. It would be impossible for the legal profession to handle a caseload comparable to my estimate of the existing needs. To cover 1 percent of these problems would mean an average of 60 hours of work per lawyer, and 10 percent would mean 600 hours or one-third of a working year.

In 1976, a public commission presented plans for reform in the legal services system in Norway. Two proposals were put forward to reduce the capacity problem, namely, to establish a few small public legal aid offices in the rural parts of the country and to subsidize lawyers who want to establish new private practices in these outlying areas. Of course, the effect of these proposals on the estimated need would be very limited. To cover 10 percent of these problems, 500 full-time lawyers would be needed. To cover 30 percent, 1500 would be needed, which would mean nearly twice as many lawyers as today. To meet these needs by establishing new private practices means a larger expansion of lawyers, and these lawyers cannot be expected to work full-time with legal aid clients. If they work half-time with these clients, twice as many lawyers are needed. Nevertheless, the Norwegian Bar Association believes that establishment of new lawyers in private practice is the *only* acceptable method of improving legal services.

POLICIES FOR CHANGE

The four above-mentioned obstacles to the delivery of legal services also limit the scope of realistic goals for development of the legal services system. It is impossible to establish institutions that can adequately cover the needs in the near future. An acceptable system demands extensive expansion during a long period. Without a comprehensive development of public legal assistance agencies, the amount of unsolved legal problems will remain about the same in the future.

On the other hand, legal aid research shows that new institutions able to fulfill the needs in a far better way than today can be developed. Trying out new models of legal services is one of the main tasks in reforming the system. The widespread need for legal assistance also means that the legal services sector is characterized by a large shortage

of resources. The allocation of significantly more money and expertise is another main task in the field. But this admission also questions the use of the scarce resources spent on the sector today. In Norway, the legal services commission emphasizes an increase in income as the main reform. But this will be of little help to the groups who are most in need of improved legal services. In Norway, the most serious legal problems are found among low-income households in social welfare law, housing law, and tax law. From the viewpoint of social justice, the services for these classes must be substantially improved before resources are allocated to groups with higher standards of living.

The combination of the large unmet need and the lack of resources in the field makes it necessary to discuss solutions other than developing and expanding legal services. Three proposals have been put forward in the debate in Norway:

1. Dissemination of more public information on legal matters. This may increase knowledge among ordinary people and also increase the actual demand for assistance. However, this proposal is obviously a limited remedy.
2. Simplification of existing legislation. This remedy may enable ordinary people to solve more problems by themselves. Of course, the effects of such reforms are also limited. Legislation must necessarily have an abstract, general form, which creates difficulties for the individual when he wants to find a solution to his specific problem.
3. More use of "self-fulfilling" legislation, that is, rules that create the intended effect without interference from the individual. An example is the Norwegian system of automatic distribution of pensions to everybody over the age of sixty-seven. However, the more "schematic" and "automatic" welfare rules are made, the weaker the redistributive effect becomes. This system of public age pensions is, of course, easy to administer, and few of the old are without pensions. But from the viewpoint of social justice, the effect would have been better if the pensions had been distributed on the basis of actual economic need instead of giving each person the same amount.

In addition to developing legal services, the following two methods are in my opinion the most important:

1. Raising the legal competence of ordinary people. A solution that makes people more able to solve their own legal problems is clearly preferable to a solution that requires dependence on legal service institutions. Of course, such a remedy can have substan-

tial effects only over a long period of time. In reality, the numerous unsolved legal problems in the population show a weakness in our educational system and represent a task for the educational authorities as well as for the administrators of justice.

2. Reduction of the lawyer's monopoly on legal assistance. With a few exceptions, only licensed lawyers are entitled to give legal aid in Norway. Both research and governmental reports show that other professions and public institutions are able to give legal advice in limited fields. Although such services may be of poorer quality than the services provided by lawyers and also prove insufficient for more complicated cases, they are still better than nothing. Today, lawyers in Norway are unable to cover the existing needs. Their monopoly of legal services represents an important obstacle to the escalation of services from other professions and institutions, which could serve as substitutes in areas in which professional lawyers are unavailable.

LIMITS OF LEGAL SERVICES

Existing legislation also represents important limits on efforts to achieve social justice through improved legal services. Most class inequities exist according to the law, not despite it. The minimum pensions offered by social welfare legislation are much less than the average wages earned in working life and the living conditions offered patients under the Mental Health Act are, of course, worse than those among average households. Important changes in the existing distribution of wealth in society cannot be achieved through improvement of traditional legal services alone.

If this is a goal, legal services must be extended to legal policy in the form of assistance in changing existing legislation. The interests of powerful groups normally dominate the legislation process, which means that law usually serves their needs rather than those of the weaker groups. It is possible that the need for legal policy assistance among the lower classes is greater than their need for ordinary legal services. Improvement of such group services should be given far more consideration in the future.

This does not mean, however, that improvement of traditional legal services is unimportant. The poorer people are, the more important is a given contribution or sanction. A social benefit or a fine that has little influence on the economy of an ordinary wage earner may be of great importance to a household living on a minimum disability pension. The

weakest groups in society have the greatest need both for ordinary legal services and for assistance in legal policymaking.

LEGAL SERVICES AND WELFARE POLICIES

Improved legal services are also important to welfare policies. Much of the need is connected to legislation with redistributive purposes. The large number of problems concerning legislation counteracts such aims and reinforces uneven economic distribution because the most serious needs are found among the lower classes. This means that welfare legislation is least effective among groups who need it most. Economically strong institutions and groups will normally profit by the deficiencies of legal services. The government receives more taxes and pays less in welfare contributions because people are unfamiliar with their legal positions. Employers save considerable sums because employees are unable to enforce their rights. Commerce profits when consumers do not utilize all of their legal possibilities. Landlords save money by not fulfilling their maintenance duties because the risk of legal sanction from tenants is low.

Such legal impotence is usually a symptom of underlying social problems. The need for legal aid in a social insurance case also indicates a health problem and an income problem. A case concerning the denial of a building permit may also encompass a housing problem because the present dwelling is too small, a family problem because the family lives too closely together, and an economic problem because construction plans are delayed.

Of course, legal services alone cannot solve such underlying problems. Certain contributions to finding solutions can be made, however. In some situations, legal services may play a key role by advising the client about professional resources necessary to solving the problem. In other cases, the contribution may be insignificant or even negative. The close connection between legal services and welfare problems should be kept in mind when improvements are discussed.

More than in other parts of the legal system, welfare legislation appears as one of several different possibilities for improving an existing problem. An economic problem may be solved by using accumulated savings, working overtime, living more cheaply, or applying for welfare benefits. Such choices do not often exist in more traditional situations such as criminal or matrimonial cases. The client is involved in the process whether or not he wants to be. The problem in legal services is to secure the best possible outcome.

In welfare cases, the assistance cannot be limited to analysis of the

legal strategies. The possibility of other problem-solving techniques must also be taken into consideration. The ability to judge alternative solutions in a broad welfare perspective and to cooperate with other parts of the social assistance system is a major requirement in a developed legal service.

LEGAL ASSISTANCE AND POLITICAL POVERTY

The connection between legal needs and welfare legislation also represents a political paradox. Welfare legislation is meant to be the answer to social problems. The existence of a large unmet legal need implies that many problems have only been transferred from the political to the legal arena without concrete improvement for the individuals concerned. The major effect is a political neutralization of social demands. When the problems cease to be political issues, the client's chances of gathering support and sympathy from the public also diminish. The problem becomes a private one of enforcing individual rights. Counterattacking such processes is an important function of a developed legal service.

The existence of a considerable difference in the possibilities of promoting and defending political demands and decisions between social classes represents a serious problem for Western democracies today. Legal policymaking is no exception to this.

The Norwegian reform commission has proposed limited access to free legal assistance for individuals who want to raise general questions, a proposal that implies changes in legislation or administrative regulations. However, legal policy assistance of this kind is only granted when the questions are closely related to an ordinary free legal aid case. This is an awkward limitation.

Often, it is obvious that ordinary legal aid is of little use to the client because the legislation itself is unsatisfactory. Nevertheless, the need for legal policymaking is important.

Legal policymaking should not be a task for legal services only when a specific client wants to raise a specific issue. It will often seem unprofitable to the individual client. A long time may pass before a reform can be brought about. Clients in straightened circumstances do not want to commit themselves to strategies that cannot influence their situation in a short time. Moreover, some underprivileged groups, such as minors under child welfare and patients in mental hospitals, are incapable of participating in legal policymaking. Nevertheless, reforms can be important to such clients as a group.

Most claims for reform also have to be based on a wide range of material showing the general weakness of legislation. To argue for reforms on the basis of single cases is often purposeless. Legal services should therefore have the responsibility of working for reforms in the legal system. Today, only the most powerful groups in society are able to use lawyers for such purposes. A developed legal service should provide this assistance to weaker groups as well.

Chapter 3

A Comment on Research into "Legal Needs"

John Griffiths

THREE QUESTIONS THAT CAN BE EXPRESSED IN TERMS OF "NEEDS"

Research into "legal needs" can be of three kinds:

Execution of Policy: If it is agreed that everyone accused in a serious criminal case or who is a party to a divorce proceeding or who is denied some kind of welfare state benefit should have the opportunity to receive legal assistance, we need to know how many such situations there are and what factors (such as the price or geographic distribution of legal services) affect the likelihood that such assistance will be given. I cannot think of any objection to such inventory-taking and assessment of the effectiveness of execution and will not discuss it further here.

Justification of Policy: Research into legal needs is often thought to provide answers relevant to the question of how legal assistance ought to be distributed. Oversimplified, the argument seems to be—unfilled need is a reason for reorganization of the distribution system. I believe such arguments are circular because the concept of "need"

contains within it an implicit policy; furthermore, I think the implicit policy is an essentially conservative one.

Sociology of Law: Research into legal needs is often thought to contribute to our understanding of the behavior of legal systems. I believe that this is not the case and that such research is—from the point of view of sociology of law—fundamentally misguided.

This comment is addressed to the latter two uses of the term legal needs. The gist of my argument is that the concept of legal needs is not and cannot be made an empirical one: there is no such thing as an empirical "need" and no such thing as an empirical "legal problem" or empirical "legal services." These concepts are all ways of expressing judgments about how the world ought to be. To say that legal services should be made available to some groups in some situations because they have a need for such services is merely to say that they ought to have the services because they ought to use them. And to say that some other social variable gives rise to a certain need for legal services explains nothing; it makes the absurd assertion that the social variable in question causes a moral judgment that legal services ought to be employed.

CONTENT OF THE CONCEPT OF LEGAL NEEDS

Legal needs resolve into two elements:

1. *Need for*
2. *(Professional) help with (legal) problems*

Both elements are nonempirical and reflect implicit policies.

NEED

Contacts Versus Needs

We know a lot about contacts with various kinds of legal assistance and about the social variables that are associated with variation in rates of contacts. Despite its title, Curran's work (Chapter 1) is an example—one of the best and most careful—of this kind of research. The idea of need for legal services is presumably intended to refer to something different from actual use. The question is precisely what is that which is

different? There are two possible approaches to an empirical concept of need: it could be something that the person in so-called need subjectively experiences, or it could be something that an observer objectively records about a person in need. The one thing it cannot be is need as reflected in behavior because legal needs research is intended to be critical of the distribution of legal services produced by the existing market for such services; that is, need may not reflect price. And that is where one encounters difficulties.

Need as Subjective Experience

It is possible that there is a distinct kind of subjective experience, unconnected with the price of a thing, that one could call need for that thing. All the difficulties that have been encountered with related concepts, such as "pain" and "pleasure," should certainly give one pause before setting out to try to define exactly what a subjective experience of need is. My own suspicion is that it is not useful to think of need as the name of a distinct experience. However that may be, none of the legal needs research I know of consistently tries to employ such a concept of need for a variety of reasons:

1. Patronizing approach of the researchers. The poor are supposed not to know how good legal services are for them, and because of such ignorance, they experience need too frequently. Curran's paper at the very least justifies great caution with a patronizing methodology.
2. Lack of connection with policy concerning legal services. Subjective experiences are as likely to reflect psychological as they are to reflect social factors, and to call for psychiatric or social rather than legal services. Measuring legal need is a matter of combining a so-called real need with an unknown element.
3. The influence of reference groups on the experience of need. Those who are "really" better off may experience more need than those worse off because they compare themselves with those still more fortunate while the group that is worse off compares itself with those still more unfortunate. Those who experience less subjective need for something may be precisely those who "really" need it more.

In short, if those who investigate legal needs are not content to accept the idea that a need is always relative to a price, and therefore to accept the assessment of individuals of their need as reflected in their behavior as consumers of legal services, they are equally unwilling to accept their subjects' subjective experiences of need unrelated to price.

Legal needs research is based on the concept of a real need for legal services that is different from need as expressed in behavior and different from need as subjectively experienced.

Need as an Objective Condition

To impose an artificial order upon a variety of usually not very distinctly articulated concepts of need as an objective condition—that is, as a state of affairs that an observer can record, independent of the appearance or behavior of his subject—we may use two basic approaches:

1. Need is the quantity that would be consumed if the price were at or near zero.
2. Need is the quantity of legal services whose benefits outweigh their costs.

The first approach is quite absurd, although one often comes across conceptions of need that seem to imply it. There is no conceivable reason for treating a scarce good as if it were not scarce, and for describing someone as needing legal services worth, for example, $100, in order to get $10 worth of satisfaction. Johnsen, in Chapter 2, nicely demonstrates the preposterous consequences of taking the notion seriously that people need what they would consume if it were free.

In the second conception, the influence of price upon the consumer is still excluded, but a possible use is not described as a need if its indulgence would be "wasteful." The problem in this approach is to ascertain the benefits of legal services.[1] The general solution is that costs are taken to be outweighed by benefits in those situations in which a prudent person would consume legal services. The researcher, or his or her panel of so-called experts, guesses when this would be, usually under the heading of a criterion such as the "seriousness" of the problem concerned. Need is, in effect, an idealized version of a middle-class consumption pattern (and the idealization is usually that of lawyers). My impression that this approach to need underlies Zander's research (Chapter 6)—for which, in other respects, I have nothing but admiration—was confirmed rather than dispelled in the course of the discussion.

In short, the "objective" conception of need leads either to the absurd idea that needs can be thought about wholly independently of the costs of satisfying them, or to a substitution of the observer's ideas about the benefits of legal services for the ideas reflected in the behavior of actual consumers.

(PROFESSIONAL) HELP WITH (LEGAL) PROBLEMS

If we were to talk about the need for chocolate bars without reference to their price, we would similarly be making the assumption that there is some basis—other than personal preference among competing goods, as reflected in behavior—for judging how much of something is good for people, that is, what their "real" benefit from the thing would be. We imply either that they cannot afford enough of those things that are good for them (in which case, the solution is to give them more income)—or that we know better than they what they should spend their money on. But at least the good we are talking about is something we can take as empirically definite. The problem of measuring legal needs is much more difficult than the problem of measuring need for chocolate bars would be because both the concept of need and the supposedly needed thing are problematic. Legal services are not a distinct entity like chocolate bars.

The kind of situation with which a legal system regularly deals, the ways in which it characteristically does so, and the role that various kinds of legal assistance play in the process together with the organization and distribution of its services are all subject to variation. There is nothing empirically given about what a legal problem is or about what legal assistance amounts to. Even within a given system there is no distinct category of legal problems for which legal services are suitable. Instead, there exist problematic situations in which resort to law is one of many available options, and resort to law may take forms other than going to see a lawyer.

The above observations may seem almost trivial, but they are deadly for legal needs research. There is no way one can even begin to talk about the costs or benefits of something without specifying what that thing is. The implicit specification in legal needs research assumes the existing organization of legal assistance and of the legal system and the problem-solving inclinations attributed to some part of the population.[2] But need so established gives no support to a policy of redistributing legal services. A gap between need and actual contacts can just as well be closed by depressing need through the reorganization of legal services and of the legal system or by redefining legal problem and legal services as through increasing contacts. The fact is that the single largest category of need is a wholly artificial creation of the state. I refer to the requirement (of varying degrees of strictness and effected in various ways) of a lawyer's services in divorce cases. To describe this as a situation of need is to confuse what is exacted of people with what they want or what benefits them. In short, a given level of measured need

may not reflect the need one would have found if lawyers offered a different range of services or if the legal system were brought to bear on a different range of situations.

Thus, the concept of need in legal needs research is based on an idea of the benefit of legal services that pretends to objectivity, but which is in fact an extension to the whole population of lawyers' idealized notions concerning the judgment of prudent members of the middle classes. Moreover, the thing supposed to be needed is a mere reflection of the existing organization of legal services and of the legal system. Legal needs research is profoundly justificatory of existing arrangements; it takes the correctness of those arrangements for granted as the basis of an argument for increases in the output of the very product that is currently being produced. No wonder that the organized bar enthusiastically finances such research![3]

CONCLUSION

I am not suggesting that research is always irrelevant to arguments about policy. I am arguing that to make it relevant one must be very careful about the terms of the argument. What facts, precisely, would count for or against a policy of redistributing lawyers' services? This depends upon whether the argument for redistribution is that legal services are a good, a merit-good, an instrument for social change, a necessary element in the implementation of various social policies, or a requirement of justice.[4] One must never lose sight of the fact that the thing to be justified is not merely redistribution, but redistribution of lawyers' services. Mere observation of inequalities between rich and poor is trivial for two reasons. In the first place, such inequalities are, ultimately, merely tautological reflections of wealth differences (the rich have to have more of things in order to be considered rich), and if they justify anything, they justify redistribution of wealth, not of the things that wealth can buy. Secondly, an inequality can just as well be cured by taking from the rich (e.g., delegalization) as by giving to the poor.

In connection with the necessity of justifying the redistribution of lawyers' services, two things should be said about legal needs. First, they are not any kind of fact at all but rather a concealed idea about policy, and thus to invoke them in support of a policy is to beg the question. Secondly, legal needs research has in fact not figured in the major policy decisions that have been made about the distribution of legal services, for example, the decision to recognize a right to counsel in criminal cases.[5] The terms of that debate were justice—fairness and

equality—not need. I believe that those terms are the proper terms of debate and that research relevant to such a debate should concern itself with the distribution of actual use of lawyers' services, the difference that such services make to outcomes of various individual situations, and the costs and effects of various redistribution schemes.[6]

NOTES

1. A preliminary problem, of course, is to explain why it is supposed that ordinary people are not now making the appropriate cost-benefit decisions. If the answer is a lack of money, surely the solution is to give them money, not legal services.
2. This section owes much to Marks (1976). There is a second sense in which legal needs research is inherently conservative, namely, in that the selection of law as the vehicle for dealing with problematic situations in itself tends to favor some social interests and disfavor others, as Handler pointed out. In Galanter's (1974) famous expression, those favored tend to be the "haves." Finally, it is also conservative in the sense noted by Glastra van Loon in the discussion, namely, that it concentrates social effort upon cure rather than upon prevention.
3. Not always with the contemplated results, however. One wonders whether the bar will be happy with Curran's substitution of the neutral concept of empirical contacts for the lucratively laden, nonempirical concept of legal needs.

   Zander's reference in discussion to the English developments described in Chapter 6 as "revolutionary" seems to me extraordinary. One may view those developments with satisfaction or with alarm, but to view them as revolutionary is to confuse some (relatively limited) extension of the status quo with basic change in the status quo. I see no evidence of the latter in the information that Zander presents. In fact, given the various limitations on the reach and use of the English programs, the only group of whom one can say without qualification has benefited are the lawyers. Within a few years, the bar has managed to arrange that half of its income comes from public funds, with a means test arranged to insure that a minimum of potential paying clients are siphoned off. In addition, many rules restricting the cultivation of business have been relaxed. I do not suggest that these developments are bad; I do think, however, that one must keep one's eye on the latent as well as the manifest purposes of such programs.
4. These arguments are distinguished and discussed in Griffiths (1977), except that to the four kinds of arguments there treated, I would now want to add a fifth possible argument for redistribution of legal services. This is, namely, the argument concerning effective implementation of other social policies, for example, those contained in legislation creating new rights, and so on, for the poor. In Chapter 14 Nonet can be read as addressed to that argument, and while I find it utterly lacking in relevance to the American context with which it purports to deal, it does seem to me that his argument deserves attention in legal systems that actually possess functioning administrative bodies of the sort he contemplates.
5. Zander argued in the discussion that England is a deviant case as far as this generalization is concerned, and that policy was in fact heavily influenced by research that purported to demonstrate the existence of unmet legal needs. While the examples that he cited tended to be of legal contacts research and of research showing the difference in outcomes between persons represented and unrepre-

sented, I certainly would not presume to dispute his statement that legal needs research was also important. If so, and if the legislative bodies concerned were in fact taken in (i.e., if Zander was right about causality), it seems to me that English social science carried off a massive fraud against the legislature and thereby against English "democracy." Whether one is for or against fraud in politics is outside the scope of my comment. All I assert is that there are facts and there are policies and that legal needs research present the latter as if it were the former.

6. Only after the conference did I have the pleasure of reading Lewis (1973) and of discovering that he had anticipated arguments made here (as well as in Griffiths, 1977, and Marks, 1976) in several ways.

Chapter 4

Types of Legal Needs and Modes of Legalization: The Example of the Berlin Tenants Initiative

Udo Reifner

LEGAL NEEDS AND SOCIAL PROBLEMS

Most studies on legal needs either imply or state explicitly that people have a number of unsolved problems that can be regarded as legal problems when a legal solution seems feasible. Sykes surveyed poor people in Denver in 1969 for unsolved problems. He then commissioned lawyers to analyze whether or not these problems could be solved by legal procedures. The resulting problems were summed up and correlated with the social status, age, religion, race, and so on, of the interviewees. However, to us the mere addition of legal problems does not lead to valid results. In these studies, it is not the poorest people who report the greatest number of legal problems, but rather those who are just above the poverty level.[1]

Social problems that can be solved by means of the law are to be defined as legal problems only if the legal definition of the problem guarantees its solution. Therefore, Griffiths is quite right in characterizing the definition of "latent legal problems" imposed on the persons concerned by researchers as politically patronizing. Whether a problem can be solved through legal processes depends not only on the

law, but also on time, money, knowledge, courage, the opponent, and the type of problem. The reluctance of people to define their problems as "legal" cannot simply be attributed to their lack of knowledge and experience in legal matters (see Schuyt et al., 1977). It might just as well be good judgment to avoid the costs and the inconvenience of legal procedures and the inadequacy of the promised results.

Therefore, social problems should not be treated as legal problems just because a legal solution would be feasible. It is also dangerous to assume that the social problems that do in fact gain legal relevance are consequently to be regarded as important problems. Tenants in Germany, for instance, have a right to examine the utility accounts of their apartment building (heating, garbage removal, etc.). When asked if their landlord always presents the accounts as required, it is clear that a number of legal problems could be found by the tenants. But most tenants are unable to understand accounts anyway, and thus the existing legal problem does not reflect a social problem. Summing up all potentially legal problems named in a survey only leads to nonsensical results. This becomes apparent when comparing the legal problems of a transient with the legal problems of a tenant.

The problem of the transient—finding a place to live—does not appear as a legal problem because there is no law guaranteeing a "right to housing." In a survey, therefore, the transient whose situation is worse than that of the tenant would appear to have no problems, whereas the tenant would be able to name a number of legally relevant problems. In addition, the problems of tenants might be on a different qualitative level; for example, a claim for rent that has been overpaid is of much less importance to the person concerned than an eviction notice.

Therefore, we have tried in our study to determine the relevance of legal problems when they had not been prejudiciously defined as legal. We based our judgment of the social problem situations on the definitions of the tenants. We also tried to separate their view of the problem from their view of the possible solution.

In evaluating their opponent, the tenants applied moral rather than legal standards in order to measure social problems. Seventy-four percent of all interviewed persons regarded their landlords as "using unscrupulous business practices"; but only 19 percent regarded him as "not law abiding," 13 percent as a "clever business man," and 4 percent as "as bad or good as any other landlord." Only a minority of people chose legal processes for problem solution from among the offered alternatives. We asked who should decide about repairs (with 76 percent the most frequent problem), evictions, new rentals, and abiding by the house regulations. Thirty-nine percent of the interviewees were

Table 4.1

Grievances to Be Solved by the Tenants Rights Group	Evaluation of Landlord: Not Law Abiding (N = 21)	Evaluation of Landlord: Unscrupulous Business Practice (N = 83)
Repairs	67%	83%
Renovation of the building	19%	41%
Damages from the landlord	5%	16%
Enforced rental of empty apartment buildings	71%	59%
Information to the public	62%	46%

in favor of an assembly of tenants, whereas 33 percent wanted a mediation board. Public agencies, courts, or lawyers each made up less than 10 percent of the answers. This figure is equivalent to Curran's results,[2] where 50 percent of the interviewees wanted to consult an attorney only after all other possibilities of problem resolution had failed.

The opinions about court procedures were similarly critical. Fifty-five percent called the results unpredictable, 60 percent said they were too expensive, and 50 percent said they took too long. Positive judgments, such as "they level social disparities" (5 percent), "thoroughness" (2 percent), or "proceed without bias" (1 percent) were rarely expressed.

Table 4.1 gives some insights into the reasons why tenants define their problems as legal. We have combined the legal and the moral evaluation of the landlord and correlated these findings with the objectives of the Tenants Rights Group (TRG). People who use the law as their standard for evaluation show a tendency not to pursue irrational objectives. They have a more general view of the task of the TRG. On the other hand, there seems to be more of a correlation between moral judgments and individual expectations of success.

The most significant difference appeared when we asked about the feasibility of the objectives. Only 47 percent of the group who judged their landlord on a moral basis expected their objectives to be feasible, as opposed to 71 percent of the group who made a legal evaluation.

Only for a minority of tenants can the law be regarded as a means of expressing their true interests. The incidence of problems being defined as legal increases, however, the more tenants expect that there is a solution to their problems.

People perceive their problems independently of whether or not they fall within certain legal categories. In addition, they do not necessarily prefer a legal resolution of their problems. Rather, they show an intensive rejection and a generalized negative evaluation of juridical

Table 4.2

Activities to Be Undertaken by the Tenants Rights Group	All Respondents (N = 112)
To inform about rights	71%
To conduct lawsuits	57%
To exert pressure on politicians and public agencies	55%
To inform the public	48%
To organize rent boycotts	32%
To collect signatures	9%
To correspond with landlords	6%

procedure and language. However, this does not imply that people would not use a legal approach. On the contrary, the functions attributed to the TRG lie mostly in the legal field, for instance, "to inform tenants about their rights" (71 percent) and "to conduct law suits" (57 percent), whereas nonlegal activities were indicated less frequently.

In letters of complaint to their landlords, 46 percent of the tenants questioned had particularly referred to their tenants rights. Forty-seven percent said they would try to solve their future problems by legal means, 41 percent indicated that they would participate in communal actions, and 42 percent in social reform groups. Eighty percent of the interviewees indicated that they would be willing to sue their landlord if necessary.

A question as to whether the courts implement the rights of tenants was answered "partly," and negative and positive opinion was equally divided (Table 4.3).

There is a contradiction between the frequent criticism of legal procedures and high evaluation of extralegal activities and institutions, on the one hand, and the high level of importance that the tenants attributed to the pursuit of interests through legal processes, on the other. This discrepancy can be explained by differing expectations of success. In spite of the fact that extralegal activities, like distributing leaflets, organizing demonstrations, submitting petitions, and collecting signatures, were named as the tasks of the social reform group against nuclear power plants as well as conducting legal actions (90 percent each), the expectations of success were mostly linked to taking legal action (66 percent). The TRG showed the same tendency; they expect success only in areas in which the pursuit of acknowledged rights is concerned (repairs, 62 percent, or meeting of legal regulations, 44 percent). They do not expect success in extralegal areas (rent prices, 12 percent, or real estate speculation, 11 percent). Expectations were particularly low in areas in which the existing laws are unfavorable to

Table 4.3

		All Respondents (N = 112)
Yes, always	5%	18%
Mostly	13%	
Partly		56%
Rarely	19%	21%
Never	2%	
No answer		5%
		100% = 112

tenants (interior repairs in apartments, 5 percent). Although people seem to have accepted this social weakness as a fact, they still have some faith in the judicial system. In actual cases, however, scepticism prevails when the practices of the judicial system are evaluated.

A higher likelihood of success is the major advantage of the legal system over other ways of interest representation. A claim that has been sanctioned by court can be enforced. Whatever has been reached through extralegal actions, however, can easily be lost again. The less social power a group of people have for the extralegal pursuit of their interests, the more their hopes focus upon the judicial system. Therefore, the legal need of the underprivileged can be defined as a constellation of the following three elements:

1. Social problems exist.
2. The persons concerned do not have enough social power to solve their problems.
3. The legal system is their only chance of pursuing their rights.

Therefore, studies on legal needs of socially underprivileged groups are not impossible. They are only useful, however, if the three basic conditions (a social problem, social powerlessness, and the chances for a legal solution) are analyzed. Legal aid is necessary only when a social problem and a situation of social powerlessness cannot be overcome by any other means. That is to say, for us legal means are only a substitute in situations in which it is not possible to achieve conditions that prevent underprivileged situations.

POVERTY AS THE BASIS OF A GENERAL LEGAL NEED

A number of empirical studies have tried to certify the validity of their results by examining only the legal problems of socially

underprivileged or poor people.[3] They assumed social powerlessness as a prerequisite for the existence of a "need." In defining poverty simply as the "lack of money," they overrate the power of money. Money is merely one means of satisfying social needs under given circumstances. It cannot solve all problems. A foreign worker with four children may have an adequate income. His chances of remaining confined to poor housing, however, are much higher than those of a German on the edge of the subsistence level. Even if we restrict ourselves to the legal solution of a problem (assuming the adequacy of this solution), the lack of money may be an important, but not the only, barrier in the pursuit of legal rights. In order to bring court action, courage, persistence, self-confidence, specific knowledge, and abilities and contacts are often more important than money, which in many cases can be substituted through "Armenrecht" (state funding of court costs for the poor), legal insurance, or membership in a tenants organization. Therefore, it would be a mistake to regard only the financial risk of a lawsuit as the "poverty barrier." A comparison of the interviewees covered by legal aid insurance with the control group of noninsured persons (Table 4.4) proves this point. The insured group is more willing to engage in a lawsuit (94 percent as opposed to 71 percent), but they too would prefer to engage in a lawsuit with others rather than alone. Although they may be indifferent about the costs of the procedure, when the social costs and social barriers of a lawsuit are considered, the alliance with equally interested persons increases the willingness for legal action. The comparison of the control groups does not show whether the higher litigiousness of the insured is due to their reduced financial risk or to an effect of recruitment, that is, the assumption that better informed and more litigious persons show a stronger tendency to buy legal insurance.[4] One common element of the two control groups can be interpreted, however. Both evaluate the outcome of a lawsuit as uncertain (54 percent and 60 percent), the procedure as too expensive (58 percent and 64 percent), too long (60 percent and 43 percent), and as "often more advantageous for the rich" (36 percent and 28 percent) (see table 4.4).

Social deprivation is tied to certain situations. Persons who are "poor within a certain situation" require help for precisely this specific problem. If deprivation is viewed in relation to vital problem areas (employment, consumption, housing, or health), handing out money can alleviate the effects of the problem but not combat the causes.

As was shown by an examination of the TRG, the exclusion of poor tenants would also sever them from important means of aid. The TRG had set up five working groups to deal with problems of rent, repairs, utility costs, publicity work, and tenants' policy. In a way, the TRG thus represented the interests of the poor tenants because these problems

Table 4.4

	% of All Persons with Legal Insurance (N = 50)	% of Persons without Legal Insurance (N = 58)	
Contact with Courts[a]			
As plaintiff	46	29	
As plaintiff with a tenant problem	16	9	
As defendant	26	28	
As witness	36	19	
Judgment about Court Procedure[b]			
Uncertain results	54	60	
Equalize social disadvantages	8	2	
In favor of the rich	36	28	
Too expensive	58	64	
Too long	60	43	
Incomprehensible	12	19	
Average of other judgments	2	1.7	
Solution of Tenant Problems in Future[a]			
By means of the legal system	50	40	
Would bring a lawsuit against landlord			
No	6	15	86% (No, Alone, Only together with others)
Alone	28	26	
Only together with others	66	45	
Don't know	—	12	
No answer	—	2	
Do the courts grant tenants their rights?			
Yes, always	2	7	94% / 92% (Yes, always through Never)
Mostly	14	10	
Partly	54	59	
Rarely	22	14	
Never	2	2	
Don't know	6	8	

[a]The answers were taken from different questions. The remaining answers to equal 100% are not shown in this table. Cumulative choices were permitted.

[b]Cumulative choices were permitted.

were also the interests of the poor, but the groups consisted mostly of nonpoor tenants. The average rent of TRG members was DM 553.67 (an average of 2.71 persons per household), whereas the average rent of nonmembers was DM 435.81 (2.16 persons per household). The average income per household was DM 2894.23, significantly higher than that of the nonmembers, who averaged DM 1950.58. The professional status of the members was also higher than of the nonmembers (Table 4.5).

Table 4.5

	Tenants' Rights Group (N = 26)	*Nonmembers* (N = 86)
Unskilled worker	4%	8%
Skilled worker	—	6%
Lower-level employee	31%	28%
Manager	12%	6%
Civil servant	11%	13%
Liberal profession	11%	4%
Pensioner	4%	13%
Students	23%	22%
No answer	4%	—

Higher education correlates with higher participation, as shown in Table 4.6.

If we compare educational level and income per capita within a household, it becomes apparent that with increasing educational level the probability of participation in the TRG increases significantly.

Thus, the average TRG member is from the middle class and has attained a relatively high educational level. Nevertheless, the majority of less-educated interviewees agreed about the usefulness of the TRG (87 percent) (97 percent of persons with Abitur and 100 percent with university education), 56 percent of them thought it effective (in comparison with 71 percent with Abitur and 96 percent with university education). Only 11 percent had a negative opinion, and the rest were undecided. Of the less-educated group, 37 percent believed that the work of the TRG had a favorable influence on the courts (45 percent with Abitur and 83 percent with university education), whereas 32 percent did not see an influence (42 percent with Abitur and 9 percent with university education), and 28 percent were undecided.

As to reasons for their nonparticipation, the less-educated group indicated that they had no time (35 percent), that the meeting dates were unfavorable for them (9 percent), or that they had nothing to contribute (9 percent).

Aid restricted only to the poor members of an interest group would therefore prove unsatisfactory to those who are the most articulate and ardent supporters of the cause; it would also foster the dissolution of the group. In this way, particularly the poor would be barred from the possibility of representing their own interests in a group or at least having a chance to voice their interests through others. The underlying cause of a problem would remain untouched if we were to examine it only with regard to the poor. Therefore, a better way to determine legal needs would be to specify interests, such as environmental and

Table 4.6

	Tenants' Rights Group	Nonmembers
	(N = 26)	(N = 86)
9 years high school	14%	26%
10 years vocational school	8%	30%
Abitur	35%	26%
University degree	35%	16%
Other	4%	2%
No answer	4%	—

consumer protection rights, civil rights, and welfare claims,[5] public and collective interests,[6] the right of self-determination for mental patients,[7] or the interests of debtors in arrears.[8]

LEGAL NEEDS AND STEPS OF LEGALIZATION

We can regard legal need as the need for power of socially deprived groups, a need that arises under certain social conditions. It is not an end in itself to instruct people about their rights, how to gain access to courts, or how to come into contact with attorneys. Tenants, consumers, or employees want to be successful in the struggle to protect their interests, that is, they want conditions that serve their interests. They generally do not care how these conditions are brought about as long as their moral beliefs are not violated. Therefore, legalization makes sense to us only when it is successful. A mere substantive legal position does not fulfill this purpose. It is only the first of a number of conditions, followed by knowledge of the law, the access to legal institutions, the handling of the apparatus of court procedures, and finally a mechanism to enforce the desired outcome.

We examined some of the conditions for legislation to determine whether or not existing legal claims have in some cases led to a positive legalization of the underlying social interests within the further steps of the legalization process. We concluded that the way in which existing rights are formulated and publicized often counteracts the actual use of a right for the concerned person's interests. The reason is that understanding the law has developed into a "secret science" and social rights in particular are formulated in a vague and complicated manner incomprehensible to the layman. The factual or legal monopoly of attorneys as well as the professional forms of action have been criticized as barriers to using the law.[9] Overformalized, incomprehensible, and expensive court procedures[10] are also seen as barriers. For each of these

cases, propositions and models have been suggested. For general legal socialization, use of a more comprehensible legal language, teaching of legal information in the elementary schools, and widespread consumer information are recommended. For granting more protective rights, the integration of welfare and legal aid, waiving of legal charges, and group representation through attorneys, the introduction of public interest lawsuits or collective suits for public organizations are suggested. For procedural improvements, deciding a settlement by final judgment and finding new forms of sanctions are advocated. Most reforms are concerned with changing only one aspect of the legal system. Granting social claims by law might be counterproductive if forces are unduly bound by the process of legalization; this method would not effectively lead to success for the persons concerned because they would probably fail to claim their rights at higher levels.

The simplification of legal procedure in the small claims courts has not led to an increase of suits by consumers, but rather to an increase of claims by businesses. This reform simplifies the collecting of debts for businesses. A study oriented to the success of interest representation through law would have to analyze the route taken by specific interests vertically through all levels of the legal process. Surveys that consider only a single level give a distorted picture. How much success changes the perception of the desirability of going to court is shown in a survey of parties in landlord-tenant cases, in which the interviewees were asked how they would evaluate the judge's attitude. Two-thirds of the winners evaluated the procedure positively, whereas two-thirds of the losers replied negatively.[11] People do not understand why they fail in court. The same holds true for legal counseling, which became apparent when observing the legal aid office in the TRG. Most people did not follow either the legal information they received about their case or the necessary court procedures. When advised that they must pursue their interests in a different way, many people failed to understand. They only wanted to know if they were "right." They felt that being right guaranteed success. If an attempt were made to change this expectation through counseling, they either accused the counselors of being misinformed or incomprehensible, or they considered the opponent's power so overwhelming that they viewed themselves as no match for it.

Caplovitz found[12] that many of the debtors involved in a lawsuit did not even know the results of the suit. Despite the fact that 44 percent of the interviewees in our study had legal insurance, 60 percent indicated that court procedures were too expensive. If a level of legalization is not reached, it may be because of problems on that particular level, but the reason may also be that the previous steps have not been taken or that failure on a later level had been anticipated. For example, a person who

believes that he has no rights at all will not make the effort to gain legal information; a person who does not want to conduct a lawsuit under any circumstances will not be interested in legal counseling; and a person who has received false advice will not understand legal procedures and will therefore give up.

FORMS OF LEGALIZATION AS A REASON FOR LEGAL NEEDS

Pursuing social interests by legal means requires a certain kind of activity and attitude by the persons concerned. Not only must they accept the law as a measuring stick for their problems and therefore view their problems as legal problems, but they must also demonstrate a particular kind of behavior on all levels of the legalization process. The law defines the problem itelf as well as the interests and expectations of the parties. Neither substantive law nor forms of legal aid and of judicial procedures have been formulated to promote the interests of those groups whose social deprivation has led to the discussion of legal needs.[13] These interests have been characterized as "diffuse" (Galanter), "collective interests" (Trubek), "group interests," or simply as "social interests."

On the other hand, the legalization process exhibits the same characteristics on all levels. These characteristics have been criticized in substantive civil law. The following might be mentioned: individualism (Raiser) and the related isolation of social conditions from "the rest of the world" (Medicus), formal abstraction (Sinzheimer), orientation toward money, and the tendency toward compensation on the level of legal regulations. These factors prevent the regulation of individual cases or exemptions, the development of a collective legal consciousness, and thus the development of new forms of legal knowledge. The fee orientation of attorneys' "services" (Rosenthal), the formalized duel in civil cases (Wassermann), and also the impotence of judicial enforcement agencies in handling nonmonetary interests exclude important dimensions of social interest representation.

Surveys on "barriers to access" neglect the limits of law when they use the existing form of legalization to measure criticism and access. Empirical surveys should add questions that suggest alternatives to existing institutions. They should open possibilities for the interviewees to express criticism about their own interests instead of measuring the institutions by their own standards. The suggestive force of nonexisting institutions could be just as great as that of the existing

institutions. This proposition will be exemplified with two formal alternatives.

Individual and Collective Means of Problem Resolution

Law classically formulates tenants' problems as individual problems. In Germany, only the individual tenant's rights can be violated. Legal aid is provided only for individuals and for specific problems. This individualization of legal forms of interest is contradicted by social needs for collective action.

When asked if they wanted to sue their landlords alone or with others, 26 percent answered "alone," whereas 55 percent wanted to sue "together with others," and 11 percent did not want to sue at all. When asked how they wanted to solve their problems with the landlord in the future, only seven percent wanted a private solution, 43 percent voted for collective action with other tenants, and 43 percent voted for a TRG. Of the tenants, 50 percent believed that because of the work of the TRG, the courts decided more favorably for tenants; 29 percent did not see a connection, and only 2 percent believed in a negative influence.

About half of the tenants who had a problem and had taken some kind of action had been supported by their neighbors. When asked why they did not work in the TRG, more than 50 percent answered that they had "no time." Of the nonactive, 21 percent said that there were already enough participants, that everybody should represent their own interests, that they could not contribute anything, or that it was useless anyway. Although 93 percent thought that the TRG was useful, 68 percent thought that it was effective. Three-fourths of the members of the TRG indicated that they would work for it even if they had no problems of their own.

Gathering information about the law, legal aid, and the conducting of a lawsuit are usually regarded as collective tasks. Certainty of action, sharing of the risk, distribution of work, financial savings, and an increase in influence as well as contacts and communication are expected of the collective form of action. The underlying interests can in many cases only be reasonably articulated as supraindividual (social) interests. They are diffuse "public" or "collective" interests. Accordingly, the expectation of success for these interests is not related to public or collective goods that could be individually consumed. Collective action is not only important to the articulation of these interests, but it is also a necessary condition for their effective pursuit. Risks can be distributed throughout the organization and thus be made bearable (Galanter), the public can be informed and encouraged to take part

(Trubek), and the pursuit of rights can be used to achieve changes within the law and individual results can be collectively verified.

Practice shows, however, that these interest organizations often break up after a short period of activity and that they are either not able to motivate their members for a longer time or that they ossify as bureaucracy and degenerate into a service delivery institution for their members. The latter leads to a monopolization of the representation of interests and to a further threatening of the individual's social interests.

The TRG in our study began to show distinct symptoms of dissolution after a year. Its survival could only be secured by integrating the group into the larger "Berlin Tenants' Association." At first this solution had been violently resisted by the members of the TRG who feared bureaucratic petrification and domination by the larger organization.

Some social interests cannot be independently organized because they are only of subordinate importance to the individual, who thus does not want to spend the time and energy necessary for organization (Galanter). "Where collective goods are at issue the rational economic man will tend to become a free rider" (Handler, Trubek). Clients are not willing to submit their cases as test cases for drawn-out law suits. Group activities fail when they do not achieve an immediate, tangible result, but only achieve a level of legalization at best (Handler). If no tangible results are achieved for the individual, he or she will leave the group. "There is no natural nexus that ties consumers together" (Trubek).

The representation of interests by specialized institutions or organizations (Galanter) or by interest representation supported by the state (Trubek) are offered as solutions to this dilemma. However, in light of the results reported above, it is doubtful if this could enhance collective action, which largely determines the willingness of the persons concerned to cooperate. If we evaluate the scale of sympathy for organizations, state agencies, and other alternatives for problem resolution, it seems to be of primary importance to the individual that he be allowed to express his opinion. This is why people reject public agencies, courts, political parties, unions, and big organizations, whereas tenants' groups restricted to specific blocks of apartment buildings, neighborhood groups, citizen rights groups, and also courts or the use of arbitration receive more sympathy.

However, although the tenant's initiative permits informal communication, it nevertheless leads to the establishment of a hierarchy within the group. In the TRG one group member with more legal knowledge than others developed into an individual counselor, answering the questions of the other members. One group had an

attorney as a member, with the effect that individual counseling sessions were held. Thus the motivations for group activity were decreased and frustrated step by step.

Existing legal processes for the pursuit of tenants' interests not only discourage collective action, but they also tend to make extralegal as well as legal alternatives for action obsolete. If we examine the objectives for the TRG as indicated by the tenants with regard to frequency (Table 4.1), we arrive at the following list of barriers to reaching these objectives: The TRG cannot give legal counseling under sanction of a misdemeanor according to paragraph 1 of the Law on Legal Counseling of 1936; it cannot act as party in a lawsuit; and it cannot even act as counselor before the district courts (paragraph 90 of the Code of Civil Procedure) because of the Law on Legal Counseling. There are no institutionalized possibilities for the TRGs to make themselves heard in public agencies or in Parliament, as for instance through a special board for housing problems.

As far as legal possibilities exist, other forms of action are illegal and are threatened with legal sanctions. The boycott of rent payments, for instance, violates contract laws, even when used in response to violations by the landlord. Propagating the violation of legal regulations is limited by the laws that prohibit the damaging of business and credit, criminal sanctions against slander and insult, and the regulations about termination of contracts. Squatting in buildings that have not been rented despite fines imposed by the housing agencies is legally still trespassing and disturbance of the public peace. Even the distribution of leaflets and collecting signatures are restricted by police laws.

For the TRG, threats of sanctions played a less important role than the uncertainty about the complicated and nontransparent legal situation. Therefore, the issue of legal restrictions on collective actions was continually brought up in the meetings of the TRG. Since the expectations for success of these actions were limited anyway, the slightest doubt about the legality of an action was often sufficient to prevent the members from attempting it. Even if a group wanted to support the individual pursuit of rights, this action was confronted with restrictions. According to the Law on Legal Counseling, it was not clear whether legal counsel could be provided for the members of the group; when a case that had subsequently been discussed in the group came into court, the group members were ordered by the judge not to discuss it among themselves or disturb the procedures through their explanations because "they were not involved."

Therefore, organization and collective action cost in terms of sacrificing time but pay in terms of encouragement. One of the main

reasons for people joining the TRG is to gain certainty. However, we find the same correlation with participation in collective action as we find for the individual pursuit of rights; that is, participation in the tenants' initiative increases with educational status and also with income.

Forms of legalization that make collective actions possible deal with social interests within their social context and guarantee for success. The forms can thus be seen as a lowering of access barriers to the law. Collectivity can reduce social powerlessness not only in the area of labor law, but also in all areas in which the use of collective goods is confronted by the prerogatives of private disposal. A system of legalization that encouraged collective actions on all levels could produce different attitudes toward action usually taken from those indicated by the current empirical studies.

Compensation and Prevention

Some of the legal limitations to tenants' pursuit of their rights have to do with the restricted possibility of compensation. Tenants may reduce or withhold rent payments if the landlord fails to honor his part of the contract. But this is of little help in cases where landlords have to deliver some service (repair, heating, etc.). The procedural steps to be taken to sue a landlord (consulting an attorney, bringing the motion for a court order, accounting of the court order, and executing it) take too much time when the heating, elevator, or water stop working in a building. The possibility of solving the problem through one's own initiative is prohibited by contract law. Preventive action by bringing an action of default is met by the barrier of the necessary threat of repetition. The main interest of the tenants is, however, protection against infringements of their rights. The legally trained observer was surprised to learn that the tenants most feared the computerized reminders. These reminders were sent out monthly by the landlord without consideration of the reasons for partial or nonpayment of rent and without pursuing the matter in other ways. Many tenants complained about these reminders as an unbearable stress for them, even though they lacked legal force. This again prevented—and it may be a calculated effect—other tenants from resisting unjustified claims or exercising their rights to reduce rent.

Other problems were, for instance, the landlord replacing gas stoves in the kitchens with electric stoves and using this action to unjustifiably increase the rent. For a while the illegal practice of demanding damage deposits from prospective tenants also existed. Only some of the tenants sued for the return of these deposits, without being able to prevent the continuation of this practice with other tenants. In many

cases of new rentals, the rent was increased in spite of the rent control regulations. Not every tenant notices this and demands information from the housing authorities, and even fewer use their right to refuse to pay excessive rent demands because people are not certain about the legal situation and are afraid of being evicted or becoming involved in lawsuits.

Preventive measures can become useful only by uniting a group of tenants. If the landlord then violates their rights, the whole group instead of only the individual will be concerned. The use of forms containing illegal conditions, for instance, could be dealt with as a threat against the whole group of tenants, because it makes tenants insecure and conceals the actual legal situation. This imminent threat, however, becomes relevant only after the rights of a tenant have been violated and this tenant wants to gain information about his contractual obligations. If a preventive possibility for all of these problems existed, it would act as an important stimulus for organization by counteracting one of the most important barriers to the pursuit of interests; that is, the insecurity of the individual about his rights.

In studying legal needs, we have to begin with the specific interests of the persons concerned and their means of exerting social power. These interests should be regarded as legal needs only if they can be satisfied through a legal process that utilizes the potential for action of the persons concerned and thus furthers their social power.

NOTES

1. Curran, 1977b; Sykes, 1969/1970; Abel-Smith et al., 1973.
2. Curran, 1977b, p. 240.
3. Sykes, 1969; Carlin, Howard, and Messinger, 1967; Marks, 1971.
4. Cf. Blankenburg and Fiedler, 1978.
5. Handler, 1978, p.2.
6. Trubek, Trubek, and Becker, in this volume.
7. Halpern, in this volume.
8. Caplovitz, 1974.
9. Rosenthal, 1974.
10. Wassermann, 1978.
11. Koch, 1976, p. 116–117.
12. Caplovitz, 1974.
13. Menger, 1968.

Chapter 5

Dilemmas in the Delivery of Legal Services

Kees Schuyt

TWO LEGAL AID MODELS

In their article, "Legal Aid: Modern Themes and Variations," Cappelletti and Gordley conclude their review of the legal aid systems in Eastern and Western Europe and in the United States with a short description of the two legal aid models that exist side by side: the "individual juridical" model and the "welfare" model. On the one hand, legal aid can be seen as a juridical right, a right granted to citizens to protect their individual interests; on the other hand, it can be seen as a welfare right, forming part of the packet of social facilities in a welfare state.

The right to legal aid is a recent concept. Under Roman law, legal aid occupied a place in the sphere of a political patronage system. During the Middle Ages, it fell within the sphere of morality. This office was performed as charity, pro deo, to the glory of God. After the French Revolution the right to legal aid fell into the juridical sphere, and the principle of equal access to the courts for all citizens was proclaimed. Nonetheless, as a result of the attitude that all citizens themselves

Note: An earlier version of this chapter written in Dutch appeared as Chapter 10 of a book I wrote with C. A. Groenendijk and B. Sloot: *De weg naar het recht* (*The road to justice*) (Kluwer: Deventer, 1976), a sociological study about relations between social inequality and legal services.

must take the initiative to defend their rights, the right to legal aid remains only a concept for many. A wide gap continues to exist between proclamation and realization. In theory, legal aid falls within the sphere of favors. Legal aid to the poor becomes a honorary duty of the lawyer. Although considerable attention was paid to the matter of representation at the end of the nineteenth century, legal aid remained in the sphere of favors until well into the twentieth century. Moreover, it is mainly limited to cases in court. In present-day Italy and Belgium, legal aid continues to fall within the sphere of favors and honorary duties. In other countries, however, the government has increasingly assumed financial responsibility for legal aid to the underprivileged in civil suits: for example, in Germany since 1919 to 1923, in England since 1949, in the Netherlands since 1957, in the United States since 1965, and in France since 1972.

The formal guarantee of legal aid for the underprivileged in the nineteenth century, which resulted in a wide discrepancy between principle and practice, has, as a result of measures taken by the state, changed to an effective guarantee in the second half of the twentieth century. Cappelletti and Gordley summarize this development as follows:

> Although its content and implications are still far from certain, this new solution can be characterized by three central themes: legal aid has become a right to be protected by positive law; this protection calls for affirmative state action; and this action must effectively rather than formally guarantee the right. . . . Such a demand inevitably raises the questions to which the modern answer to problems of legal aid has no ready response.[1]

The manner in which government intervention takes place affects the realization of the goal of equal access to the law and the risk that discrepancies should again arise between the principle of equal access and an actual situation of unequal access. Two models deserve attention in this connection. The individual juridical model still has many characteristics of the classical pattern of legal aid. It is left up to the individual to defend his rights. Individuals approach lawyers with their legal problems. The lawyers are paid by the government for their services. In order to arrive at a fair and efficient expenditure of public funds, an investigation of the individual's financial circumstances and of the nature of the case is carried out before aid is provided. If the person in question is eligible for financial aid, this person is in theory free to make his own choice of a lawyer. Because of its organizational form, this model is mainly aimed at *individuals* seeking legal aid. It is

to a large degree dependent on the initiative of the clients and the expertise of the lawyers.

The welfare model views legal aid as one aspect of a more general social policy, for example, the suppression of poverty, social insecurity, or dependence. The social rights recognized in the framework of the welfare state—with respect to housing, labor, social security, and a minimum standard of living—call for more active intervention by the state. Within this framework, legal aid is one of the means of realizing these new rights. In the welfare model, government finances legal aid bureaus staffed with lawyers who are employed either full- or part-time. The nature of aid provided by these bureaus is wider. It is part of a broad program of social policy and social reform (especially in the United States, where it is an element of the War on Poverty). There is more attention paid to group-oriented aid and a more active approach is taken by the lawyers. In this model, legal aid *may* be combined with social and political action. Neighborhood Law Offices in the United States, financed since 1965 by the Office of Economic Opportunity Legal Services Program, constitute one example of this welfare model.[2] Although some may be tempted to express a clear preference for one of the two models, each has its limitations. This makes an "either-or" choice difficult. The individual juridical model involves high administrative costs (in England during recent years more than one-fifth of the total gross cost of legal aid in civil cases). Moreover, the service is strictly juridical, which for clients from the lower social classes is not always the best solution. Language and cultural barriers constitute a hindrance as well. The advantage of free choice of a lawyer must be weighed against the responsibility of the individual to personally do something about his or her legal problems. Often this is asking too much; as Cappelletti and Gordley show:

> A lawyer treats the aid applicant or aided litigant just as he treats a normal private client. As a result, the poor man must be articulate enough to communicate his problems to a man with a different cultural background and intelligent enough to understand what he is told and to choose between the legal alternatives he is presented. Inevitably these tasks are difficult for poor men who must step into a somewhat alien world and deal with it on its own terms. Inevitably many of them will be unable to do so.[3]

In the welfare model, the special attention given to poor clients can solve problems of this sort. But here the limitations lie elsewhere. As a result of the wider goal (the solution of social problems), the danger arises that the client's problems may be neglected. The individual

responsibility of the client is relegated to the background. Considerable power rests in the hand of the professional consultant, who in addition to solving the problem of the individual is also concerned with satisfying the goals of the organization and his or her own interests. (The latter problem of course also exists among private lawyers.) The danger is that these idealistic consultants may feel that they know better what the clients want than the clients themselves. Another real danger of this model is political intervention by the subsidizing agency. This may come into play particularly in cases where the government is the defendant.

Despite these risks, the welfare model offers considerable advantages in making legal aid available especially to those groups that are least accessible. In England, in addition to the individual juridical Legal Aid and Advice Act administered by the bar, more than fifteen Neighborhood Law Centers are in operation, all of which are fashioned on the American welfare model. By this means the advantages and disadvantages of the two models compensate each other.

Cappelletti and Gordley's analytical description of some current systems of legal aid is a useful guide for making explicit choices. Nonetheless, we would like to offer criticism of two points. In the first place, their scheme is not sufficiently detailed. In particular, it is unclear which value premises or value preferences are implicit in the two models. In the second place, little attention is devoted to the relation between goals and means. What can one expect from the choice of certain means? The structuring of organizations in a particular manner almost always entails independent side effects that may counteract set goals. In the analysis of the various models of legal aid, attention will be devoted separately to such effects. An example may clarify this.

The goals of the Dutch Legal Aid for the Underprivileged Act of 1957 were fashioned on the welfare model. Legal aid was viewed as a "branch of social care." Ultimately, the organizational instrumentation was based on the individual juridical model. Thus, it is not surprising that one of the goals of the act—the elimination of inequality—was not realized. Implementation of a legal aid system in such a way that the best means are chosen continues to be a most important challenge.

FOUR QUESTIONS ABOUT THE ORGANIZATION OF SOCIAL FACILITIES

If supplying legal aid to lower income groups is viewed as a branch of social care, experience gained in the organization of other

Table 5.1. Dimensions of Choice and Value Orientations in Social Policy

Individualistic Orientation	*Choice Problem*	*Collectivist Orientation*
Cost-effectiveness ←	Allocation	→ Social effectiveness
Freedom of choice ←	Facility	→ Social control
Freedom of deviation ←	Supply	→ Efficiency
Local autonomy ←	Financing	→ Centralization

Source: Neil Gilbert and Harry Specht, *Dimensions of Social Welfare Policy,* © 1974, p. 43. Reprinted by permission of Prentice-Hall, Inc., Englewood Cliffs, N.J.

forms of social care may be helpful in achieving the optimal organization of legal aid. Moreover, social assistance for underprivileged groups and juridical aid share similar problems—spanning social distance, accessibility, professionalization, and selection of clients.

Studies of other forms of assistance sometimes give surprising insight into the problems of choice and other dilemmas encountered in legal service. For this reason, we will for the moment divert our attention from legal aid and investigate possible parallels between social and legal aid, basing our investigations on the study.

Gilbert and Specht, in their book, *Dimensions of Social Welfare Policy,* suggest that four questions must be answered for every type of social policy. They are:

1. *Who* gets what? (the question of allocation of services and resources)
2. Who gets *what?* (the question of the content of social facilities)
3. *How* are the services distributed? (the question of supply)
4. *How* is financing regulated? (the question of financial sources and grants)

Each question can be broadly answered in two ways. Each answer points to a value's orientation, and together these values point to a social philosophy. Gilbert and Specht explain the choices in the scheme shown in Table 5.1. A choice in favor of one of the two orientations must be made at the expense of equally worthwhile values in the other direction. Though different social values may often be recognized as having worth, it is not always possible to practice them simultaneously. Compromise and a dualistic system of aid may be expected to result.

Next, we will review the four problems and, as far as possible, apply them to the area of legal aid.

Who Is Entitled to Publicly Financed Legal Services?

Past findings about unequal access to legal aid that indicated that the more privileged groups in society were sooner, better, and more often in

a position to defend their interests through legal channels have resulted in a plea for better legal aid for the underprivileged. Further study of the problem, however, shows that the question involves not only improvement for the most deprived, but also for many others, for example, middle-income groups. *Justice for some* evoked a strong reaction in favor of *justice for the poor,* which in turn was followed by a call for *justice for all.*[4]

The foregoing gives some indication of the allocation question. When granting totally or partially free legal aid should the choice be for universal allocation (*all*) or for a selection of the society (e.g., *the poor*)? If a choice is made to select particular individuals or groups, what selection criterion should be employed? Universal allocation is not unknown in the welfare state. Everyone receives a practically free education; everyone, poor or rich, is entitled to an old age pension. The selection principle is often applied, however. There are special provisions for widows, the unemployed, individuals below a certain income level, and the disabled.

At present, free legal aid is granted exclusively to people below a certain income level. The selection principle is based on the precept that (financial) aid should only be given to those who are really in need of it. Those who are in a position to provide and finance their own legal aid along other channels are expected to do so. This is called *cost-effectiveness.* Every guilder is expended in such a manner that it benefits precisely those who cannot themselves afford this expenditure. In addition, this approach appeals to the sentiments of individualizing fairness, whereby the most suitable solution is sought for each case. Criteria as to need may be determined by the group or category. Often, however, selection is not made according to the group, but according to the individual. A diagnostic survey is first carried out to determine whether the person in question is indeed eligible for aid. This survey is often a combination of a financial investigation (means test) and an investigation of the merits of the case. For each case, it must be shown that the need for aid does exist. A selective allocation system is thus often discriminatory, humiliating, and stigmatizing.

Such an investigation often has a deterring effect, especially for middle-income groups or people who count themselves as belonging to the middle-income groups. The constant screening calls for an efficient and meticulous administration, as a result of which operational costs are high. The eligibility standards employed must be constantly tested and adjusted from year to year. Because many people are uncertain of their eligibility, owing to the complexity of the standards, aid often does not reach precisely those persons for whom it is intended. These disadvantages can be resolved by making aid available to all. Attention

is focused on reaching as many groups and individuals as possible, regardless of the fact that some people who could finance their own legal aid also benefit. This is termed social effectiveness. No one is deterred by an investigation of his circumstances. There is no discrimination between groups, and less administration is involved. In the Netherlands, the Law Shops opened their doors to all, implicitly applying universal allocation. However, as a consequence, clients were encouraged who did not originally qualify for assistance.

It may seem that if emphasis is placed on social effectiveness, costs will be higher than if the emphasis is on cost-effectiveness, since in the latter case funds are strictly guarded and no one who can pay his or her own way is aided. Nonetheless, the English sociologist Titmuss, who has made an extensive study of social services, is of the opinion that the emphasis on cost-effectiveness is often related to a short-term point of view:

> If access to medical provision entails a means-test investigation that is demeaning, time-consuming, or otherwise inconvenient, clients may procrastinate about seeking medical aid until the symptoms of disease are so painful that they can no longer be ignored. At this advanced stage the cost of treatment is usually more expensive. In the calculus of the long-run cost-effectiveness and social effectiveness can be brought into harmony when universal allocation of medical provision saves more in prevention than allocation saves by limiting treatment only to those in dire need.[5]

Preventative help reduces costs. Though one cannot draw an unqualified parallel between medical and juridical aid, the same social processes can be observed. Lawyers also find that clients approach them too late. Timely advice can often avert a lengthy dispute or lawsuit. In the long run, application of a universal allocation principle could prove to be less expensive. A detailed cost-benefit analysis could possibly throw light on the matter.

Nevertheless, there continue to be proponents of a selective principle, and they may even hold opposing social views. Against the liberal view that everyone should pay his or her own way as far as possible (cost-effectiveness) is the progressive view that legal aid should be made available to everyone. By restricting aid only to poor people, a certain balance is introduced. Various Law Shops in the Netherlands explicitly practice this principle.

In addition to the problems of discrimination and stigmatization, the principle of limiting aid exclusively to the underprivileged involves two further problems. The first problem is injuring the interests of

those who fall just outside of the eligibility standards. A feeling of relative deprivation and aggressive attitudes toward the socially deprived are possible side effects of aid that is exclusively for the underprivileged.

The second problem is unavoidable operationalization of the criteria. Though a selective needs criterion should not necessarily be condemned as an allocation principle, it does lead to all kinds of practical difficulties, such as visiting the social (welfare) department, waiting, being asked to return, and referral to other authorities. If selective allocation is chosen, the related disadvantages can be partially offset by the following factors:

1. Choosing a clear criterion for the right to legal aid that is known and can be recognized by all
2. Employing an administratively simple criterion or coupling the right to legal aid with an already existing and accepted criterion (such as the salary limit for compulsory health insurance)
3. Making specific groups (such as senior citizens) automatically eligible for aid

The system is then easy to understand and administrative costs are reduced. Such palliatives do not, however, remove the stigmatization.

The final problem is how hard-to-reach groups can be made to benefit more from services that have been developed precisely for their interests. In our opinion, simply extending the limits of allocation will not increase accessibility for these groups. In most instances, they already fall within the limits of existing criteria. These hard-to-reach groups can be approached only through special distribution methods.

What Facilities Are Offered?

The most important choice in making the facilities packet available is the choice between giving money or giving goods and services—*in cash or in kind.* Every packet of social facilities must be submitted to this question. In general, it has been established that services are cheaper and more effective than money. Supposing that the government is responsible for providing clothing and shoes for all poor children. In this case, it is cheaper for the government to buy these goods en masse and distribute them in kind than to give each child a certain amount of money from which to buy clothing and shoes in the neighborhood shops according to individual taste. This method opens the opportunity for good and bad bargains. Of course, the disadvantages of providing facilities in kind are also clear—no freedom of choice as well as a large risk of discrimination, especially in the case of tangible goods. For legal

services, we encounter the same problem of choice. The government can make available amounts of money for those seeking legal aid, which they can then use to employ a lawyer in the same manner as people who are not dependent on government aid. These people can then purchase their legal aid on a competitive open market. The fact that the government pays the lawyer directly and does not provide the client with cash does not detract from the principle of cash help. It is true that in this case, however, the money can only be used to pay for the services of a lawyer.

The government may also make available the services of lawyers and remunerate these lawyers either per case, by the amount of time expended, or according to other standards, usually in the form of full- or part-time employment. The remuneration of lawyers who are permanently employed by the government or other institutions is thus not dependent on the number of cases they handle. Competition from other legal aid consumers is excluded by this means.

What are the advantages and disadvantages that accompany the two forms of provision? In the United States both forms of legal aid, which are even financed by the same source, have been employed since 1965. The first system is known as *judicare*. According to this system the poor are given the right to go to any private lawyer of their choice who is affiliated with the judicare system. The lawyer receives remuneration for services rendered. The second system, employing a permanent staff of lawyers, became known through the Neighborhood Law Offices. Both forms are aimed primarily at the poor. There are fervent proponents of both systems.[6] In England since 1949 and in the Netherlands since 1957, two systems are in operation that strongly resemble judicare. The most important similarities are:

1. Only part of the population is eligible for this aid (cost-effectiveness).
2. Services are provided by private lawyers.
3. The lawyers receive remuneration from the government.

The major difference between judicare and the two Western European systems is that for judicare the right to legal aid is determined beforehand for a certain period (usually a year). Thus, for example, when a person is granted a public welfare benefit, he at the same time receives a card that makes him eligible for the services of all lawyers who participate in the system. He knows that while this card is valid he can consult a lawyer for all kinds of legal matters. When the need for legal aid arises, he is not obliged to undergo a means test first.

In England, Neighborhood Law Centers based on the American model have recently come into being. In the Netherlands, the Law

Shops resemble this model. There are a few significant differences. Most Law Shops are staffed by volunteers (law students), often assisted in the background by lawyers with other employment, whereas the American Neighborhood Law Offices are staffed by lawyers who are assisted by volunteers. Moreover, the Law Shops are only partially financed by the government. The following arguments are put forward in favor of the judicare system.[7]

1. It eliminates discrimination.
2. It increases the freedom of choice, autonomy, and thus the self-respect of persons seeking aid.
3. It precludes socialization of the legal profession and thus guarantees that the bar has greater independence.
4. No government funds are used for striving toward social reform through legal aid.

On the other hand, proponents of Neighborhood Law Offices make the following arguments:

1. Financial remuneration provided by the government cannot compete with normal lawyers' fees, and thus discrimination is not completely excluded.
2. Freedom of choice is an illusion for someone who has no knowledge of the juridical world.
3. Permanent employment of lawyers in the law offices does not necessarily mean that the government acquires authority over these lawyers or over the law profession as an institution.
4. A significant advantage of this approach is that legal aid can be provided in the context of a program that strives toward social reform.

A number of these differences of opinion are rhetorical. There are, however, other, more empirical differences. Judicare was mainly employed in rural areas where the population was acquainted with the local private lawyers. The system made use of the geographical distribution of these lawyers' offices. The Neighborhood Law Offices were established mainly in the poor neighborhoods of large cities. Lawyers employed by these bureaus had only recently been called to the bar and were often still inexperienced. Private lawyers had, of course, more experience and consequently more experience with poor clients. The caseload of the Neighborhood Law Offices often accumulated so rapidly that this led to new problems. Theoretically and ideologically, there was room for reform-oriented action, but in practice activities of this kind were estimated at no more than 5 percent of all activities.[8] The type of cases dealt with by these offices differed little

from those dealt with by judicare lawyers. Brakel makes the following observation about law-reform advocates:

> The problem is that so many law-reform advocates do not know and do not care to know about clients' needs or preferences. They deal with abstract issues, abstract strategies and abstract clients .... their perspective is more like a war perspective, a paternalistic assessment of priorities made for, not by the poor.[9]

Though the danger of paternalism is certainly present, Brakel draws an exaggerated picture. Precisely as a result of the establishment of these centers, the inadequate aid for the underprivileged and the lax attitude of established lawyers in the United States with respect to providing legal aid for these groups were exposed.[10] Though reform may be abstract, the clients from the ghettos certainly are not.

Participation by private lawyers lends the judicare system a decentralized structure in the organizational sense. Decentralization has major advantages for the client. Nonetheless, organizational decentralization does not necessarily go hand in hand with geographical distribution. The opposite is the case in many cities where law offices are often strongly concentrated in one area. The advantages of organizational decentralization are valid only when lawyers are actually distributed over various districts of city and rural areas. On this point, the Neighborhood Law Offices and the Dutch Law Shops have contributed to improving the geographical distribution of legal aid facilities. An important comparison is the costs involved in both systems. On the basis of a limited survey, Johnson came to the conclusion that the system in which lawyers are employed on a permanent basis is cheaper than the judicare system of legal aid in which legal aid is provided by private lawyers.

> This information suggests that government apparently can provide in-kind legal assistance less expensively—by a ratio of over 3 to 1—than this service can be purchased by poor people out of income transferred to them.[11]

The method of calculation that he employs has, however, not remained undisputed. Brakel points out that:

> The difference lies in recording techniques rather than in substance. The staffed-office and Judicare portions of the Meriden program handled an equal number of *clients*, but the staffed office recorded three times as many *cases*.[12]

In the Canadian province of Quebec, a system of legal services has been in operation since 1973, in which use is made both of lawyers permanently employed by legal aid bureaus and private lawyers. Comparison of the costs of both forms of legal aid showed that the average remuneration that private lawyers received per case was 50 percent higher than the average cost per case in bureaus with lawyers in permanent employment. The suggestion was made that this difference might be explained by a difference in the type of case handled.[13] We will discuss this difference later.

Thus, there is no need to make a one-sided choice between the two systems. Though proponents and opponents of both systems discuss the question heatedly, the conclusions reached often do not differ greatly. Johnsen pleads for what he terms a compromise, namely, a combination of the two systems. In other words, if the know-how of private lawyers is available, it can be put to good use. Lawyers attached to bureaus can then specialize in fields and forms of legal aid that are either not practiced or seldom practiced by private lawyers (e.g., legal aid for group and neighborhood activities).

In England such agreements exist between the lawyers employed permanently by the Neighborhood Law Centers and private lawyers of the local bar. The centers refer family matters, divorce cases, and many criminal cases to private lawyers located in the neighborhood of the centers. To compensate for this, the lawyers of the Neighborhood Law Centers are exempted from certain rules of the code of professional conduct, such as the rules about advertising, approaching clients, and sharing fees with members of other professions. Other conceivable combinations of the two systems include a geographic limitation of the range of operation of a legal aid office or the possibility that these offices limit their services to specific groups. Brakel, too, concludes by advocating a combination system in which, however, the judicare system plays a dominant role.

> We are convinced, then, that the Judicare method for delivering legal services to poor people is a sound method and should be the basis for the national attempt to help the poor use legal resources. The central office, the staffed office, the staff attorney—these should function to *supplement* Judicare, fill in the gaps, supervise, co-ordinate and in exceptional circumstances perhaps intervene in (by prohibiting or activating) local Judicare problem resolution. The role of the central offices and staff should vary with the performance of the *primary* Judicare component: perhaps in some area no office would be warranted or necessary and a staff attorney would ride circuit, whereas in other

Table 5.2 Quebec, 1974–1975, Type of Case According to Type of Lawyer

	Family Matters	*Criminal Cases*	*Other Cases*	*N*
Private lawyers	47%	34%	19%	23.819 (25%)
Lawyers in public legal aid bureaus	26%	31%	43%	72.455 (75%)
Total	31%	32%	37%	96.274 (100%)

geographic or demographic regions, offices manned by several staff attorney would be desirable.[14]

In Sweden and Quebec both systems are employed simultaneously. In Sweden, however, there is no specific division of work or agreement about cases. Public legal aid bureaus must compete with private lawyers to show that the remuneration paid by government to both groups of lawyers is sufficient for operation of their offices and a reasonable income. This involves the disadvantage that the assistance offered by the bureaus hardly differs from that of the private lawyers. In 1974 more than 80 percent of the cases dealt with by these bureaus related to family affairs. Research in several countries, however, shows that cases of this type are not the only legal problem with which the lower income groups are confronted. From Table 5.2, it appears that in Quebec a division of work has come about.

The 2270 private lawyers (approximately 60 percent of all members of the bar) who participated in this system dealt mainly with family affairs and criminal cases. The 260 lawyers employed by the 100 legal aid bureaus dealt mainly with matters that did not fall within these two branches. Moreover, Table 5.2 shows that for every 10 cases dealt with by private lawyers, lawyers in the bureaus dealt with approximately 275. This gives a fairly clear indication that the two groups of lawyers provided different kinds of legal aid. The bureaus were probably much more engaged in advisory work, whereas the private lawyers probably handled more cases in court.

How Are the Services Distributed?

Expansion of social services usually involves competition for the available financial resources. As a result of increasing competition, the relationship between the various groups and organizations that provide services becomes increasingly turbulent. Social and political differences stand out. Under such circumstances the answers in situations of choice are given more on the basis of value and ideological preferences than on the basis of the predictable effects of the various

propositions. Especially in the choice of a distribution system, ideological imagination may confuse the issue. On the basis of experience and research in social service systems, various predictions can be made regarding the probable consequences of a particular organization of legal assistance. Supply of legal services may sound strange as a concept since traditionally the providers of legal aid wait until clients approach them. Supply of services suggests a certain degree of initiative by the providers of aid. Aid to socially weak groups often requires a more active approach than is the case when dealing with stronger groups who themselves take the initiative in seeking aid. If one possesses a certain surplus of resources (financial, social, psychological, and political), aid can be found on one's own initiative. Since in the past lawyers usually rendered their services to the socially stronger groups, this professional passivity created no serious problems in the distribution of services.

Now that more and other social classes can obtain legal aid, however, the question of supply acquires a new perspective. Legal aid can be brought closer to the people simply by the way in which services are organized. The questions involved here are as follows: Should legal services be centralized or decentralized? Must there be a combined service including medical, social, and juridical aid, or is a separate service sufficient? Should the various services be situated in one building or spread over various buildings? Is a high level of coordination desirable or not? Must assistance be provided exclusively by professionals or should volunteers be allowed to participate? Should the organization be managed and controlled by experts, clients, the government, or society? These situations can be dealt with by formulating the most important problems in organizational structure of a system of aid. These problems are:

1. Fragmentation of services
2. Discontinuity of services
3. Inaccessibility of services
4. Nonaccountability and nonliability of services

By fragmentation, one means that the party seeking aid must approach various authorities for various kinds of problems. Fragmentation is a consequence of specialization. The idea of a "generalist" in legal aid, who can be approached on matters of any kind, is the opposite of fragmentation and the ideal representative of integrated aid. Fragmentation also involves a certain overlapping of services, since it is never possible to determine exactly where one field ends and the other begins. The resulting problems are taken care of by coordination.

One is confronted with the problem of fragmentation not only within one branch of aid, but also and even increasingly between various sorts of aid, for instance, medical, social, juridical, and pedagogic aid. Often a person seeking aid is confronted not with one single problem, but with a series of problems in various fields. The ideal solution would then be an integrated, nonfragmented service, whereby one institution could deal with the interrelated problems. Coordination, exchange of information, and sometimes assistance in context of a team are essential. Though coordination (the attuning of various services to each other) has become almost indispensable, certain disadvantages are nonetheless involved.

Discontinuity of assistance is encountered when a client must approach various providers of aid for the solution to one problem. For example, a client approaches a social counselor with a problem; the latter refers the client to a social worker, who in turn refers him to a lawyer, who then turns the problem over to a young colleague, who, halfway through, turns the case over to another colleague. Discontinuity is a problem encountered in the Legal Aid Offices and Law Shops when the client is confronted with a different advisor on every occasion. Discontinuity is evinced by the channels the client must go through before finally receiving assistance. These channels can be shortened by good communication between aid-givers, by a rapid and efficiently functioning referral, and by keeping check of the referrals so that the client does not get lost in between. Discontinuity is mainly an organizational problem. It is, however, clear that the risk of discontinuity increases in direct proportion to the degree of fragmentation in the services provided.

Inaccessibility of assistance may be related to the degree of bureaucratization, to the language employed by those giving assistance, or to (an unconscious) selective preference for clients from a particular social group or class. Accessibility of services is not exclusively a problem of furthering knowledge of the various channels among those seeking aid, but also to a large degree is determined by the manner in which the provision of assistance is organized.

Nonaccountability of services has to do with the limited possibilities open to clients for voicing their complaints regarding legal services. On the one hand, this problem falls under the general problem of discipline and occupational liability, and on the other hand, it has to do with the less formalized relationship between clients and providers of aid. How much say does the client have in the decisions regarding the assistance provided in his particular case and in the organization of provision of services in general? Participation by clients is seen as a possibility for increasing the accountability of the organization. In many systems of

legal aid, far less attention is devoted to accountability and professional liability than to coordination and accessibility.

The ideal service system would consequently be characterized by integration, continuity, easy accessibility, and adequate accountability. But in practice this ideal is very difficult to achieve. Gilbert and Specht point out that these four elements of an ideal aid system impose restrictions on each other. They make the following observations:

> Fragmentation and discontinuity may be diminished by better coordination (communication and referral) and by avoiding overlapping in services provided; but by so doing, the risk of inaccessibility and unaccountability is increased.
>
> The inaccessibility may be decreased by providing new approaches and by multiplying the services, but such steps would increase the risk of fragmentation.
>
> The unaccountability of the aid services can be reduced by client participation; but by permitting this, the risk of fragmentation would be increased (groups of clients may follow their own course, thus rendering coordination more difficult).

It would be possible to name more such restricting relations between the aspects of providing aid. The objectives of those who formulate policy are usually strongly focused on coordination. In this process it is sometimes forgotten that by the solution of one problem other problems may be created, which counteract the good intentions of the problem-solvers. Ultimately policy depends on the weight that is ascribed to the various problems recognized. If increased accessibility is desired, a certain fragmentation and duplication of services must not only be accepted as inevitable but must even be encouraged. From the above discussion, it can be seen that the organization of aid services is no simple matter.

The various advantages and disadvantages must be considered with a view to finding an optimum solution. Once a choice has been made, the organization of an aid system becomes easier. There are then rational answers to the various questions of supply. If high priority is ascribed to increasing accessibility (as we do), answers can be formulated to a number of questions regarding the organization of the legal aid system. We will touch on five points.

Striving Toward Coordination. The problem of coordination arises as a consequence of specialization. The fact that only a few aspects of a client's problem can be dealt with by one member of the aid system is a result of increasing technical expertise. A client may have the feeling of being torn asunder by the professional division of labor,

that is, fragmentation. Coordination attempts to counteract the negative effects of this division of labor. The ultimate goal—perhaps in a team context—is of course to help the "whole" person. This ideal of reaching the whole person has had the effect that new "alternative" aid organizations are trying, as far as possible, to provide all services in one organization. To this end, nonprofessionals are sometimes chosen in preference to dividing the labor. The Youth Advice Centers in the Netherlands have as their ideal to provide youth with a total packet of services. The aim is to deal not only with the legal but also with the social and psychological aspects of the client's case. Sometimes this is done because the client requests it, but sometimes this is simply the standard approach.

In our opinion, alternative aid has sprung up to counteract the side effects of coordination. Coordination calls for centralization, and this increases the distance between the client and consultant. Moreover, centralization entails a tendency toward monopolization of services. This monopolization has special negative effects for the client. In the first place, the accountability of the assisting organization diminishes. In the second place, the criteria for accepting and helping clients become increasingly standardized; the organization operates according to one set of rules. The chance that clients will be able to influence the determination of these criteria will also be minimized. Only one approach to the service will remain available. If one does not want to use this approach or if one has had conflicts with the central coordinating authority, there is no other way of receiving service. In the Netherlands, this has occurred in the case of rehabilitation institutions. Formerly, clients of one independent institution could sometimes, after a conflict, find another institution willing to help them. As a result of cooperation and coordination, however, this possibility has become increasingly limited. If the now united rehabilitation organization gives up on a client as incapable of being helped, there is no other institution to which he can turn.

For the organization itself the risk of inner conflict increases, especially as a result of the heterogeneity of the various departments, which formerly operated independently, but now function as parts of a larger unit. In other words, the—often economic—usefulness of coordination and cooperation may detract from the quality and variety of the services. In the long run, decentralization and preservation of autonomous units may be beneficial to the whole spectrum of aid.

Instead of attempting to achieve organizational unity, geographical unity is sometimes considered sufficient, for example, in the form of a common services center (or social supermarket). The various branches of the aid service can then more easily arrive at agreements regarding

referral and cooperation. But this geographical centralization of the various forms of aid as a solution to the problem of fragmentation involves a decrease in accessibility. According to Gilbert and Specht, it should not be too quickly assumed that services of all kinds, like the pieces of a big puzzle, can be manipulated to form one neat picture.[15] The necessity for some minimum of coordination should not give rise to the conclusion that social work and legal aid must necessarily be integrated to form one services system. These two methods of assistance sometimes have opposing approaches that need not be eliminated. Attempts to arrive at close cooperation between social workers and law students in some Dutch Law Shops have often resulted in problems for those providing help as well as for the clients.

Striving Toward a Separate Entrance. A central entrance for all persons seeking aid offers the advantage that problems receive specialized attention from the start. A recognizable institution offers its services for information, advice, and referral. In giving advice and making referrals, this institution can employ the services of experts (front-line assistance). Where clients are virtually uninformed, this separate entrance can be very valuable. In the Netherlands the television Ombudsman functions at such a separate level entrance, especially for people with a low level of education and low income and limited verbal skills. This does not mean, however, that the accessibility problems are solved all at once. For many of those seeking aid, the need for a stepping-stone remains. This stepping-stone indicates the desirability of a network of entrances that are decentralized and close to those seeking aid (in the neighborhood). We consider this comparable to a kind of legal general practitioner. Specialization in information, advice, and referral has the disadvantage that a division may come about between diagnosis and treatment of the case. Thus, a separate entrance to a certain extent solves the problem of accessibility at the expense of continuity. Moreover, it is not inconceivable that the more well known the first entrance becomes, the more other organizations (particularly government agencies) will reduce their information and advice services. Everyone is then directed to the first entrance. The local "Release" organizations and the Law Shops have repeatedly observed such a development. For this reason it would appear advisable not to shift all front-line assistance to one separate organization. The need does exist, however, for an institution that has a coordinating function within a decentralized network of front-line and follow-up assistance.

Striving Toward Pluriformity. At first glance, it seems inefficient and wasteful to allow two types of legal aid institutions to continue to exist side by side, or to set them up at the same time. The effort to achieve greater efficiency often implies an amalgamation of services that originally operated separately. The benefits of this must, however, be weighed against the social costs for the client. These social costs are more difficult to measure and are thus often not taken into account.

Multiplying services leads to a pluriform system of aid provision. The resulting competition between the institutions may exert a beneficial influence on the quality of aid provided. Attempts at pluriformity in legal aid were formerly embodied in the principle of free choice of a lawyer. In our opinion this principle must now be translated as free choice of the institution providing legal aid. The principle of freedom of choice has the following advantages:

It reduces the clients' dependence on the aid-providing institution because the client is able to check advice and has the possibility of using real alternatives (the competition touched on above).

It reduces the possibility of arbitrariness on the part of those providing aid.

It reduces the risk of bureaucratization in central legal aid bureaus (and as such reduces costs).

It constitutes recognition of the subjective choice and the personal preferences of the client and thus increases his autonomy.

An essential condition for freedom of choice is, however, that the clients are adequately informed. If this condition is not met, a combination of a central bureau with decentralized consultants is a possible in-between stage on the way to the largest possible degree of pluriformity. The idea that one type of legal service could solve the whole problem of unmet legal need is an idée fixe. According to our survey, legal aid institutions attract their own specific clientele and specific types of problems after a certain period of time.

Furthermore, pluriformity offers the extra advantage of retaining the possibility of separatism. Certain institutions that provide aid continue to operate outside of the existing system. This increases the chance that independently operating institutions, even more than the "established" institutions, will continue to promote the interests of certain social and political groups. They can fill in the gaps that are present in every system. They may direct their services at a particular geographical area or group without having to pay much attention to other groups or interests.

It is not to be expected that an aid organization that has expressed a clear preference for furthering particular interests will be suitable for

all groups seeking legal aid. For this reason alone, a system of exclusively centralized legal aid should be rejected. Every client (or group of clients) has the right to a legal advisor with whom he feels some affinity. Our survey showed that the various providers of legal aid (barristers, the Law Shops, and the television Ombudsman) evoke feelings of affinity (identification and solidarity) among some groups of people, while in other groups feelings of opposition, antipathy, and censure are evoked.

Opposing the advantages of pluriformity is the view that such a system will be more expensive and less efficient. There is competition for financial sources as well as competition for clients. Conflicts between the various authorities and reciprocal depreciation may consequently arise. But it is precisely this autonomy that makes the solution of such conflicts less problematic than when all the various institutions are simply departments of one central organization. Moreover, this very competition may lead to a reduction of the price of services (see the case of Sweden).

Client Participation. Coordination places more power in the hands of professional providers of aid and thus increases the danger of paternalism. One way in which to counteract the danger of one-sided professionalism is participation by clients, both in the way their cases are treated[16] and in decisionmaking within the organization. Moreover, client participation may lead to an increase in accessibility and accountability. If there are people in the organization who move in the same circle as (potential) clients, information about the organization and its goals will be disseminated through informal channels and will therefore probably be more effective. In spite of difficulties in achieving effective representation of clients, the Neighborhood Law Centers in England and a few Neighborhood Law Offices in the United States have succeeded in involving clients in the work of the bureaus.[17]

Participation by Volunteers in the Provision of Aid. Another possibility for avoiding the danger of paternalism is to employ nonprofessional volunteers. The professional approach often gives rise to a discrepancy between the behavior of the consultant and the expectations of the client. Professionals, particularly legal professionals, are accustomed to employing an approach that is as objective, impersonal, and businesslike as possible, while clients often expect a personal approach to their problems, that is, a human touch. The success of the Law Shops is due largely to the fact that they comply with the expectations of many clients. The advisor views the problem in the same perspective as the client and gives the client personal attention. Moreover, volunteers are independent of other (financial) interests of

the aid system. Provided it is possible to meet the necessary qualitative conditions, a combination of volunteer and professional aid is extremely valuable.

The new Legal Assistance Act in Quebec explicitly states that use can be made of volunteers (law students) in providing legal aid. The use of volunteers will, however, not always go uncontested by professionals. The question arises if and how the work of these volunteer helpers can be supervised. Should disciplinary rules be adjusted to apply to the new helpers or should they be employed to exclude them? After a period of time, the nonprofessionals too become versed in the routine and may begin to show the characteristics of professionalism. The students in the Law Shops then become lawyers without robes and to a certain degree begin to behave as such. Thus, participation by volunteers may lead to a greater variety of professional providers of aid. This would appear to us to have the advantage of furthering the dynamic development of services that could otherwise easily lose flexibility. Summarizing, it may be said that furtherance of accessibility goes hand in hand with a certain minimum of coordination. This coordination should, however, not lead to a centralistic system. Accessibility is promoted by an extensive network of organizations that complement each other on some points and overlap on other points. Participation by clients and volunteers in services also furthers accessibility.

How Are the Services Financed?

In the Netherlands—in the absence of large private funds—only a limited number of answers are possible to the question of financing. It is almost self-evident that most answers involve the general resources of the central government. Apart from political and economic circumstances, a few other questions arise—the question of partial financing by contributions from the clients, the question of the choice between financing from public funds or a national insurance, and the question as to the chances and consequences of private legal aid insurance. These questions cannot be dealt with at length in this chapter. Our research permits only a few remarks, based on statements of interviewees.

A contribution by the client to the costs of legal aid may give the client the feeling that he may expect more from the assisting services. To some clients making a personal contribution may mean applying a brake to abuse, but at the same time for other clients precisely this contribution prevents them from making use of the services. If there is some uncertainty among clients as to the size of the contribution or if the maximum contribution is a considerable amount, this may

constitute an impediment to seeking aid—even among those who are exempt from making this contribution. Apart from these possible effects, the importance of clients' contributions to the total cost of legal aid should not be overestimated. It covers only a (small) portion of the costs, but it necessitates a large amount of extra administration for collection, recording, and auditing.

In England, where since 1949 a widely differentiated system for personal contributions has been employed, the contributions paid by clients account for not more than 12 percent of the total cost of legal aid in civil cases. During the last five years nearly two-thirds of the recipients of legal aid certificates were exempted from payment of a contribution, while not even 10 percent of consumers made a contribution of £ 150 or more.[18] In Sweden in 1974 only 18 percent of all clients paid a contribution exceeding the minimum of Skr. 60. Less than 10 percent of all consumers made a contribution of more than Skr. 300.[19] The receipts administration necessary for recording and collection of this money can be weighed against the risk of discouraging just those clients one desires to reach. Up to now, such a cost-benefit analysis has not been carried out in the Netherlands or elsewhere.

A national insurance might cause the client to feel that he or she has the right to legal aid since the client has paid the premium. But in view of the more abstract nature of many legal problems in comparison with other risks of the modern welfare state and also because of the already high premiums for existing social insurance schemes, there appears to be little chance at the present of realizing a national insurance for legal services. Among the middle-income groups there is an aversion to being submitted to a means investigation in order to receive legal service financed by the government. Moreover, the members of this group are often under the misguided impression that such service is not intended for them, but only for the lowest income groups, "those who live on government aid."

Finally, there is a preference (and a tradition) among these groups to make personal provision for such contingencies in the form of private or supplementary health insurance. For these groups, personal legal aid insurance could offer the possibility of an entrance to legal aid outside of the system financed by government. A private legal aid insurance could function as a modern form of "self-help" in a society where the chances of needing legal assistance become increasingly greater. In the Federal Republic of Germany the path to legal assistance is for many via legal aid insurance (for more than one million persons in 1974). In 1973, a total of more than 760 million marks was paid for legal aid insurance. In the Netherlands, the total amount paid for such insurance is estimated at thirty-four million guilders.[20]

Among middle-income groups the need for simple advice and relatively inexpensive, easily accessible information is also felt. Middle-income and poorer groups show a similar pattern in the need for (front-line) legal advice. Most legal aid insurance plans in the Netherlands give the client the right to legal advice four times a year (maximum). This aid is usually provided by the staff of the insurance company. In Germany, the legal aid insurance companies do not themselves provide legal advice since this falls under the legal monopoly of the bar. The Dutch system does give rise to certain questions, particularly as to the quantity and quality of this legal aid and the regulation of possible conflicts of interest between those who are insured and the insurance companies.

NOTES

1. Cappelletti and Gordley, 1972, p. 363. Copyright 1972 by the Board of Trustees of Leland Stanford Junior University.
2. See Johnson, 1974.
3. Cappelletti and Gordley, 1972, p. 405. Copyright 1972 by the Board of Trustees of Leland Stanford Junior University.
4. Also see the Society of Labor Lawyers, 1968.
5. Titmuss, 1968.
6. Compare Brakel, 1974; Cahn and Cahn 1964; and Johnson 1974.
7. Compare Johnson, 1974, pp. 238–241; Brakel, 1974, pp. 123–128.
8. Compare Brakel, 1974, p. 80; Johnson, 1974, pp. 192 and 337.
9. Brakel, 1974, p. 127.
10. Compare Auerbach, 1976.
11. Johnson, 1974, p. 225.
12. Brakel, 1974, p. 122.
13. Commission des Services Juridiques, 1975, p. 21.
14. Brakel, 1974, p. 128; italics are used by Brakel.
15. Gilbert and Specht, 1974, pp. 112–115.
16. Compare Rosenthal, 1974.
17. Johnson, 1974, p. 220.
18. Legal Aid Annual Reports, 1975, p. 30.
19. Ministry of Justice, 1975, p. 15.
20. Van der Feltz and Wansink, 1975, p. 152.

Chapter 6

Public Policy for Legal Services

Michael Zander

In the past decade or two, there have been some highly significant changes in the systems of providing legal services, especially to the poor. In this chapter the nature and the implications of some of these developments are analyzed, drawing principally on the experience of England.

STATE FUNDING

For centuries, equality before the law was an ideal to which legal systems subscribed mainly in rhetoric. The courts were open to all—like the Ritz Hotel. Those who could afford to pay lawyers might succeed in securing their rights, but a substantial section of the population was not in this position. In some countries, statute permitted the waiver of court fees or formal or informal methods existed for services to be provided free of charge through the voluntary actions of individual lawyers or requests to lawyers from the courts. But charitable work by lawyers was inevitably patchy; even those who

did it could not devote much time to it and most did little or none. Waiver of court fees left the problem of lawyers' fees untouched. Lawyers were not normally appointed by the court to act without charge unless it was a serious criminal case. In many countries, the court-appointed lawyer tended to be young and therefore inexperienced. Therefore, the aggregate of these various techniques were not significant.

In recent years, however, this condition has greatly changed. In many countries, it has not been recognized that nothing less than a substantial commitment of state funds will suffice if equality before the law is to be made a realistic objective. In England and Wales, for example, the recent growth of state funding for civil and criminal legal aid may be seen from the figures in the government's expenditure plans. They show an annual expenditure on legal aid as follows, in millions of pounds (£).[1]

1972–1973	*1973–1974*	*1974–1975*	*1975–1976*	*1976–1977*
55	58	70	80	83

1977–1978	*1978–1979*	*1979–1980*	*1980–1981*	*1981–1982*
92	96	99	103	103

In the five years from 1972–1973 to 1977–1978 there was an increase of two-thirds from £55 million to £92 million. In the nine years from 1971–1972 to 1981–1982 the level of expenditure, it is expected, will have almost doubled. (These figures do not include money spent on the public sector of legal services—law centers, etc., which are discussed later.) Funding for the Legal Services Corporation in the United States rose from $71 million in 1971 to $205 million in 1977–1978. (The Office of Economic Opportunity Legal Services Program started with $27 million in 1964.) Expenditure on legal aid may be slight by comparison with that for general social services. The social security budget in 1977, including pensions, was £1.2 billion. But although legal aid may absorb a relatively small share of the total GNP, there is no question that in many countries it is a significant and increasing amount and proportion. (It is notable that in the recent efforts in England to reduce public expenditure generally, legal aid fared better than many other services.)

THE LEGAL AID SCHEME

Because delivery systems are the subject of Chapter 5, "Dilemmas in the Delivery of Legal Services," I shall do no more here than to

refer briefly to the chief examples of these systems.The two major models for the delivery of legal services to the poor have been via private practitioners (judicare) and via salaried lawyers (the staff model).

In England, the traditional mode of legal aid has been through private practitioners and this remains the dominant mode today. There are three parts to the legal aid scheme:

Civil Legal Aid: The client obtains an application from the legal aid authorities under the administrative control of the Law Society and is subject both to a means test and a merits test. Those who are eligible may be required to pay a contribution, although most people receive legal aid without having to pay anything. The assessment of the contribution depends on the applicant's means. In 1976–1977, the authorities received 307,751 applications for civil legal aid. In 1976–1977 25,768 applications (8 percent) were refused. In 9195 cases (36 percent) the refusal was based on financial grounds and in 16,573 cases it was based on failure to satisfy the merits test. A total of 225,667 certificates were issued—about three-quarters in matrimonial proceedings. The second largest category of legally aided cases was personal injury cases. The total amount of damages recovered by legally aided plaintiffs was some £44 million.

Legal Advice and Assistance (otherwise known as the Green Form scheme or the £25 scheme): The client goes into a solicitor's office, and providing the solicitor operates the scheme (most do) and the client qualifies under the severe means test, the solicitor can undertake any form of work short of advocacy up to a maximum of £25. If the solicitor wishes to exceed the £25 limit, he must obtain permission from the legal aid authorities. In 1976–1977 solicitors' bills under the scheme were paid in 291,961 cases. In 15,868 cases there was a request to exceed the £25 limit and in 12,537 cases (79 percent) this request was granted. The type of case in which assistance is sought has been reasonably consistent from one year to another. In close to 60 percent it has been matrimonial cases, in some 12 to 15 percent it has been criminal cases, and in some 5 percent landlord and tenant. The other main categories have been accidents (3 to 5 percent), hire purchase and debt (3 percent), wills (2 percent), and advice in relation to tribunals (2 percent). A client can be asked to pay a contribution, the amount of which depends on the client's takehome pay in the previous week as well as the number of dependents. About 90 percent of those who receive help under the scheme, however, are assessed as qualifying without having to pay a contribution.

During 1976–1977 the accounts for the civil legal aid and the legal advice and assistance schemes show the following figures:

Payments to barristers and solicitors for legal advice and assistance	£33.7 million	
Payments to legal aid solicitors for legal advice and assistance	5.4 million	
Administration costs	6.5 million	
Gross cost	£45.6 million	
	Carried over	£45.6 million
Less		
Contributions from assisted persons retained	£4.5 million	
Costs paid by losing parties	7.7 million	
Damages paid by losing parties and retained to meet costs of fund	0.8 million	
Miscellaneous	0.3 million	
Total		13.3 million
Overall cost		£32.3 million

(*Source: 27th Legal Aid Annual Report, 1976–1977,* and Appendix 21.)

Criminal Legal Aid Scheme: The client applies to the court and the application is decided upon, usually by the clerk. If the clerk wishes to refuse the application, it must be referred to the court itself. In other words, the clerk has only power to grant, not to refuse, an application. There is a means test and a merits test. In the higher of the two criminal courts, the Crown Court, virtually everyone qualifies for legal aid. In 1976, 96 percent of those who appeared in the Crown Court for trial were represented through legal aid. For those committed for sentence only the proportion was 97 percent. For trials before magistrates' courts, applicants have to show that they need representation because the case threatens them with a risk of losing their liberty or reputation, because there is a substantial question of law, or because they cannot follow the proceedings because of a physical, mental, or language disability. The number of grants of legal aid in magistrates' courts has gone up dramatically in the past few years. (In 1960 there were 5648 grants of legal aid in magistrates' courts; in 1976 the number of proceedings had doubled, but grants of legal aid had increased nearly fiftyfold to 269,883.) A study in seventy-six magistrates' courts in 1976, covering 782 cases, showed that the defendant was represented in

46 percent of cases. It is reasonable to assume that the great majority was represented through legal aid, although some defendants will have been paid for privately and some through organizations such as the British Automobile Association. The refusal rate for legal aid applications is about 10 percent. Contributions toward the costs can be, but rarely are, asked for by the courts. The cost to the public of criminal legal aid in 1977–1978 was some £41 million.

Strengths of the Legal Aid Scheme

1. The scheme covers all forms of advice and assistance and all forms of court advocacy (except for advocacy in tribunals and one or two classes of work such as defamation). Coverage in the higher criminal courts is now almost total and in magistrates' courts very considerable.
2. Legal aid work involves a large portion of the profession. The bar as a whole derives about half its income from public funds and for many barristers the proportion is much more. The statistics show that in 1975–1976 no less than 8159 solicitors' offices received payments for civil legal aid work
3. For those who pay nothing or only a small contribution the scheme provides very great protection.
4. Lawyers are paid either the whole of their proper taxed fees (the criminal scheme and the legal advice and assistance scheme) or 90 percent of their taxed fees (the High Court civil scheme). They are able to make ordinary profits on the work, and all the more so if they handle such work in considerable bulk. The quality of the work done may not be as high as for private work but it is not distinctly and notoriously inferior.
5. Clients have complete choice of lawyers. They will be assisted in finding a lawyer if they do not know any names, but if they wish to do so, they normally can select their own.
6. The state has committed substantial funds to legal aid, and although there will always be a need for more money, the principle of state funding for legal services is wholly accepted.

Weaknesses of the Legal Aid Scheme

1. The means test limits are too low.
2. The contributions are too high—especially in the Green Form scheme, in which they go up steeply.
3. Legal aid work is highly concentrated. Many firms do a small amount of legal aid work but the bulk of it is handled by

relatively few firms. (Thus, in 1975–1976, 5 percent of the offices had one-third of the legal aid payments under civil legal aid.) This means that many firms do not attract (or, possibly, do not encourage) legal aid work.

4. Many firms complain that the level of legal aid remuneration is not high enough, especially if the lawyers try to be conscientious about standards.
5. The range of matters taken to the legal profession remains consistently narrow—matrimonial work dominates not only ordinary civil legal aid, but also the cases brought to solicitors under the Green Form scheme.

OTHER RECENT INNOVATIONS IN METHODS OF DELIVERING LEGAL SERVICES

In recent years, the services of private practitioners have expanded beyond the legal aid scheme in various ways.

Fixed Fee Interviews: In December 1977 the Law Society published details of the firms who had agreed to provide up to half an hour's diagnostic advice for a flat rate of not more than £5—regardless of means. The lists showed that 73 percent of the 7000 offices stated that they were agreeable to participating in this new scheme.

Duty Solicitor Schemes in Courts: In many parts of the country, private practitioners have organized rotas to provide a solicitor in the magistrates' court in order to advise unrepresented defendants as to their plea, to help them apply for an adjournment, to get bail and legal aid, or if they intend to plead guilty, to make a speech in mitigation of sentence. The first such scheme was started in 1972. By 1977 there were about eighty. (There are 680 such courts, but many are very small. Of the ninety courts that had over 800 criminal legal aid applications in 1975, there were duty solicitor schemes in thirty-six.) The Law Society has recommended that these schemes should be "supported and extended." The time of the duty solicitor is paid for either under the Green Form scheme or through ordinary legal aid. The duty solicitor will usually pick up a number of ordinary legal aid cases in the course of a morning session, and this makes his time financially worthwhile. Experiments are now being tried to see whether the concept of the duty rota can be operated successfully in civil as well as in criminal courts.

Rota Schemes in Citizens' Advice Bureaus: In many areas the

Citizens' Advice Bureau (see below) has a rota of local solicitors who come to advise both bureau workers and clients of the bureau on legal problems free of charge. By special dispensation from the Law Society, the solicitors who operate in such schemes can take the client back to their own office and handle their cases on the legal aid scheme or on a paying basis. These schemes have developed only in the last few years; in 1972 there were five, but by autumn 1977 this number had increased to about 200. The Law Society estimated in 1976 that there might be 4000 solicitors involved in rota schemes throughout the country, dealing with 80,000 bureau interviews a year, of which about one-third might be referred back to solicitors' offices for further help.

Twenty-four-hour-a-day Telephone Answering Service: In one or two cities there is a scheme manned by lawyers through which clients can get advice or referrals. In Southampton, for instance, there is a rota in which a solicitor is on duty at the end of a telephone every evening from 6:00 P.M. to the next morning, and from 6:00 P.M. on Saturday to Monday morning. The name of the duty solicitor can be obtained by dialing an advertised number that has a recorded announcement. The number is advertised in the local press. The solicitors pay £8 as their annual subscription to cover the cost of the answering service and of the advertisements. The first interview given under the scheme is free. Of the first thousand people advised under the scheme, about one-third applied for legal aid; thus it is likely that there is some profit to the lawyers in participating in the scheme.

In the 27th Annual Report on Legal Aid, in February 1978, the Law Society particularly commended the arrangement in Southampton whereby the duty solicitor scheme had persuaded the local county court to send out a leaflet with each possession summons. This alerted recipients to the desirability of consulting a solicitor. It referred to the fact that all local solicitors were listed in the yellow pages of the local telephone directory and in the county court office, with their address. It also gave the number of the duty solicitor scheme.

Referral or Solicitors' Lists: In December 1976 the Law Society published lists of firms throughout the country. The lists were in twenty-eight separate booklets. Each booklet covered the offices in its area that did legal aid as well as an indication of which of fourteen categories of work the firms dealt with. The lists were paid for out of public funds and were distributed free to citizens' advice bureaus, public libraries, local authority social service departments, town halls, police stations, and so on. Some 25,000 copies were distributed. The second edition was published in December 1977, and the society plans

to republish the list annually. The second edition contains information about the firms that participate in the fixed fee scheme. The second edition also introduced the innovation that firms could list an emergency telephone number, either the number of a member of the firm or the office number if arrangements had been made for calls to be intercepted and redirected to the firm's "duty solicitor." A message recording machine is not allowed. Consideration is now being given to supplying more information in the lists about the individual solicitors in the firm, for example, number of years since qualifying, qualifications, or special interests.

Insurance Prepayment and Group Schemes as a Means of Financing Legal Service: Legal services that are financed by insurance companies are familiar in the field of motor accidents; every motorist is required by law to have an insurance policy that covers him for the risk of causing injury to a third person. Such policies provide protection against potential damages and the costs involved in defending proceedings. A comprehensive policy also covers the cost of being a plaintiff. Policies of insurance taken out by householders cover the risk of legal proceedings faced by the homeowner through accident or other incidents.

In recent years, however, a new development has been policies offering protection for general legal services. There are two companies offering such policies in England (one is the German company DAS, and the other is Paul Strover Ltd., through Lloyds). It appears that individuals have not yet taken up these general legal services policies to any great extent, but employers are beginning to do so for their employees. In the United States the proliferation of employment-related insurance prepayment or group schemes in the past few years has been phenomenal. In August 1977 the U.S. Department of Labor had notice of 2112 schemes financed wholly or in part by employers. The number of persons covered by such schemes varied from the very small (105 plans covered up to five employees) to the very large (there were seventeen plans involving more than 50,000 employees). The largest plan to date seems to be that of the Chrysler Corporation, which in 1977 negotiated with the United Auto Workers to provide a wide range of legal services for some 150,000 workers and retired workers. The plan was to be financed out of a fund of $23 million. The legal work to be covered included divorce, wills, probate, bankruptcy, consumer complaints, landlord-tenant disputes, taking or defending tort actions, and the defense of misdemeanor and juvenile court cases. Schemes of this kind may prove to be one of the most significant developments in the techniques for providing and funding legal services.

THE PUBLIC SECTOR

In addition to legal services offered by private practitioners, in England there is also a growing public sector of legal services provided by salaried lawyers. The public sector started in 1970 with the establishment of a law center in North Kensington in which solicitors were paid salaries to provide free services to local citizens. Today there are about thirty law centers. Some are funded entirely by the local authority, and some are funded entirely by the Lord Chancellor's office; many are funded 75 percent by the central government and 25 percent by the local authority under the Urban Aid Program or the Community Development Project. The typical budget for a law center is £50,000 a year for a two- to three-lawyer office, including a support staff. The centers are limited in the work they can do by the terms of the concordat worked out with the Law Society, which spells out the terms on which waivers from the practice rules will be granted.[2]

The role of the law centers is to supplement the work of the private profession. The work they do is largely in fields not covered, or not covered adequately, by private practitioners, notably landlord-tenant disputes, consumer complaints, social security, immigration problems, and so on. Law centers have also devoted a great deal of their time and energies to group or community legal work—problems that affect large numbers of people. Thus, one law center announced in February 1978 that it had persuaded the local council to establish new terms and conditions for tenants living in council accommodations, with much better provision for security of tenure and repairs by the council than would be normally available. Another law center has devoted itself to getting its local council to repair the roads and pavements and mastermind opposition to the council's plan to redevelop the neighborhood.

Another facet of the public sector has been the growing number of salaried lawyers employed by the Citizens' Advice Bureaus—to train their own workers, to advise them on actual problems, to advise clients, and to prepare kits, pamphlets, and other informational material for the benefit of bureau workers. The first lawyer of this kind was appointed in 1973. In 1977 there were ten bureaus employing salaried lawyers at a cost of £10,000 per lawyer per annum. The Council of the National Association of Citizens' Advice Bureaus resolved in September 1977 to expand the salaried lawyer component in its service.

The public sector in legal services is now fully accepted as part of the English system. The Law Society said in 1977 that law centers "act as a magnet to attract a wide variety of people with legal problems." The Lord Chancellor's Legal Aid Advisory Committee in its 1975–1976

report said that law centers were "playing a vital part in making legal services avilable in the most deprived areas, and on matters on which the poorer sections of the community most strongly feel the need for those services." It said that most centers should be established and existing centers should be supported where necessary because law centers had "established themselves as an integral and essential branch of the legal services."[3]

LEGAL SERVICES PROVIDED BY NONLAWYERS AND ALTERNATIVES TO LEGAL SERVICES

In England, legal services are provided by nonlawyers on a considerable scale. Some of these alternative forms of legal aid are discussed next.

Citizens' Advice Bureaus

Citizens' Advice Bureaus (CABs) are a major source of legal services provided to the public. They are staffed largely by voluntary workers although bureau organizers are normally paid and work full-time. There are close to 10,000 workers who man the 700 or more bureaus. The voluntary workers have to commit themselves to do at least one session a week. Training is a combination of basic introductory courses, on-the-job training, and formal courses.

The latest figures show the CABs handling about 3 million inquiries a year. According to a special survey carried out for the Royal Commission on Legal Services, at least a third have a legal component. Of these bureaus (i.e., those with a legal element), the bureaus themselves dealt with six out of ten inquiries, they referred three out of ten to lawyers of one kind or another, and sent the remaining one-tenth to other specialists.

Trade Unions

The unions have for years provided considerable legal services to their members, although primarily in the field of problems arising out of their employment. The main services have been assistance with handling claims for personal injury and tribunal cases related to unfair dismissal and the like. It has been estimated that the amount of damages collected by the unions in personal injury cases is now well over £50 million a year. They also represent their members in upward of

10,000 cases a year in tribunals, such as the Industrial Tribunals and the National Insurance Tribunal. They employ lawyers in private practice as and when they feel the need arises. Some unions in England have legal departments, but most of the people who work in these departments are nonlawyers. There are hardly any lawyers employed on a salaried basis by trade unions.

Specialist Advice Services

In recent years a number of specialist advice services have grown up, which provide legal advice and legal services to a greater or lesser extent. Consumer advice centers financed by central government provide advice to consumers. By the end of 1976 there were over a hundred such centers. (The first was started in 1969 by the Consumers' Association, publishers of "Which?") Housing Aid Centers provide help to people in the housing field—landlord-tenant law, rent fixing, public health requirements, and so on. The first such center financed by the public was opened in 1970. In 1976 it was estimated that there were some 160 such centers—two-thirds funded by local authorities and one-third financed by voluntary organizations.

There has also been a significant increase in the use of lawyers and the provision of legal services by organizations such as the Child Poverty Action Group (concerned with the position of the poor generally), MIND (which deals with the mentally handicapped), the National Council for Civil Liberties, and Release (concerned with drug offenders). The Child Poverty Action Group, for instance, runs a separate Citizens' Rights Office that handles telephone inquiries from anywhere in the country from individuals or those who advise them. It receives about 10,000 calls a year, whereas Release answers about 20,000 queries a year, a high proportion of which relate to legal cases.

Policy implications of recent developments

1. State funding on a considerable scale is inevitable and unavoidable.

2. There is no necessary incompatability between state funding and the continuing independence of the legal profession.

The English legal profession is passionately devoted to the ideal of "independence." Nevertheless, it has accepted not only the judicare

method of paying for legal services, but also the new salaried sector. Thus, for instance, although salaried barristers employed in commerce and industry or central or local government do not have a right of audience in the courts, those who work in law centers do. (Their right of audience is, however, limited to the lower courts as are those of solicitors.) The preconditions for a Law Society waiver from the practice rules for law centers is that the center be "independent." By independence it is meant that the funding authority should not have undue power in the management of the law center. Thus, the conditions state that the "management committee must be independent of the funding agency and of central and local government, none of whose representatives should be ex-officio Chairman, Vice Chairman or Secretary of the management committee." During the debates about the role of the public sector in England there has been virtually complete acceptance of the doctrine that law centers, whether funded by the central or local government, *can* be independent. "Independence" is, above all, the capacity of lawyers to do their duty for their clients without fear of consequences to themselves.[4] There is clear evidence from several countries, including the United States, Canada, Australia, as well as England, that lawyers who are paid salaries out of state funds can be as independent in this sense as private practitioners.

3. Mixed delivery systems are likely to be best.

There is virtually no one in England today who contends that legal services ought to be delivered exclusively by private practitioners or exclusively by salaried lawyers. In its commentary on the document discussing the waivers for law centers, the Law Society, for instance, stated:

> Legal services are now being increasingly provided by a variety of new methods: for instance by Honorary Legal Advisers or by rotas of private practitioners in Citizens' Advice Bureaus or by duty solicitor schemes in magistrates' courts and now also in county courts, or by salaried solicitors working in Citizens' Advice Bureaus. There are now over 20 law centers funded mainly by central or local government. . . . Some lawyers work exclusively in the "private sector," others wholly in the "public sector," and others partly in one and partly in the other.[5]

4. The respective role of the private sector and the public sector does pose some important issues of principle.

The present consensus of most of those concerned with this field in England is that the public sector ought to complement rather than to

compete with the private sector. Thus, under the terms to which they have to agree to get their waiver, law centers agree not to compete in the following terms:

(1) Apart from initial advice and assistance, and save in the circumstances mentioned in (2) below, salaried solicitors will not normally act in cases where the professional business of the client involves (i) conveyancing; (ii) commercial matters; (iii) divorce proceedings; (iv) probate matters (save for personal applications in small estates); (v) personal injury claims where the damages, as initially and approximately quantified exceed scale 2 of the county court costs band (in 1977 £500); or (vi) in criminal matters where the accused is aged 21 or over.

(2) It is understood that:

there will be exceptional circumstances in which a salaried solicitor may undertake cases falling within the categories mentioned in (1) above, for example: in cases of emergency; where the conduct of the client's case requires his professional business to be conducted by the salaried solicitor; where a solicitor in private practice is not reasonably available or where the confidence of the client would be eroded by referral of the case.

In other words, law center lawyers agree not to compete for the bulk of the legal aid work from which the professional derives a substantial income. A client who comes in with such a problem must normally be sent to a private practitioner—if there is one reasonably available.

The reasons for this division of work are:

1. To avoid unnecessary duplication of work, for example, the public sector should mainly do what the private sector cannot handle, thus making best use of scarce public funds.
2. To avoid friction between the public and private sectors. If the public sector were able to compete for paying work, it is likely that there would be considerable antagonism from the private profession. This would create bad relations between the two types of lawyers.
3. Law centers can specialize and make a contribution distinct and different from that of private practitioners.

Therefore, there has been a conscious rejection of the Swedish and Quebec models in which the work of the public and private sectors overlaps and the public has a choice between the salaried and the private practitioner model.

The workload of law centers originally was primarily "casework" (i.e., helping individuals). Increasingly, however, it has been group- and community-oriented, and in their evidence to the Royal Commission on Legal Services, the Law Centers Working Group stated that they saw their main function increasingly in this field of work. Of course, the result will be that, to the extent that law centers are not handling the landlord-tenant and other individual welfare law problems of clients, these cases must either go to private practitioners or be dealt with by alternative systems—or continue to be unmet, as in the past. There is no clear answer to this dilemma.

5. What is the size of the public sector?

There is no way of determining the "poorer" size of the public sector. In the foreseeable future there will always be a need for more law centers (and other salaried lawyers) than there will be money to provide them. How many more is largely a question of political and fiscal judgment. Even in areas with many private practitioners there will be uses for a law center—and all the more so if law centers move increasingly into work for communities and groups because this work is virtually not done by private practitioners. I would expect the public sector to grow in England in the next decade to 100 or more law centers.

6. Where should law centers be placed?

In my view it is fairly arbitrary where salaried lawyers are placed, for there are so many areas that need lawyers—or at least more lawyers. One might start with the areas of greatest deprivation in which there are likely to be few, if any, lawyers. In such areas, however, they will, perforce, be doing ordinary traditional lawyer's work—divorces, criminal defenses, and so on. In such areas law centers will be unable to make a distinct contribution.

7. Should public funds available for legal services be directed primarily to the private sector (judicare) or to the public sector?

In a sense, the English system has avoided this problem by making judicare open-ended. In other words there is no annual budget for legal services, a portion of which must be allocated to the private or to the public sector. The legal aid scheme is open-ended in that if, in a particular year, the number of accepted applications for civil and

criminal legal aid doubled or trebled, the British Treasury would *have* to provide the funds. There is no budgetary ceiling above which the certifying authorities are not permitted to go. There *is* a budget for the salaried sector, but at present it is a patchwork affair because of the many different funding authorities.

For this reason it is probable that the American debate about the comparative merits of the private versus the public sector has not occurred in Britian. A missing element in the debate in the United States has been a recognition that, even if public sector legal services are cheaper per unit of work than those provided by the private sector, it does not follow that it is cheaper to establish new law centers than to channel funds to private practitioners via judicare. Private practitioners already exist whereas law centers have to be set up. Normally, it should be much less expensive to add a legal aid component to the work of private practitioners than to set up a separate office capable of existing entirely from legal aid work. From the point of view of access for the public, it is also obvious that clients will find it much easier to reach a legal aid lawyer, if most private practitioners can provide such services, than to go to the relatively smaller number of law centers. (In England at this time there are about 8000 solicitors' offices as compared to thirty or so law centers. In the United States public sector lawyers are outnumbered by private practitioners by approximately 80 to 1.)

In countries like England, in which judicare is open-ended, the problem of allocation between the public and private sectors, therefore, does not really arise. The private sector "allocates itself." The only question is how much money can then be squeezed out for the public sector. In countries where a finite amount of money is allowed for legal services, the problem of allocation is obviously difficult. But the tendency to assume that the public sector should take the lion's share (as it has in the United States) may not be right. Judicare, supplemented by salaried firms, may provide a better spread of legal services than salaried services supplemented by a small amount of judicare.

8. What controls should exist for remuneration out of public money?

Under the English rules all fees for legal aid are allotted by processes independent of the lawyers who do the work. For work done in the higher courts and in the county courts, taxation of fees is in the hands of special officials in the courts. For both civil and criminal cases dealt with in magistrates' courts and for work done under the Green Form scheme, the taxing authority is the Law Society's Area Committee.

This committee also has jurisdiction over higher court cases in which the solicitor does not claim more than £200 in costs.

In the crown courts the basis of taxation is a guide prepared by the Lord Chancellor's office, which sets maximum and minimum normal fees based on the plea, the length of the case, and the number of pages of witness statements. The clerk then assesses the actual fee on the basis of his or her view of the difficulty of the case, the seniority of counsel, and so on. For work in magistrates' courts, the Law Society's Area Committee works mainly on the basis of an hourly rate, but consideration is also given to the amount of time that should have been taken and to the weight, complexity, and importance of the case. In civil legal aid cases the lawyers receive the fees that were reasonably incurred; however, for cases in the higher courts, there is a statutory reduction of 10 percent.

The weakness in the machinery is that there are no data from which the appropriateness of the fees allowed can be measured in terms of the lawyers' annual income or overhead. It would appear desirable to have a mechanism for sampling the income and overhead of the lawyers on a regular basis in order to assess the proper levels of remuneration paid out of public funds.

9. What controls should exist over the quality of legal work?

At present there are virtually no controls over quality, save for the marginal control exercised by the complaints and disciplinary machinery. A client of a solicitor can complain to the Law Society. In the event that he is not satisfied with the Law Society's handling of the matter, he can complain to the office of the Lay Observer set up under the provisions of the 1974 Solicitors Act. The complaint machinery is sufficient as far as it goes, but it deals only with matters that are regarded as professional misconduct, that is, very serious misbehavior by the lawyer. The ordinary case in which the lawyer's work is not as careful or as speedy as it should be is not within the scope of the complaint system.

Even if the Law Society did handle less serious complaints, it would still make little impact since most clients would never complain.

What is needed is a system in which the standards of ordinary work are monitored. The best way of doing this is to have some form of official research organization authorized to check standards of work in the profession by random sampling. The results could then be published without identifying the black sheep or without having to rely on clients' complaints. In the English system, one possible site for such an organization might be in the office of the Lay Observer.

10. To what extent should laymen be involved in the management of the legal profession?

The English system has so far experienced the following types of external participation in the affairs of the profession:

1. *Standing official bodies:*
   a. *Lord Chancellor's Legal Aid Advisory Committee,* which was set up under the Legal Aid and Advice Act 1949. Its chairman and about half the members have always been layman. It publishes an annual report and commentary on the report of the Law Society on the civil legal aid scheme.
   b. *Lay Observer* for complaints against solicitors.
   c. *Lay members of the bar's and the Law Society's disciplinary tribunals;* one out of the three members of the tribunal has to be a layman, drawn from a panel appointed by the Lord Chancellor (Legal Aid Act 1974).
   d. *Lay members of the Law Society's statutory legal aid committee,* which consists of two laymen added voluntarily by the Law Society in 1977 to a committee made up only of lawyers.
   e. *Lay members of the management committees of law centers;* virtually every law center has a local management committee and in all of them laymen form either a majority or a substantial minority. In the Law Society's statement on waivers (see above), it is provided that "although not a condition for the grant of waiver, it is considered that a majority of the voting members of the Management Committee of a salaried service should normally be able to represent the interests of the recipients of the service."
   f. *The Legal Services Committee,* established experimentally in Greater Manchester by the Law Society in 1977, with fifteen members, of whom eight are laymen and seven are lawyers.
2. *Ad hoc bodies:*
   a. *The National Prices and Incomes Board,* which made three reports on solicitors' remuneration, 1968, Cmnd. 3529; 1969, Cmnd. 4217; and 1971, Cmnd. 4624.
   b. *The Monopolies and Mergers Commission,* which made four reports in the past few years on aspects of the profession, on restrictive practices in all the professions (1970, Cmnd. 4463); on advertising by solicitors (1976, No. 558); on advertising by barristers (1976, No. 559); and on Queen's Counsel appearing alone (1976, No. 512).

c. *The Royal Commission on Legal Services*, which was appointed in February 1976 with terms of reference to inquire into all aspects of legal services. It has a lay chairman and a majority of lay members and is expected to report in 1979.

There are two main questions for consideration by the Royal Commission in this area. One is whether laymen should now be added to the central committees of the professional bodies, that is, the Senate of the Four Inns of Court and the Bar with ninety members and the Council of the Law Society with seventy members. The purpose would be to have six or eight laymen to "hold up the public interest mirror" to the members of the profession as they deliberate on the affairs of the profession.

The second is whether the Lord Chancellor's Legal Aid Advisory Committee should have its authority broadened to cover the same wide field as the Royal Commission, for example, legal services generally. This would permit it to comment on and investigate any problem in the field that appeared to require consideration. An advisory committee for legal services would be a recognition of the need to have public accountability for the profession in all aspects of its work, not merely those aspects that are paid for by the public. The concept has been accepted in the establishment of ad hoc inquiries during the past few years—the Prices and Incomes Board, the Monopolies Commission, and now the Royal Commission. What is needed is to put this development on a permanent basis.

NOTES

1. *Government Expenditure Plans, 1978–1979 to 1981–1982,* Vol.II, Cmnd. 7049–11, 1978, Table 2.9, pp. 64–65.
2. See *Law Society's Gazette,* August 31, 1977, p. 698; for a history of the negotiations leading to the settlement, see Zander, "Waivers—the end of a long story?" *New Law Journal* (1977): 1236.
3. 26th Annual Report on Legal Aid, 1975–1976, pp. 70–71.
4. See Zander, "Independence of the Legal Profession—What does it mean?" *Law Society's Gazette* (1977): 758.
5. *Law Society's Gazette* (1977): 698, col 4.

Chapter 7

Comments on Public Policy for Legal Services

Wolfgang Däubler

Two factors justify the provision of legal services:

1. They enable individuals to pursue their interests as defined and protected by the law
2. They assure that existing laws will be applied equally to all citizens, thus avoiding differences in the execution of justice

Therefore, legal services are not to be regarded as "welfare" for the individual, but rather as a contribution to the communal order, a means of promoting the public interest. The promotion of legal services implies an acceptance of the existing order, which may weaken the potential for social reform. Consequently, critical approaches to reform will be restrained from using the contradiction between normative rules and reality as an inconspicuous strategy for more far-reaching demands.

POWER BARRIERS

The costs of court procedures, which played a dominant role in Chapter 6 by Zander, are not the only barrier to access to court. There

are many subjective barriers to access, such as fear of role expectations, lack of information, and mistrust of the judicial system. These factors can be partially corrected through informational and educational measures. For instance, courses on legal instruction in the schools could play an important role.

A more important barrier to the protection of individual rights, however, are the existing power relationships, which prevent the individual from using the courts and judicial procedures to their full extent. This is particularly true for disputes between employers and employees. Only in extreme cases are these disputes brought to court during an existing employment relationship. Employees are usually so apprehensive about losing their jobs that court proceedings are started only after their employment has been terminated. This cannot be changed through financial aid or financial measures alone. It is necessary to develop forms of legal protection that are independent of the social situation of the employee. For instance, unions could be granted the right to act on behalf of employees in lawsuits. It is not desirable to simply omit the recognition of one party's dependence on the other; this omission would only serve to promote illusionary ideas about the possibilities and effectiveness of existing legal protection.

CONVERTING PUBLIC ISSUES INTO PRIVATE CONFLICTS

Furthermore, legal services cause an increase in the resolution of conflicts through legalized processes. This may not be desirable in cases in which there is an alternative form of handling conflicting interests, a form that allows all parties to at least partially effectuate their own interests. This is particularly important in labor relations. Which strategy should be chosen in this case?

In my opinion, conflict resolution through court decisions has three main disadvantages:

1. It individualizes conflicts. A case concerning a large number of people, for example, an action that results in the obsolescence of an occupational skill, is treated by the courts as an individual conflict between plaintiff X and defendant Y. This can prevent the court, either de jure or de facto, from dealing with the total background of the case. Participation by all persons concerned is prevented by the procedural codes, which are based on the liberal mode of free markets. A few approaches are developing within German law to extend the number of parties or participants

permitted within a lawsuit. Physical presence during the oral proceedings is possible, based on the "principle of publicity." It is, however, not customary and may be regarded as undue influence on the court under certain circumstances. The attempt of the Metal Workers' Union to induce a court decision on the legality of lockouts is noteworthy. By bringing 5000 simultaneous suits for back payment, they are trying to represent the employee's interest as a group interest. It remains to be seen whether this is a singular phenomenon or a first breakthrough for "collectivized" procedures.

2. The individualization of conflicts is complemented by a privatization of arguments. If a certain regulation is to be introduced through collective bargaining or Parliament, arguments are exchanged publicly. Those concerned, that is, every citizen, can follow the discussion and form their own opinions. They can implement their demands through various measures, such as demonstrations and collective refusals to cooperate. Courts, on the other hand, admit only certain arguments; "legally irrelevant" statements are barred from the courtroom or regarded as an infringement on the rules. The remaining arguments are then exchanged in a language incomprehensible to laymen. They are thus prevented from expressing their opinions. The process of defining and formulating interests becomes the private cause of lawyers.
3. When courts decide collective conflicts, this means that political questions are decided by actors who have not been sufficiently legitimized by democratic procedures. Even when judges are elected for limited periods of time, a rare practice in Western Europe, there is no control over their decisionmaking. This has become particularly apparent in the recent decisions of the German Constitutional Supreme Court. It can also be illustrated by the stop-and-go decisions on nuclear power plants. As the circle of conflicts resolved in court is extended, the democratic process recedes into the background.

ALTERNATIVES TO LEGAL STRATEGIES

The disadvantages of conflict resolution described above should not result in a general refusal to provide legal services. Where interests are not sufficiently organized (as with consumers, for instance), a renunciation of legal services would open the door to a

"dictatorship of the stronger party." The decision to provide legal services should be regarded as the lesser evil. Under certain circumstances, it is, moreover, conceivable that trend-setting test cases may sensitize the public and perhaps even induce attempts to organize interests. However, where there is an alternative between extralegal compromises and conflict resolution through the courts, the first solution is preferable. Whether there are cases in which both strategies can be applied cannot be determined theoretically. It is, therefore, necessary not to entrust legal counseling to traditional jurists, but rather to persons who are able to evaluate both alternatives in their capacity as engaged representatives of the interests involved. The workers' secretariats in Germany before World War I set an important example of this kind and there seems to be a similar approach within the English unions.

PART II

Alternative Forms of Lawyer Services

Chapter 8

The Public Interest Law Movement in the United States

Charles Halpern

Perhaps the most striking institutional innovation in the American legal community during the past fifteen years has been the development of the public interest law firm. A perusal of the Supreme Court's docket or of the leading cases in law school casebooks during this period reveals an increasing number of cases brought by lawyers in public interest law firms. Public interest lawyers have shaped and promoted the law relating to the rights of racial minorities—that is, women, children, mental patients, and prisoners—environmental protection, and consumer rights.

In 1975, the year for which the most recent data are available, approximately ninety public interest law firms existed with approximately $40 million in legal fees. These firms, some of which are committed to providing representation of the unrepresented in the legal system and others with specific focuses, existed outside the normal marketplace for legal services. They were subsidized by charitable foundations or the federal government to provide legal

Note: This chapter was edited by Erhard Blankenburg on the basis of an introductory paper by Charles Halpern, who much to our regret was kept from revising his contribution by his involvement in public interest representation.

services to groups and individuals who were otherwise unable to purchase legal services. Their commitment was not to provide legal services for indigents on day-to-day matters, but to represent them before courts and administrative agencies on large cases that promised to have a substantial impact on the resolution of broad questions of public policy.

Public interest law firms played a central role in the development of several substantive areas of the law. These firms had in common a commitment to providing representation to one or more unrepresented groups. The basic concept drew on the traditional lawyer-client relationship, but the nature of the institutions typically evolved into something quite distinctive.

BACKGROUND

The National Association for the Advancement of Colored People and the American Civil Liberties Union are the great precursors of the public interest law movement. Both systematically used the legal process to clarify and protect the rights of minorities—blacks and persons deprived of civil liberties—who would not otherwise have had adequate representation in the legal process. The public interest law firms, which began around 1970, drew on their experience. They also drew on the experience of the large corporate law firms that represented affluent clients, frequently using the courts to protect their clients' interests and at the same time affecting major policy disputes.

The period of rapid growth of public interest law coincided with the Nixon presidency, a period in which government institutions were unresponsive to the needs of disadvantaged groups and were overly responsive to big business. The organizers of public interest law firms aligned themselves with sympathetic members of the establishment bar (like former Justice Arthur J. Goldberg) or well-established institutions (like law schools), or both.

The concept of public interest law firms was developed by a few entrepreneurial lawyers who recognized that systematic advocacy could give previously unrepresented groups an effective voice in major policy decisions that affected their interests. This was neither a response to complaints lodged by the unrepresented nor to a survey showing a significant unmet legal need. Nor did law schools or the organized bar initiate this effort, although they did provide support and encouragement.

As public interest law firms were being established, the support of potential clients was solicited. They were called upon to certify, in

effect, that they would utilize the services of public interest law firms when and if they were established.

Seed money for financing was essential. Small grants from a few foundations oriented toward social action provided crucial support to a number of firms at this early stage of development.

The primary appeal of the public interest movement was stated in lawyerly terms, asserting that the public interest law firms could assure groups with a legitimate interest in an issue of an opportunity to "have their day in court." The appeal was made in value-neutral terms, that is, in terms of enhancing the effectiveness of the legal process rather than asserting substantive values.

The term "public interest law," which was coined by the press, not the public interest lawyers, was for the most part defended as a contribution to a process that would ultimately lead to more responsible decisions based on a wider range of views being heard.

Nonetheless, the ideology of most public interest law firms that began around 1970 was distinctly liberal. This alignment was predictable in the sense that the most disadvantaged groups, the traditional objects of liberal concern, had the least adequate access to legal service and to the courts.

There was some disagreement among public interest lawyers about the relative need of certain groups for legal services. For example, some critics argued that the limited subsidies available for public interest legal services should go to the poor and to racial minorities rather than to broader consumer and environmental groups, which tended to be more affluent, to have better access to representation, and to have a broader range of techniques to protect their interests. In the intervening years a number of business-oriented firms have begun calling themselves "public interest firms" and alleging that the interests of the business community as a whole and of citizens who are interested in encouraging economic growth are inadequately represented.

STRUCTURE AND FINANCING

The typical public interest law firm is established as a nonprofit, tax-exempt corporation, governed by a self-perpetuating board of trustees. Although the board often includes members of client groups and experts in relevant allied disciplines, it is usually dominated by lawyers. As is true with the boards of most profit-making and nonprofit corporations, the staff usually plays a more significant role in policy formulation than the board itself.

The subsidization of citizen groups to participate in the legal process could have gone in two directions—funding clients to hire lawyers in the commercial marketplace (or using the subsidy to finance other, possibly more effective, advocacy or organizing techniques) or funding specialized law firms to provide legal services to clients who could not afford to hire lawyers. In fact, the foundations that have put up the largest share of financing for public interest law would probably not have been willing to finance general advocacy programs relying on citizen organizations. It is clearly much less risky for them to finance organizations of professionals, especially if the establishment bar is involved; the chance of embarrassment to the foundation is reduced. And the defense is always available to the foundation that it is legitimate to give a significant group "its day in court," without the necessity of the foundation defending the substantive positions taken by its grantees.

Funding the lawyers and not the clients encourages the kind of advocacy with which lawyers are most comfortable: court litigation and advocacy in formal administrative proceedings. They are less likely to pursue other kinds of advocacy like direct action (e.g., sit-ins or demonstrations); efforts to affect policy by participating in agencies' budgeting process; or investigative reporting and disclosure. Furthermore, the approach of funding lawyers rather than the clients encourages lawyers to define their advocacy roles in conventional ways. They acquire a vested interest in the notion that lawyer advocacy in courts and agencies is distinct from other kinds of advocacy and is not part of a continuum of techniques by which interest groups pursue their objectives.

The fact that the financing of public interest law involves tax-exempt money is also significant. The Internal Revenue Code severely limits the amount of legislative activity that can be undertaken by a tax-exempt organization. While the 1976 revisions of the code significantly loosen these restrictions, there is nonetheless little legislative activity undertaken by public interest firms.

The structure of the public interest law firm, its internally generated program, and the frequent disparity in financial resources between the law firm and its clients have altered the nature of the attorney-client relationship. The traditional concept of the lawyer as the "mouthpiece," a relatively passive instrument of the client, poorly describes most lawyers' practice, especially the complex interrelationship between a corporation and its outside counsel in dealing with policy matters. But the special circumstances of their activity go still further. The lawyers' greater sophistication and experience make it hard for the client to exercise control. The situation is exacerbated by the fact that

public interest law firms often have more technical information and readier access to experts whose involvement is critical.

The relationship is tangled further by the fact that clients usually lack the financial resources to go elsewhere if they are displeased by the way the law firm handles their case.

Does this mean that a public interest law firm, freed of the control of the client, is responsible only to itself, accountable to no one? Although public interest law firms act more autonomously toward their clients than conventional law firms, they are subject to a powerful network of restraints: the foundations that support them; the courts and administrative agencies before which they appear; the clients whom they serve and on whose credibility they often rely; the experts on whom they rely for guidance and expert testimony; the bar which polices their professional conduct; and the Internal Revenue Service, which polices their tax exemption. The success of a public interest lawyer will ultimately depend on his capacity to accommodate these often conflicting pressures.

NONLITIGATION ACTIVITIES

Gradually, many public interest lawyers have come to recognize that litigation can be most effective if it is treated as an element in an advocacy process that integrates legislative activity, constituency organizing, investigative reporting, public education, promotion of scholarly interest, and regular involvement in the administrative process at all levels.

This shift has involved a move from a narrow focus on individual lawsuits to a recognition that the public interest lawyer is doing something more than simply providing traditional legal service to a new group of clients. The public interest law process is in itself distinctive, and the lawyer in public interest practice must have a wider range of skills than the lawyer in conventional practice.

Public interest law firms are not always well equipped to perform effectively in nonjudicial forums. Lobbying in Congress and in state legislatures calls for special skills, including the ability to organize politically. Most lawyers have little training in these skills. Lawyers are notably poor as community organizers. This highlights the importance of public interest law firms forming effective partnerships with broadly based client organizations so that their complementary skills can be meshed.

Another activity in which public interest lawyers are becoming involved is the design or adaptation of new dispute resolution tech-

niques that can be used as an alternative to litigation. Many public interest lawyers have been frustrated in recent years by the delay and expense of litigation; by the fact that the relief ultimately obtained often falls far short of remedying the grievances that initially motivated the lawsuit; and by the hostility and polarization often involved in litigation. The development of environmental mediation represents one such effort. Public interest law firms are interested in the development of this concept, which promises to give environmentalists an effective voice in policy. At the same time, however, they are anxious to assure their opponents that the availability of mediation is not thought to make litigation unnecessary. Access to the courts is essential to give them an effective voice in mediation.

THE FUTURE OF PUBLIC INTEREST LAW

In less than ten years, public interest law has established a record of substantial achievement and won a high degree of acceptance and respect within the legal profession. Nonetheless, its practitioners constitute a minute fraction of the lawyers in the United States. Its practitioners are clustered on the East and West Coasts. Few public interest lawyers devote their attention to representation in state and local matters, where their efforts are urgently needed.

The survival and expansion of public interest law will ultimately depend on our ability to deal with several questions, some of which are much larger than the interests of public interest lawyers.

First, there is a strong antipathy toward the "overlegalization" of American society. It is expressed in hostility toward the federal bureaucracy and the legal profession. It is difficult to maintain support for public interest law in the face of these pressures. Some of the hostility, although expressed in procedural terms (e.g., confusing legal language of regulations and bureaucratic red tape), is really opposition to underlying policies designed to redress the grievances of minorities and women, protect the environment, and assure a safe workplace. But public interest law firms must deal with this backlash in order to survive.

Second, foundation financing of public interest law firms has not expanded in recent years, and it will most probably begin to shrink. New sources of support—from the bar, the general public, government funding, and the like—should be encouraged. The growing number of unemployed lawyers poses both a challenge and an opportunity. Any government support for public interest law firms must be carefully structured to preserve their independence and diversity of viewpoint.

Third, the importance of public participation in policy formulation must be established. The current administration in Washington, D.C., has appointed many public interest law firms to governmental office. It must be understood that even well-intentioned people with strong commitments are subjected to pressures while in government. The public interest law firm can be an important countervailing force that enables such people to make balanced judgments.

Fourth, a careful look at the court system should be taken, and the role of the courts—especially the federal courts—should be clarified. I believe that the proper role of the federal courts is to handle precisely the kinds of cases brought by public interest law firms—cases involving interpretations of statutes and the Constitution that affect basic policies. Other kinds of cases should be diverted into other forums. In addition, the courts' rules and procedures should be modified to make them more hospitable to suits involving large policy issues brought by groups that would otherwise be denied as a forum.

Chapter 9

Social Movements and the Legal System: A Theoretical Perspective

Joel F. Handler

During the last two decades in the United States, there has been an enormous growth of law reform litigation via test cases for social reform groups—civil rights, environmental, consumer, poverty and minority groups, to name only the most prominent examples. The period can probably be dated from 1954, when the National Association for the Advancement of Colored People Legal Defense Fund, one of the major civil rights organizations in the United States, won the school desegregation case before the U.S. Supreme Court.[1]

Under the leadership of Chief Justice Earl Warren, the federal judiciary opened its doors to the disenfranchised in American society. Encouraged by the apparent success of civil rights groups, other groups, representing a wide variety of interests, sought out the growing number of young activist lawyers who were pushing litigation to reform the law on a broad range of issues. At first the lawyers were in civil rights; then the War on Poverty adopted law reform as a principal strategy, followed by Ralph Nader and consumerism, the environmentalists, and the latest manifestation, "public interest law."

Note: This chapter is a condensed version of *Social Movements and the Legal System: A Theory of Law Reform and Social Change* (New York: Academic Press, 1978).

For convenience, I will refer to all of these lawyers collectively as "law reformers" or "public interest" lawyers, bearing in mind that the label covers the full spectrum of lawyers engaging in test-case litigation for social reform groups.

In this chapter a theoretical framework for evaluating this reform effort is set forth. Why do these groups come to the lawyers and the legal system rather than pursuing their goals through political and social channels? What price do they have to pay for using the legal system, and under what circumstances do they succeed or fail in their efforts?

The groups and their lawyers claim three types of benefits from this reform activity, and we will evaluate their efforts in terms of their claims.

1. They seek direct, tangible benefits from judicial or administration litigation—by this they mean substantive civil rights, a cleaner environment, safer products, and improved social welfare benefits and programs.
2. They seek to further their cause through indirect benefits, such as legitimacy, publicity, and consciousness-raising.
3. They also claim that they will revitalize pluralism in the United States by opening up decisionmaking processes to the unrepresented—consumers, environmentalists, minorities, and the poor. Through litigation to reform the law, these groups and interests will be given an effective voice.

In my research, I have examined about forty cases picked from four principal areas of activity—environmental and consumer protection, civil rights, and social welfare (which includes public assistance, health and mental health, and occupational health and safety). Although these cases have not been selected randomly, they are representative of significant types of group social reform activity. In this chapter, I cannot, of course, review all of the evidence, but I will set forth only the theoretical argument with brief reference to some important illustrations.

Before proceeding, I would like to present two contrasting environmental cases that will help illustrate the argument. The first is the Trans-Alaskan Pipeline litigation (TAPS), in which a suit was initiated by environmentalists to prevent the Department of Interior from issuing permits to a consortium of oil companies to construct the pipeline. A temporary injunction was issued on the grounds that the agency and the consortium failed to file an adequate environmental impact statement as required by the National Environmental Policy Act (NEPA).[2] (There was also a technical violation of the Mineral Leasing Act.) Construction was blocked for two years until Congress

enacted legislation that authorized the permits and waived further requirements of NEPA. As part of the compromise, however, detailed environmental conditions were stipulated with administrative enforcement machinery; for example, construction at various points could not proceed unless government officials agreed that the environmental specifications were met.

At this point in the controversy, although the pipeline was authorized, the result could still be considered a victory for the environmentalists. The environmental and safety aspects of the pipeline were improved considerably.

Although the evidence on what finally happened is not complete, indications are that the construction has been an environmental disaster and a complete defeat for the environmental groups. There are many reasons for this, including the fact that the government official in charge of environmental protection was a retired U.S. Corps of Engineers officer with a long record of hostility to the environmentalists. The reason that is most relevant to our concerns, however, is that once Congress approved the pipeline, the major social reform groups and their lawyers turned to other matters. There were a few desultory attempts to raise funds to monitor construction, but they failed, and the monitoring task was left to two small groups based in Alaska who lacked the resources. The government and the developers combined to build as quickly as possible; the environmentalists were denied access to the sites as well as to public information filed with the government. The environmental stipulations were ignored or waived, and serious damage has been done due to improper stream crossings, grading, land restoration, solid waste disposal, and oil pollution, to name some of the more serious degradations.[3]

The second example can be stated more quickly. In the *Calvert Cliffs* case, an oil company building an offshore loading facility agreed under threat of a lawsuit to substitute a pipeline for a pier, move the pipeline downstream, and dedicate part of the shoreland for a public park. This was a complete victory for the environmentalists. What explains the difference between the two cases, and does our explanation shed some light on evaluating group social reform activity?

In attempting to answer this question, we will look at the characteristics of the principal actors in law reform litigation, as well as the type of activity undertaken.

1. The first variable in the theory is the characteristics of the social reform groups themselves. To be effective, all social reform groups must mobilize resources, but what leads people to become members or to contribute money, political support, or services to groups? The common

assumption is that people with mutual interests will join together to further those interests; but Mancur Olson, Jr., an economist, has challenged that assumption.[4] In his view, rational self-interested people will not join groups unless the groups are small or they are forced to contribute. The key to Olson's analysis is the distinction between collective and selective goods and the concept of the "free rider." Collective goods are goods that any member of a group can consume even if the member has not paid any of the cost of producing the goods. A consumer who does not pay is a free rider. A major example is the American labor movement in which unionization had to come about primarily through coercion. Otherwise, rational, self-interested factory workers would enjoy the benefits of negotiated working conditions without paying their union dues. If collective goods are at issue, the rational economic man will tend to become a free rider.

On the other hand, if the group is small or dominated by a small subgroup, the collective goods may be supplied if the benefits to the small group outweigh the costs of paying for the collective good. An example is a trade association dominated by a few large interests seeking a protective tariff.

Most of the groups that we will discuss fit Olson's model of the large group. Environmental, consumer, civil rights, and social welfare groups are large and seek collective goods. Cleaner air, safer products, integrated facilities, and higher welfare benefits can be consumed whether or not a particular consumer contributes to the cost of acquiring the goods.

Olson provides an important analysis, but it is obvious that he overstates the case. After all, groups seeking collective goods do form and are active. How do they overcome the problem of the free rider?

McCarthy and Zald, two sociologists, have noted the rise of what they call "funded social movements." These are organizations that have a full-time professional staff that depends primarily on contributions from "conscience constituents."[5] Conscience constituents are people and organizations that suffer grievances only vicariously. They are usually the liberal, elite individuals and foundations that support civil rights, minorities, and the poor, as well as other causes.

These so-called conscience donors pay for the collective good but they do not consume it, for example, in America, organizations to abolish the death penalty. The distinguishing characteristic of these funded social movements is that the professional leadership does not depend on the mass membership for support; in fact, in many of these groups, there may be no membership as such at all. Rather, the leaders concern themselves with appeals to their conscience constituency, mainly through manipulating the media as well as packaging grievances.

Because the main contributors to these organizations do not directly feel the grievances, their relationship to the group is tenuous; they have other choices and demands for their money.

There are other incentives that lead people to join organizations. People join for the purposes of solidarity, for purposive reasons, or for selective incentives, which can be intangible, such as prestige, or specific and material, such as enhanced career opportunities, money, tennis courts, or charter flights. Scholars think that leaders have a hard time in maintaining purposive organizations because groups rarely attain their goals; the groups that do survive become staff-led as McCarthy and Zald describe. They also feel that lower-income groups are primarily responsive to material, selective incentives—incentives that are "immediate, substantial, and personal." They are closest to Olson's rational economic man.[6]

Although it is difficult to be precise about the effects of various kinds of incentives that lead people to join and contribute to social reform groups, there is a consensus that Olson is the starting point and that groups that are large, are seeking collective goods, and cannot supply selective incentives will have to figure out a method of overcoming free riders. The most common method for these groups is to seek outside funding from liberal sources—the so-called conscience constituency.

2. The second variable is the distribution of benefits and costs of group social reform activity, which affects the strength or weakness of incentives to join in the struggle. Benefits and costs can be either concentrated or distributed.[7] For example, when small numbers of private economic interests seek protective tariffs, benefits are concentrated and incentives to seek the tariffs are strong. For those opposed to the tariffs, the consumers, the costs are distributed and incentives to join in opposition are weak.

In most group social reform activity with which we will be concerned, the distribution of benefits and costs will be unfavorable to the group. In most environmental and consumer matters, at least in the short run, the costs will be concentrated on the industry; they will have strong incentives to resist. The benefits that the environmentalists and consumers seek to obtain are distributed. They are collective goods; they face the free rider problem, and incentives to pay the cost are weaker. With civil rights and social welfare, however, costs are not private economic, but are bureaucratic, social, or political and are concentrated for government officials, politicians, and racists.

3. The third variable deals with the nature of the bureaucratic response demanded by the social reform group; what I call the

"bureaucratic contingency." The principal distinction is between an administrative change that can be accomplished at the top, that is, a one-time decision that is not overly complex, as compared to decisions that are long-term, require behavioral changes throughout a far-flung bureaucracy, or are very technical and complex. In the examples mentioned earlier, *Calvert Cliffs*—changing the pipeline for the pier, moving it down the shore, and dedicating land—the effective decision was made at the top; it was a one-time decision, and although not simple, it was not overly technical or complex. Supervising the construction of the Trans-Alaskan pipeline was the opposite kind of decision—it was long-term and involved thousands of field-level discretionary decisions.

The type of bureaucratic change necessary to accomplish group goals imposes different demands on group social reform resources. Modern, complex bureaucracies are characterized by imperfect information and varying degrees of lack of control over field-level operations. Many rule changes that involve field-level implementation are usually modified or even ignored unless carefully monitored or incentive structures are changed. These low-visibility field-level discretionary decisions, as in the pipeline example, present the single most formidable obstacle to social reform groups.

4. The fourth variable concerns the nature of the judicial remedy. Social reform groups go to court, but there are limits to what courts can or are willing to do. Generally, the effectiveness of the judicial remedy parallels the nature of the demand made on the bureaucracy. Courts are most effective if all that is required is a preventive injunction, if the problem is such that a court can impose a solution rather than remand the problem to the administrative agency, or if the order can be easily monitored. Stopping a bulldozer satisfies all three tests.

The judicial remedy is least effective if regulatory or structural injunctions are called for, if the matter has to be referred back to the agency for a further exercise of discretion, or if the court order is complex or involves large numbers of individualized cases.

There are exceptions, which we will discuss shortly, in which courts have ordered the reorganization of voting districts, implemented school desegregation plans, or supervised mental health hospitals, but these are rare. Most judges will grant only traditional remedies and are loath to interfere with administrative discretion.

5. The fifth, and final, variable concerns the reform lawyers themselves. There is great variety among law reformers, but we will focus on the dominant kind of organization—the separately organized firm

consisting of about five to seven full-time lawyers who are paid mostly by private foundations.[8] These lawyers are very different from most members of the bar. Aside from being disproportionately young, elite, highly educated, and socially committed, their most distinguishing characteristic is the attorney-client relationship. The public interest (PIL) firms survive by getting grants, and in order to do this, they have to develop a program and establish a sufficient amount of publicity and legitimacy to make them salable to funding sources. In the words of two economists, they are "publicity maximizers." This result has two consequences. It produces a litigation bias. A court injunction, especially if upheld on appeal, is newsworthy, and it legitimizes the lawyers and the clients.

Contrast this style of operation with the classical lobbyist, often also a lawyer, who quietly stays with an agency or a particular legislative committee for years and is most successful when the client's view is adopted without even a conscious awareness that the lobbyist had been pressing that position. Public interest lawyers cannot build programs and further social movements by quietly walking corridors and knocking on doors, and it is doubtful whether they have the patience or temperament to do this anyway. Occasionally, they do enter into quiet negotiations, but as one public interest lawyer wryly commented, a case without publicity is our "pro bono" work, meaning of course, no material benefit comes to the firm.

Even though lawyers tend to litigate, they are constrained by their resources. It is crucially important to keep in mind that despite what seems like generous foundation funding, the resources of these firms are tiny when compared to their adversaries—government, the largest corporations, and the largest law firms. This means that the lawyers have to avoid long-term, complex factual litigation, and of course, they have no stomach for long-term, low-visibility monitoring. If the lawyers who brought the pipeline case to litigtion had undertaken to monitor implementation, they would have been able to do nothing else, and they probably would have been out of business by now.

The second consequence of this peculiar funding arrangement is that the lawyers have to pick and choose their clients to fit their own organizational needs, that is, clients whose cases have the requisite publicity and lend themselves to litigation but not lengthy trials. From the point of view of the lawyers, the ideal situation is for the lawyers to think up the case and then select the client group as plaintiffs. With groups that fit the McCarthy-Zald model, that is, are staff-led, have a nonexistent or passive membership, and rely on manipulating the media to attract "conscience constituent" support, this arrangement fits their needs as well. The lawyers do not cost them anything. They get

publicity and hopefully legitimacy and they might even win. In real life, we do find this attorney-client relationship. But there are variations, of course. There are strong social reform groups with an active, knowledgeable membership and staff who manage lawyers to fit the group's agenda.

Generally speaking, the characteristics of the attorney-client relationship vary with the socioeconomic status of the membership. Lawyers are more in control of minority and poverty groups and less in control with environmental and consumer groups.

We have now specified some of the characteristics of the variables. Before turning to the results, we must discuss what we mean by "success." It is difficult to define and measure the success of organizations. There is often a difference between stated goals and goals actually pursued. Organizations often have multiple or even conflicting goals. They rarely achieve their goals, however defined. Success, therefore, is usually measured in terms of degree.

A further difficulty is that the examples I am using are contemporary; most of the groups are still in the middle of their struggles and outcomes have to be forecast. This means, of course, that the theory cannot be validated by historical events. Nevertheless, I hope to show that the theory is promising for predicting outcomes.

Our starting point will be with groups seeking direct, tangible benefits such as improved health standards, welfare benefits, substantive civil rights, or a cleaner environment. We focus on whether the group achieves these direct benefits, not whether society in general is better or worse off.

In order to achieve benefits, norms have to be established or validated and then implemented. If the laws produce no behavioral change, the group has failed. On the other hand, it is unrealistic to evaluate group social reform efforts in terms of complete victories. Compromise, uneven administration, and gradual change are the more common results of all political actions, and we cannot hold social reform groups to a higher standard. Sometimes groups are interested in symbolic rewards rather than tangible goods and services. The distinction between symbolic and tangible rewards is subtle, especially since tangible rewards often carry symbolic rewards as well.[9] In the real world, pure symbolic rewards are rare. There is always some enforcement and some behavior change. None of the groups that I am concerned with is interested in pursuing purely symbolic rewards, and a law that fails in implementation will be regarded as a failure for the group.

In addition to pursuing specific, tangible benefits, social reform groups use law reform for more indirect effects, such as leverage,

legitimacy, publicity, and consciousness-raising. Quite often, a particular case, statute, or administrative rule is only one aspect of a larger campaign to change public opinion or the opinion of officials and politicians. As is also noted, a third level of evaluation involves the claim of revitalizing pluralism; as a result of law reform activity, social reform groups will gain access to decision-making processes and be listened to.

As we move further away from evaluating direct, tangible benefits, problems of evaluation, definition, and causality become more difficult. Nevertheless, these more intangible, elusive goals of group social reform and law reform activity may be the most important of all, and we will have to do the best we can in examining the claims.

Finally, in evaluating success, we must recognize that social reform groups can rarely achieve success in isolation from other events. Major social change comes about through broad changes in public opinion, usually caused by dramatic events, extraordinary leadership, the accumulation of ideas filtered through the media, or on occasion, by political entrepreneurs. Once accepted, programs acquire a clientele that helps perpetuate them. Social reform groups can aid in this process, but they can rarely bring about major change. To be successful, they have to be in tune with other forces in society.[10] They and their lawyers are only one set of actors, and it is often impossible to ascertain their exact role with any degree of precision.

Evaluation, thus, must be done with caution. We can shed light, though, on whether certain combinations of characteristics of the variables are more likely to lead to certain kinds of success than other combinations, or in policy terms, whether groups interested in achieving certain kinds of results are more likely to do so if they can alter some of the characteristics of the variables.

DIRECT RESULTS FROM TRADITIONAL LAW REFORM ACTIVITY

Our first perspective is to look at direct gains or losses in the short run. In reviewing all of the case studies, it is clear that the single most important variable in determining success is the bureaucratic contingency. Practically all of the groups are large, have a dispersed membership, and rely primarily on purposive incentives. Selective incentives are weak or absent. All pursue collective goods and face free riders. In practically all cases, benefits are dispersed for the membership and costs are concentrated on their adversaries.

Outside resources from conscience constituents, which include the subsidized law reform lawyers, help the groups overcome the free rider for certain kinds of law reform activity. However, if the rule change by itself cannot solve the problem and the matter must ultimately rest on administrative discretion, the group will not achieve much direct, tangible benefit. This is especially true if administration is long-term, discretionary, and at the field level.

The unfavorable bureaucratic contingency has a number of variations. In cases like the Trans-Alaskan pipeline, social reform groups are required to monitor large numbers of low-visibility factual and judgmental determinations made on a daily basis. Errors have to be uncovered and challenged, and if not capable of negotiation, they have to be appealed.

The problem is further complicated if monitoring requires the active participation of aggrieved clients to bring errors to the attention of the group or the lawyers. Anyone who has dealt with low-income people knows the difficulty of making clients aware of their rights and instilling in them the willingness to pursue their rights.

Social reform groups also face great difficulties even if the bureaucratic contingency is not at the field level, but is long-term and complex. A prominent example is nuclear power plant licensing. By the time the social reform groups are able to enter the proceedings, the agency has already resolved the safety and environmental issues and it is up to the group to refute this judgment. The battle can last years, and it is estimated that a single challenge can cost the group well over a hundred thousand dollars. And what are the chances of success? One environmental lawyer reports that he has been unable to find a single instance in which a license was denied either by the agency or at court. "In every proceeding, the weight of influence, scientific expertise, money, and decision-making power lies with the utility and the agency."[11]

Similar difficulties occur in rate regulation. In addition to the Federal Power Commission, every state has a public utility commission. Most rate proceedings, if challenged, are costly, time-consuming matters, and even the largest environmental and consumer organizations can only take on one or at most two cases a year. There are many other major regulatory agencies that require long-term adversary participation. Social reform groups simply lack this kind of capacity.

There are ways, however, in which groups and law reformers can overcome unfavorable bureaucratic contingencies. For example, the rule change will sometimes avoid the bureaucratic contingency. In California, after a long and bitter struggle lasting over two years in a dozen courts, the California Department of Welfare was enjoined from

reducing welfare benefits.[12] This case shows the power of social reform groups and law reform when the right circumstances are present. Vast sums of money were involved. The California administration under Ronald Reagan, aided by the Nixon administration, was determined to cut benefits. Practically all of the characteristics of the variables were unfavorable to successful group social reform activity—the goods were collective, the membership was dispersed, and costs were concentrated. The only thing that the social reform group had was subsidized lawyers. This was pure law reform (motions in the trial courts and appeals), which fit the organizational needs of the law reformers exactly. The problem could thus be solved by a preventive injunction.

There are other examples in which a court order can solve or potentially solve a problem, and benefits will or should accrue to the membership. Outlawing restraints of trade, such as prohibitions on drug advertising, price fixing, or interest rates, should benefit the groups if competitive markets take hold. In the environmental field, the bulldozer has sometimes been stopped or major modifications agreed to, such as in *Calvert Cliffs*.

In sum, in situations where a court order or rule change can accomplish the desired result, the subsidized law reformers can constitute a sufficient outside resource to overcome the free rider. But it must be emphasized that, effective as preventive injunctions are, they are as equally rare. As government and developers are becoming more sophisticated, it is more difficult to convince a court that their proposed acts are outrageous and in clear violation of the law.

If law reformers and groups have to fight it out at the administrative level, they can sometimes form alliances. In an early environmental case involving the construction of a power plant on the Hudson River in New York, one of the major laboratories of the Atomic Energy Commission supplied the bulk of the scientific expertise for the environmentalists. This technical assistance was essential, and the groups could not have paid its cost.[13]

Government agencies have also helped social reform groups in civil rights and employment discrimination cases. Alliances with the government, however, can prove costly. In most group social reform activity, the government is the enemy. In several important cases, government agencies, although formally on the side of the social reform groups, have dragged their feet or covertly undercut the position of the groups. Under the Nixon administration, the pace of civil rights and employment discrimination efforts slowed considerably, but the relevant government agencies piously denied any change of position. When this occurs, the social reform groups are at an extreme disadvantage. It is very difficult to persuade a court to intervene when the government

lawyers assure the court that they are diligently working on the problem.

Alliances can also be formed with private groups. In a major effort challenging plans of the U.S. Corps of Engineers to reconstruct a substantial portion of the locks and dams on the Mississippi River, the environmental groups were joined by railroads that are opposed to improved river navigation. Without the railroads, the environmentalists could not raise the money to finance this litigation. Another famous alliance is between Nader's Center for Auto Safety and several major insurance companies interested in reducing the cost of accidents.

In theory, alliances with private interest groups provide selective incentives, or in Olson's terms, the benefits of collective goods to the private interest groups outweigh the cost of acquiring them. In addition, the distribution of benefits and costs is altered; benefits are concentrated for the private groups allied with the social reform groups.

On the other hand, alliances with private groups can cause problems for social reform groups. Purposive incentives might be weakened. In the Mississippi lock and dam case, some environmental organizations dropped out rather than ally themselves with the railroads. Courts may also become suspicious of the purity of the plaintiffs when private interests join them. Private interests may have conflicting interests. Private land developers joined in several cases with the Open Suburbs Movement, a group that attacked zoning laws designed to keep out low-income residents. The developers joined for purposes of invalidating the restrictions, but not for the next stage—the continuing struggle against local government to allow public housing to be built. As a result, in practically all of these cases the social reform group could not sustain the effort and in fact only middle- and upper-middle-income housing was built.[14]

A very important method of overcoming the bureaucratic contingency is to substitute a quantifiable measure of performance for field-level discretion. The foremost example occurred in voting rights for southern blacks. The American Civil War Amendments guaranteed the right to vote, but through various devices southern states blocked the exercise of the franchise. In time, the most blatant laws were invalidated, but blacks were still effectively barred through field-level discretionary decisions (voting registrars administered a literacy and knowledge of the Constitution test) that were discriminatorily enforced. There were, of course, other nonlegal constraints.

For a time, civil rights groups attempted to win the vote through law reform litigation, but even several Supreme Court victories failed to crack the southern system, and black voter registration remained

pitifully low. Then the federal government, under the Kennedy and Johnson administrations, began to enact legislation which step by step eliminated field-level discretion. Eventually the law provided a quantified test—if an applicant completed a certain number of years of schooling, he or she was literate enough to vote. In addition, there were also quantified provisions to check illegal field-level discretion. If a certain proportion of black residents in a particular county were not registered, the Justice Department could appoint a federal registrar to enroll the blacks. Again, the important point is that the appointment of the federal registrar rested only on an easily gathered statistic, and not on any proof of illegal acts by local officials. This last measure was Draconian by American standards, since historically and even today, voting qualifications and administration are primarily state and local matters. The new scheme worked dramatically, but only in those counties where social reform groups were active in petitioning the federal government and, more importantly, educating the local blacks and getting them to register.

The other major example of substituting a quantified standard also occurred in civil rights—in measuring the legality of school desegregation plans. For a time, southern school boards were able to evade federal court orders by discretionary decisions. Then the courts became tired and disgusted and looked only at results: proportions of students in integrated classes. They ignored protestations of "good faith" from school administrators.

For a time, efforts to combat employment discrimination proceeded along this path. Social reform groups composed of minorities and low-income workers lacked the ability to challenge individual acts of alleged discrimination. Therefore, the groups and their lawyers pressed for affirmative action agreements that contained "goals and timetables," a euphemism for quotas, and as with school integration, legality would depend only on statistical results: proportions of minorities or women hired in various positions. Recently this approach is being undercut and defenses of "good faith" are creeping back in, which means that large numbers of low-visibility discretionary decisions have to be challenged by the members of society who can least afford it.

As a general proposition, enforcing rights becomes considerably easier when substantive relationships are simplified and measured in statistics. But some problems, of course, will not lend themselves to simplification and routinization—for example, human services. Groups that have been active in establishing rights for mental health patients have a particularly formidable task in monitoring performance. In most cases, statistical tests have to be used as proxies—for

example, staffing ratios, therapy plans, and budgets. In Alabama, however, the U.S. federal court took the unusual step of establishing human rights committees composed of citizens, professionals, relatives, and former patients to monitor implementation of eighty specified standards of care. The committees had a staff and a budget as well as the power to receive complaints. Empirical studies have indicated that the committees have been effective within limits.[15]

On occasion, other courts, particularly in explosive, complex civil rights cases, have appointed committees or masters to find facts and help implement orders. But it must be emphasized that, although courts have these powers, they are reluctant to exercise them. Judges prefer to leave administration to the parties, one of which may be a weak, resource-starved social reform group.

A final method of attempting to cope with the bureaucratic contingency is relying on client groups. Using community groups has been a favorite rallying cry of radicals and liberals, but on the whole, the record has not been good. Groups given participation rights lack the resources and professional support necessary to make their voices heard. They thus often become passive. As a result of past failures, social reform groups and law reformers are becoming more sophisticated and are seeking resources and technical help as part of their settlements. For example, in some large employment discrimination cases, funds are available to the client group to monitor performance, conduct outreach, and train applicants. At the present time, there is a concerted effort to improve safety standards in nonunionized coal fields. In addition to traditional law reform work, considerable effort is going into community education, training, and providing advocacy resources. The approach is right; whether or not it will succeed is still an open question. Nonunionized coal miners are very oppressed. They live in remote areas of the country where large labor surpluses exist and thus are often at the mercy of the coal mine operators.

I have mentioned a number of ways in which social reform groups and their lawyers can overcome the important hurdle of implementation, but how important are these techniques? My cases were not randomly selected, but they do indicate that there are large areas of concern in which the bureaucratic contingency cannot be avoided. In the environmental field, particularly in energy and in air and water pollution, challenges are extremely expensive, technically complex, and long and drawn-out. Nationwide, there are very few such challenges. In the consumer area, major regulatory agencies, such as the Food and Drug Administration, are hopelessly bogged down and at the mercy of powerful industries. Similar examples abound in civil rights and social welfare; an especially acute area is health and mental heath.

The vulnerability of social reform groups to the bureaucratic contingency raises doubts about one of their most important claims—gaining access to decision-making procedures. During the past decade, there has been a remarkable increase in formal access for social reform groups, but how important is this participation? The ultimate test is not the symbolic conferring of legitimacy, but whether, as a result of participation, different points of view are listened to and outcomes are changed.

There are several ways, however, in which planning agencies are able to undermine these newly won procedural rights. Groups are still brought into the planning process much too late. They are swamped with reports and technical information; sophisticated agencies such as the Corps of Engineers comply with NEPA with a vengeance, churning out hundreds of environmental impact statements. Many other agencies employ biologists, geologists, demographers, and other kinds of environmental specialists. In these situations, reviewing courts will not be of much help. As long as the agency complies with all the procedures, the court will not intervene in the substantive decision. And if the decision is reversed, the case will be remanded to the agency for further examination. Furthermore, most important administrative decisions are ongoing, and in order for participation to be meaningful, groups still have to mobilize long-term technical and professional resources.

In sum, social reform groups will find it difficult to obtain direct, tangible benefits from law reform activity. It can be done, but special conditions have to be met, the most important of which is that the rule change must itself substantially bring about the result. Of course, there is a great deal more that is desired besides direct tangible benefits. After all, most groups are part of movements interested in broad social change rather than individual cases.

INDIRECT RESULTS FROM LAW REFORM ACTIVITY

Litigation often serves multiple purposes—legitimacy, publicity, and stimulating purposive incentives. Now we wish to focus on these more indirect effects. Although the line is artificial perhaps, we are looking at situations in which social reform groups and lawyers use litigation as part of a broader campaign, which may or may not use additional litigation, but will also use nonlitigation techniques such as lobbying, direct action, community organization, and public relations.

In many campaigns, law reform is used to *clear the underbrush,* that is, remove legal barriers to other kinds of activity. In the struggle for voting rights mentioned earlier, the principal weapons were legislation, a vigorous federal administration, and local social reform group activity. Before these tactics could be used, however, important law reform litigation was necessary to invalidate the southern primary system and poll tax and to clarify key provisions in the legislation. After that, lower court services were necessary to protect blacks from illegally imposed criminal sanctions.

Similarly, in many civil rights campaigns, principal reliance was placed on direct action, such as sit-ins and marches, but law reform litigation was needed initially, and then repeatedly, to remove or lessen the threat of criminal sanctions, which is important to most mobilization efforts.

Another indirect function of litigation is to increase bargaining leverage. In the Trans-Alaskan pipeline case, the initial court injunction served to increase the leverage. The groups could apply in negotiating with the government and the oil companies. Without the injunction, no one would have listened to the environmentalists. Temporary injunctions are often used for this purpose. The groups know that there is no real hope for a permanent injunction, but delay often increases their bargaining strength.

In a famous case in Wisconsin, the state Supreme Court invalidated the interest charged by major retailers and credit card companies as a violation of the state usury law. As the price of agreeing to an amendment to the usury law, consumer groups were able to extract a decent consumer protection statute from the legislature. Prior to the court decision, the consumers lacked the power to get their bill enacted.

The distinguishing characteristic of these *leverage cases* is that the social reform groups are not as interested in the specific results of the judicial decision as in using the court decision to increase their ability to use nonlitigation strategies.

PUBLICITY, LEGITIMACY, AND CONSCIOUSNESS-RAISING

Most law reform activity is newsworthy, and some public interest lawyers are especially adroit at manipulating the media to get the maximum public relations value out of filing complaints. This is an especially important tactic when opponents, such as banks, savings and loans associations, and large retailers, are particularly sensitive to charges of employment discrimination, as for example in California,

which has a large population with Spanish surnames. In these situations, the lawyers do not intend to obtain tangible benefits from the litigation, which would be factually complex and time-consuming. Rather, the strategy is to use the adverse publicity to drive their opponents to the bargaining table. Of course, the settlement will also be highly publicized, this time for the benefit of the employers. With the possible exception of Ralph Nader, a 20-page complaint is worth a dozen 300-page reports.

The use of courts to publicize a cause is, of course, a time-honored technique; the oldest and most dramatic example is the political trial. Environmentalists and consumers are usually not willing to go to jail, but they are acutely sensitive to the importance of publicity to reinforce purposive incentives, stimulate conscience constituency support, and gain legitimacy.

Legitimacy derived from laws, court decisions, and claims of right is supposed to have a special saliency in American political culture.[16] The particular claims of group social reform activity fall within the basic values of the Constitution—the opportunity to be heard, equality before the law, and enforcement of the law. When courts agree with the groups, their values receive the highest form of legitimacy.

Social reform group leaders and public interest lawyers lay great stress on legitimacy, but how important is legitimacy in the mobilization of resources? Theories of legitimacy tell us very little about the circumstances under which attitudes are changed, how much they are changed, and what follows from such changes. We know, for example, that attitudes toward the law vary with socioeconomic class, and that throughout history, the attitudes of responsible leaders and large segments of society were not changed by Supreme Court decisions.

It may be that legitimacy is not a powerful force, but that people are selective in the kinds of laws they will approve. It is possible that legitimacy merely bolsters prior attitudes about right and wrong and is, on the whole, weak and diffuse. This view of legitimacy would coincide with McCarthy's and Zald's opinion that conscience constituents are unstable, fickle, and easily lured to other causes.

Legitimacy also addresses the membership and society at large; it is supposed to raise consciousness. The legitimation of demands can overcome the acquiescence of oppressed groups. Court decisions convert demands into rights and raise them in status. They are expected to be granted—they are legitimated.

Again, we must ask what consciousness-raising means in concrete terms. The legitimation of grievances may make people feel better (or worse), but how important are legal symbols? In the great civil rights struggles, the Supreme Court early and clearly legitimated the

demands of southern blacks. While this was probably of great importance in mobilizing northern white support, and eventually that of the federal government, there was great difficulty in mobilizing ordinary southern blacks. Legal symbols often speak to the most powerless in society, the victims of racial, social, and political discrimination. Nevertheless, these people are the most difficult to mobilize.

It may not be fair to assess consciousness-raising in the short run. As many point out, major social change comes about through long-term changes in public opinion, and the elite, the media, and other opinion formers are affected by the pronouncement of basic constitutional values. Clearly, the dominant climate of opinion in America toward blacks and civil rights has changed dramatically as a result of the Supreme Court.

This argument has a plausible ring, but a number of questions can be raised. The theory is too broad; it does not distinguish between cases. In most of the cases that I have studied, claims were vindicated in court or before agencies, but where will legitimacy adhere to further the cause? The more general and diffuse the symbols become, the more difficult it is to assess effects, and the more it would seem that social reform groups, law reformers, and their elite support would be subject to symbolic reassurance that all is well. We have a long history of myths in abortive regulatory reform. Scholars point out that mass publics and reform groups that lack technical and professional resources are particularly susceptible to symbolic reassurance in low-visibility, technical regulatory matters, and that legal symbols are very important in this myth-making process.[17]

In the environmental area, most groups lack the capacity to analyze the outpouring of technical environmental impact statements or challenge agency claims that they are now obeying the law. If the past is a guide, conscience constituent supporters will gradually succumb to symbolic reassurance that all is well, purposive incentives will weaken, and financial contributions will diminish.

THE REVITALIZATION OF PLURALISM

Space does not permit a full analysis of the third claim of group social reform activity, that of revitalizing pluralism, but I will sketch the issue. Pluralist theory holds that interest groups are constantly forming and pressing their demands on each other as well as on government (also an interest group) in a constantly changing negotiating process. Powerful groups moderate their demands for fear of stimulating counter groups. On the other hand, new groups emerge

because of the changing conditions of society and the relatively open access to the political process. Thus pluralism allows for both change and stability.

The critics of pluralism challenge this view. As new groups, such as labor and agriculture, have emerged, they face problems of organizational maintenance and form partnerships with various levels of government. The alliances between group leaders and officials reinforce each other and advantages accumulate. Instead of fostering change, the groups become hierarchically organized to perpetuate the status quo. We have in America what is called "institutionalized pluralism" and what is called in Western Europe, "societal corporatism."[18]

Social reform groups and law reformers also face problems of organizational maintenance, which turns us to the important question of funding. Although these groups and their lawyers face tremendous odds, I think it a mistake to assume that they will die. They have widespread political and social support. However, the question remains—what kind of support and what consequences will it have for the future structure of the groups?

To the extent that the groups and lawyers are able to achieve a stable source of funding, the characteristics of the groups will change and come to resemble what McCarthy and Zald describe as "funded social movements." They will be staff-led, hierarchically organized, and eventually even lawyer-led. These are all questions of degree. Some groups already resemble this model whereas others have a vigorous, active membership. But the prognosis is that the source of funding will convert them into the hierarchical, staff-led model.

For example, one of the newly emerging sources of funding will be from the regulatory agencies themselves. Increasingly, funds are included in their budgets to finance social reform group or public interest law participation in their proceedings. But to whom will the agencies give their money? They will tend to finance those groups that satisfy the agency's need to remain procedurally honest, but not cause too much trouble. If the agencies are successful in picking and choosing the representatives of the public, existing groups will be favored over new groups, existing leaders will be favored over dissidents, who will not be recognized or financed by the agency, and law reform lawyers will be strengthened since they are the route to money, publicity, and legitimacy. The agencies will be able to nurture the leaders by giving them information, important symbols of access and concessions.

Other funding proposals, while not so fraught with danger, may have similar tendencies. For example, funding by the various state bar associations will mean only one or two law reform firms per state,

which, in order to survive, will select clients to serve their organizational needs.

The analysis, therefore, leads to three choices for social reform groups. In their natural state of evolution, many will rise, be active for awhile, languish, and then either die or become staff-led. If they choose to pursue their goals through the legal system, this process may well be hastened.

After that there will be two alternatives. Some groups will gain formal access, but because of a lack of resources and abandonment by the lawyers, they will become passive. The other alternative is that the groups will participate actively, but as part of the system of "institutionalized pluralism." Pluralism will not be revitalized, and decision making will not be democratized. Rather, as in earlier times, when the system took in and socialized radical farm and labor groups, it will take in and socialize today's social reform groups. Because socialization is often a reciprocal process, substantive decisions will probably be changed to take new members into account.

Social reform groups have turned to lawyers and the legal system because they are weak. By turning to the legal system, however, they have appealed to traditional institutions, and their claims for social justice have been based on traditional American legal and political values. Thus, it should come as no surprise that group social reform activity via law reform will not disturb the basic political and economic organization of modern American society.

NOTES

1. *Brown* v. *Board of Education,* 347 U.S. 483, 1954.
2. 42 U.S.C. § 433, 1970.
3. This account is largely based on G. M. Zemansky, "Environmental Noncompliance and the Public Interest during the Construction of the Trans-Alaska Pipeline," mimeographed (Fairbanks: Fairbanks Environmental Center, 1976).
4. M. Olson, Jr., *The Logic of Collective Action* (Cambridge, Mass., Harvard University Press, 1965).
5. J. D. McCarthy, and M. N. Zald, "Resource Mobilization and Social Movements: A Partial Theory," *American Journal of Sociology,* 82 (1977): 1212–1241.
6. J. Q. Wilson, *Political Organizations* (New York: Basic Books, 1973).
7. Ibid.
8. For detailed analysis of public interest lawyers, see J. F. Handler; E. J. Hollingsworth; and H. Erlanger, *Lawyers and the Pursuit of Legal Rights* (New York: Academic Press, 1978).
9. M. Edelman, *The Symbolic Uses of Politics* (Urbana: University of Illinois Press, 1964).
10. J. Q. Wilson, *Political Organizations.*

11. T. P. Davis, "Citizen's Guide to Intervention in Nuclear Power Plant Siting: A Blueprint for Alice in Nuclear Wonderland," *Environmental Law* (1976): 621–650.
12. P. Sitkin, "Welfare Law: Narrowing the Gap between Congressional Policy and Local Policy," in U.S. Joint Economic Committee, Subcommittee on Fiscal Policy, *Issues in Welfare Administration* (Washington, D.C.: U.S. Government Printing Office, 1973).
13. *Scenic Hudson Preservation Commission* v. *Federal Power Commission,* 354 F.2d 608 (2d Cir. 1965), cert. denied, 384 U.S. 941 (1966). See D. M. Trubek and W. J. Gillen, "Environmental Defense 2: Examining the Limits of Interest Group Advocacy in Complex Disputes," in *Public Interest Law,* edited by B. Weisbrod; J. Handler; and N. Komesar (Berkeley: University of California Press, 1978).
14. G. Shields, and L. S. Spector, "Opening up Suburbs: Notes on a Movement for Social Change," *Yale Review of Law and Social Action* 2 (1971): 300.
15. See "The Wyatt Case: Implementation of a Judicial Decree Ordering Institutional Change," *Yale Law Journal* 88 (1975): 1338.
16. L. Friedman, *The Legal System: A Social Science Perspective* (New York: Russell Sage Foundation, 1975); and S. A. Scheingold, *The Politics of Rights: Lawyers, Public Policy and Political Change* (New Haven: Yale University Press, 1974).
17. M. Edelman, *The Symbolic Uses of Politics* (Urbana: University of Illinois Press, 1964).
18. W. Connolly (ed.), *The Bias of Pluralism* (New York: Atherton, 1969); and T. J. Lowi, *The End of Liberalism* (New York: W. W. Norton, 1969).

Chapter 10

Legal Services and the Administrative State: From Public Interest Law to Public Advocacy

David M. Trubek, Louise G. Trubek, and Jonathan Becker

When lawyers speak of "legal services," they tend to mean programs that provide lawyers for the poor. Such programs are justified because they give the disadvantaged greater access to the courts, thus reducing one of the inequalities created by a specialized legal system in a stratified society. But in advanced capitalist societies, it is not only the poor who lack lawyers. And in the modern administrative state, it is not only the courts to which citizens lack access. Quite the contrary; in these societies many citizens, including members of the "middle classes," lack any effective means to vindicate important rights.

The state in capitalist society has expanded its role to include the regulation of economic activity and the provision of welfare and similar benefits to large numbers of citizens. These expanded roles lead to a proliferation of rights and benefits whose nature and scope must be determined, in the final analysis, by the officials of the administrative state. "Rights" may be created in the legislatures, and courts may continue to play a role in defining and enforcing these rights. But the central arena of definition and implementation of many crucial entitlements are the countless agencies, bureaus, and offices charged with regulating the economy and dispensing benefits.

In the United States, at least, this means that many citizens for whom formal protections, entitlements, or benefits seem to be available from the state lack any effective means to protect their "rights," or secure protections and benefits. Administrative decisionmaking, contrary to textbook models, involves considerable discretion and is subject to conflicting political pressures. When citizens are granted formal protections, but lack access to the administrative arenas in which these protections are translated into concrete policies, the rights may become meaningless. For example, if a statute requires that agencies only license factories that will not unduly harm the environment but no affected citizen can challenge a firm's request for a license, "environmental protection law" may be a hollow promise.[1]

Public interest law is a recent innovation in the United States, and it seeks to deliver legal services to groups whose rights are affected by such administrative decisions.[2] Public interest law firms are subsidized law centers that provide legal and related advocacy services to groups like consumers, environmentalists, minorities, the handicapped, and the elderly. Such client groups include the poor and the nonpoor; what they have in common is that they lack the ability to organize effectively to influence administrative decisions. Public interest lawyers seek to do that for their "clients."

The public interest law movement is relatively new in the United States; it is one of the innovations that came out of the ferment of the 1960s. But this fledgling institution has already encountered serious problems. Changes in the legal, political, social, and financial climate in the last few years have brought into question the future viability of the public interest law firm as it was originally conceptualized and operated.[3] As a result, the public interest law movement—that is, the existing firms and their supporters—is seeking new directions. In looking beyond public interest law, these groups are forced to analyze the basic causes of "underrepresentation" of some interests or groups in the administrative state, and to seek more fundamental and permanent institutional arrangements to ensure effective access to administrative forums.

This chapter has emerged from this reanalysis. It reflects our effort to generalize what we have learned in five years of conducting and studying public interest law practice in the United States. In the course of this experience, we have had to reexamine the goals and institutional needs of institutions that seek to represent unorganized interests at the local, state, or federal level. Naturally, our most specific conclusions are of primary interest to those who seek to restructure public interest law in North America. But our reappraisal suggests that the basic

problem is more general and that the propensity of the welfare-corporate state to create rights for which no effective "remedies" exist is not limited to North America. To the extent this is true, this chapter will be relevant to all those concerned with innovations in legal services in societies of this type.

THE PUBLIC INTEREST LAW MOVEMENT

Although public interest law is a relatively new phenomenon in the United States, it has been described and analyzed in numerous publications.[4] It is not our task here to trace its history or recount its successes. Chapter 8 by Halpern and Blankenburg will give the reader unfamiliar with this movement insight into what public interest law is and what public interest lawyers do. Here we merely want to highlight some major features of this approach in legal representation.

The public interest law movement must be seen in context. It should not be confused with the American "legal services" program. In the United States these programs are run by a government corporation and are limited to the poor. In addition, legal services programs tend to emphasize direct provision of legal assistance to individual clients. Public interest law, on the other hand, tends to be privately funded, to emphasize group rather than individual representation, and to work on behalf of both poor and nonpoor clients. Frequently the poor are included, but rarely are client groups exclusively made up of persons with incomes below the official poverty level.

Partly because of the areas of concern to public interest lawyers and partly because of their emphasis on "group" representation, the 600 or so lawyers who practice in public interest firms tend to concentrate on administrative issues. There is a "popular" image of public interest lawyers as litigators seeking test case and class action victories in the courts. That image is partially accurate; a significant percentage of many public interest lawyers' time will be spent in court. But even when this is the case, the *goal* of the litigation will often be to secure judicial review and reversal of the decision of an administrative body. Whether public interest lawyers are suing to protect environmental rights or to preserve the interests of welfare clients, in the end they are typically concerned with stopping, or changing, the decision of a bureau or agency like the U.S. Corps of Engineers or the Department of Health, Education and Welfare.

We should really treat public interest law as a phenomenon of the 1960s. Although the movement's origins can be traced back to the progressive legal tradition of great jurists like Louis D. Brandeis and

precursors to the public interest law firm can be found in the Legal Defense Fund of the National Association for the Advancement of Colored People, the public interest law firm as a general institutional form first emerged in the mid-1960s.[5] In that period, dozens of firms were started. They tended to specialize in a particular area, such as the environment, consumer advocacy, or women's rights. The firms were supported principally by donations from private charitable foundations, and to a much lesser degree by law schools and government agencies. Many emphasized test case litigation as their chief mode of advocacy. And most were staffed by idealistic young lawyers dissatisfied with conventional practice.

What caused this innovation? Although a full analysis lies beyond the scope of this chapter, we do suggest some of the factors that seem important to us and of interest to an international audience. These are the existence of "law to be applied," the lack of automatic benefits from that law, the emergence of a pool of politically or socially active lawyers, the effects of an activist judiciary, the defensiveness of the bar, and the presence of private foundations concerned with social issues.

Public interest law might be called the institutionalization of the ideology of rights. That is, it is based on the belief that legal rights can lead to social change, but that to do so, these rights must be translated into concrete benefits through advocacy. Thus public interest lawyers start from a body of "law to be applied," that is, there must be a body of positive law or doctrine that appears to promise benefits to a particular group of persons. And this law must require "lawyering" to work, for if the rights operated directly, legal advocacy would be unnecessary. In the late 1960s in the United States, there seemed to be a significant amount of law to be applied. At the constitutional level, the United States had witnessed a period of doctrinal innovations by the Warren Supreme Court that suggested that constitutional texts could and would be reinterpreted by an activist judiciary to expand the legal rights of "have-not" groups.[6] At the statutory level, numerous laws and programs created rights for consumers, environmentalists, minorities, and so forth, but did not guarantee that executive agencies would enforce these rights.

The existence, or potential, of this body of legal rights was attractive to several groups in the society. These were times when dissenting groups, led by activist students, challenged all the nation's institutions and values. Even relatively conservative groups sought to adjust themselves to these challenges and to respond in a limited way to the criticisms.

Public interest law might be seen as the reaction of three *basically* conservative groups to the challenge of the legitimacy of the legal order.

The public interest law firm was created by the conjunction of the interests of three groups: law students and young lawyers seeking alternatives to private practice; private foundations seeking a relatively neutral way to support certain social movements; and the organized bar seeking a relatively nonthreatening way to meet radical critics of the legal order. The law students wanted to be able to do the kind of legal work they had been trained to do in elite law schools and corporate law offices, but to do it for causes in which they believed. The foundations wanted to support efforts like the environmental, consumer, and women's movements, but do it in a nonpolitical way. And the bar wanted to restore its image of providing "equal justice under law" that had been tarnished by revelations of the role of Wall Street and Washington lawyers in manipulating and "capturing" administrative agencies.

The public interest law firm appealed to all of these "constituencies." It was suggested that these firms would merely enforce existing statutory and constitutional rights. For the young lawyers, this meant they could do the work they knew best and would not have to dirty their hands with things like lobbying or group organization, which they were neither prepared for nor attracted to. For the foundations, it meant that they could help social movements in an apolitical way, since their support for environmental law, women's rights groups, and so on, only ensured that the existing law would be enforced. And for the bar, it meant that the symbol of equal access to justice could be upheld without major risks that serious legal changes would occur.

The result was remarkable. As Americans often do, they threw themselves into this cause with great enthusiasm. New public interest law firms were set up almost every month. At the peak, there were ninety firms employing over 600 lawyers.[7] Big, dramatic test cases were brought to trial. Dams were halted. Even the Alaska Pipeline was delayed substantially by public interest litigation. Lawsuits led to reorganization of mental hospitals, forced manufacturers to pay damages to large groups of consumers, and so on. The work of the public interest firms offered visible proof that agency decisions could be changed, that the "underrepresented" could be protected, and that legal action could contribute to social change. It was an exciting time.

Today, the scene is less exhilarating. Times have changed. Fewer young lawyers seem to have the relative idealism or social concern that marked the graduates of the 1960s.[8] The judiciary, taking the lead from a more conservative Supreme Court, seems less willing to extend constitutional doctrine or second-guess agency interpretations of statutes. The foundations have either retreated from the field altogether or limited their support to maintenance of a few already

established firms. Even that limited foundation support may be cut back in the future. The organized bar has been unwilling to provide material support for the movement.[9]

Ten years ago, when people from public interest law firms got together, they talked about new cases and projects; today, likely as not, they anguish over declining budgets, dwindling staffs, and the need to find advocacy arenas to replace the courts.

This is a time of reappraisal. Although a few public interest law firms have managed to find stable forms of activity and funding, most are seeking new fields of activity and new sources of support. The litigation strategy is played out in many fields.[10] What, then, can public interest lawyers do to help the groups whose causes they champion? The foundations have retreated from the field. Where can the firms go for money?

Not surprisingly, the problem of funding tends to be dominant. And the only solution that seems viable is to look to the state for financial support that is needed to maintain a subsidized institution like a public interest law firm. But as the movement turns to the state for financial support, it is forced to deal more explicitly with the basic question of why such institutions are needed. To answer this, it is necessary to lay bare the causes of underrepresentation in the administrative forums. Thus, more attention is being given to the critical scrutiny of the working of the administrative process in the United States. Public interest law was originally conceived as a reform in systems of legal services delivery. Today, it is being seen increasingly as part of the process of reforming the administrative state.

SEEKING TO UNDERSTAND THE ADMINISTRATIVE STATE—THE PROBLEM OF UNORGANIZED POTENTIAL BENEFICIARIES OF STATE ACTION

The result of interest in state support has been an effort to move from public interest law to "public advocacy." We use this term to refer to all government programs that create, encourage, or sustain institutions whose task is to provide advocacy for unrepresented groups in administrative agency proceedings.[11] Recently, consumers, supported by the Carter administration, tried to get Congress to endorse this idea. In the 95th Congress the administration supported the establishment of an office of consumer protection (OCP) charged solely with advocacy duties.[12] The bill noted that consumers are inadequately represented in federal administrative proceedings and that vigorous representation of

consumers is necessary to the fair and efficient functioning of the market economy. It proposed a government office empowered to appear as a party on behalf of consumers in any federal administrative proceedings and to appeal adverse decisions to the courts. The defeat of this bill, following sustained lobbying by business interests, was a serious setback to the consumer movement in particular and the administrative reform effort in general.

The failure of the idea for an office of consumer protection can be attributed to many factors. At one level, the problems were political. But, at a deeper level, the problem was conceptual. Few people fully understand the nature of the problem to which the OCP was to be a response. This experience suggests that the critique of the administrative process has not gone deep enough or been disseminated widely enough to ensure a constituency for ideas that might preserve the idea of public interest law. This chapter is an effort to deepen the analysis.

Toward a Theory of "Consumer" Representation

The OCP plan was designed to provide representation in federal administrative proceedings for consumers in the normal sense of that term, that is, people who buy goods and services in the marketplace. The bill recognized that in the regulatory state, consumers are affected by what the government does as much as by the decisions of business firms. The authors of OCP accepted governmental regulation of business as a permanent and essential part of the "mixed economy." But at the same time they believed that regulatory decisions would fail to "protect" consumers if this interest were not adequately represented in administrative proceedings. And they felt the government had to provide this representation.

The OCP bill rests on a critique of the administrative state, and this critique extends well beyond the sphere of consumers. Citizens depend on the government to ensure that products are safe and prices are fair. But they also depend on the government to be sure the air is clean, that they can get adequate medical care, that they will be treated with equal dignity, and that their income will be shielded from the impact of certain catastrophes. The government promises such rights and protections just as it promises to regulate the marketplace. As the authors of OCP recognize, however, the administrative state does not always *deliver* on these promises.

OCP and similar reform proposals address the tension between the promise of benefits and their subsequent denial by the realities of politics, administration, and law. Since the reformers lack a systematic theory of the nature and causes of this tension, proposed solutions often

fail. The failure of the reform movement to produce a coherent theory of the problem means that at best we can hope for partial reform, and at worst, it means that reformers may opt for inappropriate solutions that will fail effectively to deal with the basic problem. Thus, we must ask, why are rights created but some not enforced?

The Modern State and the Creation of Potential Beneficiaries. The modern state ceaselessly expands its roles. It regulates market behavior, imposes requirements (such as pollution control) designed to curb the social costs of industrial activity, and directly provides goods and services that are unavailable through the market. Given the constitutional rules and political ideology of liberal democracies, all this intervention by the state must be justified as the pursuit of a general, collective, or "public" interest. Whether the real motive of railroad regulation is to protect railroad profits or whether the regulation of competitive practices is designed to curb monopoly or eliminate "unfair" competition, regulatory activity is *presented* as an effort to secure broad goals shared by the public as a whole.

Not only is intervention justified because it is in the public interest, but it is also frequently presented in the form of rights that are given to citizens. When the state regulates the housing market, for example, it may create, or appear to create, "rights" to adequate shelter. The process of rights creation and public interest regulation creates a class of potential beneficiaries of state action. If an industry is to be regulated by an agency in the public interest, presumably this will lead to some action that will benefit citizens who would not be so benefited by the absence of regulation. When the state declares that it is illegal for landlords to rent housing that violates health and safety standards or establishes welfare programs designed to give benefits, say, to people over sixty-five with an income below $8000, residents of dilapidated housing and the elderly poor become potential beneficiaries of state action.

Let us introduce a simplified scheme to analyze the sphere of what we call potential benefits. If the state has made no claim to act in a given area of social life, we cannot say there are any potential beneficiaries of state action. Once the state has intervened, it may or may not provide tangible gains for a given class or group of potential beneficiaries. Unless state intervention involves direct, automatic, and clear action creating benefits, the act of intervention merely creates a situation in which an "argument" may be made that action that will lead to real benefits should be taken.

What determines the likelihood that potential beneficiaries will secure real gains? This is obviously a complex question. At the purely

verbal-legal level, the answer will be influenced by the language of statutes or regulations. The more clearly the benefits are created as formal entitlements, ceteris paribus, the more likely it is that real benefits will flow to intended beneficiaries. But things are never equal, and although statutory language may have some significance, other variables are clearly more important.

Regulation of Industry—Administration and the Nonrealization of Potential Benefits. To explore the issue of potential beneficiaries in more detail, let us look more closely at one area—regulation of industrial activity by administrative regulation. This will help us understand the problem with which reformers are concerned, that is, the inability of unorganized potential beneficiaries to receive tangible gains from state action. There are several models that explain why the state regulates economic activity. We want to focus on two, which we shall call the "public interest" perspective and the "industry interest" perspective. They lead to different accounts of the causes and implications of the obvious fact of the proliferation of government regulation. They share, however, certain elementary assumptions. The most basic of these is the idea that there can be a conflict of interest between industries and the public at large. Industries seek to maximize profits, not social welfare. While these goals may coincide when the conditions of perfect competition are met, the existence of such conditions is rare, and it is not in industry's interest to preserve them. Thus it is assumed that industries will struggle for higher profits regardless of the effect of this struggle on social welfare.

The models diverge in their explanation of the role of regulation in the struggle between profits and "welfare." The public interest model sees regulation as the response of the state to market failure. Thus, public utilities may be regulated to curb the effects of "natural monopoly," or to mediate possible conflicts between the needs of consumers and producers and thus avoid suboptimal levels of investment.[13] Environmental regulations ensure that industries internalize the social costs of their activity. The public interest model, therefore, assumes that demands for such regulation are created by a political process that responds, at least in part, to concerns of citizens adversely affected by industry decisions.

The industry interest model offers a radically different explanation for regulation. It says we have regulation because industry uses state power to increase profitability. Stigler identifies four types of state policies that enhance the profitability of industry: cash subsidies, control over entry of new rivals, limitation of substitute products and subsidization of complementary products, and price maintenance.[14] In

the industry interest model, regulation is explained as a zero or negative sum game, and regulations are thought to emerge from the political efforts of business to secure policies that favor industry.

The two models differ in their view of politics. Both see the political game as involving a struggle between organized groups like industries and large numbers of unorganized citizens like consumers or victims of industrial pollution. But the public interest model assumes that the state can be, and is, responsive to the demands of large numbers of persons, even if their individual interest in a policy is small and even if the policy will harm organized groups. Proponents of the industry interest theory, on the other hand, assert that the state is more likely to respond to the demands of organized groups, like industries, especially if these groups have substantial economic resources that can be mobilized to secure favorable policies, and regardless of the fact that the resulting policies will have negative effects on large numbers of citizens.

A satisfactory explanation of the typical process of regulation requires some fusion of these two models. Some policies can clearly be explained by the industry interest model. But more frequently, the establishment of regulatory schemes involves a complex process in which both public interest and industry interest forces are at play.[15] This fact helps to explain the pervasiveness of the problem of unorganized potential beneficiaries of state regulatory activity.

If the industry interest theory were correct, there would be no rights created for consumers or other "public" groups. But there are. To understand why there are such rights is also to understand why they are often unenforced. To see this, let us examine a hypothetical case, the effort to create an agency that would ensure the safety of products sold in the marketplace. Many societies are concerned with this problem, and thus it has wide applicability.

The potential beneficiaries of such a regulatory agency are unorganized. Assume that a consumer product safety law would create economic benefits for consumers by reducing the consumer-assumed risks associated with the purchase of certain commodities. Although such a law would benefit large numbers of people, there is no organized entity that represents all the potential beneficiaries of this regulation. This means that there is no "lobbyist" for the consumer interest who can mobilize the economic resources that all consumers would be willing to contribute to securing such a law, or control their votes for or against legislators and other politicians who secure passage of it. At the same time, there *will* be such lobbyists for industry who can mobilize economic resources reflecting what industry will pay not to have such a law.

If we assume that the politicians act to maximize the votes they will receive at the next election, under what conditions will the political process respond to the demands of such unorganized groups and reject those of the industry? One might conclude that since the consumers are more numerous than the industry, the vote-maximizing propensity of the politicians would lead them to favor the consumers over the industry.

This will occur only if there is a high probability that the legislator's vote for the agency will lead potentially benefited consumers to support him at the next election. Frequently, this is not the case. The mere fact that large numbers of people will benefit from a measure does not mean that they will reward the proponents of it with votes, or that rewards will be proportional to the number of losers versus the number of gainers. In the first place, some of the potential beneficiaries may not be regular voters. In the United States, for example, the more affluent and better educated tend to vote more regularly than other groups. Secondly, even if they vote, the potential beneficiaries may lack information about the politician's acts. Unless the consumer groups are well organized, they may fail to realize that Act X initiated by Representative Y is in their interest. Thirdly, politicians must seek intermediate resources like money or endorsements as tools for securing votes in the long run. If consumers control these resources in amounts well below their numbers and producers in amounts well above their numbers, it may be very risky for a politician to exchange certain access to intermediate resources for the possible but highly uncertain votes of large, unorganized groups.[16] Finally, if the political culture encourages political actors to weigh the needs of "business" higher than other needs, either on ideological grounds or because of fiscal concern, it becomes even less likely that the numerical size of an unorganized interest will sway the politician's voting decision.[17] Since all these factors affect political decisions in the United States, it is not surprising that laws of this type are infrequent.

Although politicial responses to demands of large but unorganized groups for regulations opposed by producers are rare, they do occur. Why? The answer may lie in the relative "visibility" of certain issues. In any period of time, certain issues become more politically visible than others. Environmental issues were highly visible in the late 1960s; today they are less in the public mind. The more visible an issue is, in the sense of being debated in the media and other cultural instititutions like universities and foundations, the more likely it is that unorganized beneficiaries will become aware of both the need for regulation and the response of individual legislators to demands for regulation. In such situations of high visibility, it may become more risky *not* to respond to

the needs of numerous citizens, even if this entails the displeasure of smaller but more organized interests.

The regulations that create "unorganized potential beneficiaries" arise from such moments of high visibility. The Sherman Act came from a period of popular concern about trusts, food and drug laws from the work of muckrakers who brought abuses to the public eye, and environmental protection laws from the Earth Day movement. In a word, the democratic process only rarely works to benefit groups that are unorganized, and then only when some set of conjunctural conditions creates an unusual degree of concern over an issue that allows visibility to substitute for the normal advantages that organized groups have in politics.

If these occasional "outbursts" of legislative responsiveness led directly to concrete and tangible gains for unorganized interests, there would be no problem of "unorganized *potential* beneficiaries." We would have many laws creating organized actual beneficiaries, a few creating unorganized *actual* beneficiaries, and a zone in which there is no state action at all because producer-organized interests would have blocked any action on behalf of unorganized groups, even large ones. The problem of unorganized groups whose benefits are only potential occurs because extraordinary, high-visibility politics may lead to intervention on behalf of unorganized groups, but they rarely create immediate or direct benefits for them.

In high-visibility situations a substantial majority of the electorate is aware (or thinks it is aware) of the consequences of a decision, and the decisionmakers are accountable to voters. In such situations, decisionmakers may respond to demands of unorganized groups.[18] But in low-visibility situations—where persons affected by a decision are unaware of its impact or the decisionmakers are not electorally accountable—unorganized groups cannot win. Yet most regulatory issues have such low visibility. When an agency is being created, proposals are often widely discussed in the press, parties take stands and seek votes based on their position on a particular regulatory scheme, and the decision to establish the agency is taken by legislators and the chief executive. Thus, such decisions may achieve high visibility. But the *creation* of an agency does not directly lead to changed economic behavior by regulated industries. Most agencies are given very general charters and mandates to regulate the industry concerned in "the public interest." The task of translating this mandate into specific rules and decisions so that the regulatory scheme produces tangible economic benefits for the diffuse group whose potential political power helped bring the scheme into being is, typically, left to the agency itself.[19]

This implementation stage, however, is rarely so visible.[20] The

legislature as a whole, the parties who sponsored the legislation, and the chief executive do not concern themselves with the detailed and technical process of implementing regulatory laws. Similarly, the press has little interest in such matters. The job is left to the agency, with possible oversight from a specific legislative committee. The issue tends to disappear from the public agenda.

The move from high to low visibility dilutes the power of unorganized groups who favor strict regulation. Unorganized potential beneficiares are less aware of the impact of specific decisions, and decisionmakers are less sensitive to the latent voting power of the group. The shift enhances the relative strength of the regulated industry.

Why are administrative decisions less "visible"? A crucial aspect of the administrative process is its technical and legal complexity. Where, as is the norm, the legislature grants an agency a general authority to regulate an industry, sector, or problem, but creates no clear guidelines or substantive rules, the agency must develop policies and rules itself. This effort is technically complex. Issues turn on the analyses of detailed economic and scientific data; indeed, this is one reason legislatures tend to delegate such issues to agencies. Industry has greater access to needed information than does the agency,[21] and the agency has more than representatives of the diffuse group of potential beneficiaries.[22] Decisions are frequently taken through legally complex proceedings, including such quasijudicial proceedings as rate-making and licensing. Such adversary processes have many of the procedural trappings of trials, consume countless hours, offer endless opportunities for delay, and require the costly services of lawyers. Industry has access to the legal and technical experts needed to prevail in such processes; representatives of diffuse interests do not.[23]

Advocacy

Organization is the key to success in low-visibility arenas. Unorganized potential beneficiaries suffer from serious disadvantages in such situations. Visibility can substitute for organization. But without major transformations of the political process, the vast majority of decisions will remain administrative and of low visibility. For this reason, reformers have concentrated on changes that would directly counterbalance the advantages of organized groups in low-visibility situations. Most of the proposals for public advocacy accept the administrative process, largely as it is. What they do propose is to give unorganized groups some of the advocacy resources that already are used by organized interests.

Interest groups in the American political process have learned that

they must engage in constant efforts to get what they seek from the state. The policymaking and implementation process is a competitive struggle among various groups for limited resources allocated by government. The demand for such resources exceeds the supply. Furthermore, government agencies have limited time and money to process demands and to establish and implement programs. Every public agency, whether judicial, legislative, or administrative, must cope with two pressures—the need to consider conflicting demands from a wide variety of groups and a limited capacity to process these demands and implement programs. This limited capacity of the government to produce programs results from the large number of demands, the limited resources agencies have, and the "rules of the game" imposed upon government action

Advocacy is the overall process by which a group attempts to secure its share of limited public resources. Advocacy provides a sustained stream of coherent demands to government agencies and facilitates favorable decisions by whatever means available. Advocacy must be sustained. Sustained advocacy means the capacity to stick with a single issue for long periods of time. Very few laws or programs are self-executing. Legislative decisions become paper rights unless implemented by administrative officials. Officials have conflicting demands on their time and resources. Rights secured in the legislature are lost in the halls of bureaucracy. Policy-making involves constant readjustments and revisions as budgets change, resource availabilities fluctuate, and priorities shift; few decisions are permanent, and policies take a long time to effectuate. Unless a group can work at all levels over long periods of time, it may find its interests ignored by the officials who make the crucial daily decisions that determine the levels of effective support.[24]

Advocacy for administrative enforcement of rights and benefits must go on in the legislature and courts as well as the agencies. Legislatures set general policy and create specific mandates. The ability to be heard in the legislature has important implications, not only for the creation of rights, but also for the scope of questions open to administrative discretion.

Advocacy in the courts is important. Judicial review serves as an important check on the exercise of administrative discretion. Furthermore, the ability to threaten an appeal to the courts provides consumers and others with important leverage in dealing with administrators.

What all this means is that most decisions will be affected by advocacy. But advocacy requires organization. Advocacy costs money and takes time. If a group of people is to benefit from collective advocacy

efforts, they must pool their resources. Industry knows this. Producers and providers of all sorts of goods and services know this. That is why we have so many trade associations, professional organizations and so on, in the United States. For these groups, the pluralist system of interest group politics seems to work.

What public interest law is really all about is the problems of the groups for whom the system does not work. Or better, the groups who get halfway into the tent and become potential beneficiaries, but are then barred from moving further and actually enjoying the show because they lack an essential ticket for admission—the organizational ability to advocate their interest.

We know that the political system treats these groups as legitimate because it does enact rights and programs that benefit them. What it does not do, however, is provide the wherewithal to translate these promises into reality in the competitive struggle of the organized interests that dominate low-visibility politics in the United States.

Why There Are No Groups for Some Interests

We might say that the problem lies with the "groups." If they really wanted these rights and benefits, they should organize like everyone else. After all, no one claims that the state in any way impedes the formation of such groups. If consumers want to organize to advocate their interests in federal administrative proceedings, no one stops them. They have the same protection of free assembly, speech, and petition accorded the National Association of Manufacturers and the Socialist Labor party. If the Consumer Federation of America needs more money or if the Sierra Club is short of cash, why should they come to the federal treasury—or to private foundations? Let them organize the unorganized. Is not that the answer? And if it is, there is, in fact, no "problem," at least not for the policymakers.

But there is a problem. To understand it, we have to distinguish between interests, rights, and groups. Large number of citizens, taken as individuals, may share interests. Sometimes these interests will be translated into "rights" of one degree of specificity or another. But it does not follow that individuals with similar interests or shared rights are, or can be, joined together in a group, that is, in a formal organization that can mobilize resources from its members and participate in advocacy.[25]

In a nutshell, the problem to which public interest law is addressed is that groups actually determine the output of the political process. Yet our political ideology recognizes that many interests that are not

represented by groups are legitimate and deserve state protection. Moreover, our political process at least occasionally creates rights that appear to benefit numerous unorganized citizens with common interests, but which remain paper promises. Thus there is a tension between what is legitimate and what actually happens, and between the appearance of rights and the reality of state action.

Although groups control political decisions, groups cannot be created, or at least they cannot be created easily, to represent all the interests we recognize as legitimate or even the rights we created through our law-making process. Americans are good at creating groups for many purposes, including political representation. In many cases, shared economic interests, such as those of farmers, industrial workers, businessmen, or teachers, lead citizens to form groups. But the existence of such common goals may not even be a necessary cause for organization, and it certainly is not a sufficient one. Thus, it has been shown that some groups that have come to serve the function of political representation were originally created to deal with a purely economic need, such as a desire for insurance benefits, and it was only after an organization had come into being that it was found to be usable for political representation as well.[26] Furthermore, the mere fact that citizens share interests or even have common rights does not mean they can be brought together in a group. Often the only thing such people have in common is an interest in some kind of state action; otherwise they may live apart, work in different trades, and so forth. One may not know that the other exists, let alone that they share interests. Sometimes the shared interest becomes so important that organizational barriers are overcome. For example, the only thing that the parents of handicapped children have in common is their shared affliction, but this is so serious for their lives, and state action so crucial for each family, that these citizens do form relatively cohesive and effective groups.

Other interests, however, may be less central, or the potential benefits less significant. Take the interest in environmental protection. There may be millions and millions of people who would prefer, at the margin, more environmental conservation. But for each of them, this concern is small, relative to other needs, and the results of altered policies will have a minute effect on the lives of each. Thus, the environmental interest may be one interest for which it is nearly impossible to create a full-blown group, in the sense of an actual organization that includes all the potential beneficiaries of environmental conservation or which can tap the full resources these individuals would, hypothetically, be willing to contribute to the support of environmental advocacy.[27]

PUBLIC ADVOCACY: PROVIDING STATE ASSISTANCE TO ADVOCATES FOR INTERESTS WITHOUT GROUPS

Pluralist theory demonstrates how interest groups can promote democratic ideals in complex, modern societies. There is, however, no theory that would allow a democratic state to ignore the needs of large numbers of citizens because the interests they share cannot be translated into an interest *group*. Thus, the issue posed by public interest law and the problem of unorganized consumers and other potential beneficiaries is how to offset the negative effects of group politics and low-visibility administrative decisions.

At a theoretical level, there are several approaches to this question. One answer is to restructure the process of lawmaking and implementation so that group organization becomes less salient in influencing outcomes. Some think, for example, that if legislatures delegated fewer decisions to administrative bodies, policymaking would be more responsive to widely shared interests of unorganized citizens.[28] A second answer is that political parties might serve the role of advocating the interests of such citizens.[29] To allow this to occur in the United States, the party system would have to be substantially reorganized.

There is much to be said for these basic reforms. But both of them require major structural changes, and neither is on the political agenda in the United States today. What is on the agenda, and thus of active concern to policymakers, is what we have called "public advocacy"—governmental assistance to advocates for unrepresented groups. A number of proposals for this kind of aid have been presented, and some have been tried. In this section, we canvass the principal forms of public advocacy.[30]

All public advocacy proposals accept the basic structure of the administrative state and political process. Thus all recognize that organized groups will have systematic advantages over unorganized ones in the low-visibility arenas where key decisions will continue to be made. To deal with this, all propose a strategy identical to that contained in the approach of the public interest law firm. This might be called "advocacy equalization." That is, the suggested policy response to the unequal power of organized and unorganized groups is for the government to provide equalizing resources for advocates of unorganized interests.

Public advocacy proposals and programs start from the assumption that there are some interests for which it is difficult, or impossible, to form advocacy groups. They attempt to correct this situation by

measures that ensure that *interest advocacy* will occur even if there is no interest group. Two basic approaches are taken. First, the government itself can provide advocacy for a given interest. This approach leads to the creation of government agencies or offices that become *surrogate representatives* for all the citizens who share the environmental interest, the consumer interest, and so on. Secondly, the government can *facilitate private groups* that will provide advocacy on behalf of the unorganized interest. The facilitation approach to public advocacy is similar to public interest law, except that needed financial resources would come from public rather than private sources. Naturally, this is an important difference.

Surrogate Representatives

The ill-fated office of consumer protection is an example of surrogate representation. This agency would have appeared in federal administrative proceedings and argued for whatever outcome would favor the consumer interest. Since consumers are not well organized, the agency would have become the principal, if not the only, voice for this interest in such proceedings. Thus it would have been a surrogate representative of the interest each citizen has as a consumer of goods and services.

While the OCP plan seems dead, some surrogate agencies have been set up to represent unorganized interests. Most are at the state level. In Wisconsin the public intervenor represents environmental interests. New Jersey's cabinet-level public advocate represents a variety of interests, including those of mental patients, the elderly, and consumers of utility services. Under federal law, all states have state councils for the developmentally disabled to represent the interest of handicapped persons. In the federal government, the Interstate Commerce Commission has public counsel who speak for the interests of consumers of transportation services.

Surrogate representatives are official governmental bodies supported by the government budget. This gives them some advantages in interest advocacy. First, they have relatively stable sources of funding. This allows them to plan long-term advocacy campaigns and devote most of their resources to advocacy. Secondly, as official members of the government, surrogate advocates may have channels of access to decisionmakers not available to outside groups. This can facilitate certain forms of advocacy.

The official status of surrogate intitutions may also hamper advocacy efforts. Some may be constrained by formal or informal limits on their powers. For example, the OCP bill explicitly prohibited the agency from lobbying. This provision might have restricted a full program of

multiarena advocacy. Similarly, state law prohibits some state agencies from suing other entities of the same government. This has meant that litigation is not available to the state developmental disabilities (DD) councils.[31] Even if there are no *formal* barriers to litigation and lobbying, the official status and relationship of surrogate agencies may hamper their advocacy efforts. At times, advocacy must take the form of a contest between opponents. People with long-term working relations may be hesitant to take strong advocacy stances, such as litigation. The state DD councils, for example, have hesitated to use some available advocacy tools because of their possible impact on long-term relations with state agencies whose decisions affect the handicapped.[32]

In Wisconsin the public intervenor is an example of a relatively successful surrogate advocacy agency.[33] Established in the state's Department of Justice, the office is empowered to appear as a representative for "conservation" interests, principally in licensing proceedings of the Department of Natural Resources, which controls the use of the state's water and mineral resources. The public intervenor is an assistant attorney general appointed by the attorney general and serving at his pleasure. The office is independent of the Department of Natural Resources, receiving its funding through the Justice Department budget. While the principal role of the office is to appear in specific administrative proceedings, the public intervenor also has the power to seek judicial review of administrative decisions.[34] Although the authorizing statute is silent on the intervenor's power to appear in legislative proceedings, there seems to be no barrier to such appearances, and the intervenor has supported and opposed various bills that would affect the environment.

In its first nine years, the office was not very effective.[35] It took few cases, established no clear advocacy strategy, often took a neutral rather than truly advocacy stance, focused principally on administrative issues of personal concern to the several incumbents of the position, and did not develop close relationships with private environmental advocacy groups.

When a new attorney general was elected in 1974, however, major changes occurred. The status of the intervenor was upgraded, and additional personnel were hired. The new incumbent of the office adopted a strong advocacy stance, employing all available resources, including the media, courts, and lobbying. An advisory committee was set up to improve communication between the intervenor and private environmental groups in the state. Although no systematic evaluation of the effects of this change has been conducted, it is clear that the interest in conserving the state's natural resources is now being vigorously articulated in all relevant forums.

The effectivess of surrogate representation will depend on a variety of factors. These include the legal structure of the surrogate agency as well as its relationship to political decisionmakers and other parts of government. Formal independence from the agency(s) whose decisions must be effected is generally necessary if advocacy is to be effective. Some budgetary autonomy is needed if it is to be sustained. And surrogates must be free of formal or informal restrictions that would unduly hamper their choice of advocacy arenas and tactics.

Too little is known about these institutions to permit any but the most general conclusions about whether surrogate representation will achieve the goals of the strategy of advocacy equalization. However, there is one feature of the surrogate route that should trouble those who believe that equalization is a viable goal. All approaches to equalization and public advocacy accept the fact that it is hard to form "private" groups to represent certain interests. But most would agree that the formation of such groups is desirable, even if it is difficult. The problem with surrogate representation as a policy is that it may mean giving up completely the goal of forming or strengthening private groups to perform these tasks. The decision to deal with interest representation through surrogates can *increase,* rather than decrease, the barriers to creation of viable private groups. The surrogate competes with private groups for limited public resources. Its presence can convince people that the difficult task of group formation is unnecessary. To the extent that strengthened private groups could do a better job than government agencies can, the surrogate route can prove costly.

Facilitating Private Advocacy

For these and other reasons, proponents of the public advocacy approach for equalization have shifted their attention to measures that would strengthen, rather than replace, private advocacy groups that can serve as interest advocates. It would be misleading to see the interests of consumers, environmentalists, and so on, as totally unorganized. There are numerous private groups in the United States that speak for these interests. Rather, we might say that such interests are "suboptimally organized." That is, the existing level of organization does not adequately reflect the number ofpersons who hold these interests, or the value these persons would place on furthering environmental conservation, consumer protection, and so forth. Since policy results are directly influenced by the *degree* of interest organization, when an interest's actual organization is in this sense suboptimal, policymakers will be *relatively* insensitive to this set of needs or demands.[36]

The goal of all the reform efforts, and of public advocacy in particular, is to see that these interests are given their fair weight in policy decisions. Since there is usually some degree of organization, the *facilitation* strategy seeks to strengthen these existing groups so that their efforts will more fully reflect the extent of public concern for the values they seek to promote.[37] If, as many believe, private groups will tend to be more flexible in advocacy strategy, better informed on the true interests of the citizens for whom they speak, and at the same time will be perceived as more legitimate spokesmen for those citizens, the facilitation approval has much to commend it.

Therefore, substantial attention has been given to devising public advocacy strategies that would facilitate the creation of private groups and support their efforts to advocate for various interests in administrative and related policy arenas. These can be groupėd into two basic types of policies. The government may take measures that make it easier to organize an unorganized or underorganized group. By facilitating organization, the government makes it possible for advocates to secure the resources they need to defend the interest in question. Alternatively, the government may provide direct subsidies to advocacy groups who demonstrate a capacity to speak for an unorganized interest. Limited experimentation with both approaches has begun.

Reducing Advocate-Constituent Barrier—RUCAG. In a 1976 law review article,[38] Robert Leflar and Martin Rogol proposed the creation of Residential Utility Consumers Action Groups (RUCAGs). A RUCAG would be a not-for-profit membership corporation, organized on the state level. It would represent the interests of consumers of the services of utilities such as gas, water, and electricity. These services are usually provided by private corporations whose rates and terms of service are controlled by state regulatory agencies. RUCAGs could appear before these agencies as well as before the courts and state and local legislative bodies.

The corporation would be financed largely through consumer contributions that would be made via a checkoff mechanism included with utility bill payments. The contributions would then be forwarded to RUCAG by the utiities receiving payments. RUCAG would also be authorized to accept governmental and foundation grants, but it would receive no support from legislative appropriations. Any residential utility consumer, aged sixteen or older, could obtain membership in RUCAG by contributing a specified amount each year.

A state RUCAG would be governed by a board of directors elected on a geographic basis for staggered three-year terms. Candidates would

have to meet strict spending limits and disclosure requirements, and membership on the board would be barred to persons employed by or associated with utilities or holding stock in them.

RUCAG is an imaginative approach to the problem of organizing interest groups. Its basic strategy is to reduce the barriers that impede the natural formation of consumer groups, thus narrowing the gap between an interest and the group that represents it. The key to RUCAG is the checkoff system. By providing an easy mechanism by which citizens with this interest can be located, and by which they can directly contribute to advocacy on their behalf, the checkoff system directly attacks some of the major obstacles to group formation. Since the RUCAG leadership must be elected and since the corporation will depend on a continuing flow of funds for consumers, the scheme should ensure strict advocate accountability.

While RUCAG seems to be an ideal approach to the problem of an unorganized interest, the scheme has distinct limitations. In the first place, it does not overcome the so-called free rider problem that plagues many groups of this type. That is, all utility consumers will benefit from RUCAG's work, whether they contribute to it or not. Thus donations may be inadequate.[39] More seriously, RUCAG seems to depend on a particular and unique regulatory structure—a regulated industry that regularly bills its customers. No similar mechanism exists by which checkoffs could be created for consumers of most goods and services, or by which other interests, say those in environmental protection or defense of women's rights, could be mobilized. The RUCAG approach may have promise in a few limited areas, but it does not seem to be generally applicable. Wisconsin recently became the first state to try this approach. Legislation was passed in 1979 creating a Wisconsin Consumer Utility Board, modeled on the RUCAG plan.

Direct Subsidies to Private Advocacy Groups Financing Consumer Intervention. Today most of the interest in the public advocacy area is centered around programs and proposals for direct government subsidies to private organizations that wish to participate in administrative proceedings as advocates for consumers and other unorganized groups. These programs are generally referred to as "financing consumer intervention" (FCI) even though they include many types of unorganized interests. Programs of this type have been adopted by several federal administrative agencies; federal FCI funds are currently available for consumer, environmental, and other advocacy groups.

The largest and most formal FCI system was set up at the Federal Trade Commission (FTC) by the Magnuson-Moss FTC Improvement

Act.[40] This statute provides the FTC with the authority to compensate eligible persons for reasonable attorneys' fees, expert witnesses' fees, and other costs of participating in FTC rule-making proceedings. The act provides that compensation may be awarded to any person

(a) who has, or represents an interest (i) which would not otherwise be adequately represented in such proceeding, and (ii) representation of which is necessary for a fair determination of the rule-making proceeding taken as a whole, and
(b) who is unable effectively to participate in such proceeding because such person cannot afford to pay costs of making oral presentations, conducting cross-examination, and making rebuttal submissions in such proceeding.[41]

The commission is responsible for determining whether these criteria are met in particular cases.

Some doubts have arisen whether agencies can create these programs without legislative approval,[42] but many have done so nevertheless. Moreover, the Carter administration has endorsed the FCI approach, and legislation has been introduced in Congress to allow all federal administrative agencies to subsidize private advocacy groups that have something substantive to contribute to administrative decisions, but which lack the financial resources needed to participate effectively in these proceedings.

The FCI approach has proven quite popular with federal agencies, and it has received support from important groups in the administration and Congress. Moreover, it has been enthusiastically received by the public interest law movement, for obvious reasons. FCI relies on private advocacy groups. It is focused toward appearances in federal administrative agency proceedings, and thus of necessity it provides funds for skilled lawyers who can deal with these complex situations. It is little wonder that FCI administrators look to public interest law firms to provide subsidized advocacy, and the firms to FCI as a solution for their budgetary dilemmas.

There is much of promise in the FCI approach. It offers the possibility that government subsidies can simultaneously support advocacy for interests that are not now organized, *and* help reduce the barriers that impede such organization. FCI funds are given out only for specific advocacy interventions, and thus they do not directly go to support interest *groups* as such. But the receipt of funds to participate in important federal proceedings, some of which are well publicized, can increase the ability of advocacy organizations to secure support from individual citizens. If this occurred, FCI would have substantial advantages over either surrogate representation or RUCAG. Unlike

the surrogate strategy, FCI relies on private groups who have specialized in the representation of an interest. Although these groups may be small now and may not have a membership base, they could form the nucleus for expanded interest advocacy institutions that could ultimately generate support from citizens. Unlike RUCAG, on the other hand, FCI can be applied in any administrative area and support advocacy for any interest thought to be underrepresented.

While FCI has substantial promise, the current approach to administering FCI leaves much to be desired. The ultimate goal of any public advocacy program shoud be to ensure that all important interests are represented by advocacy organizations that are accountable to persons whose interests they advocate and are capable of maintaining an independent, sustained, multiarena advocacy effort. The constraints of the present FCI system make it unlikely that it will produce such organizations.

In the first place, there is nothing in the FCI system that encourages advocate accountability. None of the statutes or regulations that govern funding allocation speaks to this issue. While agencies might use this as a criterion for allocating monies among competing groups, there is no evidence that they have done so. Indeed, the opposite danger is more serious; that is, the agencies will become the real constituency for FCI intervenors. While agencies have tried, to one degree or another, to insulate FCI awards from the immediate process of decision on the substantive policies on which the intervenor is to advocate, final funding decisions rest with the agency involved, and funds are given out on a case-by-case basis. Is it unreasonable to fear that this system may lead intervenors, who must return to the agency for future funding, to tailor their advocacy to what is acceptable to agency decisionmakers? Final agency control of FCI funds is a threat to advocate independence.

If the FCI does not ensure independent advocates, it also does little to guarantee sustained or multiarena advocacy. Most FCI awards are for participation in specific rule-making proceedings in which the issues have already been framed and final decision rests with the agency. There is little provision for funding advocates to initiate policy issues or challenge agencies in court or Congress. Many of the important issues for unrepresented interests are the ones that are now never decided at all. Thus, an interest advocate constrained only to oppose or support measures already adopted by agencies may be ineffective. Limitation of FCI funds to the administrative arena may also hamstring effective advocacy. Many so-called administrative questions are ultimately decided in the courts or Congress, and an advocate with money to appear in a rule-making proceeding, but

unable to follow this up with further advocacy, may find his efforts frustrated.

A fully satisfactory FCI system must meet several criteria. It must be sufficiently independent of particular agencies so that intervenors do not become "captive" appendages of agency decisionmakers. It must provide funds in such a way that advocates can make an independent choice between various advocacy strategies, including the strategy of petitioning for agency action, and not be constrained merely to appear for or against policies already formulated in the bowels of the agency. Furthermore, a satisfactory system must permit advocacy in all relevant arenas, including the Congress and the media, and ensure that advocates will not be penalized for taking choices that may be painful to the agency but effective for the represented interest. Finally, an effective system must encourage the creation of advocacy groups that are accountable to the citizens whose interests they speak for and capable of mobilizing the resources of these citizens for advocacy efforts. Unless FCI can achieve these goals, it may become no better and perhaps worse than surrogate representation.

CONCLUSION

The public interest law movement put the issue of unorganized interests on the agenda in the United States. The public interest law firms demonstrated that the American political system works best in responding to organized groups that represent specific interests, and they showed that advocacy for unorganized but socially important interests can offset some of these biases. As private funds for public interest representation dry up, supporters of this activity look to the state to continue the work started by the foundation-supported firms. A strategy of "advocacy equalization," through public subsidization or other forms of advocacy facilitation, has been adopted as the solution. Experiments in public provision of advocacy, facilitation of group organization, and subsidies for private advocates have been proposed and in some cases tried. The results of these experiments are mixed, but the public advocacy movement continues to seek innovative ways to deliver the legal and other services needed to give unorganized interests a greater voice in the policy decisions of the administrative state.

This chapter has focused on the current policy debate in the United States and the proposals now on the agenda for discussion and

experimentation. These proposals all assume that some combination of public and private action can eliminate observed bias in the decisions of the administrative state by equalizing the resources available to advocates of different and competing interests. It has not examined the question of the need for more basic reform in the administrative process or the political system that might render decisions less susceptible to the power and pressure of organized interests. That issue still remains with us.

True equalization may well be a chimera. It is important to remember that the amounts of money proposed by the strongest advocates of public advocacy are infinitesimal in comparison with the funds spent by industry and other organized groups to influence administrative decisions. The entire OCP budget was probably not much larger than the annual revenue of only one of the hundreds of large law firms that represent corporate interests in Washington. This fact must give us pause. Perhaps the most basic question to be asked is not whether one approach to public advocacy is better than another, whether we should prefer surrogates or private groups with public subsidies, but whether even a well-designed and adequately funded public advocacy program can make much of an impact on an administrative state that today is responsive basically to organized interests.

We support the existing public advocacy efforts and hope that larger and better designed programs will follow. At the same time, however, we hope that this fundamental question will not be forgotten. Public advocacy is a promising innovation in the delivery of legal services and the operation of the administrative state. But it is, at best, a limited skirmish in a much larger and more protracted battle to realize the ideal of democratic control of government in societies like ours.

NOTES

1. D. G. Trubek, "Environmental Defense," in *Public Interest Law, an Economic and Institutional Analysis,* edited by B. Weisbrod; J. Handler; and N. Komesar, 1978; subsequently cited as Weisbrod.
2. For a detailed description of the public interest law movement, including case studies of specific areas of activity, see Weisbrod, supra note 1.
3. See D. Trubek's book review, *Wisconsin Law Review* (1977): 303.
4. See, for example, Weisbrod, supra note 1; Rabin, "Lawyers for Social Change: Perspectives on Public Interest Law," *Stanford Law Review* 28 (1976): 207.
5. For a history of public interest representation, see Council for Public Interest Law, *Balancing the Scales of Justice: Financing Public Interest Law in America,* 1976 (subsequently cited as *Balancing the Scales of Justice*).
6. For an example of the hopes created by this atmosphere, see Sager, "Tight Little Islands: Exclusionary Zoning, Equal Protection, and the Indigent," *Stanford Law*

Review 21 (1969): 767. Subsequent retrenchment by the U.S. Supreme Court dashed these hopes. See Komesar, "Housing and Zoning," in Weisbrod, supra note 1.

7. *Balancing the Scales of Justice,* supra note 5.
8. See Erlanger, "Young Lawyers and Work in the Public Interest," *American Bar Foundation Research Journal* (1978).
9. An effort to have the American Bar Association raise money for public interest law through a checkoff system failed. A few local bar groups do provide some support for public interest law activities.
10. See Trubek, "Environmental Defense," in Weisbrod, supra note 1.
11. For a survey, see Center for Public Representation, *Public Advocacy in the Administrative State* (Madison, Wis.: 1976).
12. The major bill before the 95th Congress was S1262, 95th Cong., 1st Sess., 1977.
13. See Goldberg, "Regulation and Administered Contracts," *Bell Journal of Economics* 7 (1976):426.
14. G. Stigler, *The Citizen and the State,* 1974.
15. It has been pointed out, for example, that support for the establishment of the Interstate Commerce Commission came mostly from commercial interests and farmers. See Huntington, "The Marasmus of the ICC: The Commission, The Railroads, and The Public Interest," *Yale Law Journal* 61 (1952): pp. 467, 472; and M. Nadel, *The Politics of Consumer Protection* (1971): 607.
16. See Peltzman, "Toward a More General Theory of Regulation," *Journal of Law and Economics* 19 (1977): 211.
17. See C. Lindblom, "Politics and Markets," 170–189 (1977).
18. Recent empirical evidence suggests the legislators are highly responsive to visible or perceived voter preferences, especially as elections approach. See L. Mayhew, *The Electoral Connection* (1974). American democratic theory has held stubbornly that leaders will respond to followers' interests if appropriate information about leaders' activities is made available to voters. See R. Dahl and C. Lindblom, *Politics, Economics and Welfare* (1954). This literature is immense. A good general statement relevant to the concerns in this chapter can be found in R. Dahl, *A Preface to Democratic Theory* (1956). T. Lowi, *The End of Liberalism* (1969) offers a critique of the limits of pluralist theory suggested by Dahl and others (T. Lowi, at pp. 41–93) but concludes that high-visibility (legislative) political assertiveness can solve the liberal state's dilemma, idem, pp. 310–315.
19. K. C. Davis, *Administrative Law Text,* ch. 1 (1976); Stewart, "The Reformation of American Administrative Law," *Harvard Law Review* 88 (1975): 1688; T. Lowi, supra note 18, pp. 128–155; H. Simon, *Administrative Behavior* (1945); and A. Downs, *Inside Bureaucracy,* ch. 8 (1967).
20. Sabatier, "Social Movements and Regulatory Agencies: Toward a More Adequate—and Less Pessimistic—Theory of 'Clientele Capture,'" *Policy Sciences* 6 (1975): 301, 306–310; W. Cary, *Politics and the Regulatory Agencies,* ch. 4 (1967); F. Rourke, *Bureaucracy, Politics, and Public Policy* (1969); and I. Sharkansky and A. Wildausky, *Implementation* (1975).
21. M. Bernstein, *Regulating Business by Independent Commissions* (1953); R. Niskanen, *Bureaucracy and Representative Government,* ch. 4 (1973); and Sabatier, supra note 20 pp. 330–336.
22. Sabatier, supra note 20, pp. 304–306; Stewart, supra note 6, pp. 1762–1781, 1803–1997.
23. See generally, Trubek, "Environmental Defense," in Weisbrod, supra note 1. See also S. Eblin and R. Kasper, *Citizen Groups and the Nuclear Power Controversy,* ch. 1 (1974); Leflar and Rogol, "Consumer Participation in the Regulation of Public

Utility: A Model Act," *Harvard Journal of Legislation* 13 (1976): 235.

24. Joel Handler has stressed this feature of advocacy in numerous articles. See, for example, his chapter in this volume.
25. This issue is thoroughly examined in Weisbrod, supra note 1. The diffuse nature of such interests makes it hard to organize groups to defend them. Persons who share some specific economic or ideological interest may lack other ties that could reduce the costs of organizing them into a group. They may not live or work together, and their common interest involves only a small portion of their lives and interests—they may not perceive themselves as members of a single "group."

One major barrier to group formation is information. It is hard to secure data about who actually fits in these categories. Moreover, the cost of such information may exceed the benefits to each individual of participating in a representative organization. Thus, each consumer of electric power might gain X dollars from the efforts of an advocacy group for power consumers, but it may cost the organizers of such a group $\$X + \$Y$ to identify and inform the potential recipients of these possible benefits.

Another major barrier is the famous "free rider" problem. See M. Olson, *The Logic of Collective Action* (1971). Each potential member of an organized consumer group may calculate that he or she can secure benefits from the group without contributing to the group's effort. The product of such advocacy organizations are usually what economists call "collective goods," that is, goods which, if provided for one member of a class, must be provided to all. See also Samuelson, "Pure Theory of Public Expenditures," *Review of Economics and Statistics* 37 (1955): 347; and Coase, "The Lighthouse in Economics," *Journal of Law and Economics* 6 (1971), especially 283-289. Contrast J. Buchanan, *The Demand and Supply of Public Goods* (1968) chs. 1 and 2; and Head, "Public Goods and Public Policy, *Public Finance* 17(1962): 197. If a rate increase is halted by the efforts of a consumer advocacy organization, all consumers will benefit whether they contributed to the organization or not. Thus, even if one knew who might benefit from advocacy and could persuade these potential beneficiaries that they would gain more than they are asked to contribute to the advocacy effort, it is not necessarily the case that the response of the (economically) rational consumer would be to make the contribution.

There is, however, substantial debate about the extent of the barriers to organization and the effectiveness of public policy in reducing these barriers. One school of analysis contends that the barriers are so great that no policy can be devised to make it possible to create genuine representative organizations for consumers, environmentalists, and so on. This group stresses the importance of the "free rider" principle in deterring formation of groups to pursue collective interests. The classic of this school is Olson's *Logic of Collective Action*. Olson suggests individuals will not find it in their best interest to support collective attempts to secure desired benefits since they may obtain collective benefits without contributing. In such cases, individuals lack motivation to organize (see generally, M. Olson, ch. 2). Moreover, the larger the number of persons who share an interest, the less likely they will form an interest *group*, since organization costs increase with size (see Peltzman, supra note 16).

Allied with Olson are the organization theorists who suggest that, even if some organizations are formed, internal group stratification, the development of internal oligarcy, will prevent groups from being truly representative of group views. Kariel, *The Decline of American Pluralism* (1961); Mayhew and Loevinger, "On the Emergence of Oligarchy in Human Interaction," *American Journal of*

Sociology 81 (1976): 1017.

Another shcool is more optimistic. This body of thought notes that political "entrepreneurs" have a motivation to create advocacy groups to represent diffuse interests and that these professionals can create "social-movement organizations" that can effectively aggregate the views of diffuse individuals with common interests and mobilize the resources needed to represent these interests in all policy arenas.

This more "optimistic" aproach includes three rather different trends of analysis. "Political exchange" theorists suggest that individual entrepreneurs will always be motivated to develop political "capital" by forming organizations to advance their position in the political power hierarchy. The capital involved is the group itself, or more particularly, the probability that the group will act cohesively to force the stream of public policy in their direction. See Salisbury, "An Exchange Theory of Interest Groups," *Midwest Journal of Politics* 13; P. Blau, *Exchange and Power in Social Life* (1964).

The "leadership" school is more hesitant about the liquidity of political capital, but they agree with the pure exchange theorists that there are substantial private and collective incentives that stimulate group formation, resource production, and sustained activity. Frolich, Oppenheimer, and Young suggest that the key elements in the model of group formation are the presence of some interest, value, or good that numbers of people will value highly enough to make contributions, the set of leaders who organize (mobilize) these interests to generate private and collective payoffs, and the competitiveness of this market; see *Political Leadership and Collective Goods* (1971). In their theory, large groups need not be ineffective or grossly inefficient, given the interdependent utility calculations of interested citizens.

The "resource mobilization" school, the third of the more optimistic approaches to group formation, departs from analytic economics, but concludes that the key element to evaluating reform is to understand the growth and decline of the social movement sector of society. While this approach also stresses the role of leaders in mobilizing, organizing, and directing collective endeavors, their analysis also identifies the different roles various subgroups play in social reform movements. The social movement sector grows and declines as a function of economic and social conditions in society, tempered by the ability of leaders in the sector to develop social movement industries around the production of collective goals—civil rights, welfare, benefits, or bread; see McCarthy and Zald, "Resource Mobilization and Social Movements: A Partial Theory," *American Journal of Sociology* 82 (1977): 1212. Moreover, representatives of this perspective contend that governmental policies can be designed to encourage the creation of such social movement organizations. These policies include direct provision of government subsidies, indirect support through technical asistance or provision of information, as well as specific actions to reduce the information and search costs of locating and communicating with potential members and supporters of such advocacy organizations. Sabatier, supra note 20. In "Consumerism and Legal Services: The Merging of Movements," *Law and Society Review* 11 (1976): 247–256, Ralph Nader describes a system of checkoffs to fund and facilitate the organization of consumer groups that would implement the approach suggested by Sabatier.

26. M. Olson, supra note 25.
27. See D. Trubek, "Environmental Defense," in Weisbrod, supra note 1.
28. T. Lowi, supra note 18.
29. The rise of the "green parties" in Europe suggests how this might work in the

environmental area.

30. For recent survey, see Senate Committee on Governmental Affairs, 95th Cong., 1st Sess., Study on Federal Regulation: Public Participation in Regulatory Agency Proceedings 17–22 (Committee Print 1977).
31. H. Erlanger, *Strategies for Action: Developmental Disabilities and State Government* (Madison, Wis.: Center for Public Representation, 1978).
32. Idem.
33. See P. Dubois and A. Christensen, *Public Advocacy and Environmental Decision-making: The Wisconsin Public Intervenor* (Madison, Wis.: Center for Public Representation, 1977).
34. Wisconsin Stat. § 165.07 (1975).
35. See P. Dubois and A. Christensen, supra note 33, pp. 35–49.
36. The reasons for suboptimal organization are discussed in note 25, supra.
37. The facilitation approach is supported by the "optimistic" school of organizational theorists who think that suboptimal organization can be overcome; see note 25, supra.
38. Leflar and Rogol, supra note 23.
39. See note 25, supra, for a discussion of the "free rider" effect.
40. 15 U.S.C. § 57A.
41. Idem.
42. Compare Opinion of the Comptroller General, B-139703; 31 Ad. L. 2d 474 (1972) with *Greene County Planning Board* v. *FPC,* 559 F. 2d 1227 (2nd Cir. 1977).

Chapter 11

Comments on Legal Services and the Administrative State: From Public Interest Law to Public Advocacy

Wolfgang Däubler

Our discussions often gave the impression that the success or failure of citizens' rights groups or other organized interests occurs more or less at random. For example, with luck, a railway company can be found that opposes the straightening of the Mississippi River for competitive reasons and therefore will provide the necessary funds; if no such ally can be found, the group would have to give up. Although I do not want to deny that these kinds of alliances can be useful, they do not allow for planned policies. It seems necessary to reflect upon the basic conditions of effectuating interests and reforms.

In a general sense, only organized interests can be carried through. However, the concept of organization should not be defined too narrowly because the existence of a socially or legally independent force is not an absolute precondition for organization. An interest is to be regarded as organized when a substantial number of concerned persons agree on uniform actions that are structured by common objectives. This precondition is given, for example, when consumers cast their votes during elections in favor of consumer protection laws or more state supervision for certain products. This kind of organized behavior can only result in immediate short-term success; it cannot sustain a long-term reform process. Unorganized interests cannot be

successfully pursued. To install a commissioner for consumer questions or to fund a legal counsel alone cannot be effective. It is impossible to reduce conflicting interests, as for instance the interests of entrepreneurs, in order to increase consumer protection without thereby applying social pressure.

This mechanistic model can describe struggles within society in an exact way, particularly the struggles between capital and labor. An unorganized minority group of employees will hardly succeed in pursuing their interests by merely appealing to their employer. This model is modified, however, by the existence of the state. The state reacts not only to more or less strongly articulated interests, but it also needs to legitimize its actions. Within this framework, unorganized interests can play a certain role. This explains, for instance, the existence of successful initiatives for the rights of mental patients; the constant neglect of their interests would be an abuse with undesirable sociopsychological results. It would shake public belief in the justice of society, without which society cannot retain the loyalty of the masses. This holds true particularly for the demands directly related to the governmental system that can be realized without excessive financial costs. The pursuit of interests becomes a good deal more difficult when governmental intervention within certain sociological structures (as, for instance, the prohibition of certain technologies in favor of environmental protection) is demanded. There has to be extreme abuse to achieve progress in these cases without the support of organized interests.

The fact that interests can be better promoted through organization suggests that the proper course of action is not to establish new institutions, but rather to expand the functions of the existing ones. It can, for instance, be very effective, as examples in France and Italy have shown, to entrust the union organization with representing the interests of employees as consumers. This would have the advantage that conflicting interests between individual occupational sectors and the general interest of employees for equitable compensation and benefits could be integrated within one organization. Thus a serious controversy between different groups of employees would be avoided. To give an example, employees in the retail business certainly have an interest in finishing work at 3 or 4 P.M., and not at 6:30 P.M. The total group of employees in their capacity as consumers, however, have an interest in being able to shop longer than 3 or 4 P.M. If one would confront the employees in the retail business with the consumer associations, it would de facto mean employees fighting other employees. It should be possible to find compromises within an organization in order to avoid a public confrontation and its negative effects with regard to solidarity

among all employees. There is evidence supporting the assumption that the development of independent consumer and environmental organizations can be explained by insufficient union policies, even by a failure of the labor movement, which has been reduced to understanding its function as simply negotiating for better wages and working conditions.

Finally, the possibility of pursuing organized interests is limited by the functional principles of the capitalist system. This means that demands can no longer be satisfied if individual economic units are made unprofitable or profitability is reduced to an extent that would render a company unable to compete on the market. Within this framework, the network of national economies in the world market gains decisive importance. Because it is not possible to pursue workers' interests or other interests in a coordinated way against profit interests across national borders, the competitive capability on the world market remains the outermost limit even for the demands of a very active labor movement. Secondly, the fact has to be considered that certain interests cannot be safeguarded within the existing economic order and, moreover, that the neglect of these interests is a necessary precondition for the production of goods and the provision of services. I am talking about the employees' interest in personal fulfillment and existential security. This cannot be protected as long as the decisions of the entrepreneurs are determined by necessities of the market and are oriented by profit as opposed to other interests. It would narrow the ideological focus, which would serve to legitimize the status quo, if these structural limits in the pursuits of interests were to be denied. One should not project the image of a pluralistic society, which basically recognizes every interest as long as that interest is articulated strongly and with sufficient engagement. These concepts of pluralism limit knowledge and impede the demand for changes within the whole society, causing science to lose a major part of its function.

Chapter 12

The Working Group on Legal Aid for Immigrants: A Public Interest Law Organization in the Netherlands

Kees Groenendijk

The public interest law firms described in the chapters by Halpern and Trubek appear to be a uniquely American phenomenon. The wave of experiments with legal services in Western Europe during the last ten years did not give rise to organizations financed mainly by private funds and primarily conducting litigation aimed at law reform. Law reform, of course, was high on the agenda of many recent experiments in the legal services in Europe. The law centers in England, the Jus Bus in Norway, and the law shops and the lawyers collectives in the Netherlands all considered law reform as one of their principal aims. In fact, however, it turned out to be a small part of their activities. Most of their work is service and problem solving for individual clients.

Trubek[1] pointed to five typical elements of public interest law firms:

1. Law to be applied while the potential beneficiaries are disorganized

2. Lack of automatism, a discrepancy between law on the books and law in practice
3. Socially active and politically oriented lawyers
4. An activist judiciary
5. Private foundations supplying the funds

The first and second elements he presumed to be common to most countries. The last three elements, however, happen to be absent in many places. Even in the United States, these elements are not always present. Some public interest law firms operate in states with a passive judiciary or receive only a small part of their funds from private foundations. This suggests that even if not all five conditions are met, a law firm similar to a public interest law firm could exist in Europe, too. Possibly a closer look at the European situation will reveal the existence of organizations with aims and activities like those of public interest law firms. In this chapter a Dutch experiment is described in which legal services for immigrants are organized, and this group is compared with some of the projects described as "public interest law."

ORIGIN OF THE WORKING GROUP

The origin of the working group is related to the arrival of two different groups of immigrants in the Netherlands in the late 1960s—migrant workers and their families from Mediterranean countries[2] and a new type of refugee. Refugees are an elite group among immigrants. In the Netherlands, the influx of refugees from Eastern Europe during the cold war made it clear to the public that the legal status of aliens was very weak. This realization eventually caused a complete renewal of Dutch immigration legislation.[3] Refugees also gave rise to a major innovation in the organization of legal aid in this field.

Around 1970, a large number of Portuguese and Greek refugees and U.S. Vietnam War deserters arrived in Western Europe. The established Dutch refugee organizations, used to assisting mainly Eastern European refugees, did not (with one notable exception) extend their assistance to these new refugees from allied (NATO) countries. The new organizations (Amnesty International, Release, several ad hoc committees, and the law shops) that took care of these refugees, could, however, find very few lawyers willing and able to assist them. There was an unmet need for specialized knowledge and the ability to render assistance on very short notice. In many refugee

cases (and immigrant cases in general), the aid of a lawyer must be available very quickly if it is to be of any help at all; otherwise the client will have already been expelled from the country or been refused entry and sent back home.

At the request of these organizations, in 1973 a few lawyers wrote to all local bar associations in the country and asked which members of the bar had had experience with immigration cases, and if none had had experience, who would be prepared to handle such cases. The result of this letter was that lawyers practicing in twenty different cities came together and founded the "Working Group on Legal Aid for Immigrants." At its first meeting, the group decided not to restrict its activities to refugees, bu to extend the work to all immigrants. The group formulated three aims:

1. To enlarge the knowledge of immigration law and practice among lawyers by pooling and exchanging experience and information
2. To make their specialized knowledge better and more quickly available to immigrants and organizations that assist immigrants
3. To improve the legal position of immigrants through collective action aimed at changing the rules and practices in this field (special emphasis was put on the prevention of abuse of discretionary power by the Aliens' Police)

The secretariat of the group was run by a member of the staff of the National Center for Immigrants, a government-financed but independent foundation. The membership of the group was not restricted to lawyers. Today the group has 200 members, including 140 attorneys working either in private law offices or in lawyers' collectives. Among them are students from several law shops, lawyers from official legal aid bureaus, journalists, research assistants from law faculties, and staff members of the television stations. The Ombudsman and other organizations that assist immigrants also participate in the work of the group. The members practice in forty-five different cities covering all regions of the country. Many members have made arrangements with local immigrants' organizations to hold special office hours for immigrants when interpreters are available.

ACTIVITIES

The group has four kinds of activities.

1. There is a meeting each month in a central place in the country (Utrecht). On the average, one-quarter of the members are

present. All members receive a detailed written report of the meeting. At these meetings, members discuss unsolved problems they have experienced in individual cases and try to find solutions to these problems. They exchange good and bad experiences. Members also tell of their mistakes and discuss ways of limiting the damage or preventing the recurrence of such mistakes. This kind of systematic quality control is unique to the Dutch legal profession. In other countries, it takes place only behind the doors of some of the larger lawyers' offices.

At these meetings, information is also provided about recent changes in immigration legislation or governmental practice, new treaties, and so forth. Special attention is paid to possibilities of free (i.e., government-subsidized) legal aid to foreigners. Without financial compensation, one can hardly expect lawyers to maintain an active interest in this work over the long run.[4] In addition, there is always a lecture on a specific item of the law concerning immigrants (e.g., detention, naturalization, procedural rules, work permits, or private international law) or on the culture of the home countries of immigrants. The group often invites an official from a government agency or appeal body. This guarantees first-hand information and provides an opportunity for the members to become acquainted with the officials with whom they often have to deal. Finally, plans for collective action are discussed.

2. A second important feature is the distribution of a list of names and addresses (both office and private) of group members to organizations and persons working for immigrants. This makes it easy to know which nearby lawyers have had at least some experience in this field. Consequently, these lawyers get even more experience because they get more immigrants' cases. Inclusion in the list of private addresses is important, since the Aliens' Police sometimes seems to have a strange preference for deportation of foreigners on Saturday morning (or for giving notice on Friday afternoon of deportation on Monday morning). Since both lawyers' and government offices are closed over the weekend, it is hard to get legal aid at such times.

The publication of this list is contrary to the policy of the bar concerning advertisement and specialization. So far, the bar has not interfered with the activities of the working group. This might be because most immigration cases are not very lucrative, the group is relatively open (in principle, every lawyer can become a member), and also because the bar wants to demonstrate that its members do "social" as well as profitable work.

3. The group also provides for the publication of official statements, rules, and instructions regarding immigrants. Some of these sources of immigration law are more or less "confidential" and most of them are very hard to obtain.

   With the financial support of the National Center for Immigrants, the group has stimulated the publication of a selection of court decisions concerning immigration. While preparing this publication it became apparent that cases are not selected in a purely impartial manner. It was discovered, for instance, that in other publications, edited by officials of the Ministry of Justice, many decisions favorable to immigrants had been deleted.
4. Finally, part of the activities of the working group were directed at improvement of the legal position of immigrants in general.

LAW REFORM ACTIVITIES

The group has frequently written to Parliament or to governmental agencies. Some of these actions were occasioned by the discovery at a group meeting that several members had experienced the same problem. Next to these accidental actions, the group has presented to Parliament its opinion on every proposal for a new law about the rights of immigrants. Each year the group comments on the report of the budget of the Ministry of Justice concerning the Dutch Immigration Service. Because the opinions are based on the practical experiences of a large group of lawyers, these concerted efforts have, on the whole, been quite successful.

Three examples of such collective actions may illustrate this part of the group's activities. These three actions were all more or less successful. This gives, of course, a too optimistic picture of the group's activities. It would be interesting to compare the successful with the unsuccessful actions and look for the causes of the different outcomes.

The first example occurred in 1975, when a proposal for a law to restrict the job mobility of immigrant workers was introduced in Parliament. At three subsequent stages of the parliamentary procedure, the group wrote to the responsible parliamentary commissions about the practical effects of this bill and about its incompatibility with obligations under several international treaties. These treaties were not mentioned by the government in its explanatory statements. Members of the group prepared thirty amendments to the bill. The most important amendment limited the period during which a foreign worker must have a labor permit to three instead of five years. While other organizations staged demonstrations against the bill and ap-

peared on television, the working group provided the legal arguments and concrete texts for specific changes, carrying on, in fact, a sort of legal lobbying.

The second example concerns workers who involuntarily lose their jobs. In the Netherlands these workers are normally entitled to two and one-half years of unemployment benefits. Until 1974, immigrant workers received such benefits for a maximum period of six months. The Dutch unemployment legislation does not contain any rule that limits the benefits for legally employed immigrants. It was, however, an administrative practice to expel such workers if they had not found a new job within six months. In 1974, the working group wrote to Parliament about this practice. After a long discussion, the minister agreed to liberalize the policy. But the officials at the ministry implemented the new policy in such a way that the legal position of unemployed foreigners became very insecure. Following a suggestion from members of the group, a member of Parliament addressed an oral inquiry to the government on the subject. When he got an evasive answer from the minister, a member of the group drafted written questions for the same member of Parliament. His questions finally received a positive answer. The effect of this action was that immigrant workers who have worked for less than five years can now enjoy up to two years of unemployment benefits. If they have worked in the country for more than five years, they are entitled to these benefits for the full two and one-half years.

From 1974 to 1976, while the general economic situation deteriorated, the rights of immigrant workers to unemployment benefits were thus considerably extended. In the same period, the number of registered unemployed immigrant workers rose from 4,000 to 13,000. The rise partly reflects the delay in the "export" of unemployment. Today, it takes more time for an unemployed foreigner to be expelled from the country and thus disappear from the Dutch unemployment statistics.

The third example occurred in 1953, when the member states of the Council of Europe signed a treaty, in which each state accords the citizens of the other states equal treatment in granting social welfare benefits paid from public funds.[5] The treaty also restricts expulsion of an immigrant who has become dependent on public social welfare. Such expulsion is prohibited after five years of residence.

Three members of the group tried to read all official government publications to see whether they contained any information concerning the legal position of foreigners. One of them discovered in a publication of the Ministry of Foreign Affairs that Turkey had ratified this treaty in January 1977. This was important news for the 80,000 Turks in the

Netherlands. The group asked the Ministry of Social Welfare whether they had informed the local welfare agencies of this change. The group was told that the ministry was unaware of the ratification. They flatly refused to inform the agencies. The group then informed its members, began some test cases at the local level, and published announcements in newspapers, a social workers' journal, and a Turkish magazine. A Member of Parliament read one of these articles and presented written questions to the minister about the application of the treaty. In July, the minister announced that the Turks had equal rights. He also informed the local agencies of this fact. The group thus brought about the conditions to make this new right effective; it might otherwise have existed only on paper for quite a while, and the Turks would have remained dependent on the discretion of social welfare agencies. Today, social welfare benefits are no longer a favor, but a right. The officials in the ministry who know about the treaty evidently took no interest in dissemination of the information. They have, however, learned from this experience. When Portugal ratified the same treaty in 1978, the ministry spontaneously informed the local agencies.

These three examples of action of the group aimed at improvement of the legal position of immigrants were directed either toward the legislature or the administration. The process of rule change through the courts appears to take much more time. Usually it results only in small changes. Only one test case was, with assistance of the group, pursued all the way to the Supreme Court. The case was lost.[6] Nonetheless, the possibility of access to local courts and the extensive use of administrative appeal tribunals in immigration cases have limited the discretion and power of the authorities in two ways. First, the threat of a civil action for an injunction is often sufficient to get an expulsion postponed. It gives the otherwise powerless immigrant (or his lawyer) a bargaining position against the administration. Secondly, the courts have repeatedly asked officials to state the internal rules concerning the use of discretionary power granted to the administration by the Aliens Act. These explicit policy statements are then incorporated into their decisions by the courts. When these decisions are published, the statements can be used as a basis for claiming equal treatment in other cases.

EFFECTS OF THE WORKING GROUP

For the members of the group, the informal specialization brought much new information and many new clients. The publica-

tions of the group made it possible to use more diverse legal techniques in immigrants' cases. It also provided an opportunity to discuss difficult problems, which is important for unexperienced or young lawyers working on their own or in small offices. In addition, the group meetings are a source of motivation to continue with this sometimes frustrating work, which includes difficult relations with clients and many hopeless cases, that is neither very prestigious nor very remunerative. The existence of the group may have made some young members more self-confident in tackling the problems posed by the opponent government agencies.

For the *bar*, the group sets an example of the advantages of publicized specialization for both lawyers and clients. The group has also stimulated the bar to take an active position on the improvement of the legal position of immigrants. In the past few years the bar has on several occasions written to the minister of justice and the Parliament on this subject. The group initiated the use of the political influence of the bar in favor of immigrants.

For the *clients*, the group has resulted in easier access to legal aid and better quality of the aid given. Because most members of the group work in private lawyers' offices, the experience accumulated in these offices could also be applied in immigrants' cases. A newly founded legal aid organization with a full-time staff could never have built up a similar network covering the whole country and possessing so much general know-how about legal techniques within a few years. The improved access to legal aid in immigration cases resulted in an increase of legal aid in other cases, too. In recent research on the uses of social security tribunals, it appeared that immigrants come before these tribunals twice as often as Dutchmen.

The existence of the group also prevented a boom of unqualified or mala fide "immigration consultants" such as has occurred in some other countries.[7] Finally, the activities of the group have led to some changes in rules and practices to the advantage of immigrants. It may also have changed the conduct of the Aliens' Police, who are aware of the increased risk that their conduct could be subject to outside scrutiny.

For the *courts*, the group has generated a lot of new business. Many judges have thus had their first confrontation with immigration law. For the administrative tribunals, the group's activities have caused a major increase in their caseload. One of the most visible effects of the group is the increased use of the appeal system of the Aliens Act.

Before 1971, the State Council received ten to twenty immigration appeals a year. In 1977, these appeals made up one-sixth of it total caseload. The number of injunctions against deportation applied for in

Number of Appeals to:	*Minister of Justice*	*State Council*
1971	100	20
1972	400	100
1973	650	115
1974	760	165
1975	1400 (500)[a]	170
1976	2030 (900)	1045 (800)
1977	1390	650

[a]The numbers in parentheses indicate the appeals concerning the legalization of illegal immigrant workers. These appeals constituted more than half of the caseload in 1976 and thus created an incidental peak in that year. (*Source:* Report on the Budget of the Ministry of Justice for 1978, p. 44.)

civil courts was 7 in 1975, 30 in 1976, 77 in 1977, and about 100 in the first half of 1978.

For the *administration,* the increased involvement of lawyers means a loss of discretionary power but an increase in its status within the bureaucratic hierarchy. The various control mechanisms (court, parliament, and press) are now used to a much larger extent. The ministry has therefore intensified its organizational control of the local Aliens' Police. The number of civil servants in the Foreigners Section at the Ministry of Justice increased sharply between 1973 and 1977. This increase cannot be explained solely by the increased number of immigrants in the country. Furthermore, ex-army officers at the top of that section were replaced by lawyers. The civil servants increasingly have had to deal with lawyers instead of immigrants (or foreigners sentenced by criminal courts). This change in the "clientele" (or opponents) of the organization has caused a change in its status and probably also in the attitude of the officials in the organization. All these effects, of course, are not only due to the existence of the group. They also reflect the increased interest in legal aid in general and the sharp increase in the number of immigrants since 1969.

TWO LEGAL CULTURES: SIMILARITIES AND DIFFERENCES

A comparison of the public interest law firms described by Trubek and the Working Group on Legal Aid for Immigrants shows several obvious similarities between the two legal cultures. The client groups of both have a marginal social position. Both tackled underdeveloped areas of the law with the expectation that the law and legal techniques could improve the actual conditions of the client group. In

both cases, the organization of lawyers functioned as a substitute for the inability of their clients to organize themselves. As to the effects of the clients, they both caused an (informal) specialization among members of the bar. Both led to the legalization of social relations thus far characterized by arbitrariness, dependence on the part of the immigrants, and bad treatment. In the Netherlands, we observed an often unnoticed by-product of the extension of legal services; that is, the employment of more lawyers helping individual clients created a need for more lawyers in other institutions (in opponent organizations, administrative agencies and in the courts).

There are, however, some important differences between the two movements. Public interest law is clearly a lawyers' initiative, while the Working Group on Legal Aid for Immigrants originated from a pressing demand by a growing number of individual clients for legal services and the initiative of some client (refugee) organizations. This difference in origin is also reflected in the different structures and activities of both projects. The principal aim of public interest law was to shape law in a legal vacuum, whereas the working group wanted to discover and implement existing legislation, rules of practice, and court decisions. Its main purpose was the implementation of existing rules at the local level combined with action to improve these rules. The group can thus be seen as a method of law enforcement. Muir[8] has suggested that legislators, when proposing new laws, should ask themselves: "Which group of lawyers will assist in enforcing this law, in what ways, on behalf of which persons and for what reasons?"

Until 1973, the Dutch Aliens Act was only partially enforced, almost exclusively by civil servants (among them relatively few lawyers) who worked on behalf of the state. The group created a group of lawyers who enforced other parts of the law, the parts intended to protect immigrants. They increased the level of compliance with the law by governmental agencies.

The group acts like a clearinghouse with two-way traffic: (1) collection of lawyers' experiences at the local level for use in law reform activities by the secretariat of the group at the national level and (2) implementation at the local level of results of law reform activities through distribution of information, training, and support in individual cases. The working group is an example of an effort to combine the two approaches in legal services—the service orientation and the law reform approach. For the public interest firms, law reform is the governing perspective. Both showed, however, that the two different approaches to legal service do not exclude but rather often complement or even support each other.

Thus, the differences between the two projects should not be overestimated. The comparison shows that even in the absence of two of the five elements mentioned by Trubek (an activist judiciary and rich private foundations) in the Netherlands, it was possible to establish a legal service organization providing independent, sustained, and multiarena advocacy to an unorganized clientele. Lacking private foundations, the necessary funds were acquired partly through direct government subsidies (with a threat to independence) and partly indirectly through compensations paid to lawyers handling individual cases in a "judicare" system of public legal aid. When the judiciary proved unresponsive to claims for law reform, it was possible to direct the law reform advocacy to other arenas such as administrative agencies and Parliament.

Immigration law has much in common with other fields of law that are typical products of the modern welfare state in Western Europe. The position of immigrants is comparable not only to the situation of inmates of mental institutions but also to that of many recipients of social welfare, unemployed workers, or persons in old-age homes. All of them are dependent, suffer from social isolation, are confronted with complicated and detailed legislation or the lack of information, or face a system of monopoly, that is, little is known about the relevant rules outside the public institutions that handle these "client" groups.

Possibly similar strategies for the organization of legal services and law reform have actually been applied in other Western European countries. If so, the public interest law firm would turn out to be the American name for a more widespread phenomenon.

NOTES

1. In an oral summary of his paper in this volume.
2. In 1978 the number of foreigners living in the Netherlands was approximately 350,000 (i.e., 2.5% of the total population). One-third of them were citizens of other Common Market countries. In 1960, only a few hundred people from Mediterranean countries (outside the Common Market) lived in the Netherlands. Today, in 1978, they number almost 200,000 and make up the majority of the foreign population. These immigrant workers (mainly from Turkey and Morocco) work in unpleasant, inferior, and dangerous jobs. In the Netherlands, however, the reliance on foreign labor is not (yet) as great as in some other European countries.
3. The Vreemdelingenwet (Aliens Act) of 13.1.1965, Staatsblad 1965, Nr. 40, which became effective in 1967.
4. The official legal aid system in the Netherlands has a structure similar to the system of the English Legal Aid and Advice Act. Both are similar to the judicare

model. The total amount of compensation paid in 1976 from public legal aid funds to members of the group for legal services in immigration cases can be estimated as between $200,000 and $300,000.

5. "European Convention on Social and Medical Assistance," Paris, 11.12.1953, 218 U.N. Treaties Series, p. 255.
6. *Muskita* v. *Staat, Hoge Raad* (1977), Nederlandse Jurisprudentie 1977 411. The same issue was brought before that court again in 1978. The second case has not yet been decided.
7. P. Schuler, "Immigration Consultants," *University of California at Davis Law Review* 8 (1975): 85–105.
8. W. K. Muir, *Law and Attitude Change* (University of Chicago Press, 1973), p. vii.

PART III

The Basic Issue of Legalization and Delegalization

Chapter 13

Some Reasons for Not Legalizing

Erhard Blankenburg

"Legalization" in our terms usually refers to areas of social life in which the law has either been absent or ineffective so far and in which legal services have contributed to increasing the use of the law. This is the case both with legal aid for the poor and with public interest law. Whereas the first movement tried to compensate for the social deprivations of the lower classes as well as of marginal groups, the latter movement has taken up a number of issues that reach into the realm of middle-class interests, for example, consumer protection, environmental control, or checks on administrative discretion. Here, too, the law is used as a means to compensate for social weakness. In both cases the deprivation is transformed into a problem that a single individual experiences, being subject to the consequences of political decisions, economic developments, and decisions of large organizations. Whereas legal aid in the context of the War on Poverty was seen as a way to combat overall deprivation, public interest issues take up a pluralistic array of issues in which individuals stand against organized powers.

Although such compensatory use of the law might be claimed to be part of "social policy" or in the "public interest," this use of the law makes it necessary to define individual claims. Even though the

American law provides for such legal instruments as bringing class action suits (which the German law does not), most public interest cases are categorized before being taken to court in terms of a single case, thus an individual case becomes a precedent for general policy decisions. Hopefully, as lawyers increasingly mobilize the courts to gain compensation for damages incurred to their clients, either for faulty products or for administrative decision, the institutions that are sued react by anticipating being sued and change some of their behavior patterns. The result is partly in the desired direction of increasing the responsiveness of organizations to the needs of their clients and of those affected by their decisions. Therefore, litigation is an effective means of feedback if the impact of the law is not restricted only to the cases actually brought to trial, but if it is anticipated and complied with without each time escalating to an open conflict. Increased litigation, however, leads partly to purely defensive actions; for example, when doctors ask patients to sign a waiver of liability before starting an operation or when insurance firms use lawyers to regulate claims. In such cases litigation strategies lead to a "legalization" of social relations, often making them more rigid, cumbersome, and costly.

The degree to which social relations are implicitly regulated by the law may vary. In everyday relations the law may almost never be made explicit because life tends to be regulated by implicit consensus. However, so-called legalization can be introduced by one side and forced upon the other. If a party begins to refer to the legal regulation underlying everyday interaction, the other side might find it difficult to avoid the law from thereon because legalization presupposes a legal norm underlying social relations. Sophisticated lawyers will always find these legal norms if a particular party desires it. Therefore, I would prefer to define legalization in behavioral terms—it begins with a party bringing up legal norms as an issue in social relations, and it continues in steps, consulting legal experts, threatening legal action, and going to court.

It should be clear by now that by legalization I do not refer simply to the act of formulating a law, but rather I include the processes of its implementation and the conditions of it being used in this concept. One of the conditions is that information and perception by those affected, as well as some activity to use the law, must be present. Sometimes this can be observed in pathological forms, for example, in a harmless way with students in their first year of legal training. As a form of learning they begin to see the legal quality of interactions in everyday life; thus, buying a beer appears to be a contract, cheating appears to be a fraud, and jaywalking an offence. Hopefully, law students (like most people)

will not consistently derive behavioral consequences from all of their intellectual conclusions and attitudinal preferences. If law students formally acted on the consequences of their behavior, legalization might soon become a nuisance. Only by using the law selectively can its rigidity and formality be tolerated. Therefore, it might be useful *not* to inform the public about legal norms and not to lower the costs of going to court. As data show that the likelihood of mobilizing the law increases with legal competence, the need for expertise in legal institutions functions to limit the use of law. The less legal competence people have, the less they perceive of interactions in legal terms and the less they are inclined to mobilize the law if they have problems or enter into conflicts.

Even if the actors are aware of the possible uses of the law, they may make a well-informed, rational choice to settle conflicts without the law, for the law tends to be costly in time and money, and also in complicating problems. Even if people were acting rationally and with full information, they would still calculate costs and benefits before invoking the law. Being partly irrational, they might avoid the costs of the law by barring themselves from perceptional choices and by not accepting information that a problem or a conflict is legally relevant. Both perceptional and behavioral choices add to a process in which the scope of effective legalization is defined. As in the process of criminalization, which is not automatically invoked by a particular act of deviance, there are a number of actors, agencies, and institutional conditions that determine the extent of actual implementation of legal norms. There is nonmobilizing in all kinds of law. As in criminology, we might regard the "labeling process" as that which determines when the law is called into action.

The fields of law differ with respect to the agents who define the law. In penal law, the police and prosecutors are considered as the main labeling agents, even if most of the crimes are reported to the police by a private party, most often the victim. In cases of conflict about contracts, liability, and property issues, the mobilization of courts may be initiated by several parties, and it might depend on social conditions of a number of actors whether lawyers and courts are invoked or whether alternative means of conflict resolution are chosen. The barriers to access to private law largely depend on what kind of competence and legal advice is offered by lawyers and legal counseling agencies. Lawyers who concentrate on their traditional fields of activity factually define the boundaries of effective "legal" action. How much the profession traditionally limits its scope of labeling can be demonstrated by arguing with reverse examples under the pressure of increased lawyer competition. In many countries an enlargement of the

range into which the bar gets involved has been experienced, such as lawyers being engaged in public law matters or increasingly showing up in labor courts. These activities are indications of a change in professional labeling.

Labeling, however, not only takes place at the level of the agents, who mobilize and implement the law, but also at the level of what is designed by legislation. Substantive law defines the claims that can be made, procedural law sets the conditions (and the barriers as well) under which they can be realized, and parties and also implementation agencies choose to what degree they make use of them.

We thus arrive at a definition of the law on three levels—what has been laid down as a legal framework by *legislation* has to be filled out by an institutional infrastructure for *implementation,* again being dependent on the *mobilization* of the law by particular parties. On each of the three levels, there is selectivity as to the issues that are brought to the law and as to the conditions of making them effective. On each of the three levels there are alternatives to legalization: *not* passing laws on certain issues, *not* providing a sufficient institutional infrastructure to implement the law, or the parties *not* taking legal action.

However, the alternative to legalization must not always be altogether alegal. The law can take more or less rigid forms, that is to say, it can be formal or discretionary in substance. With increasing legalization of policy issues by the legal profession, there is a concomitant attempt to develop alternative forms of the law that could avoid some of its dysfunctions. Philippe Nonet develops a normative position to this effect, whereas Paul Geerts gives an overview of the theoretical positions that have been taken in this "third wave" of discussions on the conditions of access to legal institutions, thus changing the behavioral definition of the law.

Chapter 14

What Price Rights?

Philippe Nonet

This chapter is concerned with the relationship between legal services and public services. The question it addresses may be stated as follows: how should legal services be designed if they are to contribute to the quality and effectiveness of public services? A large part of the work lawyers do for their clients has little to do with "public services" in any significant sense of the word. To be sure, the resolution of disputes arising from accidents, contracts, domestic relations, and the like, does involve a public service of sorts, that is, the administration of justice. And much can be gained from assessing the contributions lawyers make to the quality of this service. For example, it is a recurrent complaint—almost an item of folklore—in most Western countries that the lawyer tends to aggravate private disputes and to make their resolution needlessly brutal and chancy, at great expense to all. In neglecting this facet of legal services, I do not wish to discount its importance. Rather, I want to draw attention to the special problems that arise in the relationship between legal services and the public services that distinguish the modern, active, "welfare" state from its historical predecessors. In services of this type, government undertakes an affirmative responsibility to regulate or to deploy resources in pursuit of such public purposes as health, education, or environmental protection. Special problems arise in this context, mainly because of massive legal inexperience. By and large, despite the growth of administrative law in the last few decades, public services remain a relatively uncharted legal terrain.

Perhaps the point of my initial question will be sharpened if we consider the following hypothetical proposal. Suppose the provision of legal services for criminal defendants were designed to increase the effectiveness of penal law enforcement. In that context we are apt to think that the proper criterion for evaluating legal services is how good they are at protecting the rights of the accused. Indeed we have come to regard legal representation itself as an essential ingredient of these rights, and we are quite prepared to accept that the right to counsel, like other guarantees of fairness, results in some impairment of efficiency in the apprehension and conviction of offenders. Put more abstractly, this is an area in which we feel most inclined to heed the Kantian advice that persons should not be treated as means to the ends of others and in which we resist embracing any principle that smacks of unrestricted utilitarianism.

The example of criminal law highlights an important, albeit obscure and problematic, meaning of the idea of "right." Rights are interests we wish to be protected without (or with less) regard for considerations of social costs and benefits. The same logic applies to legal services insofar as they are (more or less indispensable) instruments for the assertion of rights, and thus tend to be regarded as a kind of secondary right, a right to rights. If this analysis is correct, in asking what legal services contribute to the effectiveness of public services, we are posing a question to which that institution should perhaps not be exposed. In effect, we seem to be challenging the appropriateness of allowing a place in that context for the institution of rights.

LAW AND GOVERNMENT

In fact, however, despite a secular expansion of rights to public services, even in the most liberal Western democracies administrative law has been less than fully receptive to legal action against government institutions. Everywhere, out of an apparent regard for the prerogatives of the state, it imposes a variety of restrictions (such as exemptions from liability in torts or contracts and limitations of judicial review) on the capacity of citizens to seek legal remedies against injurious government actions. Of course, different legal systems vary in their approaches to these issues. On the whole, it is probably fair to say that, for a variety of historical reasons, the legal traditions of continental Europe have given more weight—and more thought—to the special status of public services than has the common law, especially its American version. American administrative law

has been almost obsessively preoccupied with procedures for the assertion of rights and almost careless of the administrative needs of public institutions. To American jurists, "large questions of administrative organization," such as agency autonomy and the roles of executive and legislative control, "are more in the realm of political theory and practice than of administrative law,"[1] and "apart from judicial review, the manner in which public officers handle business unrelated to adjudication or rule-making is not a part of administrative law," which is "confined to arrangements involving rights of private parties."[2]

Needless to say, such comparisons across legal systems are elusive. Differences of perspective are more striking than variations in concrete legal outcomes. In Europe also, the rhetoric of rights has challenged the legitimacy of traditional principles limiting the legal accountability of the government. More important, we should not presume that the *law's* preoccupation with (or indifference to) rights offers any good indication of the amount or quality of the services *government* provides. In the United States, a highly rights-centered law coexists with a "welfare state" that, by European standards, remains relatively ungenerous and poorly administered. Perhaps this seeming paradox is only a by-product of the American propensity to deflect toward the courts the social demands and controversies to which legislatures and the political order do not respond. In that context, to the extent legal thought is attuned to the work of the courts, its focus upon rights will reflect the troubles and frustrations, rather than the virtues, of the larger system. But perhaps the assertion of legal rights has also directly corrosive effects upon the proper functioning of public institutions. And perhaps after all there is some latent administrative wisdom in the traditional immunities and prerogatives of the state that American scholars tend to dismiss as mere privileges of an authoritarian officialdom. Some recent American experience suggests that the question warrants reexamination.

About fifteen years ago, American law reviews of all persuasions began publishing, disguised as scholarly papers, the manifestos of a movement aimed at expanding legal services and legal rights.[3] Feeding on changes that were already occurring in administrative and criminal procedure, the movement triggered a veritable explosion of advocacy. Provisions for the right to counsel in criminal proceedings set the model for a federally subsidized program of noncriminal legal services for the indigent.[4] Rules of "standing" that restricted the capacity of organized groups to undertake legal action on behalf of their members or of the "public," were dramatically liberalized.[5] In all settings, administrative or judicial, public or private, demands for

"due process of law"—procedural rights to notice, hearing, and judicial review—were the priority items on the agenda for reform. Everywhere the goal was to secure "entitlements"; official discretion was the obstacle to overcome. Not only would legal action conquer new rights in welfare, housing, education—all of which are now the subjects of new law school courses—but it would also offer expanded opportunities for self-assertion and for democratic participation in the making of public policy.

Times have changed. Today we hear the sounding of retreat. There is widespread concern that a "creeping legalism" is suffocating public and private institutions;[6] that the courts, pressed by excessive demands, have exceeded their competence to the point of awaking the specter of an "imperial judiciary";[7] that officials, deprived of discretion, are lapsing into irresponsible deference to legal rules imposed from without; and that this whole pattern is the product of excessive "lawyering" on behalf of persons and groups who do not understand the limits of what law can accomplish.[8]

There are two distinct strands in current criticism of the abuses of lawyering. Some, in the spirit of classical liberalism, complain of how legal action has enlarged the scope of government control at the expense of private initiative and individual freedom.[9] Meanwhile, others complain of how legal action has diminished the competence of government.[10] The two strands may combine, of course, because government intrusions are all the more objectionable in that they appear less able to achieve their own ends. But this apparent convergence of right and left should not make the two issues less distinguishable.

First, there is no question that lawyers and judicial proceedings do serve as instruments for claiming the benefits and securing the enforcement of government regulations of all sorts. If this is so, resources allocated to legal services must help raise the level of government control. This result is somewhat troubling, for in the past law and lawyers have ordinarily been thought to play just the opposite role, that of helping resist government interference with autonomous individual choice. There was a time when the "rule of law" was the antinomy of government; when A. V. Dicey could contrast English legality with the lawless regime of French "droit administratif";[11] when Georges Ripert characterized social legislation as signaling a "déclin du droit";[12] and when the Supreme Court of the United States found most government restrictions on freedom of contract to be violations of the constitutional right to "due process of law."[13] Accordingly, those who then sought to enlarge the powers of government found it necessary to develop new public institutions that were in some

sense beyond the reach of law. Administrative law grew in part from the early effort to free the legislative authority of the modern state from the restrictive effects of a liberal understanding of individual rights that, by the end of the nineteenth century, had permeated legal doctrine and the professional consciousness of lawyers and judges. Since then, of course, legal thought has by and large assimilated the premises, aspirations, and policies of the welfare state. Perhaps, therefore, we should not be surprised that persons and groups who have a stake in the implementation of these policies now feel free to turn to a highly conservative institution, the legal profession, and enlist it to claim the new "rights" they have gained from government regulation.

In lending themselves to these new claims, legal services seem to remain, as in the past, in the service of rights. Legal advocacy remains centered on the individual grievant and the protections to which he is "entitled" by law. There is a continuing appeal to the symbols of legal individualism. But the symbolism is strained. With exceptions, such as in criminal law, where the liberal imagery has retained much of its integrity, modern public law litigants can hardly be characterized as seeking protection of an inviolable private domain against government intrusion. More likely, they are seeking a benefit, the right to which is contingent upon government having adopted a detailed program of regulation or public services. In support of their claim, they may well argue that such benefits and programs are due to them by virtue of one of the basic rights to health, education, or employment, which a few modern constitutions and the statutory laws of most Western countries purport to guarantee.

This rhetorical gambit, however, cannot distract us from the fact that rights of this kind are more aptly described as *purposes,* the achievement of which requires a deployment of governmental resources, than as domains upon which the government may not encroach. Where such rights exist, citizens may well be entitled to expect that the government will try as hard as it can to achieve these purposes. But it does not follow that citizens are entitled to any specific program or level of effort, for other interests may have equally legitimate claims on government resources, and the choice among them must ultimately depend upon complex and elusive political judgments. The rights that are claimed in public law actions presume that these judgments have been made. Ordinarily they assert only that the government be bound by the rules it has already established to design its own programs, or that other parties subject to those programs comply with their obligations under them. In the first case, claimants recall the government to the responsibilities it has officially

assumed, as, for example, when they claim welfare benefits to which they are entitled by existing regulations; in the second case, claimants may be thought of as lending a helping hand to the enforcement of regulations against recalcitrant subjects, as when they complain of a violation of industrial safety rules that government inspectors have failed to discover or prosecute. Either way, claimants help make public policy more effective, and perhaps, as some critics complain, more oppressive.

If this is true, how can it also be that, as other critics fear, the growth of public law litigation may undermine the competence of public services? The answer to this question lies in the dynamics of legalization. The assertion of rights tends to transform government policies into more rigidly binding rules that reduce the element of discretion in administrative decisions. If the claimant has a legally protected title to benefits derived from government regulation, there grows a presumption against tampering with the rules. Here, too, the vesting of interests makes it more difficult to change the status quo. More important, however, is the effect of legalization on the day-to-day implementation of policy. Because they are held more strictly accountable to rules, officials discover they have lost the authority to interpret and qualify established policy in light of their professional judgment. An increasingly large array of practical issues are taken out of the hands of responsible administrators and experts. They are now to be decided by (or in anticipation of the opinions of) judges and lawyers who are removed from the field of action, have distorted perceptions of policy questions, and bear no responsibility for the consequences of their decisions.

In effect, government becomes the victim of its own medicine, that is, oppressive regulation. The explosion of legal advocacy tightens the regulation of the regulators, as well as of the regulated. It should be no surprise that complaints of a paralyzing bureaucratization, a continuing theme in criticism by business of the abuses of regulation, are now echoed in the lamentations of responsible public servants. Insofar as modern government purports to become a creative actor in society—capable of deploying resources, offering services, and creating viable organizations—it requires some of the same freedom of initiative and adaptation that "private"enterprise had secured under the banner of property and liberty. The abuses and the rhetoric of "free enterprise" have obscured a truth we are apt to find obvious in many other contexts, including the management of our private lives and the pursuit of moral aspirations, namely, that "legal rules are not an effective device for directing human energies to those places where they can be most creatively and effectively applied."[14]

We should indeed recall that the fear of a suffocating "legalism" was a major spur to the emergence of a specialized field of "administrative law."[15] In that sense, Dicey was basically right in suspecting that the model of French "droit administratif" threatened to subvert, or at least erode, the institutions of strict legality.[16] Administrative law was more than a temporary expedient for circumventing a legal order overly committed to liberal ideology. It also reflected a more durable understanding of what public *enterprise* would require, including some liberation from the "frigid legal atmosphere"[17] induced by accountability to rules, some room to solve problems in the light of public purpose, and some authority to balance fairness against administrative imperatives.

At this point, however, I should like to depart from the assumption, often too readily accepted, that there is an irreconcilable tension between the requirements of legality and administrative enterprise. Not only does that assumption put us on the horn of an unpleasant dilemma, but also the choice it seems to force upon us may not be altogether necessary. After all, the proponents of administrative law did not envision a regime of official lawlessness or of casual disregard for the interests of citizens. Rather, they had in mind institutions that would cultivate a certain form of legal sensibility compatible with a competent discharge of governmental responsibilities. Administrative law was to be a species of law. But it had to be a law that made purpose and policy the key sources of legal guidance and restraint, and hence one that encouraged the creative exercise of discretionary judgment and treated rules as subordinate and instrumental. For that reason, it was at odds with a style of legal thought, derived largely from criminal law, that presumed a radical distrust of official discretion and centered on securing close accountability to rules.[18]

ACCOUNTABILITY AND RESPONSIVENESS

Distrust of what some call "the official perspective"[19] was indeed a main force in the explosion of a consciousness of rights during the last decade and in the corollary expansion of legal services. We need not consider here how much warrant there was for this breakdown of confidence. Discretion always entails a risk of arbitrariness, though the seriousness of that risk varies considerably in different contexts. But a high price is paid for strategies of reform that move from a *posture* of mistrust. Having pressed for close accountability, rule-conscious lawyers are likely to find that in curing abuses they

have also stifled initiative and devalued responsible judgment. An alternative to that approach, of course, is to discover what an institution may need to regain the integrity and competence upon which our confidence in its judgments must depend. The more rights in public services are contingent upon the vigor with which government institutions seek to discharge their mandates, the more urgent it is for legal reformers to be mindful of what effective administration requires.

What is needed, then, is a theory of legal action appropriate to the special context of administrative law and capable of guiding the provision of legal services in that context. Such a theory need not give up the idea of rights any more than it need give up the idea of lawful government. But it must be prepared to locate rights in the more basic *purposes* of public institutions and to regard specific entitlements as means the worth of which must be assessed on practical grounds, including considerations of institutional effectiveness. The following paragraphs outline some of the questions a theory of this kind would have to address.[20]

The first question, and the most fundamental, is implicit in the preceding remarks: how should one weigh and balance the institutional costs and benefits of legal accountability? Put another way, in words that parallel and rephrase the title of this chapter, what price accountability? For the sake of brevity, I shall use "accountability" to mean legal or bureaucratic accountability, that is, accountability to rules. This is not to deny the existence of other forms of accountability, such as the political accountability of an elected official to his constituency. In any case, no serious confusion should follow from this usage. The heart of the idea remains—one is accountable when one is liable to be called upon to account for, or justify, one's actions in the light of recognized standards of evaluation. The stronger the demand for accountability, the closer is the required justification, the more the standards of judgment must become stringent and detailed. Thus even electoral accountability, as it becomes more pressing, takes on the character of accountability to narrow prescriptions, in this case the specific demands of the electorate—a fact the force of which even Edmund Burke's eloquence was not able to overcome.[21]

A system of legal services that focuses on securing entitlements assumes there is no limit beyond which we should stop wanting more accountability. But consider the following examples. In their efforts to give effect to the constitutional ideal of racial integration in public schools, the American federal courts developed a set of rules requiring that in any school district the racial composition of classes reflect the racial composition of the population of the district. There followed, in

most large cities, a serious decline of school quality and morale, with an exodus of middle-class children to private schools and of white families to suburbs with fewer blacks. But the rules remain, and they continue to produce "integrated" schools that are ever more exclusively black.[22]

Suits by advocates of conservation have led the federal courts to try and give teeth to a statute requiring government agencies that plan major construction to assess the "environmental impact" of the project. The effect was a series of court decisions that faulted environmental impact studies for neglecting some issues or for exhibiting some bias in their policy conclusions. Now, to satisfy the courts, agencies find themselves compelled to write voluminous reports that omit no detail, however trivial, and make no policy judgment, however helpful it might be. The environmental impact report is becoming not a source of enlightenment, but yet another cause of bureaucratic irritation.[23]

The pathological quest for accountability is of course not uniquely the product of excessive lawyering. Any pattern of "close supervision" works in the same direction. If a government employment service expects its success to be assessed by a fixed measure of efficiency, such as "cost per placement," we may safely expect it will work more on readily employable clients and will neglect those most in need of its services.[24] "Operational goals" are to the management expert what rules are to lawyers and courts. In all these cases, underlying the quest for tighter accountability, there was an eagerness to reach quicker results in a recalcitrant environment. But whether the unemployed, black pupils, or conservationists gained any true benefit from the accountability they secured in this way remains an obscure and debatable question. The point is that we cannot assume the rightness of any move in the direction of stronger entitlements, tighter accountability, or of more widely accessible legal services in the service of such ends. Like other policy changes, these changes require a careful weighing of costs and benefits.

The central problem is that, in fact, any increment of accountability must generally be purchased at the price of a corresponding loss of *responsiveness*. An organization, public or private, requires a system of decision such that a large number of actions will be informed at once by the *same* purpose and by knowledge of factual conditions that *vary* across situations and over time. Problems arise because distant purposes are ineffective in guiding conduct. Their meaning is complex and elusive, and their pursuit involves a multiplicity of participants whose understanding and commitment are normally shallow, partial, and uneven. For that reason, purpose must be translated into proximate goals to which there are more clearly delineated means and to

which participants can therefore be more effectively held *accountable*. The authority of purpose is thus transferred to specific rules or policies that embody a theory of what means are appropriate under determinate conditions. The trouble is that these rules should also be adaptable enough to remain *responsive* to variations of context. In other words, their authority should in principle be conditional upon their problematic instrumental merits. But authority so qualified is rendered vulnerable. In effect the burden of direction is returned to precisely those general ends whose impotence was to be cured. Hence the dilemma. Either authority is given to rules capable of ensuring accountability, but at the price of diminished inquiry into, and responsiveness to, variations of context; or the source of authority is found in general purposes, which encourage inquiry and facilitate adaptation, but undermine accountability.

Borrowing some language from statistics, we may speak of two types of error or arbitrariness in systems of legal and administrative decision. Type I error follows from uncritically *departing from* authoritative policy. Type II error is induced by uncritically *adhering to* authoritative policy. Either way purpose is frustrated. Accountability protects us from the risk of Type I errors by biasing the system in favor of Type II errors. Responsiveness does exactly the opposite. Although these two virtues are in obvious conflict, they must nevertheless be combined, for neither is worth much without the other. Accountability loses its value when it assures only continued adherence to policies that are out of touch with context, and hence irrelevant to their purpose. This is the condition we have in mind when we criticize an institution for its excessive "formalism" or "legalism." The examples discussed above are just a few of countless instances of formalism induced by legal action.

THE AUTHORITY OF PURPOSE

But suppose it were demonstrated, after a careful assessment of costs and benefits, that the administration of a particular public service would benefit from tighter accountability to rules. (Note that normally this conclusion would have to be held subject to reconsideration, as conditions may eventually require a relaxation of accountability to induce greater responsiveness.) Before we could move further and argue for a program of legal services, we would have to consider a second question—who should bear the burden of identifying and correcting lapses of accountability?

In raising this question, I have in mind a situation not uncommon in

the poverty law offices of large American cities, which spend a large part of their meager resources handling the complaints of disgruntled applicants for public welfare benefits. Much of the work of the few attorneys and numerous volunteers specializing in "welfare law" consists of fighting to correct the clerical mistakes of a local welfare office plagued by rampant incompetence and ill-will, in varying mixes. A mistaken entry was made on the application form (sometimes only because the applicant was illiterate and got no help in filling out the papers); a clerk made the wrong subtraction in computing a benefit formula; or the office "forgot" about some more or less obscure clause of the relevant federal rules. A very large part of this so-called legal work involves nothing that could not be done perfectly well by a decent old-fashioned bureaucracy. Of course, any complex organization will find that grievances of all sorts help it uncover problems and mistakes that would otherwise have gone by unnoticed. For this reason, and quite apart from any concern for rights, institutions may (and probably should) encourage the assertion of claims as an administrative resource to supplement internal mechanisms of control. But there is a point beyond which reliance on that resource shifts upon claimants the burden of maintaining administrative regularity and fosters what amounts to an abdication of institutional responsibilities. Legal action, even with "free" legal assistance, is always a costly imposition upon the individual claimant. Used as a way of doing business, its costs include the erosion of what we should regard as a basic principle of institutional design, namely, that institutions be capable of self-correction.

This principle is especially salient when individual claims point to pervasive patterns of official arbitrariness. If there is a role for legal services in cases of this kind, it should be to render themselves unnecessary by seeking not only satisfaction for the aggrieved individual, but also, and indeed primarily, correction of the institutional flaws from which problems arise. Lawyers may find themselves uncomfortable with this approach, for it may seem to conflict with a deeply rooted sense of professional loyalty to the special interests of individual clients. In the long run, however, the risk is that an apparent concern for justice and fairness to the individual will disguise a system of legal services that indulges administrative irresponsibility.

This problem leads us to a third question, which is much larger and much more elusive. Whenever a claim of right is asserted against a public institution, we need to ask what that institution's responsibility should be for the interest that is demanding protection? Put another way, how does the asserted interest relate to the purposes that

define the special mandate of the institution? Consider two contrasting cases. A student suffers injuries from falling down a staircase in a school building that the student claims was negligently maintained. A former student, who has just graduated, complains that the school district was negligent in failing to teach him to read, though it had him for twelve years in its custody. Clearly, schools have an obligation to teach, as well as a duty to exercise reasonable care in maintaining their buildings. But the former case strikes at the heart of the schools' special mission, whereas the latter case is better conceived as a constraint to which any person or institution is subject, whatever the purpose of its activities may be. So far, American courts have, I think wisely, declined to extend the law of torts to claims of school negligence in the discharge of educational responsibilities. The point I want to stress is that, in general, the closer an interest lies to the core of an institution's special mandate, the more we should be concerned that legal remedies maintain and enhance the institution's capacity to fulfill its mission. The law has a propensity to intervene by formulating specific duties to which sanctions can readily be attached. But this mode of "regulation by legal orders"[25] is of doubtful effectiveness when the true problem is how to restore, nurture, or enhance a sense of purpose within the complex system of decisionmaking and cooperation that constitutes an institution.

Students of law-in-action have long noted the many ways—sometimes quite subtle, hardly visible at first—in which legal intervention can demoralize institutions. As lines are drawn in preparation for legal battles, the beneficiaries of a public service come to be perceived, and to perceive themselves, as its adversaries, at great costs to all.[26] Officials adopt a self-protective posture, become preoccupied with minimizing the risks of censure and liability, and lose their freedom to be candid in discussing or reporting their problems. By a slow drift, a point is reached where the requirements of institutional purpose have been reduced to superficial observance of the rough and minimal standards law imposes from without. In the words of Lon Fuller, a morality of duty takes the place of the morality of aspiration.[27]

This pattern of demoralization is most noticeable when a public agency is vulnerable to the intervention of the courts, or of other reviewing bodies that do not share in the exercise of its special responsibility. Under this kind of external supervision, the agency loses the authority to set and correct its own standards and becomes resigned to merely following orders. This tendency can be moderated if the agency provides an internal forum with sufficient legitimacy and effectiveness to resolve disputed claims and to earn judicial deference

to its judgments. In this respect, experience has confirmed the wisdom of an invention of modern administrative law, the specialized administrative tribunal. But even here the abuses of legal action weaken the authority of institutional purpose. I have documented elsewhere the dynamics of a pattern of "judicialization," quite common in American regulatory agencies, whereby an administrative authority retreats into the role of a passive, impartial "court" standing in judgment of claims and policies that, by its mandate, it should arguably have been championing.[28] When administrators are allowed to arbitrate disputes involving their own policies, our first impulse is to fear for the fairness and integrity of their arbitration. But also to be feared is that, pressed into the role of arbitrators, they will become altogether too neutral toward their policies, and thus weaken their effectiveness as administrators.

Can legal action avoid, or at least reduce, such institutional costs, that is, detrimental effects upon the institutional sense of purpose? The answer, I believe, is a qualified and cautious affirmative. Yes, if we manage to reduce its bluntness, including its commitment to the vindication of particular claims, and its dependence upon the imposition of gross, invariant obligations. There is, to be sure, much room for legal services of the routine sort, in which the focus is upon claims, entitlements, and upholding recognized duties. But the pursuit of these traditional lawyerly objectives needs to be (a) moderated by a greater regard for their institutional effects, especially when it moves into unexplored terrain; and (b) supplemented by other tools—other modes of proceeding and other remedies—better suited to the complex fabric of administrative experience and capable of making purpose and policy more effective.

What public services need from lawyers today is a sharper awareness of administrative conditions affecting *the authority of purpose* in decisionmaking. Giving authority to purpose is not just a matter of elaborating policies and fixing the rules that will govern their implementation. Also required is a kind of social engineering: creating organizational units with special skills and commitments, distributing authority so that critical decisions are made where purpose is best understood, and managing incentives so that energies are enlisted and initiative is released. When legal action reaches into the working administrative enterprise, it should take account of the dynamics of this complex social system so that it can trace the sources of the problems it seeks to correct and can identify the appropriate institutional remedies. What is truly needed may not be a new rule, or a tougher sanction, but the creation of a new organization, a change in the distribution of authority, or a restructuring of incentives. In any

case, whatever the appropriate remedy may be, the focus of inquiry must be not on censuring and restricting, but rather on enabling and facilitating.

THE QUESTION OF COMPETENCE

From the above it follows that the practical worth of legal services will depend upon what expertise is present, or may develop, in the art of institutional evaluation and institutional design. This is not the kind of expertise we ordinarily think of as a distinctive lawyerly skill. In concluding, we must therefore confront a fourth question, that is, the question of competence. May we expect legal services to develop the competence required for legal action in the domain of public services? or have we reached the point "where the law ends"[29] for want of the needed intellectual resources?

The controversy that is currently raging in the United States on and around this question has focused upon the competence of the courts and of lawyers in litigation before courts. The courts, critics argue, are unable to conduct the comprehensive studies of policy and administration that are needed to plan viable reforms. This intellectual disability is a by-product of the fact that policy issues come before them only as incidents of particular disputes; the latter define and limit the scope of judicial inquiry. In addition, courts and lawyers have cultivated a style of analysis that aims at narrowing issues, separating them from one another, and limiting the exploration of facts by stringent criteria of relevance. Given such an approach, the policy judgments of courts are bound to do violence to the realities of administrative experience. In this area, no problem can be taken out of context because everything is relevant to everything else. Furthermore, even if courts managed to be wise in making policy, they would still lack the political and administrative resources necessary to monitor the implementation of their judgments. The conclusion is clear—lawyers and courts should stay away from policy issues.

On the whole, I believe, this conclusion is true, though it needs important qualifications. The characteristics of lawyerly intelligence to which our critics point are associated with a specific function of courts, that is, the adjudication of disputes. In the exercise of this function, the limitations of legal inquiry serve important values and contribute greatly to the effectiveness of courts as makers of peace, if only because they help narrow the differences to be resolved. At the same time, it is important for the integrity and fairness of adjudication that in settling disputes courts avoid extending their policy concerns

beyond the limited amount of interpreting and clarifying that may be necessary for the case at hand. The policy-conscious court is apt to be seriously unfair, as well as to make bad policy.

It is possible, however, that the courts are being called upon to assume functions other than adjudication, requiring a more direct involvement in policy evaluation and administrative reform. And it is also quite possible, as some observers of American federal courts have suggested, that in due course they will evolve procedures, modes of analysis, and remedies appropriate to such new functions.[30] Perhaps, then, we should temper our criticism and help courts learn that different tasks require different intellectual resources. There is, of course, always some risk that an institution with multiple functions will not be able to avoid confusing its roles. But maybe this risk can be controlled. In this regard, it may be worth studying more closely the experience of the French Conseil d'Etat, which has long managed to combine separate responsibilities for adjudication and for advice on matters of policy.

Nevertheless, insofar as adjudication remains the primary vehicle through which lawyers and courts tackle the problems of public institutions—insofar as a "strategy of rights" keeps inspiring legal action—the critics of lawyerly intelligence are amply warranted. But it is a serious mistake to think that advocacy embraces the full range of services lawyers provide or that activist courts are the model of the law's contribution to policy. They may be the most visible (perhaps more so in the United States than anywhere else), but their importance can hardly compare with the obscure but critical contributions lawyers make to the drafting of statutes, to the design of charters of association and complex contractual arrangements, to the conduct of negotiations, and to the management and oversight of public affairs. Perhaps the services of the counselor, rather than the advocate, and the skills of the negotiator and draftsman, rather than the adjudicator, offer a more viable model of what the law can contribute to public services. In these activities, the lawyer shares in, as well as facilitates, the responsibilities and commitments of the executive, the planner, or the evaluator. Perhaps there is also greater promise in the critical work of legal scholarship, especially when it manages to overcome its intellectual isolation.[31]

In any event, the question of competence can be recast to encompass the *facilitative* roles of the lawyer. Put in this light, the question is at once more pertinent and less easy to answer. Clearly it no longer permits the sweeping negatives that critics of legalism seem to prefer. For every instance where a foolish policy can be traced to lawyerly overreaching, countless others can be found where legal counsel

helped to moderate the single-ended prescriptions of "professional" ideologies, to educate naive and superficial "management" analysts, or to countervail the latent cynicism of social science interpretations. In fact, there is much administrative knowledge in the inherited wisdom of the legal mind. The conditions and limits of authority, the variety and the problems of decision procedures, the dilemmas posed by conflicting ends, the maintenance of objectivity in moral and policy debate, and the art of principled judgment are all matters to which law cultivates a special alertness. Public institutions cannot do without this kind of sensibility. Perhaps lawyers—and those who study them—should worry more about how to train that sensibility than about how people will sue when hurt by insensitive "experts" in administration. General and elusive as they are, these qualities of mind may in the end be the main, if not the only, enduring contribution lawyers can make to the competence of public services.

NOTES

1. L. L. Jaffe, "Administrative Law," in *Talks on American Law,* edited by Harold J. Berman (New York: Vintage Books, 1961), p. 122.
2. K. C. Davis, *Administrative Law Text* (St. Paul: West Publishing Co., 1959), p. 2.
3. Among the chief documents of the period are Edgar S. Cahn and Jean C. Cahn, "The War on Poverty: A Civilian Perspective," *Yale Law Journal* 73 (1964): 1317; Charles Reich, "The New Property," *Yale Law Journal* 73 (1964): 233; Jerome E. Carlin, Jan Howard, and Sheldon L. Messinger, "Civil Justice and the Poor," *Law and Society Review* 2 (1966): 9.
4. The origins and formative years of the program are discussed in Earl Johnson, Jr., *Justice and Reform* (New York: Russell Sage Foundation, 1974).
5. This evolution is reviewed in Richard Stewart, "The Reformation of American Administrative Law," *Harvard Law Review* 88 (1975): 1966.
6. The phrase "creeping legalism" is from Lon L. Fuller, "Two Principles of Human Association," in *Voluntary Associations,* edited by J. Roland Pennock and John W. Chapman (New York: Atherton Press, 1969), p. 3.
7. Nathan Glazer, "Towards an Imperial Judiciary?" *The Public Interest* (Fall 1975): 104. See also Donald Horowitz, *The Courts and Social Policy* (Washington, D.C.: Brookings Institution, 1977).
8. L. H. Silberman, "Will Lawyering Strangle Democratic Capitalism," *Regulation* (March and April 1978), p. 15.
9. Op. cit., p. 15.
10. Examples are R. M. Titmuss, "Welfare Rights, Law and Discretion," *Political Quarterly* 42 (1971): 113; Nathan Glazer, "Should Judges Administer Social Services?" *The Public Interest* (Winter 1978), p. 64; Gary Bellow: "A Paradox of Due Process," *5 Working Papers for a New Society* (Spring 1977), p. 8; J. S. Fuerst and Roy Petty, "Bleak Housing in Chicago," *The Public Interest* (Summer 1978), p. 103.
11. A. V. Dicey, *Introduction to the Law of the Constitution* (London: Macmillan, 1885, 1961), pp. 328–405.

12. Georges Ripert, *Le declin du droit* (Paris, 1949).
13. The most famous case is *Lochner* v. *New York,* 198 U.S. 45 (1905), famous mostly for the dissent of Justice O. W. Holmes.
14. L. L. Fuller, "Two Principles of Human Association," p. 13.
15. A classic statement of that view is James Landis, *The Administrative Process* (New Haven: Yale University Press, 1938).
16. A. V. Dicey, *Introduction to the Law of the Constitution* (London: Macmillan, 1885, 1961), pp. 328–405.
17. L. L. Fuller, "Two Principles of Human Association," p. 21.
18. The distrust of discretion is a leitmotiv of Kenneth Culp Davis, *Discretionary Justice* (Baton Rouge: Louisiana State University Press, 1969).
19. The phrase was coined by Edmond Cahn, "Law in the Consumer Perspective," *University of Pennsylvania Law Review* 112 (1963): 1.
20. A broader statement of the perspective underlying this discussion is Philippe Nonet and Philip Selznick, *Law and Society in Transition: Toward Responsive Law* (New York: Harper Colophon Books, 1978).
21. E. Burke, "Speech to the Electors of Bristol, November 1774," in *Works,* 3rd ed. (Boston: Little, Brown, 1869), vol. II, pp. 81–98.
22. Ph. B. Kurland, *The Quality of Inequality* (Chicago: University of Chicago Press, 1968); David Kirp, "School Desegregation and the Limits of Legalism," *The Public Interest* (Spring 1977), p. 101.
23. E. Bardach and L. Pugliaresi, "The Environmental Impact Statement versus the Real World," *The Public Interest* (Fall 1977), p. 22.
24. M. Johnson, *Counterpoint: The Changing Employment Service* (Salt Lake City: Olympic Publishing Co., 1973).
25. B. Ackerman et al., *The Uncertain Search for Environmental Quality* (New York: Free Press, 1974), p. 221.
26. J. F. Handler, "Controlling Official Behavior in Welfare Administration," *California Law Review* 54 (1966): 479.
27. L. L. Fuller, *The Morality of Law* (New Haven: Yale University Press, 1964), pp. 3–32.
28. Ph. Nonet, *Administrative Justice: Advocacy and Change in a Government Agency* (New York: Russell Sage Foundation, 1970).
29. C. D. Stone, *Where the Law Ends: The Social Control of Corporate Behavior* (New York: Harper and Row, 1975). This work discusses the limits of law in the regulation of private administrative contexts.
30. A. Chayes, "The Role of the Judge in Public Law Litigation," *Harvard Law Review* 89 (1976): 1281; and Richard B. Stewart, "The Reformation of American Administrative Law," *Harvard Law Review* 88 (1975): 1669.
31. An outstanding example is the study of B. Ackerman et al., *The Uncertain Search for Environmental Quality* (New York: Free Press, 1974), p. 221.

Chapter 15

Some Conditions Restricting Innovativeness of Legal Services in Germany

Erhard Blankenburg

Some classical legal sociologists as well as many legal historians present the history of law as an evolution of ever-increasing formalism and positivism. Max Weber ordered legal systems into steps of development from charismatic prophetism as the source of law to the case and precedence law of elite notables, ranking the systematic codification of law by the legal profession as the "highest" state of evolution. Niklas Luhmann uses an evolutionary theory of ever-increasing differentiation in society as a descriptive as well as a normative reason for increasing positivism (i.e., legitimation by the legal procedures of legislation and changeability as a result thereof).

Although such theories most often refer to the way in which legal norms are formulated and legitimized, there is a parallel evolutionary thesis for the use of litigation for conflict resolution. According to this theory, with increasing urbanization and mobility informal means of conflict resolution are replaced by formal means, the courts being the most prominent example. Indeed, the number of court cases increases in direct proportion to the degree of urbanization in the countries studied. However, as much as this theory holds true for a structural comparison at a specific time, it does not necessarily hold true for comparisons over a long time. Some authors concluded from overall

court data that there is a "breaking point" in the frequency of litigation in postindustrial societies as compared to industrial societies. However, observations of this effect are based on insufficient court statistics; they would presuppose a broader effort in comparative court studies, which would break down the litigation figures by the types of courts and types of cases. My own observation of German courts indicates growing litigation rates for some issues and constant rates for others, without a universal explanation for these trends.

Much of this controversy amounts to "grand theorizing" and is hard to validate. In addition, our hypotheses lack the comparative dimensions to justify generalizations across national legal cultures. In this chapter I shall give some suggestions as to the direction and operationalization that the formulation of hypotheses may take. The question of whether or not there is a development away from litigation as a response to some of the challenges of postindustrial societies might find contradictory responses. Any such trend may show a different form, depending on the legal culture in which it manifests itself.

TWO CHALLENGES OF POSTINDUSTRIAL SOCIETIES

The challenges of postindustrial societies can be characterized as increasingly replacing informal ways of insuring against life risks by formal means. With a loss of the economic functions of the family, there is an increasing dependence of the individual upon larger organizations, such as social security, health insurance, and unemployment benefits. Lower social classes are especially deprived of the possibilities of attaining their rights from public administration, large cmployers, or housing corporations. Institutions and big business have more frequently used courts against private parties than individuals have mobilized the law in their own defense. Lawyers are ill-prepared to advise the poor of their needs, having been traditionally preoccupied with the legal problems of the property-owning middle classes.

Regarding the legal system as an institution for solving conflicts between individuals who are basically equal has repeatedly been proven incorrect. There are too many economic and social costs and barriers to overcome before a personalized conflict can be brought to court. Courts are usually invoked if a conflict refers to an anonymous social relation; in a personal relationship, invoking the law is almost tantamount to ending the relationship.

Courts are not a major institution through which social weakness is compensated. In most civil lawsuits they function as debt collectors and

rule enforcers for (big) organizations. Thus, the courts are in many respects a part of organized society instead of a countervailing power to it. However, such a statement does not always hold true; it has to be substantiated by research into the particular types of courts and the types of cases, a task that raises a number of theoretical as well as operational problems. Nevertheless, we wish to state a general hypothesis that a system of codified law, such as that which exists in Germany, is better prepared to protect the interests of individuals by means of court litigation than the traditional American system of case law, which therefore calls for the development of alternative institutions for conflict resolution.

A second challenge to courts in postindustrial societies arises from what has been called "diffuse interest" cases. Consumer protection, pollution control, and industrial and urban planning are all collective issues. They affect interests shared by larger social groups, but they are not vital enough for any one individual to make the costs of litigation worthwhile or even feasible. The American "class action" suit is a model for making such issues judiciable; law firms specializing in public interest litigation meet some of the challenges of diffuse interest situations. Our second hypothesis is that the lawyer-centered American legal system, with its adversary procedural tradition, is better prepared to meet such challenges, while the judge-centered German legal system, with its patriarchal procedural tradition, is more likely to develop responses by governmental regulation. I shall elaborate on these hypotheses in the following pages.

IN-COURT ALTERNATIVES TO A LEGAL DECISION

The statistics of the German and American legal profession give some rough, but obvious indicators about the differences between the two legal cultures. Both countries have approximately the same number of legally trained people per capita. However, in the United States three-fourths of all jurists are practicing lawyers. In Germany the legal profession consists of four groups that used to be about equal in size:

Judges
Lawyers
Civil servants
Employees of private firms

Every fifth member of the profession is a judge; every fourth jurist

works as a civil servant in the public administration. The group of jurists engaged by private firms has traditionally been as large as that of practicing lawyers. However, in recent years, admissions to the bar have risen, leading to fears that increasing competition might threaten the norms of conduct of lawyers. That practicing lawyers outnumber each of the three other groups is a recent phenomenon; they now represent about one-third of the legal profession. In spite of these recent changes, the German legal profession is still characterized by an almost equal distribution of jurists in the private and public sectors. Furthermore, legal training centers around the role of the judge, whose tenured career begins immediately upon termination of his legal studies.

The emphasis on the judge's role is reflected in some of the features of procedural law. German court procedures are dominated by the judge whose role is more active than his or her counterpart in the American adversary system. In civil as well as in criminal courts, the German judge is obliged to fully investigate all the facts pertaining to the case. In this investigation, the judge does not rely upon the arguments presented by either the concerned parties or the legal counsel, but prepares the case and especially the oral proceedings upon the basis of well-documented files and briefs. Observation of the courts shows a variety of behavior by judges, ranging from authoritarian to patriarchal, but rarely does it show a judge allowing the parties or the legal counsel to dominate the course of the oral proceedings.

The combination of these characteristics serves to explain why the American legal system has to look for additional alternatives to litigation in court. The reasons are related to the deficiencies of the American court system that act as barriers to litigation. The great number of lawyers, their relative freedom to advertise their services (which now has been legalized), and the possibilities of arranging for contingency fees all make the "input organization" of the litigation system very strong. On the other hand, the limited personnel in the courts leads to delays that act as a barrier to filing cases for litigation. Although complaints are heard in Germany about delays in court as well as the costs of cases, this problem is not nearly as serious as in the American courts. Thus the pressure to look for alternatives for conflict resolution is much lower in Germany. Even among businessmen, court settlements can be cheaper and more expedient than having a mediator take up the case (with the possible continuation of the case to a judicial decision). This explains not only why fewer alternative forms of conflict resolution are considered, but it also explains why German courts are often seen as a mediatory institution in which

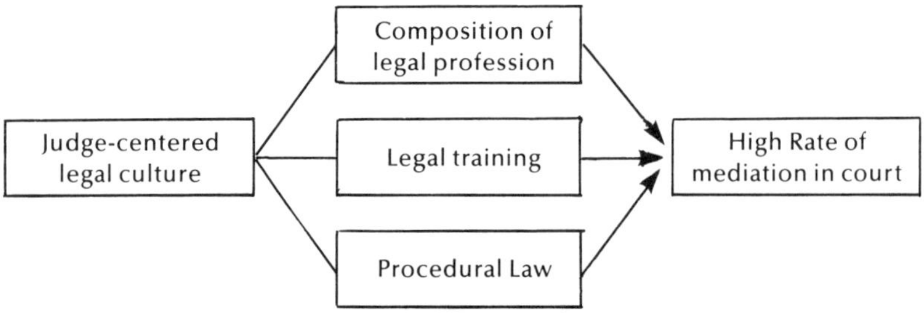

Figure 15.1

settlements can be reached with the help of a judge. The predominant pattern of reaching settlements in a German court involves the judge as a mediator within the procedural setting; the equivalent of it in the American legal setting takes place as pretrial bargaining.

The paternalistic behavior patterns of German judges reinforce the tendency to reach a settlement; because procedural law grants them investigatory powers, the judges very often assume a mediatory role during the oral proceedings. Our observational studies show that in acting as mediators as well as adjudicators, the judges are able to consider extralegal factors and consequences. This would not be possible if their sole function were to arrive at a legally correct decision. Thus, extralegal institutions of conflict resolution, which might lead to alternative forms of institutionalization in the United States, are built-in components of the oral proceedings in German courts. Therefore, in characterizing the German legal culture as being judge-centered and the American legal culture as being lawyer-centered, we refer to the large number of judges in Germany and the predominance of lawyers in the American legal profession as well as to differences in their procedural roles and to the orientation of the legal training. We see these differences as being related to a higher degree of mediation by judges in German courts as opposed to a higher degree of pretrial bargaining and adjudication in American courts (see Figure 15.1).

ALTERNATIVES TO COURT PROCEEDINGS IN DIFFUSE INTEREST ISSUES

There is a functional relationship between the dominance of lawyers in the American legal profession and the fact that the scope of their activities extends beyond that of German lawyers. Some of the functions American lawyers have in registering real estate or building

contracts are partly administrative and partly court responsibilities in Germany. German lawyers do not have any authority to question witnesses in cases that they represent in court, and they rarely enter into extensive investigations such as American lawyers do. Just as they are more passive in court sessions, so are they less active outside of court in looking for cases and in organizing ways of presenting their clients' interests. German lawyers are more restricted to handling legal matters; they do not provide all-around services for their clients as some American lawyers do. Again, we may argue that there is a correspondence between the comparatively small number of lawyers in Germany, the limited authority given them by the procedural code, and the restricted understanding that they have of their functions. These factors can explain why public interest lawyers are nonexistent, and they might also explain why legal possibilities to bring diffuse interest cases before the courts—such as the American class action suit—are unknown in German law.

These are some of the reasons in German legal culture that explain why product liability and consumer protection issues are less developed than in the United States. German legal culture makes it very difficult to organize such diffuse interests. Extralegal movements have developed in recent years around issues such as town planning and protests against nuclear power plants. They have largely used symbolic political means by organizing issue campaigns and mass demonstrations. The campaigns usually involve some symbolic legal issues that are brought before administrative courts. Local administrative decisions such as construction permits, the control of antipollution requirements, or the observance of residual participation rights of citizens to be affected by town planning can be contested only by an individual who has been affected by such decisions.

Politicizing such issues by using legal strategies (among others) confronts an administrative culture that in Germany is largely bound by legal regulations. While American agencies often have discretion in lower-level decisions, German administration has traditionally been legally bound by a cascade of federal laws supplemented by executive guidelines issued by the states, which can be used to challenge administrative decisions in court. Recently there has been a sharp increase in cases brought before administrative courts, most of which deal with regulations restricting access to universities or cases concerning town planning or construction permits. Lower-level judges tend to decide in favor of the individual more frequently than do the administrative agencies.

This increased mobilization of administrative courts has had an effect on the administration as well as on legislation. Town planners

and also industrial investors start out with campaigns of their own, thus opening up possibilities of early participation that might render legal action unnecessary at a later stage. At the same time, administrators look for ways to avoid decisions that would bring them into political conflicts. Attempts are being made to let legislative bodies on the local and regional levels decide on town planning and industrial investment, making it impossible to involve administrative courts. Thus the burden of decisionmaking will rest with the political parties. We can see this movement as a result of a legally bound administrative culture; that is, a narrow range of administrative discretion and a high degree of control over administrative decisions lead to the incapacity of such a system to decide in cases of collective interest conflicts. Therefore, alternatives are being sought in the direction of participatory decision processes.

> A model for participation as an alternative to adversary conflict resolution might be seen in the German "Mitbestimmung" in industrial conflicts: recruitment as well as dismissals of employees, changes of occupational status due to rationalization as well as changes in work rules have to pass the works councils in plants and firms. Even if these do not have veto powers, but only informative rights, such participation leads to anticipation of protest and early bargaining. Once a decision is taken, works councils and thereby trade unions are so involved in the conflicts that they cannot avoid helping to legitimize them.
>
> Comparing labor conflicts in Germany with those of other countries reveals a high degree of conflict anticipation, which correlates to the German notion of "legality" as a means of avoiding adversary conflicts. It shows one of the preconditions of participatory conflict management. The collective interests in industrial disputes are well organized. Individuals can leave the representation of their interests in the hands of functionaries, thus allowing them to develop patterns of oligarchical cooperation.

If alternatives to legal strategies in diffuse interest issues are to have any chance of success in a legal and administrative culture such as Germany's, they would have to organize interest representation. If our hypothesis holds true, German administration is likely to promote the organization of such interests in order to free itself of the burden of legitimizing controversial decisions, but it is not likely to develop mobilization of the courts for collective action on a large scale. It is most likely to choose "governmental" alternatives as opposed to class actions in court, which in our opinion as well as that of many observers results

Figure 15.2

in reducing the innovative capacity of the German legal system when compared to the American public interest movement.(see Figure 15.2).

However, what the legal profession is lacking in innovativeness is substituted by legal accountability of the administration. There is no administrative decision that might not be challenged in court by those who are affected. As is the case with the legal regulation of the "Mitbestimmung," German institutions internalize protest much more than their counterparts in Anglo-Saxon countries do. This, however, means that all interests that are not organized are left with legal procedures that do not provide incentives for responsiveness. Whoever wants to challenge an administrative decision has to do so in the proper ways of administrative complaint or litigation in the administrative courts. Not knowing how to handle such a legal procedure is a serious handicap for any form of influence by the clients of the administration. As there is no tradition of active issue campaigns by lawyers, there is not much encouragement to do so from the legal system. Thus, internalizing protest within institutions seems to have the effect of legitimizing administrative power (in the sense of the belief in legality that Max Weber described) more than in making the administration more responsive.

Chapter 16

The Issue of Delegalization

Paul Geerts

In this chapter I will attempt to answer two questions. First, why are social problems (conflicts) and interests legalized, that is, why do they become formulated in a way that a legal solution may be chosen to resolve or to realize them? And, secondly, what are the consequences (and merits) of such a "legalization"? It is obvious that a full consideration of all aspects of both questions (which, in fact, asks for a theory of "law in a modern society") goes far beyond the scope of this chapter. I only wish to trace some basic guidelines for further research.

I do not intend to treat the subject from the approach of an "access to justice"; which implies that an increase, diversification, and reform of legal services delivery systems do not suffice to guarantee an "equal access to justice," or what Galanter calls an equal distribution of "legality." We need, the argument continues, new systems for processing disputes (informal, etc.), neighborhood justice centers, and more responsive government agencies.[1] These approaches at least have the advantage of not considering legal services as the deus ex machina, which, if only correctly assembled, will restore equality to the legal system.

However, these proposals do not question the merits as such of a legal strategy in solving social problems. They look only for alternative

solutions to already legalized problems and interests, for ways of facilitating access to the law, and for making this access more equal. In fact, most of them still do look for a deus ex machina.

THE CONCEPT OF "LEGAL NEEDS" OR "LEGAL PROBLEMS"

There is no difference between the meaning of these concepts, although "problem" seems to be less "subjective" than "need." The type of analysis I propose and the questions I want to answer are the result of a problematization of the concepts of legal need and of legal problems.

Until recently, research has been concentrated on these concepts. It was assumed that they were neutral concepts that could be defined in an objective way. Researchers in several countries tried to measure and list legal needs and problems, often assuming that if these needs were not met, or these problems not solved, there was a (unmet) need for legal services.[2] As Marks rightly states, "the paradigm of legal need implicitly held in most of the early surveys is: persons who encounter a problem that others routinely have taken to lawyers, have an unfulfilled need for the services of lawyers."[3]

A further assumption was often made that legal problems need to be multiplied, especially among the poor. The eradication of poverty becomes reducible to defining the problems of the poor as legal problems, and thus open to a final solution in courts.[4]

The most recent, and I think the most sophisticated, study of unmet legal needs was done in the Netherlands by Schuyt, Groenendijk, and Sloot.[5] These authors extracted from the existing research four basic explanatory strategies, "four sociological theories on the lack in legal services":[6]

Economic resources theory: unequal access to legal services is determined by the available wealth (income and property).

Sociosychological resources theory: need is determined by a set of sociopsychological qualities.

Participation theory: the degree to which one participates in the socioeconomical life and the legal risks one has to face are emphasized; poor people have fewer legal problems, and thus they have less need for a lawyer.

The organization theory: The gap between needs and legal services is attributed to the selective attention that the bar pays to specific legal problems, that is, problems of property and contract.

Schuyt and others combine these elements.[7] The lack of legal aid can be explained by considering three elements: the type of legal problem, the particular people involved, and the characteristics of the legal services available. Such a model accepts the idea that a problem becomes legal because it is defined as such by the legal profession and because a specific legal solution to the problem is presented. This means that the authors accept that a legal problem as such is not given, but rather is the result of a certain type of organization of the legal system and the delivery of legal services.

Such circular reasoning or tautology (legal problem—delivery of legal services—legal problem) falsifies the problems we face because it suggests that a better delivery system of legal services is the solution.[8] Indeed, if we accept that there is a set of problems that are legal "by definition," or defined as such by the respondents to a questionnaire, our analysis becomes superfluous; if a problem is legal, the solution has to be legal, too.

Mayhew[9] reacts rightly in a recent article against the idea that there are claims and rights "which fail to be met because legal services are unavailable." He writes:

> Neither surveys of the experiences of the public nor the patterns of cases brought to legal agencies produce a particularly valid measure of the "legal needs" of the citizenry, needs for legal services and opportunities for beneficial legal action cannot be enumerated as if they were too many diseases or injuries in need of treatment. Rather, we have a vast array of disputes, disorders, vulnerabilities, and wrongs which contain an enormous potential for generating legal actions. Whether any given situation becomes defined as a "legal" problem, or, even if so defined, makes its way to an attorney or other agency for possible aid or redress, is a consequence of the social organization of the legal system and the organization of the larger society—including shifting current of social ideology, the available legal machinery, and the channels for bringing perceived injustices to legal agencies.

According to this view, the "legal nature" of a problem becomes questionable. It becomes a variable that can be "manipulated" to a certain extent.[10] Developing a "legal strategy" becomes a matter of choosing one of a number of possible strategies. We may question the mechanism by which certain types of problems become legal (especially property related matters as explained by Mayhew), or under certain circumstances, we can push for further legalization if we are convinced of its merits. If the rent or the electricity rates increase, we could

challenge the increases with legal arguments, and perhaps eventually go to court. We could, however, also try to organize a rent strike.[11]

The mobilization of the legal system to solve a problem or a conflict is in this sense not so much an answer to a legal need as it is a conscious strategy to solve the problem, taking into account all the circumstances of the situation. Formulated in this way, the problem is not to determine what kinds of unmet legal needs exist and how they may be met. Rather, the question then becomes to consider the merits of a legal strategy in solving problems and how to mobilize the law for this purpose. The problem is not to gain "access to the law," but to "mobilize the legal system." "Access" is only a part of this process.

It should be clear that this approach no longer considers the individual, with his or her perceived "unmet needs" and "unsolved problems" as a starting point for research on the delivery of legal services, but instead considers the delivery system itself and, in a broader sense, the organization of the legal system (*le droit*). For example, Marks states,

> Our approach to legal services delivery systems has focused for too long on the client, to the neglect of the lawyer. How society selects, educates, socializes, and organizes its lawyers are relevant questions about legal services delivery systems.[12]

Nader's[13] remarks on the subject are relevant:

> The merger of consumerism and legal services needs to be treated with a sensitivity to the functions of formal legal services, an awareness of the shortcomings of our legal system as presently structured, and with a realization that some problems are amenable to solution only through a redistribution of power and wealth in the society. . . . We in the legal profession too often tend to see legal problems in terms of individualized justice—in terms of an individual tenant, an individual consumer, or an individual laborer, with a particular grievance that can be resolved by pursuing an individual "case" if only that case can somehow be engaged by the legal system. The concentration has alway been on "access," how do people get access to the legal system. . . . I find a great difference between the concept of access and the concept of power. . . . If we are going to make access meaningful, it has to be part of a general redistribution of legal, political, social, and economic power.

On a theoretical level, we can further develop this idea, using the recent works of Illich (on the link between professionalism and "induced" needs) and the writing of Heller (on the marxist theory of "Bedürfnis").

WHY ARE CERTAIN PROBLEMS LEGALIZED?

My preliminary remarks may be summarized as follows:

> Need will be seen as relative, and it may then be useful to point out how, and why, in specific situations, one set of definitions (or combination of definitions) prevails over others, and to illustrate the way in which this relates to the authority structure in society, since the definition of need likely to be adopted in terms of the service provided will reflect the power and status of those providing the service rather than the definition of those receiving it.[14]

Therefore, two elements and their interrelationship become central—the legal profession and "the authority structure in society." In view of the "dynamic role that lawyers play in the creation of legal problems,"[15] we must now define how and why this occurs. My thesis is that changes in the delivery of legal services will generate new legal problems or, at least, will bring more people to define their problems as legal. I will try to explain why these innovations have occurred and also refute the legal needs–legal problems theory.

I will argue that they might be considered a consequence of the struggle between segments of the legal profession.[16] This is of considerable interest, both on a theoretical and a practical level. From a theoretical point of view, it enables us to surpass the equation of legal needs with legal problems. And it is of practical importance to question the "professionalization"[17] of a particular field of social conflicts. This again may have consequences in changing the legal profession itself. The legal profession, however, although a necessary factor, is not in itself a sufficient explanation.

The history of legal aid shows that innovations have always occurred in times of rapid social change. We also have to consider and to appraise the function of law in our society. In the final section of this chapter, I will discuss this function briefly and schematically as well as indicate the direction in which research on this point might be continued. The emphasis in this chapter, however, is on the legal profession.

THE LEGAL PROFESSION

As already mentioned, I will use a segmentation approach to the legal profession. This approach has been primarily developed by

Bucher and Strauss[18] and Bucher[19] who consider the "professions as loose amalgamations of segments pursuing different objectives in different manners and more or less delicately held together under a common name at a particular period in history." It is clearly a reaction to the functionalist approach to the profession as an occupational community based on consensus.

Mok[20] indicates three basic conditions of segmentation, the most general of which is the duality of every occupation; that is, every occupational system creates an antisystem. An example of this duality is the concentration of one segment mainly on the development of knowledge (theory), whereas the other segment applies this knowlege (practice). A second, more specific condition is the increasing division of labor, which leads to specialization and thus to horizontal segmentation.[21] The third, and most specific, condition is the inability of the professional mechanisms of control to make the ideology of the professional community acceptable to all members.[22] Mok[23] refers to the Dutch and Belgian law shops as the possible "seed for segmentation of the legal profession." The way in which segmentation affects the delivery of legal services can be shown by analyzing two aspects of the legal profession—the economic requirements of the profession and the "myth of rights" as part of the lawyers "world view."

Market Requirements

We can develop this argument, which is typical of the organized profession though not limited to it, along two lines:

First, lawyer's skills are mainly concentrated on property-related matters,[24] areas in which there is a good chance of making money.[25] This explains to a certain extent why certain fields are legalized and others are not, or more exactly, why a legal solution is offered and used for certain types of problems (this refers to Mayhew's problem-solving patterns).

For instance, it is a well-known phenomenon that lawyers, even though they present themselves as "generalists," are, in fact, specialists. In a small country such as Belgium (or the Netherlands) with a much less stratified bar than the United States or England, we see a very strong tendency toward specialization. According to Cardijn-De Salle,[26] Belgian lawyers are specialized in:

1. Commercial and company law
2. Inheritance, bankruptcy, and divorce law
3. Social law (labor law and social security law)

And in Brussels, an international commercial center, the lawyers are specialized in:

1. Commercial and company law
2. Insurance and liability
3. Inheritance, bankruptcy, and divorce law (idem, pp. 52–53)[27]

Excluding inheritance law and divorce (which are a traditional lucrative field for lawyers), we can state without exaggeration that lawyers are most interested in the fields in which organizations rather than individuals are concerned.[28] For Griffiths,[29] this is a variation on the "resource impetus," that is, only organizations are capable of paying lawyers' fees on a regular basis. The high number of lawyers specializing in social law does not change this fact because these lawyers work for trade unions, the social security administration, or for business. A specialization not mentioned by Cardijn-De Salle, but also very important, is automobile injury claims. In Belgium, this may be explained by the fact that most car owners have legal aid insurance,[30] and in the United States by the fact that probably most lawyers work for "contingency fees."[31]

Critiques on this unilateral specialization were (and arc) made especially from within the profession. I believe that they are used as a lever for extension (or redistribution) of the market and for the creation of new job opportunities by different segments of the profession. Although I do not want to suggest that innovations in legal services can be explained completely by the economic interests of(some segments of) the organized legal profession, a strenghtening of these interests has always been the result. As noted by Bankowski and Mungham:[32]

> Although solicitors speak of a "service," it is a service given entirely on their terms. The concept of "public interest" is still one defined by lawyers and by no-one else. Lawyers set about defining the "public interest" and then think of the best way they can "satisfy" it. In other words, the limits of the so-called "public interest" come to correspond mysteriously with the ability of the profession to "serve" this "interest." The claim to "know" the public interest is, of course, inseparable from the legal profession's claim to a special knowledge and expertise.

Indeed, lawyers are often prompted by political ideals or philanthropic motives and are sincerely convinced of the importance of these innovations to the so-called public interest. We might particularly refer to some developments of the last twenty years in which segments of the legal profession were influenced by and became involved in several

social reform movements, which gave rise to new professional models and ideologies.[33]

In the United States, this culminated in the neighborhood law firms, developed under the War on Poverty, and in the public interest law movement. In Great Britain, it gave rise to the Neighborhood (or Community) Law Centers, in Holland and Belgium to the law shops, and in Norway to the Juss Buss. I consider these institutions as very valuable innovations or experiments, or both, although their potential for social reform (and sometimes even their origins)[34] can be questioned. The argument is as follows:

> Given the fact that "social reform" lawyers pointed to a particular client group (roughly "the poor" or "the disadvantaged") and sometimes developed alternative methods, they needed external support, both for money and for legitimacy. As they did not occupy powerful positions—they were in fact a tiny minority within the powerful organized profession—they had only the force of their arguments. Their arguments were heard because many young jurists were active in several governmental administrations and because they were involved in governmental programs such as the War on Poverty or the Community Development Program.
>
> One set of arguments ("the myth of rights") was widely shared by the whole profession, or at least it was very useful to it, as I will argue. The second set of arguments, a critique on the actual functioning of the legal profession, was supported by a growing number of legal need studies and by academic jurists. These arguments could be very well used by lawyers who, without the political or humanitarian motives of the "social reform" lawyers, were in search of new job opportunities, market extension, and redistribution of work within the profession.
>
> Smith and Thomas (1977) and Bankowski and Mungham (1976) describe how public funds and support were used to these ends in the duty solicitor scheme, which was above all a restructuring and extension of the legal job market. To break down a monopoly of criminal cases by a few law firms (the "barons"), other segments used the service argument and public funds. Official bar policies, which are in general defined by the higher ranks of the organized profession, were probably to a great extent inspired by a need for legitimization, although the so-called higher ranks recognized the financial advantages of *some* innovations.
>
> This phenomenon is described by Bellow, with specific reference to the issue of creating publicity, and by Bankowski and Mungham,[35] with reference to the duty solicitor scheme. Although *power* is a central issue

in the concept of legitimization,[36] *knowledge*[37] and the notion of *public service*[38] are also important factors.

If the profession is under attack on the basis of these two elements, the legitimacy of the profession as such is then in danger. Different reactions are possible. The bar can try to deny both of these criticisms and the results of legal needs studies.[39] Or it can challenge the legitimacy of the innovators, involving the "incompetence" of the social reform lawyers, the high ethical standards of the profession, and the guarantee this includes for the client in terms of responsibility, independence, and discipline.[40]

This strategy is often combined with other new proposals that do not challenge the professional interests or model.[41] If this strategy fails, because of popular governmental or scientific support, or both, for the innovations or because the innovators are independent of professional control (e.g., law students in the law shops), a modus vivendi can be worked out. It consists of a conditional acceptance of the innovations plus a division of labor between the "alternative" and "traditional" segments of the organized profession. We can refer to the analysis of Peters (1974), who called the legal services provided by the Dutch law shops "additional" instead of "alternative," and who warned of the fact that the legal profession could thus avoid a redefinition of its role and function. The history of the British Neighborhood Law Center is another good example.

In exchange for waivers from the Law Society (or for reasons of principle), the neighborhood law centers refused cases and clients that could be served by private solicitors, thus increasingly involving them in the legal aid scheme.

Second, the organized legal profession looks for new job opportunities, especially if there is a decrease in its normal activities. This is the way Smith and Thomas (1977) explain the growth of duty solicitor schemes in Cardiff (Wales). The same phenomenon is described by Widdiss[42] in Massachusetts, which occurred after the introduction of a no-fault insurance compensation plan for road accidents. When a large number of young people enter the profession, we see a similar movement, which is eventually achieved by curtailing other professionals[43] or by statutory legalization. It is striking, for example, that discussions on legal aid in Belgium are always accompanied (and mainly motivated) by concern with the financial problems of young lawyers. This is not a new phenomenon, as the following quotation shows:

> At its annual meeting in 1933 the Association of American Law Schools considered at length the economic condition of the Bar. The questions

> asked concerned not merely the welfare of the lawyers, but also the service they were rendering to the public. . . . The Committee interpreted its obligation as primarily that of working out a methodology for conducting surveys of the bar which . . . should show how the needs of the commuity for legal service were being met.[44]

How does the organized profession gain support for the implementation of or resistance to legal services delivery systems and in general for changes in the legal system? This would require an analysis of the organized legal profession as a pressure group.[45]

Although I do not intend to develop such an analysis, it might be useful to discuss at least some elements that are of particular interest. The legal profession "occupies a unique political and social position in the community,"[46] which results in a "proverbial"[47] overrepresentation of lawyers in Parliament and in the civil service professions.[48] This makes lobbying by the organized legal profession highly efficient. A large number of members of Parliament and civil servants are former lawyers or at least share the same beliefs (which from a particular point of view can be called "the myth of rights").

"The Legal profession," writes Morris[49] "controls access to the formal processes of adjudication, and, because of the interaction [between them, it controls] the judicial, the legislative and administrative bodies as well."[50] Alcock[51] provides some data on the "close relationship" of the Law Society to the Lord Chancellor's Office in matters concerning legal aid. And it might be easy to find similar relations in other countries, or at least, to prove the predominance of the legal profession in the development of legal services. Because the influence of the legal profession is closely linked with the appeal it makes for the myth of rights and the so-called public interest, legitimization becomes a central issue.[52]

Furthermore, the political strength of the organized profession lies in its role as implementer of legal aid schemes.[53] If the organized legal profession has to have a key function in providing legal aid (as is generally assumed), a certain degree of cooperation between innovators and traditionalists must be present before a scheme can be implemented.

The Myth of Rights

Lawyers, molded by their education and by the socialization process through which they have become "full" members of the organized profession,[54] are caught in the legal paradigm that is, in the words of

Scheingold,[55] at the core of the myth of rights: "a social perspective which perceives and explains human interaction largely in terms of rules and of the rights and obligations inherent in rules." This results in two overestimations—on the one hand, an overestimation of the "social engineering" function (or potency) of the law, and on the other hand an overaccentuation of the "access theme." The first overestimation is typical of the Law Centre and similar approaches; that is, the law is used as a means of eradicating poverty and of balancing power, in short, as a vehicle for social change. The second overestimation, in which access to the law becomes an end in itself, is typical of the more traditional and so-called liberal approaches to the legal services issue.

First Overestimation: Social Engineering. "Social engineering is an applied social science which informs the practitioner how to find effective means of realizing intended social goals when a given set of values is accepted and a given body of tested propositions describing human behavior is accessible."[56] Lawyers often use such a model in which the law becomes instrumental as a more or less efficient means of reform or of realizing policy issues, either in a progressive or a conservative sense. A careful analysis of the literature on neighborhood law offices and the early public interest law movement in the United States, on neighborhood or community law centers in Great Britain, on law shops in Holland and Belgium, and also on the "radical" movement of judges in France and Italy shows the importance and the dissemination of this "paradigm." Also worth mentioning is a very similar movement at the end of the nineteenth and beginning of the twentieth century in Europe. It became known under the name "socialisme juridique" or "Juristensozialismus," and it was represented in Germany by Menger, in Italy by Labriola, and in France by Andler, Mater, and Lévy.[57]

The aim of this movement was "to give to the class struggle a legal formular" (Lévy): "La socialisme juridique ne doit pas avoir pour but de déformer le collectivisme pour l'adapter au droit bourgeois, mais de manipuler le très souple droit bourgeois pour l'adapter au collectivisme."[58]

One of the means was the court. "L'idée générale du socialisme juridique . . . autorise le juge à faire en quelque sorte de la loi pour instaurer, par voie de soi-disant interprétation, un système juridique socialiste . . . (à la limite, c'est) du socialisme révolte contre le pouvoir législatif et même le pouvoir exécutif, autrement dit contre l'ordre social," is the evaluation of the famous French scholar Bonnecase.[59] It was also the period of "le bon juge Magnaud" in France, a judge who systematically favored the weak (women, the poor, and workers).[60]

This trend was quite influential in the Social Democratic workers movement of that time, which can be illustrated by the fact that the German Social Democrats referred in 1903 to the "eminent Viennese legal scholar Menger" to justify its electoral aims.[61] In France Andler was a close collaborator of the socialist leader Jean Jaurès. It should be interesting to see how the legal policies of trade unions were influenced by this trend, and what effect it had on their policies. In the last few years a renaissance of "legal socialism" can be noted, particularly in Germany.[62]

As the lawyers for social reform in the United States and in Europe and the so-called radical judges in France and Italy shared the same ideas, an examination of this tradition seems worthwhile. It also seems valuable from a theoretical point of view because one of the "classical" Marxian texts on law[63] is a very hard critique of Menger's "Das Recht auf den vollen Arbeitsertrag in geschichtlicher Darstellung."[64] Although I do not want to criticize this paradigm as such, I do want to indicate why a number of lawyers began with a certain type of practice. As research shows, their attempts at effecting substantial changes were not successful. This point will be further considered when evaluating the legalization of social problems.

Second Overestimation: The Access Theme. A model of law generally accepted among lawyers (at least as part of the professional ideology) considers the law (*le droit*) as a system of intrinsic values (let us say "justice") that, from a formal point of view, can be called "the rule of law" (Selznick and his school). Even those who do not agree with the ideals of justice (or ideology?) of our legal system generally do accept the basic features of the rule of law (especially characteristic of so-called political processes). Sometimes these ideals are also considered as a condition or as a lever for criticism of the functioning of legal systems.[65] As a result, the access to justice often becomes a goal in itself instead of a means of attaining that goal.

This model is an obvious factor in most approaches starting from the equality theorem; that is, the law pretends to be equal for everyone, and by giving people access to the law, we can realize this principle. This is expressed clearly by Cappelletti and Gordley:[66]

> The words "access to justice" . . . are not easily defined, but they serve to focus on two basic purposes of the legal system—the system by which people may vindicate their rights and/or resolve their disputes under the general auspices of the state. First, the system must be equally accessible to all, and second, it must lead to results that are individually

> and socially just. Our focus here will be primarily on the first component, access, but we will necessarily bear in mind the second. Indeed, a basic premise will be that social justice, as sought by our modern societies, presupposes effective access. [And further] Optimal effectiveness in the context of a given substantive law could be expressed as complete "equality of arms"—the assurance that the ultimate result depends only on the relative legal merits of the opposing positions, unrelated to the differences which are extraneous to legal strength and yet, as a practical matter, affect the assertion and vindication of legal rights. This perfect equality, of course, is utopian . . . ; the differences between parties can never be completely eradicated. The question is how far to push toward the utopian goal, and at what cost.

Although less obvious, this is also true of most of the literature emphasizing the importance of access in making rights effective. A further assumption, obvious in most of the literature of the public interest law movement, is that an implementation of the rule of law (for which access to the decisionmaking process is a central feature) will guarantee fair treatment or balance of power.[67] From this belief emerges the claim toward the "juridicialization" of every decision-making process.[68] Nader[69] warns of the limits of such an approach:

> We will raise the expectations of a whole generation only to have people realize that access is a very small part of the mechanism involved in bringing power to bear in institutional behavior.

Until now, I have argued that the legal profession had (and has) a crucial role in defining problems as legal problems (an approach comparable to the labeling theory in criminology) and in the organization of legal ways to process disputes. And although innovations in legal services are not a new concern,[70] an analysis of the innovations of the last twenty years will suffice to substantiate this thesis. The lobby for legal services is located within the legal profession itself.[71] These innovations were not a response to needs of the public, community, or neighborhood, but to needs perceived or induced by the profession. This mechanism is also seen when other professions define and handle exactly the same problems. A supposed legal problem becomes a psychiatric[72] or a medical problem,[73] depending on the profession involved.

Although this is an interesting theoretical issue, it should not be criticized on a practical level if the results are of value. If a problem or a conflict is solved in a satisfactory way, it does not matter in which terms

or by which profession it is achieved. But here again it is necessary to be critical. First, although much of the lawyers' attempts to increase the servicing and the representation of the weak and underrepresented members of society was done because of sincere philanthropic or political grounds (the myth of rights), it fitted in well with professional anxieties about new job opportunities,[74] market extension, legitimation of the legal profession, redistribution of work within the profession, and a bureaucratic device for a better functioning of the courts. If we can prove that the philanthropic and political reasons were primarily based on an overestimation of the myth of rights,[75] what remains is, above all, a strengthening of the legal profession.[76] This leads as well to a further dependency of already dependent people on a new "helping profession."[77]

Secondly, the legalization of social problems and conflicts can have, and often has had,[78] the consequence that a particular problem or conflict was reduced to "manageable" size,[79] and that its political aspects disappeared or were underestimated.[80] The legal strategy thus becomes a substitute for social reform (as noted by Scheingold[81]):

> . . . only those who accept the myth of rights could think seriously about an approach to change which is based exclusively on rights. Rights are no more than a political resource which can be deployed, primarily through litigation, to spark hopes and indignation.[82]

A further development of this argument in the last part of my analysis will show the dangers of this approach of improving a given "legal order." As stated by Alcock:[83]

> . . . (legal aid) was produced to justify ideologically the operation of the legal system, which was primarily concerned with property interests, by giving the appearance of making equal access to the legal system available to the lower classes.

THE ROLE OF LAW IN CAPITALIST SOCIETY

Following Morris, I use the term "authority structure" to indicate the structural elements in society that bring about the legalization of certain problems, interests, and conflicts. In other words, I pose the following question—what is the role of law in a capitalist society? I suggest a double approach:

Law as an ideological apparatus
Law as a mechanism of social control

Although these approaches overlap, a separate treatment seems indicated. Common to both approaches is that the law is considered in its formal aspect, as a distinct form of structuring social relations. The first approach focuses on the role of law guaranteeing the exchange of commodities in a capitalist society.[84] I will illustrate this argument with the analysis of Edelman (1973) and of Mayhew and Reiss (1969). Law as a mechanism, a tool of social control, emphasizes that laws are often used to control conflicts by reformulating them and by reducing them. This can be illustrated by the history of the worker movement and legal aid movements.[85]

There is a third approach to law, which goes beyond the previous models. Law as an ideological apparatus and as a mechanism of social control is not the emanation of one particular class or power group, but reflects to a certain extent the contradictory forces in our society.[86] Within certain limits (the so-called relative autonomy of the law), a legal strategy can further develop these contradictions. The basic lines of what Trubek (1977c) calls a "critical legal theory" can thus be traced.

On an empirical level, this evaluation must consider at least two sets of arguments. Galanter's analysis[87] will be very helpful in doing this.

> First, what were the consequences of the legal strategy adopted by trade unions almost a century ago (and more recently by consumer organizations) in dealing with working conditions, power relations in the modern capitalist society and with the structure and functioning of trade-unions? This will include an examination of historical material and an inquiry into the functioning and organization of the legal services of trade unions. Secondly, what are the results of innovations in the delivery of legal services over the last 20 years? This will focus on the disparity between programmatic ideals of those innovations and their realization (a typical feature of a good deal of American literature), and on the broader influence these programs have had from a professionalism-dependency point of view.

NOTES

1. M. Galanter, "Why the 'Haves' Come Out Ahead: Speculations on the Limits of Legal Change," *Law and Society Review* 9 (1974): 95ff; R. Lempert, "Mobilizing Private Law: An Introductory Essay," *Law and Society Review* 11 (1976): 173ff; R. Lempert, "Questions for Research," *Law and Society Review* 11 (1976): 387ff; L. Nader and L. R. Singer, "Dispute Resolution in the Future: What Are the Choices?"

California State Bar Journal 51 (1976): 281ff; also compare the small claims literature, e.g., B. Yngvesson and P. Hennessey, "Small Claims, Complex Disputes: A Review of the Small Claims Literature," *Law and Society Review* 9 (1975): 219ff. See also, R. Dantzig and M. J. Lowy, "Everyday Disputes and Mediation in the U.S.: A reply to Professor Felstiner," *Law and Society Review* 9 (1975): 675ff.

2. The identification of unmet legal needs with the need for legal services is striking in the Dutch translation of "unmet legal needs": "leemte in de rechtshul" meaning "Lack of legal services." "The definition of unmet need currently being used is that of the lawyer—legal problems are those problems for which there is at present a legal solution. By a relatively simple headcounting operation which determines how many people have such problems yet do not consult a lawyer, and which discovers to what socio-economic class they belong, it is argued that one can assess at least in a crude form, the extent and type of unmet need for legal services," writes P. Morris, "A Sociological Approach to Research in Legal Services," in *Social Needs and Legal Action* (London: 1973), pp. 51–52. See also P. Lewis, "Unmet Legal Needs," in *Social Needs and Legal Action* (London: 1973), p. 75. See also Z. Bankowski and G. Mungham, *Images of Law* (London: 1976), p. 39. For a critical discussion of these "unmet legal needs" studies, see F. R. Marks, "Some Research Perspectives for Looking at Legal Need and Legal Services Delivery Systems: Old Forms or New?" *Law and Society Review* 11 (1976): 191ff. See also J. E. Griffiths, "The Distribution of Legal Services in the Netherlands," *British Journal of Law and Society* 4 (1977): 260ff.
3. F. R. Marks, op. cit., p. 198.
4. As noted by Bankowski and Mungham, op.cit., p. 146: "The trouble with this view—which is one especially popular among 'liberal' lawyers and any legal professional anxious to push law to the people— is 1. it implies that the balm of law is an effective antidote for the inequalities generated by basic structural cleavages in society, and 2. that the 'law strategy' for conflict resolution and dispute settlement is the best." Both issues will be discussed at length in this chapter.
5. C. J. M. Schuyt; K. Groenendijk; and B. Sloot, *De Weg naar het Recht* (Deventer, 1976), pp. 18–35.
6. J. E. Griffiths, "The Distribution of Legal Services in the Netherlands," *British Journal of Law and Society* 4(1977): 260ff.
7. Schuyt et al., op. cit., 1976, pp. 281–291.
8. I will not stress the methodological problems one has to overcome in measuring "unmet" legal needs or problems. Griffiths, op. cit., p. 280, writes, " 'Access', 'need', 'legal problem' and the like are not empirical concepts because they refer not to things in the world but to judgements about things. There is nothing non-empirical about *feelings* of 'need', or *opinions* that one has a 'legal problem' etc. and still less about *statements* that one lacks 'access'. Feelings, opinions and statements exist in the sense that they can in principle be counted. Counting *statements about 'access'* is utterly different from measuring 'access'—a point that seems embarrassingly obvious and yet more often than not overlooked, as it is the most of the time, for example, by the authors of the present book" (i.e., the book by Schuyt et al.).
9. Mayhew, op. cit., 1975, p. 404.
10. Note, however, that Mayhew's analysis stresses the importance of "routine" in the perception of a problem as legal, and in the form of action developed. This will be a serious limitation to the "manipulation" we intend. See also J. M. Broekman, "Zietke en gezondheid als politieke begrippen," *De Nieuwe Maand* 18 (1975):

477ff.

11. See E. Cherki and M. Wieviorka, "Luttes sociales en Italie: les mouvements d'autor éduction à Turin," *Les temps Modernes* (1975): 1793ff. See E. Cherki and M. Wieviorka, "Luttes sociales en Italie: Magistrats et autor éducteurs." *Les Temps Modernes* (1976): 635ff. See J. M. Fitzgerald, "The Contract Buyers League and the Courts: A Case Study of Poverty Litigation," *Law and Society Review* 9 (1975) 165ff.
12. Marks, op. cit., p. 203. This theoretical shift can be compared with a similar change in European political theory. Until a few years ago, research on political movements and parties concentrated primarily on the members and voters and their various characteristics and affiliations as explanatory factors for the type of organization and their electoral success. Now, however, researchers focus more and more on structural factors; the party itself is analyzed in an attempt at explaining its impact on (potential) members and voters. For a similar attempt in the consumer field, see M. Wieviorka, *L'Etat, le Patronat et les Consommateurs* (Paris: 1977).
13. R. Nader, "Consumerism and Legal Services: The Merging of Movements," *Law and Society Review* 11 (1976): 247–249.
14. P. Morris, "A Sociological Approach to Research in Legal Services," in *Social Needs and Legal Action,* edited by P. Morris; R. White; and P. Lewis (London: Martin Robertson, 1973), p. 51.
15. R. Lempert, "Mobilizing Private Law: An Introductory Essay," *Law and Society Review* 11 (1976): 178.
16. By "legal profession," I mean all the people who have had a legal education, whether they work as a solicitor (lawyer), a judge, an academic, a civil servant, or as an employee of an organization. The word becomes a synonym for the French *jurist.* When I speak of lawyers (who are often considered *the* legal profession), I will use the term "organized legal profession," to indicate the more institutionalized features of that part of the profession (self-regulation and financial autonomy)—see A. L. Mok, *Beroepen in Aktie* (Meppel, 1973), pp. 54–55 and 85–89. This does not mean that the other parts of the profession lack organization or institutionalization!
17. For the different meanings professionalization has in the literature see Mok, op. cit., pp. 71–72. I use it here in the sense of an increased involvement of specialists in solving vital problems, a phenomenon that has roots in the technocratic model of "the end of ideologies."
18. R. Bucher and A. Strauss, "Professions in Process," *American Journal of Sociology* 66 (1961): 325.
19. R. Bucher, "Pathology: A Study of Social Movements within a Profession," *Social Problems 10,* 40 (1962).
20. A. L. Mok, *Beroepen in Aktie* (Meppel, 1973), pp. 69–70, and 1974, p. 20.
21. R. L. Akers, "The Professional Association and the Legal Regulation of Practice," *Law Society Review* 2 (1968): 472ff.
22. D. Rueschemeyer, "Lawyers and Doctors: A Comparison of Two Professions," in *Sociology of Law,* edited by V. Aubert (Harmondsworth: Penguin, 1969), pp. 273–277.
23. A. L. Mok, op. cit., 1973, p. 68.
24. See Mayhew, 1975.
25. For a very striking example, see R. Luckham, "The Market for Legal Services in Ghana," *Review of Ghana Law* 8 (1973): 7ff, 116ff, and 186ff.
26. B. Cardijn-De Salle, *La Profession d'Avocat* (Brussels: Larcier, 1972), pp. 35–38.
27. Belgian lawyers do not handle land transfers, wills, and so on, as British and

American lawyers do. A specialized branch of the legal profession, the "notaries," does this.

28. M. Galanter, op. cit., 1974 and 1976.
29. J. E. Griffiths, op. cit., 1977, p. 280.
30. See G. Michel, "Beschouwingen over het beroep van advokaat," *De Nieuwe Maand* (1973): 246ff. See H. Lebeau, SOS-Barreau, *Journal des Tribunaux* (1966): 25ff.
31. See J. O'Connell, *The Injury Industry and the Remedy of No-Fault Auto-Insurance* (New York: 1971), p. 131. It is interesting to note the "aggressive and nearly hysterical" resistance of the bar to no-fault compensation for traffic accidents in the United States. See M. S. Dukakis, "Legislators Look at Proposed Changes," *University of Illinois Law Review* (1967): 558ff. See D. Dimoens, *De Hervorming van het verkeersongevallenrecht* (Leuven: Katholieke Universiteit, 1978) pp. 167ff. See J. Fuchsberg, "Lawyers View Proposed Changes," *University of Illinois Law Review* (1967): 574ff. See E. Kuhn, "In Defence of the Tort System," *University of Illinois Law Review* (1967): 1ff. See American Bar Association, *Report of the ABA Special Committee on Automobile Accident Reparation* (Chicago: ABA, 1971). This resistance was partly based on arguments invoking the "client's" interest, while experience proved the "client's" interest of no-fault compensation. See A. I. Widiss, "Massachusetts No-fault Automobile Insurance; Its Impact on the Legal Profession," in *No Fault Automobile Insurance in Action: The Experiences in Massachusetts, Florida, Delaware and Michigan,* edited by A. I. Widiss; J. W. Little; R. S. Clark; and T. C. Jones (New York: 1977). See also a similar resistance, but less passionate, in New Zealand (J. M. Matheson, "Compensation for Personal Injury in New Zealand: The Woodhouse Report," *International and Comparative Law Quarterly* 18 (1969): 205ff. and in France (A. Tunc, "Un Bilan Provisoire," *Droit Social* (1967): 71ff).
32. Z. Bankowski and G. Mungham, op. cit., p. 53.
33. For an illustration, see the articles collected in R. Lefcourt, *Law Against the People: Essays to Demystify Law, Order and the Courts* (New York: 1971); and in B. Wasserstein and M. J. Green, *With Justice for Some: An Indictment of the Law by Young Advocates* (Boston: 1970). For a rather critical account, see S. Wexler, "Practicing Law for Poor People," *Yale Law Journal* 79 (1970): 1049ff. This is probably not a new phenomenon, as the history of the British Settlement movement proves. See D. Leat, "The Rise and Role of the Poor Man's Lawyer," *British Journal of Law and Society* 2 (1975): 166ff. Nor is it a phenomenon limited to the legal profession. See, for example, I. J. Goldenberg, *The Helping Professions in the World of Action* (Lexington, Mass.: Lexington Books, 1973). And F. F. Piven and R. A. Cloward, *Regulating the Poor: The Functions of Public Welfare* (New York: 1971).
34. J. Katz, "Lawyers for the Poor in Transition: Involvement, Reform, and the Turnover Problem in the Legal Services Program," *Law and Society Review* 12 (1978): 25, who in an article on the "involvement" problem of legal services lawyers, and the important turnover, writes that, whether or not motivated by ideological preferences for reform, legal services lawyers interested in sustaining experiences of personal growth are channeled by the social structure of their institution into reform activity.
35. Z. Bankowski and G. Mungham, op. cit., pp. 51–53.
36. T. J. Johnson, *Professions and Power* (London: 1972); J. Habermas, *Technik und Wissenschaft als "Ideologie"* (Frankfurt/M.: 1968), pp. 52ff; see also Mok, op. cit., pp. 27–32 and 108.
37. T. Parsons, "Professions," in *International Encyclopedia of the Social Sciences,* vol. 12 (New York: 1968), p. 536; and D. Rueschemeyer, "Lawyers and Doctors: A

Comparison of Two Professions," in *Sociology of Law,* edited by V. Aubert (Harmondsworth: Penguin, 1969), pp. 270–271.
38. Mok, op. cit., pp. 32–36.
39. H. P. Stumpf; H. P. Schroerluke; and F. D. Dill, "The Legal Profession and Legal Services: Explorations in Local Bar Politics," *Law and Society Review* 6 (1971): p. 47. *Jura Falconis,* De rechtshulp in Belgie. Verslag van een Kongres. *Jura Falconis,* nr. 4, 1975–1976.
40. For a very good example, see the controversy between René Victor Knight, *éminence grise* of the Belgian legal profession, and the Leuven Law Shop (J. Theunis, "De taal van de advokaat en zijn plaats in de rechtsbijstand; gesprek met Prof. Mr. Ridder R. Victor," *Jura Falconis* (1973): 169ff; and Wetswinkel Leuven,"Antwoord op Ridder Victor," *Jura Falconis* (1974): 363ff.
41. See Stumpf; Schroerluke; and Dill, op. cit., 1971. As noted by Mok, op. cit., p. 46, "The use of the professional ideology promotes in general the maintenance of a given situation: the status claims of the established profession are honored, while those of new professions are usually dismissed" (my translation). See also Rueschemeyer, op. cit., p. 267ff.
42. A. I. Widiss, "Massachusetts No-Fault Automobile Insurance—Its Impact on the Legal Profession," in *No-Fault Automobile Insurance in Action. The Experiences in Massachusetts, Florida, Delaware and Michigan,* edited by A. I. Widiss; J. W. Little; R. S. Clark; and T. C. Jones (New York: Oceana Publishing, 1977).
43. See two recent bills in Belgium ("Proposition de loi tendant à compléter le Code judiciaire par un article 440 bis," Sénat de Belgique, 674–675, nr. 1, 1975. See on this, *Advokatenkollektieven en wetswinkels: De advokatuur, meer stand dan Bijstand. De Rechtshulp in Belgie ontleed.* Leuven, 1976) and in France (see "Actes: organisons la lutte contre la création d'un délit d'exercice illégal du droit." *Actes* 15 (1977): 3ff.
44. C. E. Clark and E. Corstvet, "The Lawyer and the Public: An A.A.L.S. Survey," *Yale Law Journal* 47 (1938): 1272.
45. For such an analysis regarding the Dutch legal aid scheme of 1957, see L. Spigt and J. Westhoff, *Voorgeschiedenis Wet Rechtsbijstand on en minvermogenden 1957. Twee geslaagde buitenparlementaire akties van de Nederlandse balie* (Amsterdam: 1974). See also C. J. M. Schuyt; K. Groenendijk; and B. Sloot, *De Weg naar het Recht* (Deventer, 1976), pp. 18–35. For a fascinating illustration, see also O. Garceau, *The Political Life of the American Medical Association* (Handen, 1961).
46. P. Morris, "A Sociological Approach to Research in Legal Services," in *Social Needs and Legal Action,* edited by P. Morris; R. White; and P. Lewis (London: Martin Robertson, 1973), p. 53.
47. D. Rueschemeyer, *Lawyers and Their Society* (Cambridge, Mass.: Harvard University Press, 1973), p. 71.
48. D. Podmore, "Lawyers and Politics," *British Journal of Law and Society* 4 (1977): 55; M. Cohen, "Lawyers and Political Careers," *Law and Society Review* 3 (1969): 563.
49. P. Morris, op. cit., p. 53, 1973.
50. Z. Bankowski and G. Mungham, *Images of Law* (London: Routledge and Keagan Paul, 1976), pp. 40–44.
51. P. C. Alcock, "Legal Aid—Whose Problem?" *British Institute of Law and Society* 3 (1976): 151.
52. G. Bellow, "Which Lawyers Urn?" *Working Papers for a New Society* 4 (1976).
53. Alcock, op. cit., 1976, p. 168.
54. But here as well we must take the segmentation approach into account. "Socialization" is a typical issue for a functionalist model in which the "role"

concept is central. But roles do change and are often contradictory (see Mok, op. cit., pp. 97–102). As I mentioned before, socialization becomes particularly important (and problematic) when a great many newcomers enter the profession in combination with the difficult economic situation of most of the "stagiairs."

55. S. A. Scheingold, *The Politics of Rights: Lawyers, Public Policy and Political Change* (New Haven: Yale University Press, 1974).
56. Podgorecki and Schulze, cited in C. J. M. Schuyt, *Rechtssociologie, een terreinverkenning* (Rotterdam: Universitaire Press, 1971).
57. For a good review of "legal socialism," see the special issue of *Guaderni Fiorentini per la Storia del Pensiero prividico moderno* 3 (1975). See also A. I. Arnaud, *Les Juristes Face à la Société du XIXe siècle à nos jours* (Paris: 1975), pp. 87–90.
58. A. Mater, "Le Socialisme Juridique," *La Revue Socialiste* (1904): 190.
59. J. Bonnecase, *La pensée juridique francaise, de 1804 à l'heure présente. Les variations et ses traits essentiels* (Paris: 1932).
60. See, e.g., Arnaud, op. cit., pp. 103–105, Bonnecase, op. cit., Vol. II, p. 389ff. and F. Gény, *Méthode d'interprétation et sources en droit privé positif,* Vol. II (Paris: 1919), pp. 287–307.
61. P. Schöttler, "Arbeiderbeweging en Rechtsideologie," *Rechten Kritiek* (1977): 161 and 366.
62. N. Reich, "Anton Menger und die demokratische Rechtstheorie," *Recht und Politik* 8 (1972): 93.
63. Engels-Kautsky, 1975.
64. Schöttler, op. cit., 1977.
65. A. A. G. Peters, "Recht als vals bewustzijn," in *Recht, Macht en Manipulatie,* edited by C. Kelk et al. (Utrecht: 1976), pp. 189ff.; and M. Wieviorka, "Les Magistrats et la Défense des Consommateurs," *Les Temps Modernes* 33 (1977): 273ff.
66. M. Cappelletti and J. Gordley, "Legal Aid: Modern Themes and Variations," *Stanford Law Review* 24 (1972): 347–421. Copyright 1972 by the Board of Trustees of Leland Stanford Junior University.
67. D. M. Trubek, "Complexity and Contradiction in the Legal Order: Balbus and the Challenge of Critical Social Thought about Law," *Law and Society Review* 11 (1977): 529.
68. See the claims of "legal rights" of the patients in a medical or psychiatric hospital and of the clients of social services. See also E. Cahn and J. L. Cahn, "The War on Poverty: A Civilian Perspective," *Yale Law Journal* 73 (1964): 1317.
69. R. Nader, "Consumerism and Legal Serviçes: The Merging of Movements," *Law and Society Review* 11 (1976): 247.
70. Before World War I there already were movements in several countries that may be regarded as prototypes of the "new" systems of delivering legal services. For Great Britain see, e.g., R. Egerton, *Legal Aid* (London: 1945); S. Pollack, *Legal Aid: The First 25 Years* (London:1975), pp. 9–25. For the United States see, e.g., E. Johnson, *Justice and Reform: The Formative Years of the OEO Legal Services Program* (New York: 1974), pp. 5–19. Also R. H. Smith, *Justice and the Poor* (New York: 1919); L. Deitch and D. Weinstein, *Prepaid Legal Services: Socioeconomic Impacts* (Lexington, Mass.: Lexington Books, 1976), pp. 6–42. For West Germany see, e.g., U. Reifner and I. Gorges, *Alternativen zur Rechtsberatung* (Berlin: Wissenschaftszentrum, 1977). For a very interesting account on the prototype of a Neighborhood Law Center in England, see Leat, op. cit.
71. S. K. Huber, "Thou Shalt Not Ration Justice: A History and Bibliography of Legal Aid in America," *George Washington Law Review* 44 (1976): 768.
72. I. J. Goldenberg (ed.), *The Helping Professions in the World of Action* (Lexington,

Mass.: D. C. Heath, 1973), pp. 9–38.

73. Z. Bankowski and G. Mungham, *Images of Law* (London: Routledge and Keagan Paul, 1976), pp. 41–44.
74. A striking example is offered in Katz, op. cit., pp. 276–277, note 2.
75. I submit that an analysis of American literature on the "public interest" and "legal services" movements will give enough evidence of this hypothesis. See also Galanter's critical approach to such strategies, M. Galanter, "Why the 'Have' Come Out Ahead: Speculations on the Limits of Legal Change," *Law and Society Review* 9 (1974): 95ff; and M. Galanter, "Delivering Legality: Some Proposals for the Direction of Research," *Law and Society Review* 11 (1976): 225ff.
76. Leat, op. cit., pp. 176–177, notes that "(t)he extent to which the provision of equal access to the law can be seen as an effective method of dealing with the problems of disadvantaged groups in society depends, of course, in large measure upon the actiological theory of those problems to which one subscribes. Insofar as such problems are seen as the result of the imperfect working of a potentially just social system or as a result of a disjunction between the (adequate) theory and the (inadequate) practice of current social institutions then the provision of equal access to the law would seem to go some way toward the elimination of such problems. If, however, one sees such problems as rooted not merely in the gap between theory and practice but in the deficiency of the theory itself, then solution in terms of equal access to the law must also be deficient. The provision of equal access to the law would undoubtedly by definition, go some way towards remedying structurally based inequalities in the application of the law. But the extent to which such changes may be seen as likely to bring about any real reduction in social inequality, must depend upon an analysis of, first, the extent to which such changes merely serve to increase the power of professional groups (including, and in this context most notably, the legal profession) and, second, the potential role of law in reducing inequalities within the existing social and economic structure of society."
77. E. Cahn and J. L. Cahn, "The War on Poverty: A Civilian Perspective," *Yale Law Journal* 73 (1964):1317.
78. J. M. Fitzgerald, "The Contract Buyers League and the Courts: A Case Study of Poverty Litigation," *L.S.R.* 9 (1975):165; E. Cherki and M. Wieviorka, "Luttes sociales en Italie: Les mouvements d'autor éduction à Turin," *Les Tempes Modernes* (1975): 1793ff.
79. Bankowski and Mungham, op. cit., pp. 82–83, refer to this by citing Wright Mills, " . . . several types of persons—such as judges and social workers— . . . think in terms of 'situations'. Their activities and mental outlook are set within the existent norms of society; in their professional work they tend to have an occupationally trained incapacity to rise above series of 'cases'. It is in part through such concepts as 'situation' and through such methods as 'the case approach' that social pathologists have been intellectually tied to social work with its occupational position and political limitations. And, again, the similarity of origin and the probable lack of any continuous 'class experience' of the group of thinkers decrease their chances to see social structures rather than a sealter of situations. The mediums of experience and orientation through which they respectively view society are too similar, too homogenous, to permit the clash of diverse angles which, through controversy, might lead to the construction of a whole."
80. P. Lewis, "Unmet Legal Needs," in *Social Needs and Legal Action,* edited by Pauline Morris; Richard White; and Philip Lewis (London: Martin Robertson, 1973).

81. S. A. Scheingold, *The Politics of Rights: Lawyers, Public Policy and Political Change* (New Haven: Yale University Press, 1974), p. 204.
82. D. M. Trubek, "Book Review of 'Balancing the Scales of Justice: Financing Public Interest Law in America'," *Wisconsin Law Review* (1977): 303.
83. P. C. Alcock, "Legal Aid—Whose Problem?" *British Institute of Law and Society* 3 (1976): 151.
84. Cf. I. Balbus, "Commodity Form and Legal Form: An Essay on the 'Relative Autonomy' of the Law," *Law and Society Review* 11 (1977): 571–587; also, P. Schöttler, op. cit., pp. 161 and 366.
85. F. F. Piven and R. A. Cloward, *Regulating the Poor: The Functions of Public Welfare* (New York: Pantheon, 1971).
86. L. Basso, "De rol van het recht in de overgangsfase naar het Socialisme," Kosmodoc 6, 3 (1973) (originally published in *Problemi del Socialismo* 13/14, 1873).L. Basso, "Maatschappij en staat in de theorie van Marx," *Recht en Kritiek* (1975): 216–245 (originally published in *Problemi del Socialismo,* 13/14, 1873).
87. Galanter, op. cit., 1974 and 1976.

PART IV

A Look Back on the Topic

Chapter 17

Why Historical Precedents of the "Access to Law" Movement in Germany Were Not Followed up

Erhard Blankenburg

Our discussions on access to law seem to develop a basic contradiction: on the one hand, research into legal contacts has discovered a large unexplored field that has normatively been called "unmet legal needs." There was consensus in our discussions that part of the reason that some people do not use legal services is that they do not have equal access to law. On the other hand, legal institutions are criticized for being too costly, for taking too much time, and for being socially dysfunctional. That is, on the one hand we call for increasing legal access, and on the other hand we call for avoiding law and for providing alternative solutions. Cappelletti (1978) has published an impressive series of four volumes with contributions from many countries, all of which argue for reforms of legal services in both these directions. And as long ago as the turn of the century in Germany, precedents for both were set: increasing the mobilization of law by giving free legal advice to socially underprivileged people, and providing alternative forms of mediation at the same time. It is worth looking at this predecessor of an "access-to-law" movement to see the dangers involved in trying to reconcile the two contradictory strands of thought too rapidly.

Before entering into this discussion, however, I should emphasize

some of the differences between these two historical movements. The recent discussion in America about "access to law" includes the legal profession's attempt to organize what has been called "diffuse interests." This "public interest law movement" does not have similar protagonists in any of the European countries. It seems to stem from deficiencies that are specific to the American political system, and it seems to rest on innovative capacities that are specific to the American legal profession. Therefore, one has to argue carefully about the conditions under which innovations in the American legal services can be transferred to European legal cultures. However, even if the "three waves" that Cappelletti discussed refer to the American succession of issues, the basic goal of improving access to law and of finding alternative forms to legal procedures is common in all our countries, and we profit from the effects of its imitation in the international community of scholarship.

Even in the United States the attempt to improve legal aid for the poor in the 1960s had a precedent, which was set as early as the turn of the century. The classic book by Reginald Herber Smith, *Justice and the Poor* (1919),[1] develops most of the arguments that call for eliminating barriers of access to law. Smith mentions the first attempts of organizing legal aid made by German immigrants to New York, who tried to help their countrymen manage some of the problems of newcomers who wanted to integrate into the New World. That it was Germans who brought their belief in legalism to the new country does not seem sheer accident: at the same time (around the turn of the century), legal aid in Germany had a rapidly growing institutional infrastructure. However, not much of that infrastructure remains in modern Germany.

The ideas of the turn-of-the-century legal aid societies as well as the classical arguments by R. H. Smith fell into disuse until they were rediscovered in the 1960s. That is, they had a recurring but not continuous impact. The same does not hold true of the legal aid movement that gained considerable strength in pre-World War I Germany: starting with some of the problems of the emerging working class, trade unions instituted legal advice centers for their members as early as 1890, the churches soon followed with charitable legal aid institutions, and local governments later established public institutions. The competition of private as well as public legal aid societies in the German Reich of the early 1900s exactly mirrors the societal forces that were competing for dominance in the ideological development of industrialization. However, the pre-World War I legal aid institutions experienced only a short revival in the Weimar Republic, were turned around later by corporatist

ideology and for purposes of the fascist state, and were forgotten after the Second World War in both of the successors of the German Reich. While in the United States a renaissance of the "justice and the poor" discussion occurred in the 1960s, in the Federal Republic of Germany no such recurrence of any significance has taken place.

In this chapter, I want to indicate some of the sociological reasons for this absence of problem awareness in Germany in spite of the early legal aid tradition. Second, I want to draw some conclusions from these arguments as to which form legal aid could take if it were institutionalized under the present conditions in the Federal Republic of Germany.

THE SOCIAL CONDITIONS OF THE ACCESS TO LAW MOVEMENT

The Innovative Cases: The United States, England, and the Netherlands

The discussion about "access to justice" in the 1960s and 1970s has been dominated by Anglo-Saxon scholars. The basis of it has been a pragmatic interest in innovating institutions: the oldest and most far-reaching ones being the legal aid and neighborhood law centers in England,[2] the most widely publicized being the "legal services" spawned by the American "War on Poverty" in the 1960s,[3] and the most diverse being continental attempts to import some of the legal aid schemes of the neighborhood law shops. (The Dutch neighborhood law shops have been very successful, and they have been imitated throughout Belgium, France, and Switzerland.)[4]

We might consider this movement a response to some of the challenges of postindustrial Western countries. The most apparent of them, if we look at the clientele of neighborhood law centers in London, Los Angeles, or Amsterdam, is the problem of urban slum populations. England, the United States, the Netherlands, and the French-speaking countries on the European continent experienced a massive economic immigration during the 1950s and 1960s. Immigration from Latin American countries to the United States, from former Asian colonies to Great Britain, from Indonesia to the Netherlands, and from Northern Africa to France and Belgium can be considered to be the latest consequence of an imperialistic past. Because these largely unskilled, non-Caucasian workers had access only to low-paying jobs and because they migrated mainly to industrialized population centers, bringing with them their own

family structures and cultural ties, they aggravated the problems of urban infrastructures (which were further accelerated when the native populations fled to suburbia). The immigrant quarters in big cities tended to become ghettos with massive problems of unemployment, criminalization, and cultural and economic deprivations.

In the 1970s all these countries introduced stricter measures to control and prevent immigration, thus causing legal controls to penetrate further into unemployment and immigration procedures. Legal controls also were introduced into the regulation of public welfare, and they multiplied with increasing landlord-tenant problems and with racial tensions in the emerging slums. It is no wonder, then, that legal aid institutions have developed to try to defend the poor against controlling institutions.

However, immigration problems were not the only impetus behind the first wave of new legal aid institutions. They account for some specific forms of legal aid, like neighborhood law centers, but they do not account for the growth of legal aid schemes in England or "Judicare" in some of the more rural parts of the United States. Legal aid has been a broader movement, answering various latent needs in different social environments.

Nevertheless, legal aid institutions have been imitated across social (and national) boundaries, and they have progressed from innovative beginnings to more stable and more everyday activities. The developmental cycle from early innovativeness to the routine-like institutionalization that the legal aid movement of the U.S. Office for Economic Opportunity (OEO) went through resembles what Max Weber (with respect to charismatic leadership) called the process of *Veralltäglichung*. When in 1974 the Legal Services Corporation was founded in Washington, many of the former collaborators of OEO-Legal Services saw it as the end of the War on Poverty attempts to improve the situation of the poverty population through legal means. However, even if the enthusiastic expectations of the innovative years have waned, the Legal Services Corporation Act signifies a stabilization of institutions that provide "legal assistance to those who would otherwise be unable to afford adequate legal counsel." (In 1977 it funded 320 legal services programs, which are operating in about 700 neighborhood offices throughout the United States.)[5] The bar had accepted in principle the need for specific forms of legal services aimed at specific legal needs—even though local bar associations in some places were still afraid of any competition from federally subsidized lawyers.

The routinization of the legal aid movement went hand in hand with a broadening of needs, to which the Legal Services Corporation

responds. We can characterize these needs as a general challenge to postindustrial societies. Informal ways of insuring against life risks are increasingly replaced by institutional ones. With a loss of the family's economic functions, the individual increasingly depends on larger organizations and programs, such as social security, health insurance, and unemployment benefits. Lower social classes, especially, are deprived of the possibilities of attaining their rights from public administrators, large employers, or housing corporations. Civil courts traditionally have been used to enforce claims of big organizations against individuals rather than vice versa. Because traditional lawyers are ill prepared to advise the poor of their needs—having been traditionally preoccupied with legal problems of the property-owning middle classes—neighborhood law centers have compensated for the lack of services to lower classes, and they have taken up issues that might not pay a business-minded lawyer well enough. Subsidized legal services have become involved in areas of legal activity that subsequently could become regular lawyer services as well. Rather than competing with traditional lawyers, the law centers have fulfilled the functions of exploring new "markets" for legal services.

Similar arguments can be brought forward with respect to the development of legal aid in England, in the Netherlands, or in Sweden: today about half of the forensic income of barristers in England stems from legal aid clients. Their business has not replaced a formerly private clientele: rather, it is largely additional income to the barristers' offices. The same holds true of the "second wave" of the American access-to-law movement: public interest issues considerably extend the scope of lawyers' activities.

In searching for the social conditions that explain changes in the infrastructure of legal services, I shall adopt two types of arguments: (1) seeing them as a *response* to social problems and *demands* for legal help and (2) seeing them as a *supply* of services that are available because the legal profession is *interested* in offering them. Thus, I believe that the rise of the legal aid movement and its routinization can be explained by the following:

The increasing demand for defensive legal action in a world that is increasingly regulated by big organizations, administration, and, consequently, legal regulations

The (objective) interests of a growing legal profession in finding additional areas of competence in which to diversify its services (even when many of the established lawyers do not perceive such interests subjectively).

A Conservative Case: The Federal Republic of Germany

Both these social conditions hold true for all the Western postindustrial countries. However, whereas some of them have led in the development of legal aid, others—such as the Federal Republic of Germany—are very conservative in their access-to-law policies. Can it be that the social conditions that led to the development of legal aid in Anglo-Saxon countries are absent in Germany, or that other reasons prevent innovations in legal institutions?

In part, lawyers justify the lack of German legal policy with respect to legal aid by referring to traditional institutions. They point to the *Armenrecht,* a provision of the Civil Procedure Code of 1877 that allows the courts to cover the court and lawyer costs for a party who cannot afford them, with the condition that the case have some likelihood of success in court.[6] Lawyers for some time complained that their remuneration for such cases was lower than for ordinary cases; finally, in 1972, they achieved the goal of raising their Armenrecht fees to the level of normal legal fees.[7] This could hardly be called an access-to-law reform, however, as it does not involve any attempt to improve the availability of before-court counseling or to mobilize law for cases in which the party does not yet know whether it has any rights or how to use them. Armenrecht is accessible only after a law suit has been filed, its use requires legal information, and it presupposes legal counsel rather than encouraging it. Consequently, it has been used mainly in divorce cases where the parties are compelled to use the law and to hire counsel. (Wider use of the Armenrecht is reported only from Hamburg, where the ÖRA—public legal counseling bureaus—provided clients with information and access to the Armenrecht in cases involving a number of other issues.[8] This shows how much all procedural solutions to lower the barriers of access to courts depend on concomitant improvements of extracourt institutions for counseling.)

Although the ruling consensus of the German legal discussion has been satisfied with the modest and inefficient subsidization of court cases by Armenrecht,[9] there has been some criticism of any more far-reaching access-to-law policy.[10] Lawyers in the Social Democratic Party, especially, have proposed to install more Public Legal Counseling Offices according to the ÖRA model in Hamburg. (A legal counseling scheme of local government exists in Berlin, too.) The Bar Association reinforced its pro bono work during special

hours in the lower district courts, and some of the West German states (most widely publicized in Bavaria and Saarland) offered counseling services in their courts as well.[11] The federal government took these "model experiments" as a basis for a "law on legal aid" that is currently before Parliament, with little chance of being enacted.

All in all, however, these attempts to reform the conditions of access to law are exclusively directed at lowering the cost barrier for people with moderate economic means. They do not address any of the informational and social barriers of access to law, but rather increase them by devising bureaucratic procedures of checking on the entitlement to public legal aid. The German discussion among lawyers has not taken notice of the vast scope of social problems that legal aid schemes in other countries have brought before court, nor has it reflected the need to offer a different kind of institution (starting with the physical location and layout of offices) that, like the Neighborhood Law Centers, lowers the barriers of access for lower-class clients.

Trying to explain this difference in problem awareness brings us back to the historical conditions that initiated the "charismatic phase" of legal services in the United States, England, and the Netherlands. Some of the social problems of these countries are far less serious than those in the Federal Republic of Germany: there is no urban immigration comparable to that in the postimperialistic countries, which sped up local innovations. Germany is free of any significant colonial past, and it has drawn its immigrant labor force from Eastern European countries throughout the nineteenth century and the beginning of the twentieth century. After World War II, Germans experienced a forced remigration, which was followed by a twenty-year period of slow economic and political migration from East to West.

The Federal Republic of Germany consequently was very late in encouraging immigration from the Mediterranean countries. Starting late in the 1950s, Italian workers came to southern Germany, followed by Yugoslavian workers and, to a lesser extent, Greek and Spanish workers. Finally, a large wave of Turkish workers arrived. With succeeding immigrant groups, the cultural gap between Germans and the immigrants widened, and at the same time immigrants moved farther and farther into northern West Germany (including West Berlin). Because the influx of foreign workers from the Mediterranean has always been controlled by the German federal employment agency, it could be drastically halted according to changing employment policies. In fact, while there were indica-

tions that (mainly Turkish) slums were forming in Berlin and in the larger urban areas of the Ruhr and the Rhine/Main area, the unemployment shock of 1973 led to an immediate cessation of this immigration. A final wave of family members immigrated from 1973 to 1975, but as a whole, the foreign worker employment decreased from 2.8 million in 1973 to 1.8 million in 1978. Thus, one could say that the Federal Republic of Germany managed to control the immigration movement administratively and to prevent many of the social problems that would have resulted. Nevertheless, social and legal problems of integrating the immigrant population into West Germany form an important issue of political concern, but they involve far fewer deprivations than do the immigration problems of Germany's western neighbors.[12]

Even if urban poverty and immigrant slums do not form comparable social problems in West Germany, this cannot altogether explain the absence of a legal aid movement. It would be an oversimplification to attribute the access-to-law movement in the United States, in Britain, and on the continent wholly to the urban problems caused by immigration (even though these problems might have been its most dramatic source). Legal aid in Great Britain started at the same time as did the local Citizens' Advice Bureaus, which were designed in the first place to help reintegrate World War II veterans, and most of the "second wave" of representing diffuse interests by legal means responded to social problems of the indigent population, largely of its middle classes. Public interest law is not restricted to large metropolitan areas nor does it take up the problems of its immigrant population. It treats problems of consumers, of clients of administrations, and of those who are subject to institutions such as mental hospitals or homes for the aged. It takes sides for underprivileged groups, such as worker clients and tenants, but it extends also to such general diffuse interest as consumer problems and environmental concerns.

While such "diffuse interest" issues are universal to all postindustrial countries (not only the Western ones), the specific form in which they are represented in public interest law is genuine to the American legal tradition. It is a movement that needs lawyer elites (or, rather, counterelites) as protagonists, and it has developed around such legal institutions as adversarial litigation, case law traditions, and specific instruments such as class action suits and plea bargaining. Public interest law firms have been promoted by liberals in law schools as well as by research foundations, and they are embedded in the genuinely American phenomenon of lobbying institutions that replace some of the functions that the party system

fulfills on the continent. Thus legal as well as political institutions explain why similar interests are represented in different forms in different countries. Lawyers do take part in public interest campaigns in the Federal Republic of Germany as well. They are not prominent in them, however, and their means are not predominantly legal, as they are in the public interest law movement. In the FRG, environmentalists, especially, and people objecting to town planning, nuclear energy, or industrial investment organize around spontaneous action groups (*Bürgerinitiativen*) that use political pressure inside and outside the established party organizations as well as legal means of administrative complaints and procedures. Litigation (especially before administrative courts) is only one of their means, and it is usually a last-ditch attempt to prolong decision procedures and thus make them more costly. Consequently, public interest issues in Germany are seen as something that endangers the establishment of the political parties, not as a movement that changes the patterns of access to law.[13]

Similarly, what Cappelletti, with respect to the American situation, calls the "third wave" of the access-to-law discussion refers to problems that are specific to the American legal tradition. Even though there are complaints about the long duration of law suits in Germany,[14] German courts look like prime examples of speed and efficiency compared with American courts.[15] Institutional innovations—such as the Stuttgart model of handling the Civil Procedural Code—have been effective in reducing the orientation of German judges to the written files of a case and in involving the parties more in oral proceedings, in speeding up law suits even further, and in encouraging judges to reach settlements rather than go all the way to final judgments.[16] This is within the scope of procedural discretion, just as the delegation of judicial powers to paraprofessionals (in Germany, the *Rechtspfleger*) is a step toward treating routine cases in a bureaucratized way.[17] The German default action (*Mahnverfahren*) is a bureaucratic procedure of providing creditors with a legal title to collect debts—an automatic legal stamp without substantive control when the debtor contradicts and thus calls for a law suit to clarify the case. It is a precourt institution to enforce small (and large) claims, rather than an encouragement to contest them.

German courts, therefore, are to a large extent part of the institutional setup that leaves the individual with no choice but to defend by legal means, if he knows how to go about it. It is more speedy and more efficient than the judiciary in many other countries, and it employs many more judges and considerably fewer attorneys than does either the English or the American legal

system. Comparative indicators show that its output organization is much more developed, and its input organization much less developed than that of other Western legal systems.[18]

This is even more astonishing when one considers that the German legal system had a very elaborate system of legal institutions at the turn of the century. We shall have to look at the social conditions for this early legal aid movement in Germany, its history and the events that led to its breakdown, and finally the social conditions that might explain that there has been no revival of legal aid institutions in the Federal Republic of Germany so far.

THE GERMAN PEACE-OF-LAW MOVEMENT AS AN ATTEMPT TO PACIFY SOCIAL ANTAGONISMS OF INDUSTRIALIZATION

One side of our argument is that legal aid movements emerge only in response to some social issue. At the end of the nineteenth century, the German Reich was in the process of industrialization and the rapid rise of a workers' movement. Industrialization came later in Germany than it did in England, and especially in Prussia it was characterized by the alliance of big landowners, big industry, and the state. Workers' unions as well as workers' parties were oppressed by economic as well as legal means: Bismarck's 1878 outlawing of "all associations which aimed to turn over the order of the state and society by social democratic, socialist or communist means" was only the highlight of the legal repression of the workers' movement. Shortly thereafter, however, Bismarck introduced the illness insurance law (1883), the accident insurance law for industrial workers (1884), and insurance for retired and handicapped people (1889)—all of which were designed to solve some of the social problems of the industrial proletariat as well as to prevent them from organizing themselves in Socialist parties and in unions.[19]

In this way the Prussian state of Bismarck's time became a forerunner in social policy, and it managed to prepare the workers' movement for making peace with the state. When by 1890 the Social Democratic Party was successful in the general elections (in which this party was still allowed to participate), the anti-Socialist law had to be dropped, but the social security legislation remained as a feature of a paternalistic understanding that the "state" was above the antagonism of class interest.[20]

Table 17.1. Legal Aid in Germany in 1912: Number of Offices and Their Activities

	Legal Aid Offices	*Number of Counselings*	*Number of Written Actions on Behalf of Clients*
Public legal aid	119	337,071	57,563
Denominational			
1. Protestant	23	30,838	13,434
2. Catholic	122	235,638	90,713
Legal aid by workers' associations			
1a. Workers' Secretaries of the Free Trade Unions	119	701,648	173,897
1b. Legal aid by Trade Unions Cartel	211	51,772	18,748
2. Federations of Artisans (*Deutsche Gewerkvereine*)	55	58,365	11,185
3. Christian Trade Unions	55	40,056	22,490
4. Polish Union of Professions	8	21,081	12,224
5. Other Workers' Associations	6	3,166	1,516
Legal aid by associations of employees	23	58,703	1,319
Legal aid by rural cooperatives	9	17,056	584
Legal aid by entrepreneurs	9	12,461	5,017
Legal aid by political associations	32	33,732	14,463
Women's legal aid	93	45,485	8,859
Other Nonprofit organizations	32	194,292	36,016
Total	916	1,841,364	468,028

Source: Reichsarbeitsblatt 11, Beiheft 7 (Berlin, 1913), p. 4.

When the social welfare legislation was first enacted, the task of counseling on these new rights—the social security laws, the installment credit protection act (1894), and the labor protection acts (1891)—had been fulfilled by the workers' secretariats of the unions.[21] When, in 1904, 226,260 persons had already come to the forty-eight worker secretariats, bourgeois politicians recognized that legal aid for the workers would be a necessary part of their attempt to integrate the working class by means of social policy institutions. The former minister of trade, Möller, represented the public opinion when he said, in the Prussian parliament, "The propaganda activities through legal counseling administered by the Social Democratic Party are exceedingly effective and we would be gravely negligent if we failed in satisfying this need by offering different services."[22] With the support of the government, the communities and denominational nonprofit organizations institu-

ted legal aid offices that offered free legal advice to all citizens. In the Legal Advice Centers, laymen worked with public functionaries, especially those who were concerned with legal affairs in public administration courts. The legal advice was to be given objectively and not partially. The goal of counseling was to uphold the social peace and to prevent "unnecessary litigation."[23]

The competitive system of legal aid institutions had led within a few years to the development of an infrastructure of legal aid provided by the associations of three of the main societal forces: trade unions, churches, and public authorities. The survey also tells which type of legal issues have been raised in the counseling activities:[24]

Labor and training contracts	15%
Other civil law	29%
Social security law	25%
Civil courts	7%
Penal courts	5%
Public law	12%
Others	7%

Clearly, the problems of lower social classes are overrepresented when compared to the legal matters handled by attorneys. Traditionally, labor law as well as social insurance issues had been alien to the lawyers' practice as well as to their training. The legal aid institutions—of the trade unions first, but later those of public authorities and the church—helped develop fields of law that otherwise might not have been implemented as early as they were in the German Reich.

ACCESS TO LAW AND THE GERMAN LEGAL CULTURE

Structural Restriction to Innovativeness

The German bar's fixation on keeping its monopoly of legal counsel has to be seen in relation to its weak position in the legal profession altogether. This can already be demonstrated by the small percentage of advocates: about one-third of the German legal profession, contrasted to about three-fourths of the American legal profession (this is only one obvious indicator of the differences between the two legal cultures). Another difference is the emphasis on the judge's role in the socialization of German lawyers and in procedural law.

German court procedures are dominated by the judge, who has a more active role than does his counterpart in the American adversary system. In civil as well as criminal courts, the German judge is obliged to investigate fully all the facts pertaining to the case. In his investigation, he does not rely on the arguments presented either by the concerned parties or the legal counsel, but prepares his cases and especially the oral proceedings on the basis of well-documented files and briefs.[25]

The combination of these characteristics serves to explain why the American legal system has to look for more alternatives to litigation in court. The reasons are related to some deficiencies of the American court system that act as barriers against litigation. The great number of lawyers, their relative freedom to advertise for their services (which has been legalized by the Supreme Court), and the possibilities of arranging for contingency fees make the "input organization" of the litigation system very strong. On the other hand, the limited personnel capacity of the court leads to delays, which act as a barrier against filing cases for litigation. Thus the pressure to look for alternatives to conflict resolution is much lower in Germany. Even among businessmen, settlements can be less expensive and more expedient if a judge in court is the mediator (with the possible continuation up to a judicial decision).[26] The dying away of the mediation institution of the "Schiedsmann" demonstrates as well that there is no demand in the German legal system for extracourt alternatives (even if they are provided with legal status in the civil procedural code).[27] Having been active mainly for private penal prosecutions and interpersonal conflicts, in charges of insult the Schiedsmann lost its clientele with the fading away of rules of status, and with that, the need for "saving face" and defending one's honor through legal means. Alternative forms of conflict resolution are not considered to be an urgent need in Germany, because German courts are successfully acting as a mediator and settlements can be reached with a judge's help. The predominant pattern of reaching settlements in Germany takes place in court with the judge as mediator, while in the American legal setting bargaining prevails, largely out of court.

There is a functional relationship between the dominance of lawyers in the American legal profession and the fact that the scope of their activities extends beyond that of German lawyers. Some of the functions American lawyers have in registering real estate or building contracts are in Germany partly administrative, partly court responsibilities. German lawyers do not have any authority to question witnesses in cases that they represent before court, and

they rarely enter into extensive investigations such as American lawyers do. Just as they are more passive in court sessions, so are they less active outside the court in looking for cases and in organizing ways of presenting their clients' interest. The understanding of German lawyers is more restricted to handling legal matters; they do not provide all-around services for their clients as do some American lawyers. Again, we may argue that there is a correspondence between the comparatively small number of lawyers in Germany, the limited authority given them by procedural code, and the restricted understanding that they have of their functions. These factors can explain why public interest lawyers are nonexistent, and they might explain why legal possibilities to bring diffuse interest cases before courts—such as the American "class action" suits—are unknown in German law.

These are some of the reasons that explain why product liability and consumer protection issues are less often presented in German courts than they are in U.S. courts. German legal culture makes it very difficult to organize such diffuse interests. Extralegal movements have developed in recent years around the issues such as town planning and protests against nuclear power plants. They have largely used symbolic legal cases that are brought before administrative courts. However, administrative decisions—such as construction permits, the control of antipollution requirements, and the observance of residual participation rights of citizens to be affected by town planning—can be contested only by an individual who has been directly affected by such decisions.

A Possible Alternative: Integrating Legal Aid into Existing Institutions

We have seen some reasons why the discussion of legal aid has not led to as much institutional innovation as it has in the Anglo-Saxon countries. For once, social antagonisms are less sharp in the Federal Republic of Germany than they are in countries with mass immigration and urban deterioration. This explains why there is no similar demand for legal aid institutions of the "first wave." Second, we have argued that the legal profession in Germany is much more integrated into state bureaucracies (including the very large judiciary), and that lawyers have neither the tradition of being adversary advocates in the public interest nor the same legal instruments as lawyers in the American legal culture. This explains why the "second wave" of improving access to law has chosen different institutional channels from seeking access to justice. This corre-

sponds to the ideological tradition of German political culture to amalgamate adversary interests into existing institutions rather than to establish counterinstitutions such as an active lawyer advocacy. Using legal strategies contesting administrative policy (as do public interest lawyers in the United States) would confront the German administration with political decisions they are not accustomed to handling: German administrative law guarantees a maximum of accountability at the cost of minimizing political responsibility.[28]

While American agencies often have discretion in lower-level decisions, German administration traditionally has been legally bound by a cascade of federal laws supplemented by executive guidelines issued by the states. These laws can be used to challenge administrative decisions in court, and there has recently been an increase in cases brought before administrative courts, most of which deal with regulations restricting access to universities or cases concerning town planning or construction permits. Lower-level judges tend to decide in favor of the individual more frequently than do the administrative agencies. This increasing mobilization of administrative courts has caused some anticipatory reactions on the part of the administration as well as on the part of the legislature. Town planners as well as industrial inventors start out with campaigns of their own, thus opening possibilities early participation that might render exceptions possible at a later stage. At the same time, administrators look for ways to avoid decisions that would involve them in conflicts of interest. Attempts are being made to let local and regional legislative bodies decide on town planning and industrial investment, so that administrative courts cannot be invoked and so that the burden of decisionmaking rests with the political parties. We can see this as a result of a legally bound administrative culture: a narrow range of administrative decisions leads to the incapacity of such a system to decide in cases of politicized conflicts. Therefore, alternatives are being sought in the direction of participatory decision processes.

A model for participation as an alternative to adversary conflict resolution might be seen in the German participation laws in industrial conflicts (*Betriebsverfassungsgesetz* and *Mitbestimmung*): recruitment as well as dismissals, changes of occupational status due to rationalization, and changes in work rules have to pass the works councils in plants and firms. Even if these councils do not have veto powers, but only informative rights, such participation leads to anticipation of protest and early bargaining. Once a decision is made, works councils and thereby trade unions are so

involved in the conflicts that they cannot avoid helping legitimize them.

Comparing labor conflicts in Germany with those of other countries reveals a high degree of conflict anticipation, which correlates to the German notion of "legality" as a means of avoiding adversary conflicts. However, participatory conflict management rests on one precondition: the collective interests in industrial disputes are well organized, and individuals leave the representation of their interests in the hands of functionaries, thus allowing them to develop patterns of oligarchical cooperation.

German history gives us reasons to warn against integrating social antagonisms under some ideology of "peace of law." However, the Fascists did not seize power by means of corporate institutions, but rather by using party elections and parliamentary legitimation. Strengthening the adversary potential within institutions might, under the conditions of German legal culture, lead to a functional equivalent to "access to justice" as does legal aid in the Anglo-Saxon countries. This, however, rests on two preconditions:

There must be some capacity for giving organization to the interests to be represented (which is true for labor conflicts, but apparently not for the interests of foreign workers or of housewives, to take two examples out of many).

There must be some autonomy of internal adversary institutions, which again is best provided by external interest organizations backing them.

This puts the discussion of the legal profession into the framework of a theory of political organizability: where organizational capacity and conflict potential of socially weak groups are not given, there is still a need for a strong legal profession backing legal aid and thus providing some organizational means for otherwise unrepresented groups. Where these needs of organizability are located socially, and in which form they can be compensated by the legal profession, differs from one legal political culture to another.

NOTES

Note: An extended version of this paper was presented at the Colloquium on "Access to Law" under the chairmanship of Professor Mauro Cappelletti in Florence, in October 1979. I am grateful for this opportunity to develop further some of the arguments that were brought forward at our meeting in Berlin 1978.

I greatly profited from the discussions with Udo Reifner on his manuscript "The Ideology of Public Legal Advice in Germany from 1904 to 1930" (Berlin 1978). Even

though we differ somewhat in interpretation, I largely base my arguments on his analysis.

1. Reginald Heber Smith, *Justice and the Poor* (New York: Carnegie Foundation, 1919; reprint, 1964).
2. Cf. Michael Zander, *Legal Services for the Community* (London: Temple Smith, 1978).
3. Cf. Earl Johnson, *Justice and Reform—The Formative Years of the OEO Legal Services Program* (New York: Russell Sage, 1974).
4. For the Netherlands, see Kees Schuyt, Kees Groenendijk, and Ben Sloot, *De Weg naar het Recht* (Deventer: Kluwer, 1976), esp. pp. 35–42; for France, *Boutiques de droit, ouvrage collectif redigé par Chr. Revon* (Paris: Solin, 1978).
5. Legal Services Corporation, *Annual Report 1977* (Washington, D.C., 1978).
6. German Civil Procedural Code, §§ 114–127 ZPO.
7. Up to the value of a case of DM 3200, the Armenrecht fees for lawyers became equal to their normal fees; beyond that, they are still lower. Cf. Gesetz zur Änderung der Bundesgebührenordnung für Rechtsanwälte, October 24, 1972, Bundesgesetzblatt I 2013.
8. Josef Falke, Günter Bierbrauer, and Klaus-Friedrich Koch, "Legal Advice and the Non-Judicial Settlement of Disputes," in Cappelletti, ed., *Access to Justice,* Vol. II, Book 1, pp. 105-152.
9. Cf. Gottfried Baumgärtel, *Gleicher Zugang zum Recht für Alle* (Cologne: Heymanns, 1976); W. Grunsky and N. Trocker, *Empfehlen sich im Interesse einer effektiven Rechtsverwirklichung für alle Bürger Änderungen des Systems des Kosten- und Gebührenrechts?* (Gutachten A and B of the 51st Deutscher Juristentag, Munich, C. H. Beck, 1976).
10. "Arbeitsgemeinschaft Sozialdemokratischer Juristen," *Recht und Politik* 10 (1974): 98.
11. For Berlin, see Udo Reifner, "Unentgeltliche Rechtsberatung in West-berlin," in Erhard Blankenburg and Wolfgang Kaupen, eds., *Rechtsbedürfnis und Rechtshilfe, Jahrbuch für Rechtssoziologie und Rechtstheorie,* Vol. 5 (Wiesbaden: Westdeutscher Verlag, 1978), pp. 43–93; for the ÖRA, see Falke, Bierbrauer, and Koch, op. cit., and Josef Falke, "Zugang zum Recht-Fallstudie zur ÖRA in Hamburg," in Blankenburg and Kaupen, eds., pp. 13–42.
12. See the documentation in Baumgärtel, op. cit., pp. 43–56.
13. Cf. I. Ansay and U. Gessner, eds., *Gastarbeiter in Gesellschaft und Recht* (Munich: C. H. Beck, 1974). The extent of legal deprivation of foreign workers in West Berlin is currently being studied by Ulrich Spies at the Science Center Berlin, report forthcoming in 1980.
14. See the court file study of Gottfried Baumgärtel et al., *Rechtstatsachen zur Dauer des Zivilprozesses* (Cologne: Heymanns, 1972); and our evaluation of these data in Bundesrechtsanwaltskammer, ed., *Tatsachen zur Reform der Zivilgerichtsbarkeit,* Vol. I (Tübingen: C. B. Mohr, 1975). Compare with data from the United States, such as H. Kalven and B. Buchholz, *Delay in Court* (Boston: Little, Brown, 1959), or from Italy, such as C. Castellano, C. Pace, and G. Palomba, *L'Effizienzia della Giustizia Italiana* (Bari: Editori Laterza, 1965).
15. Cf. Bundesrechtsanwaltskammer, ed., op. cit., Vol. II: *Strukturenanalyse der Zivilgerichtsbarkeit.*
16. Rolf Bender, "The Stuttgart Model," in Cappelletti, ed., op. cit., Vol. II, Book 2, pp. 431–475.

17. Cf. Rolf Bender and Helmut Eckert, "The Rechtspfleger in the FRG," in Cappelletti, ed., op. cit., Vol. II, Book 2, esp. pp. 486–487.
18. Cf. Earl Johnson et al., "A Comparative Analysis of the Justice System of Seven Industrial Democracies," (unpublished report, University of Southern California, Los Angeles, 1977).
19. Edward Bernstein, Geschichte der Berliner Arbeiterbewegung, 3. Teil, Berlin 1910, p. 2.
20. Franz Neumann, *Behemoth: Struktur und Praxis des Nationalsozialismus 1933–1944* (reprint, Cologne and Frankfurt: Neudruck, 1977), p. 468.
21. Udo Reifner and Irmella Gorges, *Alternativen der Rechtsberatung—Dienstleistung, Fürsorge oder kollektive Selbsthilfe* (Science Center Berlin, IIM dp/78-42), p. 13 ff.; Soudek, *Die deutschen Arbeitersekretariate* (Leipzig, 1902); Müller, *Arbeitersekretariate und Arbeiterversicherung in Deutschland* (Munich, 1904).
22. Brunner, "Die deutschen Arbeitersekretariate im Jahre 1905," in *Correspondenzblatt der Generalkommission der Gewerkschaften Deutschlands* (Berlin, 1906), p. 401.
23. See Link, "Rechtskonsulenten und Rechtsauskunftsstellen," in *Die Arbeiterversorgung* 9 (March 20, 1907), p. 173ff.; "Juristische Rundschau," in *Deutsche Juristen-Zeitung,* 1907, p. 576 and 1362.
24. Reichsarbeitsblatt 11, Beiheft 7, July 1913.
25. See Chapter 15, "Some Conditions Restricting Innovativeness in the Legal Services in Germany."
26. Klaus Kohler, *Die moderne Praxis des Schiedsgerichtswesens in der Wirtschaft, Ergebnisse einer Untersuchung in Frankfurt/Main* (Berlin: Duncker and Humblot, 1967).
27. Günter Bierbrauer, Josef Falke, and Klaus-Friedrich Koch, "Conflict and Its Settlement: Legal Basis Function and Performance of the Institution of the Schiedsmann," in Cappelletti, ed., op. cit., Vol. II, Book 1, pp. 41–51.
28. Fritz Scharpf, *Die politischen Kosten des Rechtsstaates* (Tübingen: C. B. Mohr, 1970).

Bibliography

Abel-Smith, B. Y., Zander, M., and Brooke, R. 1973. *Legal Problems and the Citizens*. London: Heinemann.
Ackerman, B., et al. 1974. *The Uncertain Search for Environmental Quality*. New York: Free Press.
Advokatenkollektieven en Wetswinkels van Belgie 1976. *De Advokatuur, meer stand den bijstand. De rechtshulp in Belgie ontleed.* Leuven: Wetswinkel.
Akers, R. L. 1968. "The Professional Association and the Legal Regulation of Practice." *Law Society Review* **2,** 463.
Alcock, P. C. 1976. "Legal Aid—Whose Problem?" *British Institute of Law and Society* 3, 151.
American Bar Association 1971. *Report of the American Bar Association Special Committee on Automobile Accident Reparation.* Chicago: American Bar Association.
Anderson, F. R. 1973. *NEPA in the Courts: A Legal Analysis of the National Environmental Policy Act.* Baltimore: Johns Hopkins University Press.
Andrews, R. N. 1976. "Agency Responses to NEPA: A Comparison and Implications." *Natural Resources Journal* **16,** 301–308.
Ansay, I., and Gessner, U. (eds.) 1974. *Gastarbeiter in Gesellschaft und Recht.* Munich: Beck.
Arnaud, A. I. 1975. *Les Juristes Face à la Société du XIX siècle à nos jours.* Paris: Presses Universitaires de France.
Auerbach, J. S. 1976. *Unequal Justice, Lawyers and Social Change in Modern America.* New York: Oxford University Press.

Aulock, G. von. 1977. *Rechtshilfe für untere soziale Schichten*. Munich: Tuduv Verlagsgesellschaft.

Balbus, I. 1977. "Commodity Form and Legal Form: An Essay on the Relative Autonomy of the Law." *Law and Society Review* **11,** 571–588.

Bankowski, Z., and Mungham, G. 1976. *Images of Law*. London: Routledge & Kegan Paul.

Bardach, E., and Pugliaresi, L. 1977. "The Environmental Impact Statement versus the Real World." *The Public Interest,* 22.

Basso, L. 1973. "De rol van het recht in de overgangsfase naar het Socialisme." *Kosmodoc* **6,** 3. (Originally published in *Problemi del Socialismo* **13/14,** 1873.)

———. 1975. "Maatschappij en staat in de theorie van Marx." *Recht en Kritiek,* 216–245. (Originally published in *Problemi del Socialismo* **13/14,** 1673.)

Baumgärtel, G. 1976. *Gleicher Zugang zum Recht für Alle*. Cologne: Heymanns.

Baumgärtel, G., et al. 1972. *Rechtstatsachen zur Dauer des Zivilprozesses*. Cologne: Heymanns.

Bellow, G. 1976. "Which Lawyers Earn?" *Working Papers for a New Society* **4,** 4.

———. 1977. "A Paradox of Due Process." *Working Papers for a New Society* **5,** 8.

Bender, R. 1979. "The Stuttgart Model." In M. Cappelletti (ed.), *Access to Justice,* Vol. 2, Book 2, 431–475.

Bender, R., and Eckert, H. 1979a. "The Rechtspfleger in the FRG." In M. Cappelletti (ed.), *Access to Justice: A World Survey,* Vol. 2, Book 2. Milan: Giuffré; and Alphen an der Rijn: Süthoff and Nordhoff, 1978.

Bernstein, E. 1910. *Geschichte der Berliner Arbeiterbewegung,* 3. Teil, Berlin.

Bierbrauer, G., et al. 1978. "Conflict and Its Setttlement: Legal Basis Function and Performance of the Institution of the Schiedsmann." In M. Cappelletti (ed.), *Access to Justice: A World Survey,* Vol. 2, Book 1, 41–51. Milan: Giuffré; and Alphen an der Rijn: Süthoff and Nordhoff, 1978.

Bernstein, M. 1955. *Regulating Business by Independent Commissions*. Princeton, N.J.: Princeton University Press.

Blankenburg, E., and Fiedler, J. 1978. *Die Rechtsschutzversicherungen und der Geschäftsanfall der Gerichte*. Berlin: Science Center Berlin, IIM Discussion Paper, 78–90.

Blankenburg, E., and Kaupen, W. (eds.). 1978. *Rechtsbedürfnis und Rechtshilfe. Jahrbuch für Rechtssoziologie und Rechtstheorie,* Vol. 5. Wiesbaden: Westdeutscher Verlag.

Blankenburg, E. and Reifner, U. 1979. "Rechtshilfe als Teil eines Beratungssystems." IIM, 78–91. In T. Rasehorn (ed.), *Rechtsberatung als Lebenshilfe,* 21–42. Neuwied and Darmstadt: Luchterhand.

Blau, P. 1964. *Exchange and Power in Social Life*. New York: John Wiley.

Bonnecase, J. 1933. *La pensée juridique francaise, de 1804 à l'heure présente. Les variations et ses traits essentiels*. Bordeaux: Delmas.

Brakel, S. J. 1974. "Judicare: Public Funds, Private Lawyers and Poor People." Chicago: American Bar Association.

Broekman, J. M. 1975. "Ziekte en gezondheit als politieke begrippen." *De nieuwe Maand* **18,** 477.

Brunner, L. 1906. "Die deutschen Arbeitersekretariate im Jahre 1905." *Correspondenzblatt der Generalkommission der Gewerkschaften Deutschlands* **25,** 485–501. Berlin.

Buchanan, J. 1968. *The Demand and Supply of Public Goods.* Chicago: Rand McNally.

Bucher, R. 1962. "Pathology: A Study of Social Movements within a Profession." *Social Problems* **10,** 40.

Bucher, R., and Strauss, A. 1961. "Professions in Process." *American Journal of Sociology* **66,** 325.

Bundesrechtsanwaltskammer (ed.). 1975. *Tatsachen zur Reform der Zivilgerichtsbarkeit,* Vol. 1 Tübingen: C. B. Mohr.

Burke, E. 1869. "Speech to the Electors of Bristol, November 3, 1774." In *Works,* 3rd ed., Vol. 2, pp. 81–98. Boston: Little, Brown.

Cahn, E. 1963. "Law in the Consumer Perspective." *University of Pennsylvania Law Review* **112,** 1.

Cahn, E., and Cahn, J. L. 1964. "The War on Poverty: A Civilian Perspective." *Yale Law Journal* **3,** 1317.

———. 1966. "What Price Justice: The Civilian Perspective Revisited." *Notre Dame Lawyer* **41,** 927.

Caplovitz, D. 1974. *Consumers in Trouble.* New York: Free Press.

Cappelletti, M. (ed.). 1978. *Access to Justice: A World Survey,* 4 vols. Milan: Giuffré; and Alphen an der Rijn: Süthoff and Nordhoff.

Cappelletti, M., and Gordley, J. 1972. "Legal Aid: Modern Themes and Variations." *Stanford Law Review* **24,** 347–421.

Cappelletti, M., and Garth, B. 1978. "Access to Justice: The Newest Wave in the Worldwide Movement to Make Rights Effective." In M. Cappelletti (ed.), *Access to Justice: A World Survey,* Vol. 1, Book 1, 3–124. Milan: Giuffré; and Alphen an der Rijn: Süthoff and Nordhoff.

Cardyn–de Salle, B. 1972. *La Profession d'Avocat.* Brussels: Larcier.

Carlin, J. E. 1973. "Store Front Lawyers in San Francisco." In A. Blumberg (ed.), *The Scales of Justice.* New Brunswick, N.J.: Transaction Books.

Carlin, J. E., Howard, J., and Messinger, S. *Civil Justice and the Poor.* New York: Russell Sage Foundation.

Cary, W. *Politics and the Regulatory Agencies.* New York: McGraw-Hill.

Casamayor, L. *La Justice pour Tous.* Paris: Flammarion.

Castellano, C. 1965. L'Effizienzia della Giustizia Italiana. Bari: Edizione Laterni.

Center for Public Representation. 1976. *Public Advocacy in the Administrative State.* Madison, Wis.: Center for Public Representation.

Chayes, A. 1976. "The Role of the Judge in Public Law Litigation." *Harvard Law Review* **89,** 1281.

Cherki, E., and Wieviorka, M. 1975. "Luttes sociales en Italie: Les

Mouvements d'autoréduction à Turin." *Les Temps Modernes* **30,** 1793.

Chilton Research Services. 1971. *Legal Services Evaluation Study: Literature Search Report.* Prepared for Office of Planning, Research and Evaluation, Office of Economic Opportunity. Philadelphia: Chilton Research Services.

Christensen, B. F. 1971. *Lawyers for People of Moderate Means: Some Problems of Availability of Legal Services.* Chicago: American Bar Association.

Clark, C. E., and Corstvet, E. 1938. "The Lawyer and the Public: An A.A.L.S. Survey." *Yale Law Journal* **47,** 1272.

Cloward, R. A., and Piven, F. F. 1977. "A Strategy to End Poverty." *The Nation: Poor People's Movements.* New York: Pantheon.

Coase. 1971. "The Lighthouse in Economics." *Journal of Law and Economics* **6,** 283–289.

Cohen, M. 1969. "Lawyers and Political Careers." *Law and Society Review* **3,** 563–574.

Commission des Services Juridiques. 1975. *Rapport Annuel,* 3rd ed. Montreal: Commission des Services Juridiques.

Committee of the Judiciary. 1969. "The Criminal Justice Act in the Federal District Courts—Report of the Subcommittee on Constitutional Rights." U.S. Senate, 1968. Washington, D.C.: U.S. Government Printing Office.

Council for Public Interest Law. 1976. *Balancing the Scales of Justice: Financing Public Interest Law in America.* Washington, D.C., Council for Public Interest Law.

Curran, B. 1977a. "Legal Services for Special Groups." *Encyclopedia of Social Work,* pp. 828–835. New York: National Association of Social Workers.

———. 1977b. *The Legal Needs of the Public: The Final Report of a National Survey,* pp. 1–9. Chicago, American Bar Association.

Dahl, R. 1956. *A Preface to Democratic Theory.* Chicago: University of Chicago Press.

———, and Lindblom, C. 1953. *Politics, Economics and Welfare.* New York: Harper & Brothers.

Danzig, R., and Lowy, M. J. 1975. "Everyday Disputes and Mediation in the U.S.: A Reply to Professor Felsteiner." *Law and Society Review* **9,** 675.

Davis, K. 1959. *Administrative Law Text,* p. 2. St. Paul, Minn.: West Publishing Co.

———. 1969. *Discretionary Justice.* Baton Rouge: Louisiana State University Press.

Davis, T. P. 1973. "Legislative Restriction of Creditor Powers and Remedies: A Case Study of the Negotiation and Drafting of the Wisconsin Consumer Act." *Michigan Law Review* **72,** 3.

———. 1976. "Citizen's Guide to Intervention in Nuclear Power Plant Siting: A Blueprint for Alice in Nuclear Wonderland." *Environmental Law* **6,** 621–650.

Deitch, L., and Weinstein, D. 1976. *Pre-paid Legal Services: Socioeconomic Impacts.* Lexington, Mass.: Lexington Books, D. C. Heath.

Dicey, A. V. 1961. *Introduction to the Law of the Constitution,* pp. 328–405. London: Macmillan.

Di Mento, J. F. 1977. "Citizen Environmental Litigation and the Administrative Process. Empirical Findings, Remaining Issues and a Direction for Future Research." *Duke Law Review,* 409–448.

Dolbeare, K. M. 1969. *Power and Change in the United States: Empirical Findings and Their Implications.* New York: John Wiley.

Downs, A. 1967. *Inside Bureaucracy.* Boston: Little, Brown.

Dubois, P., and Christensen, A. 1977. *Public Advocacy and Environmental Decisionmaking: The Wisconsin Public Intervenor.* Madison, Wis.: Center for Public Representation.

Dukakis, M. S. 1967. "Legislators Look at Proposed Changes." *University of Illinois Law Forum,* 558.

Ebbin, S., and Kaspar, R. 1974. *Citizen Groups and the Nuclear Power Controversy.* Cambridge, Mass.: M.I.T. Press.

Edelman, B. 1973. *Le Droit saisi par la Photographie.* Paris: Maspéro.

Edelman, M. 1964. *The Symbolic Uses of Politics.* Urbana: University of Illinois Press.

———. 1974. "The Political Language of the Helping Professions." *Research on Poverty,* Discussion Paper 195–74. University of Wisconsin, Madison.

Egerton, R. 1945. *Legal Aid.* London: Routledge & Kegan Paul.

Erlanger, H. 1978. *Strategies for Action: Developmental Disabilities and State Government.* Madison, Wis.: Center for Public Representation.

———. 1978. "Young Lawyers and Work in the Public Interest." *American Bar Association Research Journal.*

"European Convention on Social and Medical Assistance." 1953. *U.N. Treaties Review,* p. 255. Paris: United Nations.

Falke, J. 1978. "Zugang zum Recht—Eine Fallstudie über die öffentliche Rechtsauskunfts—und Vergleichsstelle in Hamburg." In E. Blankenburg and W. Kaupen (eds.), *Rechtssoziologie und Rechtstheorie* 5. Wiesbaden: Westdeutscher Verlag.

Feltz, F., and Wansink, H. J. 1975. "De rechtsbijstandverzekering in Nederland." *Verzekerings-Archief* **53,** 148–173.

Fitzgerald, J. M. 1975. "The Contract Buyers League and the Courts: A Case Study of Poverty Litigation." *Law and Society Review* **9,** 165.

Friedman, L. 1975. *The Legal System: A Social Science Perspective.* New York: Russell Sage Foundation.

Fröhlich et al. 1971. *Political Leadership and Collective Goods.* Princeton, N.J.: Princeton University Press.

Fuchsberg, J. 1967. "Lawyers View Proposed Changes." *University of Illinois Law Forum,* 574.

Fuerst, J. S., and Petty, R. 1978. "Bleak Housing in Chicago." *The Public Interest,* 103.

Fuller, I. 1964. *The Morality of Law.* New Haven: Yale University Press.

———. 1969. "Two principles of Human Association." In J. Roland Pennocks and John W. Chapman (eds.), *Voluntary Associations,* p. 3. New York: Atherton Press.

Galanter, M. 1974. "Why the 'Haves' Come Out Ahead: Speculations on the Limits of Legal Change." *Law and Society Review* **9,** 95.

———. 1976. "Delivering Legality: Some Proposals for the Direction of Research." *Law and Society Review* **11,** 225.

Gamson, W. 1975. *The Strategy of Social Protest.* Homewood, Ill.: Dorsey Press.

Garceau, O. 1961. *The Political Life of the American Medical Association.* Handen: Archon Books.

Geerts, P. 1977. "De Rechtshulp in Belgie." *Recht und Kritiek,* 308.

Geny, F. 1919. *Méthode d'interprétation et sources en droit privé positif,* Vol. 2, pp. 287–307. Paris.

Gilbert, N., and Specht, H. 1974. *Dimensions in Social Welfare Policy.* Englewood Cliffs, N.J.: Prentice-Hall.

Glazer, N. 1975. "Towards an Imperial Judiciary?" *The Public Interest* Fall, 104.

———. 1978. "Should Judges Administer Social Service?" *The Public Interest,* 64.

Goldberg, W. 1976. "Regulation and Administered Contracts." *Bell Journal of Economics* **7,** 426.

Goldenberg, I. J. (ed.). 1973. *The Helping Professions in the World of Action.* Lexington, Mass.: Lexington Books, D. C. Heath.

Görlitz, A. 1976. *Politische Funktionen des Rechts.* Wiesbaden: Akademische Verlagsgesellschaft.

Green, M. J. 1970. *With Justice for Some: An Indictment of the Law by Young Advocates,* edited by Bruce Wasserstein and M. J. Green. Boston: Beacon Press.

Griffiths, J. E. 1977. "The Distribution of Legal Services in the Netherlands." *British Journal of Law and Society* **4,** 260

Groenendijk, C. A. 1974. "Juss-Buss: alternatieve en actieve rechtshulp." In *Rechtshulp, een bewijs van onvermogen,* pp. 72–84. Amsterdam: Rechtswinkel.

Habermas, J. 1968. *Technik und Wissenschaft als 'Ideologie'.* Frankfurt: Suhrkamp Verlag.

Halpern, C., and Cunningham, J. 1971. "Reflections on the New Public Interest Law: Theory and Practice at the Center for Law and Social Policy." *Georgetown Law Journal* **59,** 1095–1126.

Handler, J. 1966. "Controlling Official Behavior in Welfare Administration." *California Law Review* **54,** 479.

———. 1978. *Social Movements and the Legal System: A Theory of Law Reform and Social Change.* New York: Academic Press.

Handler, J., Ginsberg, B., and Snow, A. 1977. "The Public Interest Law Industry." In B. Weisbrod, J. F. Handler, and N. Komesar, (eds.), *Public Interest Law.* Berkeley, Calif.: University of California Press.

Handler, J., Hollingsworth, E. J., and Erlanger, H. 1978. *Lawyers and the Pursuit of Legal Rights.* New York: Academic Press.

Head. 1962. "Public Goods and Public Policy." *Public Finance* **17,** 197.

Höffner. 1971. "Was ist Sozialpolitik?" In Külp and Schreiber (eds.), *Soziale Sicherheit,* p. 27. Berlin and Cologne: Kiepenheller and Witsch.

Horowitz, D. 1977. *The Courts and Social Policy.* Washington, D.C.: Brookings Institution.

Huber, S. K. 1976. "Thou Shalt Not Ration Justice: A History and Bibliography of Legal Aid in America." *George Washington Law Review,* **44,** 754.

Huntington. 1952. "The Marasmus of the ICC: The Commission, the Railroads and the Public Interest." *Yale Law Journal* 61, 467 and 472.

Jaffe, L. 1961. "Administrative Law." In Harold J. Berman (ed.), *Talks on American Law,* p. 122. New York: Vintage Books.

Jenkins, J. C. and Perrow, C. 1976. "Insurgency of the Powerless: Farm Workers Movements 1946–1972." *American Sociological Review,* **42,** 249–268.

Johnsen, J. 1978. *Rettshjelp i utkanstrøk.* Oslo: Institute for Sociology of Law, University of Oslo.

Johnson, E. Jr. 1974. *Justice and Reform.* New York: Russell Sage Foundation.

Johnson, M. 1973. *Counterpoint: The Changing Employment Service.* Salt Lake City: Olympic Publishing Co.

Johnson, T. J. 1972. *Professions and Power.* London: Macmillan.

Jura Falconis. 1975–1976. "De rechtshulp in Belgie. Verslag van een Kongres." *Jura Falconis* 4.

Kalven, H., and Buchholz, B. 1959. *Delay in Court.* Boston: Little, Brown.

Kariel, H. S. 1961. *The Decline of American Pluralism.* Stanford, Calif.: Stanford University Press.

Katz, J. 1978. "Lawyers for the Poor in Transition: Involvement, Reform and the Turnover Problem in the Legal Services Program." *Law and Society Review* **12,** 275.

Kirp, D. 1977. "School Desegregation and the Limits of Legalism." *The Public Interest,* 101.

Kirp, D., Boss, C., and Kurilof, R. 1974. "Legal Reforms of Special Education: Empirical Studies and Procedural Proposals." *California Law Review* **62,** 40 and 62.

Kohler, K. 1967. *Die moderne Praxis des Schiedsgerichtswesens in der Wirtschaft.* Ergebnisse einer Untersuchung in Frankfurt/Main. Berlin: Cuncker and Humblot.

Koch, H. 1976. "Das Gerichtsverfahren als Konfliktlösungsprozess—Einstellung von Klägern und Beklagten zu Mietprozessen." Phil. Diss., Darmstadt 1974. Published by Arbeitskreis für Rechtssoziologie e.V. Hannover: Materialien zur Rechtssoziologie.

Komesar, N., and Weisbrod, B. 1978. "The Public Interest Law Firm: A Behavioral Analysis." In B. Weisbrod, J. Handler, and N. Komesar

(eds.), *Public Interest Law*. Berkeley: University of California Press.

Krupp. 1975. "Arm und Reich: Wie man die Unterschiede misst." In *Transfer 1, Gleiche Chancen im Sozialstaat*. Opladen: C. Böhret, G. D. Brewer.

Kuhn, E. 1967. "In Defense of the Tort System." *Illinois Bar Journal* **55,** 1.

Kurland, P. B. 1968. *The Quality of Inequality*. Chicago: University of Chicago Press.

Landis, J. 1938. *The Administrative Process*. New Haven: Yale University Press.

Large, D. W. 1972. "Is Anybody Listening? The Problem of Access in Environmental Litigation." *Wisconsin Law Review,* 72, 229.

Leach, P. A. 1974. "Legal Advice Centres and Neighbourhood Law Offices." *Law Society Gazette* **7,** 726.

Leat, D. 1975. "The Rise and Role of the Poor Man's Lawyer." *British Journal of Law and Society* **2,** 166.

Lebeau, H. 1966. "S.O.S.–Barreau." *Journal des Tribunaux* **81,** 25.

Leflar and Rogol. 1976. "Consumer Participation in the Regulation of Public Utility: A Model Act." *Harvard Journal of Legislation* **13,** 235.

Lefourt, R. (ed.). 1971. *Law Against the People. Essays to Demystify Law, Order and the Courts*. New York: Random House.

Legal Action Group (LAG). 1974. *LAG Bulletin,* 2.

Legal Aid Annual Reports (25th). 1975. London: Her Majesty's Stationery Office.

Lempert, R. 1976a. "Mobilizing Private Law: An Introductory Essay." *Law and Society Review* **11,** 1730.

———. 1976b. "Questions for Research." *Law and Society Review* **11,** 387.

Lewis, A., and *The New York Times*. 1964. *Portrait of a Decade: The Second American Revolution*. New York: Random House.

Lewis, P. 1973. "Unmet Legal Needs." In Pauline Morris, Richard White, and Philip Lewis (eds.), *Social Needs and Legal Action*. London: Martin Robertson.

Lindblom, C. 1977. *Politics and Markets,* pp. 170–189. New York: Basic Books.

Link, H. 1909. "Rechtskonsulenten und Rechtsauskunftsstellen." *Die Arbeiterversorgung* **9,** 173.

Liroff, R. A. 1976. *A National Policy for the Environment*. Bloomington: Indiana University Press.

Lowi, J. J. 1969. *The End of Liberalism*. New York: W. W. Norton.

Luckham, R. 1973. "The Market for Legal Services in Ghana." *Review of Ghana Law* **8,** 7–27, 116–139.

Lukes, S. 1974. *Power: A Radical View*. London: Macmillan.

Marks, R. 1971. *The Legal Needs of the Poor: A Critical Analysis*. Chicago: American Bar Association.

———. 1976. "Some Research Perspectives for Looking at Legal Need and Legal Services Delivery Systems: Old Forms or New?" *Law and Society Review* **11,** 191.

Mater, A. 1904. "Le Socialisme Juridique." *La Revue Socialiste,* 190.

Matheson, J. M. 1969. "Compensation for Personal Injury in New Zealand, The Woodhouse Report." *International & Comparative Law Quarterly* **205.**

Mayen, L. H. 1975. "Institutions of Representation: Civil Justice and the Public." *Law and Society Review* **9,** 401.

Mayhew, D. R. 1974. *Congress: The Electoral Connection.* New Haven: Yale University Press.

Mayhew, L. H., and Loevinger. 1976. "On the Emergence of Obligarchy in Human Interaction." *American Journal of Sociology* **81,** 1017.

Mayhew, L. H., and Reiss, A. J. 1969. "The Social Organization of Legal Contacts." *American Sociological Review* **34,** 309.

McCarthy and Zald. 1973. *The Trend of Social Movements in America: Professionalization and Resource Mobilization.* Morristown, N.J.: The General Learning Press.

———. 1977. "Resource Mobilization and Social Movements: A Partial Theory." *American Journal of Sociology* **82,** 1212.

Mechanic, D. 1962. "Sources of Power of Lower Participants in Complex Organizations." *Administrative Science Quarterly* **7,** 349–364.

Medicus. 1974. "Durchblick: Drittbeziehungen im Schuldverhältnis." *Juristische Schulung,* 613.

Menger. 1968. *Das bürgerliche Recht und die besitzlosen Volksklassen.* Darmstadt: Neudruck.

Michel, G. 1973. "Beschouwingen over het beroep van advokaat." *De Nieuwe Maand* **3,** 246.

Ministry of Justice. 1975. *The New Legal Aid System in Sweden.* Stockholm: Ministry of Justice.

Mok, A. L. 1973. Beroepen in Aktie. Meppel: Boom.

———. 1974. "De Advokatuur als georganiseerde beroepsgroep." In *Rechtshulp, een Bewijs van Onvermogen.* Amsterdam: Rechtswinkel.

Morris, P. 1973. "A Sociological Approach to Research in Legal Services." In P. Morris, R. White, and P. Lewis (eds.), *Social Needs and Legal Action,* p. 47. London: Martin Robertson.

Müller. 1904. *Arbeitersekretariate und Arbeiterversicherung in Deutschland.* Munich.

Muir, W. K. 1973. *Law and Attitude Change.* Chicago and London: University of Chicago Press.

Muskita, V. 1977. Staat, Hoge Raad, 22.4.1977. *Nederlandse Jurisprudentie,* 411.

Nadel, M. 1971. *The Politics of Consumer Protection,* p. 607. Indianapolis: Bobbs-Merrill.

Nader, L., and Singer, L. R. 1976. "Dispute Resolution in the Future: What are the Choices?" *California State Bar Journal* **57,** 281.

Nader, R. 1976. "Consumerism and Legal Services: The Merging of Movements." *Law and Society Review* **10,** 247.

Nagel, S. S. 1975. "Minimizing Costs and Maximizing Benefits in Providing Legal Services to the Poor." In *Improving Legal Process.* Lexington, Mass.: Lexington Books, D. C. Heath.

Niskanen, W. A. 1971. *Bureaucracy and Representative Government.* Chicago: Aldine–Atherton.

Nonet, P. 1970. *Administrative Justice: Advocacy and Chance in a Government Agency.* New York: Russell Sage Foundation.

Nonet, P., and Selznick, P. 1978. *Law and Society in Transition: Toward Responsive Law.* New York: Harper Colophon Books.

Oberschall, A. 1973. *Social Conflict and Social Movements.* Englewood Cliffs, N.J.: Prentice-Hall.

O'Connell, J. 1971. *The Injury Industry and the Remedy of No-Fault Auto Insurance.* New York, Chicago, and Washington, D.C.: Commerce Clearing House.

Olson, M. Jr. 1965. *The Logic of Collective Action.* Cambridge, Mass.: Harvard University Press.

Parsons, T. 1968. "Professions." In D. Sills (ed.), *International Encyclopedia of the Social Sciences* Vol. 12, p. 536. New York: Macmillan.

Peltzman. 1977. "Toward a More General Theory of Regulation." *Journal of Law and Economics* **19,** 211.

Peters, A. A. G. 1974. "Officiële en Alternatieve Rechtshulp" In *Rechtshulp: een Bewijs van Onvermogen,* p. 4. Amsterdam: Rechtswinkel Amsterdam.

———. 1976. "Recht als vals Bewustzijn" In C. Kelk et al. (eds), *Recht, Macht en Manipulatie.* Utrecht and Antwerpen: Spectrum.

Piven, F. F. 1977. *Poor People's Movements: Why They Succeed, How They Fail.* New York: Pantheon.

Piven, F. F., and Cloward, R. A. 1971. *Regulating the Poor: The Functions of Public Welfare.* New York: Pantheon.

Podmore, D. 1977. "Lawyers and Politics." *British Journal of Law and Society* **4,** 55.

Pollock, S. 1975. *Legal Aid–The First 25 Years.* London: Oyer Publishers.

Pressman, J., and A. Wildavsky. 1973. *Implementation.* Berkeley and Los Angeles: University of California Press.

Rabin, R. 1976. "Lawyers for Social Change: Perspectives on Public Interest Law." *Stanford Law Review* **28,** 207–261.

Raiser, L. 1971. *Die Zukunft des Privatrechts.* Berlin and New York: de Gruyter.

Reich, C. 1964. "The New Property." *Yale Law Journal* **73,** 733.

Reich, N. 1972. "Anton Menger und die demokratische Rechtstheorie." *Recht und Politik* **8,** 93.

Reichsarbeitsblatt. 1913. *Die Rechtsberatung der minderbemittelten Volkskreise im Jahre 1912,* edited by Kaiserliches Statistisches Amt, Reichsarbeitsblatt 11.

Reifner, U. 1978a. "Die Schutzwürdigkeit des Verbrauchers und der Schutzbereich von Verbraucherschutzgesetzen." *Zeitschrift für Verbraucherpolitik* 3.

———. 1978b. *The Ideology of Public Legal Advice in Germany from 1904 to 1936.* Science Center Berlin, IIM, 78–88.

———. 1978c. "Unentgeltliche Rechtsberatung in West Berlin." In E. Blankenburg and W. Kaupen (eds.), *Jahrbuch für Rechtssoziologie und Rechtstheorie* 5. Wiesbaden: Westdeutscher Verlag.

Reifner, U., and Goerges, I. 1977. "Alternativen der Rechtsberatung." Berlin: Science Center Berlin (unpublished).

Ridgway, P. 1974. "Law Centre Crisis." *Law Society Gazette* **7,** 46.

Ripert, G. 1949. *Le Declin du Droit.* Paris: Pichon & Durand Auzias.

Rodgers, H. R., and Bullock, C. 1972. *Law and Social Change: Civil Rights Laws and Their Consequences.* New York: McGraw-Hill.

Rosenberg, M. 1971. "Devising Procedures That Are Civil to Promote Justice That Is Civilized." *Michigan Law Review* **69,** 797.

Rosenthal, D. E. 1974. *Lawyer and Client: Who's in Charge?* New York: Russell Sage Foundation.

Rourke, F. 1969. *Bureaucracy, Politics and Public Policy.* Boston: Little, Brown.

Rueschemeyer, D. 1969. "Lawyers and Doctors: A Comparison of Two Professions." In V. Aubert (ed.), *Sociology of Law,* p. 267. Harmondsworth: Penguin.

———. 1973. *Lawyers and Their Society.* Cambridge, Mass.: Harvard University Press.

Sabatier, P. 1975. "Social Movements and Regulatory Agencies: Toward a More Adequate and Less Pessimistic Theory of 'Clientele Capture'." *Policy Sciences* **6,** 301–342.

———. 1976. "Consumerism and Legal Services: The Merging of Movements." *Law and Society Review* **11,** 247–256.

Sager. 1969. "Tight Little Islands: Exclusionary Zoning, Equal Protection and the Indigent." *Stanford Law Review* 21, 767.

Samuelson, P. 1955. "Pure Theory of Public Expenditures." *Review of Economics and Statistics* **37,** 347.

Sarat, A., and Grossman, J. 1975. "Courts and Conflict Resolution: Problems in the Mobilization of Adjucation." *American Political Science Review* **69,** 1200–1217.

Scharpf, F. 1970. *Die politischen Kosten des Rechtsstaates.* Tübingen: C. B. Mohr.

Scheingold, S. A. 1974. *The Politics of Rights: Lawyers, Public Policy and Political Change.* New Haven: Yale University Press.

Schöreit, T. A. 1974. *Rechtsberatung Unentgeltlich.* Karlsruhe: Müller Juristischer Verlag.

Schöttler, P. "Arbeiderbeweging en Rechtsideologie." *Recht en Kritiek.*

Schuler, P. 1975. "Immigration Consultants." *University of California at Davis Law Review* **8,** 85–105.

Schuyt, C. J. M. 1971. *Rechtssociologie, een terreinverkenning.* Rotterdam: Universitaire Press.

Schuyt, K., Groenendijk, K., and Sloot, B. 1976. *De Weg Naar Het Recht.* Deventer: Kluwer.

Senate Commission on Governmental Affairs. 1977. *Study on Federal Regulation: Public Participation in Regulatory Proceedings,* 95th Congress, 1st Session, pp. 17–22. Washington, D.C.

Silberman, L. H. 1978. "Will Lawyering Strangle Democratic Capitalism?" *Regulation* **15.**

Simoens, D. 1978. *De Hervorming van het verkeersongvallenrecht,* p. 167. Leuven: Katholieke Universiteit.

Simon, H. 1945. *Administrative Behavior.* New York: Macmillan.

Sinzheimer, H. 1976. "Das Weltbild des bürgerlichen Rechts." Reprinted in *Arbeitsrecht and Rechtssoziologie,* Vol. 2. Frankfurt and Cologne: Europaische Verlagsanstalt.

Sloot, B. 1973. "Einige sociologische beschouwingen over de effectiviteit de wet op de gratis rechtsbijstand." Ph.D. Dissertation (doctoraalscriptie), Groningen.

Smith, P., and Thomas P. A. 1977. *Evidence to the Royal Commission on Legal Services: The Duty Solicitor Scheme in the Cardiff Central Charge Unit.* Cardiff: Faculty of Law, University College.

Smith, R. H. 1919. *Justice and the Poor.* New York: Carnegie Foundation.

Snow, A., and Weisbrod, B. 1978. "Consumerism, Consumers and Public Interest Law." In B. Weisbrod, J. Handler, and N. Komesar (eds.), *Public Interest Law.* Berkeley: University of California Press.

Society of Labour Lawyers. 1968. *Justice for All.* Fabian Research Series Nr. 273. London: Society of Labour Lawyers.

Spigt, L., and Westhoff, J. 1974. *Voorgeschiedenis Wet Rechtsbijstand onen minvermogenden 1957. Twee geslaagde buitenparlementaire akteis van de Nederlandse balie.* Amsterdam.

"Statistics of Legal Aid and Defender Work in the United States and Canada." 1969. Chicago: National Legal Aid and Defender Association.

Stewart, R. 1975. "The Reformation of American Administrative Law." *Harvard Law Review* **88,** 1667, 1669, 1688.

———. 1977. "The Development of Administrative and quasi-Constitutional Law in Judicial Review of Environmental Decision-Making: Lessons from the Clean Air Act." *Iowa Law Review* **62,** 713.

Stigler, G. 1975. *The Citizen and the State.* Chicago: University of Chicago Press.

Stolz, P. 1968. *The Legal Needs of the Public: A Survey Analysis.* Chicago: American Bar Association.

Stone, C. D. 1975. *Where the Law Ends: The Social Control of Corporate Behavior.* New York: Harper & Row.

Stumpf, H. P., Schroerluke, H. P., and Dill, F. D. 1971. "The Legal Profession and Legal Services: Explorations in Local Bar Politics." *Law and Society Review* **6,** 47.

Sykes, N. 1969–1970. "Legal Needs of the Poor in the City of Denver." *Law and Society Review* **4,** 225.

Theunis, J. 1973–1974. "De taal van de advokat en zijn plaats in Rechtsbijstand, gesprek mit Prof. Dr. Ridder R. Victor." *Jura Falconis,* 169.

Titmuss, R. M. 1968. *Commitment to Welfare.* London: Allen and Unwin.

———. 1971. "Welfare Rights, Law and Discretion." *Political Quarterly* **42.**

Trubek, D. M. 1977a. "Book Review of 'Balancing the Scales of Justice: Financing Public Interest Law in America'." *Wisconsin Law Review,* 303.

———. 1977b. "Complexity and Contradiction in the Legal Order: Balbus and the Challenge of Critical Social Thought about Law." *Law and Society Review* **11,** 529.

———. 1978. "Environmental Defence 1: Introduction to Interest Group Advocacy in Complex Disputes." In B. Weisbrod, J. Handler, and N. Komesar (eds.), *Public Interest Law*. Berkeley: University of California Press.

Trubek, D. M., and Gillen, W. J. 1978. "Environmental Defence 2: Examining the Limits of Interest Group Advocacy in Complex Disputes." In B. Weisbrod, J. Handler, and N. Komesar (eds.), *Public Interest Law*. Berkeley: University of California Press.

Tunc, A. 1967. "Un bilan Provisoire." *Droit Social* **71.**

U.S. Council on Environmental Quality. 1976. "Environmental Impact Statements: An Analysis of Six Years Experience by Seventy Federal Agencies." Washington, D.C.: U.S. Government Printing Office.

U.S. General Accounting Office. 1976. "Trans-Alaska Oil Pipeline—Progress of Construction through November, 1975." Washington, D.C.: U.S. Government Printing Office.

Vogel, D., and Nadel, M. 1977. "Who Is a Consumer? An Analysis of the Politics of Consumer Conflict." *American Political Quarterly* **5,** 27–56.

Vose, C. 1972. *Constitutional Change*. Lexington, Mass.: Lexington Books, D. C. Heath.

Wassermann, R. 1978. *Der Soziale Zivilprozess*. Darmstadt and Neuwied: Lachterhaud.

Wasserstein, B., and Green, M. J. 1970. *With Justice for Some: An Indictment of the Law by Young Advocates*. Boston: Beacon Press.

Weisbrod, B. A., in collaboration with J. F. Handler and N. K. Komesar (eds.). 1978. *Public Interest Law*. Berkeley: University of California Press.

Wetswinkel, Leuven. 1973–1974. "Antwoord of Ridder Victor." *Jura Falconis,* 363.

Wexler, S. 1970. "Practicing Law for Poor People." *Yale Law Journal* **79,** 1049.

Widiss, A. I. 1977. "Massachusetts No-Fault Automobile Insurance: Its Impact on the Legal Profession." In A. I. Widiss, J. W. Little, R. S. Clark, and T. C. Jones (eds.), *No-Fault Automobile Insurance in Action. The Experiences in Massachusetts, Florida, Delaware and Michigan*. New York: Oceana Publishing.

Wieacker, T. 1960. "Das bürgerliche Recht im Wandel der Gesellschaftsordnungen." In *Hundert Jahre Deutsches Rechtsleben,* Vol. 2, 6. Karlsruhe: Müller.

———. 1974. *Industriegesellschaft und Privatrechtsordnung*. Frankfurt.

Wieviorka, M. 1977a. *L'État, le Patronat et les Consommateurs*. Paris: Presses Universitaires de France.

———. 1977b. "Les Magistrats et la défense des Consommateurs." *Les Temps Modernes* **33,** 273.

Williams, G. 1973. *Learning the Law*. London: Stevens.

Wilson, J. Q. 1973. *Political Organization*. New York: Basic Books.

———. 1974. "The Politics of Regulation." In J. W. McKie (ed.), *Social Responsibility and the Business Predicament,* pp. 135–168. Washington, D.C.: Brookings Institution.

Yale Law Journal. 1975. "Comment: The Wyatt Case: Implementation of a Judicial Degree Ordering Institutional Change." *Yale Law Journal* **88,** 1338.

Yngvesson, B., and Hennessey, P. 1975. "Small Claims, Complex Disputes: A Review of the Small Claims Literature." *Law and Society Review* **9,** 219.

Zander, M. 1978. *Legal Services for the Community*. London: Maurice Temple Smith.

Zander, M., and Russel, P. 1976. "Law Centres Survey." *Law Society Gazette* **9,** 208–214.

Zemansky, G. M. 1976. "Environmental Non-Compliance and the Public Interest during the Construction of the Trans-Alaska Pipeline." Mimeographed. Fairbanks, Alaska: Fairbanks Environmental Center.

List of Contributors

Erhard Blankenburg	Research Fellow, Science Center Berlin; Professor of Sociology, University of Freiburg
Barbara A. Curran	Research Director, American Bar Association, Chicago
Wolfgang Däubler	Professor of Labor Law, University of Bremen
Paul Geerts	Doctoral Fellow, European University Institute, Florence; Dr. des., University of Leuven
John Griffiths	Professor of Sociology of Law, University of Groningen
Kees Groenendijk	Lawyer; Researcher, Faculty of Law, Catholic University of Nijmegen
Joel F. Handler	Professor of Law, Law School, University of Wisconsin, Madison
Charles Halpern	Professor of Law, Georgetown University; Executive Director, Council for Public Interest Law, directing the Institute for Public Interest Representation, Washington, D.C.

Jon T. Johnsen	Professor, University of Oslo, Institute for Sociology of Law
Phillipe Nonet	Professor of Law, Center for Law and Society, University of California, Berkeley
Udo Reifner	Dr. jur.; Researcher, Science Center Berlin; Assistant at the Law Department, Free University of Berlin
Kees Schuyt	Professor of Sociology of Law, Catholic University of Nijmegen
David M. Trubek	Professor of Law, Law School, University of Wisconsin at Madison; Codirector, Center for Public Representation, Madison, Wisconsin
Louise Trubek	Codirector, Center for Public Representation, Madison, Wisconsin
Michael Zander	Professor of Law, London School of Economics; Legal Correspondent, *The Guardian*

About the Science Center Berlin

The Wissenschaftszentrum Berlin (Science Center Berlin), a non-profit corporation, serves as a parent institution for institutes conducting social science research in areas of significant social concern.

The following institutes are currently operating within the Science Center Berlin:

1. The International Institute of Management,
2. The International Institute for Environment and Society,
3. The International Institute for Comparative Social Research.

They share the following structural elements: a multinational professional and supporting staff, multidisciplinary project teams, a focus on international comparative studies, a policy orientation in the selection of research topics and the diffusion of results.